# The Cash Constituents of Congress

# *The Cash Constituents of Congress*

**Larry Makinson**

**Center for Responsive Politics**

**Congressional Quarterly Inc.**
**1414 22nd Street N.W.**
**Washington, D.C. 20037**

Printed in the United States of America

**Library of Congress Cataloging-in-Publication Data**

Makinson, Larry.
    The cash constituents of Congress / Larry Makinson.
      p.    cm.
    "A paperback distillation of Open secrets:   the encyclopedia of
congressional money & politics"--P.
    Includes index.
    ISBN 0-87187-690-6
    1. United States.  Congress--Elections, 1990.  2. Campaign funds-
-United States.   3. Political action committees--United States.
I. Makinson, Larry.  Open secrets.  II. Title.
JK1991.M257   1992
324.7'8'0973--dc20                           92-22751
                                             CIP

# Editorial, Research & Production Staff

| | |
|---|---|
| Author and Editor: | Larry Makinson |
| Assistant Editor: | Joshua Goldstein |
| Production and Research Assistants: | David Mendeloff<br>Carol Mallory |
| Intern Assistants: | Kevin Huffman<br>Allison Lee<br>Mark Emerson<br>Jennifer Richardson |

## Acknowledgments

Countless hours, days, weeks and months of painstaking research and production went into the publication of this reference work and dozens of people and organizations were extremely helpful in the process. *Cash Constituents* is an outgrowth of the Open Secrets project of the Center for Responsive Politics. The information contained in this book would never have emerged in this form or any other without the untiring efforts of the Center's director, Ellen Miller, in winning the enthusiasm and support of the foundations whose grants made it possible. The staff of the Federal Election Commission's Public Records Office provided invaluable assistance, as usual. The office's director, Kent Cooper, has offered advice, assistance and encouragement at every step of this project from its earliest days to its completion. His second-in-command, Michael Dickerson, has deftly guided successive waves of Center researchers through the labyrinth of filing cabinets, computer terminals and microfilm readers to the riches that lie within. Bob Biersack, the FEC's Supervisory Statistician and chief computer guru, provided critical assistance at many points in the project — and deserves special thanks for making vast improvements to the FEC's on-line database. Matt Costello, of the National Library on Money & Politics, assisted numerous times in the often cantankerous task of translating the FEC computer tapes into Macintosh-compatible files. Sharon Sand turned her eagle eye to proofing and her steady hand to making pie charts for this paperback edition. Particular thanks go to the small but amazingly hard-working staff of the Center for Responsive Politics, which endured many trying moments during the completion of this project. Josh Goldstein, who gave up six months of weekends and uncountable hours above and beyond the call of duty is deserving of particular thanks. The author is also grateful to Brooks Jackson of CNN, whose illuminating book, *Honest Graft*, introduced the concept of "cash constituents" that this book adopts as its title and theme.

The funding that made this book possible came from major grants from the John D. and Catherine T. MacArthur Foundation, the Joyce Foundation, the Mary Reynolds Babcock Foundation and the Deer Creek Foundation. Computer equipment used in compiling and presenting the data was provided through a grant from Apple Computer.

## The Center for Responsive Politics

The Center for Responsive Politics is a non-profit bipartisan research group in Washington, D.C. that studies Congress and related issues. Founded in 1983 by Senators Frank Church (D-Idaho) and Hugh Scott (R-Pa), it was designed to study Congress and examine potential reforms that could improve both its internal operation and its responsiveness to the American public. Over the years, the Center has become one of the nation's leading institutions studying the role of money in American politics. It is affiliated and works closely with the National Library on Money & Politics, a research facility which performs computerized research on campaign data, combining the Center's research with extensive computerized files of federal campaign records. The Center's funding comes from a variety of foundations. It serves as a non-partisan resource for the public, the academic community and the news media.

# Contents

# 4. Member Profiles ................................................................. 171

**State Delegations**

# 5. PAC Profiles ...................................................................... 305

# Appendix: Classification Categories ........................................ 340

# Index .................................................................................. 350

# Introduction

Many Americans view politics as a necessary nuisance, tuning in each election season only long enough to make their choices — or to decide they'd rather not participate. But within the Washington beltway, among the permanent political community of interest groups, lobbyists, fundraisers, political consultants, and members of Congress, politics has a different image and a different purpose than it does for most voters — one that is almost never talked about on the campaign trail or in 30-second TV spots. Quite apart from all the rhetoric about war and peace, handguns and abortion clinics, the business of government has much to do with the governing of business. And inside Washington, the worlds of business and government converge on Capitol Hill.

Decisions are made in committee rooms and around conference tables that can mean billions of dollars to industries and tens of millions to individual companies. Pressures from all sides in competing interest groups can be intense, as lobbyists buttonhole lawmakers and try to win nuances in legislative amendments that can make or break business — as well as political — fortunes. In this pressure-cooker world, one of the most potent tools in the lobbyist's arsenal is money. The prohibitive cost of modern campaigning has dictated that dollars are crucial to electoral victory, and nearly every member of Congress spends more time than they'd like courting it, raising it, stockpiling it for the next election.

All this is well known to the political community inside Washington. It is less well known outside Washington, where many people these days assume the worst. Voters may be wrong when they think that all members of Congress are crooks, but they are not far off the mark when they worry that their own representatives may be listening to two competing sets of constituents — the *real* constituents back home in the district, and the *cash* constituents who come calling in Washington, DC. This book attempts to bring the realities of that world — and the identity of those cash constituents — to a wider audience.

The facts on these pages will no doubt be useful to political practitioners inside the beltway, but this book was not written for them. It was written for the great majority of Americans who live hundreds or thousands of miles from Washington. It was written to show everyone where their own members of Congress get the money that keeps them in office, and to reveal the specific industries and interest groups that are most generous to Congress as a whole.

In pursuit of that goal, *Cash Constituents* provides a concise and affordable reference for those wishing to track political money in Congress. The book has been distilled from a larger work, the 1300-page hardcover *Open Secrets: The Encyclopedia of Congressional Money & Politics* (also published by Congressional Quarterly). Where *Open Secrets* includes two-page contribution profiles of each member of Congress, *Cash Constituents* offers mini-profiles of members, six to a page, arranged by state and district. The opening Big Picture section, as well as the profiles of industries and congressional committees are identical in both books. The PAC profile section at the back of this book covers all PACs that gave $50,000 or more in the 1990 elections, while *Open Secrets'* PAC profiles include all PACs giving $20,000 or more. Both books are based on the same research, which traced PAC and individual contributions to members of Congress in the 1990 elections.

Much additional work remains to be done in identifying contributors and tracking their influence, and future editions of *Cash Constituents* will continue to expand and refine the analysis. Meantime, this book is offered as a state-of-the-art guide to the realities of money and politics on Capitol Hill. You can read it like an encyclopedia, picking out pages at random and skipping back and forth between committee profiles, member profiles, industry profiles and the Big Picture section in front. Every page has something that may raise eyebrows or give pause for thought.

Readers will note that the narrative in this book is sparse. The facts have been presented as directly and simply as possible so that each reader can absorb and interpret them on their own, without the need for outside experts or a grand unifying theory. It is the author's hope that in the process of browsing through these pages, attentive readers will gain many new insights into the way government works in the real world of our modern American democracy.

*Larry Makinson*
*Center for Responsive Politics*
*May 1992*

# Scope, Limitations & Methodology

*Cash Constituents* is a paperback distillation of *Open Secrets: The Encyclopedia of Congressional Money & Politics.* The larger book is over 1300 pages long and includes detailed two-page campaign finance profiles for every member of Congress. The Big Picture section, Industry Profiles and Committee Profiles are identical in both books. The PAC Profile section uses the same format in both books, though in *Open Secrets* the list includes all PACs that gave $20,000 or more in 1990. In *Cash Constituents,* the PAC profiles cover only those PACs that gave $50,000 or more.

The biggest difference is in the Member Profiles, which have been abbreviated here and arranged state-by-state. Given that the information provided here had to be greatly abbreviated from the larger book, every effort was made to provide the most important information about each member's financial supporters and present it in a clear and useful format. So that readers can understand the procedures that were used, and the limitations that apply, the following section explains how the data which forms the basis of both books was collected and analyzed.

The starting point for this book was the official record of campaign contributions made to congressional candidates in the 1990 elections. That data was provided both by candidates and by political action committees, and was collected and computerized by the Federal Election Commission in Washington, D.C. Using those computer tapes, the author, assistant editor and several intern assistants undertook the laborious task of identifying the contributors — both PACs and individuals — by industry and interest group.

## What's Included in this Study

The primary focus of this book is on the 535 members of the U.S. Congress. Each member has a capsule contribution profile that details the leading industries and interest groups that contributed to his or her campaign. Those profiles are arranged by state and district and begin on page 174.

Profiles of each of the 37 standing committees of the House and Senate are also presented, showing which industries and interest groups contributed most heavily to members of that committee. Those listings begin on page 96.

An industry-by-industry breakdown of contributor groups (beginning on page 42) examines in detail which segments of the business, labor and ideological communities give the biggest share of dollars to members of Congress. The top contributors within each sector are listed, as are the top recipients in the House and Senate.

At the end of the book, a directory of political action committees is included. This brief statistical overview shows the general patterns by which each PAC that gave $50,000 or more distributed its money. The PAC profiles begin on page 305.

## What's Missing

**Small individual contributors** — those giving $200 or less — are not itemized on federal campaign reports, so no analysis was done of the origin of the money in this book. The proportion of campaign revenues received from small individual contributions is listed, however, in each member's mini-profile.

**Money that went to losers.** Because of the large number of contributors, the small size of our staff, and the difficulty in identifying the financial interests of tens of thousands of individual companies, the authors did not attempt to categorize individual contributions made to losing candidates. This would have been desirable — especially in the case of well-funded incumbents who lost — but it was simply not possible, given the restraints of time and personnel. Because of this, the total dollar volume of individual contributions attributed to specific companies is unquestionably low. Since the PAC community is comparatively small — around 3,300 PACs actually gave money in the 1990 elections — this report *did* analyze PAC contributions to both winning and losing candidates, so those totals can be considered complete.

**Unknown contributors.** Federal law requires that candidates identify all contributors who gave $200 or more to their campaign. Individual contributors are supposed to be identified by name, address, occupation and employer. In many cases, however, they are not. In researching the federal records, the authors found many thousands of cases of unidentified (or under-identified) contributors. In almost every case, names and addresses were provided, but quite often information on employer and occupation was left blank, incomplete, or so generic as to be useless in identifying the contributor's financial interest.

In all, of the approximately $101 million in individual contributions that went to winning candidates for Congress in the 1990 elections, the authors were able to classify just over 75 percent. The breakdown for the missing dollars is as follows:

- **No employer listed or found:** ...................................................................................................**$8.5 million**

Over 15 percent of that amount came from a single candidate — Senator Jesse Helms of North Carolina. Helms failed to provide occupation or employer information for more than $1.3 million in large individual contributions — far more than any other member of Congress. That total does not include contributors who were subsequently identified through information provided by other candidates.

- **Employer listed but category unknown:** ...............................................................**$11.6 million**

With over 40,000 individual companies to identify, the task of finding them all and filling in their classifications was simply impossible, given our limitations of staff and time. As the Center refines and updates its database, we hope to reduce this figure in future editions of *Cash Constituents.*

- **Homemakers, students and other non-income earners:** .......................................**$3.9 million**

Where contributors' occupations were listed as "homemaker," "housewife," or some equivalent, the Center tried to match them with an income-earning spouse. In many, many cases this was possible. It is a common practice for wealthy contributors to double their effective limit by giving both personally and with their spouse. In some cases this even extends to children, who are usually identified by occupation as "student." Whenever the source of the family's income could not be determined, the contribution was put into this category — with one exception. Persons with no income who contributed both to candidates and to political action committees — whether corporate or ideological — were assigned the classification of the PAC they contributed to.

- **Generic occupation/impossible to assign category:** ...............................................**$970,000**

When a candidate identifies a contributor as "businessman" or "entrepreneur," classifying them in the right category becomes a hopeless task. Fortunately, many of these generic contributors gave to more than one candidate, sometimes enabling us to discover their employer or occupation.

**Contributions from individuals who gave before 1989.** Members of the U.S. Senate run for reelection every six years. Classifying their PAC contributions from previous election cycles was a difficult, but possible task. Identifying their *individual* contributors in those previous cycles, however, was beyond the capability of our limited time and staff. Consequently, contribution profiles of senators in this book include only PACs for the years prior to 1989.

## How this Book Was Prepared

The first step in this project — and one that began in 1989 with the original edition of *Open Secrets* — was creating a classification system for the industries and interest groups that make political contributions. Since a majority of PACs and individual contributors come from the business world, the starting point was the system of Standard Industrial Codes (SIC codes) developed by the U.S. government's Office of Management and Budget. The SIC codes are used widely by reference organizations, such as Standard & Poors, that publish business directories. The codes were then streamlined to eliminate fine lines of distinction between industries and to make them more relevant to the political realities of congressional committee jurisdictions.

No similar codes cover non-business groups, so the Center developed its own, both for labor unions and for ideological and single-issue PACs. During the course of the project the classification system underwent a continual evolution, as the real world patterns of political giving gradually became apparent. A complete list of the categories — with the totals each contributed — is included in the Appendix, beginning on page 340.

### Classifying the Contributions

The contemporary American business world does not lend itself to simple classification. Modern corporations are often extremely diversified in their lines of business — and in their political interests — and in recent years many have been buying and selling subsidiaries almost routinely. To allow for this, the Center developed a multi-level system for classifying corporate PACs and other diversified contributors. A primary code was assigned, based on the company's primary business or profit center. Secondary codes were then added to account for subsidiary interests contributing more than 10 percent of the company's revenues or profits.

These multiple codes were then matched against the committee assignments of the candidates who received contributions. If the committee's jurisdiction did not relate to the PAC's main category, but did relate to a secondary code, that secondary code was used to classify the contribution. For example, a contribution from the Boeing PAC to a member of the Armed Services Committee was classified as a defense contribution. A similar contribution to a non-incumbent, or to someone sitting on a non-defense committee, would be classified under Boeing's primary category as an aircraft manufacturer. This system was used to determine unique codes for each contribution made to congressional candidates during the 1989-90 election cycle.

Classifying contributions from individuals presented a new level of complexity. While it is generally safe to assume that a PAC is giving to further its economic interests, it is quite another matter to try to divine the motivations behind an individual's contribution to a politician. The Center's approach was not even to try. Rather, *the classifications in this book are based on the economic interests of the contributor's employer or line of business.* The only exception to this rule is in the case of individuals who have contributed to ideological or single-interest PACs. In that case, the contributor was generally assigned the same category as the PAC *if* they contributed to a candidate who received money from the PAC as well.

The following example illustrates the methodology: If a real estate developer contributes both to a pro-Israel PAC and to a candidate who received direct contributions from one or more pro-Israel PACs, the contribution would be classified under "pro-Israel." If the donor gave to someone who got no money from pro-Israel PACs, it would be classified under "real estate."

### "Homemakers" and other non-income earners

If one to were take at face value the occupations and employers listed on federal campaign finance reports, one would quickly come to the conclusion that the biggest political interest group in the nation was made up of "homemakers" and "housewives." In fact, the use of contributions by spouses and other family members is common practice among wealthy contributors. Whenever a connection could be found between students, homemakers, or other non-income earners and a member of the household who did earn an income, the breadwinner's classification was used for all family members. Thus, a bank president, his wife and children would all be classified under "commercial banking" unless the wife listed a different occupation or employer, in which case she would be classified separately.

The only exception to this rule was in the case of ideological contributors. Non-income earning family members are not classified as ideological givers unless they themselves have contributed to an ideological PAC.

### Compilation and Publication

Once all the data was collected and categorized, the final step was to arrange it in some order that would make it comprehensible — both for our own analysis and for readers of this book. Viewing the mountains of data that this book covers from only one angle would be limiting at best, so the information is presented here from a number of perspectives. Profiles cover not only the finances of individual members of Congress, but of PACs, congressional committees and specific industries as well. Wherever possible, the data is presented graphically, so readers can view not just the detail in the numbers, but also the patterns.

## Technical Notes

This entire project, from the first drafts of foundation proposals to the compiling of the databases, the charting and final desktop publishing, was done using Apple Macintosh™ computers. A large ensemble of software was used to gather and report the data. The workhorses included: FoxBase+/Mac™ and Panorama II™ for database work, DeltaGraph Professional™ for the charts and graphs, Microsoft Word™ for word processing, and Aldus PageMaker™ for final page layout.

The research to identify the thousands of PACs and individual contributors was done in libraries (primarily the Library of Congress), over the telephone, and in the Center's own growing library of reference materials. Standard & Poor's *Register of Corporations, Directors and Executives* was an invaluable reference work in identifying companies and matching the names of corporate officials and directors. *Washington Representatives*, published by Columbia Books, is the definitive guide to Washington lobbyists and was a constantly-appreciated reference tool. Also immensely useful were the *Almanac of Federal PACs* by Edward Zuckerman of Amward Publishing and the *Yellow Book* series of business and congressional directories published by Monitor Publishing.

Even with the vast resources of the Library of Congress, and the dozens of business directories the Center consulted, the classification of the thousands of small businesses whose owners and officials gave money would not have been possible without the newly emerging tool of electronic reference works. Two CD-ROMs in particular proved to be worth more than their weight in gold: *MarketPlace Business* from MarketPlace Information Corp. of Cambridge, Mass. and *Business Lists-On-Disc* from American Business Information of Omaha, Neb. Without those CD-ROMs, thousands of small businesses identified on these pages would have been impossible to classify.

# 1.

# The Big Picture

# The Price of Admission

Winning election to the U.S. Congress has never been easy, but in recent years it has become so expensive as to effectively preclude all but the wealthiest — or most well-connected — from waging a competitive campaign. The cost of the average winning U.S. House campaign was $407,000 in the 1990 elections. Successful Senate campaigns ranged from the $533,000 spent by Nancy Kassebaum in Kansas to Jesse Helms' record-breaking $17.7 million effort in North Carolina. On average, Senate winners spent $3.9 million to win their seats in 1990.

But while the trend towards ever more expensive races has continued to build over the years, the 1990 elections saw the beginning of a counter-trend that could become a dominant factor in 1992: a volatile electorate angry at Congress has begun voting against incumbents, no matter how much money they spend. The first signs of that trend could be seen in 1990. While reelection rates still hovered in the high stratosphere in that election (96 percent in both the House and Senate), the cost of *defeating* incumbents began to decline. Since 1990, both the House and Senate have been tarnished by a string of scandals — from the Keating Five investigation to the resignation of House Speaker Jim Wright to the check-bouncing scandal at the House bank. Key questions in the 1992 elections will be whether incumbent members of Congress can collect enough money to insulate themselves against the voters' ire, and whether challengers can attract enough contributions to present themselves as viable alternatives.

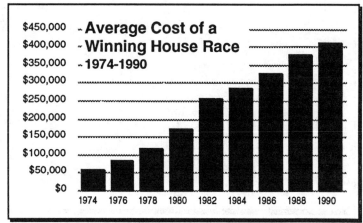

## Mismatched Races

Few House incumbents faced serious challenges in the 1990 elections — at least financially. Of the 406 House incumbents who sought reelection, all but 16 won. And, as this chart illustrates, the great majority of races were financial runaways. Most challengers spent less than $100,000 in their bids to win a seat in Congress, while the greatest number of winning candidates (predominantly incumbents) spent between $100,000 and $700,000. In 250 of the nation's 435 congressional districts, the winning candidate outspent the loser by a factor of 10-to-one or greater. In nearly all those cases the winner was an incumbent seeking reelection.

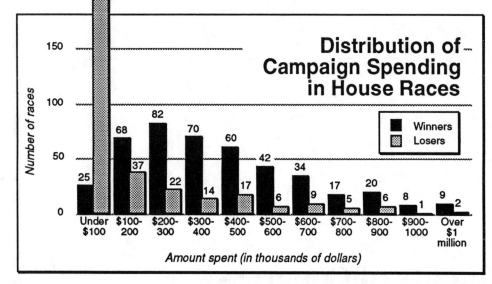

# The Widening Spending Gap in House Races

Since the mid 1980s a growing dichotomy has been evident in spending for U.S. House races. While spending by incumbents continues to rise with each new election, spending by challengers has slowly but steadily declined. By 1990 the gulf in spending between incumbents and challengers had widened to more than $308,000. The chart at right shows the contrasting pattern. The chart below plots the ever-increasing size of the gap in spending versus those who are already in the U.S. House versus those trying to break in.

The rise in the spending gap — and the rising inability of challengers to raise funds — has much to do with the growing power of political action committees or PACs. PACs now account for nearly half the campaign dollars raised by winning House candidates, and those dollars go overwhelmingly to incumbents. Of the $110 million in PAC contributions that went to House candidates in the 1990 elections, more than $89 million went to incumbents. Less than $8 million went to challengers and the rest went to candidates in open seat races where no incumbent was running.

Business PACs are the most reluctant to contribute to challengers. Labor and ideological PACs, while more likely to give to newcomers, still give most of their dollars to incumbent office holders as well. As a result, candidates seeking to unseat incumbent members of Congress have an almost impossible task raising the funds it takes to wage a competitive race. Unless they have considerable personal funds of their own, personal ties with the Washington-based fundraising community, or an exceptionally vulnerable opponent, challengers for the U.S. House of Representatives face an increasingly uphill battle.

The only exceptions are the relative handful of Democratic challengers who win large-scale support from Labor PACs, and an even smaller handful of Republicans who draw support from business and ideological PACs. In the 1990 elections only 25 challengers — 17 Democrats and eight Republicans — drew $100,000 or more from PACs. Eleven of them (nine Democrats and two Republicans) won on election day.

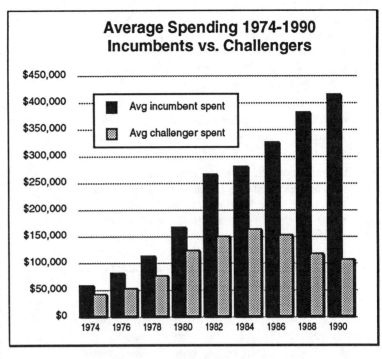

| Year | Avg incumbent spent | Avg challenger spent | Spending gap |
|------|---------|----------|---------|
| 1974 | $56,537 | $40,015 | $16,523 |
| 1976 | $79,398 | $50,776 | $28,622 |
| 1978 | $111,159 | $74,802 | $36,358 |
| 1980 | $165,082 | $121,751 | $43,330 |
| 1982 | $265,001 | $148,013 | $116,988 |
| 1984 | $279,044 | $161,994 | $117,050 |
| 1986 | $324,768 | $150,766 | $174,002 |
| 1988 | $380,010 | $115,906 | $264,104 |
| 1990 | $413,231 | $105,017 | $308,214 |

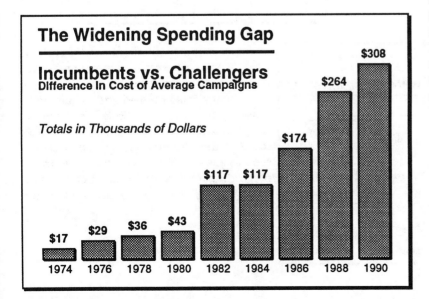

# The Dollars & Cents of Incumbency

Incumbents, for any office at any level of government, have always enjoyed a natural advantage at election time. Their names are already well known, they have established a record of service for all to see, and if they have served their constituents well, the voters are likely to be reminded of it come election time. Congressional incumbents also have the benefit of regular news coverage during their term in office — coverage which often gives them credit for federal grants and projects in their districts. And they have the congressional franking privilege, enabling them to send correspondence and periodic newsletters to their constituents postage free.

Members of Congress also have the inside track on contributions from political action committees. In 1990 PACs accounted for nearly half of all the dollars received by House incumbents and almost one-quarter of total contributions to Senators. More than 79 percent of the dollars contributed by PACs in 1990 went to incumbents.

What all this adds up to is an overwhelming advantage by incumbents over challengers, particularly in races for the House of Representatives. The vast majority of candidates opposing House incumbents, financially speaking, were never in the race. Even those who spent large amounts of money (see table on the facing page) found tough odds against them. In the 1990 elections, 96 percent of the House and Senate incumbents who sought reelection were successful at the polls.

There was one bright side to the otherwise cloudy outlook for House challengers in the last election. Though the great majority of challengers were vanquished at the polls, the 16 who did manage to win in 1990 did it with considerably less money than their counterparts two years earlier. In 1990, the cost of beating incumbents ranged from a low of just over $178,000 (by Republican Scott Klug in Wisconsin's 2nd district) to the $883,000 campaign of Democrat Jim Moran in northern Virginia's 8th district. Two years earlier only six incumbents fell to challengers and the cost of those campaigns ranged from $316,000 to $1.3 million.

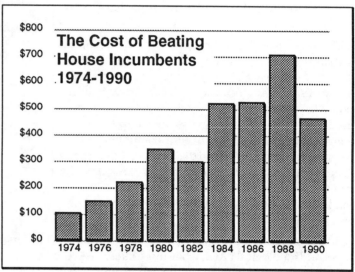

The Cost of Beating House Incumbents 1974-1990

| Year | Avg Challenger | Avg Incumbent | No. |
|------|---------------|---------------|-----|
| 1974 | $100,435 | $101,102 | 40 |
| 1976 | $144,720 | $154,774 | 12 |
| 1978 | $217,083 | $200,607 | 19 |
| 1980 | $343,093 | $286,559 | 31 |
| 1982 | $296,273 | $453,459 | 23 |
| 1984 | $518,781 | $463,070 | 17 |
| 1986 | $523,308 | $562,139 | 6 |
| 1988 | $703,740 | $876,678 | 7 |
| 1990 | $462,546 | $631,025 | 16 |

More House incumbents faced close calls in 1990 than two years earlier, though most still won with relative ease. Still, the whiff of anti-incumbency was in the air and beginning to cause problems even for long-time lawmakers. Following two years of almost non-stop scandals, the 1992 elections were expected to see this anti-incumbent mood grow to maturity, with an unusually large number of incumbents finding their careers cut short by the voters.

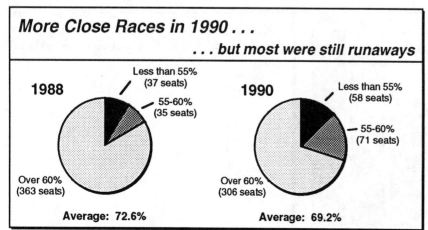

More Close Races in 1990 . . .
. . . but most were still runaways

**1988**
Less than 55% (37 seats)
55-60% (35 seats)
Over 60% (363 seats)
Average: 72.6%

**1990**
Less than 55% (58 seats)
55-60% (71 seats)
Over 60% (306 seats)
Average: 69.2%

# Reelection Rates through the Years

Reelection rates for incumbents in both the House and Senate were 96 percent in 1990, indicating the extreme difficulty faced by challengers trying to break into Congress. The Senate figure was the highest in 30 years, with only one incumbent out of 32 who sought reelection losing his seat. But in the House, the 96 percent reelection rate was actually a *drop* from the rates in the last two elections.

As the charts at right show, reelection has historically been more of a sure thing for House members than for Senators. Reelection rates for the House have rarely dipped below 90 percent in the past 30 years, while Senate rates have risen and fallen in response to national political trends.

The 1980 election, which brought Ronald Reagan to the White House, saw the defeat of nine Senate incumbents — all of them Democrats. In the same year, even though Democrats did lose 33 seats in the House, some 91 percent of House incumbents were reelected.

The last time the reelection rate for House members dropped below 80 percent was in 1948, when it was 79 percent. In every election since 1976 the rate has been 90 percent or above.

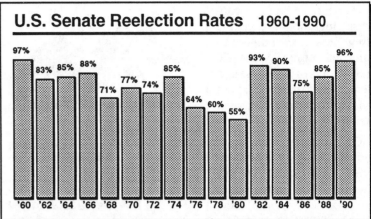

**U.S. Senate Reelection Rates** 1960-1990

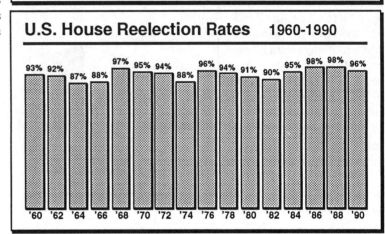

**U.S. House Reelection Rates** 1960-1990

## The 10 Top-Spending Challengers in House Races

| Challenger | Spent | Vote Pct | Party | District | Outcome |
|---|---|---|---|---|---|
| Reid Hughes | $1,067,366 | 44.0% | Dem | Fla 4 | Lost |
| John H. Carrington | $890,838 | 42.0% | Rep | NC 4 | Lost |
| James P. Moran Jr. | $883,216 | 51.7% | Dem | Va 8 | Won |
| Mike Kopetski | $844,797 | 55.0% | Dem | Ore 5 | Won |
| G. Robert Williams | $817,944 | 46.0% | Rep | Wash 3 | Lost |
| John Arthur Johnson | $781,224 | 47.0% | Rep | Ind 5 | Lost |
| John A. Boehner | $732,765 | 61.1% | Rep | Ohio 8 | Won |
| John Linder | $696,859 | 48.0% | Rep | Ga 4 | Lost |
| Richard Allen Waterfield | $679,117 | 44.0% | Rep | Texas 13 | Lost |
| Manny Hoffman | $642,391 | 41.0% | Rep | Ill 4 | Lost |

## The High Cost of Losing

While having enough money to wage a serious campaign is a clear prerequisite for winning a seat in Congress, money alone won't guarantee victory — as the chart on the left plainly shows. Of the 10 highest-spending challengers in 1990 House races, seven lost at the polls. Still, that was an improvement from 1988, when nine out of 10 lost.

# Where the Money Came From

The dollars that drove winning campaigns in 1990 came from different mixtures of sources depending on the office and the status of the candidate. These pie charts highlight the differences.

Political action committees were most important to incumbent House members, who collected nearly half their revenues from PACs. In contrast, incumbent Senators drew less than one-fourth their dollars from PACs, while newcomers to the House and Senate each received about one-third of their campaign dollars from PACs.

Contributions from individuals giving $200 or more were important to all groups — particularly Senate incumbents, who drew 38 percent of their dollars from that source. Small individual contributions accounted for less than 20 percent of the dollars for winning House candidates, and a slightly higher proportion among Senate winners. Senate incumbents had the biggest percentage of all, though this was skewed somewhat by Jesse Helms' reelection campaign, which relied heavily on small donations raised through a nationwide direct mail effort.

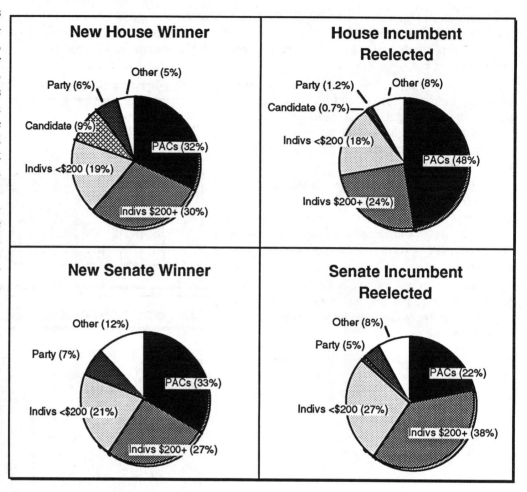

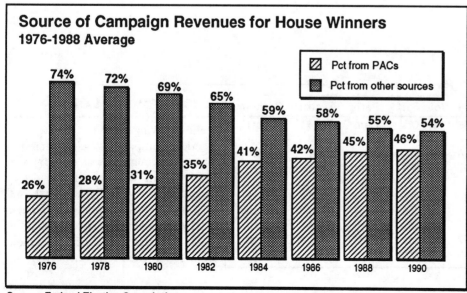

## A Rising Dependence on PACs

With each new election cycle, more and more candidates for Congress — particularly for the House of Representatives — are becoming dependent on ever larger sums from political action committees. The chart at left shows the slow but steady progression in the importance of PACs for House winners. Senators raise higher dollar totals from PACs, but their biggest share of funds comes from individual contributors.

Source: Federal Election Commission
Note: Base data includes contributions to non-voting House Delegates.

# Source of PAC Funds — House Freshmen vs. Incumbents

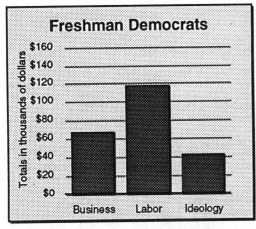

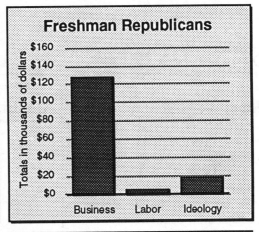

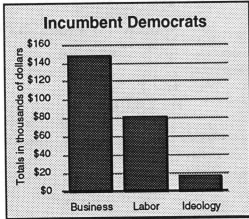

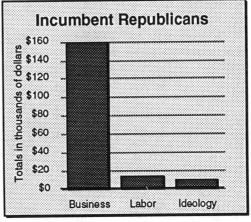

When PAC receipts are combined into three distinct groups — business, labor and ideological — significant contrasts in the source of PAC funds can be seen between Democrats and Republicans, and between freshman members of Congress versus incumbents. The biggest source of funds for newly-elected Democrats comes from Labor PACs, which gave an average of more than $115,000 per Democratic winner in the 1990 elections. That is considerably more than the freshmen Democrats got from all business PACs combined. Ideological and single-issue PACs are also an important source of funds for newly-elected Democrats.

Once the House Democrats have served one or more terms in Congress, the complexion of their PAC contributions undergoes a significant change. Labor dollars are still an important source of campaign revenues, but they are swamped by the combined dollars collected from business PACs. Ideological PACs, meanwhile, play only a minor part in the reelection war chests collected by Democratic incumbents in the House.

Republicans — whether freshmen or incumbents — collect the preponderance of their PAC dollars from business interests. Labor PACs are almost non-existent for newly-elected Republicans, and ideological PACs provide only about half the dollars for freshman Republicans as they do for Democrats. As Republicans take office and seek reelection, their proportion of business dollars rises even higher. The Labor contributions, while still small, overtake ideological donations as the second-leading source of PAC funds for incumbent Republicans.

# Where Newcomers Found the Money . . .

## Freshman Democrats

PAC contributions from organized Labor were the key to success for most freshman Democrats who broke into the House of Representatives in 1990. On average, the new Democratic members received just over $115,000 from Labor PACs. Ideological PACs were another important source of funds for this group. Many of the most promising challengers and open seat candidates drew contributions from "leadership PACs" operated by Democratic members of Congress. Financial interests and lawyers were the other leading sources of funds for freshman Democrats. Most of those dollars came through individual contributions.

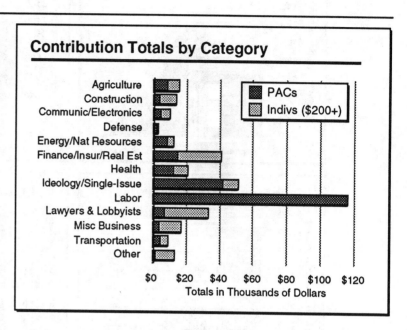

## Freshman Republicans

Newly-elected Republicans had a markedly different contribution profile from their Democratic colleagues. Financial interests and miscellaneous business contributors were the two leading sources of campaign cash for the GOP freshman. Both those groups gave about half their money through PACs and half through large contributions from individuals. The remainder of the Republicans' dollars came from a wide cross-section of business groups.

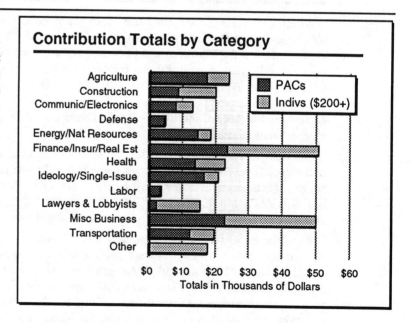

# Where Incumbents Found the Money . . .

## Contribution Totals by Category

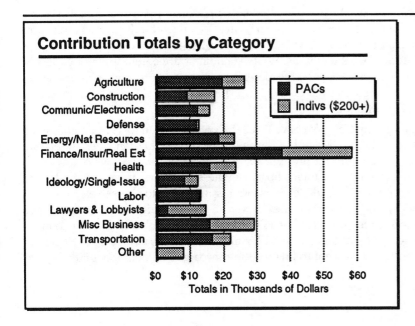

| | |
|---|---|
| ■ PACs | |
| ▨ Indivs ($200+) | |

Agriculture
Construction
Communic/Electronics
Defense
Energy/Nat Resources
Finance/Insur/Real Est
Health
Ideology/Single-Issue
Labor
Lawyers & Lobbyists
Misc Business
Transportation
Other

$0 $10 $20 $30 $40 $50 $60 $70 $80
Totals in Thousands of Dollars

## Incumbent Democrats

Once they've been elected to Congress — and received their committee assignments — Democrats begin to receive contributions from many business groups that rarely give to non-incumbents. Organized labor continues to be an important source of campaign funds, but not nearly as important as it is to freshman Democrats. The finance/insurance/real estate sector is by far the most important source among business groups for incumbent Democrats. On average, other business sectors are roughly equal in importance to Democrats, though the industry patterns to individual members tend to closely parallel their committee assignments. Contributions from ideological PACs — an important source of funds for freshman Democrats — are a relatively minor source for most Democratic incumbents.

## Incumbent Republicans

## Contribution Totals by Category

Agriculture
Construction
Communic/Electronics
Defense
Energy/Nat Resources
Finance/Insur/Real Est
Health
Ideology/Single-Issue
Labor
Lawyers & Lobbyists
Misc Business
Transportation
Other

| | |
|---|---|
| ■ PACs | |
| ▨ Indivs ($200+) | |

$0 $10 $20 $30 $40 $50 $60
Totals in Thousands of Dollars

By a wide margin, the finance/insurance/real estate sector is the leading industry giving campaign funds to incumbent House Republicans. Other important industries include agriculture, energy, health, transportation, and miscellaneous business — though Republican incumbents drew significant funds from all other business sectors as well. Like their Democratic colleagues, most Republican incumbents get only a small proportion of their funds from ideological groups. Their share of Labor PAC dollars, while still small in comparison to Democrats, is significantly higher than that received by Republican freshmen.

# Rules of the Game

The rules that govern the financing of elections can be complicated enough to keep a small army of Washington lawyers perpetually employed. But federal election laws are not so complicated that the average voter can't figure out the basics. Outlined below is an overview of the rules.

## Who Can Contribute and Who Cannot

Any American citizen can contribute funds to candidates for federal office or to political parties. There is only one exception to this broad rule: individuals and owners of sole proprietorships that have contracts with the federal government. (That prohibition does not extend to employees, partners, officers or shareholders of larger businesses with federal contracts — many of whom are active contributors).

Foreign nationals who do not have permanent residence in the United States are prohibited from contributing to *any* political candidates in the U.S. — at the federal, state, or local level.

Cash contributions exceeding an aggregate of $100 are also prohibited, no matter where they come from. And no candidate can accept an anonymous donation of more than $50.

Corporations, labor unions, national banks and federally chartered corporations are also prohibited from contributing to federal campaigns or parties — though they may make unlimited contributions to the parties' "soft money" accounts (see page 16). They may also organize political action committees or "PACs" that enable the employees of the company, or members of the union, to pool their resources and deliver their funds as a bloc. The prohibition against direct corporate giving has been a part of federal law since the passage of the Tillman Act in 1907. The ban was extended to labor unions in 1943.

In recent years, the issue of political action committees operated by foreign-owned corporations has become contentious — particularly since a growing number of American companies have been acquired by Japanese and European investors. The Federal Election Commission has ruled that such companies *may* operate political action committees as long as American citizens are the only contributors to the PAC.

## The Birth of PACs

When Congress acted in 1943 to ban direct contributions from labor unions to federal candidates, organized labor was quick to react. That same year, the first modern "political action committee" was formed by the Congress of Industrial Organization (which later merged with the American Federation of Labor to form the AFL-CIO). The dollars the PAC distributed came not from the union treasury, but from voluntary contributions by its members. While such an arrangement was not explicitly sanctioned by federal law, neither was it prohibited. Over the next 30 years the idea gradually caught on as other labor unions, then corporations and business groups, formed PACs of their own. But many groups held back. PACs were still a loophole in federal election laws — tolerated, but not officially sanctioned.

In 1974, amid the post-Watergate climate of political reform, Congress gave PACs the green light. In its 1974 amendments to the Federal Election Campaign Act, Congress specifically sanctioned the formation of "political committees" to enable employees of corporations, members of labor unions, or members of professional groups, trade associations or any other political group to pool their dollars and give to the candidates of their choice. At the same time, it gave PACs higher contribution limits than individual contributors, and set up the Federal Election Commission (FEC) to oversee elections and to collect and monitor campaign finance reports filed by PACs and candidates. It was an opening of the floodgates. By the end of 1974, 608 political action committees were officially recognized by the FEC. By 1990 that number had grown to more than 4,700. The dollars they pumped into federal elections mushroomed from $12.5 million in 1976 to more than $159 million in 1990. The great majority of those dollars — then and now — went to finance the campaigns of incumbent members of Congress.

# Contribution Limits

Candidates for Congress can spend as much money as they can raise, whether from their own pockets or from those of contributors. No spending limits apply. Contributors to federal campaigns, on the other hand, do face limits in what they can give to a federal candidate or a national political party. The limits were set as part of the 1974 Federal Election Campaign Act, and they are summarized in the chart below:

## Federal Campaign Spending Limits

| | To any candidate or candidate committee | To any national party committee | To any PAC or other political committee | Total |
|---|---|---|---|---|
| Time period | per election* | per calendar year | per calendar year | per calendar year |
| Individual can give... | $1,000 | $20,000 | $5,000 | $25,000 |
| Multicandidate Committee† can give... | $5,000 | $15,000 | $5,000 | No limit |
| Other Political Committee can give... | $1,000 | $20,000 | $5,000 | No limit |

SOURCE: Federal Election Commission

* Primary and general elections count as two separate elections; so this contribution can be effectively doubled during a normal election year in states with primaries.

† Multicandidate committees are those with more than 50 contributors, that have been registered for at least six months, and (with the exception of state party committees) have made contributions to five or more federal candidates.

# Enforcement of the Campaign Laws

Enforcement of the federal campaign laws lies in the hands of the six-member Federal Election Commission in Washington, D.C. Appointed by the president to serve staggered six-year terms, the commission members are traditionally split 3-3 between Republicans and Democrats.

The 3-3 split is also common in many of the commission's votes on rulings that would likely benefit one party over the other. Many analysts and commentators have contended that the institutional paralysis which sometimes results was exactly what the drafters of the Federal Election Campaign Act had in mind — namely, to keep the commission from being too vigilant or activist in its enforcement.

Over the years, the commission has come under considerable attack by critics on both sides of the political fence for its lack of direction in enforcing and interpreting the campaign finance law. While the commissioners have fairly regularly cited candidates and fined their campaigns for relatively minor offenses (and occasionally for serious ones), they have been unable to reach consensus on many larger issues affecting the conduct of federal elections.

One area for which the FEC has received well-deserved praise, however, is in its role as a provider of campaign finance information to the public. The FEC has collected millions of pages of detailed records since 1975 on the financing of federal elections, and citizens curious about the identity of their representatives' financial backers can find a wealth of information in the FEC's files.

# Public Disclosure

By law, every candidate for federal office must file periodic reports with the Federal Election Commission in Washington, D.C., detailing both the income and expenditures of their campaign. Copies of these reports, which are timed to coincide with various high points in the two-year election cycle, must also be filed in the candidate's home state with the state election commission or equivalent agency.

Individual contributors who give an aggregate of $200 or more must be identified by name, address, occupation and employer. All PAC and party contributions, no matter how large or small, must also be itemized.

In addition, PACs themselves must file reports four times a year with the FEC in Washington, detailing both the contributions received by the PAC and the names of candidates and other groups that received the PAC's donations. While PACs are required to file at least quarterly, they may choose to file monthly if they wish — and many of the larger PACs do.

When it compiles the official records of PAC contributions, and records them on its computers, the FEC uses the reports filed by the PACs — *not* those filed by the candidates. Because of this, occasional discrepancies are inevitable between the contributions reported by the candidates and those recorded in the FEC's official records.

# Filing Deadlines

Members of Congress and candidates for Congress must file their FEC reports according to the schedules shown in the following charts. Each report must list the candidate's contributions and expenditures during the reporting period. As the charts show, the schedules vary during election years and off years. In the course of a typical election year, a candidate for Congress may file as many as seven reports. In other years, only two reports are required.

## Election Year Reporting Deadlines

| Reports | Deadline | Period covered |
|---|---|---|
| Pre-election reports | 12 days before primary election | Up to 20 days before the election |
| | 12 days before general election | Up to 20 days before the election |
| Post-general report | 30 days after general election | Up to 20 after the election |
| Quarterly reports | Apr 15 | Jan 1 - Mar 31 |
| | Jul 15 | Apr 1 - Jun 30 |
| | Oct 15 | Jul 1 - Sep 30 |
| | Jan 31 | Oct 1 - Dec 31 of previous year |

NOTE: If two of the above deadlines closely coincide, a single report may be sufficient.

## Non-election Year Reporting Deadlines

| Reports | Deadline | Period covered |
|---|---|---|
| Semi-annual reports | Jul 31 | Jan 1 - Jun 30 |
| | Jan 31 | Jul 1 - Dec 31 of previous year |

# Where to Find a Candidate's Reports

Any member of the public can view current and past campaign spending reports filed by their own representatives in Congress — or any other candidate for federal office. The central repository for these reports is the Public Records office of the Federal Election Commission at 999 E Street NW, Washington, D.C. 20463. The FEC's toll-free phone number is 1-800-424-9530. In the Washington area, the number is 202-219-4140.

The FEC also maintains a number of remote computer terminals around the country, generally in the offices of the secretary of state or the state election commission. As of March 1992, some 24 states were equipped with FEC terminals. Computer printouts of candidate or PAC reports can be ordered either from the FEC in Washington or from these state offices with terminals. A nominal charge is made for the materials, generally calculated on the cost of reproducing each page. One caveat: itemized contribution reports for major campaigns, such as those for the U.S. Senate, can be quite lengthy, even when reduced to computer printouts. Browsing through them (and in some cases even picking them up and carrying them out the door) can be quite an effort.

Federal campaign records are also available on-line to anyone with a computer, a modem, and an interest in obtaining the information. The on-line fee is $25 an hour and new subscribers must first request the service in writing and include a deposit before receiving their password. Among the reports available on-line are full contribution reports for any candidate or group of candidates (such as the congressional delegation from a particular state) and any PAC or groups of PACs. Recent FEC news releases are also available on line.

Copies of the candidates' FEC filings are also available in the candidate's home state. The reports are filed with the secretary of state's office or the state election commission, or whichever other agency in the state monitors elections.

In addition to campaign reports, the FEC also publishes pre-election and post-election reports listing summary statistics on campaign spending and fundraising by federal candidates, as well as a number of informative brochures outlining federal campaign laws and how they apply to candidates, PACs and contributors.

# National Library on Money & Politics

The Federal Election Commission is no longer the only source for campaign finance data. The non-profit, non-partisan National Library on Money & Politics (a group affiliated with the Center for Responsive Politics) takes the raw FEC data and classifies the contributions by the same system of industry and interest group categories used throughout this book.

The Library was established primarily to work with news organizations, academic researchers and others who want to follow the trends and specifics of who's funding federal elections. It can prepare custom reports analyzing the contributions of any member of Congress or other federal candidate. Reports can also be compiled on the spending patterns of a particular company, industry, or interest group.

The Library's computerized databases include FEC data going back several election cycles. It also has access to congressional voting records, so reports can be compiled comparing a member of Congress' voting pattern with his or her contributions.

Standard reports are priced from $5 to $25, depending on their complexity. Custom reports can be done on an hourly fee schedule.

For more information or to place an order for a report, the Library can be reached at 202-857-0318.

# Deciphering the Candidates' FEC Reports

Sifting through a candidate's FEC reports is not always an enlightening experience. Many candidates, instead of entering the full name of a PAC, often enter the PAC's informal acronym. Even if you knew, for example, that the Association of Trial Lawyers of America was the nation's largest PAC representing lawyers, you might not be able to decode the PAC's shorthand name — ATLA — when it appears on a candidate's report.

Making matters worse, there are no conventions to PAC acronyms and no FEC guidelines to ensure that each PAC uses a unique name. In fact, there are many duplications of shortened PAC names. "APAC," for example, is the informal acronym of at least three PACs: The Alltell Corporation PAC, the American Society of Association Executives PAC, and the Armco Employees PAC. Many other duplicates can also be found among the more than 4,700 currently-registered political action committees.

Aside from the acronyms, most PAC names are fairly self-explanatory — at least in naming the organization that sponsors them. There is nothing mysterious, for example, about the Boeing Company PAC or the Mid-America Dairymen PAC. Identification becomes more difficult when the PAC sponsor is less well known and the company's name offers no hint of its line of business. Without consulting a corporate directory on the shelves of the nearest library, for example, one might have difficulty knowing that Malone & Hyde is a major food wholesaler, that the Kaman Corporation is a defense contractor, or that the Summa Corporation runs a Las Vegas hotel and casino.

Many other PACs, particularly ideological or single-issue PACs, have names that can be maddeningly obscure. Few casual observers would guess, for example, that the "Valley Education Fund" is actually the leadership PAC of former Democratic Congressman Tony Coelho of California, or that the "Committee for a Level Playing Field" represents banks that want Congress to allow them to begin offering stock brokerage services.

To assist those wanting to decipher the mysteries of PAC names that appear on candidates' FEC filings, the final section of this book (beginning on page 305) identifies the primary interests of each PAC that gave $50,000 or more in the 1990 election cycle. But new PACs do spring up each election year, so the job of classifying the more obscure ones is a never-ending task.

Individual contributors present a different set of problems. Though candidates are required by law to list the name, address, occupation and employer of each contributor who gives $200 or more, this information is often incomplete. In the process of analyzing individual contributions undertaken for this book, these shortcomings stood out in stark relief. Some typical problems:

- **Missing information.** Federal election law requires that candidates for federal office make their "best effort" to obtain full information on employers and occupations of their contributors, and to report this information on their campaign filings for all contributors giving $200 or more. When formally asked to define what "best effort" actually means, the FEC ruled that it means candidates must ask for the information once. Most candidates are conscientious and do list the information for the great majority of their contributors. A few do not. Yet candidates who habitually omit this information from their filings rarely receive any penalties from the FEC.

- **Incomplete information.** Sometimes the information listed by candidates is so generic that it is impossible to trace the economic interest of the contributor. "Businessman" or "Executive" is one example. "Self-employed" is another. Another commonly used euphemism is to identify contributors only by the term "consultant." The Center's analysis has found that many of these "consultants" — particular those from the Washington, DC area — turn out to be lobbyists.

- **Unemployed spouses and children.** If one were to take at face value the reports filed by candidates, one might come to the conclusion that the single most powerful constituency in America today is that of "homemakers" and "housewives." According to the reports filed by winning candidates for Congress in the 1990 elections, "housewives, homemakers, home managers, *executive* home managers" and various other variations on the theme contributed some $8.4 million — higher than any other listed occupation. In reality, the money that supplied these donations came overwhelmingly not from the "homemaker" but from her (or his) spouse. The same can be said of contributors identified as "students." In the research that went into this book, the Center took great pains to try to identify the spouses (or parents) of unemployed contributors. In many cases this was possible by comparing addresses, dates of contributions, etc. Where the connection with the income-earner was found, the contribution was classified as having the same economic interest as that of the person earning the family income.

# Independent Expenditures

Direct contributions to candidates are not the only outlet for political action committees wishing to influence elections. "Independent expenditures" — funds spent independently by PACs to either support or oppose a candidate — offer another potentially powerful option. Unlike regular PAC gifts to campaigns, which cannot exceed $10,000 for an election cycle, independent expenditures can total any amount at all. They may directly attack or support a candidate by name, but the expenditures (or the advertising they support) cannot be made in conjunction or coordination with the campaign or staff of any candidate. In all, some 110 PACs spent a total of more than $5.1 million on independent expenditures during the 1990 elections. That was a steep drop from the $20.8 million spent during the 1988 campaigns — but it reflects the fact that independent expenditures are most heavily used not at the congressional level, but in the race for President.

The most controversial independent expenditure campaign in 1988 was also the most expensive — the $8.5 million campaign run by the National Security PAC to produce the "Willie Horton" ads attacking Michael Dukakis. A complaint was filed with the Federal Election Commission after the ads appeared, charging they were coordinated with members of the Bush campaign, but the FEC eventually closed its investigation without ruling in the matter.

In the 1990 races, most independent expenditure campaigns were small and localized, giving token amounts in support of local congressional candidates. Only 35 groups gave $10,000 or more and only 11 ran campaigns exceeding $100,000. The chart below lists the chief contributors of independent expenditures in 1990 and the top beneficiaries and targets of their funds.

## Top PACs making Independent Expenditures in 1990

| PAC Name | Total | Top Beneficiaries/Targets | Amount | For/Agn | Office |
|---|---|---|---|---|---|
| National Assn of Realtors | $1,049,585 | Hank Brown (R-Colo) | $186,589 | For | Senate |
| | | J. Bennett Johnston (D-La) | $158,811 | For | Senate |
| | | Robert C. Smith (R-NH) | $141,774 | For | Senate |
| | | Larry E. Craig (R-Idaho) | $109,363 | For | Senate |
| | | Daniel G. Heath (R-Ind) | $105,360 | For | House |
| | | Peter Hoagland (D-Neb) | $95,779 | For | House |
| | | Ben Jones (D-Ga) | $93,516 | For | House |
| | | Jack Buechner (R-Mo) | $91,447 | For | House |
| | | Ileana Ros-Lehtinen (R-Fla) | $66,946 | For | House |
| Auto Dealers & Drivers for Free Trade | $653,915 | Smith, Robert C. (R-NH) | $357,600 | For | Senate |
| | | Rudy Boschwitz (R-Minn) | $202,565 | For | Senate |
| | | J. Bennett Johnston (D-La) | $93,750 | For | Senate |
| National Right to Life PAC | $508,450 | Helms, Jesse (R-NC) | $136,901 | For | Senate |
| | | George Bush | $82,010 | For | Pres |
| Natl Cmte to Preserve Social Security | $402,666 | Harvey B. Gantt (D-NC) | $40,178 | For | Senate |
| | | Tom Harkin (D-Iowa) | $34,808 | For | Senate |
| | | Baron Hill (D-Ind) | $32,795 | For | Senate |
| | | Mark O. Hatfield (R-Ore) | $25,435 | For | Senate |
| Louisiana Coalition | $287,135 | David E. Duke (R-La) | $287,135 | Against | Senate |
| Council for National Defense | $263,328 | Jesse Helms (R-NC) | $72,842 | For | Senate |
| | | Robert K. Dornan (R-Calif) | $29,510 | For | House |
| American Citizens for Political Action | $247,032 | Edward M. Kennedy (D-Mass) | $59,147 | Against | Senate |
| | | George Bush | $30,979 | For | Pres |
| | | Joseph P. Kennedy II (D-Mass) | $28,007 | Against | House |
| National Security PAC | $204,495 | George Bush | $199,529 | For | Pres |
| National Rifle Assn | $173,248 | Jolene Unsoeld (D-Wash) | $46,942 | For | House |
| National Education Assn | $130,000 | Harvey B. Gantt (D-NC) | $100,000 | For | Sen |
| | | Reid Hughes (D-Fla) | $30,000 | For | House |
| Conservative Campaign Fund | $115,409 | Jim Wright (D-Texas)† | $66,042 | Against | House |
| | | Jesse Helms (R-NC) | $47,914 | For | Senate |

† Wright resigned his seat June 30, 1989

# "Soft Money" — The Sky's the Limit

In the eyes of many observers — and many political practitioners who make use of it — the principal loophole in the federal campaign spending law is something that has come to be called "soft money." In the broadest sense, soft money encompasses any contributions not regulated by federal election laws. The biggest single pockets of soft money are contributions made to state and local party organizations, and to the national parties when earmarked for their local affiliates. Under the terms of the federal campaign laws, these contributions are exempted from the limitations that apply to other contributions. Their use, however, is restricted.

Technically, soft money contributions may only be used to support state and local political activities, such as voter registration, get-out-the-vote drives, and the distribution of voter materials such as bumper stickers, campaign buttons and yard signs. The funds can also be used to finance political activities that jointly benefit state, local and federal candidates.

In practice, soft money funds have seeped into federal races in a big way, and have become an important means of supporting the parties' candidates for president and Congress — particularly in key battleground states. During the 1988 presidential campaign, the Democratic and Republican parties are estimated to have raised between $25 million and $50 million each in soft money contributions — though the exact figures will never be known (except to the parties) since there were no requirements that the donations be publicly disclosed. Under new rules which took effect Jan. 1, 1991, soft money contributions to the national parties are finally being reported to the Federal Election Commission.

Even though it must now be reported, soft money can still be given with virtually no strings attached. This offers four main benefits to soft money contributors and recipients:

- **Soft money is not subject to any contribution limits.** Contributions to candidates or federal party committees are subject to specific limits (outlined in the chart on page 11). Soft money contributions can be made for any amount at all. In 1987, for example, a $1 million soft money contribution was given to the Democratic Party by Joan Kroc, heiress to the McDonald's Hamburger fortune.

- **Soft money contributions can be made by anyone — including groups prohibited from making contributions to federal candidates or parties.** In federal campaigns, corporations and labor unions are explicitly prohibited from making direct contributions to federal candidates, federal parties, or federal PACs. Their soft money contributions are subject only to the restrictions passed by the legislatures in the individual states where the contributions are made. Many states currently allow corporate and labor union contributions.

- **Soft money offers an extra means of political giving for individuals who've already given the maximum to candidates and federal parties.** Under the federal election laws, individual contributors are limited to an annual maximum of $25,000 in contributions to all candidates, PACs and national parties. Once they've "maxed out" they can give no more — except in soft money. Using this device, wealthy contributors, often with the encouragement of the national parties, have been able to give substantially more than the nominal limit.

- **Soft money offers a way for corporations, unions and wealthy contributors to support presidential candidates in the fall elections.** Since 1974, when Congress authorized the $1 checkoff on federal income tax returns, presidential elections have been publicly financed. While presidential candidates can (and do) raise millions during the primary election battles for the nomination, once the parties have officially nominated their candidate at their party conventions, no more private contributions are allowed. Because of the soft money loophole, however, the period during the fall campaign has turned into the most intensive period of political fundraising in American politics. In 1988 the Republicans even organized an exclusive club — called "Team 100" — made up of soft money contributors who gave $100,000 or more. Several Team 100 members were later appointed ambassadors to foreign nations after the Bush administration took office. The Democrats, not to be outdone, created a top-dollar group of their own in 1988. For the 1992 elections, the Democrats have raised the ante with a new circle of "Managing Trustees." Admission to this blue-chip group requires giving or raising at least $200,000 in soft money.

# Top Soft Money Contributors in 1989-90*

| Name | City | Amount | To Dems | To Repubs |
|---|---|---|---|---|
| Assn of Trial Lawyers of America | Washington, DC | $540,000 | $540,000 | $0 |
| United Auto Workers | Detroit, Mich. | $325,700 | $325,700 | $0 |
| Amer Fedn of State/County/Munic Employees | Washington, DC | $322,550 | $322,550 | $0 |
| Atlantic Richfield Co | Los Angeles, Calif. | $308,360 | $12,000 | $296,360 |
| National Education Assn | Washington, DC | $290,000 | $285,000 | $5,000 |
| United Steelworkers of America | Pittsburg, Pa. | $283,518 | $283,518 | $0 |
| Mary C. Bingham | Louisville, Ky. | $281,000 | $281,000 | $0 |
| RJR Nabisco | Atlanta, Ga. | $201,755 | $42,825 | $158,930 |
| American Federation of Teachers | Washington, DC | $170,000 | $170,000 | $0 |
| Irvine Co | Newport Beach, Calif. | $165,100 | $15,000 | $150,100 |
| AFL-CIO | Washington, DC | $163,734 | $163,734 | $0 |
| Roy M. Huffington | Houston, Tex. | $151,000 | $0 | $151,000 |
| American Financial Corp | Cincinnati, Ohio | $150,460 | $0 | $150,460 |
| Occidental Petroleum | Los Angeles, Calif. | $149,780 | $50,000 | $99,780 |
| Machinists/Aerospace Workers Union | Washington, DC | $147,000 | $147,000 | $0 |
| Thomas A. Dennis | Chicago, Ill. | $137,000 | $137,000 | $0 |
| Philip Morris | New York, N.Y. | $134,650 | $43,150 | $91,500 |
| Frederick W. Field | Los Angles, Calif. | $131,400 | $131,400 | $0 |
| Mark B. Dayton | Minneapolis, Minn. | $131,000 | $131,000 | $0 |
| Joseph J. Bogdanovich | Rolling Hills, Calif. | $130,000 | $0 | $130,000 |
| Teamsters Union | Washington, DC | $125,350 | $104,850 | $20,500 |
| Gary Winnick | Beverly Hills, Calif. | $125,000 | $0 | $125,000 |
| Auto Dealers & Drivers for Free Trade | Jamaica, N.Y. | $120,000 | $50,000 | $70,000 |
| Sheet Metal Workers | Washington, DC | $114,300 | $114,300 | $0 |
| Service Employees Intl Union | Chicago, Ill. | $112,500 | $112,500 | $0 |
| Albert B. Glickman | Beverly Hills, Calif. | $110,000 | $0 | $110,000 |
| Archer-Daniels-Midland | Decatur, Ill. | $108,500 | $58,500 | $50,000 |
| Bruce D. Benson | Golden, Colo. | $107,000 | $0 | $107,000 |
| Intl Brotherhood of Electrical Workers | Washington, DC | $106,250 | $105,250 | $1,000 |
| Agenda for the 90s | San Francisco, Calif. | $106,000 | $106,000 | $0 |
| Henley Group | Hampton, N.H. | $106,000 | $50,000 | $56,000 |
| Monte Friedkin | Boca Raton, Fla. | $105,000 | $105,000 | $0 |
| Richard J. Dennis | Chicago, Ill. | $105,000 | $105,000 | $0 |
| Lawyers Involved for Texas | Austin, Tex. | $104,832 | $104,832 | $0 |
| Sunrise Co | Palm Desert, Calif. | $102,374 | $0 | $102,374 |
| Milton Petrie | Secaucus, N.J. | $102,010 | $100,000 | $2,010 |
| Trammell Crow | Dallas, Tex. | $101,150 | $0 | $101,150 |
| Growth Industries Inc | Grandview, Mo. | $100,300 | $0 | $100,300 |
| Alexander P. Papamarkou | New York, N.Y. | $100,000 | $0 | $100,000 |
| Beatrice Corp | Chicago, Ill. | $100,000 | $0 | $100,000 |
| Bertram R. Firestone | Waterford, Va. | $100,000 | $0 | $100,000 |
| Hibbard Brown & Co | New York, N.Y. | $100,000 | $0 | $100,000 |
| James F. Keenan | Aiken, S.C. | $100,000 | $0 | $100,000 |
| James W. Walter | Tampa, Fla. | $100,000 | $0 | $100,000 |
| Jerome V. Ansel | New York, N.Y. | $100,000 | $0 | $100,000 |
| John W. Harris | Charlotte, N.C. | $100,000 | $0 | $100,000 |
| Moey Segal | Las Vegas, Nev. | $100,000 | $0 | $100,000 |
| Monty Hundley | New York, N.Y. | $100,000 | $0 | $100,000 |
| Mr. & Mrs. Bill Cosby | Santa Monica, Calif. | $100,000 | $100,000 | $0 |
| Robert I. MacDonnell | Hillsborough, Calif. | $100,000 | $0 | $100,000 |
| Salem Leasing Corp | Winston Salem, N.C. | $100,000 | $0 | $100,000 |
| Sonic Communications | Walnut Creek, Calif. | $100,000 | $0 | $100,000 |

* This list was compiled by the Center for Responsive Politics and includes contributions made to the Democratic and Republican National Committees, as well as to state parties in nine states that had key congressional races in the 1990 elections. The states included Colorado, Hawaii, Illinois, Iowa, Kentucky, Minnesota, North Carolina, Oregon and Texas.

# The Rising Tide of PACs

Political action committees were born in the 1940s out of a perceived political necessity. When labor unions were prohibited from spending union treasury funds to contribute to federal candidates, they invented the idea of pooling donations from their members and presenting *that* money to the candidates instead. The idea appealed not only to labor unions, but to business and ideological groups as well, though the lack of a formal federal sanction for PACs kept many groups from setting up their own committees. When Congress passed the 1974 amendments to the Federal Election Campaign Act, officially sanctioning the concept of "political committees," the great PAC rush began. In recent years, the number of political action committees has stabilized, and even begun to decline. Total PAC dollars have also stabilized, though the amounts going to incumbents — particularly in the House of Representatives — continues to rise with each new election.

Nearly 4,700 political action committees were officially registered at the close of the 1990 election year. Of those, just over 3,000 actually contributed funds to federal candidates. Many of those PACs were small-scale operations, sponsored by small businesses, political clubs, or labor union locals, and contributed only to candidates in their own state or region. Only one out of four of the registered PACs gave $20,000 or more to federal candidates, but those that did accounted for over 93 percent of all PAC giving. The chart below shows the relative distribution of small, medium and large sized PACs, and their respective spending power in the 1990 elections.

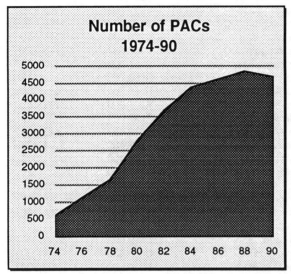

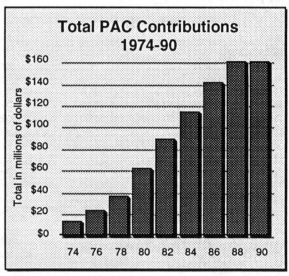

## Biggest PACs deliver the Biggest Punch

| This many PACs... | Gave this much money... | for this total impact... |
|---|---|---|
| 1636 | $0 | |
| 1598 | Less than $10,000 | |
| 415 | $10,000-$19,999 | |
| 443 | $20,000-$49,999 | |
| 255 | $50,000-$99,999 | |
| 352 | $100,000 or more | |

As is evident from this chart, the real power of PACs lies not in their numbers, but in the dollars they can deliver. In 1990, as in every year since PACs emerged as an important force in congressional politics, a comparatively small number of large PACs delivered the biggest share of the money. Less than one-tenth of the total PAC community provided more than two-thirds of all the dollars in the 1989-90 election cycle. On the other side of the spectrum, over 1,600 PACs — more than a third of all registered political action committees — made no contributions at all to congressional candidates.

# With outstretched hands . . .

The financial clout of PACs is not something that has been forced upon members of Congress over their objections. Modern campaign techniques, centered around 30-second TV spots and highly targeted direct mail appeals, have prompted many incumbents to hire campaign consultants, pollsters, media advisors, fund-raisers and a retinue of specialists who are the behind-the-scenes operatives of today's high-tech campaigns. The pressures of raising the money it takes to pay for them all have forced nearly every incumbent to spend an increasing amount of time appealing to PACs and other large contributors for funds. Because of their higher contribution limits ($5,000 per election, versus $1,000 per election for individuals), PACs offer the most convenient means of raising large sums of campaign cash quickly.

While many incumbents faced only token opposition in the 1990 elections, many others had cause to use those funds to fend off aggressive challengers. The following charts show the members of Congress who relied the most heavily — and the least — on contributions from political action committees in the 1990 elections.

## Top Recipients of PAC Contributions

### House Members (1989-90)

| Name | PAC Rcpts | Total Rcpts |
|------|-----------|-------------|
| Richard A. Gephardt (D-Mo) | $852,848 | $1,647,415 |
| David E. Bonior (D-Mich) | $686,854 | $1,189,127 |
| Jill L. Long (D-Ind) | $669,084 | $1,159,045 |
| John D. Dingell (D-Mich) | $624,276 | $843,579 |
| Peter Hoagland (D-Neb) | $623,459 | $945,952 |
| Jolene Unsoeld (D-Wash) | $593,706 | $1,297,700 |
| Robert T. Matsui (D-Calif) | $571,737 | $1,207,843 |
| Pete Geren (D-Texas) | $568,658 | $1,434,684 |
| Butler Derrick (D-SC) | $534,694 | $849,338 |
| Wayne Owens (D-Utah) | $517,716 | $1,014,489 |

### Senate Members (1985-90)

| Name | PAC Rcpts | Total Rcpts |
|------|-----------|-------------|
| Lloyd Bentsen (D-Texas) | $2,488,545 | $9,550,410 |
| Slade Gorton (R-Wash) | $2,286,752 | $6,328,567 |
| Dave Durenberger (R-Minn) | $1,892,868 | $6,761,094 |
| Arlen Specter (R-Pa) | $1,880,933 | $9,032,615 |
| Phil Gramm (R-Texas) | $1,812,176 | $16,268,341 |
| Tom Harkin (D-Iowa) | $1,748,081 | $5,715,839 |
| Tom Daschle (D-SD) | $1,720,159 | $4,802,957 |
| Paul Simon (D-Ill) | $1,714,221 | $9,643,884 |
| Frank Lautenberg (D-NJ) | $1,703,442 | $8,337,711 |
| Steve Symms (R-Idaho) | $1,660,761 | $3,929,597 |

## Heaviest Reliance on PAC Dollars

### House Members (1989-90)

| Name | PAC Pct |
|------|---------|
| William J. Coyne (D-Pa) | 89.3% |
| Bernard J. Dwyer (D-NJ) | 86.2% |
| Mary Rose Oakar (D-Ohio) | 85.6% |
| Morris K. Udall (D-Ariz) | 85.4% |
| Jim McDermott (D-Wash) | 84.3% |
| Joel Hefley (R-Colo) | 83.3% |
| Joseph M. Gaydos (D-Pa) | 82.7% |
| Joe Kolter (D-Pa) | 81.2% |
| William L. Clay (D-Mo) | 80.0% |
| Carl C. Perkins (D-Ky) | 78.7% |

### Senate Members (1985-90)

| Candname | PACPct |
|----------|--------|
| James M. Jeffords (R-Vt) | 65.2% |
| Robert C. Byrd (D-WVa) | 63.0% |
| Malcolm Wallop (R-Wyo) | 60.9% |
| Quentin N. Burdick (D-ND) | 59.8% |
| Ted Stevens (R-Alaska) | 57.0% |
| Jim Exon (D-Neb) | 56.9% |
| Kent Conrad (D-ND) | 56.4% |
| Jake Garn (R-Utah) | 56.2% |
| Max Baucus (D-Mont) | 54.0% |
| Wendell H. Ford (D-Ky) | 53.7% |

Nine House members drew 80 percent or more of their 1990 campaign funds from PAC contributions. All but one were Democrats. Among incumbent senators, only 10 — six Democrats and four Republicans — relied on PACs for more than half their contributions. Both patterns are reflective of overall trends. Democrats are more dependent on PACs than Republicans, and House members on average received nearly twice as high a proportion of PAC dollars as senators.

| House Members | Total Receipts |
|---------------|----------------|
| Bill Archer (R-Texas) | $241,863 |
| Anthony C. Beilenson (D-Calif) | $231,386 |
| Philip M. Crane (R-Ill) | $178,141 |
| Andrew Jacobs Jr. (D-Ind) | $28,712 |
| Jim Leach (R-Iowa) | $115,051 |
| William H. Natcher (D-Ky) | $6,768 |
| Ralph Regula (R-Ohio) | $110,331 |
| Mike Synar (D-Okla) | $622,454 |
| *Senators* | Total Receipts |
| David L. Boren (D-Okla) | $1,716,590 |
| John Kerry (D-Mass) | $8,041,413 |
| Herb Kohl (D-Wis) | $8,035,208 |

## . . . And Eleven Members Who Said "No"

Eight House incumbents reported taking no PAC funds in the 1990 elections. They were joined by Senators David Boren and John Kerry, who also ran in 1990, and Senator Herb Kohl, who ran in 1988. In nearly all those cases, a handful of individual PACs did report making contributions to the members, but the totals in most cases were small.

Refusing PAC funds does not necessarily mean members refused all money from contributors with a direct interest in legislation. Sen. Boren, for example, got $177,000 from oil and gas interests, while Sen. Kerry received more than $570,000 from lawyers and lobbyists.

# The Patterns in PAC Contributions

Pragmatism — not partisanship and not political philosophy — appears to be the guiding principle behind many PAC contributions to congressional candidates, at least in the world of business PACs. Of the 1,050 PACs that gave $20,000 or more in the 1990 elections, 95 percent gave to members of both parties. About one third of those top-spending PACs — nearly all of them within the business community — split their dollars fairly evenly between Democrats and Republicans, giving no more than 60 percent of their money to either side. Ideological and labor PACs were far more likely to concentrate their funds with candidates of a single political party, as seen in the chart below.

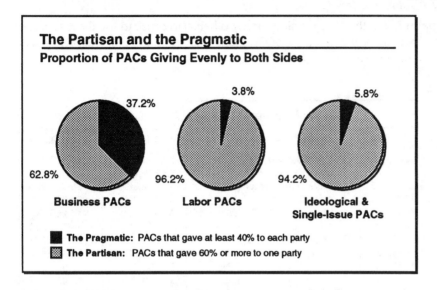

## The Big Three Sectors:
## Business, Labor & Ideological/Single-Issue

While it is certainly possible to learn something about PAC behavior by looking at the overall patterns of PACs, it can be far more revealing to examine the many different segments of the PAC community one by one. It quickly becomes apparent that different groups of PACs behave differently. Labor and ideological PACs, for instance, distribute their money in a quite a different pattern from business PACs — as the charts on this page show.

Business PACs gave almost exactly the same amount to Democrats as Republicans. Ideological PACs favored Democrats two-to-one. And labor PACs, long the stalwarts of the Democratic Party, favored. the parties candidates by a ratio of nearly ten-to-one. when handing out their contributions.

The overwhelming proportion of labor contributions to Democratic candidates tips the scale in favor of that party in overall PAC contributions, even though business PACs as a group gave nearly three times as much as labor PACs, and nearly twice as much as labor and ideological PACs combined. (See the chart on the facing page).

Within these three main categories of PACs many other patterns can be found. The rest of the book explores their differences and similarities in detail.

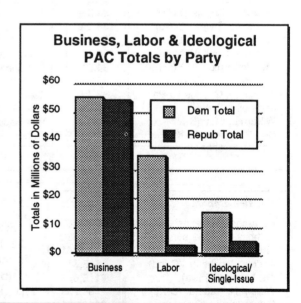

| | Total | To Dems | To Repubs | Dem Pct | Repub Pct |
|---|---|---|---|---|---|
| Business | $108,187,654 | $54,708,726 | $53,476,943 | 50.6% | 49.4% |
| Labor | $36,799,438 | $33,856,234 | $2,882,497 | 92.0% | 7.8% |
| Ideology | $14,329,179 | $9,765,830 | $4,544,699 | 68.2% | 31.7% |
| Total | $159,316,271 | $98,330,790 | $60,904,139 | 61.7% | 38.2% |

# The World of PACs from Three Different Angles

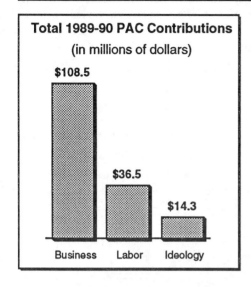

**Total 1989-90 PAC Contributions**

(in millions of dollars)

$108.5

$36.5

$14.3

Business    Labor    Ideology

The dollar power of business PACs can be clearly seen in the chart at left. With $108.5 million in contributions to federal candidates in the 1990 election cycle, PACs representing every industry from car dealers to morticians sought to help their political friends and win their favor. Compared to labor and ideological/single-issue PACs, their dollar power was overwhelming.

A different story emerges when you turn the chart on its ear and break apart the business PACs into their individual sectors. No business sector comes close to offering either party the dollars that labor PACs produce for Democrats. While business PACs were giving relatively equal amounts to members of both parties, labor put 92 percent of its PAC dollars into Democratic campaigns. Even ideological and single-issue PACs rank high compared with the many diverse components of business PACs.

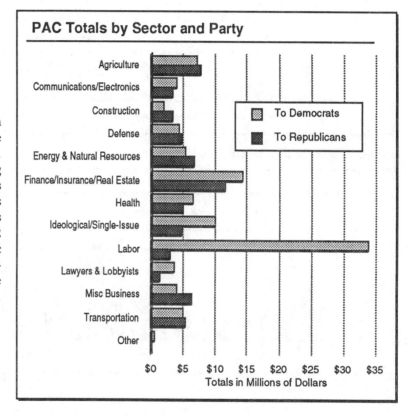

**PAC Totals by Sector and Party**

Agriculture
Communications/Electronics
Construction
Defense
Energy & Natural Resources
Finance/Insurance/Real Estate
Health
Ideological/Single-Issue
Labor
Lawyers & Lobbyists
Misc Business
Transportation
Other

☐ To Democrats
■ To Republicans

$0    $5    $10    $15    $20    $25    $30    $35
Totals in Millions of Dollars

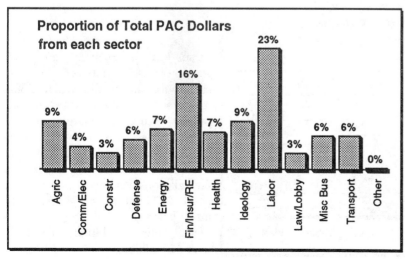

**Proportion of Total PAC Dollars from each sector**

9%    4%    3%    6%    7%    16%    7%    9%    23%    3%    6%    6%    0%

Agric  Comm/Elec  Constr  Defense  Energy  Fin/Insur/RE  Health  Ideology  Labor  Law/Lobby  Misc Bus  Transport  Other

After labor, the financial sector was the biggest PAC contributor to congressional campaigns, supplying 18 percent of all PAC dollars given in the 1990 elections. Banks, investment firms, insurance companies and Realtors combined to make it the biggest segment by far within the community of business PACs. What the charts on these pages don't show (but what can be seen in the pages that follow) is that PACs are only one source of campaign cash for members of Congress. When large individual contributions are counted as well the picture changes again. Financial interests move to the top, lawyers rise to financial prominence from almost nowhere, and the dollars from organized labor are buried under an avalanche of dollars from business interests.

# PACs and Individual Contributions Compared

The charts below illustrate the similarities and contrasts in spending patterns between individual contributors and PACs. Two sectors in particular are strikingly different — organized labor and lawyers and lobbyists. Nearly all the Labor dollars are delivered through political action committees. Looking only at PAC contributions therefore strongly overstates the political punch of labor unions. The charts at the bottom of the page underline this even more.

Lawyers and lobbyists, on the other hand, are dramatically undercounted when looking only at PACs. Some 75 percent of the legal community's contributions come from individuals, not PACs.

## Individual Contributions by Sector

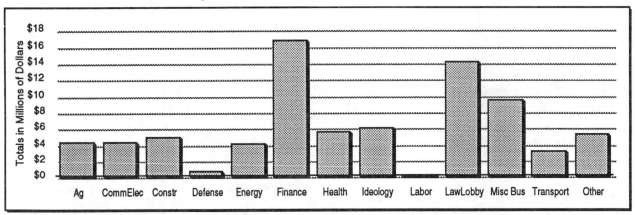

## PAC Contributions by Sector

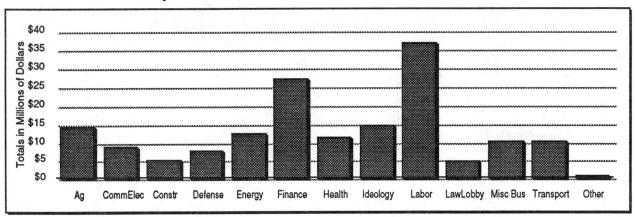

## From PACs

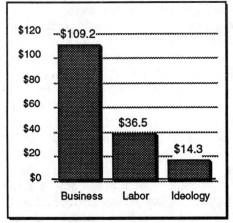

## From Individuals

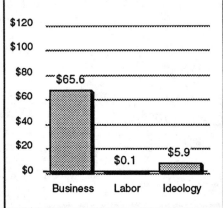

Comparing the individual dollars versus PAC dollars in the three large sectors of business, labor and ideological groups, shows the overall dominance of the business sector. Among political action committee contributions, business outspends labor about three-to-one. In individual contributions, the ratio is considerably higher. Overall, business contributors gave nearly $175 million in 1989-90. Organized labor gave $36.6 million. Ideological groups' combined total was just over $20 million.

## Where the Individual Dollars* Came From: Top Metro Areas

Totals in Millions of Dollars

| Metro Area | Total |
|---|---|
| New York | $25.8 |
| Washington | $19.3 |
| Los Angeles | $17.4 |
| Chicago | $10.5 |
| Boston | $8.4 |
| Houston | $7.2 |
| Philadelphia | $6.8 |
| Dallas | $5.8 |
| San Francisco | $5.3 |
| Detroit | $4.8 |
| Miami | $4.3 |
| Newark/Northern NJ | $4.2 |
| Anaheim, Calif | $3.8 |
| Minneapolis | $3.8 |
| Atlanta | $3.7 |
| San Diego | $3.6 |
| Bridgeport/Fairfield, Conn | $3.6 |
| St. Louis | $3.4 |
| Denver | $3.0 |
| West Palm Beach | $2.6 |

The top 20 metro areas providing campaign cash to candidates, parties and PACs in the 1990 election roughly parallels the population of the nation's largest cities. The one exception is Washington, DC, which — not surprisingly — is second only to New York as a center for political fundraising.

* Contributions of $200 and above

## Where the PAC Dollars Came From: Top Metro Areas

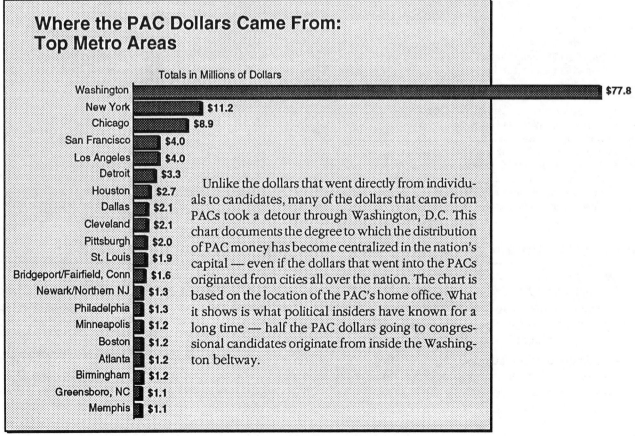

Totals in Millions of Dollars

| Metro Area | Total |
|---|---|
| Washington | $77.8 |
| New York | $11.2 |
| Chicago | $8.9 |
| San Francisco | $4.0 |
| Los Angeles | $4.0 |
| Detroit | $3.3 |
| Houston | $2.7 |
| Dallas | $2.1 |
| Cleveland | $2.1 |
| Pittsburgh | $2.0 |
| St. Louis | $1.9 |
| Bridgeport/Fairfield, Conn | $1.6 |
| Newark/Northern NJ | $1.3 |
| Philadelphia | $1.3 |
| Minneapolis | $1.2 |
| Boston | $1.2 |
| Atlanta | $1.2 |
| Birmingham | $1.2 |
| Greensboro, NC | $1.1 |
| Memphis | $1.1 |

Unlike the dollars that went directly from individuals to candidates, many of the dollars that came from PACs took a detour through Washington, D.C. This chart documents the degree to which the distribution of PAC money has become centralized in the nation's capital — even if the dollars that went into the PACs originated from cities all over the nation. The chart is based on the location of the PAC's home office. What it shows is what political insiders have known for a long time — half the PAC dollars going to congressional candidates originate from inside the Washington beltway.

# Serious Money: The Top 100 Contributors

| Rank | Contributor | Total | PAC Pct | Dem Pct | Rep Pct | Principal Category |
|---|---|---|---|---|---|---|
| 1 | National Assn of Realtors | $3,094,228 | 100% | 56% | 44% | Real Estate |
| 2 | American Medical Assn | $2,647,981 | 100% | 49% | 51% | Doctors |
| 3 | Teamsters Union | $2,438,184 | 99%+ | 92% | 8% | Teamsters |
| 4 | National Education Assn | $2,334,715 | 99%+ | 93% | 7% | Teachers Unions |
| 5 | United Auto Workers | $1,801,772 | 99%+ | 99% | 1% | Manufacturing Unions |
| 6 | Letter Carriers Union | $1,755,478 | 99%+ | 86% | 14% | Postal Unions |
| 7 | American Fedn of State/County/Munic Employees | $1,549,720 | 99%+ | 98% | 2% | Local Govt Unions |
| 8 | National Assn of Retired Federal Employees | $1,545,122 | 100% | 76% | 24% | Fedl Worker Unions |
| 9 | Assn of Trial Lawyers of America | $1,539,550 | 100% | 87% | 13% | Lawyers |
| 10 | Carpenters Union | $1,526,534 | 99%+ | 96% | 4% | Constr Unions |
| 11 | National Assn of Life Underwriters | $1,487,800 | 100% | 51% | 49% | Life Insurance |
| 12 | Machinists/Aerospace Workers Union | $1,487,495 | 99%+ | 98% | 1% | Manufacturing Unions |
| 13 | AT&T | $1,477,200 | 98% | 57% | 43% | Long Distance |
| 14 | American Bankers Assn | $1,473,061 | 100% | 55% | 45% | Commercial Banks |
| 15 | National Assn of Home Builders | $1,362,550 | 99%+ | 48% | 52% | Resid Construction |
| 16 | Laborers Union | $1,359,119 | 99%+ | 92% | 8% | Constr Unions |
| 17 | National Auto Dealers Assn | $1,313,900 | 100% | 38% | 62% | Auto Dealers |
| 18 | Intl Brotherhood of Electrical Workers | $1,257,920 | 99%+ | 97% | 2% | Communication Unions |
| 19 | Air Line Pilots Assn | $1,167,797 | 100% | 81% | 19% | Air Transport Unions |
| 20 | American Institute of CPA's | $1,089,294 | 99%+ | 56% | 44% | Accountants |
| 21 | AFL-CIO | $1,075,142 | 99%+ | 97% | 2% | Manufacturing Unions |
| 22 | Marine Engineers Union | $1,066,125 | 100% | 62% | 38% | Sea Transport Unions |
| 23 | American Federation of Teachers | $1,043,616 | 99%+ | 97% | 3% | Teachers Unions |
| 24 | American Postal Workers Union | $976,403 | 100% | 92% | 8% | Postal Unions |
| 25 | American Academy of Ophthalmology | $961,411 | 100% | 52% | 48% | Eye Doctors |
| 26 | Seafarers International Union | $955,796 | 99%+ | 85% | 15% | Sea Transport Unions |
| 27 | National PAC | $953,500 | 100% | 61% | 39% | Pro-Israel |
| 28 | Food & Commercial Workers Union | $945,281 | 100% | 98% | 2% | Food Svc Unions |
| 29 | National Cmte to Preserve Social Security | $914,052 | 99%+ | 91% | 9% | Elderly/Soc Security |
| 30 | United Steelworkers | $897,675 | 100% | 100% | 0% | Manufacturing Unions |
| 31 | Operating Engineers Union | $881,809 | 99% | 91% | 8% | Constr Unions |
| 32 | American Dental Assn | $824,578 | 100% | 54% | 46% | Dentists |
| 33 | RJR Nabisco | $823,337 | 98% | 50% | 50% | Tobacco |
| 34 | Communications Workers of America | $807,737 | 100% | 99% | 0% | Communication Unions |
| 35 | Associated Milk Producers | $769,800 | 100% | 67% | 33% | Dairy |
| 36 | Federal Express Corp | $765,225 | 99% | 63% | 37% | Express Delivery |
| 37 | National Rifle Assn | $749,493 | 100% | 39% | 61% | Pro-Gun Control |
| 38 | Plumbers/Pipefitters Union | $740,750 | 100% | 93% | 7% | Constr Unions |
| 39 | United Transportation Union | $710,350 | 99%+ | 92% | 8% | Railroad Unions |
| 40 | BellSouth | $699,974 | 95% | 51% | 49% | Phone Utilites |
| 41 | American Council of Life Insurance | $692,743 | 99%+ | 58% | 42% | Life Insurance |
| 42 | Independent Insurance Agents of America | $676,335 | 100% | 58% | 42% | Insurance |
| 43 | Sheet Metal Workers Union | $673,058 | 100% | 98% | 1% | Constr Unions |
| 44 | United Parcel Service | $659,732 | 99%+ | 60% | 40% | Express Delivery |
| 45 | ACRE (Action Cmte for Rural Electrification) | $654,769 | 100% | 69% | 31% | Rural Electric |
| 46 | Associated General Contractors | $654,194 | 99% | 22% | 78% | Heavy Construction |
| 47 | General Motors | $650,056 | 95% | 45% | 55% | Auto Manufacturers |
| 48 | Auto Dealers & Drivers for Free Trade | $644,450 | 100% | 33% | 67% | Japanese Auto Dlrs |
| 49 | National Beer Wholesalers Assn | $633,150 | 100% | 57% | 43% | Liquor Wholesalers |
| 50 | Philip Morris | $623,411 | 97% | 53% | 47% | Tobacco/Food Prod |

## Labor PACs, Financial Interests Dominate Top 100 Contributor List

These 100 corporations, labor unions, trade associations, professional societies and assorted interest groups were the top contributors in the 1990 elections. Together, they gave a combined $79.2 million to congressional candidates. The total includes some $77 million in PAC contributions — nearly half the total given by all PACs in the 1989-90 election cycle. Nearly all the top contributors gave the bulk of their funds through PACs. Only three — Time Warner, Goldman, Sachs and Salomon Brothers — gave more than half their funds through contributions from individuals.

Labor unions were the leading sector, accounting for 28 positions in the Top 100 and seven in the Top 10. In all, the leading unions gave over $31 million in direct contributions to candidates — almost all of it delivered through political action committees. The figure is particularly remarkable given that all labor PACs combined gave just $36.6 million.

| Rank | Contributor | Total | PAC Pct | Dem Pct | Rep Pct | Principal Category |
|------|-------------|-------|---------|---------|---------|-------------------|
| 51 | National Cmte for an Effective Congress | $598,575 | 100% | 100% | 0% | Dem/Liberal |
| 52 | National Restaurant Assn | $582,492 | 100% | 20% | 80% | Restaurants |
| 53 | National Cable Television Assn | $574,475 | 99% | 63% | 37% | Cable TV |
| 54 | Union Pacific Corp | $552,164 | 93% | 42% | 58% | Railroads |
| 55 | Aircraft Owners & Pilots Assn | $513,900 | 100% | 49% | 51% | General Aviation |
| 56 | Amalgamated Transit Union | $512,630 | 100% | 95% | 5% | Misc Transport Union |
| 57 | Credit Union National Assn | $512,098 | 100% | 57% | 43% | Credit Unions |
| 58 | American Hospital Assn | $506,639 | 99%+ | 68% | 32% | Hospitals |
| 59 | Mid-America Dairymen | $485,950 | 100% | 71% | 29% | Dairy |
| 60 | Human Rights Campaign Fund | $479,371 | 99% | 84% | 16% | Gay/Lesbian |
| 61 | Chicago Mercantile Exchange | $475,875 | 97% | 66% | 34% | Commodity Investment |
| 62 | General Electric | $473,142 | 82% | 61% | 39% | Aerospace/Nuclear |
| 63 | Dow Chemical | $468,225 | 69% | 12% | 88% | Chemicals |
| 64 | Barnett Banks of Florida | $466,250 | 99% | 44% | 56% | Commercial Banks |
| 65 | Goldman, Sachs & Co | $449,650 | 38% | 74% | 26% | Investmtent Banking |
| 66 | American Family Corp | $447,968 | 96% | 54% | 46% | Health Insurance |
| 67 | Waste Management Inc | $434,962 | 90% | 58% | 42% | Waste Mgmt |
| 68 | National Rural Letter Carriers Assn | $430,875 | 100% | 87% | 13% | Postal Unions |
| 69 | Lockheed Corp | $428,409 | 99% | 42% | 58% | Air Defense |
| 70 | Ford Motor Co | $425,675 | 87% | 51% | 49% | Auto Manufacturers |
| 71 | Northrop Corp | $421,463 | 98% | 37% | 63% | Air Defense |
| 72 | American Express | $421,064 | 55% | 71% | 29% | Stock Investment |
| 73 | Ironworkers Union | $419,999 | 100% | 96% | 4% | Constr Unions |
| 74 | GTE Corp | $413,425 | 99% | 49% | 51% | Phone Utilites |
| 75 | JP Morgan & Co | $412,925 | 98% | 55% | 45% | Commercial Banks |
| 76 | Citicorp | $412,178 | 93% | 60% | 40% | Commercial Banks |
| 77 | Sierra Club | $410,210 | 99%+ | 91% | 9% | Environment Policy |
| 78 | American Crystal Sugar Corp | $408,125 | 100% | 63% | 37% | Sugar |
| 79 | McDonnell Douglas | $404,300 | 92% | 52% | 48% | Air Defense |
| 80 | Metropolitan Life | $402,482 | 92% | 65% | 35% | Insurance |
| 81 | Salomon Brothers | $394,925 | 39% | 48% | 52% | Stock Investment |
| 82 | Textron Inc | $390,625 | 96% | 57% | 43% | Air Defense |
| 83 | Akin, Gump, Hauer & Feld | $389,400 | 69% | 79% | 21% | Lawyers |
| 84 | US League of Savings Assns | $388,418 | 100% | 59% | 41% | Savings & Loans |
| 85 | Time Warner | $388,075 | 31% | 91% | 9% | Broadcast/Movies |
| 86 | Chicago Board of Trade | $388,011 | 96% | 69% | 31% | Commodity Investment |
| 87 | National Abortion Rights Action League | $385,495 | 99%+ | 89% | 11% | Pro-Choice |
| 88 | Martin Marietta Corp | $383,610 | 99% | 46% | 54% | Air Defense |
| 89 | General Dynamics | $378,279 | 98% | 58% | 42% | Air Defense |
| 90 | Transportation Communication Intl Union | $377,401 | 100% | 97% | 3% | Misc Transport Union |
| 91 | Food Marketing Institute | $376,572 | 100% | 35% | 65% | Food Stores |
| 92 | Rockwell International | $375,085 | 97% | 38% | 62% | Air Defense |
| 93 | Burlington Northern | $371,246 | 88% | 49% | 51% | Railroads |
| 94 | US West | $357,485 | 93% | 43% | 57% | Phone Utilites |
| 95 | Prudential Insurance | $356,816 | 75% | 67% | 33% | Stock Investment |
| 96 | Atlantic Richfield | $339,389 | 88% | 41% | 59% | Oil & Gas |
| 97 | FMC Corp | $337,690 | 99%+ | 26% | 74% | Chemicals |
| 98 | Transport Workers Union | $335,615 | 100% | 96% | 4% | Misc Transport Union |
| 99 | Amoco Corp | $334,373 | 97% | 20% | 80% | Oil & Gas |
| 100 | KidsPAC | $334,350 | 100% | 88% | 12% | Health/Welfare |

NOTE: Contributors with PAC percents of "99%+" gave more than 99.5% but less than 100% of their contributions through PACs.

Financial interests were the second leading group on the Top 100 list. Nineteen companies from the Finance, Insurance & Real Estate sector dispensed a total of $14 million. Leading the list — both in the finance sector and among all other contributors — was the National Association of Realtors, whose Realtors PAC contributed nearly $3.1 million to some 510 congressional candidates.

Transportation companies were next on the list. Nine transport-related contributors gave a total of $5.9 million. They were led by the National Auto Dealers Association and Auto Dealers and Drivers for Free Trade, a PAC representing dealers of Japanese imports.

Eight ideological and single-issue groups made the Top 100 list. Biggest of all was National PAC, the largest of the pro-Israel political action committees.

# Individual Givers: A Counterpoint to the PACs

While most attention by the public and the news media is concentrated on contributions from political action committees, an entirely different community of contributors has received almost no notice at all. Individual contributors giving $200 or more accounted for more than $101 million in contributions to winning House and Senate candidates in the 1990 elections. Until now, little has been known about the details of that money — where it came from, who were the top contributors, and what were the patterns by which it was dispensed. The Center's research, which eventually resulted in the identification and classification of approximately 75 percent of that $101 million, shows that many of the same industries and interest groups that have come to dominate the PAC world also give heavily through individual contributions.

The Finance, Insurance & Real Estate sector was the biggest contributing group overall, accounting for some $16.5 million in individual donations to winning candidates. Lawyers & Lobbyists ranked second, with just over $14 million in contributions. Overall, three-quarters of the dollars from lawyers and lobbyists were delivered through individual contributions. In contrast to its high profile in the world of PACs, organized labor was scarcely in evidence among individual donors; nearly all of labor's dollars were delivered through PACs. Defense contractors were also very small players compared with other industries. A chart comparing each sector's PAC and individual contributions can be found on page 22.

## Who Gives Individually

One notable pattern that emerges from a study of individual versus PAC giving is that, by and large, PACs are an instrument of large organizations, while individual givers tend to be connected with smaller companies. A clear example of this can be seen in the oil industry, where a discernible split can be found in the spending patterns of large oil companies versus small ones. Nearly all the dollars delivered by major oil companies — such as Exxon, Atlantic Richfield, or Mobil — are funneled through PACs. Few oil executives from these companies make substantial contributions directly to candidates. Among smaller companies — known in the trade as "independents" — PACs are rare and most of the dollars are given as individual contributions.

That trend is consistent among a cross-section of American industries. Firms that are big enough to form PACs tend to use those PACs as their primary means of delivering campaign dollars. Firms that are smaller tend to rely on individual donations. The one exception to the rule is in the case of small businesses connected with nationwide organizations — such as doctors, Realtors, or trial lawyers. Those groups often give both ways — directly through individual contributions, and through the PAC of their national affiliate.

## Wall Street, Hollywood and Washington Lobbyists Lead Individual Givers

Another pattern that emerges from examining individual contributions is that certain industries, whether large or small, tend to prefer individual contributions to PACs. Most noteworthy among these are the securities industry based in Wall Street, the film industry, based in Hollywood and New York, and the influential community of lobbyists and lawyers concentrated in Washington, DC.

Some of the biggest contributors (seen in the chart on the facing page) give both through PACs and individually. Some of them also tend to deliver large bundles of contributions to selected candidates. The "bundling" of individual contributions from a group of executives within a particular company has become a popular means of supporting favored candidates. PACs alone are limited to a maximum $10,000 contribution during a normal election cycle. But a group of, say, a dozen vice presidents or partners in a law firm, can easily give much more than that, particularly if their spouses (and sometimes children) add contributions of their own. A list of the biggest "bundled" contributions to candidates in the 1990 elections can be found on pages 28 and 29.

The chart on the opposite page shows the biggest individual contributors in 1989-90. Goldman, Sachs & Co., the Wall Street investment firm, was the biggest of all, giving nearly $280,000 to congressional winners. Time Warner, the giant media conglomerate, ranked second. Third on the list was Salomon Brothers, another leading New York securities firm. Walt Disney Co., with an interest both in motion picture production, cable TV and the world's most popular resorts, was fourth. American Express held fifth place; most of its dollars came from its securities subsidiary, Shearson Lehman Hutton.

A number of other Wall Street investment houses — including Morgan Stanley, Bear Stearns and Merrill Lynch — also made the Top 50 list. The top recipient of the Wall Street money was New Jersey Senator Bill Bradley, who collected $25,000 or more from nine different investment firms. Most of those dollars came through individual contributions.

Washington law firms and lobbying groups were also well-represented on the Top 50 list. Leading the list was Cassidy & Associates, a D.C. lobbying firm whose partners included Bob Farmer, chief fundraiser for Michael Dukakis in his 1988 bid for the presidency. Farmer has since left Cassidy & Associates to raise funds for Democratic presidential candidate Bill Clinton. In all, six of the 12 largest contributors of individual contributions are legal or lobbying firms with Washington offices.

# Top 50 Individual Contributors

| Rank | Contributor | Individual Total | Grand Total | Category |
|------|-------------|------------------|-------------|----------|
| 1 | Goldman, Sachs & Co | $279,850 | $449,650 | Investmtent Banking |
| 2 | Time Warner | $258,725 | $388,075 | Broadcast/Movies |
| 3 | Salomon Brothers | $242,775 | $394,925 | Stock Investment |
| 4 | Walt Disney Co | $190,515 | $277,034 | Movies/Resorts |
| 5 | American Express | $188,300 | $421,064 | Stock Investment |
| 6 | Cassidy & Associates | $176,877 | $176,877 | Lobbyists |
| 7 | Akin, Gump, Hauer & Feld | $121,798 | $389,400 | Lawyers |
| 8 | Skadden, Arps et al | $120,050 | $200,400 | Lawyers |
| 9 | E&J Gallo Winery | $118,426 | $118,426 | Wine & Liquor |
| 10 | Williams & Jensen | $114,100 | $193,311 | Lawyers |
| 11 | Camp, Barsh, Bates & Tate | $105,950 | $130,700 | Lawyers |
| 12 | Neill & Co | $102,130 | $102,130 | Lobbyists |
| 13 | Morgan Stanley & Co | $100,925 | $277,175 | Investmtent Banking |
| 14 | Bear, Stearns & Co | $99,975 | $146,825 | Investmtent Banking |
| 15 | MCA Inc | $94,550 | $277,950 | Broadcast/Movies |
| 16 | NL Industries | $91,250 | $161,250 | Chemicals |
| 17 | Prudential Insurance | $89,401 | $356,816 | Stock Investment |
| 18 | General Electric | $87,409 | $473,142 | Aerospace/Nuclear |
| 19 | Dow Chemical | $86,950 | $468,225 | Chemicals |
| 20 | Stephens Inc | $85,150 | $138,400 | Investmtent Banking |
| 21 | Merrill Lynch | $74,575 | $196,130 | Stock Investment |
| 22 | Paramount Communications | $71,520 | $185,570 | Broadcast/Movies |
| 23 | Emily's List | $69,300 | $140,313 | Womens Issues |
| 24 | USX Corp | $62,850 | $230,550 | Oil & Gas/Steel |
| 25 | Arkla Inc | $62,100 | $135,300 | Natural Gas |
| 26 | Sears | $59,833 | $290,532 | Retail/Insurance |
| 27 | Occidental Petroleum | $59,450 | $297,850 | Oil & Gas/Meat Prod |
| 28 | Chrysler Corp | $57,950 | $301,300 | Auto Manufacturers |
| 29 | Mobil Oil | $57,550 | $267,350 | Oil & Gas |
| 30 | Ford Motor Co | $56,230 | $425,675 | Auto Manufacturers |
| 31 | Archer-Daniels-Midland Corp | $54,700 | $297,700 | Grain Traders |
| 32 | Anheuser-Busch | $53,700 | $187,470 | Beer |
| 33 | Arthur Andersen & Co | $51,850 | $176,325 | Accountants |
| 34 | Ernst & Young | $50,950 | $187,361 | Accountants |
| 35 | Deloitte & Touche | $48,865 | $184,525 | Accountants |
| 36 | Equitable Life | $45,600 | $220,350 | Insurance/Securities |
| 37 | Burlington Northern | $45,500 | $371,246 | Railroads |
| 38 | Eli Lilly & Co | $43,400 | $219,140 | Pharmaceuticals |
| 39 | Tyson Foods | $43,000 | $169,950 | Poultry |
| 40 | First Boston Corp | $42,700 | $127,200 | Investmtent Banking |
| 41 | Waste Management Inc | $42,582 | $434,962 | Waste Mgmt |
| 42 | Coopers & Lybrand | $40,667 | $187,953 | Accountants |
| 43 | Union Pacific Corp | $39,550 | $552,164 | Railroads |
| 44 | Atlantic Richfield | $39,125 | $339,389 | Oil & Gas |
| 45 | Corning Glass Works | $38,800 | $203,260 | Communications Equip |
| 46 | BellSouth | $37,974 | $699,974 | Phone Utilites |
| 47 | Blue Cross/Blue Shield | $36,575 | $272,210 | Health Insurance |
| 48 | Hill & Knowlton | $35,230 | $150,764 | Lobbyists/PR |
| 49 | McDonald's Corp | $35,050 | $226,550 | Restaurants |
| 50 | Beneficial Management Corp | $33,000 | $162,775 | Credit/Loans |

# Bundles of Money: Biggest Contributions in the 1990 Elections

## In the Senate . . .

Despite the fact that political action committees are limited to a maximum of $10,000 in one election cycle and individuals are limited to $2,000, a total of 18 Senators received contributions of $20,000 or more from a single company or interest group in the 1990 elections. Most of the dollars were given through individual contributions from company executives and their families, supplemented in many cases by PAC funds.

New Jersey Democrat Bill Bradley was the king of bundled contributions. Bradley collected $20,000 or more from nine securities firms, five law firms and three film studios. His biggest contributor — and the biggest donor to any Senate campaign in the 1990 elections — was Shearson Lehman Hutton, the Wall Street brokerage firm. Other major contributors to the Bradley campaign were the investment houses of Goldman, Sachs & Co., Salomon Brothers, Bear, Stearns & Co., Smith Barney, Prudential-Bache Securities, Morgan Stanley, First Boston Corp. and Merrill Lynch. Communications giant Time Warner was his leading entertainment industry contributor, followed by Walt Disney Co. and Paramount Communications. His top law firm contributors were Skadden, Arps and Bryan, Cave.

Bradley wasn't the only one to cash in on large gifts in 1990. Indiana Republican Dan Coats drew more than $51,000 from pharmaceutical executives, their families, and the company PAC at Indianapolis-based Eli Lilly & Co. Democrat Sam Nunn of Georgia collected over $48,000 from Goldman, Sachs. Massachusetts Democrat John Kerry, who declined to take PAC donations, did take more than $40,000 from members of the Boston law firm of Mintz, Levin and their families. He collected another $38,500 from individuals connected with Time Warner.

Overall, the Wall Street investment firm of Salomon Brothers was the most prolific bundler of campaign dollars, giving $20,000 or more to five U.S. Senators — Bill Bradley, Pete Domenici, Dan Coats, Mark Hatfield and Carl Levin. Time Warner gave $20,000 or more to four Senators — Bill Bradley, John Kerry, Jay Rockefeller and Sam Nunn.

## Biggest Contributions to Senators

| Contributor | Total | Type | Recipient |
|---|---|---|---|
| Shearson Lehman Hutton | $71,800 | Indiv | Bill Bradley (D-NJ) |
| Eli Lilly & Co | $51,700 | PAC/Ind | Daniel R. Coats (R-Ind) |
| Goldman, Sachs & Co | $50,100 | Indiv | Bill Bradley (D-NJ) |
| Goldman, Sachs & Co | $48,550 | PAC/Ind | Sam Nunn (D-Ga) |
| Time Warner | $48,525 | PAC/Ind | Bill Bradley (D-NJ) |
| Salomon Brothers | $47,550 | Indiv | Bill Bradley (D-NJ) |
| Salomon Brothers | $46,800 | PAC/Ind | Pete V. Domenici (R-NM) |
| Bear, Stearns & Co | $44,225 | PAC/Ind | Bill Bradley (D-NJ) |
| Mintz, Levin et al | $40,496 | Indiv | John Kerry (D-Mass) |
| Walt Disney Co | $40,040 | PAC/Ind | Bill Bradley (D-NJ) |
| Smith Barney | $39,350 | PAC/Ind | Bill Bradley (D-NJ) |
| Time Warner | $38,500 | Indiv | John Kerry (D-Mass) |
| Prudential-Bache Securities | $38,142 | PAC/Ind | Bill Bradley (D-NJ) |
| Skadden, Arps et al | $37,700 | PAC/Ind | Bill Bradley (D-NJ) |
| JMB Realty Corp | $36,100 | PAC/Ind | Paul Simon (D-Ill) |
| Willkie, Farr & Gallagher | $34,250 | Indiv | Bill Bradley (D-NJ) |
| Time Warner | $34,000 | Indiv | John D. Rockefeller IV (D-WVa) |
| First City Bancorp/Texas | $31,428 | Indiv | Phil Gramm (R-Texas) |
| Morgan Stanley & Co | $31,425 | PAC/Ind | Bill Bradley (D-NJ) |
| First Boston Corp | $30,450 | PAC/Ind | Bill Bradley (D-NJ) |
| Union Pacific Railroad | $30,300 | Indiv | Jim Exon (D-Neb) |
| Chicago Board of Trade | $28,950 | PAC/Ind | Paul Simon (D-Ill) |
| Baker & Botts | $28,675 | PAC/Ind | Phil Gramm (R-Texas) |
| Salomon Brothers | $28,225 | PAC/Ind | Daniel R. Coats (R-Ind) |
| Arkla Inc | $26,850 | PAC/Ind | J. Bennett Johnston (D-La) |
| Bryan, Cave et al | $26,753 | Indiv | Bill Bradley (D-NJ) |
| Merrill Lynch | $26,550 | PAC/Ind | Bill Bradley (D-NJ) |
| Warner-Lambert | $25,500 | PAC/Ind | Bill Bradley (D-NJ) |
| Cyprus Minerals Co | $25,177 | PAC/Ind | Hank Brown (R-Colo) |

# In the House . . .

The biggest bundle of cash delivered to any candidate in the 1990 election went to freshman Republican House member Dave Camp of Michigan. Camp, whose hometown of Midland, Mich. is also the headquarters of Dow Chemical, received over $100,000 from Dow's PACs, its employees and officials, and their families. The total does not include contributions under $200, since small donations are not itemized on federal campaign reports.

Another freshman House member, Democrat Ray Thornton of Arkansas, drew $67,200 in contributions from Stephens Inc., an investment banking firm located in Little Rock. Nearly all the money came from Stephens executives and their families. Thornton had previously served three terms in the House during the 1970s, before running unsuccessfully for the U.S. Senate in 1978.

House Majority Leader Dick Gephardt (D-Mo) was another top-dollar recipient in 1990. He collected over $62,000 from the St. Louis law firm of Thompson & Mitchell — all in individual contributions. Gephardt also received nearly $50,000 from Anheuser-Busch executives and the company PAC.

Washington state Democrat Jolene Unsoeld drew more than $61,000 in contributions from Emily's List, a PAC that supports progressive women candidates. Though the PAC itself was limited to the maximum $10,000, it was able to direct several dozen "earmarked" contributions from Emily's List contributors who specifically requested that their contributions go to Unsoeld. Even though the PAC was the conduit for delivering the funds, federal law treats earmarked contributions as individual gifts which do not count against the PAC's $10,000 limit.

Democrat Pete Geren of Texas collected $49,000 from members of the oil-rich Bass family during his two campaigns in 1989-90. He first won his seat in Congress in a 1989 special election following the resignation of House Speaker Jim Wright, then ran for reelection in 1990.

In all, some 46 House members drew contributions of $15,000 or more from a single source in the 1990 elections.

## Biggest Contributions to House Members

| Contributor | Total | Type | Recipient |
|---|---|---|---|
| Dow Chemical/Dow Corning | $100,200 | PAC/Ind | Dave Camp (R-Mich) |
| Stephens Inc | $67,200 | PAC/Ind | Ray Thornton (D-Ark) |
| Thompson & Mitchell | $62,510 | Indiv | Richard A. Gephardt (D-Mo) |
| Emily's List | $61,205 | PAC/Ind | Jolene Unsoeld (D-Wash) |
| Anheuser-Busch | $49,250 | PAC/Ind | Richard A. Gephardt (D-Mo) |
| Bass Brothers Enterprises/Bass International | $49,000 | PAC/Ind | Pete Geren (D-Texas) |
| Latham & Watkins | $27,200 | Indiv | C. Christopher Cox (R-Calif) |
| Corning Inc | $25,450 | Indiv | Amo Houghton (R-NY) |
| Teamsters Union | $25,000 | PAC | Jill L. Long (D-Ind) |
| National Assn of Realtors | $24,999 | PAC | Greg Laughlin (D-Texas) |
| Kelly, Hart & Hallman | $23,659 | Indiv | Pete Geren (D-Texas) |
| Morgan Stanley & Co | $22,350 | PAC/Ind | Nita M. Lowey (D-NY) |
| Federal Express Corp | $21,000 | PAC/Ind | Harold E. Ford (D-Tenn) |
| E&J Gallo Winery | $20,626 | Indiv | Gary Condit (D-Calif) |
| JT Moran & Co | $20,225 | Indiv | Joseph P. Kennedy II (D-Mass) |
| American Bankers Assn | $20,000 | PAC | Peter Hoagland (D-Neb) |
| American Medical Assn | $20,000 | PAC | Nita M. Lowey (D-NY) |
| Intl Brotherhood of Electrical Workers | $20,000 | PAC | Jill L. Long (D-Ind) |
| National Assn of Realtors | $20,000 | PAC | Ileana Ros-Lehtinen (R-Fla) |
| National Education Assn | $20,000 | PAC | Pete Geren (D-Texas) |
| New Enterprise Stone & Lime | $20,000 | Indiv | Bud Shuster (R-Pa) |
| United Auto Workers | $20,000 | PAC | Pete Geren (D-Texas) |
| USX Corp* | $19,700 | PAC/Ind | John P. Murtha (D-Pa) |
| RJR Nabisco | $19,187 | PAC/Ind | Stephen L. Neal (D-NC) |
| United Auto Workers | $18,900 | PAC | Glen Browder (D-Ala) |
| Archer-Daniels-Midland Corp | $18,500 | PAC/Ind | Robert H. Michel (R-Ill) |
| Intl Brotherhood of Electrical Workers | $18,500 | PAC | Glen Browder (D-Ala) |
| National Education Assn | $18,300 | PAC | Glen Browder (D-Ala) |
| McDonnell Douglas* | $18,250 | PAC/Ind | Ike Skelton (D-Mo) |
| Sun-Diamond Growers* | $18,000 | PAC | Gary Condit (D-Calif) |
| Amer Fedn of State/County/Munic Employees | $17,500 | PAC | Jill L. Long (D-Ind) |
| Assn of Trial Lawyers of America | $17,500 | PAC | Nita M. Lowey (D-NY) |
| National Education Assn | $17,500 | PAC | Craig Washington (D-Texas) |

* Contributions came from more than one PAC affiliated with this sponsor

# Leading Categories of Individual Contributions

Contributions from lawyers towered over all other industries and interest groups among individual contributions made to congressional candidates in the 1990 elections. In all, attorneys gave just over $11 million — three and a half times as much as the second leading category, physicians.

Close behind the doctors were lobbyists — many of whom are also attorneys. The total includes only registered lobbyists and employees of lobbying firms. Because of the nature of lobby registration laws in the nation's capital, however, many attorneys and other professionals who function as lobbyists never officially register. These de facto lobbyists are classified elsewhere, depending on their occupation.

Pro-Israel contributors were the fourth leading group of individual contributors. This total was compiled by counting individuals who had contributed $200 or more both to a pro-Israel PAC and to a candidate who was supported by pro-Israel PACs.

| Category | Total from Individuals | Grand Total |
|---|---|---|
| Attorneys & law firms | $11,053,117 | $15,425,424 |
| Physicians | $3,066,512 | $5,947,306 |
| Lobbyists & public relations | $2,948,676 | $3,168,285 |
| Pro-Israel | $2,707,456 | $6,747,554 |
| Retired | $2,660,255 | $2,660,255 |
| Security brokers & investment companies | $2,543,243 | $3,775,778 |
| Real Estate developers & subdividers | $2,058,261 | $2,369,556 |
| Real estate, diversified | $1,823,656 | $1,823,656 |
| Misc finance, diversified or unclassified | $1,604,229 | $1,604,229 |
| Insurance companies, brokers & agents, diversified | $1,528,486 | $6,126,838 |
| Commercial banks & bank holding companies | $1,473,078 | $7,775,819 |
| Construction, unclassified or diversified | $1,429,455 | $1,429,455 |
| Real estate agents & managers | $1,034,276 | $4,265,904 |
| Motion picture production & distribution | $954,495 | $1,303,815 |
| Conservative/Republican | $939,297 | $1,351,283 |
| Independent oil & gas producers | $934,012 | $1,501,245 |
| Investment banking | $903,675 | $1,392,356 |
| Liberal/Democrat | $871,991 | $2,202,277 |
| Accountants | $840,166 | $2,550,917 |
| Public works, industrial & commercial construction | $737,618 | $2,219,773 |
| Misc business services | $720,769 | $782,069 |
| Building operators and managers | $715,605 | $741,455 |
| Oil & gas, diversified | $667,411 | $945,811 |
| Crop production & basic processing | $649,347 | $699,547 |
| Auto dealers, new & used | $630,125 | $1,944,025 |
| Civil servant/public employee | $623,745 | $623,745 |
| Schools & colleges | $577,673 | $581,973 |
| Restaurants & drinking establishments | $565,159 | $1,760,397 |
| Book, newspaper & periodical publishing | $554,697 | $672,197 |
| Livestock | $531,048 | $947,903 |
| Industrial/commercial equipment & materials | $530,578 | $1,019,022 |
| Engineering, architecture & construction mgmt services | $514,088 | $945,451 |

Retirees were another important sector of individual contributors. The total includes all individuals who described themselves as "retired," except those who were classified as ideological contributors because of contributions to ideological or single-issue PACs.

Securities brokers accounted for $2.5 million in individual contributions, while another $900,000 came from individuals connected with investment banking houses. Together, these securities professionals comprised one of the most important industry groups making individual contributions. Many of the larger Wall Street firms bundled numerous contributions from partners, brokers and their families, to deliver sizable contributions to individual candidates. Those donations were often supplemented by PAC contributions from the parent firm.

Real estate brokers, developers and investors were also very much in evidence with individual contributions. Developers in particular were much more likely to give individually than through political action committees. Other financial sector categories with substantial individual contributions were bankers and insurance agents, but both those groups delivered the vast majority of their campaign dollars through PACs.

# Industry Support of Democrats & Republicans

The widespread assumption that labor unions support Democrats while business groups support Republicans is only partially true — and in many cases is downright wrong. Organized labor is indeed heavily Democratic in its politics and its campaign contributions, though Republicans on committees important to labor often receive substantial financial support from unions. But the world of business is much more diverse in its political orientation than most casual observers realize. Overall, business groups split their dollars nearly evenly between Democrats and Republicans in Congress. It is common even for individual companies to support both parties — sometimes even in the same race.

Even among industries and individual businesses that are Republican in their politics, there is a tendency —presumably born of hard-headed pragmatism — to ensure a favorable reception on Capitol Hill by giving to members on both sides of the aisle. That inclination is strengthened by the fact that Democrats hold strong majorities in both the House and Senate. In that environment, virtually no bill becomes law without wide support among Democratic members — a fact that business groups must take into account, whatever their political orientation.

A glance at the charts at right illustrates several patterns in congressional contributions. Most obvious is the contrast in Labor dollars between Republicans and Democrats. Also clear, from both the charts and the bottom line below is that congressional Democrats received considerably more money overall than Republicans in the 1990 elections.

Other interesting findings can be seen by looking more closely. The finance, insurance and real estate sector, for example, is clearly the heaviest business contributor to both parties. Moreover, the bankers, Realtors, insurance agents and others that make up that sector gave considerably more to Democrats than to Republicans. Lawyers and lobbyists were even more strongly Democratic in their contributions, as were ideological and single-issue contributors.

A more detailed examination of the spending patterns in each of these sectors can be found in the Industry Profiles section beginning on page 41. A closer look at the individual categories most important to members of each party appears on the following two pages.

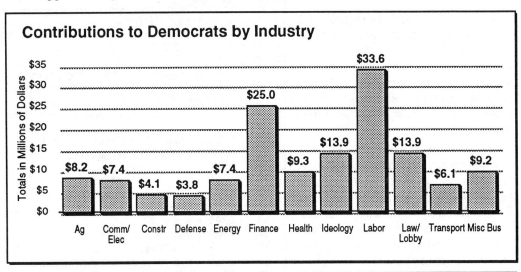

Contributions to Democrats by Industry

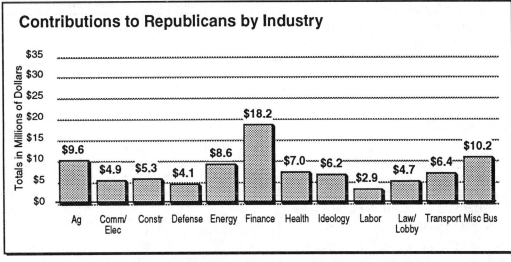

Contributions to Republicans by Industry

| Sector | To Democrats | To Republicans |
|---|---|---|
| Agriculture | $8,206,840 | $9,265,251 |
| Communications/Electronics | $7,365,932 | $4,904,348 |
| Construction | $4,134,583 | $5,341,418 |
| Defense | $3,833,272 | $4,050,081 |
| Energy & Natural Resources | $7,371,577 | $8,618,709 |
| Finance, Insurance & Real Estate | $24,973,503 | $18,167,437 |
| Health | $9,303,032 | $6,987,048 |
| Ideology/Single-Issue | $13,924,578 | $6,224,773 |
| Labor | $33,647,405 | $2,880,667 |
| Lawyers & Lobbyists | $13,893,577 | $4,698,732 |
| Transportation | $6,122,135 | $6,376,019 |
| Misc Business | $9,209,979 | $10,245,259 |
| **GRAND TOTAL** | **$94,414,430** | **$79,014,302** |

# Top-Dollar Categories to Each Party

Listed below are the industry and interest group categories that gave the most money to congressional Democrats and Republicans in the 1990 elections. A complete listing of categories used throughout this book, and the totals they provided in contributions, can be found in the Appendix, which begins on page 340.

## To Democrats . . .

Labor unions and lawyers provided the biggest financial assistance to Democratic candidates in the 1990 elections. Attorneys and law firms were by far the leading single category giving to Democrats, though taken as a whole, unions contributed more heavily than any other sector.

Of the top 20 categories contributing to Democrats, eight came from the Labor community, two (Pro-Israel and Liberal/Democrat) were ideological, and the remaining 10 were from the world of business. Among the business categories, five were from the finance, insurance & real estate sector.

The category totals in this list include contributions both from PACs and indi-

| Rank | Category | To Democrats | Dem Pct |
|---|---|---|---|
| 1 | Attorneys & law firms | $11,541,116 | 75% |
| 2 | Construction unions | $5,920,053 | 94% |
| 3 | Manufacturing unions | $5,270,812 | 98% |
| 4 | Pro-Israel | $5,042,408 | 75% |
| 5 | Commercial banks & bank holding companies | $4,349,862 | 56% |
| 6 | US Postal Service unions & associations | $3,274,119 | 86% |
| 7 | Teachers unions | $3,202,106 | 95% |
| 8 | Insurance companies, brokers & agents, diversified | $3,074,172 | 50% |
| 9 | Physicians | $3,013,116 | 51% |
| 10 | Security brokers & investment companies | $2,431,748 | 64% |
| 11 | Real estate agents & managers | $2,408,401 | 56% |
| 12 | Lobbyists & public relations | $2,352,461 | 74% |
| 13 | Teamsters | $2,243,149 | 92% |
| 14 | Defense areospace contractors | $2,192,977 | 50% |
| 15 | Liberal/Democrat | $2,180,027 | 99% |
| 16 | Life insurance | $2,100,121 | 57% |
| 17 | Mechant marine & longshoremen unions | $1,834,661 | 74% |
| 18 | Telephone utilities | $1,744,353 | 50% |
| 19 | Federal employees unions | $1,568,475 | 79% |
| 20 | State & local govt employee unions | $1,510,820 | 97% |

viduals. In this list, and throughout the book, PAC classifications are based on the industry or interests of the sponsoring organization or company. Contributions from individuals are classified based on the occupation/employer of the contributor. Individuals are classified as ideological givers only if they made contributions to an ideological/single-issue PAC.

## To Republicans . . .

Attorneys and law firms also topped the Republicans' Top 20 list of leading categories, though lawyers gave only one-third as much to Republicans as they did to Democrats.

Seventeen of the top 20 categories were business related. The two ideological categories were Pro-Israel and Conservative/Republican. Retirees, who gave nearly 60 percent of their dollars to Republicans, ranked tenth on the list.

The finance, insurance & real estate sector accounted for six of the Republicans' top 20 categories — more than any other sector.

| Rank | Category | To Republicans | Repub Pct |
|---|---|---|---|
| 1 | Attorneys & law firms | $3,881,908 | 25% |
| 2 | Commercial banks & bank holding companies | $3,418,207 | 44% |
| 3 | Insurance companies, brokers & agents | $3,052,666 | 50% |
| 4 | Physicians | $2,931,988 | 49% |
| 5 | Defense areospace contractors | $2,232,538 | 50% |
| 6 | Real estate agents & managers | $1,857,303 | 44% |
| 7 | Telephone utilities | $1,759,473 | 50% |
| 8 | Pro-Israel | $1,705,146 | 25% |
| 9 | Major (multinational) oil & gas producers | $1,683,350 | 70% |
| 10 | Retired | $1,570,591 | 59% |
| 11 | Life insurance | $1,553,713 | 43% |
| 12 | Public works, industrial & commercial construction | $1,370,558 | 62% |
| 13 | Security brokers & investment companies | $1,338,855 | 35% |
| 14 | Conservative/Republican | $1,322,286 | 98% |
| 15 | Defense electronic contractors | $1,243,443 | 51% |
| 16 | Restaurants & drinking establishments | $1,221,449 | 69% |
| 17 | Auto dealers, new & used | $1,196,077 | 62% |
| 18 | Tobacco & tobacco products | $1,117,275 | 53% |
| 19 | Accountants | $1,090,183 | 43% |
| 20 | Pharmaceutical manufacturing | $1,078,450 | 54% |

# The Most Heavily Partisan Categories

These were the categories that gave most heavily to one party or the other during the 1989-90 election cycle. The categories have been pared to include only those that accounted for $50,000 or more in contributions to one party.

## To Democrats . . .

Labor unions dominate the list of most-partisan categories giving to Democrats. As a group, organized labor delivered 92 percent of its campaign dollars to Democratic candidates, making it by far the most important sector for Democrats. In fact, the strong partisanship of labor unions accounts for much of the overall edge in fundraising that congressional Democrats enjoyed over their Republican opponents.

In all, 15 of the 20 most partisan categories on the Democrats' list were from the Labor sector. Of the remaining five, three were from ideological & single-issue groups — Liberal/Democrat, Democratic leadership PACs, and Pro-Peace groups.

| Rank | Category | To Democrats | Dem Pct |
|---|---|---|---|
| 1 | Democratic leadership PACs | $1,484,312 | 99.5% |
| 2 | Misc unions | $84,040 | 99.4% |
| 3 | Liberal/Democrat | $2,180,027 | 99.0% |
| 4 | Labor unions, diversified | $829,427 | 98.9% |
| 5 | Communications & hi-tech unions | $1,104,103 | 98.6% |
| 6 | Manufacturing unions | $5,270,812 | 98.3% |
| 7 | Outpatient health services (incl drug & alcohol) | $61,550 | 97.5% |
| 8 | State & local govt employee unions | $1,510,820 | 97.5% |
| 9 | Retail trade unions | $923,222 | 97.4% |
| 10 | IBEW (Intl Brotherhood of Electrical Workers) | $1,224,495 | 97.3% |
| 11 | Misc commercial unions | $294,796 | 97.2% |
| 12 | Misc transportation unions | $1,175,971 | 95.9% |
| 13 | Welfare & social work | $201,530 | 95.5% |
| 14 | Food service & related unions | $329,253 | 95.1% |
| 15 | Pro-Peace | $320,769 | 94.7% |
| 16 | Teachers unions | $3,202,106 | 94.6% |
| 17 | Mining unions | $300,090 | 94.5% |
| 18 | Construction unions | $5,920,053 | 94.0% |
| 19 | Railroad unions | $1,135,991 | 93.6% |
| 20 | Teamsters | $2,243,149 | 92.0% |

The dearth of business categories on the list of partisan categories is not surprising, given the tendency of most business groups to spread their dollars relatively evenly between Democrats and Republicans.

## To Republicans . . .

Ideological and single-issue contributors accounted for the five most heavily partisan categories giving to Republicans, and seven of the top 20. But a number of business categories were also heavily Republican in their giving.

The construction industry was the friendliest to Republicans. Overall, the industry gave 56 percent of its dollars to GOP candidates. It also accounted for four of the most partisan categories on this list.

| Rank | Category | To Republicans | Repub Pct |
|---|---|---|---|
| 1 | Republican leadership PACs | $854,612 | 99.3% |
| 2 | Republican officials, candidates & former members | $61,191 | 99.2% |
| 3 | Anti-Union | $445,878 | 98.0% |
| 4 | Conservative/Republican | $1,322,286 | 97.9% |
| 5 | Fiscal & tax policy | $72,954 | 97.6% |
| 6 | Builders associations | $100,662 | 93.7% |
| 7 | Pro-business organizations | $106,266 | 93.4% |
| 8 | Household appliance manufacturers & dealers | $107,090 | 85.7% |
| 9 | Pro-Defense | $209,304 | 85.0% |
| 10 | Small business organizations | $316,484 | 82.8% |
| 11 | Plumbing, heating & air conditioning contractors | $247,395 | 79.7% |
| 12 | Direct mail advertising services | $75,875 | 79.2% |
| 13 | Computer software manufacturers & dealers | $67,904 | 78.2% |
| 14 | Pro-Life | $154,406 | 77.9% |
| 15 | Construction equipment | $120,995 | 77.7% |
| 16 | Farm machinery & equipment | $201,575 | 77.6% |
| 17 | Greeting card publishing | $70,000 | 75.6% |
| 18 | Paper & pulp mills and paper manufacturing | $785,858 | 75.1% |
| 19 | Stone, clay, glass & concrete products | $379,135 | 73.6% |
| 20 | Defense shipbuilders | $197,350 | 73.1% |

# In-State vs. Out-of-State Contributions

## Highest Percent of Out-of-State Contributions: US House*

| Rank | Name | Out-of-state Pct | Out-of-state Total |
|------|------|------------------|--------------------|
| 1 | Dick Swett (D-NH) | 96.3% | $226,400 |
| 2 | Thomas S. Foley (D-Wash) | 93.4% | $60,573 |
| 3 | Lee H. Hamilton (D-Ind) | 87.8% | $62,348 |
| 4 | Pat Williams (D-Mont) | 84.2% | $43,025 |
| 5 | Les Aspin (D-Wis) | 83.5% | $187,115 |
| 5 | David R. Obey (D-Wis) | 83.5% | $111,797 |
| 7 | John Conyers Jr. (D-Mich) | 83.4% | $60,150 |
| 8 | John D. Dingell (D-Mich) | 80.6% | $106,288 |
| 9 | Byron L. Dorgan (D-ND) | 80.3% | $28,900 |
| 10 | James L. Oberstar (D-Minn) | 76.8% | $31,900 |
| 11 | Gus Yatron (D-Pa) | 76.5% | $28,700 |
| 12 | Pete Stark (D-Calif) | 75.4% | $54,800 |
| 13 | Sam M. Gibbons (D-Fla) | 73.8% | $43,615 |
| 14 | William D. Ford (D-Mich) | 73.5% | $22,200 |
| 15 | Nick J. Rahall II (D-WVa) | 72.1% | $76,358 |
| 16 | Dan Rostenkowski (D-Ill) | 68.7% | $20,800 |
| 17 | Charlie Rose (D-NC) | 68.6% | $28,750 |
| 18 | Bernard Sanders (I-Vt) | 67.2% | $67,825 |
| 19 | Ron Wyden (D-Ore) | 67.1% | $140,771 |
| 20 | Sidney R. Yates (D-Ill) | 65.2% | $253,227 |

* Among members with $10,000 or more in individual contributions

Most House members drew the bulk of their large individual contributions (about 75 percent on average) from within their own state. Many collected less than 10 percent of their cash from out-of-state contributors. Of the 435 members of the House of Representatives, only 63 drew the majority of their large individual contributions from outside their home states. The 20 members in the chart at left had the highest proportion of out-of-state contributions from large individual contributors.

Freshman Democrat Dick Swett of New Hampshire got the most out-of-state money in the House in the 1990 elections. Swett is the son-in-law of California Democrat Tom Lantos and Lantos provided a helping hand in rounding up contributors for the Swett campaign.

All the totals on this page include only large individual contributions ($200 and above). Smaller contributions are not itemized, so it is not possible to check where they came from. PAC contributions are not counted, since many PACs with local affiliates maintain their headquarters in Washington, DC or other major cities.

## Highest Percent of Out-of-State Contributions: US Senate

| Rank | Name | Out-of-state Pct | Out-of-state Total |
|------|------|------------------|--------------------|
| 1 | Quentin N. Burdick (D-ND) | 98.5% | $500,913 |
| 2 | Tom Daschle (D-SD) | 93.0% | $697,137 |
| 3 | Joseph R. Biden Jr. (D-Del) | 92.7% | $1,226,170 |
| 4 | Orrin G. Hatch (R-Utah) | 92.4% | $1,094,433 |
| 5 | Kent Conrad (D-ND) | 91.9% | $165,750 |
| 6 | Bob Packwood (R-Ore) | 91.6% | $2,105,347 |
| 7 | Patrick J. Leahy (D-Vt) | 90.8% | $404,054 |
| 8 | Daniel K. Inouye (D-Hawaii) | 88.4% | $338,574 |
| 9 | Larry Pressler (R-SD) | 87.7% | $744,712 |
| 10 | Bob Dole (R-Kan) | 87.1% | $983,015 |

Senators were much more likely than House members to draw substantial support from out-of-state contributors — particularly those senators from small states. The more prominent senators have developed national constituencies that help out with campaign cash at election time. Even those less well known can often corral dollars from party loyalists in major financial and political centers such as New York, Los Angeles, Washington and Chicago.

The importance of large individual contributions is much greater for senators than for House members, since PACs — the mainstay of many House campaigns — account for only about one-quarter of Senate contributions.

## Highest Percent of In-State Contributions: US Senate

The 10 senators on the list at right got the highest proportion of large individual contributions from within the borders of their own states. Phil Gramm's in-state fundraising was particularly noteworthy. Of the ten biggest metro areas that provided cash to his campaign only one was outside Texas. That exception was New York City, which ranked ninth among Gramm's most fruitful cities — between Amarillo and Waco.

| Rank | Name | In-state Pct | In-state Total |
|------|------|--------------|----------------|
| 1 | Phil Gramm (R-Texas) | 83.2% | $6,348,756 |
| 2 | Bob Graham (D-Fla) | 81.3% | $3,201,348 |
| 3 | Richard C. Shelby (D-Ala) | 79.9% | $536,090 |
| 4 | Alfonse M. D'Amato (R-NY) | 79.1% | $3,496,754 |
| 4 | Daniel R. Coats (R-Ind) | 79.1% | $1,167,489 |
| 6 | Connie Mack (R-Fla) | 78.4% | $1,430,761 |
| 7 | Nancy Kassebaum (R-Kan) | 78.0% | $129,199 |
| 8 | Don Nickles (R-Okla) | 77.1% | $862,176 |
| 9 | Alan J. Dixon (D-Ill) | 76.2% | $616,709 |
| 10 | Thad Cochran (R-Miss) | 76.0% | $302,180 |

# Unidentified Contributors

While nearly every political action committee was identified and categorized by the Center, many thousands of *individual* contributors remain unclassified. Of the $101 million in large individual contributions that went to members of Congress in the 1989-90 election cycle, the Center was able to identify and classify just over 75 percent. Of the remaining $25 million which was not identified . . .

• $11.6 million was given by contributors who did list their employers. The Center, however, was unable to identify the types of business these companies were engaged in — mainly due to limitations of staff and time.

• $3.9 million came from homemakers, students and other non-income earners whose income-earning spouses or parents were not found.

• $970,000 came from individuals whose listed occupations were so generic they could not be classified. Examples are "businessman," "entrepreneur" and "self-employed."

• $8.5 million came from people whose occupation and employer was not listed at all. In many cases, the Center was able to discover the missing information by searching for other contributions by the same individuals. But most of these contributors remain unclassified.

Federal law requires candidates to disclose the name, address, occupation and employer of each contributor giving $200 or more to their campaign. Most members of Congress complied with that requirement, providing information on all but a small fraction of their contributors. Some members, however, were less forthcoming. The following members failed to disclose occupations and employers of at least 20 percent of their large individual contributors.

## Senators Who Disclosed the Least

| Rank | Name | Pct with No Employer Listed | Total No Employer Listed | Total Identified by Center | Final Total with No Employer Known | Final Pct with No Employer Known |
|------|------|------|------|------|------|------|
| 1 | Jesse Helms (R-NC) | 65.9% | $1,936,685 | $630,180 | $1,306,505 | 44.5% |
| 2 | Paul Wellstone (D-Minn) | 48.4% | $126,252 | $42,621 | $83,631 | 32.0% |
| 3 | Larry E. Craig (R-Idaho) | 42.0% | $153,520 | $120,120 | $33,400 | 9.1% |
| 4 | Daniel R. Coats (R-Ind) | 40.6% | $602,216 | $228,864 | $373,352 | 25.1% |
| 5 | Tom Harkin (D-Iowa) | 37.4% | $658,115 | $410,046 | $248,069 | 14.1% |
| 6 | Hank Brown (R-Colo) | 35.0% | $499,940 | $213,285 | $286,655 | 20.1% |
| 7 | Paul Simon (D-Ill) | 30.9% | $1,008,015 | $536,758 | $471,257 | 14.4% |
| 8 | Daniel K. Akaka (D-Hawaii) | 27.5% | $165,860 | $67,500 | $98,360 | 16.3% |
| 9 | Al Gore (D-Tenn) | 26.7% | $286,203 | $166,253 | $119,950 | 11.2% |
| 10 | Phil Gramm (R-Texas) | 21.6% | $1,648,464 | $700,109 | $948,355 | 12.4% |

## House Members Who Disclosed the Least

| Rank | Name | Pct with No Employer Listed | Total No Employer Listed | Total Identified by Center | Final Total with No Employer Known | Final Pct with No Employer Known |
|------|------|------|------|------|------|------|
| 1 | Gary Franks (R-Conn) | 74.5% | $99,470 | $21,200 | $78,270 | 58.6% |
| 2 | John Conyers Jr. (D-Mich) | 52.4% | $37,800 | $15,200 | $22,600 | 31.3% |
| 3 | Neil Abercrombie (D-Hawaii) | 52.2% | $40,225 | $3,500 | $36,725 | 47.6% |
| 4 | William J. Jefferson (D-La) | 51.9% | $114,711 | $15,811 | $98,900 | 44.7% |
| 5 | Robert K. Dornan (R-Calif) | 46.1% | $112,152 | $69,013 | $43,139 | 17.7% |
| 6 | Dick Armey (R-Texas) | 44.5% | $67,300 | $33,450 | $33,850 | 22.4% |
| 7 | Jim McCrery (R-La) | 44.2% | $86,650 | $41,850 | $44,800 | 22.9% |
| 8 | H. Martin Lancaster (D-NC) | 43.6% | $42,590 | $3,205 | $39,385 | 40.3% |
| 9 | Maxine Waters (D-Calif) | 42.0% | $104,853 | $37,848 | $67,005 | 26.9% |
| 10 | Dan Burton (R-Ind) | 40.5% | $76,207 | $29,100 | $47,107 | 25.0% |
| 11 | Dean A. Gallo (R-NJ) | 38.9% | $133,425 | $53,775 | $79,650 | 23.2% |
| 12 | John T. Doolittle (R-Calif) | 31.2% | $52,242 | $19,300 | $32,942 | 19.7% |
| 13 | Newt Gingrich (R-Ga) | 31.0% | $174,050 | $79,650 | $94,400 | 16.8% |
| 14 | Craig T. James (R-Fla) | 28.9% | $49,218 | $11,244 | $37,974 | 22.3% |
| 15 | Gary Condit (D-Calif) | 26.0% | $76,500 | $31,200 | $45,300 | 15.4% |
| 16 | Dana Rohrabacher (R-Calif) | 25.7% | $66,684 | $26,425 | $40,259 | 15.5% |
| 17 | Dick Swett (D-NH) | 25.2% | $59,700 | $28,950 | $30,750 | 13.0% |
| 18 | Wayne Owens (D-Utah) | 24.8% | $77,112 | $42,712 | $34,400 | 11.1% |
| 19 | Helen Delich Bentley (R-Md) | 23.8% | $73,783 | $20,340 | $53,443 | 17.3% |
| 20 | Les Aspin (D-Wis) | 23.4% | $60,155 | $39,155 | $21,000 | 8.2% |
| 21 | Susan Molinari (R-NY) | 21.8% | $64,835 | $8,300 | $56,535 | 19.0% |

# Targeting the Committees

One of the first patterns that becomes apparent when reviewing the political contributions to incumbents in Congress is that the member's profile of contributors tends to parallel his or her committee assignments. Members of the Banking Committees of the House or Senate, for example, typically receive substantial contributions from commercial banks, savings & loans, as well as related (and sometimes competing) industries, like securities firms or insurance companies. Members sitting on industry-specific committees (like the House Merchant Marine and Fisheries Committee) often receive funds both from business interests involved in the industry and from Labor PACs whose members provide the industry's workforce. The consistency of these patterns can be seen on the member profile pages (beginning on page 171) and in the committee profiles that begin on page 94.

It can also be seen in the following charts that show the average contributions given by selected industry groups to members of various committees in the House of Representatives. The charts focus on House committees because industry contribution patterns are clearer there than in the Senate. House members generally have only one or two major committee assignments, while most senators must split their attention among three or four different committees. In addition, because senators face the voters only once every six years, the volume of dollars flowing to specific Senate committees tends to have more to do with the number of committee members seeking reelection than with the overall agenda of either the committee or the contributors.

## Agriculture

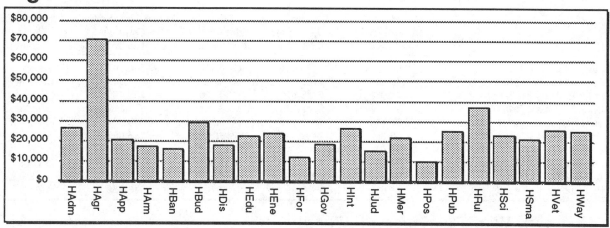

### House Committee Key

| | |
|---|---|
| HAdm | House Administration |
| HAgr | House Agriculture |
| HApp | House Appropriations |
| HArm | House Armed Services |
| HBan | House Banking, Finance & Urban Affairs |
| HBud | House Budget |
| HDis | House District of Columbia |
| HEdu | House Education & Labor |
| HEne | House Energy & Commerce |
| HFor | House Foreign Affairs |
| HGov | House Government Operations |
| HInt | House Interior & Insular Affairs |
| HJud | House Judiciary |
| HMer | House Merchant Marine & Fisheries |
| HPos | House Post Office & Civil Service |
| HPub | House Public Works & Transportation |
| HRul | House Rules |
| HSci | House Science, Space & Technology |
| HSma | House Small Business |
| HVet | House Veterans' Affairs |
| HWay | House Ways and Means |

The chart above illustrates the correlation between industry spending and members' committee assignments. Agricultural industry contributors concentrated the biggest portion of their campaign dollars on the committee that most affects their business. Members of the House Agriculture Committee received an average of $70,000 from farmers, ranchers, pesticide manufacturers, and other agricultural interests during the 1989-90 election cycle.

# Communications/Electronics

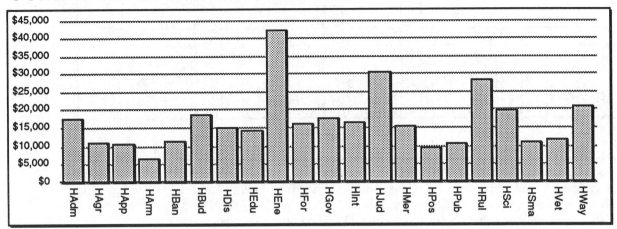

The House Energy and Commerce committee attracted the biggest share of contributions from the communications and electronics sector. The Telecommunications and Finance subcommittee of that panel is of particular importance to telephone utilities and TV and radio broadcasters — major contributors within that sector. Hollywood film studios also showed a strong interest in the House Judiciary Committee, which rules on such matters as copyright laws affecting the motion picture industry.

# Defense

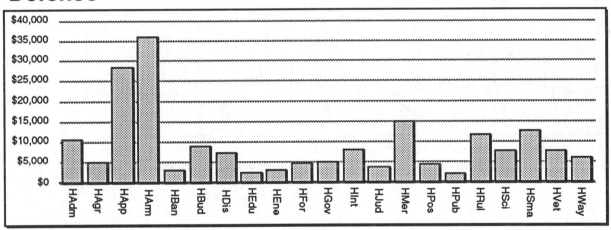

Defense contractors took careful aim at the Appropriations and Armed Services Committees when dispensing their dollars in the 1990 election. Armed Services makes crucial decisions on weapons systems and overall military budget priorities. Appropriations allocates the money to pay for it all. Both are crucial to the defense industry, particularly as defense spending winds down after the close of the Cold War and the dissolution of the former Soviet Union.

# Energy & Natural Resources

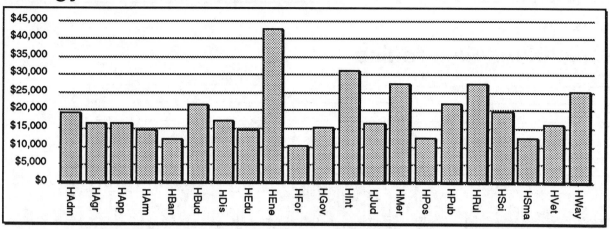

The Energy and Commerce Committee, with direct responsibility for the nation's energy policy, was the biggest beneficiary of campaign funds from the oil and gas industry and related energy interests. Other important committees were the Interior Committee, which sets policies affecting leasing of federal lands, and the Merchant Marine and Fisheries Committee, which oversees offshore oil drilling on the continental shelf.

# Finance, Insurance & Real Estate

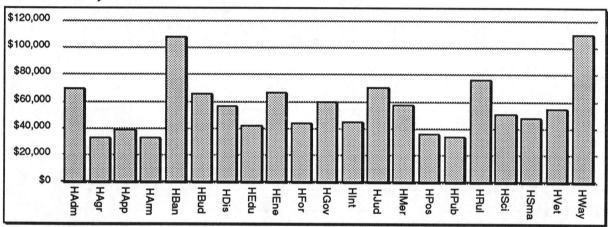

Commercial and savings banks concentrated their dollars on the Banking Committee. Insurance interests gave heavily to the tax-writing Ways & Means Committee. Real estate interests gave heavily to all members, regardless of committee assignment.

# Health

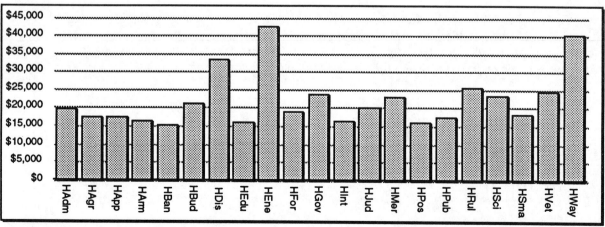

Both Energy and Commerce and Ways & Means have subcommittees dealing with Health matters. Both panels got generous funding from doctors, hospitals, pharmaceutical companies and other health care interests.

# Labor

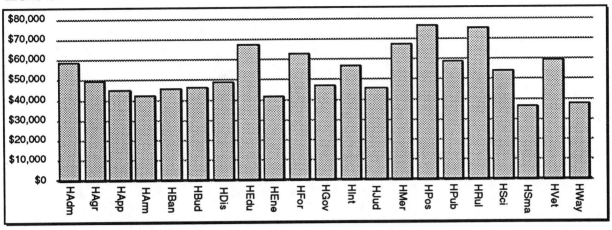

With 92 percent of its campaign dollars going to Democrats, organized Labor for the most part gave its dollars to Democratic members without regard to their committee assignments. But there were exceptions. Postal workers and federal employee unions gave heavily to members — both Democrat and Republican — on the Post Office and Civil Service Committee. Sea transport unions gave liberally to members of both parties who sit on the Merchant Marine and Fisheries Committee.

# Lawyers & Lobbyists

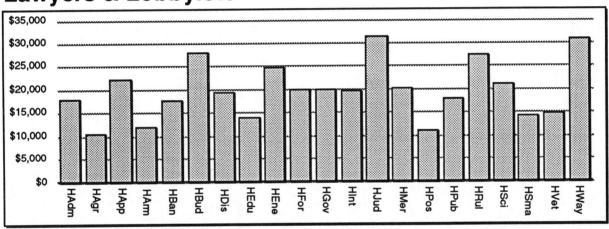

The House Judiciary Committee and Ways & Means drew the heaviest contributions from lawyers and lobbyists. Trial lawyers are most interested in combatting any movement toward tort reform. Lobbyists, perhaps the most pragmatic group of all, give to ensure access on behalf of their clients.

# Transportation

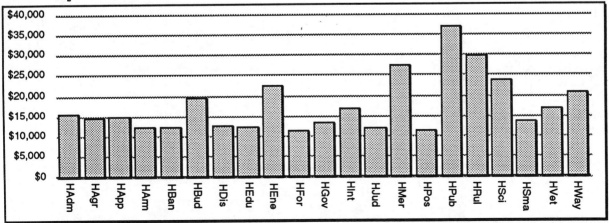

Not surprisingly, the Public Works and Transportation Committee was the biggest recipient of transport industry dollars. The Merchant Marine & Fisheries Committee got the most from shipping interests.

# 2.

# Industry Profiles

# Industry Profiles in Brief

With today's expensive election campaigns, and the almost infinite spectrum of legislation considered on Capitol Hill, members of Congress draw their campaign funds from dozens of different industries and interests. The industry profiles on the following pages provide the details on which industries are the biggest givers and which members are the biggest recipients of their funds. The profiles have two sections: one shows graphically where the money comes from and where it goes. The other gives more detail in the smaller categories within each industry. Following is a thumbnail sketch of each industry and interest group classification:

## Agriculture ...................................................................................................................$17.8 million

An important player on Capitol Hill that has maintained its longtime influence despite the decline of the American farm, agricultural contributors gave nearly $18 million in contributions to congressional candidates in 1989-90. Crop production and processing is the largest sector within the industry, but it accounts for only one-fourth of the total agriculture dollars. Other major sectors are food processors, agricultural services and products (including everything from veterinarians to pesticide and fertilizer manufacturers), tobacco companies, dairy producers, poultry and livestock producers, and the forest products industry.

## Communications/Electronics ...........................................................................................$12.3 million

The big money here comes from two main sources: the telecommunications industry (primarily local and long distance telephone utilities), and the broadcasting and motion picture industries. The phone company money comes predominantly from AT&T and the regional Bell systems. Nearly all of it is delivered through political action committees. The broadcasting and movie money comes both through PACs and through individual contributions — those individual dollars come mainly from the film community in and around Hollywood.

## Construction ..................................................................................................................$9.5 million

Despite the persistent slump in both housing and commercial construction, the building industry remains an important source of campaign funds. The industry divides into two primary groups — general contractors who concentrate primarily on commercial and industrial construction, and those who concentrate on the residential market. These two sectors' legislative interests are often quite different. The housing industry pays close attention to the House and Senate banking committees, while the heavy construction sector looks to the public works committees for highways and other federal construction projects. Supporting both sectors are three other major construction industry contributors — subcontractors, architects, engineers and other construction services, and building material suppliers and manufacturers. A close partner of the construction industry is the real estate industry, which is included in the finance, insurance & real estate sector, described below.

## Defense ..........................................................................................................................$7.9 million

The decline and eventual demise of the cold war and the Soviet Union have signaled gloomy days for defense contractors. Many large corporations (like Ford Motor Co.) have divested themselves of defense subsidiaries. Many other big contractors have seen hard times and thin profits. But their dollars continue to flow to congressional candidates, particularly incumbents on the armed services and appropriations committees.

## Energy & Natural Resources ..........................................................................................$16.0 million

Oil & gas is the big industry here. Companies and individuals involved in the production of petroleum products gave $6.9 million to federal candidates in 1989-90. Firms engaged in the distribution of natural gas added another $1.9 million. Power utilities were the second leading source of campaign dollars, giving $3.8 million in all — most of it through PACs. The major demarcation line in the oil & gas industry is between the major multinational oil companies and "independent" operators — based largely in Texas, Oklahoma and Louisiana. The "majors" tend to give most of their dollars through PACs; the "independents" give primarily through individual contributions.

## Finance, Insurance & Real Estate ...............................................................................$43.2 million

The leading sector in both PAC and individual contributions, the finance, insurance and real estate industries provided more than twice as many campaign dollars as any other industry. Each of the three sectors — finance, insurance, and real estate — were major contributors in their own right. Insurance was the biggest industry of all, giving $10.8 million. Real estate brokers and developers were close behind, with just under $10 million in contributions. Commercial banks gave $7.8 million and the securities industry added another $5.9 million.

## Health ...............................................................................................................................$16.3 million

The dominant source of campaign contributions from this industry came from physicians, both individually and through PACs operated by professional groups such as the American Medical Association. Doctors, dentists, psychologists and other health professionals gave just over $11 million to federal candidates in the 1990 elections, about two-thirds of it from PACs. Pharmaceutical manufacturers were another major source of campaign funds, as were hospitals and nursing homes.

## Lawyers and Lobbyists ................................................................................................$18.6 million

If one were looking at PAC dollars alone, no industry would be as under-represented as the legal profession, where three-quarters of the dollars came not from PACs but from individual lawyers and lobbyists. A top priority for many lawyers is the blocking of any "tort reform" legislation that would curtail cash settlements (and lawyers' fees) against corporations found liable for faulty products. This is the major interest of the Association of Trial Lawyers of America, whose PAC is the single biggest contributor in the legal community (and one of the largest PACs in the nation). Many other lawyers — particularly those based in Washington, D.C. — give both on their own behalf and to smooth the way as they lobby members of Congress on behalf of a wide variety of clients interested in passing or blocking federal legislation.

## Miscellaneous Business ..............................................................................................$19.5 million

This is a catchall category that includes a variety of business services — from billboard companies to beer wholesalers — and a potpourri of manufacturing companies producing everything from textiles to handguns. The manufacturing sector is the biggest within this classification. Other major contributors are the food and beverage industry, beer, wine & liquor manufacturers and distributors, chemical companies and retailers.

## Transportation ...........................................................................................................$12.5 million

The automotive and air transport industries were the leaders among transportation contributors in the 1990 elections — though the top contributors in each field might be surprising to a casual observer. In the air transport sector, it was not the airlines or aircraft manufacturers that led the spending, but rather the nation's two leading express delivery services — Federal Express and UPS. In the automotive sector, the big three auto makers combined to give a relatively modest $1.2 million. The leaders there were not the auto manufacturers, but auto *dealers*. Two PACs in particular gave the biggest share of funds: The National Auto Dealers Association, and Auto Dealers & Drivers for Free Trade, a PAC that represents dealers of Japanese cars.

## Labor ...............................................................................................................................$36.6 million

No other industry or interest is as loyal to a single party as organized labor, which delivered 92 percent of its funds in 1989-90 to Democratic candidates. Labor unions have long been the Democrats' strongest supporters, providing both dollars and campaign volunteers, but their overall importance to Democratic candidates may have begun to decline — particularly among established incumbents. Since the early 1980s, congressional Democrats have drawn ever increasing proportion of their dollars from business PACs. And those PAC dollars are supplemented with millions more in individual contributions from business leaders. Overall, business interests outspent organized labor by a factor of nearly five to one in the 1990 elections.

## Ideological/Single-Issue ............................................................................................$20.2 million

Among ideological and single-interest groups, those concerned with US policy towards Israel were by far the biggest contributors, delivering more than $6.7 million to federal candidates in the 1990 elections. The second leading source — though far behind — was a collection of "leadership PACs" operated by members of Congress or other prominent Democratic and Republican figures. The remaining PACs in this group covered every conceivable position along the ideological spectrum from right to left. Also included here are PACs interested in specific issues — from abortion to gun control, tax policy to gay and lesbian rights.

# Business Contributors

## Where the money came from . . .

By far the largest source of campaign contributions for members of Congress are the corporations, trade associations and professional groups that are loosely classified under the label "business" contributors. The PACs and individual contributors represented in this group come from every sector of American industry — sectors which are explored in greater detail on the following pages. Together, giving both through PACs and individuals, business groups delivered more than $173 million to candidates for Congress in the 1990 elections.

The financial sector was the leader by a large margin — both in PAC giving and from individuals. Lawyers and lobbyists, the smallest group of all in PAC giving, was the only sector to come close to the financial givers in individual contributions. In sharp contrast to all the other sectors, lawyers delivered three out of every four dollars in contributions through individuals instead of PACs.

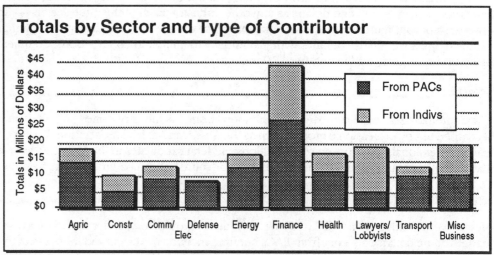

### Totals by Sector and Type of Contributor

| Category | Total | From PACs | PAC Pct | From Indivs | Indiv Pct |
|---|---|---|---|---|---|
| Agriculture | $17,836,291 | $13,673,599 | 77% | $4,162,692 | 23% |
| Construction | $9,476,751 | $4,807,741 | 51% | $4,669,010 | 49% |
| Comm/Electronics | $12,275,110 | $8,216,235 | 67% | $4,058,875 | 33% |
| Defense | $7,882,384 | $7,385,527 | 94% | $496,857 | 6% |
| Energy/Nat Resource | $15,990,937 | $12,120,379 | 76% | $3,870,558 | 24% |
| Finance/Insur/Real Estate | $43,160,575 | $26,611,513 | 62% | $16,549,062 | 38% |
| Health | $16,293,612 | $10,945,182 | 67% | $5,348,430 | 33% |
| Lawyers/Lobbyists | $18,594,709 | $4,591,916 | 25% | $14,002,793 | 75% |
| Transportation | $12,505,004 | $9,737,619 | 78% | $2,767,385 | 22% |
| Misc Business | $19,460,038 | $10,045,503 | 52% | $9,414,535 | 48% |
| **GRAND TOTAL** | **$173,475,411** | **$108,135,214** | **62%** | **$65,340,197** | **38%** |

Totals include PAC contributions to all candidates and individual contributions to winners only

## Top 20 Business Contributors

| Rank | Total | Contributor | Category | PAC Pct | Dem Pct | Repub Pct | To Dems / To Repubs |
|---|---|---|---|---|---|---|---|
| 1 | $3,094,228 | National Assn of Realtors | Real Estate | 100% | 56% | 44% | |
| 2 | $2,647,981 | American Medical Assn | Doctors | 100% | 49% | 51% | |
| 3 | $1,539,550 | Assn of Trial Lawyers of America | Lawyers | 100% | 87% | 13% | |
| 4 | $1,487,800 | National Assn of Life Underwriters | Life Insurance | 100% | 51% | 49% | |
| 5 | $1,477,200 | AT&T | Long Distance | 98% | 57% | 43% | |
| 6 | $1,473,061 | American Bankers Assn | Comml Banks | 100% | 55% | 45% | |
| 7 | $1,362,550 | National Assn of Home Builders | Resid Constr | 100% | 48% | 52% | |
| 8 | $1,313,900 | National Auto Dealers Assn | Auto Dealers | 100% | 38% | 62% | |
| 9 | $1,089,294 | American Institute of CPA's | Accountants | 100% | 56% | 44% | |
| 10 | $961,411 | American Academy of Ophthalmology | Eye Doctors | 100% | 52% | 48% | |
| 11 | $824,578 | American Dental Assn | Dentists | 100% | 54% | 46% | |
| 12 | $823,337 | RJR Nabisco | Tobacco/Food | 98% | 50% | 50% | |
| 13 | $769,800 | Associated Milk Producers | Dairy | 100% | 67% | 33% | |
| 14 | $765,225 | Federal Express Corp | Air Freight | 99% | 63% | 37% | |
| 15 | $699,974 | BellSouth | Phone Utilites | 95% | 56% | 44% | |
| 16 | $692,743 | American Council of Life Insurance | Life Insurance | 100% | 58% | 42% | |
| 17 | $676,335 | Independent Insurance Agents of America | Insurance | 100% | 58% | 42% | |
| 18 | $659,732 | United Parcel Service | Air/Land Freight | 100% | 60% | 40% | |
| 19 | $654,769 | ACRE (Action Cmte for Rural Electrification) | Rural Electric | 100% | 69% | 31% | |
| 20 | $654,194 | Associated General Contractors | Heavy Constr | 99% | 22% | 78% | |

## Where the money went . . .

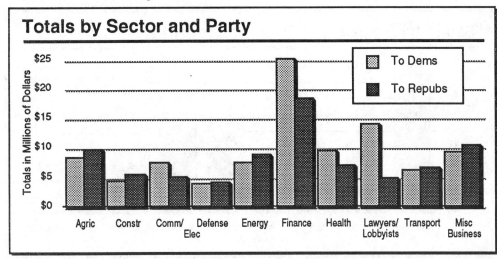

### Totals by Sector and Party

| Category | Total | To Dems | Dem Pct | To Repubs | Repub Pct |
|---|---|---|---|---|---|
| Agriculture | $17,836,291 | $8,206,840 | 46% | $9,625,251 | 54% |
| Construction | $9,476,751 | $4,134,583 | 44% | $5,341,418 | 56% |
| Comm/Electronics | $12,275,110 | $7,365,932 | 60% | $4,904,348 | 40% |
| Defense | $7,882,384 | $3,833,272 | 49% | $4,050,081 | 51% |
| Energy/Nat Resource | $15,990,937 | $7,371,577 | 46% | $8,618,709 | 54% |
| Finance/Insur/Real Estate | $43,160,575 | $24,973,503 | 58% | $18,167,437 | 42% |
| Health | $16,293,612 | $9,303,032 | 57% | $6,987,048 | 43% |
| Lawyers/Lobbyists | $18,594,709 | $13,893,577 | 75% | $4,698,732 | 25% |
| Transportation | $12,505,004 | $6,122,135 | 49% | $6,376,019 | 51% |
| Misc Business | $19,460,038 | $9,209,979 | 47% | $10,245,259 | 53% |
| **GRAND TOTAL** | **$173,475,411** | **$94,414,430** | **54%** | **$79,014,302** | **46%** |

Overall, Democrats attracted a slight majority of the dollars from within the business community — a fact that might surprise many people, since most business groups tend to be more Republican in their political outlook than Democratic. Whatever their personal preferences, however, the one quality that marks nearly all business groups is their pragmatism. Bluntly speaking, the Democrats control both houses of Congress with comfortable majorities. Business leaders know well that if legislation is to succeed, the majority party is going to have to go along with it.

Most sectors within the business community split their dollars fairly evenly between the Republicans and Democrats. The exception, however, was the legal community which gave three-quarters of its dollars to Democrats. Lawyers tend to have two distinct reasons for giving to members of Congress. Trial lawyers have long been active in blocking tort reform legislation that could drastically reduce cash settlements in product liability cases (thereby reducing attorney's fees). The trial lawyers operate one of the biggest PACs in the nation and have strongly supported Democrats through direct contributions, independent expenditures and "soft money" contributions to the Democratic party. The other group within the legal community that has a particular interest in congressional politics are those lawyers and law firms engaged in lobbying on Capitol Hill. Washington law firms were among the biggest contributors within the legal community. The great majority of their dollars are delivered through individual, as opposed to PAC, contributions.

The combined financial clout of the business community vastly exceeds that of the two other major sectors giving to congressional candidates — labor unions and ideological/single-issue groups. And within the business sector the largest volume of dollars comes from the financial, insurance and real estate industries. Like most businesses, those groups split their dollars between Democrats and Republicans, but the Democrats' advantage was relatively substantial — as can be seen from the chart above. The sheer volume of those financial sector contributions were another factor giving Democrats the overall edge in business dollars in the 1990 elections.

# Agriculture

## *Where the money came from . . .*

The Agriculture sector encompasses thousands of independent farmers, ranchers, and dairy producers from Maine to California, but that's just the half of it. Also included in this widely diversified category are commodities brokers, lumber companies, grocery wholesalers, pesticide manufacturers and giant food industry conglomerates making everything from cigarettes to frozen pizzas. In all, the industry contributed nearly $18 million to congressional campaigns in the 1990 elections. More than three-quarters of the money came from political action committees and just over half went to Republicans.

Within the farming community, the heaviest crop of dollars came from sugar growers and dairy producers, though detailed classifications were not always possible since many contributors described themselves simply as "farmers." Nearly all the tobacco and dairy money was delivered through PACs, while ranchers and meat processors were the groups most likely to make individual contributions.

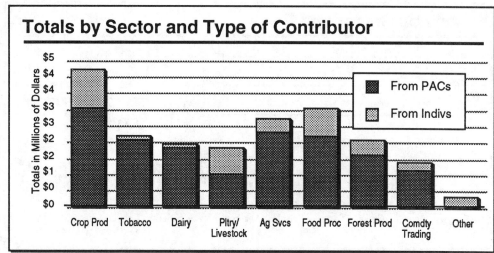

| Category | Total | From PACs | PAC Pct | From Indivs | Indiv Pct |
|---|---|---|---|---|---|
| Crop Production/Processing | $4,159,300 | $2,997,039 | 72% | $1,162,261 | 28% |
| Tobacco | $2,126,974 | $2,011,766 | 95% | $115,208 | 5% |
| Dairy | $1,887,117 | $1,773,041 | 94% | $114,076 | 6% |
| Poultry & Livestock | $1,755,233 | $961,535 | 55% | $793,698 | 45% |
| Agricultural Services/Products | $2,665,769 | $2,241,751 | 84% | $424,018 | 16% |
| Food Processing & Sales | $2,978,904 | $2,139,055 | 72% | $839,849 | 28% |
| Forest Products | $2,008,560 | $1,549,412 | 77% | $459,148 | 23% |
| Commodity Trading* | $1,323,500 | $1,080,000 | 82% | $243,500 | 18% |
| Other & Unclassified | $254,434 | $0 | 0% | $254,434 | 100% |
| **TOTAL** | **$17,836,291** | **$13,673,599** | **77%** | **$4,162,692** | **23%** |

\* Listed for information only. Total is included under Finance/Insurance/Real Estate

## Top 20 Agriculture Contributors

| Rank | Total | Contributor | Category | PAC Pct | Dem Pct | Repub Pct | To Dems / To Repubs |
|---|---|---|---|---|---|---|---|
| 1 | $823,337 | RJR Nabisco | Tobacco/Food | 98% | 50% | 50% | |
| 2 | $769,800 | Associated Milk Producers | Dairy | 100% | 67% | 33% | |
| 3 | $613,011 | Philip Morris† | Tobacco/Food | 97% | 52% | 48% | |
| 4 | $485,950 | Mid-America Dairymen | Dairy | 100% | 71% | 29% | |
| 5 | $408,125 | American Crystal Sugar Corp | Sugar | 100% | 63% | 37% | |
| 6 | $376,572 | Food Marketing Institute | Food Stores | 100% | 35% | 65% | |
| 7 | $327,057 | American Sugarbeet Growers Assn | Sugar | 100% | 59% | 41% | |
| 8 | $315,150 | United States Tobacco Co | Tobacco | 97% | 31% | 69% | |
| 9 | $299,737 | National Cattlemens Assn | Livestock | 100% | 36% | 64% | |
| 10 | $297,700 | Archer-Daniels-Midland Corp | Grain Traders | 82% | 56% | 44% | |
| 11 | $273,137 | Pepsico Inc | Food & Bevg | 97% | 28% | 72% | |
| 12 | $248,501 | Dairymen Inc | Dairy | 100% | 63% | 37% | |
| 13 | $235,500 | Westvaco Corp | Paper/Pulp | 100% | 21% | 79% | |
| 14 | $235,000 | American Veterinary Medical Assn | Veterinary | 100% | 54% | 46% | |
| 15 | $224,190 | International Paper Co | Paper/Pulp | 100% | 18% | 82% | |
| 16 | $215,825 | Southern Minnesota Beet Sugar Co-op | Sugar | 100% | 52% | 48% | |
| 17 | $208,699 | ConAgra Inc | Food Products | 98% | 23% | 77% | |
| 18 | $205,375 | Tobacco Institute | Tobacco | 100% | 42% | 58% | |
| 19 | $197,715 | American Sugar Cane League | Sugar | 100% | 63% | 37% | |
| 20 | $189,306 | National Cotton Council | Cotton | 99% | 53% | 47% | |

† Includes only food and tobacco operations

## Where the money went . . .

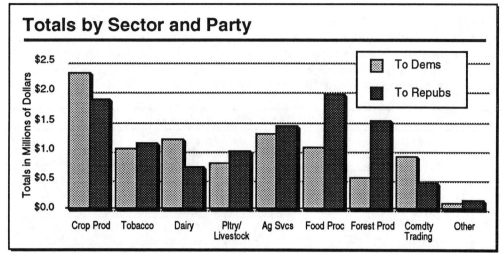

### Totals by Sector and Party

Legend: To Dems, To Repubs

Y-axis: Totals in Millions of Dollars — $0.0, $0.5, $1.0, $1.5, $2.0, $2.5

X-axis categories: Crop Prod, Tobacco, Dairy, Pltry/Livestock, Ag Svcs, Food Proc, Forest Prod, Comdty Trading, Other

Overall, the agriculture contributors tilted slightly toward Republican candidates, but there were wide variations within the industry. Dairy farmers and commodities brokers were the most likely to support Democrats, while timber companies and paper manufacturers gave nearly three out of four of their campaign dollars to Republicans.

| Category | Total | To Dems | Dem Pct | To Repubs | Repub Pct |
|---|---|---|---|---|---|
| Crop Production/Processing | $4,159,300 | $2,308,210 | 55% | $1,850,590 | 44% |
| Tobacco | $2,126,974 | $1,009,699 | 47% | $1,117,275 | 53% |
| Dairy | $1,887,117 | $1,186,894 | 63% | $700,023 | 37% |
| Poultry & Livestock | $1,755,233 | $773,886 | 44% | $981,347 | 56% |
| Agricultural Services/Products | $2,665,769 | $1,260,104 | 47% | $1,405,665 | 53% |
| Food Processing & Sales | $2,978,904 | $1,034,484 | 35% | $1,940,920 | 65% |
| Forest Products | $2,008,560 | $527,414 | 26% | $1,481,146 | 74% |
| Commodity Trading* | $1,323,500 | $884,780 | 67% | $438,260 | 33% |
| Other & Unclassified | $254,434 | $106,149 | 42% | $148,285 | 58% |
| **TOTAL** | **$17,836,291** | **$8,206,840** | **46%** | **$9,625,251** | **54%** |

\* Listed for information only. Total is included under Finance/Insurance/Real Estate

Farm-state lawmakers — from both sides of the aisle — were the top recipients of agriculture dollars in 1990. Republican Senator Phil Gramm raised particularly large amounts from Texas ranchers, while House Democrat Gary Condit drew heavily from fruit and vegetable growers in central California. Condit's total was inflated by the fact that he ran twice in 1989-90, the first time in a special election when he first won the seat in 1989.

Six of the top Senate recipients and nine of the top 10 House recipients held seats on the Agriculture committees of their respective houses.

### Top 10 Senate Recipients

| Rank | Name | Amount | Status | W/L |
|---|---|---|---|---|
| 1 | Phil Gramm (R-Texas) | $484,959 | Incumb | W |
| 2 | Howell Heflin (D-Ala) | $367,372 | Incumb | W |
| 3 | Mitch McConnell (R-Ky) | $366,860 | Incumb | W |
| 4 | Jesse Helms (R-NC) | $290,048 | Incumb | W |
| 5 | Thad Cochran (R-Miss) | $272,325 | Incumb | W |
| 6 | Rudy Boschwitz (R-Minn) | $272,299 | Incumb | L |
| 7 | Mark O. Hatfield (R-Ore) | $230,999 | Incumb | W |
| 8 | Larry E. Craig (R-Idaho) | $218,083 | Open | W |
| 9 | Hank Brown (R-Colo) | $202,268 | Open | W |
| 10 | William D Schuette (R-Mich) | $199,984 | Chall | L |

### Top 10 House Recipients

| Rank | Name | Amount | Status | W/L |
|---|---|---|---|---|
| 1 | Gary Condit (D-Calif) | $191,334 | Incumb | W |
| 2 | Bill Emerson (R-Mo) | $145,331 | Incumb | W |
| 3 | Wally Herger (R-Calif) | $129,809 | Incumb | W |
| 4 | Arlan Stangeland (R-Minn) | $111,351 | Incumb | L |
| 5 | Clyde C. Holloway (R-La) | $100,500 | Incumb | W |
| 6 | Bill Alexander (D-Ark) | $100,425 | Incumb | W |
| 7 | Charles Hatcher (D-Ga) | $92,205 | Incumb | W |
| 8 | Fred Grandy (R-Iowa) | $92,000 | Incumb | W |
| 9 | Mike Espy (D-Miss) | $91,915 | Incumb | W |
| 10 | Charlie Rose (D-NC) | $91,700 | Incumb | W |

# Closeup on Agriculture

## Crop Production & Basic Processing ......................................................... $4.1 million

Though this category includes farmers raising every crop under the sun, five of the top six contributors were sugar producers. Fruit and vegetable growers — particularly those based in California — were also big givers. The top three congressional recipients of farm contributions in the House and Senate were all from southern agricultural states. The three leading Senators were all members of the Senate Agriculture Committee, but none of the top House recipients held agriculture seats. Agricultural subsidies from the federal government are crucial to the nation's farmers.

### Top Contributors

| Rank | Contributor | Total | Category |
|------|-------------|-------|----------|
| 1 | American Crystal Sugar Corp | $408,125 | Sugar |
| 2 | American Sugarbeet Growers Assn | $327,057 | Sugar |
| 3 | Southern Minnesota Beet Sugar Co-op | $215,825 | Sugar |
| 4 | American Sugar Cane League | $197,715 | Sugar |
| 5 | National Cotton Council | $189,306 | Cotton |
| 6 | Florida Sugar Cane League | $176,150 | Sugar |
| 7 | Ocean Spray Cranberries Inc | $118,782 | Fruit/Veg |
| 8 | California Almond Growers Exchange | $89,989 | Fruit/Veg |
| 9 | Hawaiian Sugar Planters Assn | $89,420 | Sugar |
| 10 | Sun-Diamond Growers | $87,949 | Fruit/Veg |

### Top Senate Recipients

| Rank | Recipient | Total |
|------|-----------|-------|
| 1 | Howell Heflin (D-Ala) | $143,861 |
| 2 | Thad Cochran (R-Miss) | $126,625 |
| 3 | David Pryor (D-Ark) | $77,449 |

### Top House Recipients

| Rank | Recipient | Total |
|------|-----------|-------|
| 1 | Gary Condit (D-Calif) | $108,819 |
| 2 | Clyde C. Holloway (R-La) | $58,300 |
| 3 | Jerry Huckaby (D-La) | $53,225 |

## Tobacco ......................................................................................... $2.1 million

Tobacco companies gave a combined $2.1 million to federal candidates in the 1990 elections. RJR Nabisco led the industry, delivering more than $820,000. Most of that money came through the company's political action committee, which nearly tripled its giving from two years earlier. Like RJR, many of the other top tobacco companies have diversified into food products. Five of the top six House and Senate recipients of tobacco money came from major tobacco growing states.

### Top Contributors

| Rank | Contributor | Total | Category |
|------|-------------|-------|----------|
| 1 | RJR Nabisco | $738,937 | Tobacco |
| 2 | Philip Morris | $588,411 | Tobacco |
| 3 | United States Tobacco Co | $315,150 | Tobacco |
| 4 | Tobacco Institute | $205,375 | Tobacco |
| 5 | Batus Inc | $65,476 | Tobacco |

### Top Senate Recipients

| Rank | Recipient | Total |
|------|-----------|-------|
| 1 | Mitch McConnell (R-Ky) | $60,150 |
| 2 | Jesse Helms (R-NC) | $53,530 |
| 3 | Hank Brown (R-Colo) | $27,000 |

### Top House Recipients

| Rank | Recipient | Total |
|------|-----------|-------|
| 1 | Thomas J. Bliley Jr. (R-Va) | $32,699 |
| 2 | Stephen L. Neal (D-NC) | $29,387 |
| 3 | Don Sundquist (R-Tenn) | $25,700 |

## Dairy ............................................................................................. $1.9 million

The dairy industry has long been a major contributor to congressional campaigns, a reflection of the importance to the industry of federal milk supports. Overall, nearly two-thirds of the dairy industry's dollars went to Democrats.

### Top Contributors

| Rank | Contributor | Total | Category |
|------|-------------|-------|----------|
| 1 | Associated Milk Producers | $769,800 | Dairy |
| 2 | Mid-America Dairymen | $485,950 | Dairy |
| 3 | Dairymen Inc | $248,501 | Dairy |
| 4 | Milk Industry Foundation | $94,150 | Dairy |
| 5 | Milk Marketing Inc | $72,300 | Dairy |

### Top Senate Recipients

| Rank | Recipient | Total |
|------|-----------|-------|
| 1 | Mitch McConnell (R-Ky) | $27,100 |
| 2 | Jim Exon (D-Neb) | $24,000 |
| 3 | Rudy Boschwitz (R-Minn) | $22,425 |

### Top House Recipients

| Rank | Recipient | Total |
|------|-----------|-------|
| 1 | Jim Jontz (D-Ind) | $23,900 |
| 2 | Jill L. Long (D-Ind) | $21,850 |
| 3 | Gary Condit (D-Calif) | $21,305 |

## Agricultural Services & Products .........................................................................$2.7 million

The support industries that provide everything from fertilizers and pesticides to crop insurance form a major segment of the agriculture industry's contributions to Congress. In contrast to food growers, this sector of the agriculture industry gave nearly two-thirds of its contributions to Democrats. Archer-Daniels-Midland, the giant grain trader that is the nation's largest supplier of gasohol, is also a major "soft money" contributor, particularly to the Republican Party.

### Top Contributors

| Rank | Contributor | Total | Category |
|---|---|---|---|
| 1 | Archer-Daniels-Midland Corp | $297,700 | Grain Traders |
| 2 | American Veterinary Medical Assn | $235,000 | Veterinary |
| 3 | American Assn of Crop Insurers | $145,900 | Ag Services |
| 4 | Deere & Co | $127,900 | Farm Equip |
| 5 | National Council of Farmer Co-ops | $126,396 | Farm Orgs |
| 6 | Farm Credit Council | $105,107 | Ag Services |
| 7 | Land O'Lakes Inc | $92,200 | Ag Chemicals |
| 8 | Alabama Farm Bureau Federation | $86,511 | Farm Orgs |
| 9 | CF Industries | $68,700 | Ag Chemicals |
| 10 | Rhone-Poulenc Inc | $64,700 | Ag Chemicals |

### Top Senate Recipients

| Rank | Recipient | Total |
|---|---|---|
| 1 | Rudy Boschwitz (R-Minn) | $75,200 |
| 2 | Howell Heflin (D-Ala) | $67,425 |
| 3 | Bill Schuette (R-Mich) | $63,449 |

### Top House Recipients

| Rank | Recipient | Total |
|---|---|---|
| 1 | Fred Grandy (R-Iowa) | $35,800 |
| 2 | Bill Emerson (R-Mo) | $33,250 |
| 3 | George E. Brown Jr. (D-Calif) | $28,850 |

## Food Processing & Sales ...................................................................................$3.0 million

These are the middlemen who process the raw materials from farmers and deliver them to the shopping baskets of consumers in supermarkets. More Republican than most other sectors within agriculture, their spending patterns more closely resemble those of other manufacturing interests.

### Top Contributors

| Rank | Contributor | Total | Category |
|---|---|---|---|
| 1 | Food Marketing Institute | $376,572 | Food Stores |
| 2 | Pepsico Inc | $273,137 | Food & Bevg |
| 3 | ConAgra Inc | $208,699 | Food Prod |
| 4 | Winn-Dixie Stores | $137,250 | Food Stores |
| 5 | Flowers Industries | $135,550 | Food Prod |
| 6 | American Meat Institute | $133,471 | Meat Prod |
| 7 | General Mills | $100,000 | Food Prod |
| 8 | Nabisco Brands Inc | $84,400 | Food Prod |
| 9 | Malone & Hyde Inc | $82,250 | Food Whlsale |
| 10 | National Wholesale Grocers Assn | $77,400 | Food Whlsale |

### Top Senate Recipients

| Rank | Recipient | Total |
|---|---|---|
| 1 | Phil Gramm (R-Texas) | $121,165 |
| 2 | Mitch McConnell (R-Ky) | $71,375 |
| 3 | Daniel R. Coats (R-Ind) | $63,025 |

### Top House Recipients

| Rank | Recipient | Total |
|---|---|---|
| 1 | Bill Emerson (R-Mo) | $24,850 |
| 2 | Newt Gingrich (R-Ga) | $23,300 |
| 3 | Bill Barrett (R-Neb) | $21,200 |

## Forest Products ...................................................................................................$2.0 million

Ongoing battles between timber companies and environmentalists over logging policies on federal lands is one of the major issues that drive these companies' interest in federal campaigns. Among paper mills, clean air legislation is another. Overall, this sector was the most conservative within agriculture — 74 percent of its dollars went to Republicans.

### Top Contributors

| Rank | Contributor | Total | Category |
|---|---|---|---|
| 1 | Westvaco Corp | $235,500 | Paper Prod |
| 2 | International Paper Co | $224,190 | Paper Prod |
| 3 | Union Camp Corp | $123,500 | Paper Prod |
| 4 | Georgia-Pacific Corp | $112,599 | Forest Prod |
| 5 | Champion International Corp | $101,767 | Paper Prod |
| 6 | Weyerhaeuser Co | $101,717 | Paper Prod |
| 7 | Boise Cascade | $94,250 | Forest Prod |
| 8 | Manville Corp | $93,250 | Forest Prod |
| 9 | Mead Corp | $76,000 | Paper Prod |
| 10 | National Forest Products Assn | $61,524 | Forest Prod |

### Top Senate Recipients

| Rank | Recipient | Total |
|---|---|---|
| 1 | Mark O. Hatfield (R-Ore) | $174,600 |
| 2 | Larry E. Craig (R-Idaho) | $79,820 |
| 3 | Lynn Martin (R-Ill) | $56,597 |

### Top House Recipients

| Rank | Recipient | Total |
|---|---|---|
| 1 | Les AuCoin (D-Ore) | $37,834 |
| 2 | Bob Smith (R-Ore) | $37,047 |
| 3 | G Robert Williams (R-Wash) | $33,520 |

# Communications & Electronics

## Where the money came from . . .

Increasingly, the thread that ties the American nation together is an electronic one. We plug into television for the day's news, weather, football games and soap operas. We flash faxes by the millions across the continent each business day. Our telephones are never far from reach, whether we're in the backyard, the interstate, or 30,000 feet up in the air. And our computers — desktop, laptop, or palm-of-the-hand varieties — are becoming more ubiquitous and more necessary every day. We are a nation plugged in, and our unceasing appetites for instant news, communications and entertainment have spawned industries that have become an increasingly important sector of the American economy.

Since much of the telecommunications industry comes under federal regulation, decisions made in Congress can mean billions to the industry. Both sides know it, and the flow of dollars to federal campaigns reflects that fact. In the 1990 elections, the communi-

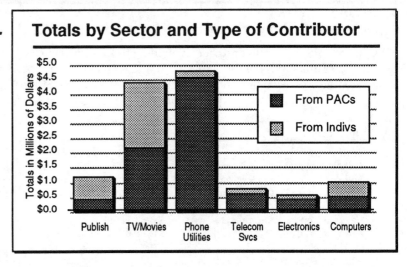

### Totals by Sector and Type of Contributor

| Category | Total | From PACs | PAC Pct | From Indivs | Indiv Pct |
|---|---|---|---|---|---|
| Printing & Publishing | $1,104,384 | $328,200 | 30% | $776,184 | 70% |
| TV, Movies & Recorded Music | $4,309,154 | $2,105,777 | 49% | $2,203,377 | 51% |
| Telephone Utilities | $4,717,480 | $4,472,735 | 95% | $244,745 | 5% |
| Telecom Services & Equip | $707,222 | $518,055 | 73% | $189,167 | 27% |
| Electronics Mfg & Services | $488,201 | $336,709 | 69% | $151,492 | 31% |
| Computer Equipment & Svcs | $927,969 | $454,759 | 49% | $473,210 | 51% |
| Other & Unclassified | $20,700 | $0 | 0% | $20,700 | 100% |
| **TOTAL** | **$12,275,110** | **$8,216,235** | **67%** | **$4,058,875** | **33%** |

cations and electronics industry gave $12.2 million to congressional candidates.

Within the sector, there were significant variations both in the source and distribution of campaign funds. The telecommunications industry, dominated by AT&T and the regional Bell telephone companies, gave nearly all its dollars through political action committees. AT&T, in fact, supports the largest corporate PAC in the nation, and dispensed nearly $1.5 million in contributions in 1989-90. The motion picture industry, centered in Hollywood, gave half its dollars through individual contributions — mainly from studio executives, agents and producers.

## Top 20 Communications & Electronics Contributors

| Rank | Total | Contributor | Category | PAC Pct | Dem Pct | Repub Pct | To Dems / To Repubs |
|---|---|---|---|---|---|---|---|
| 1 | $1,477,200 | AT&T | Long Distance | 98% | 57% | 43% | |
| 2 | $641,724 | BellSouth† | Phone Utilites | 96% | 56% | 44% | |
| 3 | $574,475 | National Cable Television Assn | Cable TV | 99% | 63% | 37% | |
| 4 | $413,425 | GTE Corp | Phone Utilites | 99% | 49% | 51% | |
| 5 | $399,795 | Time Warner | TV/Movies/Publ | 28% | 90% | 10% | |
| 6 | $357,485 | US West | Phone Utilites | 93% | 43% | 57% | |
| 7 | $314,386 | Ameritech | Phone Utilites | 98% | 47% | 53% | |
| 8 | $291,625 | Westinghouse Electric | Electronics Mfg | 93% | 57% | 43% | |
| 9 | $285,445 | Contel | Phone Utilites | 98% | 29% | 71% | |
| 10 | $278,268 | National Assn of Broadcasters | TV/Radio | 100% | 47% | 53% | |
| 11 | $277,950 | MCA Inc | TV/Movies | 66% | 89% | 11% | |
| 12 | $277,034 | Walt Disney Co | Movies | 31% | 82% | 18% | |
| 13 | $265,997 | Bell Atlantic | Phone Utilites | 98% | 58% | 42% | |
| 14 | $239,054 | Pacific Telesis Group | Phone Utilites | 100% | 62% | 38% | |
| 15 | $237,600 | Harris Corp | Electronics Mfg | 95% | 6% | 94% | |
| 16 | $231,582 | United Telecommunications | Long Distance | 98% | 40% | 60% | |
| 17 | $209,090 | NYNEX | Phone Utilites | 97% | 49% | 51% | |
| 18 | $203,260 | Corning Glass Works | Communic Equip | 81% | 44% | 56% | |
| 19 | $193,250 | Southwestern Bell | Phone Utilites | 100% | 51% | 49% | |
| 20 | $185,570 | Paramount Communications | TV/Movies | 61% | 71% | 29% | |

† Includes only telecommunications operations

# Where the money went . . .

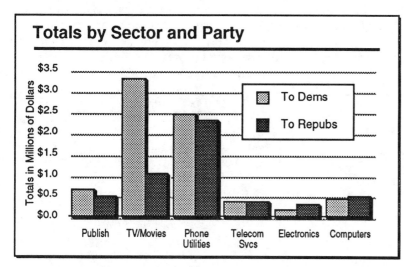

## Totals by Sector and Party

Totals in Millions of Dollars

Publish | TV/Movies | Phone Utilities | Telecom Svcs | Electronics | Computers

☐ To Dems
■ To Repubs

The Hollywood film community — both the studios and the stars — have always shown a strong preference for Democrats, a fact clearly reflected in the chart on the left. Telephone utilities split their dollars down the middle, taking a more pragmatic approach and paying particular attention to the members who sit on committees that oversee telecommunications policy.

| Category | Total | To Dems | Dem Pct | To Repubs | Repub Pct |
|---|---|---|---|---|---|
| Printing & Publishing | $1,104,384 | $630,076 | 57% | $473,158 | 43% |
| TV, Movies & Recorded Music | $4,309,154 | $3,295,665 | 76% | $1,011,389 | 23% |
| Telephone Utilities | $4,717,480 | $2,449,502 | 52% | $2,267,698 | 48% |
| Telecom Services & Equip | $707,222 | $362,252 | 51% | $344,970 | 49% |
| Electronics Mfg & Services | $488,201 | $182,703 | 37% | $305,498 | 63% |
| Computer Equipment & Svcs | $927,969 | $433,384 | 47% | $493,285 | 53% |
| Other & Unclassified | $20,700 | $12,350 | 60% | $8,350 | 40% |
| TOTAL | $12,275,110 | $7,365,932 | 60% | $4,904,348 | 40% |

Though few would consider him telegenic or particularly charismatic, Democratic Senator Bill Bradley of New Jersey had the golden touch with the Hollywood film community. Bradley collected nearly $570,000 from the Los Angeles area in his 1990 reelection campaign — much of that came from the film community. John Kerry of Massachusetts was another big recipient both of Hollywood money and communications money. He was the top recipient of funds from the Cable TV industry.

Mel Levine, whose district is just a short freeway hop from Hollywood, was the biggest House recipient of communications money, most of it from the film community. John Dingell is chairman of the powerful House Energy and Commerce Committee, which oversees telecommunications policy. Republican Tom Campbell is the congressman from Silicon Valley in California. He received more computer industry funds in 1990 than anyone else in Congress.

## Top 10 Senate Recipients

| Rank | Name | Amount | Status | W/L |
|---|---|---|---|---|
| 1 | Bill Bradley (D-NJ) | $519,505 | Incumb | W |
| 2 | John Kerry (D-Mass) | $312,096 | Incumb | W |
| 3 | Tom Tauke (R-Iowa) | $200,818 | Chall | L |
| 4 | Paul Simon (D-Ill) | $181,222 | Incumb | W |
| 5 | Hank Brown (R-Colo) | $172,525 | Open | W |
| 6 | John D. Rockefeller IV (D-WVa) | $166,157 | Incumb | W |
| 7 | Al Gore (D-Tenn) | $165,249 | Incumb | W |
| 8 | Phil Gramm (R-Texas) | $155,092 | Incumb | W |
| 9 | Howell Heflin (D-Ala) | $146,194 | Incumb | W |
| 10 | Jim Exon (D-Neb) | $145,977 | Incumb | W |

## Top 10 House Recipients

| Rank | Name | Amount | Status | W/L |
|---|---|---|---|---|
| 1 | Mel Levine (D-Calif) | $174,950 | Incumb | W |
| 2 | John D. Dingell (D-Mich) | $101,430 | Incumb | W |
| 3 | Jack Brooks (D-Texas) | $100,091 | Incumb | W |
| 4 | Tom Campbell (R-Calif) | $92,932 | Incumb | W |
| 5 | Richard A. Gephardt (D-Mo) | $87,950 | Incumb | W |
| 6 | Robert J. Mrazek (D-NY) | $80,464 | Incumb | W |
| 7 | Edward J. Markey (D-Mass) | $73,950 | Incumb | W |
| 8 | Mike Synar (D-Okla) | $72,100 | Incumb | W |
| 9 | Al Swift (D-Wash) | $69,000 | Incumb | W |
| 10 | Don Ritter (R-Pa) | $68,925 | Incumb | W |

# Closeup on Communications & Electronics

## Printing & Publishing ............................................................................ $1.1 million

The leading contributor in the publishing sector is West Publishing, the nation's top supplier of legal texts. The top recipient of publishing dollars in Congress was Bill Bradley of New Jersey — just across the Hudson River from the center of the U.S. publishing industry in Manhattan. Many of the best known publishers don't appear on this list, however, because they are no longer independent companies. Rather, they are owned by communications conglomerates (like Time Warner) that get the biggest share of their revenues not from books, but from motion pictures and television.

### Top Contributors

| Rank | Contributor | Total | Category |
|------|-------------|-------|----------|
| 1 | West Publishing | $101,900 | Books |
| 2 | Printing Industries of America | $95,900 | Printing |
| 3 | Hallmark Cards | $91,550 | Greeting Cards |
| 4 | RR Donnelley & Sons | $40,600 | Publishing |
| 5 | Assn of American Publishers | $20,650 | Books & Mags |

### Top Senate Recipients

| Rank | Recipient | Total |
|------|-----------|-------|
| 1 | Bill Bradley (D-NJ) | $95,887 |
| 2 | John Kerry (D-Mass) | $34,250 |
| 3 | Howell Heflin (D-Ala) | $29,832 |

### Top House Recipients

| Rank | Recipient | Total |
|------|-----------|-------|
| 1 | Ileana Ros-Lehtinen (R-Fla) | $19,289 |
| 2 | Nita M. Lowey (D-NY) | $11,450 |
| 3 | Chester G. Atkins (D-Mass) | $9,400 |

## TV & Movies Production/Distribution ................................................ $2.6 million

Two distinct categories of contributors make up this sector — the Hollywood-based TV and movie industry that produces much of the nation's mass-market entertainment, and the nationwide network of TV and radio broadcasters, represented politically by the National Association of Broadcasters. While the broadcasters delivered almost all their dollars through political action committees, a major share of the movie money came from individuals. Time Warner and Disney were among the nation's leading companies in individual contributions. Another important dichotomy: while the station owners gave heavily to both Democrats and Republicans, the film community was decidedly Democratic in its contributions.

Many of Hollywood's big name stars contributed to political causes in the 1990 election, but a significant portion of their money went not to candidates, but to a single PAC — the Hollywood Womens Political Committee.

By and large, however, the big money came not from box office stars, but from the producers and directors behind the cameras. They too tended to prefer Democrats. Overall the industry gave 76 percent of its dollars to Democratic candidates, and only 23 percent to Republicans.

### Top Contributors

| Rank | Contributor | Total | Category |
|------|-------------|-------|----------|
| 1 | Time Warner | $388,075 | TV/Movies |
| 2 | National Assn of Broadcasters | $278,268 | TV/Radio |
| 3 | MCA Inc | $277,950 | Movies |
| 4 | Walt Disney Co | $277,034 | Movies |
| 5 | Paramount Communications | $185,570 | TV/Movies |
| 6 | Motion Picture Assn of America | $87,520 | Movies |
| 7 | Interscope Group | $64,250 | Movies |
| 8 | Fox Inc | $62,400 | Movies |
| 9 | Creative Artists Agency | $48,510 | Movies |
| 10 | Act III Communications | $33,500 | TV Prod |

### Top Senate Recipients

| Rank | Recipient | Total |
|------|-----------|-------|
| 1 | Bill Bradley (D-NJ) | $271,400 |
| 2 | John Kerry (D-Mass) | $149,950 |
| 3 | Paul Simon (D-Ill) | $73,972 |

### Top House Recipients

| Rank | Recipient | Total |
|------|-----------|-------|
| 1 | Mel Levine (D-Calif) | $143,800 |
| 2 | Robert J. Mrazek (D-NY) | $68,250 |
| 3 | Howard L. Berman (D-Calif) | $46,150 |

The biggest recipient of Hollywood money in the 1990 elections was New Jersey Senator Bill Bradley, who collected nearly twice as much as anyone else. Bradley was considered Hollywood's favorite for President in 1992, until his embarrassingly close 1990 Senate reelection race effectively eliminated him from presidential contention in '92.

Two of the top three House recipients of TV and movie contributions — Mel Levine and Howard Berman — represent Los Angeles area districts not far from Hollywood. Robert Mrazek, of New York, caught the film community's attention by introducing a bill in Congress to prevent colorization of old black-and-white movies.

# Cable TV .................................................................................................$1.4 million

This classification includes only those firms whose business is wholly or primarily concerned with cable TV. Many of the biggest names (and contributors) in the industry are more diversified media companies and are included in the previous page under TV & Movie production. The cable TV industry has been an active player in Washington politics in recent years — partly trying to fend off tighter federal regulation of the industry in the face of consumer complaints about high fees and poor service, and also combatting the efforts of telephone utilities to expand into the home entertainment industry through telephone lines as opposed to TV cables.

**Top Contributors**

| Rank | Contributor | Total | Category |
|------|-------------|-------|----------|
| 1 | National Cable Television Assn | $574,475 | Cable TV |
| 2 | Tele-Communications Inc | $131,918 | Cable TV |
| 3 | Home Shopping Network Inc | $84,000 | Cable TV |
| 4 | Viacom International | $75,400 | Cable TV |
| 5 | Turner Broadcasting System | $68,908 | Cable TV |

**Top Senate Recipients**

| Rank | Recipient | Total |
|------|-----------|-------|
| 1 | John Kerry (D-Mass) | $73,425 |
| 2 | Ted Stevens (R-Alaska) | $52,360 |
| 3 | Paul Simon (D-Ill) | $44,500 |

**Top House Recipients**

| Rank | Recipient | Total |
|------|-----------|-------|
| 1 | Dan Schaefer (R-Colo) | $24,283 |
| 2 | Mike Synar (D-Okla) | $21,200 |
| 3 | Thomas J. Manton (D-NY) | $20,250 |

# Telephone Utilities ...............................................................$4.7 million

The breakup of the Bell System in 1984 did little to dampen the telephone companies' political participation. Nearly every major telephone utility was a contributor — both to candidates in their own area and to lawmakers sitting on committees important to the telecommunications industry.

AT&T, which supports the nation's largest corporate-sponsored political action committee, towered over all other contributors in the field. State and regional Bell companies were also big contributors. In this chart, and throughout the book, contributions by local phone utilities — such as Illinois Bell or Chesapeake & Potomac phone company — have been combined into their regional affiliates (Ameritech and Bell Atlantic to use those examples).

**Top Contributors**

| Rank | Contributor | Total | Category |
|------|-------------|-------|----------|
| 1 | AT&T | $1,477,200 | Long Distance |
| 2 | BellSouth | $640,224 | Phone Utilites |
| 3 | GTE Corp | $413,425 | Phone Utilites |
| 4 | US West | $357,485 | Phone Utilites |
| 5 | Ameritech | $314,386 | Phone Utilites |
| 6 | Contel | $285,445 | Phone Utilites |
| 7 | Bell Atlantic | $265,997 | Phone Utilites |
| 8 | Pacific Telesis Group | $239,054 | Phone Utilites |
| 9 | United Telecommunications | $231,582 | Long Distance |
| 10 | NYNEX | $206,386 | Phone Utilites |

**Top Senate Recipients**

| Rank | Recipient | Total |
|------|-----------|-------|
| 1 | Tom Tauke (R-Iowa) | $104,270 |
| 2 | Jim Exon (D-Neb) | $60,610 |
| 3 | Hank Brown (R-Colo) | $54,505 |

**Top House Recipients**

| Rank | Recipient | Total |
|------|-----------|-------|
| 1 | Don Ritter (R-Pa) | $38,100 |
| 2 | David E. Bonior (D-Mich) | $35,140 |
| 3 | Al Swift (D-Wash) | $34,850 |

On Capitol Hill, the primary center for debate on telecommunications issues comes in the House Energy and Commerce Committee. The members of that panel's Telecommunications and Finance subcommittee were among the leaders in contributions from both the regional phone companies and long-distance carriers.

# Construction

## *Where the money came from . . .*

Home builders, public works contractors, project management firms, architects, engineers and a host of assorted subcontractors supplying everything from plumbing to air conditioning to cement make up this segment of American business — the nation's construction industry.

Many construction firms — particularly the largest ones — are dependent for major portions of their work on decisions made in Washington. Government contracts to build new highways, bridges, dams and other public works projects can bring substantial amounts of business to a host of construction-related contractors and suppliers as well.

Home builders have a somewhat different perspective on federal policies. Instead of keeping an eye on the public works committees of Congress, they're more affected by the Banking committees, which set policies that deeply affect the housing market.

The pattern of construction industry contributions reflects the nature of the industry. Unlike some industries that are dominated by

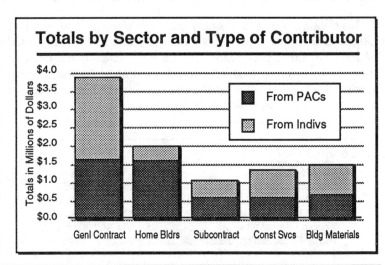

large corporations, many contractors and subcontractors run relatively small shops that operate independently. Because of this, only half the industry's campaign dollars came from political action committees. The rest came from individual contributors. Even the two PACs that dominated the top contributors list — the National Association of Homebuilders and Associated General Contractors — are nationwide trade associations that represent thousands of independent builders and suppliers.

Differentiating between home builders and public works contractors is not always easy, when analyzing campaign finance reports. Many contributors simply put "builder" as their occupation, giving no clue whether they concentrate on commercial or residential construction. Many other construction firms are diversified and do both. In classifying such contributors, this report classified them in the "general contractors" category.

| Category | Total | From PACs | PAC Pct | From Indivs | Indiv Pct |
|---|---|---|---|---|---|
| General Contractors | $3,813,865 | $1,589,567 | 42% | $2,224,298 | 58% |
| Home Builders | $1,936,680 | $1,547,425 | 80% | $389,255 | 20% |
| Special Trade Contractors | $1,007,240 | $528,530 | 52% | $478,710 | 48% |
| Construction Services | $1,286,837 | $527,863 | 41% | $758,974 | 59% |
| Building Materials & Equip | $1,432,129 | $614,356 | 43% | $817,773 | 57% |
| **TOTAL** | **$9,476,751** | **$4,807,741** | **51%** | **$4,669,010** | **49%** |

## Top 20 Construction Contributors

| Rank | Total | Contributor | Category | PAC Pct | Dem Pct | Repub Pct | To Dems | To Repubs |
|---|---|---|---|---|---|---|---|---|
| 1 | $1,362,550 | National Assn of Home Builders | Resid Constr | 100% | 48% | 52% | | |
| 2 | $654,194 | Associated General Contractors | Genl Contract | 99% | 22% | 78% | | |
| 3 | $332,268 | National Utility Contractors Assn | Genl Contract | 100% | 41% | 59% | | |
| 4 | $307,393 | Fluor Corp | Genl Contract | 99% | 39% | 61% | | |
| 5 | $201,000 | National Electrical Contractors Assn | Subcontractors | 100% | 10% | 90% | | |
| 6 | $195,560 | Sheet Metal/Air Conditioning Contractors | Subcontractors | 100% | 8% | 91% | | |
| 7 | $147,712 | Associated Builders & Contractors | Builders Assns | 99% | 7% | 93% | | |
| 8 | $111,595 | Caterpillar Tractor | Constr Equip | 98% | 11% | 89% | | |
| 9 | $104,657 | CH2M Hill | Engineers | 99% | 36% | 64% | | |
| 10 | $91,875 | American Consulting Engineers Council | Engineers | 100% | 36% | 64% | | |
| 11 | $86,750 | Stone & Webster | Engineers | 70% | 68% | 32% | | |
| 12 | $80,945 | Owens-Corning Fiberglas | Bldg Materials | 98% | 16% | 84% | | |
| 13 | $78,200 | American Supply Assn | Pipe Products | 100% | 17% | 83% | | |
| 14 | $78,100 | National Concrete Masonry Assn | Stone/Concrete | 99% | 32% | 68% | | |
| 15 | $70,800 | Brown & Root | Genl Contract | 87% | 41% | 59% | | |
| 16 | $63,000 | American Institute of Architects | Architects | 100% | 64% | 36% | | |
| 17 | $57,550 | Wall & Ceiling/Gypsum Drywall Contr | Subcontractors | 100% | 5% | 95% | | |
| 18 | $54,202 | National Society of Professional Engineers | Engineers | 100% | 33% | 67% | | |
| 19 | $51,750 | National Multi Housing Council | Resid Constr | 100% | 55% | 45% | | |
| 20 | $46,300 | Manufactured Housing Institute | Mobile Homes | 100% | 43% | 57% | | |

## Where the money went . . .

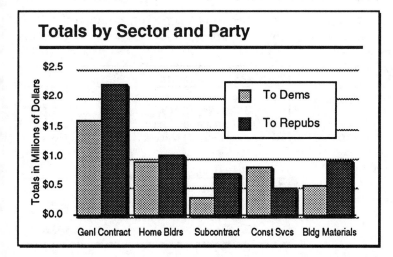

### Totals by Sector and Party

To Dems
To Repubs

Totals in Millions of Dollars

$2.5
$2.0
$1.5
$1.0
$0.5
$0.0

Genl Contract | Home Bldrs | Subcontract | Const Svcs | Bldg Materials

By and large, builders prefer Republicans. Fifty-six percent of the construction industry's dollars went to Republican candidates in the 1990 elections, this despite the fact that Democrats hold strong majorities in both the House and Senate. Only the construction services sector — which includes architects, engineers and construction management companies — gave the majority of their donations to Democrats.

| Category | Total | To Dems | Dem Pct | To Repubs | Repub Pct |
|----------|-------|---------|---------|-----------|-----------|
| General Contractors | $3,813,865 | $1,604,211 | 42% | $2,209,404 | 58% |
| Home Builders | $1,936,680 | $915,013 | 47% | $1,021,667 | 53% |
| Special Trade Contractors | $1,007,240 | $301,706 | 30% | $705,034 | 70% |
| Construction Services | $1,286,837 | $818,917 | 64% | $467,920 | 36% |
| Building Materials & Equip | $1,432,129 | $494,736 | 35% | $937,393 | 65% |
| TOTAL | $9,476,751 | $4,134,583 | 44% | $5,341,418 | 56% |

Senators Phil Gramm and Bill Bradley led the list of construction industry recipients in Congress in the 1990 elections. The high ranking may have had more to do with the general cost of their campaigns; Gramm raised over $16 million for his reelection contest, Bradley collected nearly $13 million.

Among House leaders, Miami Republican Ileana Ros-Lehtinen ran two elections — a special election in 1989 when she won her seat and a reelection race in November 1990. The number two recipient, Bud Shuster of Pennsylvania, is the ranking Republican on the Public Works and Transportation Committee's Surface Transportation Subcommittee — the panel that oversees highway construction. Most of his construction dollars came from road builders and gravel suppliers.

### Top 10 Senate Recipients

| Rank | Name | Amount | Status | W/L |
|------|------|--------|--------|-----|
| 1 | Phil Gramm (R-Texas) | $251,386 | Incumb | W |
| 2 | Bill Bradley (D-NJ) | $194,450 | Incumb | W |
| 3 | Daniel R. Coats (R-Ind) | $174,367 | Incumb | W |
| 4 | Hank Brown (R-Colo) | $139,400 | Open | W |
| 5 | Mitch McConnell (R-Ky) | $138,825 | Incumb | W |
| 6 | John Kerry (D-Mass) | $127,300 | Incumb | W |
| 7 | John W. Warner (R-Va) | $110,325 | Incumb | W |
| 8 | Jesse Helms (R-NC) | $103,775 | Incumb | W |
| 9 | Daniel K. Akaka (D-Hawaii) | $94,075 | Incumb | W |
| 10 | Robert C. Smith (R-NH) | $93,850 | Open | W |

### Top 10 House Recipients

| Rank | Name | Amount | Status | W/L |
|------|------|--------|--------|-----|
| 1 | Ileana Ros-Lehtinen (R-Fla) | $98,545 | Incumb | W |
| 2 | Bud Shuster (R-Pa) | $88,819 | Incumb | W |
| 3 | Robert A. Roe (D-NJ) | $77,107 | Incumb | W |
| 4 | Bill Paxon (R-NY) | $71,140 | Incumb | W |
| 5 | Richard A. Gephardt (D-Mo) | $69,500 | Incumb | W |
| 6 | Robert E. Andrews (D-NJ) | $63,700 | Open | W |
| 7 | Dean A. Gallo (R-NJ) | $60,850 | Incumb | W |
| 8 | Mel Levine (D-Calif) | $60,600 | Incumb | W |
| 9 | Dick Zimmer (R-NJ) | $56,475 | Open | W |
| 10 | Pete Geren (D-Texas) | $54,790 | Incumb | W |

# Closeup on Construction

## General Contractors ..................................................................$3.8 million

The leading contributor in this category, the Associated General Contractors, is the nation's largest organization of builders concentrating mainly on commercial, industrial and public works construction. Though there are a number of large nationwide construction firms — like Fluor and Brown & Root — most of the industry is made up of smaller local contractors. Their dollars tend to come primarily through individual contributions, since their companies are generally too small to operate political action committees of their own.

Overall, general contractors gave 58 percent of their campaign dollars to Republicans — unlike many industries that may be Republican in philosophy but pragmatic in their donations. The Democrats currently hold strong majorities in both Houses of Congress and thereby control all committee and subcommittee chairmanships.

**Top Senate Recipients**

| Rank | Recipient | Total |
|---|---|---|
| 1 | Bill Bradley (D-NJ) | $99,100 |
| 2 | Phil Gramm (R-Texas) | $94,925 |
| 3 | John Kerry (D-Mass) | $58,900 |

**Top House Recipients**

| Rank | Recipient | Total |
|---|---|---|
| 1 | Ileana Ros-Lehtinen (R-Fla) | $50,095 |
| 2 | Bud Shuster (R-Pa) | $43,119 |
| 3 | Bill Paxon (R-NY) | $35,535 |

**Top Contributors**

| Rank | Contributor | Total |
|---|---|---|
| 1 | Associated General Contractors | $654,194 |
| 2 | National Utility Contractors Assn | $332,268 |
| 3 | Fluor Corp | $307,393 |
| 4 | Associated Builders & Contractors | $147,712 |
| 5 | Brown & Root | $70,800 |

## Home Builders ..................................................................$1.9 million

This segment of the construction industry closely follows the ups and downs of interest rates and federal housing policies, as opposed to the pace and scale of public works projects. In that sense, home builders' legislative interests are similar to those of the real estate industry — particularly real estate developers. In many cases, the line between real estate and construction is a thin one; many companies engage in both. This book makes a distinction between the two, however, as does the federal government's Standard Industrial Classification index. The real estate industry deals primarily in the financial end of the business and is classified under Finance in this book. Builders deal more in hammers, nails and road graders, and are classified in construction.

The National Association of Home Builders is the industry's main trade association, and by far its leading contributor. Both the PAC and individual contributors split their dollars fairly evenly between the parties, with Republicans collecting slightly more than Democrats.

**Top Senate Recipients**

| Rank | Recipient | Total |
|---|---|---|
| 1 | Daniel R. Coats (R-Ind) | $43,400 |
| 2 | Phil Gramm (R-Texas) | $29,750 |
| 3 | Mitch McConnell (R-Ky) | $25,475 |

**Top House Recipients**

| Rank | Recipient | Total |
|---|---|---|
| 1 | Dean A. Gallo (R-NJ) | $21,800 |
| 2 | Ileana Ros-Lehtinen (R-Fla) | $20,200 |
| 3 | Chalmers P. Wylie (R-Ohio) | $15,731 |

**Top Contributors**

| Rank | Contributor | Total | Category |
|---|---|---|---|
| 1 | National Assn of Home Builders | $1,362,550 | Resid Constr |
| 2 | National Multi Housing Council | $51,750 | Resid Constr |
| 3 | Manufactured Housing Institute | $46,300 | Mobile Homes |
| 4 | Fleetwood Enterprises | $33,150 | Mobile Homes |
| 5 | Walter Industries | $29,750 | Resid Constr |

## Special Trade Contractors ..................................................................$1.0 million

Sharing in the fortunes — and cyclical perils — of the construction industry are not only the general contractors who build houses, highways and office towers, but the thousands of subcontractors who install the plumbing, electrical wiring, air conditioning and heating systems and a myriad of other finishing touches to buildings of every size and type. Of all construction industry segments, this was the most heavily Republican, giving 70 percent of its contributions to GOP candidates.

**Top Contributors**

| Rank | Contributor | Total | Category |
|---|---|---|---|
| 1 | National Electrical Contractors Assn | $201,000 | Electr Contr |
| 2 | Sheet Metal/Air Conditioning Contractors | $195,560 | Plumb/Air |
| 3 | Wall & Ceiling/Gypsum Drywall Contr | $57,550 | Subcontract |
| 4 | American Subcontractors Assn | $42,500 | Subcontract |
| 5 | Forest Electric Corp | $38,500 | Electr Contr |

**Top Senate Recipients**

| Rank | Recipient | Total |
|---|---|---|
| 1 | Hank Brown (R-Colo) | $33,000 |
| 2 | Daniel R. Coats (R-Ind) | $29,900 |
| 3 | Phil Gramm (R-Texas) | $29,200 |

**Top House Recipients**

| Rank | Recipient | Total |
|---|---|---|
| 1 | Mel Levine (D-Calif) | $16,000 |
| 2 | James M. Inhofe (R-Okla) | $14,250 |
| 3 | Jim Nussle (R-Iowa) | $13,050 |

## Construction Services ..................................................................$1.3 million

Architects, engineers and construction management specialists are an important (and politically active) segment of the construction industry. Big engineering firms are often competing for federal contracts. They are also clearly affected by upturns and downturns in construction cycles. The leading contributor in this category, the engineering firm of CH2M Hill is involved not only in construction engineering, but in environmental services. The company is a major federal contractor for hazardous waste cleanup projects.

One practical problem in classifying donors from this category is the lack of specificity in contributors' declared occupations. Contributors who put down "engineer" as their occupation could be involved in any number of industries — from construction to chemicals to oil & gas or aerospace. For that reason, only "structural engineers", "civil engineers" or others clearly identified with the construction industry were classified under this category. The overall total from this category, therefore, is likely to be understated.

**Top Contributors**

| Rank | Contributor | Total | Category |
|---|---|---|---|
| 1 | CH2M Hill | $104,657 | Engineers |
| 2 | American Consulting Engineers Council | $91,875 | Engineers |
| 3 | Stone & Webster | $86,750 | Engineers |
| 4 | American Institute of Architects | $63,000 | Architects |
| 5 | National Society of Professional Engineers | $54,202 | Engineers |

**Top Senate Recipients**

| Rank | Recipient | Total |
|---|---|---|
| 1 | Daniel K. Akaka (D-Hawaii) | $77,375 |
| 2 | Phil Gramm (R-Texas) | $43,675 |
| 3 | J. Bennett Johnston (D-La) | $32,500 |

**Top House Recipients**

| Rank | Recipient | Total |
|---|---|---|
| 1 | Robert E. Andrews (D-NJ) | $32,600 |
| 2 | Robert A. Roe (D-NJ) | $32,307 |
| 3 | William J. Jefferson (D-La) | $24,000 |

## Building Materials & Equipment ..................................................................$1.4 million

These are the companies that supply everything from gravel to earth movers to high-speed elevators in skyscrapers. Those involved in road building projects are particularly affected by federal decisions, especially those on the public works committees.

**Top Contributors**

| Rank | Contributor | Total | Category |
|---|---|---|---|
| 1 | Caterpillar Tractor | $111,595 | Constr Equip |
| 2 | Owens-Corning Fiberglas | $80,945 | Bldg Materials |
| 3 | American Supply Assn | $78,200 | Pipe Products |
| 4 | National Concrete Masonry Assn | $78,100 | Stone/Concrete |
| 5 | Vulcan Materials Co | $41,450 | Bldg Materials |

**Top Senate Recipients**

| Rank | Recipient | Total |
|---|---|---|
| 1 | Phil Gramm (R-Texas) | $53,836 |
| 2 | Daniel R. Coats (R-Ind) | $42,142 |
| 3 | Mitch McConnell (R-Ky) | $41,000 |

**Top House Recipients**

| Rank | Recipient | Total |
|---|---|---|
| 1 | Bud Shuster (R-Pa) | $31,700 |
| 2 | Bill Paxon (R-NY) | $15,655 |
| 3 | Joe L. Barton (R-Texas) | $14,100 |

# Defense

## *Where the money came from . . .*

Defense contractors have always been major players in congressional politics, and the dollars they dispense (primarily through corporate PACs) show it. Aerospace and electronics firms were by far the biggest segment of the defense industry, accounting for 87 percent of the $7.9 million in defense contributions delivered to candidates in the 1990 elections.

That total figure can be considered to be quite conservative. Few U.S. corporations rely on defense work for the majority of their income, but many firms do some defense work or have defense-related subsidiaries. Under the system used to compile this book, contributions from PACs or employees of those firms were counted as defense-related *only if they were given to a member sitting on the Armed Services or Appropriations committees* — panels that deal specifically with defense matters. Most contributions from Boeing, for example, are classified under Air Transport, since Boeing makes most of its money from the sale of commercial aircraft. Many other major defense contractors — from General Motors to General Electric to AT&T — fall in the same category.

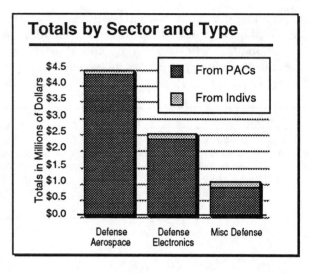

**Totals by Sector and Type**

| Category | Total | From PACs | PAC Pct | From Indivs | Indiv Pct |
|----------|-------|-----------|---------|-------------|-----------|
| Defense Aerospace | $4,424,015 | $4,263,520 | 96% | $160,495 | 4% |
| Defense Electronics | $2,444,906 | $2,289,724 | 94% | $155,182 | 6% |
| Misc Defense | $1,013,463 | $832,283 | 82% | $181,180 | 18% |
| **TOTAL** | **$7,882,384** | **$7,385,527** | **94%** | **$496,857** | **6%** |

## Top 20 Defense Contributors

| Rank | Total | Contributor | Category | PAC Pct | Dem Pct | Repub Pct | To Dems / To Repubs |
|------|-------|-------------|----------|---------|---------|-----------|---------------------|
| 1 | $428,409 | Lockheed Corp | Air Defense | 99% | 42% | 58% | |
| 2 | $421,463 | Northrop Corp | Air Defense | 98% | 37% | 63% | |
| 3 | $415,070 | AT&T† | Def Electronics | 100% | 60% | 40% | |
| 4 | $404,300 | McDonnell Douglas | Air Defense | 92% | 53% | 47% | |
| 5 | $390,625 | Textron Inc | Air Defense | 96% | 57% | 43% | |
| 6 | $383,610 | Martin Marietta Corp | Air Defense | 99% | 46% | 54% | |
| 7 | $378,279 | General Dynamics | Air Defense | 98% | 58% | 42% | |
| 8 | $375,085 | Rockwell International | Air Defense | 97% | 38% | 62% | |
| 9 | $323,975 | United Technologies | Air Defense | 100% | 46% | 54% | |
| 10 | $273,900 | Hughes Aircraft | Def Electronics | 100% | 49% | 51% | |
| 11 | $267,275 | Grumman Corp | Air Defense | 99% | 59% | 41% | |
| 12 | $251,500 | Raytheon | Def Electronics | 98% | 53% | 47% | |
| 13 | $237,550 | Tenneco Inc | Naval Ships | 92% | 15% | 85% | |
| 14 | $236,500 | Allied-Signal | Air Defense | 95% | 47% | 53% | |
| 15 | $196,025 | LTV Aerospace & Defense | Def Electronics | 100% | 65% | 35% | |
| 16 | $177,748 | Litton Industries | Def Electronics | 99% | 32% | 68% | |
| 17 | $171,850 | TRW Inc | Def Electronics | 98% | 46% | 54% | |
| 18 | $165,107 | Boeing Co† | Air Defense | 93% | 51% | 49% | |
| 19 | $155,559 | General Electric† | Air Defense | 84% | 58% | 42% | |
| 20 | $151,050 | BDM International | Defense R&D | 84% | 36% | 64% | |

† Includes defense operations only

# Where the money went . . .

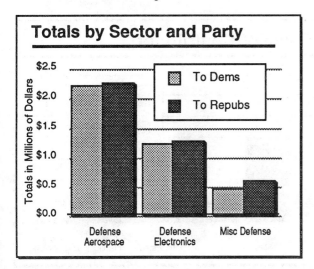

## Totals by Sector and Party

Totals in Millions of Dollars

$2.5
$2.0
$1.5
$1.0
$0.5
$0.0

☐ To Dems
■ To Repubs

Defense Aerospace | Defense Electronics | Misc Defense

Considering the traditionally conservative slant to the defense industry and the military services it is worthy of note that the industry split its dollars almost evenly between Democrats and Republicans. This is a classic example of political pragmatism at work. Democrats control both houses of Congress and as such hold the power of the purse over the industry. Whatever their personal political preference, defense contractors have learned to accommodate both sides of the aisle when pulling out their checkbooks.

| Category | Total | To Dems | Dem Pct | To Repubs | Repub Pct |
|---|---|---|---|---|---|
| Defense Aerospace | $4,424,015 | $2,192,977 | 50% | $2,232,538 | 50% |
| Defense Electronics | $2,444,906 | $1,200,932 | 49% | $1,243,443 | 51% |
| Misc Defense | $1,013,463 | $439,363 | 43% | $574,100 | 57% |
| **TOTAL** | **$7,882,384** | **$3,833,272** | **49%** | **$4,050,081** | **51%** |

Though the federal government's annual defense budget is voted on by the entire House and Senate, defense industry lobbyists spend most of their time concentrating on the Armed Services and Appropriations committees in each house. Armed Services sets the military policy, but Appropriations — particularly the Defense Appropriations subcommittees — actually allocates the hundreds of billions of dollars the federal government spends annually on defense. Consequently, members of those committees receive by far the biggest proportion of defense industry contributions. Of the top 20 House and Senate recipients of defense dollars in 1990, 13 served on the Armed Services committees and seven held seats on Appropriations.

Congress's leading recipient of defense dollars was not a Senator, but a Congressman — Democrat John Murtha of Pennsylvania, who chairs the Defense Appropriations subcommittee in the House. Murtha faced an unusually competitive fight for the Democratic primary in 1990, winning his seat with just 51 percent of the vote against a virtually unknown opponent. An important issue in the campaign was Murtha's dependence on out-of-state contributions from defense contractors and other interests with government business. Murtha eventually spent more than a million dollars on his reelection campaign.

## Top 10 Senate Recipients

| Rank | Name | Amount | Status | W/L |
|---|---|---|---|---|
| 1 | John W. Warner (R-Va) | $196,982 | Incumb | W |
| 2 | J. Bennett Johnston (D-La) | $187,714 | Incumb | W |
| 3 | Daniel R. Coats (R-Ind) | $183,239 | Incumb | W |
| 4 | Phil Gramm (R-Texas) | $169,642 | Incumb | W |
| 5 | Ted Stevens (R-Alaska) | $163,275 | Incumb | W |
| 6 | Jim Exon (D-Neb) | $158,337 | Incumb | W |
| 7 | Carl Levin (D-Mich) | $122,774 | Incumb | W |
| 8 | Sam Nunn (D-Ga) | $112,460 | Incumb | W |
| 9 | Strom Thurmond (R-SC) | $109,400 | Incumb | W |
| 10 | Al Gore (D-Tenn) | $100,812 | Incumb | W |

## Top 10 House Recipients

| Rank | Name | Amount | Status | W/L |
|---|---|---|---|---|
| 1 | John P. Murtha (D-Pa) | $212,550 | Incumb | W |
| 2 | Charles Wilson (D-Texas) | $179,550 | Incumb | W |
| 3 | Bill Dickinson (R-Ala) | $124,640 | Incumb | W |
| 4 | Les Aspin (D-Wis) | $115,985 | Incumb | W |
| 5 | W. G. "Bill" Hefner (D-NC) | $104,550 | Incumb | W |
| 6 | Joseph M. McDade (R-Pa) | $104,000 | Incumb | W |
| 7 | Herbert H. Bateman (R-Va) | $94,350 | Incumb | W |
| 8 | Robert W. Davis (R-Mich) | $75,525 | Incumb | W |
| 9 | C. W. Bill Young (R-Fla) | $68,000 | Incumb | W |
| 10 | Ike Skelton (D-Mo) | $67,065 | Incumb | W |

# Energy & Natural Resources

## Where the money came from . . .

In a nation that grew to world prominence by exploiting its abundant natural resources, then building new industries on the strength of its home-grown oil, gas, minerals and electricity, it is not surprising that energy producers still pack a powerful political punch on Capitol Hill.

Between them, the oil and gas industry and electric utilities dominated the giving within the sector. Companies and individuals engaged in the production and marketing of oil & gas provided more than $6.9 million to congressional candidates in 1989-90. Interstate gas pipeline companies added $1.9 million more. Power utilities, many of which must spend heavily on pollution control expenses to comply with Clean Air Act standards, gave $3.8 million.

About three-quarters of the dollars overall came from political action committees. The only sector with a substantial share of individual contributions was oil

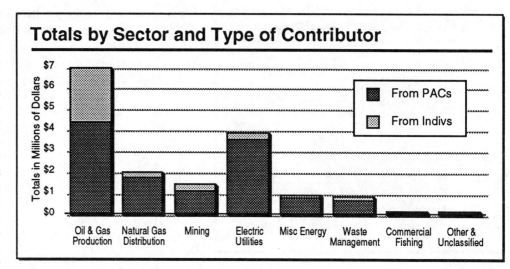

**Totals by Sector and Type of Contributor**

| Category | Total | From PACs | PAC Pct | From Indivs | Indiv Pct |
|---|---|---|---|---|---|
| Oil & Gas Prod/Marketing | $6,935,684 | $4,337,720 | 63% | $2,597,964 | 37% |
| Natural Gas Distribution | $1,935,226 | $1,702,011 | 88% | $233,215 | 12% |
| Mining | $1,370,646 | $1,046,212 | 76% | $324,434 | 24% |
| Electric Utilities | $3,819,037 | $3,537,655 | 93% | $281,382 | 7% |
| Misc Energy | $861,758 | $716,408 | 83% | $145,350 | 17% |
| Waste Management | $809,854 | $635,806 | 79% | $174,048 | 21% |
| Commercial Fishing | $119,892 | $61,367 | 51% | $58,525 | 49% |
| Other & Unclassified | $138,840 | $83,200 | 60% | $55,640 | 40% |
| **TOTAL** | **$15,990,937** | **$12,120,379** | **76%** | **$3,870,558** | **24%** |

& gas. In that instance, the major oil companies gave nearly all their dollars through PACs, while smaller "independents" contributed individually. The presence of so many individual contributors was likely bolstered by two expensive reelection campaigns of oil state Senators in 1990 — Bennett Johnston of Louisiana and Phil Gramm of Texas. Gramm in particular raised large sums from hundreds of Texas oil producers, large and small.

## Top 20 Energy & Natural Resource Contributors

| Rank | Total | Contributor | Category | PAC Pct | Dem Pct | Repub Pct | To Dems To Repubs |
|---|---|---|---|---|---|---|---|
| 1 | $654,769 | ACRE (Action Cmte for Rural Electrification) | Rural Electric | 100% | 69% | 31% | |
| 2 | $434,962 | Waste Management Inc | Waste Mgmt | 90% | 58% | 42% | |
| 3 | $339,889 | Atlantic Richfield | Oil & Gas | 90% | 41% | 59% | |
| 4 | $334,373 | Amoco Corp | Oil & Gas | 97% | 20% | 80% | |
| 5 | $317,443 | Chevron Corp | Oil & Gas | 98% | 27% | 73% | |
| 6 | $282,600 | Southern Co | Electric Utilities | 97% | 55% | 45% | |
| 7 | $277,200 | Occidental Petroleum† | Oil & Gas | 79% | 54% | 46% | |
| 8 | $267,350 | Mobil Oil | Oil & Gas | 78% | 24% | 76% | |
| 9 | $266,332 | Columbia Gas System | Natural Gas/Oil | 100% | 50% | 50% | |
| 10 | $246,500 | Coastal Corp | Natural Gas | 95% | 75% | 25% | |
| 11 | $231,050 | Cooper Industries | Power Plant Constr | 100% | 5% | 95% | |
| 12 | $230,550 | USX Corp | Oil & Gas | 73% | 57% | 43% | |
| 13 | $229,352 | Phillips Petroleum | Oil & Gas | 94% | 28% | 72% | |
| 14 | $210,760 | Exxon Corp | Oil & Gas | 90% | 24% | 76% | |
| 15 | $202,825 | Petroleum Marketers Assn | Gas Stations | 100% | 34% | 66% | |
| 16 | $195,850 | Southern California Edison | Electric Utilities | 96% | 66% | 34% | |
| 17 | $194,100 | Texas Utilities Electric Co | Electric Utilities | 99% | 41% | 59% | |
| 18 | $191,915 | Pacific Gas & Electric | Gas/Electric Util | 100% | 54% | 46% | |
| 19 | $187,724 | Ashland Oil | Refining/Mkting | 87% | 31% | 69% | |
| 20 | $180,389 | Browning-Ferris Industries | Waste Mgmt | 95% | 66% | 34% | |

† Includes energy operations only

## Where the money went . . .

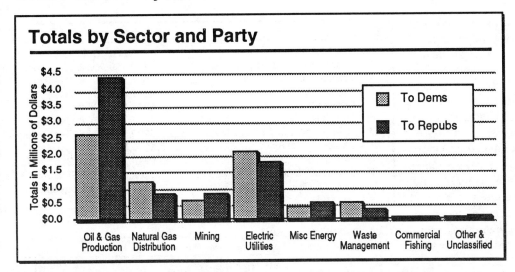

### Totals by Sector and Party

Totals in Millions of Dollars

$4.5
$4.0
$3.5
$3.0
$2.5
$2.0
$1.5
$1.0
$0.5
$0.0

To Dems
To Repubs

Oil & Gas Production | Natural Gas Distribution | Mining | Electric Utilities | Misc Energy | Waste Management | Commercial Fishing | Other & Unclassified

Oil & gas producers clearly prefer Republicans when they sign their campaign checks. Natural gas pipeline companies, in contrast, gave nearly 60 percent of their money to Democrats. Electric utilities tended to straddle both sides of the political fence.

| Category | Total | To Dems | Dem Pct | To Repubs | Repub Pct |
|---|---|---|---|---|---|
| Oil & Gas Prod/Marketing | $6,935,684 | $2,604,936 | 38% | $4,330,497 | 62% |
| Natural Gas Distribution | $1,935,226 | $1,135,784 | 59% | $799,442 | 41% |
| Mining | $1,370,646 | $580,210 | 42% | $790,436 | 58% |
| Electric Utilities | $3,819,037 | $2,067,628 | 54% | $1,751,509 | 46% |
| Misc Energy | $861,758 | $370,347 | 43% | $491,161 | 57% |
| Waste Management | $809,854 | $509,689 | 63% | $300,165 | 37% |
| Commercial Fishing | $119,892 | $58,208 | 49% | $61,684 | 51% |
| Other & Unclassified | $138,840 | $44,775 | 32% | $93,815 | 68% |
| TOTAL | $15,990,937 | $7,371,577 | 46% | $8,618,709 | 54% |

Two oil state Senators — Republican Phil Gramm of Texas and Democrat Bennett Johnston of Louisiana — towered over all other energy industry recipients in 1990. Gramm's campaign raised more than $16 million, though his reelection race was never considered close. Johnston raised $4.8 million in his high-profile contest against ex-Ku Klux Klansman David Duke. Aside from his roots in oil-rich Louisiana, Johnston is also chairman of the Senate Energy & Natural Resources Committee and chief architect of a major energy bill that could affect billions of dollars in profits for oil companies, power utilities and a host of other industries.

Most of the top House recipients of energy money hail from oil-rich districts. The exceptions are notable: John Dingell of Michigan chairs the House Energy and Commerce Committee, Phil Sharp of Indiana chairs that committee's Energy and Power subcommittee, and Norman Lent of New York is Ranking Republican for the full committee.

### Top 10 Senate Recipients

| Rank | Name | Amount | Status | W/L |
|---|---|---|---|---|
| 1 | Phil Gramm (R-Texas) | $819,481 | Incumb | W |
| 2 | J. Bennett Johnston (D-La) | $629,050 | Incumb | W |
| 3 | Mitch McConnell (R-Ky) | $371,516 | Incumb | W |
| 4 | Pete V. Domenici (R-NM) | $367,564 | Incumb | W |
| 5 | Howell Heflin (D-Ala) | $262,859 | Incumb | W |
| 6 | Hank Brown (R-Colo) | $248,118 | Open | W |
| 7 | Larry E. Craig (R-Idaho) | $234,864 | Open | W |
| 8 | John D. Rockefeller IV (D-WVa) | $219,924 | Incumb | W |
| 9 | David L. Boren (D-Okla) | $194,960 | Incumb | W |
| 10 | Tom Tauke (R-Iowa) | $186,075 | Chall | L |

### Top 10 House Recipients

| Rank | Name | Amount | Status | W/L |
|---|---|---|---|---|
| 1 | Pete Geren (D-Texas) | $195,400 | Incumb | W |
| 2 | Craig Thomas (R-Wyo) | $145,070 | Incumb | W |
| 3 | Philip R. Sharp (D-Ind) | $138,172 | Incumb | W |
| 4 | Joe L. Barton (R-Texas) | $123,307 | Incumb | W |
| 5 | Don Young (R-Alaska) | $121,025 | Incumb | W |
| 6 | John D. Dingell (D-Mich) | $102,300 | Incumb | W |
| 7 | W. J. "Billy" Tauzin (D-La) | $98,400 | Incumb | W |
| 8 | James M. Inhofe (R-Okla) | $86,249 | Incumb | W |
| 9 | Greg Laughlin (D-Texas) | $81,748 | Incumb | W |
| 10 | Norman F. Lent (R-NY) | $75,650 | Incumb | W |

# Closeup on Energy & Natural Resources

## Oil & Gas Production & Marketing ...............................................$4.3 million

The oil industry looks at itself as having two main divisions: the "major" multinational oil companies — like Exxon, Mobil or Amoco — and the smaller independent operators called "independents." In the world of campaign finance both sides tend to give to the same candidates, for the most part preferring Republicans to Democrats. But they deliver the dollars through different means. The major oil companies give almost all their donations through corporate PACs, while the independents give as individuals. Mainly, this is a matter of scale. Large companies are much more likely to support their own political action committees and mount in-house fundraising drives among their employees. Smaller firms often bypass the paperwork and deliver the funds directly from company officials to their candidates of choice.

All the top recipients of oil industry money come from oil producing states. Pete Geren of Texas ranks so much higher than anyone else both because he is a favorite of the oil industry (particularly the Bass Brothers that gave him more than $65,000) and because he ran two campaigns in the last election cycle, including a 1989 special election to fill the seat vacated by former House Speaker Jim Wright when he resigned. Over those two elections Geren drew at least $49,000 from individuals connected with Bass Brothers Enterprises and another $16,250 from the Robert M. Bass Group.

### Top Contributors

| Rank | Contributor | Total | Category |
|------|-------------|-------|----------|
| 1 | Atlantic Richfield | $339,889 | Oil & Gas Prod |
| 2 | Amoco Corp | $334,373 | Oil & Gas Prod |
| 3 | Chevron Corp | $317,443 | Oil & Gas Prod |
| 4 | Occidental Petroleum | $277,200 | Oil & Gas Prod |
| 5 | Mobil Oil | $267,350 | Oil & Gas Prod |
| 6 | USX Corp | $230,550 | Oil & Gas Prod |
| 7 | Phillips Petroleum | $229,352 | Oil & Gas Prod |
| 8 | Exxon Corp | $210,760 | Oil & Gas Prod |
| 9 | Petroleum Marketers Assn | $202,825 | Gas Stations |
| 10 | Ashland Oil | $187,724 | Refining/Mkting |

### Top Senate Recipients

| Rank | Recipient | Total |
|------|-----------|-------|
| 1 | Phil Gramm (R-Texas) | $608,866 |
| 2 | J. Bennett Johnston (D-La) | $222,650 |
| 3 | Pete V. Domenici (R-NM) | $188,687 |

### Top House Recipients

| Rank | Recipient | Total |
|------|-----------|-------|
| 1 | Pete Geren (D-Texas) | $161,450 |
| 2 | Craig Thomas (R-Wyo) | $81,350 |
| 3 | James M. Inhofe (R-Okla) | $76,499 |

## Natural Gas Distribution ...............................................$1.7 million

Quite apart from drilling for oil, refining it and marketing it in gas stations, there is another distinct industry involved in the interstate transportation of natural gas. Gas pipelines criss-cross the nation, connecting the energy-rich oil patch states with the energy-hungry Northeast, Midwest and Southeast. Because of the interstate nature of the business, pipeline carriers are heavily regulated by the federal government. In contrast to the strongly Republican tilt of oil producers, the natural gas industry gives the majority of its money to Democrats.

### Top Senate Recipients

| Rank | Recipient | Total |
|------|-----------|-------|
| 1 | J. Bennett Johnston | $113,900 |
| 2 | Phil Gramm (R-Texas) | $74,250 |
| 3 | Pete V. Domenici (R-NM) | $42,248 |

### Top House Recipients

| Rank | Recipient | Total |
|------|-----------|-------|
| 1 | Philip R. Sharp (D-Ind) | $28,923 |
| 2 | Martin Frost (D-Texas) | $16,650 |
| 3 | Charles Wilson (D-Texas) | $16,500 |

### Top Contributors

| Rank | Contributor | Total |
|------|-------------|-------|
| 1 | Columbia Gas System | $266,332 |
| 2 | Coastal Corp | $246,500 |
| 3 | Pacific Enterprises | $176,450 |
| 4 | Arkla Inc | $152,720 |
| 5 | Internorth Inc | $150,750 |
| 6 | Enserch Corp | $139,228 |
| 7 | Panhandle Eastern Corp | $120,200 |
| 8 | American Gas Assn | $98,500 |
| 9 | Interstate Natural Gas Assn | $93,910 |
| 10 | Michigan Consolidated Gas | $74,320 |

## Mining ..................................................................................................$1.4 million

### Top Contributors

| Rank | Contributor | Total | Category |
|------|-------------|-------|----------|
| 1 | Freeport-McMoRan Inc | $179,900 | Metal Mining/Process |
| 2 | National Coal Assn | $141,374 | Coal |
| 3 | Cyprus Minerals Co | $110,177 | Metal Mining/Process |
| 4 | Peabody Coal | $100,485 | Coal |
| 5 | Reynolds Metals | $78,401 | Metal Mining/Process |
| 6 | Drummond Co | $61,050 | Coal |
| 7 | Alcoa | $55,050 | Metal Mining/Process |
| 8 | Phelps Dodge Corp | $52,150 | Metal Mining/Process |
| 9 | Cleveland-Cliffs Iron Co | $32,950 | Metal Mining/Process |
| 10 | Ashland Oil | $27,968 | Coal |

Two distinct branches of the mining industry provide the bulk of its campaign dollars — the coal mining industry gave about $550,000 in the last election, while companies dealing with metal mining and processing gave $680,000. Diversified interests, non-metal miners and mining services and equipment gave the rest. By far the top recipient of their money in Congress was Kentucky Republican Senator Mitch McConnell, who drew heavily from coal miners in the eastern Kentucky mountains.

Not included in these totals — but important in areas concerning federal regulation of mine safety and other issues — is the United Mine Workers Union, classified under Labor. The UMW's political action committee gave $313,000 during the 1989-90 election cycle. The money overwhelmingly went to Democrats. Mine operators, on the other hand, gave 58 percent of their dollars to Republicans.

### Top Senate Recipients

| Rank | Recipient | Total |
|------|-----------|-------|
| 1 | Mitch McConnell (R-Ky) | $112,124 |
| 2 | Larry E. Craig (R-Idaho) | $59,756 |
| 3 | Howell Heflin (D-Ala) | $56,500 |

### Top House Recipients

| Rank | Recipient | Total |
|------|-----------|-------|
| 1 | Nick J. Rahall II (D-WVa) | $21,500 |
| 2 | Craig Thomas (R-Wyo) | $20,370 |
| 3 | Barbara F. Vucanovich (R-Nev) | $16,900 |

## Electric Utilities ..................................................................................$3.8 million

### Top Contributors

| Rank | Contributor | Total | Category |
|------|-------------|-------|----------|
| 1 | ACRE (Action Cmte for Rural Electrification) | $654,769 | Rural Electric |
| 2 | Southern Co | $282,600 | Electric Utilities |
| 3 | Southern California Edison | $195,850 | Electric Utilities |
| 4 | Texas Utilities Electric Co | $194,100 | Electric Utilities |
| 5 | Pacific Gas & Electric | $191,915 | Gas & Electric Util |
| 6 | Entergy Corp | $130,600 | Gas & Electric Util |
| 7 | Consumers Power Co | $103,188 | Gas & Electric Util |
| 8 | Public Service Electric & Gas | $101,835 | Gas & Electric Util |
| 9 | American Electric Power | $95,750 | Electric Utilities |
| 10 | Duke Power Co | $77,410 | Electric Utilities |

Cleaning up their smokestacks in compliance with Clean Air legislation is a major preoccupation of many electric utilities, particularly those whose clouds of pollution have been responsible for much of the acid rain in the Northeast. The federal government's many rules governing the operation of utilities are another important issue, as is the perennial issue of nuclear power and the disposal of nuclear waste.

Big metropolitan area utilities are not the only ones with a strong voice on Capitol Hill. The largest single political contributor in the industry is the Action Committee for Rural Electrification (or ACRE), a PAC that represents the interests of the nation's rural electric cooperatives. The national ACRE PAC gave contributions to more than 381 congressional candidates in the 1990 elections —nearly 90 percent of the dollars went to incumbents. Local affiliated PACs often added extra contributions to candidates in their areas.

The top recipients of electric utility contributions in 1990 were the chairmen of two panels crucial to the industry. In the Senate, Bennett Johnston heads the Energy and Natural Resources Committee. In the House, Phil Sharp chairs the Energy and Power subcommittee of the Energy and Commerce committee.

### Top Senate Recipients

| Rank | Recipient | Total |
|------|-----------|-------|
| 1 | J. Bennett Johnston (D-La) | $168,850 |
| 2 | Pete V. Domenici (R-NM) | $59,350 |
| 3 | Phil Gramm (R-Texas) | $48,700 |

### Top House Recipients

| Rank | Recipient | Total |
|------|-----------|-------|
| 1 | Philip R. Sharp (D-Ind) | $62,299 |
| 2 | Joe L. Barton (R-Texas) | $36,000 |
| 3 | John D. Dingell (D-Mich) | $31,250 |

# Finance, Insurance & Real Estate

## Where the money came from . . .

If doctors, lawyers, oil companies and defense contractors are tidy pots of gold to congressional candidates, the financial sector is the mother lode. The combined giving by banks, insurance companies, real estate interests, the securities industry and other finance-related businesses amounted to more than $43.1 million in the 1989-90 election cycle — more than double any other industry in the business sector. It was more even than all labor unions combined. No other group of contributors can match the dollar clout of this one, and that fact is not lost either on the industry or the members of Congress who rely on their largesse.

Within the sector, the methods of delivering dollars varied considerably. Commercial banks and other financial institutions gave most of their money through political action committees. Securities dealers gave mostly through individual contributions — often collected from numerous employees of the same firm and delivered

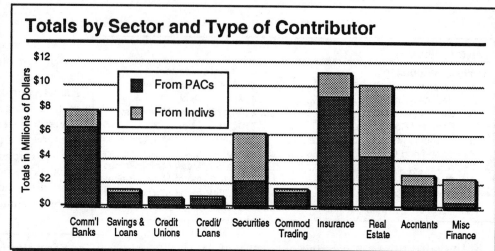

### Totals by Sector and Type of Contributor

| Category | Total | From PACs | PAC Pct | From Indivs | Indiv Pct |
|---|---|---|---|---|---|
| Commercial Banks | $7,775,819 | $6,302,741 | 81% | $1,473,078 | 19% |
| Savings & Loans | $1,284,666 | $976,293 | 76% | $308,373 | 24% |
| Credit Unions | $597,848 | $575,748 | 96% | $22,100 | 4% |
| Finance/Credit Companies | $687,310 | $543,272 | 79% | $144,038 | 21% |
| Securities & Investment | $5,874,887 | $2,073,455 | 35% | $3,801,432 | 65% |
| Commodity Trading | $1,323,500 | $1,080,000 | 82% | $243,500 | 18% |
| Insurance | $10,857,307 | $8,959,070 | 83% | $1,898,237 | 17% |
| Real Estate | $9,956,516 | $4,048,573 | 41% | $5,907,943 | 59% |
| Accountants | $2,550,917 | $1,710,751 | 67% | $840,166 | 33% |
| Misc Finance | $2,251,805 | $341,610 | 15% | $1,910,195 | 85% |
| **TOTAL** | **$43,160,575** | **$26,611,513** | **62%** | **$16,549,062** | **38%** |

to candidates in an impressive bundle. Big insurance companies gave mostly from PACs, though local agents often added their own individual contributions. Real estate salespeople funneled most of their money to the giant Realtors PAC. Real estate developers tended to write their own checks and deliver them directly to candidates. Overall, 62 percent of the financial industry money came from political action committees, the rest came from individuals.

## Top 20 Finance, Insurance & Real Estate Contributors

| Rank | Total | Contributor | Category | PAC Pct | Dem Pct | Repub Pct | To Dems / To Repubs |
|---|---|---|---|---|---|---|---|
| 1 | $3,094,228 | National Assn of Realtors | Real Estate | 100% | 56% | 44% | |
| 2 | $1,487,800 | National Assn of Life Underwriters | Life Insurance | 100% | 51% | 49% | |
| 3 | $1,473,061 | American Bankers Assn | Comml Banks | 100% | 55% | 45% | |
| 4 | $1,089,294 | American Institute of CPA's | Accountants | 100% | 56% | 44% | |
| 5 | $692,743 | American Council of Life Insurance | Life Insurance | 100% | 58% | 42% | |
| 6 | $676,335 | Independent Insurance Agents of America | Insurance | 100% | 58% | 42% | |
| 7 | $512,098 | Credit Union National Assn | Credit Unions | 100% | 57% | 43% | |
| 8 | $475,875 | Chicago Mercantile Exchange | Commodities | 97% | 66% | 34% | |
| 9 | $466,250 | Barnett Banks of Florida | Comml Banks | 99% | 44% | 56% | |
| 10 | $449,650 | Goldman, Sachs & Co | Invest Banking | 38% | 74% | 26% | |
| 11 | $447,968 | American Family Corp | Health Insur | 96% | 54% | 46% | |
| 12 | $420,564 | American Express | Stocks/Credit | 55% | 72% | 28% | |
| 13 | $412,925 | JP Morgan & Co | Comml Banks | 98% | 55% | 45% | |
| 14 | $412,178 | Citicorp | Comml Banks | 93% | 60% | 40% | |
| 15 | $402,482 | Metropolitan Life | Insur/Real Est | 92% | 65% | 35% | |
| 16 | $394,925 | Salomon Brothers | Securities | 39% | 48% | 52% | |
| 17 | $388,418 | US League of Savings Assns | Savings & Loans | 100% | 59% | 41% | |
| 18 | $388,011 | Chicago Board of Trade | Commodities | 96% | 69% | 31% | |
| 19 | $356,816 | Prudential Insurance | Insur/Stocks | 75% | 67% | 33% | |
| 20 | $296,226 | National Venture Capital Assn | Venture Capital | 100% | 64% | 36% | |

## Where the money went . . .

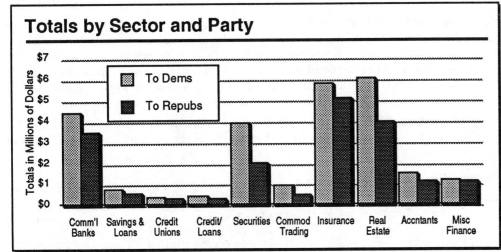

### Totals by Sector and Party

Legend:
- ▨ To Dems
- ▩ To Repubs

Y-axis: Totals in Millions of Dollars ($0–$7)

X-axis categories: Comm'l Banks, Savings & Loans, Credit Unions, Credit/ Loans, Securities, Commod Trading, Insurance, Real Estate, Accntants, Misc Finance

Democrats took the biggest share of the money — 58 percent in all. Nearly every sector within the group preferred Democrats to Republicans, though many split the dollars fairly evenly between the parties. The most heavily partisan were securities and commodities dealers; they delivered roughly two dollars to Democrats for every one dollar they gave to Republicans.

| Category | Total | To Dems | Dem Pct | To Repubs | Repub Pct |
|---|---|---|---|---|---|
| Commercial Banks | $7,775,819 | $4,349,862 | 56% | $3,418,207 | 44% |
| Savings & Loans | $1,284,666 | $732,956 | 57% | $550,710 | 43% |
| Credit Unions | $597,848 | $346,845 | 58% | $251,003 | 42% |
| Finance/Credit Companies | $687,310 | $403,681 | 59% | $283,529 | 41% |
| Securities & Investment | $5,874,887 | $3,879,022 | 66% | $1,990,690 | 34% |
| Commodity Trading | $1,323,500 | $884,780 | 67% | $438,260 | 33% |
| Insurance | $10,857,307 | $5,768,846 | 53% | $5,087,461 | 47% |
| Real Estate | $9,956,516 | $6,015,772 | 60% | $3,938,094 | 40% |
| Accountants | $2,550,917 | $1,460,734 | 57% | $1,090,183 | 43% |
| Misc Finance | $2,251,805 | $1,131,005 | 50% | $1,119,300 | 50% |
| TOTAL | $43,160,575 | $24,973,503 | 58% | $18,167,437 | 42% |

Democratic Senator Bill Bradley of New Jersey was far and away the biggest recipient of financial industry money in the 1990 elections, drawing over $1.8 million in identified contributions. More than half that came from the securities industry, primarily through individual checks from dealers, brokers and partners in the leading Wall Street investment houses. Though no one else in Congress came close to Bradley's $935,000 from the securities industry, many incumbents attracted impressive sums from bankers, insurance brokers, and real estate investors. Phil Gramm led Congress in dollars from both commercial banks and savings & loans. Bradley was the leading recipient of insurance contributions. He also led in real estate money, though John Kerry of Massachusetts and Carl Levin of Michigan were close behind.

One thing that many of the top recipients had in common was strategic committee assignments. Bradley and Jay Rockefeller sit on the tax-writing Senate Finance Committee. Gramm, Kerry and Larry Pressler hold seats on the Senate Banking Committee.

In the House, five of the top 10 recipients are members of the House Banking Committee.

### Top 10 Senate Recipients

| Rank | Name | Amount | Status | W/L |
|---|---|---|---|---|
| 1 | Bill Bradley (D-NJ) | $1,834,551 | Incumb | W |
| 2 | Phil Gramm (R-Texas) | $1,162,026 | Incumb | W |
| 3 | John Kerry (D-Mass) | $729,667 | Incumb | W |
| 4 | Carl Levin (D-Mich) | $608,764 | Incumb | W |
| 5 | John D. Rockefeller IV (D-WVa) | $602,008 | Incumb | W |
| 6 | Hank Brown (R-Colo) | $564,286 | Open | W |
| 7 | Paul Simon (D-Ill) | $515,940 | Incumb | W |
| 8 | Larry Pressler (R-SD) | $419,682 | Incumb | W |
| 9 | Tom Harkin (D-Iowa) | $415,721 | Incumb | W |
| 10 | Sam Nunn (D-Ga) | $415,445 | Incumb | W |

### Top 10 House Recipients

| Rank | Name | Amount | Status | W/L |
|---|---|---|---|---|
| 1 | Charles E. Schumer (D-NY) | $348,402 | Incumb | W |
| 2 | Richard A. Gephardt (D-Mo) | $330,403 | Incumb | W |
| 3 | Tom Campbell (R-Calif) | $287,014 | Incumb | W |
| 4 | Frank Annunzio (D-Ill) | $236,724 | Incumb | W |
| 5 | Ileana Ros-Lehtinen (R-Fla) | $224,252 | Incumb | W |
| 6 | Mel Levine (D-Calif) | $209,550 | Incumb | W |
| 7 | Stephen L. Neal (D-NC) | $207,050 | Incumb | W |
| 8 | Robert T. Matsui (D-Calif) | $206,582 | Incumb | W |
| 9 | Doug Barnard Jr. (D-Ga) | $206,062 | Incumb | W |
| 10 | Steve Bartlett (R-Texas) | $200,910 | Incumb | W |

# Closeup on Finance, Insurance & Real Estate

## Commercial Banks .................................................................$7.8 million

Banking deregulation — allowing banks to begin to operate freely across state lines and to offer a wider array of financial services — is one of the items high on the agenda of the nation's largest banks. The proposals have met great opposition in Congress from competing interests, particularly insurance companies who want to keep the banks out of the securities brokerage business — something that's become a major sideline of insurance companies themselves. Non-industry critics oppose deregulation for quite different reasons. It was the loosening of rules in the savings & loan industry that led to rampant speculation and the eventual near-collapse of the industry, which is now being bailed out at taxpayer expense.

All three of the top House recipients of commercial banking money are members of the House Banking Committee. Phil Gramm is on the Senate Banking panel and Bill Bradley sits on the Senate Finance Committee, which oversees changes in the tax laws.

### Top Contributors

| Rank | Contributor | Total |
|------|-------------|-------|
| 1 | American Bankers Assn | $1,473,061 |
| 2 | Barnett Banks of Florida | $466,250 |
| 3 | JP Morgan & Co | $412,925 |
| 4 | Citicorp | $412,178 |
| 5 | Independent Bankers Assn | $238,080 |
| 6 | C&S/Sovran Corp | $194,355 |
| 7 | Chase Manhattan | $178,130 |
| 8 | NCNB Corp | $167,000 |
| 9 | Bankers Trust | $165,600 |
| 10 | First Chicago Corp | $162,206 |

### Top Senate Recipients

| Rank | Recipient | Total |
|------|-----------|-------|
| 1 | Phil Gramm (R-Texas) | $218,371 |
| 2 | Bill Bradley (D-NJ) | $133,000 |
| 3 | Howell Heflin (D-Ala) | $75,475 |

### Top House Recipients

| Rank | Recipient | Total |
|------|-----------|-------|
| 1 | Stephen L. Neal (D-NC) | $104,400 |
| 2 | Doug Barnard Jr. (D-Ga) | $96,300 |
| 3 | Peter Hoagland (D-Neb) | $72,850 |

## Savings & Loans .................................................................$1.3 million

The massive S&L bailout and the Keating Five scandal have combined to give the surviving savings & loan industry a somewhat muted profile on Capitol Hill. Savings & loan PAC contributions dropped by half in the 1990 elections over what they were two years earlier and some members of Congress seem to have gone out of their way to avoid S&L contributions for fear of the reaction from voters. Nonetheless, the U.S. League of Savings Associations — the nation's chief lobbying group for savings & loans — dispensed nearly $390,000 in 1989-90. Like their counterparts at the commercial banks, thrift industry contributors gave a majority of their dollars to Democrats.

### Top Senate Recipients

| Rank | Recipient | Total |
|------|-----------|-------|
| 1 | Phil Gramm (R-Texas) | $33,750 |
| 2 | Alfonse M. D'Amato (R-NY) | $20,730 |
| 3 | Tom Harkin (D-Iowa) | $16,250 |

### Top House Recipients

| Rank | Recipient | Total |
|------|-----------|-------|
| 1 | Carroll Hubbard Jr. (D-Ky) | $21,077 |
| 2 | Mel Levine (D-Calif) | $18,000 |
| 3 | Howard L. Berman (D-Calif) | $17,100 |

### Top Contributors

| Rank | Contributor | Total |
|------|-------------|-------|
| 1 | US League of Savings Assns | $388,418 |
| 2 | National Council of Savings Institutions | $95,787 |
| 3 | Great Western Financial Corp | $87,850 |
| 4 | Home Federal Savings & Loan | $25,650 |
| 5 | World Savings & Loan | $19,550 |

## Securities & Investment .................................................................................................$5.9 million

In contrast to most other politically-active industries, the securities and investment community makes most of its contributions not through political action committees, but through direct contributions from investment executives. Because the money is not directed through PACs, it is much less visible to the observers of campaign finance records. But the dollars that can be delivered when members of the same firm band together are impressive.

In 1990 no member of Congress found that out more than Senator Bill Bradley of New Jersey. Bradley collected at least $986,000 from the securities industry — five times more than the second-leading recipient, John Kerry of Massachusetts. Bradley's contributions came from dozens of investment firms, large and small. The biggest contributors were a who's who of Wall Street:

| | |
|---|---|
| Shearson Lehman Hutton | $72,300 |
| Goldman, Sachs & Co | $50,100 |
| Salomon Brothers | $47,550 |
| Bear, Stearns & Co | $44,225 |
| Prudential-Bache Securities | $43,142 |
| Smith Barney | $39,350 |
| Morgan Stanley & Co | $31,425 |
| First Boston Corp | $30,450 |
| Merrill Lynch | $26,550 |

The totals include contributions from company PACs, executives and their families. Not included in the totals are contributions of less than $200 (which are not itemized on Federal Election Commission reports) or contributions from individuals who did not completely identify their employer.

Bradley was by far the largest recipient of securities industry contributions, but he was hardly alone. As the list of top recipients shows, most of the biggest contributors came from states or districts that are key financial centers. Bradley, Charles Schumer and Nita Lowey are all in or near New York City. John Kerry's investment money came heavily from Boston. Tom Campbell collected most of his money from venture capital investors in and around his Silicon Valley district south of San Francisco.

# Insurance ...................................................................................$10.9 million

Another giant of the financial world, the nation's insurance industry was one of the biggest contributors to congressional campaigns in the 1990 elections. The money came predominantly from political action committees and much of it was targeted specifically at the tax-writing committees in Congress, as seen in the chart below.

The industry has numerous items on its political agenda. Tax policy is a major one. So is the steady campaign by health care reformers to move in the direction of national health insurance — a move that would have a major impact on health insurance carriers. Other issues come and go, as this is a highly-regulated industry, and one that many analysts fear is currently on thin financial ice.

## Top Contributors

| Rank | Contributor | Total |
|---|---|---|
| 1 | National Assn of Life Underwriters | $1,487,800 |
| 2 | American Council of Life Insurance | $692,743 |
| 3 | Independent Insurance Agents of America | $676,335 |
| 4 | American Family Corp | $447,968 |
| 5 | Travelers Corp | $274,925 |
| 6 | Blue Cross/Blue Shield | $272,210 |
| 7 | National Assn of Prof Insurance Agents | $271,778 |
| 8 | Metropolitan Life Insurance | $271,202 |
| 9 | National Assn of Independent Insurers | $255,047 |
| 10 | Prudential Insurance | $226,154 |

## Top Senate Recipients

| Rank | Recipient | Total |
|---|---|---|
| 1 | Bill Bradley (D-NJ) | $243,526 |
| 2 | Phil Gramm (R-Texas) | $184,547 |
| 3 | Hank Brown (R-Colo) | $182,589 |

## Top House Recipients

| Rank | Recipient | Total |
|---|---|---|
| 1 | Barbara B. Kennelly (D-Conn) | $103,825 |
| 2 | Richard A. Gephardt (D-Mo) | $96,800 |
| 3 | Byron L. Dorgan (D-ND) | $85,256 |

## Ways and Means Committee Draws Bonanza in Insurance Industry Contributions

Many industries and individual companies direct a large share of their campaign dollars to members of committees that are particularly important to their business. Few show patterns as dramatic as the insurance industry, however, and none delivers as heavy a financial clout to the members of a single committee. Though insurance contributors did spread their dollars to members of every House and Senate committee, their main effort was clearly aimed at the tax-writing House Ways and Means Committee. Insurance contributors spent more than $1.7 million on contributions to members of that panel — an average of over $47,000 per member. The list below identifies the 16 Ways and Means Committee members who drew $50,000 or more from insurance contributors in the 1990 elections.

### Top Ways & Means Recipients of Insurance Contributions

| | |
|---|---|
| Hank Brown (R-Colo)† | $182,589 |
| Barbara B. Kennelly (D-Conn) | $103,825 |
| Byron L. Dorgan (D-ND) | $85,256 |
| Marty Russo (D-Ill) | $80,700 |
| Don Sundquist (R-Tenn) | $77,899 |
| Raymond J. McGrath (R-NY) | $72,420 |
| Thomas J. Downey (D-NY) | $69,350 |
| Jim Moody (D-Wis) | $68,850 |
| Beryl Anthony Jr. (D-Ark) | $67,300 |
| Robert T. Matsui (D-Calif) | $67,300 |
| Charles B. Rangel (D-NY) | $63,795 |
| Nancy L. Johnson (R-Conn) | $61,524 |
| Dick Schulze (R-Pa) | $59,718 |
| Rod Chandler (R-Wash) | $54,350 |
| Frank J. Guarini (D-NJ) | $54,000 |
| Michael A. Andrews (D-Texas) | $53,850 |

† Ran for Senate in 1990

# Real Estate ...........................................................................$10.0 million

Investing in land, and developing it with new and valuable buildings has been a thriving business fueling the American economy since the vast Eastern forests first began to be peeled back to make way for the villages, towns and farms of colonial settlers. The 1980s saw development at a pace extraordinary even by American standards, as shopping malls, skyscrapers, industrial parks and subdivisions sprang like mushrooms from Texas to California, Florida to Maine.

Today's vacancy rates are a testimony to the frantic pace of office building in the boom years of the 80s. Filling that space, and keeping the market moving has become an ever more challenging task, particularly as the economy has soured and boom has given way to bust. Developers, real estate agents, investors and government officials have all been groping with the problem. And $10 million in campaign contributions were no doubt persuasive in enlisting the assistance of many members of Congress to the industry's plight.

The real estate dollars came heavily both from individuals and political action committees. In the PAC world, the biggest by far was the Realtors PAC — the largest political action committee in the country, with nearly $3.1 million in contributions to 510 congressional candidates in the 1989-90 election cycle. The PAC, like the industry, gave to virtually every member of Congress, regardless of committee assignment. Like most PACs, however, it did not spend much of its time with challengers. Overall, 90.5 percent of the Realtors' dollars went to incumbents.

## Top Contributors

| Rank | Contributor | Total |
|---|---|---|
| 1 | National Assn of Realtors | $3,094,228 |
| 2 | Mortgage Bankers Assn of America | $236,000 |
| 3 | Century 21 Real Estate | $131,280 |
| 4 | JMB Realty Corp | $91,850 |
| 5 | Trammell Crow Co | $84,850 |
| 6 | Forest City Enterprises Inc | $67,500 |
| 7 | Federal National Mortgage Assn | $66,200 |
| 8 | American Land Title Assn | $65,300 |
| 9 | American Resort & Residential Devel Assn | $62,050 |
| 10 | First Union Corp | $61,700 |

## Top Senate Recipients

| Rank | Recipient | Total |
|---|---|---|
| 1 | Bill Bradley (D-NJ) | $305,508 |
| 2 | John Kerry (D-Mass) | $293,072 |
| 3 | Carl Levin (D-Mich) | $285,300 |

## Top House Recipients

| Rank | Recipient | Total |
|---|---|---|
| 1 | Mel Levine (D-Calif) | $118,550 |
| 2 | Ileana Ros-Lehtinen (R-Fla) | $81,662 |
| 3 | Charles E. Schumer (D-NY) | $80,050 |

# Health

## *Where the money came from . . .*

As the long-building drive toward some form of national health insurance moves inexorably forward, the health care industry's powerful voices on Capitol Hill are preparing for a long, and expensive, engagement. Health industry lobbyists have long been familiar figures in the halls of the Capitol and the battle over the industry's future is about to be joined. For years, campaign dollars from medical PACs and from thousands of individual doctors, dentists, chiropractors, pharmacists, nursing home operators and all other manner of medical professionals have been flowing generously toward Washington. In the 1989-90 campaign season, the industry provided $16.3 million in contributions to congressional candidates.

Its most recognizable vehicle for delivering those dollars has been the political action committee of the American Medical Association. Along with its many statewide affiliates, the AMA PAC gave more than $2.6 million in the 1990 elections, second only to the Realtors PAC in total con-

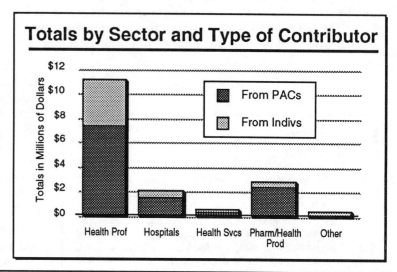

**Totals by Sector and Type of Contributor**

| Category | Total | From PACs | PAC Pct | From Indivs | Indiv Pct |
|----------|------:|----------:|--------:|------------:|----------:|
| Health Professionals | $11,031,110 | $7,173,662 | 65% | $3,857,448 | 35% |
| Hospitals/Nursing Homes | $1,889,565 | $1,348,504 | 71% | $541,061 | 29% |
| Health Services | $376,492 | $221,190 | 59% | $155,302 | 41% |
| Pharmaceuticals/Health Prod | $2,690,231 | $2,201,826 | 82% | $488,405 | 18% |
| Other & Unclassified | $306,214 | $0 | 0% | $306,214 | 100% |
| **TOTAL** | **$16,293,612** | **$10,945,182** | **67%** | **$5,348,430** | **33%** |

tributions. But the AMA PAC is hardly alone, as a glance at the Top 20 contributors list below makes clear. Many more medical professionals — from ophthalmologists to root canal specialists — have PACs of their own. In all, health professionals and their membership organizations accounted for over $11 million in political donations — by far the largest portion of the health care industry's giving. Other important sectors were pharmaceutical manufacturers, hospitals and nursing homes. Two thirds of the industry's donations came from political action committees. Most of the rest came from individual doctors.

## Top 20 Health Contributors

| Rank | Total | Contributor | Category | PAC Pct | Dem Pct | Repub Pct | ☐ To Dems  ▨ To Repubs |
|-----:|------:|-------------|----------|--------:|--------:|----------:|----|
| 1 | $2,647,981 | American Medical Assn | Doctors | 100% | 49% | 51% | |
| 2 | $961,411 | American Academy of Ophthalmology | Eye Doctors | 100% | 52% | 48% | |
| 3 | $824,578 | American Dental Assn | Dentists | 100% | 54% | 46% | |
| 4 | $506,639 | American Hospital Assn | Hospitals | 100% | 68% | 32% | |
| 5 | $330,850 | American Optometric Assn | Eye Doctors | 100% | 63% | 37% | |
| 6 | $290,360 | American Nurses Assn | Nurses | 100% | 93% | 7% | |
| 7 | $263,630 | American Health Care Assn | Nursing Homes | 100% | 68% | 32% | |
| 8 | $256,750 | American Podiatry Assn | Doctors | 100% | 71% | 29% | |
| 9 | $230,025 | American Chiropractic Assn | Chiropractors | 100% | 70% | 30% | |
| 10 | $219,140 | Eli Lilly & Co | Pharmaceut | 80% | 25% | 75% | |
| 11 | $174,350 | Federation of American Hospitals | Hospitals | 100% | 68% | 32% | |
| 12 | $169,250 | Abbott Laboratories | Pharmaceut | 100% | 29% | 71% | |
| 13 | $168,283 | Assn for the Advancement of Psychology | Psychology | 100% | 88% | 12% | |
| 14 | $163,810 | National Assn of Pharmacists | Pharmacists | 100% | 68% | 32% | |
| 15 | $160,410 | Bristol-Myers Squibb | Pharmaceut | 93% | 42% | 58% | |
| 16 | $149,850 | American Physical Therapy Assn | Health Pract | 100% | 63% | 37% | |
| 17 | $143,900 | Pfizer Inc | Pharmaceut | 95% | 54% | 46% | |
| 18 | $136,184 | Schering-Plough Corp | Pharmaceut | 94% | 42% | 58% | |
| 19 | $130,340 | Amer College of Emergency Physicians | Doctors | 100% | 75% | 25% | |
| 20 | $126,000 | Henley Group Inc | Med Supplies | 78% | 53% | 47% | |

# *Where the money went . . .*

## Totals by Sector and Party

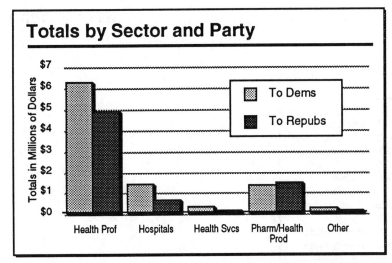

Overall, 57 percent of the campaign dollars went to Democrats. The proportion was strongest among hospitals and nursing homes and providers of health services such as outpatient clinics, home health care and HMOs. Pharmaceutical manufacturers were the only sector to give more dollars to Republicans, though the ratio was close to 50:50.

| Category | Total | To Dems | Dem Pct | To Repubs | Repub Pct |
|---|---|---|---|---|---|
| Health Professionals | $11,031,110 | $6,199,578 | 56% | $4,828,200 | 44% |
| Hospitals/Nursing Homes | $1,889,565 | $1,327,758 | 70% | $561,807 | 30% |
| Health Services | $376,492 | $269,475 | 72% | $107,017 | 28% |
| Pharmaceuticals/Health Prod | $2,690,231 | $1,303,846 | 48% | $1,386,385 | 52% |
| Other & Unclassified | $306,214 | $202,375 | 66% | $103,639 | 34% |
| **TOTAL** | **$16,293,612** | **$9,303,032** | **57%** | **$6,987,048** | **43%** |

Texas Republican Phil Gramm drew the highest total from health industry contributors — nearly $470,000. Jay Rockefeller, the West Virginia Democrat who chairs the Medicare subcommittee of the tax-writing Senate Finance Committee, was second with $412,000. Though lower than Gramm's total, it was a much higher proportion of his total campaign dollars. Rockefeller's reelection campaign raised $3.6 million; Gramm's exceeded $16 million.

Among top House recipients, Ileana Ros-Lehtinen drew an unusually large share of health industry funds considering she sits on no health-related committees. She did run two campaigns in 1989-90 however, the 1989 special election when she won her seat and a 1990 reelection for another two-year term. Allowing for the extra race, Henry Waxman would have led the House. Waxman is chairman of the Health and Environment subcommittee of the powerful Energy & Commerce Committee. Fellow Californian Pete Stark is Waxman's counterpart on the Ways and Means Committee's Health subcommittee — the other major House panel that focuses on the health care industry.

## Top 10 Senate Recipients

| Rank | Name | Amount | Status | W/L |
|---|---|---|---|---|
| 1 | Phil Gramm (R-Texas) | $469,004 | Incumb | W |
| 2 | John D. Rockefeller IV (D-WVa) | $412,327 | Incumb | W |
| 3 | Bill Bradley (D-NJ) | $294,686 | Incumb | W |
| 4 | Daniel R. Coats (R-Ind) | $244,492 | Incumb | W |
| 5 | Tom Harkin (D-Iowa) | $244,190 | Incumb | W |
| 6 | Paul Simon (D-Ill) | $229,824 | Incumb | W |
| 7 | Mitch McConnell (R-Ky) | $208,925 | Incumb | W |
| 8 | Carl Levin (D-Mich) | $169,427 | Incumb | W |
| 9 | Max Baucus (D-Mont) | $159,640 | Incumb | W |
| 10 | Jesse Helms (R-NC) | $127,154 | Incumb | W |

## Top 10 House Recipients

| Rank | Name | Amount | Status | W/L |
|---|---|---|---|---|
| 1 | Ileana Ros-Lehtinen (R-Fla) | $190,522 | Incumb | W |
| 2 | Henry A. Waxman (D-Calif) | $172,000 | Incumb | W |
| 3 | Robert T. Matsui (D-Calif) | $149,508 | Incumb | W |
| 4 | Pete Stark (D-Calif) | $121,600 | Incumb | W |
| 5 | Ron Wyden (D-Ore) | $103,460 | Incumb | W |
| 6 | Richard A. Gephardt (D-Mo) | $94,150 | Incumb | W |
| 7 | Jim Moody (D-Wis) | $88,800 | Incumb | W |
| 8 | Edward Madigan (R-Ill) | $80,604 | Incumb | W |
| 9 | Michael Bilirakis (R-Fla) | $80,504 | Incumb | W |
| 10 | J. Roy Rowland (D-Ga) | $76,265 | Incumb | W |

# Closeup on Health

## Health Professionals.....................................................................$11.0 million

**Top Contributors**

| Rank | Contributor | Total | Category |
|------|-------------|-------|----------|
| 1 | American Medical Assn | $2,647,981 | Doctors |
| 2 | American Academy of Ophthalmology | $961,411 | Eye Doctors |
| 3 | American Dental Assn | $824,578 | Dentists |
| 4 | American Optometric Assn | $330,850 | Eye Doctors |
| 5 | American Nurses Assn | $290,360 | Nurses |
| 6 | American Podiatry Assn | $256,750 | MD Specialists |
| 7 | American Chiropractic Assn | $230,025 | Chiropractors |
| 8 | Assn for the Advancement of Psychology | $168,283 | Psych |
| 9 | National Assn of Pharmacists | $163,810 | Pharmacists |
| 10 | American Physical Therapy Assn | $149,850 | Health Pract |

Doctors, dentists, chiropractors, pharmacists and a host of other health professionals form the segment of the medical industry that is far and away the biggest contributor to political campaigns. And while the political action committees in this sector are among the largest in the nation, one-third of the dollars came from individual contributions, not PACs.

Eclipsing all other groups in this category were physicians and physician specialists. Among those specialties, ophthalmologists (eye doctors) were particularly generous, giving a total of more than $1.5 million. Dentists added another $1.1 million. Psychologists and psychiatrists gave $389,000 and other physician specialists gave a total of just under $690,000. All those groups gave the majority of their dollars through political action committees.

Among health care PACs none is nearly as large as the AMA's PAC, which ranked second overall in the nation in 1990 with over $2.6 million in contributions to nearly 500 candidates. (The figures include contributions from a number of AMA state-level affiliates).

The overriding issue of importance to the medical community in Congress has to do with the federal government's participation in health care — currently through the Medicare and Medicaid programs and potentially later through some form of national health insurance. While there are few complaints about the competency of health care in the U.S. there are widespread concerns about its affordability. The cost of treatment has grown so rapidly that those without some form of insurance — and that number includes tens of millions of Americans — can face financial ruin if afflicted with a serious illness or injury. Though the AMA has resisted national health insurance for years, there are signs that position is changing as the political will of the nation moves politicians toward promises of action. The battles ahead will likely be over what form a national health care plan will take, and what the relationship will be between the government and existing private health care providers and insurers.

**Top Senate Recipients**

| Rank | Recipient | Total |
|------|-----------|-------|
| 1 | Phil Gramm (R-Texas) | $385,449 |
| 2 | John D. Rockefeller IV (D-WVa) | $243,102 |
| 3 | Mitch McConnell (R-Ky) | $177,125 |

**Top House Recipients**

| Rank | Recipient | Total |
|------|-----------|-------|
| 1 | Ileana Ros-Lehtinen (R-Fla) | $143,220 |
| 2 | Henry A. Waxman (D-Calif) | $95,500 |
| 3 | Robert T. Matsui (D-Calif) | $87,175 |

# Hospitals & Nursing Homes.................................................................$1.9 million

**Top Contributors**

| Rank | Contributor | Total | Category |
|------|-------------|-------|----------|
| 1 | American Hospital Assn | $506,639 | Hospitals |
| 2 | American Health Care Assn | $263,630 | Nursing Homes |
| 3 | Federation of American Hospitals | $174,350 | Hospitals |
| 4 | National Medical Enterprises Inc | $85,383 | Hospitals |
| 5 | Natl Assn of Private Psychiatric Hospitals | $74,150 | Hospitals |
| 6 | Humana Inc | $47,900 | Hospitals |
| 7 | Manor Healthcare Corp | $44,882 | Nursing Homes |
| 8 | Hospice Care Inc | $38,000 | Nursing Homes |
| 9 | Voluntary Hospitals of America | $37,550 | Hospitals |
| 10 | Beverly Enterprises | $35,775 | Nursing Homes |

Physicians are not the only ones with a stake in the current and future state of health care. Hospitals and nursing homes are also major players in the industry, with billions of dollars at stake in the details of federal health care policy. During the 1989-90 election cycle, hospital PACs and individual administrators and officials gave more than $1.3 million to congressional candidates. Nursing home operators gave an addition $535,000. In both cases, more than 70 percent of the dollars went to Democrats.

**Top Senate Recipients**

| Rank | Recipient | Total |
|------|-----------|-------|
| 1 | John D. Rockefeller IV (D-WVa) | $94,675 |
| 2 | Paul Simon (D-Ill) | $46,375 |
| 3 | John Kerry (D-Mass) | $38,550 |

**Top House Recipients**

| Rank | Recipient | Total |
|------|-----------|-------|
| 1 | Robert T. Matsui (D-Calif) | $41,533 |
| 2 | Henry A. Waxman (D-Calif) | $31,000 |
| 3 | Richard A. Gephardt (D-Mo) | $27,800 |

# Pharmaceuticals & Health Products .....................................$2.7 million

**Top Contributors**

| Rank | Contributor | Total | Category |
|------|-------------|-------|----------|
| 1 | Eli Lilly & Co | $219,140 | Pharmaceuticals |
| 2 | Abbott Laboratories | $169,250 | Pharmaceuticals |
| 3 | Bristol-Myers Squibb | $160,410 | Pharmaceuticals |
| 4 | Pfizer Inc | $143,900 | Pharmaceuticals |
| 5 | Schering-Plough Corp | $136,184 | Pharmaceuticals |
| 6 | Henley Group Inc | $126,000 | Medical Supplies |
| 7 | Ciba-Geigy Corp | $121,275 | Pharmaceuticals |
| 8 | SmithKline Beecham | $117,350 | Pharmaceuticals |
| 9 | Glaxo Inc | $114,650 | Pharmaceuticals |
| 10 | Upjohn Co | $111,000 | Pharmaceuticals |

Pharmaceutical manufacturers are the one segment of the health care community that gave more money to Republicans in the 1990 elections than to Democrats. In that sense, their pattern of giving more closely reflects that of the manufacturing sector than the health care industry. Drug companies contributed just over $2 million to congressional candidates. Eighty-eight percent of the dollars came from political action committees.

Medical supply manufacturers were also politically active, though on a much smaller level. In all, they gave just over $370,000 in the 1990 elections. Some 62 percent of the dollars went to Democrats.

Manufacturers of other health care products accounted for just under $220,000 in contributions. Slightly more than half that amount went to Democrats.

**Top Senate Recipients**

| Rank | Recipient | Total |
|------|-----------|-------|
| 1 | Bill Bradley (D-NJ) | $108,760 |
| 2 | Daniel R. Coats (R-Ind) | $106,970 |
| 3 | Phil Gramm (R-Texas) | $49,550 |

**Top House Recipients**

| Rank | Recipient | Total |
|------|-----------|-------|
| 1 | Dick Zimmer (R-NJ) | $34,600 |
| 2 | John D. Dingell (D-Mich) | $32,900 |
| 3 | Edward Madigan (R-Ill) | $28,414 |

# Lawyers & Lobbyists

## Where the money came from . . .

Lawyers, lobbyists and lawmakers have had a long and close relationship ever since modern democracy made its emergence on the world political scene. Indeed, many individuals have passed through all three professions in succession: lawyers winning election and becoming lawmakers, then retiring from office and becoming high-paid lobbyists. Congress has always had more lawyers than members of any other single profession, and the number of former lawmakers who make the transition from Capitol Hill to K Street — the heart of Washington's lobbying district — is large and continually growing.

But little of that can be seen from tracking PAC contributions. Indeed, compared with other major industries, the legal community seems quite small. Legal industry PACs, led by the Association of Trial Lawyers of America, gave just $4.3 million in contributions in 1990. But in this case, following the PACs leads to a misleading conclusion. In fact, lawyers and lobbyists were responsible for at least $18.5 million in contributions in the 1990 election cycle — more than any other business sector except finance. But 75 percent of those dollars were delivered in individual contributions, not through PACs. To journalists and other observers keeping a close watch on campaign dollars, the contributions were all but invisible.

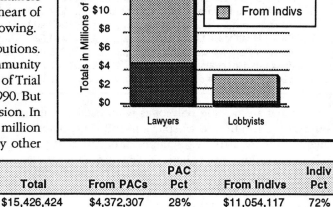

**Totals by Sector and Type**

| Category | Total | From PACs | PAC Pct | From Indivs | Indiv Pct |
|---|---|---|---|---|---|
| Lawyers | $15,426,424 | $4,372,307 | 28% | $11,054,117 | 72% |
| Lobbyists | $3,168,285 | $219,609 | 7% | $2,948,676 | 93% |
| **TOTAL** | **$18,594,709** | **$4,591,916** | **25%** | **$14,002,793** | **75%** |

Even with the research that went into this book, many questions about the role of lawyers and lobbyists are unanswered. Many lawyers failed to put the name of their law firm, but simply filled in "attorney" as their employer. And federal lobbying laws are so porous that the number of registered lobbyists is widely considered to be only a fraction of the number of Washington-area lawyers who routinely perform lobbying services for clients.

Certainly, not all lawyers are lobbyists — even those in the nation's capital. Aside from lobbying activities, attorneys are also deeply involved in legislation affecting their profession. Lawyers have long opposed any attempts at "tort reform" that would reduce corporate liability for faulty products (and reduce lawyers' fees for winning product liability lawsuits).

## Top 20 Lawyer & Lobbyist Contributors

| Rank | Total | Contributor | Category | PAC Pct | Dem Pct | Repub Pct | To Dems | To Repubs |
|---|---|---|---|---|---|---|---|---|
| 1 | $1,539,550 | Assn of Trial Lawyers of America | Lawyers | 100% | 87% | 13% | | |
| 2 | $389,400 | Akin, Gump, Hauer & Feld | Law/Lobby | 69% | 79% | 21% | | |
| 3 | $200,400 | Skadden, Arps et al | Law/Lobby | 40% | 83% | 17% | | |
| 4 | $193,311 | Williams & Jensen | Law/Lobby | 41% | 63% | 37% | | |
| 5 | $176,877 | Cassidy & Associates | Lobbyists | 0% | 76% | 24% | | |
| 6 | $150,764 | Hill & Knowlton | Lobbyists/PR | 77% | 72% | 28% | | |
| 7 | $145,540 | Powell, Goldstein et al | Law/Lobby | 91% | 89% | 11% | | |
| 8 | $134,419 | Verner, Liipfert et al | Law/Lobby | 91% | 81% | 19% | | |
| 9 | $130,700 | Camp, Barsh, Bates & Tate | Law/Lobby | 19% | 80% | 20% | | |
| 10 | $120,924 | Vinson, Elkins, Searls et al | Law/Lobby | 76% | 73% | 27% | | |
| 11 | $117,337 | Preston, Thorgrimson et al | Law/Lobby | 78% | 72% | 28% | | |
| 12 | $107,825 | Arnold & Porter | Law/Lobby | 88% | 86% | 14% | | |
| 13 | $104,425 | Dickstein, Shapiro & Morin | Lawyers | 100% | 58% | 42% | | |
| 14 | $102,712 | Jones, Day, Reavis & Pogue | Lawyers | 100% | 47% | 53% | | |
| 15 | $102,130 | Neill & Co | Lobbyists | 0% | 72% | 28% | | |
| 16 | $93,737 | Kirkpatrick & Lockhart | Law/Lobby | 60% | 71% | 29% | | |
| 17 | $89,200 | Holland & Knight | Lawyers | 92% | 68% | 32% | | |
| 18 | $86,119 | Patton, Boggs & Blow | Law/Lobby | 0% | 74% | 26% | | |
| 19 | $84,150 | Kutak, Rock & Campbell | Lawyers | 85% | 83% | 17% | | |
| 20 | $84,000 | King & Spalding | Law/Lobby | 55% | 82% | 18% | | |

# Where the money went . . .

## Totals by Sector and Party

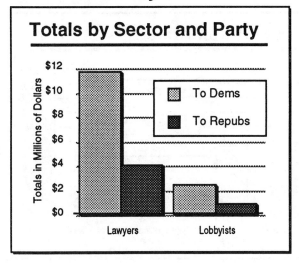

By a three-to-one margin, individual lawyers and their PACs contributed to congressional Democrats rather than Republicans. That is the strongest proportion of any business sector to go to any one political party. The proportion was consistent between lawyers and lobbyists, though the dollars from attorneys who are not registered lobbyists was five times as great as those who were.

| Category | Total | To Dems | Dem Pct | To Repubs | Repub Pct |
|---|---|---|---|---|---|
| Lawyers | $15,426,424 | $11,541,116 | 75% | $3,882,908 | 25% |
| Lobbyists | $3,168,285 | $2,352,461 | 74% | $815,824 | 26% |
| TOTAL | $18,594,709 | $13,893,577 | 75% | $4,698,732 | 25% |

The biggest recipients of contributions from the legal community were nearly all Democrats. Of the top 10 recipients in the House and Senate only two — Sen. Phil Gramm of Texas and freshman House member Dick Zimmer of New Jersey — were Republicans.

Leading the list by a large margin was Bill Bradley, the New Jersey Democrat who raised nearly $13 million in what turned out to be a much closer than expected reelection race. Bradley collected more than a million dollars from lawyers, law firms and lobbyists. Most of it came in individual contributions. Bradley collected $10,000 or more from 18 different law firms. Leading the way were Skadden Arps ($37,700) and Wilkie, Farr & Gallagher ($34,250).

Among House members, Democratic majority leader Dick Gephardt collected the biggest amount from lawyers. The biggest chunk of that — some $62,510 — came from one law firm, the St. Louis-based Thompson & Mitchell. The firm does not have a political action committee, so all the money came from individual contributions from lawyers within the firm and their families.

## Top 10 Senate Recipients

| Rank | Name | Amount | Status | W/L |
|---|---|---|---|---|
| 1 | Bill Bradley (D-NJ) | $1,047,673 | Incumb | W |
| 2 | Paul Simon (D-Ill) | $619,730 | Incumb | W |
| 3 | Phil Gramm (R-Texas) | $597,750 | Incumb | W |
| 4 | John Kerry (D-Mass) | $572,482 | Incumb | W |
| 5 | Carl Levin (D-Mich) | $506,808 | Incumb | W |
| 6 | Howell Heflin (D-Ala) | $486,564 | Incumb | W |
| 7 | J. Bennett Johnston (D-La) | $304,150 | Incumb | W |
| 8 | John D. Rockefeller IV (D-WVa) | $270,720 | Incumb | W |
| 9 | Al Gore (D-Tenn) | $264,203 | Incumb | W |
| 10 | Tom Harkin (D-Iowa) | $258,236 | Incumb | W |

## Top 10 House Recipients

| Rank | Name | Amount | Status | W/L |
|---|---|---|---|---|
| 1 | Richard A. Gephardt (D-Mo) | $222,003 | Incumb | W |
| 2 | Pete Geren (D-Texas) | $193,288 | Incumb | W |
| 3 | Craig Washington (D-Texas) | $183,860 | Incumb | W |
| 4 | John Bryant (D-Texas) | $153,157 | Incumb | W |
| 5 | Mel Levine (D-Calif) | $145,600 | Incumb | W |
| 6 | Nita M. Lowey (D-NY) | $129,200 | Incumb | W |
| 7 | Jerry F. Costello (D-Ill) | $105,725 | Incumb | W |
| 8 | Greg Laughlin (D-Texas) | $100,857 | Incumb | W |
| 9 | Jim Bacchus (D-Fla) | $98,599 | Open | W |
| 10 | Dick Zimmer (R-NJ) | $97,833 | Open | W |

# Miscellaneous Business

## Where the money came from . . .

This catchall category encompasses a variety of disparate businesses from a wide range of industries — from steel manufacturers to travel agencies, beer distributors to funeral directors. Most of the industries here have an interest in a wide variety of legislative matters, but — aside from tax laws — few of those issues are concentrated under the jurisdiction of a particular committee.

Miscellaneous manufacturers and distributors comprised the largest single group within the sector, both in PAC and individual contributions. The companies in this group manufacture everything from machine tools to textiles. Other large groups were the food & beverage industry (which includes restaurants, soft drink manufacturers and bottlers — but not food manufacturers, who are classified under agriculture), the beer & liquor industry, retail sales and "business services," which covers such fields as advertising, business consulting and employment agencies. Overall, just over half the dollars given by miscellaneous businesses came from political action committees.

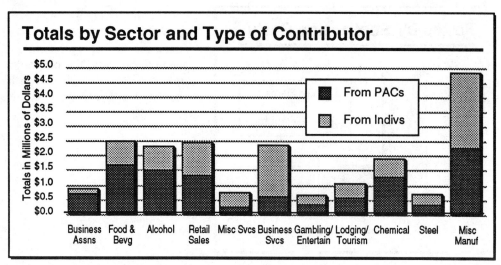

| Category | Total | From PACs | PAC Pct | From Indivs | Indiv Pct |
|---|---|---|---|---|---|
| Business Associations | $805,819 | $633,781 | 79% | $172,038 | 21% |
| Food & Beverage | $2,397,367 | $1,625,322 | 68% | $772,045 | 32% |
| Beer, Wine & Liquor | $2,230,400 | $1,418,191 | 64% | $812,209 | 36% |
| Retail Sales | $2,371,320 | $1,235,922 | 52% | $1,135,398 | 48% |
| Misc Services | $640,327 | $186,161 | 29% | $454,166 | 71% |
| Business Services | $2,264,586 | $511,128 | 23% | $1,753,458 | 77% |
| Gambling/Live Entertainment | $581,581 | $260,619 | 45% | $320,962 | 55% |
| Lodging/Tourism | $972,948 | $481,390 | 49% | $491,558 | 51% |
| Chemicals | $1,812,021 | $1,211,981 | 67% | $600,040 | 33% |
| Steel/Smelting | $628,886 | $267,021 | 42% | $361,865 | 58% |
| Misc Manufacturing & Distrib | $4,754,783 | $2,213,987 | 47% | $2,540,796 | 53% |
| **TOTAL** | **$19,460,038** | **$10,045,503** | **52%** | **$9,414,535** | **48%** |

## Top 20 Miscellaneous Business Contributors

| Rank | Total | Contributor | Category | PAC Pct | Dem Pct | Repub Pct | To Dems / To Repubs |
|---|---|---|---|---|---|---|---|
| 1 | $633,150 | National Beer Wholesalers Assn | Liquor Whlsale | 100% | 57% | 43% | |
| 2 | $582,492 | National Restaurant Assn | Restaurants | 100% | 20% | 80% | |
| 3 | $468,225 | Dow Chemical | Chemicals | 80% | 12% | 88% | |
| 4 | $420,034 | General Electric | Diversified Mfg | 86% | 60% | 40% | |
| 5 | $337,690 | FMC Corp | Chemicals | 100% | 26% | 74% | |
| 6 | $316,710 | National Fedn of Independent Business | Small Business | 100% | 11% | 89% | |
| 7 | $267,975 | JC Penney Co | Dept Stores | 100% | 61% | 39% | |
| 8 | $226,550 | McDonald's Corp | Restaurants | 85% | 29% | 71% | |
| 9 | $225,279 | Burlington Industries | Textiles | 99% | 56% | 44% | |
| 10 | $198,800 | International Council of Shopping Centers | Retail Trade | 100% | 38% | 62% | |
| 11 | $190,869 | Coca-Cola Co | Soft Drinks | 96% | 60% | 40% | |
| 12 | $187,470 | Anheuser-Busch | Beer | 71% | 74% | 26% | |
| 13 | $170,048 | Dun & Bradstreet | Market Rsch | 90% | 34% | 66% | |
| 14 | $163,700 | Wine & Spirits Wholesalers of America | Liquor Whlsale | 100% | 60% | 40% | |
| 15 | $161,250 | Contran Corp | Chemicals | 43% | 13% | 88% | |
| 16 | $160,000 | S&A Restaurant Corp | Restaurants | 100% | 6% | 94% | |
| 17 | $144,242 | Marriott Corp | Hotels/Motels | 93% | 41% | 59% | |
| 18 | $140,800 | American Hotel & Motel Assn | Hotels/Motels | 100% | 51% | 49% | |
| 19 | $139,900 | American Textile Manufacturers Institute | Textiles | 100% | 55% | 45% | |
| 20 | $138,550 | Hoechst Celanese Corp | Synthetic Fibers | 99% | 37% | 63% | |

# Where the money went . . .

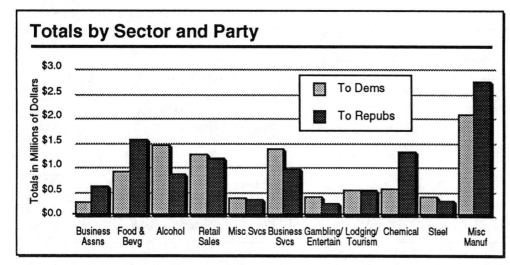

## Totals by Sector and Party

Totals in Millions of Dollars

$3.0
$2.5
$2.0
$1.5
$1.0
$0.5
$0.0

To Dems
To Repubs

Business Assns | Food & Bevg | Alcohol | Retail Sales | Misc Svcs | Business Svcs | Gambling/ Entertain | Lodging/ Tourism | Chemical | Steel | Misc Manuf

Democrats fared best among gambling and liquor industry contributors, winning 63 percent of the dollars from both those groups. Republicans were supported most heavily by chemical manufacturers, general business associations, and the restaurant and soft drink industry.

| Category | Total | To Dems | Dem Pct | To Repubs | Repub Pct |
|---|---|---|---|---|---|
| Business Associations | $805,819 | $239,777 | 30% | $567,042 | 70% |
| Food & Beverage | $2,397,367 | $863,916 | 36% | $1,533,451 | 64% |
| Beer, Wine & Liquor | $2,230,400 | $1,415,291 | 63% | $814,109 | 37% |
| Retail Sales | $2,371,320 | $1,234,251 | 52% | $1,136,069 | 48% |
| Misc Services | $640,327 | $342,083 | 53% | $298,244 | 47% |
| Business Services | $2,264,586 | $1,327,476 | 59% | $936,660 | 41% |
| Gambling/Live Entertainment | $581,581 | $366,842 | 63% | $212,239 | 36% |
| Lodging/Tourism | $972,948 | $490,627 | 50% | $482,171 | 50% |
| Chemicals | $1,812,021 | $531,088 | 29% | $1,280,933 | 71% |
| Steel/Smelting | $628,886 | $359,800 | 57% | $269,086 | 43% |
| Misc Manufacturing & Distrib | $4,754,783 | $2,038,828 | 43% | $2,715,255 | 57% |
| TOTAL | $19,460,038 | $9,209,979 | 47% | $10,245,259 | 53% |

Leading recipients in this category most typically are candidates who raised large sums from all groups of contributors. Phil Gramm and Bill Bradley top the list, as they do in many of the industry categories. Jesse Helms also makes the Top 10 list — largely due to funds he received from textile manufacturers. Though Helms raised more than any other member of Congress in 1990 (an estimated $18 million), he appears on few lists of top recipients. This is due to two main reasons: first, a substantial portion of Helms' funds came from small donors whose contributions are not itemized. Second, only a small proportion of his large contributors (those giving $200 or more) are identified by occupation and employer — despite the federal requirement that this information be listed. Nearly all members of Congress had some contributors with missing occupations; Helms had $1.3 million in that category.

## Top 10 Senate Recipients

| Rank | Name | Amount | Status | W/L |
|---|---|---|---|---|
| 1 | Phil Gramm (R-Texas) | $617,994 | Incumb | W |
| 2 | Bill Bradley (D-NJ) | $472,309 | Incumb | W |
| 3 | John Kerry (D-Mass) | $333,560 | Incumb | W |
| 4 | Carl Levin (D-Mich) | $321,405 | Incumb | W |
| 5 | Hank Brown (R-Colo) | $299,446 | Open | W |
| 6 | Jesse Helms (R-NC) | $294,757 | Incumb | W |
| 7 | Paul Simon (D-Ill) | $279,935 | Incumb | W |
| 8 | Mitch McConnell (R-Ky) | $279,892 | Incumb | W |
| 9 | Daniel R. Coats (D-Ind) | $257,272 | Incumb | W |
| 10 | John D. Rockefeller IV (D-WVa) | $256,690 | Incumb | W |

## Top 10 House Recipients

| Rank | Name | Amount | Status | W/L |
|---|---|---|---|---|
| 1 | Richard A. Gephardt (D-Mo) | $190,667 | Incumb | W |
| 2 | Newt Gingrich (R-Ga) | $162,038 | Incumb | W |
| 3 | Ileana Ros-Lehtinen (R-Fla) | $127,633 | Incumb | W |
| 4 | Dave Camp (R-Mich) | $122,867 | Open | W |
| 5 | Jim Ramstad (R-Minn) | $109,217 | Open | W |
| 6 | Mel Levine (D-Calif) | $108,200 | Incumb | W |
| 7 | John A. Boehner (R-Ohio) | $89,964 | Chall | W |
| 8 | Robert T. Matsui (D-Calif) | $86,757 | Incumb | W |
| 9 | John P. Murtha (D-Pa) | $85,125 | Incumb | W |
| 10 | Joseph P. Kennedy II (D-Mass) | $82,800 | Incumb | W |

# Closeup on Miscellaneous Business

## Food & Beverage ...................................................................$2.4 million

This group includes restaurants and drinking establishments, soft drink manufacturers and bottlers, fish processors, candy manufacturers and companies that make food additives. More general food processors and manufacturers are classified under Agriculture.

### Top Contributors

| Rank | Contributor | Total | Category |
|------|-------------|-------|----------|
| 1 | National Restaurant Assn | $582,492 | Restaurants |
| 2 | McDonald's Corp | $226,550 | Restaurants |
| 3 | Coca-Cola Co | $190,869 | Soft Drinks |
| 4 | S&A Restaurant Corp | $160,000 | Restaurants |
| 5 | General Mills Restaurants | $77,999 | Restaurants |
| 6 | Hardee's Food Systems | $55,300 | Restaurants |
| 7 | Morrison Inc | $54,550 | Food Services |
| 8 | Pepsi-Cola Bottlers Assn | $35,100 | Bevg Bottling |
| 9 | National Soft Drink Assn | $34,350 | Soft Drinks |
| 10 | National Confectioners Assn | $30,340 | Candy |

### Top Senate Recipients

| Rank | Recipient | Total |
|------|-----------|-------|
| 1 | Phil Gramm (R-Texas) | $66,435 |
| 2 | Hank Brown (R-Colo) | $40,250 |
| 3 | Tom Tauke (R-Iowa) | $37,847 |

### Top House Recipients

| Rank | Recipient | Total |
|------|-----------|-------|
| 1 | Bill Zeliff (R-NH) | $37,350 |
| 2 | Newt Gingrich (R-Ga) | $35,849 |
| 3 | Steve Bartlett (R-Texas) | $23,600 |

## Beer, Wine & Liquor ...................................................................$2.2 million

Beer & liquor wholesalers were the biggest contributors in this group, accounting for nearly $1.3 million. Wine & spirit manufacturers gave $642,000. Beer manufacturers, led by Anheuser-Busch, contributed $246,000.

### Top Contributors

| Rank | Contributor | Total |
|------|-------------|-------|
| 1 | National Beer Wholesalers Assn | $633,150 |
| 2 | Anheuser-Busch | $187,470 |
| 3 | Wine & Spirits Wholesalers of America | $161,200 |
| 4 | Joseph E Seagram & Sons | $133,575 |
| 5 | E&J Gallo Winery | $118,426 |
| 6 | Brown-Forman Distillers | $86,750 |
| 7 | Distilled Spirits Council | $66,838 |
| 8 | Adolph Coors Co | $58,808 |
| 9 | Wine Institute | $45,030 |
| 10 | Smirnoff/Inglenook Distributors | $39,700 |

### Top Senate Recipients

| Rank | Recipient | Total |
|------|-----------|-------|
| 1 | Max Baucus (D-Mont) | $47,822 |
| 2 | Mitch McConnell (R-Ky) | $42,422 |
| 3 | Hank Brown (R-Colo) | $39,508 |

### Top House Recipients

| Rank | Recipient | Total |
|------|-----------|-------|
| 1 | Richard A. Gephardt (D-Mo) | $75,250 |
| 2 | Robert T. Matsui (D-Calif) | $42,250 |
| 3 | Jack Brooks (D-Texas) | $33,100 |

## Retail Sales ...................................................................$2.4 million

Department and variety stores led the spending in this category, which includes retail stores of all types as well as catalog and direct mail houses, vending machine operators and door-to-door sales companies.

### Top Contributors

| Rank | Contributor | Total |
|------|-------------|-------|
| 1 | JC Penney Co | $267,975 |
| 2 | International Council of Shopping Centers | $198,800 |
| 3 | May Department Stores | $129,800 |
| 4 | Montgomery Ward | $79,700 |
| 5 | Sears† | $70,350 |
| 6 | K Mart Corp | $64,550 |
| 7 | Dayton Hudson Corp | $42,100 |
| 8 | National Assn of Chain Drug Stores | $41,800 |
| 9 | National Assn of Convenience Stores | $38,450 |
| 10 | Valmont Industries | $38,082 |

### Top Senate Recipients

| Rank | Recipient | Total |
|------|-----------|-------|
| 1 | Phil Gramm (R-Texas) | $83,412 |
| 2 | Bill Bradley (D-NJ) | $73,756 |
| 3 | Carl Levin (D-Mich) | $56,940 |

### Top House Recipients

| Rank | Recipient | Total |
|------|-----------|-------|
| 1 | Richard A. Gephardt (D-Mo) | $21,250 |
| 2 | Mel Levine (D-Calif) | $20,750 |
| 3 | Jack Brooks (D-Texas) | $16,250 |

† Does not include non-retail subsidiaries

## Chemical & Related Manufacturing ...................................................$1.8 million

Because of strict federal regulations on pollution control, clean air standards and other matters that affect the chemical industry, this has long been one of the most politically active segments of the manufacturing sector. It is also one of the most conservative, delivering two-thirds of its dollars to Republican candidates. The leading recipient of chemical industry money in 1990, freshman Republican Dave Camp of Michigan, collected over $100,000 from individuals and PACs connected with Dow Chemical and its subsidiary Dow Corning. That amount was the most given by any single contributor to any member of Congress in the 1990 elections. Camp's district includes Dow's headquarters city — Midland, Mich.

### Top Contributors

| Rank | Contributor | Total | Category |
|------|-------------|-------|----------|
| 1 | Dow Chemical | $440,475 | Chemicals |
| 2 | FMC Corp | $337,690 | Chemicals |
| 3 | Greyhound Dial | $121,175 | Hhld Chem |
| 4 | WR Grace & Co | $119,547 | Chemicals |
| 5 | Contran Corp | $116,750 | Chemicals |
| 6 | Monsanto Co | $91,100 | Chemicals |
| 7 | du Pont | $64,500 | Chemicals |
| 8 | Air Products & Chemicals Inc | $54,800 | Chemicals |
| 9 | Nalco Chemical Co | $45,750 | Chemicals |
| 10 | NL Industries | $44,500 | Chemicals |

### Top Senate Recipients

| Rank | Recipient | Total |
|------|-----------|-------|
| 1 | Phil Gramm (R-Texas) | $74,425 |
| 2 | Hank Brown (R-Colo) | $56,999 |
| 3 | Lynn Martin (R-Ill) | $47,500 |

### Top House Recipients

| Rank | Recipient | Total |
|------|-----------|-------|
| 1 | Dave Camp (R-Mich) | $102,050 |
| 2 | Jim Ramstad (R-Minn) | $18,650 |
| 3 | Don Ritter (R-Pa) | $17,250 |

## Misc. Manufacturing & Distributing ...................................................$4.8 million

### Top Contributors

| Rank | Contributor | Total | Category |
|------|-------------|-------|----------|
| 1 | General Electric | $420,034 | Manufacturing |
| 2 | Burlington Industries | $225,279 | Textiles |
| 3 | American Textile Manufacturers Institute | $139,900 | Textiles |
| 4 | Hoechst Celanese Corp | $138,550 | Synthetic Fibers |
| 5 | Stone Container Corp | $135,750 | Paper Packaging |
| 6 | Minnesota Mining & Manufacturing (3M) | $96,005 | Industl/Comml Equip |
| 7 | American Furniture Manufacturers Assn | $85,350 | Furniture |
| 8 | National Tooling & Machining Assn | $83,425 | Industl/Comml Equip |
| 9 | Owens-Illinois | $81,301 | Glass Products |
| 10 | Xerox Corp | $79,500 | Office Machines |

The leaders in this diverse category are textile manufacturers ($790,000), clothing and shoe makers ($400,000), and dozens of companies that manufacture industrial and commercial equipment ranging from machine tools to gears and sprockets. General Electric is the biggest single contributor in this category, though many of GE's contributions have been classified in other categories — such as nuclear power, defense, communications and transportation. Only if their dollars went to a non-incumbent or a member of Congress sitting on committees with no jurisdiction over those other categories did the contribution get counted here.

### Top Senate Recipients

| Rank | Recipient | Total |
|------|-----------|-------|
| 1 | Phil Gramm (R-Texas) | $144,925 |
| 2 | Jesse Helms (R-NC) | $144,294 |
| 3 | Bill Bradley (D-NJ) | $140,564 |

### Top House Recipients

| Rank | Recipient | Total |
|------|-----------|-------|
| 1 | Newt Gingrich (R-Ga) | $52,815 |
| 2 | Howard Coble (R-NC) | $51,279 |
| 3 | Cass Ballenger (R-NC) | $45,917 |

# Transportation

## Where the money came from . . .

In a nation that spans more than 2,000 miles from coast to coast, and another 1,000 from border to border, the transportation of goods, services and people from one location to another has always been a major industry. From the days when the railroads opened up the American West, transportation companies have relied on allies in Congress to keep their business rolling along. Likewise, competing segments within the industry— railroads versus truckers, for example—have often sought to improve their market position at their competitors' expense.

In the 1990 elections the automotive and air transport industries were the biggest contributors to congressional campaigns, though most of the dollars did not come from airlines and auto manufacturers. Rather, it was the two biggest overnight delivery carriers — Federal Express and UPS — that gave the largest amounts in air transport. And it was auto dealers and not auto manufacturers that led the way in spending in the automotive sector.

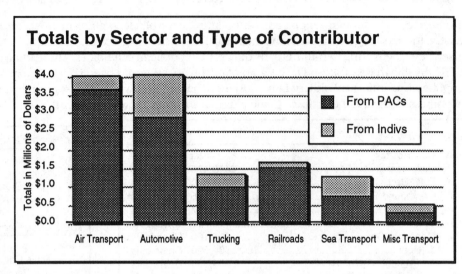

**Totals by Sector and Type of Contributor**

| Category | Total | From PACs | PAC Pct | From Indivs | Indiv Pct |
|---|---|---|---|---|---|
| Air Transport | $3,964,638 | $3,605,774 | 91% | $358,864 | 9% |
| Automotive | $3,976,677 | $2,823,862 | 71% | $1,152,815 | 29% |
| Trucking | $1,269,479 | $916,613 | 72% | $352,866 | 28% |
| Railroads | $1,604,480 | $1,455,805 | 91% | $148,675 | 9% |
| Sea Transport | $1,221,359 | $689,123 | 56% | $532,236 | 44% |
| Misc Transport | $468,371 | $246,442 | 53% | $221,929 | 47% |
| **TOTAL** | **$12,505,004** | **$9,737,619** | **78%** | **$2,767,385** | **22%** |

Contributions through political action committees were the most common form of delivering dollars from transportation interests. More than three dollars out of every four came through PACs, though individual auto dealers gave substantial sums directly, as did many individuals in the sea transport sector.

## Top 20 Transportation Contributors

| Rank | Total | Contributor | Category | PAC Pct | Dem Pct | Repub Pct | To Dems / To Repubs |
|---|---|---|---|---|---|---|---|
| 1 | $1,313,900 | National Auto Dealers Assn | Auto Dealers | 100% | 38% | 62% | |
| 2 | $765,225 | Federal Express Corp | Delivery Svcs | 99% | 63% | 37% | |
| 3 | $659,732 | United Parcel Service | Delivery Svcs | 100% | 60% | 40% | |
| 4 | $644,450 | Auto Dealers & Drivers for Free Trade | Auto Dealers | 100% | 33% | 67% | |
| 5 | $552,164 | Union Pacific Corp | Railroads | 93% | 42% | 58% | |
| 6 | $513,900 | Aircraft Owners & Pilots Assn | Genl Aviation | 100% | 49% | 51% | |
| 7 | $327,050 | Texas Air | Airlines | 97% | 30% | 70% | |
| 8 | $311,647 | CSX Corp | RR/Sea Trans | 95% | 55% | 45% | |
| 9 | $305,046 | Burlington Northern† | Railroads | 93% | 50% | 50% | |
| 10 | $301,840 | American Trucking Assns | Trucking | 100% | 56% | 44% | |
| 11 | $287,565 | General Motors† | Auto Manuf | 90% | 39% | 61% | |
| 12 | $287,207 | Boeing Co | Aircraft Mfr | 96% | 54% | 46% | |
| 13 | $262,000 | Ford Motor Co† | Auto Manuf | 88% | 56% | 44% | |
| 14 | $255,350 | Chrysler Corp † | Auto Manuf | 92% | 72% | 28% | |
| 15 | $206,200 | Norfolk Southern | Railroads | 99% | 61% | 39% | |
| 16 | $173,925 | United Airlines | Airlines | 95% | 54% | 46% | |
| 17 | $159,200 | Eaton Corp | Truck/Auto Parts | 100% | 8% | 92% | |
| 18 | $147,619 | American Airlines | Airlines | 96% | 76% | 24% | |
| 19 | $124,475 | Yellow Freight System | Trucking | 100% | 64% | 36% | |
| 20 | $123,619 | American President Lines | Sea Transport | 98% | 69% | 31% | |

† Includes only transportation industry operations

## *Where the money went . . .*

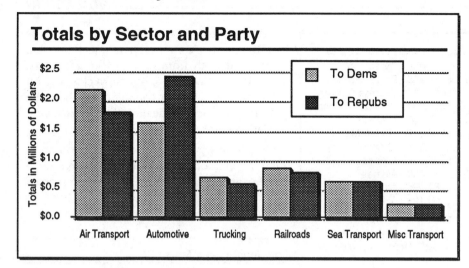

### Totals by Sector and Party

Totals in Millions of Dollars

Legend: To Dems | To Repubs

Air Transport | Automotive | Trucking | Railroads | Sea Transport | Misc Transport

Overall, the transportation industry split its campaign dollars almost straight down the middle between Democrats and Republicans. Even within the industry, the rates were fairly consistent, with the exception of the automotive industry — led by car dealers — who gave 60 percent of their dollars to Republicans.

| Category | Total | To Dems | Dem Pct | To Repubs | Repub Pct |
|---|---|---|---|---|---|
| Air Transport | $3,964,638 | $2,168,634 | 55% | $1,790,654 | 45% |
| Automotive | $3,976,677 | $1,595,523 | 40% | $2,381,154 | 60% |
| Trucking | $1,269,479 | $688,149 | 54% | $579,830 | 46% |
| Railroads | $1,604,480 | $834,064 | 52% | $770,416 | 48% |
| Sea Transport | $1,221,359 | $609,350 | 50% | $612,009 | 50% |
| Misc Transport | $468,371 | $226,415 | 48% | $241,956 | 52% |
| **TOTAL** | **$12,505,004** | **$6,122,135** | **49%** | **$6,376,019** | **51%** |

Several committees in Congress deal specifically with transportation matters, and their members were among the top recipients from the industry. In the upper chamber, the Senate Commerce and Transportation Committee is the focal point. Three of the top four recipients of transport funds — Jim Exon, Larry Pressler, and Jay Rockefeller — hold seats on that committee.

In the House, the Public Works and Transportation Committee is the industry's chief overseer. Eight of the top 10 recipients are members of that committee. The House Merchant Marine and Fisheries Committee handles sea transport matters and it accounted for two of the top 10 recipients — John Miller and Don Young. Greg Laughlin, who ranks eighth on the list, holds a seat on both committees.

### Top 10 Senate Recipients

| Rank | Name | Amount | Status | W/L |
|---|---|---|---|---|
| 1 | Jim Exon (D-Neb) | $261,087 | Incumb | W |
| 2 | Phil Gramm (R-Texas) | $241,118 | Incumb | W |
| 3 | Larry Pressler (R-SD) | $140,300 | Incumb | W |
| 4 | John D. Rockefeller IV (D-WVa) | $138,099 | Incumb | W |
| 5 | Hank Brown (R-Colo) | $127,710 | Open | W |
| 6 | Carl Levin (D-Mich) | $126,693 | Incumb | W |
| 7 | Bill Bradley (D-NJ) | $121,685 | Incumb | W |
| 8 | J. Bennett Johnston (D-La) | $120,150 | Incumb | W |
| 9 | John W. Warner (R-Va) | $114,300 | Incumb | W |
| 10 | Mark O. Hatfield (R-Ore) | $109,050 | Incumb | W |

### Top 10 House Recipients

| Rank | Name | Amount | Status | W/L |
|---|---|---|---|---|
| 1 | Norman Y. Mineta (D-Calif) | $118,820 | Incumb | W |
| 2 | Glenn M. Anderson (D-Calif) | $101,550 | Incumb | W |
| 3 | Bud Shuster (R-Pa) | $86,750 | Incumb | W |
| 4 | Robert A. Roe (D-NJ) | $86,150 | Incumb | W |
| 5 | Pete Geren (D-Texas) | $85,204 | Incumb | W |
| 6 | Richard A. Gephardt (D-Mo) | $79,750 | Incumb | W |
| 7 | James M. Inhofe (R-Okla) | $76,300 | Incumb | W |
| 8 | Greg Laughlin (D-Texas) | $76,230 | Incumb | W |
| 9 | John Miller (R-Wash) | $69,509 | Incumb | W |
| 10 | Don Young (R-Alaska) | $66,975 | Incumb | W |

# Closeup on Transportation

## Air Transport ...................................................................$4.0 million

### Top Contributors

| Rank | Contributor | Total | Category |
|------|-------------|-------|----------|
| 1 | Federal Express Corp | $765,225 | Express Delivery |
| 2 | United Parcel Service | $659,732 | Express Delivery |
| 3 | Aircraft Owners & Pilots Assn | $513,900 | General Aviation |
| 4 | Texas Air | $327,050 | Airlines |
| 5 | Boeing Co | $287,207 | Aircraft Mfr |
| 6 | United Airlines | $173,925 | Airlines |
| 7 | American Airlines | $147,619 | Airlines |
| 8 | Delta Airlines | $87,800 | Airlines |
| 9 | Northwest Airlines | $81,698 | Airlines |
| 10 | Eastern Airlines | $65,190 | Airlines |

Besides being among the most frequent fliers on the domestic airline system, as they wing back and forth from their far-flung districts, members of Congress also keep a close eye on the industry, with subcommittees in both the House and Senate dealing specifically with aviation issues.

The industry returns the attention, contributing a total of $4 million to congressional campaigns in the 1990 elections. Commercial airlines gave just over $1 million of that. Air freight and express delivery services gave $1.5 million — the bulk of which came from United Parcel Service and Federal Express.

Jim Exon, the top Senate recipient of air transport contributions, sits on the Senate Commerce Committee's Aviation subcommittee. All three of the top House recipients have committee assignments important to the industry. All three serve on the Public Works and Transportation Committee, and Norman Mineta and James Oberstar sit on the Aviation subcommittee. Robert Roe chairs the House Science, Space and Technology Committee, which oversees the aerospace industry.

### Top Senate Recipients

| Rank | Recipient | Total |
|------|-----------|-------|
| 1 | Jim Exon (D-Neb) | $68,300 |
| 2 | Phil Gramm (R-Texas) | $63,168 |
| 3 | John W. Warner (R-Va) | $46,500 |

### Top House Recipients

| Rank | Recipient | Total |
|------|-----------|-------|
| 1 | Robert A. Roe (D-NJ) | $55,800 |
| 2 | Norman Y. Mineta (D-Calif) | $52,000 |
| 3 | James L. Oberstar (D-Minn) | $45,400 |

## Automotive ...................................................................$4.0 million

### Top Contributors

| Rank | Contributor | Total | Category |
|------|-------------|-------|----------|
| 1 | National Auto Dealers Assn | $1,313,900 | Auto Dealers |
| 2 | Auto Dealers & Drivers for Free Trade | $644,450 | Japanese Auto Dlrs |
| 3 | General Motors | $287,565 | Auto Manufacturers |
| 4 | Ford Motor Co | $262,000 | Auto Manufacturers |
| 5 | Chrysler Corp | $238,850 | Auto Manufacturers |
| 6 | Eaton Corp | $159,200 | Truck/Auto Parts |
| 7 | Ryder System Inc | $29,400 | Car/Truck Rental |
| 8 | Alamo Rent-a-Car | $29,300 | Car/Truck Rental |
| 9 | Ingersoll-Rand | $19,198 | Truck/Auto Parts |
| 10 | Budd Co | $17,450 | Truck/Auto Parts |

The Big Three automakers take a back seat to the Big Two auto dealer PACs when dispensing dollars to members of Congress. The National Auto Dealers Association has members all across the nation, as does Auto Dealers and Drivers for Free Trade, a PAC that represents dealers of Japanese imports. Many foreign car dealers belong to both organizations.

In recent years, the increasing incursion of Japanese autos on American highways have made trade issues — and import quotas — paramount in the minds of GM, Ford, Chrysler, and their numerous suppliers and support industries. Emission controls, safety standards and requirements for fuel economy are other perennial issues that keep the path well-worn between Detroit and Washington.

### Top Senate Recipients

| Rank | Recipient | Total |
|------|-----------|-------|
| 1 | Phil Gramm (R-Texas) | $94,800 |
| 2 | Carl Levin (D-Mich) | $73,700 |
| 3 | Daniel R. Coats (R-Ind) | $50,500 |

### Top House Recipients

| Rank | Recipient | Total |
|------|-----------|-------|
| 1 | Richard A. Gephardt (D-Mo) | $33,500 |
| 2 | Ileana Ros-Lehtinen (R-Fla) | $28,500 |
| 3 | James M. Inhofe (R-Okla) | $25,850 |

## Trucking ...................................................................$1.3 million

### Top Contributors

| Rank | Contributor | Total |
|------|-------------|-------|
| 1 | American Trucking Assns | $301,840 |
| 2 | Yellow Freight System | $124,475 |
| 3 | Consolidated Freightways | $102,050 |
| 4 | Roadway Services | $79,850 |
| 5 | North American Van Lines | $62,650 |
| 6 | National Assn of Truck Stop Operators | $41,000 |
| 7 | Arkansas Best Corp | $31,900 |
| 8 | Paccar Inc | $24,200 |
| 9 | Central Freight Inc | $23,650 |
| 10 | Owner-Operator Independent Drivers Assn | $19,250 |

### Top Senate Recipients

| Rank | Recipient | Total |
|------|-----------|-------|
| 1 | Jim Exon (D-Neb) | $47,352 |
| 2 | Hank Brown (R-Colo) | $31,300 |
| 3 | Phil Gramm (R-Texas) | $22,600 |

### Top House Recipients

| Rank | Recipient | Total |
|------|-----------|-------|
| 1 | Norman Y. Mineta (D-Calif) | $30,970 |
| 2 | Glenn M. Anderson (D-Calif) | $26,000 |
| 3 | Bud Shuster (R-Pa) | $24,350 |

When trucking companies lobbied Congress in 1991 to allow giant triple-trailer rigs on American interstates, the truckers ran into an onslaught of negative publicity from their rivals in the railroad industry. It's an example of the inter-industry competition that's often played out in the halls of Congress. Both sides lobbied heavily, but in the end the railroads successfully derailed the proposal.

## Railroads ...................................................................$1.6 million

### Top Contributors

| Rank | Contributor | Total | Category |
|------|-------------|-------|----------|
| 1 | Union Pacific Corp | $552,164 | Railroads |
| 2 | Burlington Northern | $305,046 | Railroads |
| 3 | CSX Corp | $155,233 | Railroads |
| 4 | Norfolk Southern | $143,550 | Railroads |
| 5 | Kansas City Southern | $106,470 | Railroads |
| 6 | ITEL Corp | $82,916 | RR Svcs |
| 7 | Santa Fe Southern Pacific | $76,200 | Railroads |
| 8 | Consolidated Rail Corp | $54,775 | Railroads |
| 9 | Chicago & North Western Transport | $50,150 | Railroads |
| 10 | Southern Pacific Transportation Co | $48,600 | Railroads |

### Top Senate Recipients

| Rank | Recipient | Total |
|------|-----------|-------|
| 1 | Jim Exon (D-Neb) | $97,815 |
| 2 | Larry Pressler (R-SD) | $45,800 |
| 3 | Max Baucus (D-Mont) | $39,150 |

### Top House Recipients

| Rank | Recipient | Total |
|------|-----------|-------|
| 1 | Pete Geren (D-Texas) | $20,000 |
| 2 | Bud Shuster (R-Pa) | $17,900 |
| 3 | John D. Dingell (D-Mich) | $15,950 |

## Sea Transport ...................................................................$1.2 million

The American Merchant Marine fleet has seen more prosperous days, but shipping companies still managed to give $1.2 million to congressional candidates in the 1990 elections. Sea transport unions nearly doubled that amount. Both labor and management are struggling to keep the merchant marine afloat in the face of fierce foreign competition.

### Top Contributors

| Rank | Contributor | Total |
|------|-------------|-------|
| 1 | American President Lines | $123,619 |
| 2 | Sea-Land Corp | $116,014 |
| 3 | Alexander & Baldwin Inc | $66,850 |
| 4 | American Waterways Operators | $48,800 |
| 5 | American Pilots Assn | $44,750 |
| 6 | Southwest Marine | $43,325 |
| 7 | American Commercial Barge Line Co | $40,400 |
| 8 | Lykes Bros Steamship Co | $39,800 |
| 9 | Crowley Maritime | $34,999 |
| 10 | Outboard Marine Corp | $28,250 |

### Top Senate Recipients

| Rank | Recipient | Total |
|------|-----------|-------|
| 1 | J. Bennett Johnston (D-La) | $44,500 |
| 2 | Phil Gramm (R-Texas) | $25,850 |
| 3 | Mark O. Hatfield (R-Ore) | $24,500 |

### Top House Recipients

| Rank | Recipient | Total |
|------|-----------|-------|
| 1 | Helen Delich Bentley (R-Md) | $38,000 |
| 2 | Don Young (R-Alaska) | $36,575 |
| 3 | John Miller (R-Wash) | $27,523 |

# Labor

## *Where the money came from . . .*

The 17 million Americans who are members of organized labor unions represent a cross-section of the workforce that is as diverse as one can imagine. Union members drive trucks, deliver mail, build skyscrapers, teach children, print newspapers, and manufacture everything from bombers to safety pins. Even individual unions can be amazingly diverse. Teamsters, for example, can be found not only behind the wheels of tractor-trailers, but in canneries, dairies, building sites and even in police departments.

Despite their diversity, however, the political action committees operated by labor unions are rock solid supporters of the Democratic Party. Of the $36.6 million handed out by labor PACs in the 1990 election, 92 percent went to Democrats. No other segment of the PAC community, with the exception of party-specific ideological PACs and those run by members of Congress, is as partisan in its distribution of funds.

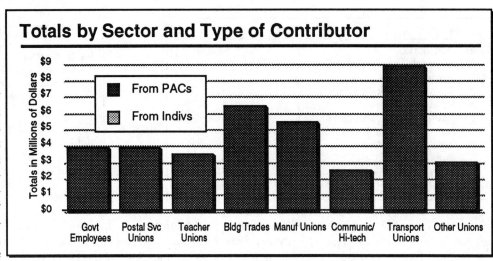

Totals by Sector and Type of Contributor

| Category | Total | From PACs | PAC Pct | From Indivs | Indiv Pct |
|---|---|---|---|---|---|
| Govt Employee Unions | $3,765,537 | $3,761,077 | 100% | $4,460 | 0% |
| Postal Service Unions | $3,785,819 | $3,779,769 | 100% | $6,050 | 0% |
| Teachers Unions | $3,384,691 | $3,376,631 | 100% | $8,060 | 0% |
| Construction Unions | $6,295,554 | $6,260,204 | 99% | $35,350 | 1% |
| Manufacturing Unions | $5,363,157 | $5,355,257 | 100% | $7,900 | 0% |
| Communications/Hi-tech | $2,377,905 | $2,373,905 | 100% | $4,000 | 0% |
| Transportation Unions | $8,708,214 | $8,702,814 | 100% | $5,400 | 0% |
| Other Unions | $2,921,021 | $2,899,921 | 99% | $21,100 | 1% |
| **TOTAL** | **$36,601,898** | **$36,509,578** | **100%** | **$92,320** | **0%** |

Nor does any segment give as high a proportion of its dollars through political action committees. In the study undertaken for this book, less than $100,000 was identified as individual contributions by labor union members. Partly this reflects the

## Top 20 Labor Contributors

| Rank | Total | Contributor | Category | PAC Pct | Dem Pct | Repub Pct | To Dems / To Repubs |
|---|---|---|---|---|---|---|---|
| 1 | $2,438,184 | Teamsters Union | Teamsters | 100% | 92% | 8% | |
| 2 | $2,334,715 | National Education Assn | Teachers | 100% | 93% | 7% | |
| 3 | $1,801,772 | United Auto Workers | Manuf Unions | 100% | 99% | 1% | |
| 4 | $1,755,478 | Letter Carriers Union | Postal Unions | 100% | 86% | 14% | |
| 5 | $1,549,720 | Amer Fedn of State/County/Munic Empl | Govt Unions | 100% | 97% | 2% | |
| 6 | $1,545,122 | Natl Assn of Retired Federal Employees | Govt Unions | 100% | 76% | 24% | |
| 7 | $1,526,534 | Carpenters Union | Constr Unions | 100% | 96% | 4% | |
| 8 | $1,487,495 | Machinists/Aerospace Workers Union | Manuf Unions | 100% | 98% | 1% | |
| 9 | $1,359,119 | Laborers Union | Constr Unions | 100% | 92% | 8% | |
| 10 | $1,257,920 | Intl Brotherhood of Electrical Workers | Electrical | 100% | 97% | 2% | |
| 11 | $1,167,797 | Air Line Pilots Assn | Transpt Unions | 100% | 81% | 19% | |
| 12 | $1,075,142 | AFL-CIO | Manuf Unions | 100% | 97% | 2% | |
| 13 | $1,066,125 | Marine Engineers Union | Transpt Unions | 100% | 62% | 38% | |
| 14 | $1,043,616 | American Federation of Teachers | Teachers | 100% | 97% | 3% | |
| 15 | $976,403 | American Postal Workers Union | Postal Unions | 100% | 92% | 8% | |
| 16 | $955,796 | Seafarers International Union | Transpt Unions | 100% | 85% | 15% | |
| 17 | $945,281 | Food & Commercial Workers Union | Food Svc Unions | 100% | 98% | 2% | |
| 18 | $897,675 | United Steelworkers | Manuf Unions | 100% | 100% | 0% | |
| 19 | $881,809 | Operating Engineers Union | Constr Unions | 99% | 91% | 8% | |
| 20 | $807,737 | Communications Workers of America | Communic Unions | 100% | 99% | 0% | |

## Where the money went . . .

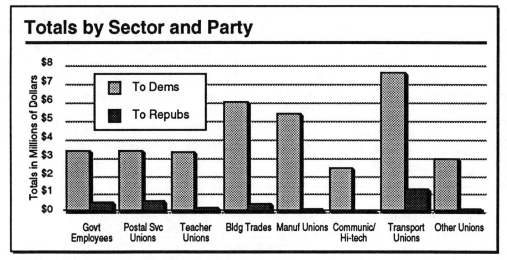

### Totals by Sector and Party

Totals in Millions of Dollars

- To Dems
- To Repubs

$8
$7
$6
$5
$4
$3
$2
$1
$0

Govt Employees | Postal Svc Unions | Teacher Unions | Bldg Trades | Manuf Unions | Communic/Hi-tech | Transport Unions | Other Unions

| Category | Total | To Dems | Dem Pct | To Repubs | Repub Pct |
|---|---|---|---|---|---|
| Govt Employee Unions | $3,765,537 | $3,284,385 | 87% | $474,552 | 13% |
| Postal Service Unions | $3,785,819 | $3,274,119 | 86% | $511,700 | 14% |
| Teachers Unions | $3,384,691 | $3,202,106 | 95% | $180,585 | 5% |
| Construction Unions | $6,295,554 | $5,920,053 | 94% | $352,251 | 6% |
| Manufacturing Unions | $5,363,157 | $5,270,812 | 98% | $77,835 | 1% |
| Communications/Hi-tech | $2,377,905 | $2,328,598 | 98% | $40,350 | 2% |
| Transportation Unions | $8,708,214 | $7,527,942 | 86% | $1,175,272 | 13% |
| Other Unions | $2,921,021 | $2,839,390 | 97% | $68,122 | 2% |
| TOTAL | $36,601,898 | $33,647,405 | 92% | $2,880,667 | 8% |

fact that it is virtually impossible to tell who is or is not a union member by looking at their occupation (unless they work for the union itself). But it is also likely, given the economic makeup of the individuals who do make large individual contributions, that few union members have the resources to write $500 or $1,000 checks to politicians.

Indeed, pooling small individual donations into large contributions from political action committees was an invention of labor unions. Only later did the idea catch on in the business world.

Within the labor community, there was a general consistency in spending patterns, though transport unions were the most likely to cross the aisle and give to Republicans who sit on committees important to the industry. That was particularly true of merchant marine unions.

In picking their candidates, labor PACs tend to concentrate their dollars on races where strong pro-union incumbents are facing a serious challenge. Unions are also far more likely than business PACs to underwrite campaigns of promising challengers. Still, nearly three of every four labor dollars went to incumbents in the 1990 elections. Seventeen percent went to challengers and nine percent went to candidates in open-seat races.

Though they tend to give as a bloc, labor unions can be classified into several distinct classes. Public sector unions — representing local, state and federal government workers, as well as postal employees and teachers — are a growing segment of the labor community. Transportation unions are another major sector. Construction and manufacturing unions are the mainstream of the popular image of union members, though their numbers, in the face of growing anti-union sentiment among businesses and successive Republican administrations, are dwindling.

### Top 10 Senate Recipients

| Rank | Name | Amount | Status | W/L |
|---|---|---|---|---|
| 1 | Paul Simon (D-Ill) | $421,742 | Incumb | W |
| 2 | Carl Levin (D-Mich) | $401,680 | Incumb | W |
| 3 | Tom Harkin (D-Iowa) | $361,730 | Incumb | W |
| 4 | Daniel K. Akaka (D-Hawaii) | $356,450 | Incumb | W |
| 5 | Baron Hill (D-Ind) | $293,050 | Chall | L |
| 6 | Jim Exon (D-Neb) | $286,100 | Incumb | W |
| 7 | Claiborne Pell (D-RI) | $285,050 | Incumb | W |
| 8 | Harvey Sloane (D-Ky) | $284,625 | Chall | L |
| 9 | Joseph R. Biden Jr. (D-Del) | $272,149 | Incumb | W |
| 10 | Harvey Gantt (D-NC) | $271,512 | Chall | L |

### Top 10 House Recipients

| Rank | Name | Amount | Status | W/L |
|---|---|---|---|---|
| 1 | Jill L. Long (D-Ind) | $360,604 | Incumb | W |
| 2 | Roy Dyson (D-Md) | $312,398 | Incumb | L |
| 3 | Jolene Unsoeld (D-Wash) | $283,626 | Incumb | W |
| 4 | Glen Browder (D-Ala) | $273,641 | Incumb | W |
| 5 | David E. Bonior (D-Mich) | $257,630 | Incumb | W |
| 6 | Richard A. Gephardt (D-Mo) | $228,775 | Incumb | W |
| 7 | Wayne Owens (D-Utah) | $227,850 | Incumb | W |
| 8 | George J. Hochbrueckner (D-NY) | $223,950 | Incumb | W |
| 9 | Peter Hoagland (D-Neb) | $223,844 | Incumb | W |
| 10 | Howard Wolpe (D-Mich) | $212,775 | Incumb | W |

# Closeup on Labor

## Public Sector Unions ..................................................................................$10.9 million

| Top Contributors | | | |
|---|---|---|---|
| Rank | Contributor | Total | Category |
| 1 | National Education Assn ...................................... | $2,334,715 | Teachers |
| 2 | Letter Carriers Union .............................................. | $1,755,478 | Postal Unions |
| 3 | Amer Fedn of State/County/Munic Employees ... | $1,549,720 | Local Govt Unions |
| 4 | National Assn of Retired Federal Employees ..... | $1,545,122 | Fedl Worker Unions |
| 5 | American Federation of Teachers ........................ | $1,043,616 | Teachers |
| 6 | American Postal Workers Union .......................... | $976,403 | Postal Unions |
| 7 | National Rural Letter Carriers Assn ..................... | $430,875 | Postal Unions |
| 8 | National Assn of Postmasters ............................. | $319,551 | Postal Unions |
| 9 | International Assn of Firefighters .......................... | $208,630 | Public Safety |
| 10 | National Treasury Employees Union ..................... | $192,531 | Fedl Worker Unions |

One of the surprising features of public sector unions — particularly those representing postal workers — is that there are so many of them. There is only one U.S. Postal Service, but its employees are represented by no fewer than 10 different PACs that contributed to candidates in the 1990 elections. Teachers have two main unions, each of which support PACs, the National Education Association and the American Federa-

tion of Teachers. Of the many PACs representing federal workers, the largest is the National Association of Retired Federal Employees. Among state and local government workers, the biggest union and the biggest PAC is AFSCME: the American Federation of State, County and Municipal Employees.

On Capitol Hill, the public sector unions pay particular attention to deliberations of the House Post Office and Civil Service Committee. Wage rates and work rules decided there directly affect millions of federal workers and committee members from both parties tend to draw considerable union support.

| Top Senate Recipients | | |
|---|---|---|
| Rank | Recipient | Total |
| 1 | Paul Simon (D-Ill) .......................... | $100,250 |
| 2 | Daniel K. Akaka (D-Hawaii) .............. | $94,150 |
| 3 | Carl Levin (D-Mich) .......................... | $93,990 |

| Top House Recipients | | |
|---|---|---|
| Rank | Recipient | Total |
| 1 | Jill L. Long (D-Ind) ........................ | $100,704 |
| 2 | William D. Ford (D-Mich) ................. | $79,698 |
| 3 | Jolene Unsoeld (D-Wash) ............... | $73,950 |

## Transportation Unions ..........................................................................$8.7 million

| Top Contributors | | | |
|---|---|---|---|
| Rank | Contributor | Total | Category |
| 1 | Teamsters Union ......................................... | $2,438,184 | Teamsters |
| 2 | Air Line Pilots Assn ..................................... | $1,167,797 | Air Transport Unions |
| 3 | Marine Engineers Union .............................. | $1,066,125 | Sea Transport Unions |
| 4 | Seafarers International Union ........................ | $955,796 | Sea Transport Unions |
| 5 | United Transportation Union .......................... | $710,350 | Railroad Unions |
| 6 | Amalgamated Transit Union ......................... | $512,630 | Misc Transport Union |
| 7 | Transportation Communication Intl Union ...... | $377,401 | Misc Transport Union |
| 8 | Transport Workers Union ............................... | $335,615 | Misc Transport Union |
| 9 | Brotherhood of Locomotive Engineers ........... | $241,050 | Railroad Unions |
| 10 | Maintenance of Way Employees .................... | $177,141 | Railroad Unions |

The Teamsters Union is the biggest of the transportation unions by a large margin. Its political action committee ranks among the nation's very biggest PACs every election cycle. But many other transport unions also are major contributors.

This is the one sector of the labor community that is most likely to support Republicans as well as Democrats. Two groups in particular — air transport unions and merchant marine unions — support members of Congress from both parties among those that sit on committees important to their interests. Most "bipartisan" of all were the sea transport unions, which gave 26 percent of their funds to Republicans.

| Top Senate Recipients | | |
|---|---|---|
| Rank | Recipient | Total |
| 1 | Jim Exon (D-Neb) .......................... | $104,300 |
| 2 | Carl Levin (D-Mich) ....................... | $100,650 |
| 3 | Daniel K. Akaka (D-Hawaii) ............. | $91,500 |

| Top House Recipients | | |
|---|---|---|
| Rank | Recipient | Total |
| 1 | Roy Dyson (D-Md) .......................... | $72,400 |
| 2 | Jolene Unsoeld (D-Wash) ............... | $67,750 |
| 3 | Richard A. Gephardt (D-Mo) ........... | $59,500 |

## Building Trades, Manufacturing & Miscellaneous Unions ...............$17.0 million

### Top Contributors

| Rank | Contributor | Total | Category |
|------|-------------|-------|----------|
| 1 | United Auto Workers | $1,801,772 | Manufacturing Unions |
| 2 | Carpenters Union | $1,526,534 | Constr Unions |
| 3 | Machinists/Aerospace Workers Union | $1,487,495 | Manufacturing Unions |
| 4 | Laborers Union | $1,359,119 | Constr Unions |
| 5 | Intl Brotherhood of Electrical Workers | $1,257,920 | IBEW |
| 6 | AFL-CIO | $1,075,142 | Manufacturing Unions |
| 7 | Food & Commercial Workers Union | $945,281 | Food Svc Unions |
| 8 | United Steelworkers | $897,675 | Manufacturing Unions |
| 9 | Operating Engineers Union | $881,809 | Constr Unions |
| 10 | Communications Workers of America | $807,737 | Communication Unions |

In the minds of most Americans, these are the meat and potatoes unions, the ones that still provide the kind of jobs people associate with unions: carpenters, steelworkers, auto assembly line operators. Ironically, it's the one sector of the American labor movement that seems most in peril, given the decline of our smokestack industries and the gradual migration by corporations away from the rustbelt and toward the non-union sunbelt.

Topping the list of PAC contributors is one of the most imperiled unions of all, the United Auto Workers, which is facing thousands of layoffs as the Big Three automakers face increasing competition from Japanese imports. Overall, this group of unions — particularly the building trades and manufacturing unions — is the biggest sector within the union community. In the 1990 elections, their PACs delivered nearly $17 million in contributions to congressional candidates. It was also the most dependably partisan. Nearly 97 percent of their dollars went to Democrats.

### Top Senate Recipients

| Rank | Recipient | Total |
|------|-----------|-------|
| 1 | Paul Simon (D-Ill) | $231,250 |
| 2 | Carl Levin (D-Mich) | $207,040 |
| 3 | Tom Harkin (D-Iowa) | $191,350 |

### Top House Recipients

| Rank | Recipient | Total |
|------|-----------|-------|
| 1 | Jill L. Long (D-Ind) | $211,700 |
| 2 | Roy Dyson (D-Md) | $176,498 |
| 3 | Glen Browder (D-Ala) | $160,175 |

# Ideological/Single-Issue

## Where the money came from . . .

A world apart from the pragmatic and largely bipartisan business PACs, and the Democratically-aligned PACs that represent organized labor, are the third family of political action committees — those organized not around a business or a union, but around an idea, cause, or political party. Ideological and single-issue PACs have become significant players on the political landscape. They gave more than $14 million to congressional candidates in the 1990 election.

Within this diverse community are political activists who represent every shade of political viewpoint, and many of them spend much of their money and time seeking to counteract the efforts of their adversaries. For issues which stir deep divisions within the American public — such as abortion, gun control, or defense spending — PACs have coalesced around both sides.

In addition to the PACs, the study that led to this book examined giving by individuals aligned

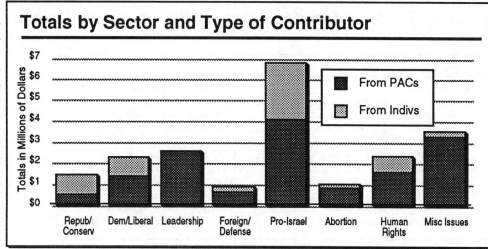

### Totals by Sector and Type of Contributor

| Category | Total | From PACs | PAC Pct | From Indivs | Indiv Pct |
|----------|-------|-----------|---------|-------------|-----------|
| Republican/Conservative | $1,351,283 | $411,986 | 30% | $939,297 | 70% |
| Democratic/Liberal | $2,202,277 | $1,330,286 | 60% | $871,991 | 40% |
| Leadership PACs | $2,482,913 | $2,476,163 | 100% | $6,750 | 0% |
| Foreign & Defense Policy | $816,719 | $572,251 | 70% | $244,468 | 30% |
| Pro-Israel | $6,747,554 | $4,040,098 | 60% | $2,707,456 | 40% |
| Pro-Life | $198,260 | $181,685 | 92% | $16,575 | 8% |
| Pro-Choice | $701,858 | $570,258 | 81% | $131,600 | 19% |
| Human Rights | $2,259,420 | $1,524,764 | 67% | $734,656 | 33% |
| Misc Issues | $3,430,993 | $3,221,688 | 94% | $209,305 | 6% |
| **TOTAL** | **$20,191,277** | **$14,329,179** | **71%** | **$5,862,098** | **29%** |

with PACs who make individual contributions of their own directly to candidates. To be classified as an "ideological" giver, a contributor had to give $200 or more both to an ideological or single-issue PAC and $200 or more to a candidate who received funds from that PAC. Using that conservative criteria, the authors were able to identify another $5.9 million of ideological contributions.

## Top 20 Ideological/Single-Issue Contributors

| Rank | Total | Contributor | Category | PAC Pct | Dem Pct | Repub Pct | To Dems / To Repubs |
|------|-------|-------------|----------|---------|---------|-----------|---------------------|
| 1 | $953,500 | National PAC | Pro-Israel | 100% | 61% | 39% | |
| 2 | $914,052 | National Cmte to Preserve Social Security | Elderly | 100% | 91% | 9% | |
| 3 | $749,493 | National Rifle Assn | Pro-Guns | 100% | 39% | 61% | |
| 4 | $598,575 | National Cmte for an Effective Congress | Dem/Liberal | 100% | 99% | 0% | |
| 5 | $479,371 | Human Rights Campaign Fund | Gay/Lesbian | 99% | 84% | 16% | |
| 6 | $410,210 | Sierra Club | Environment | 100% | 91% | 9% | |
| 7 | $385,495 | National Abortion Rights Action League | Pro-Choice | 100% | 89% | 11% | |
| 8 | $334,350 | KidsPAC | Health/Welfare | 100% | 88% | 12% | |
| 9 | $305,497 | Campaign America (Bob Dole) | Repub Leaders | 99% | 0% | 100% | |
| 10 | $262,375 | Washington PAC | Pro-Israel | 100% | 75% | 25% | |
| 11 | $252,000 | Effective Govt Cmte (Dick Gephardt) | Dem Leaders | 100% | 100% | 0% | |
| 12 | $239,575 | Public Service Research Council | Anti-Union | 100% | 1% | 99% | |
| 13 | $231,254 | Hudson Valley PAC | Pro-Israel | 100% | 57% | 43% | |
| 14 | $206,000 | Joint Action Cmte for Political Affairs | Pro-Israel | 100% | 94% | 6% | |
| 15 | $204,719 | House Leadership Fund (Tom Foley) | Dem Leaders | 100% | 99% | 1% | |
| 16 | $197,904 | Right to Work PAC | Anti-Union | 100% | 3% | 97% | |
| 17 | $191,000 | Citizens Organized PAC | Pro-Israel | 100% | 76% | 24% | |
| 18 | $180,490 | Independent Action | Dem/Liberal | 100% | 99% | 0% | |
| 19 | $173,263 | Voters for Choice/Friends of Family Plan | Pro-Choice | 100% | 92% | 8% | |
| 20 | $171,850 | Council for a Livable World | Pro-Peace | 88% | 96% | 4% | |

# *Where the money went . . .*

## Totals by Sector and Party

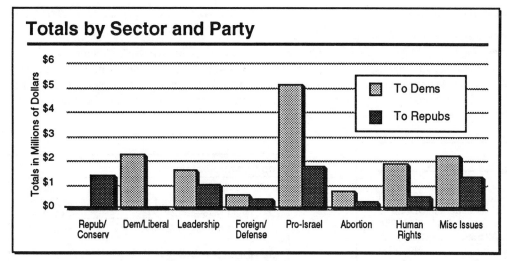

Totals in Millions of Dollars

$6
$5
$4
$3
$2
$1
$0

Legend: ▨ To Dems  ■ To Repubs

Repub/Conserv, Dem/Liberal, Leadership, Foreign/Defense, Pro-Israel, Abortion, Human Rights, Misc Issues

| Category | Total | To Dems | Dem Pct | To Repubs | Repub Pct |
|----------|-------|---------|---------|-----------|-----------|
| Republican/Conservative | $1,351,283 | $15,347 | 1% | $1,322,286 | 98% |
| Democratic/Liberal | $2,202,277 | $2,180,027 | 99% | $14,250 | 1% |
| Leadership PACs | $2,482,913 | $1,553,924 | 63% | $923,489 | 37% |
| Foreign & Defense Policy | $816,719 | $489,081 | 60% | $317,488 | 39% |
| Pro-Israel | $6,747,554 | $5,042,408 | 75% | $1,705,146 | 25% |
| Pro-Life | $198,260 | $43,854 | 22% | $154,406 | 78% |
| Pro-Choice | $701,858 | $629,433 | 90% | $71,675 | 10% |
| Human Rights | $2,259,420 | $1,821,577 | 81% | $437,043 | 19% |
| Misc Issues | $3,430,993 | $2,148,927 | 63% | $1,278,990 | 37% |
| **TOTAL** | **$20,191,277** | **$13,924,578** | **69%** | **$6,224,773** | **31%** |

The single biggest interest group within this community — in terms of dollars delivered to candidates — were those interested in strong U.S. ties with the state of Israel. Pro-Israel PACs and individuals gave a combined $6.7 million to candidates in the 1990 elections, twice as much as any other group of interests. "Leadership PACs" operated by members of Congress and other noted political figures gave nearly $2.5 million — a respectable amount, but only half what leadership PACs gave in the 1988 elections.

Other major contribution groups included general conservative and liberal PACs, PACs supporting environmental issues and animal rights, groups opposing organized labor, defending the rights of gays and lesbians, promoting women's issues, supporting or attacking the right to abortion, and groups involved in every issue from historical preservation to gun control to toxic wastes. There are also a variety of ethnic and minority PACs whose interests revolve around a specific segment of the American population — as well as the interests of the citizens in their homelands. Armenian-Americans, for example, support no fewer than five individual PACs. Others promote the interests of Albanian-, Greek-, Lithuanian-, Korean-, Turkish-, Italian- and African-Americans; and there are PACs representing both American Indians and Indians from India.

Though they may represent every issue under the sun (and a few, like the SpacePAC, *beyond* the sun) one thing most single-issue and ideological PACs do have in common is a tendency to back candidates from one political party or the other. They also have a higher-than-normal tendency to give money to challengers — something the more pragmatic business PACs do only a tiny proportion of the time.

## Top 10 Senate Recipients

| Rank | Name | Amount | Status | W/L |
|------|------|--------|--------|-----|
| 1 | Carl Levin (D-Mich) | $864,090 | Incumb | W |
| 2 | Paul Simon (D-Ill) | $815,613 | Incumb | W |
| 3 | Tom Harkin (D-Iowa) | $700,113 | Incumb | W |
| 4 | Claiborne Pell (D-RI) | $395,044 | Incumb | W |
| 5 | Jesse Helms (R-NC) | $343,085 | Incumb | W |
| 6 | Mitch McConnell (R-Ky) | $316,700 | Incumb | W |
| 7 | Bill Bradley (D-NJ) | $279,324 | Incumb | W |
| 8 | John Kerry (D-Mass) | $278,129 | Incumb | W |
| 9 | Max Baucus (D-Mont) | $236,095 | Incumb | W |
| 10 | Daniel K. Akaka (D-Hawaii) | $233,702 | Incumb | W |

## Top 10 House Recipients

| Rank | Name | Amount | Status | W/L |
|------|------|--------|--------|-----|
| 1 | Jolene Unsoeld (D-Wash) | $284,070 | Incumb | W |
| 2 | Rosa DeLauro (D-Conn) | $186,441 | Open | W |
| 3 | Jill L. Long (D-Ind) | $184,496 | Incumb | W |
| 4 | Sidney R. Yates (D-Ill) | $165,520 | Incumb | W |
| 5 | Wayne Owens (D-Utah) | $140,213 | Incumb | W |
| 6 | Nita M. Lowey (D-NY) | $139,515 | Incumb | W |
| 7 | Mike Kopetski (D-Ore) | $137,858 | Chall | W |
| 8 | Howard Wolpe (D-Mich) | $136,640 | Incumb | W |
| 9 | George E. Brown Jr. (D-Calif) | $131,507 | Incumb | W |
| 10 | Ileana Ros-Lehtinen (R-Fla) | $125,604 | Incumb | W |

# Closeup on Ideology/Single-Issue

## Pro-Israel......................................................................................$6.7 million

The biggest single source of contributions among ideological and single-issue groups came from PACs that support strong US relations with Israel. In all, some 52 pro-Israel PACs contributed to congressional campaigns in the 1990 elections, as did many more individuals who gave to the PACs and also gave to favored candidates in tight races. The money went mainly, but not exclusively, to Democrats. Instead of spreading the wealth thinly among dozens of candidates, the pro-Israel groups tend to concentrate their contributions in a handful of key races — generally in the Senate. Carl Levin of Michigan led all others in 1990 with over $570,000 in pro-Israel constributions.

### Top Contributors

| Rank | Contributor | Total |
|---|---|---|
| 1 | National PAC | $953,500 |
| 2 | Washington PAC | $262,375 |
| 3 | Hudson Valley PAC | $231,254 |
| 4 | Joint Action Cmte for Political Affairs | $206,000 |
| 5 | Citizens Organized PAC | $191,000 |
| 6 | Desert Caucus | $166,379 |
| 7 | Delaware Valley PAC | $157,250 |
| 8 | Women's Alliance for Israel | $151,500 |
| 9 | Americans for Good Government | $147,250 |
| 10 | Florida Congressional Committee | $130,000 |

### Top Senate Recipients

| Rank | Recipient | Total |
|---|---|---|
| 1 | Carl Levin (D-Mich) | $570,648 |
| 2 | Paul Simon (D-Ill) | $453,567 |
| 3 | Tom Harkin (D-Iowa) | $344,300 |

### Top House Recipients

| Rank | Recipient | Total |
|---|---|---|
| 1 | Mel Levine (D-Calif) | $86,529 |
| 2 | Sidney R. Yates (D-Ill) | $75,750 |
| 3 | David R. Obey (D-Wis) | $58,699 |

## Leadership PACs.............................................................................$2.5 million

So-called "Leadership PACs" are PACs run by members of Congress and other prominent political figures. Originally designed to curry favor among members in the voting for leadership positions, they have become a major fundraising device for House and Senate incumbents. Most of the money is directed at close races, either for new open seats or for an incumbent in a particularly difficult re-election race. Though leadership PACs did contribute nearly $2.5 million in the '90 elections, that was a steep decline from 1988, when they gave $4.9 million.

### Top Contributors

| Rank | Contributor | Total | Category |
|---|---|---|---|
| 1 | Campaign America (Bob Dole) | $305,497 | Repub Leaders |
| 2 | Effective Government Committee (Dick Gephardt) | $252,000 | Dem Leaders |
| 3 | House Leadership Fund (Tom Foley) | $204,719 | Dem Leaders |
| 4 | Republican Leader's Fund (Bob Michel) | $163,500 | Repub Leaders |
| 5 | Cmte for Democratic Opportunity (William Gray) | $155,785 | Dem Leaders |
| 6 | America's Leaders' Fund (Dan Rostenkowski) | $121,350 | Dem Leaders |
| 7 | Fund for a Democratic Majority (Ted Kennedy) | $117,000 | Dem Leaders |
| 8 | 24th Congr Dist of Calif PAC (Henry Waxman) | $110,000 | Dem Leaders |
| 9 | Cmte for a Democratic Consensus (Alan Cranston) | $99,500 | Dem Leaders |
| 10 | Valley Education Fund (Tony Coelho) | $70,740 | Dem Leaders |

### Top Senate Recipients

| Rank | Recipient | Total |
|---|---|---|
| 1 | Tom Harkin (D-Iowa) | $53,000 |
| 2 | Jim Exon (D-Neb) | $41,000 |
| 3 | Harvey Gantt (D-NC) | $39,498 |

### Top House Recipients

| Rank | Recipient | Total |
|---|---|---|
| 1 | George E. Brown Jr. (D-Calif) | $39,370 |
| 2 | Jill L. Long (D-Ind) | $36,525 |
| 3 | Howard Wolpe (D-Mich) | $29,750 |

# 1990 Leadership PAC Roster

Since members of Congress often raise funds for their Leadership PACs at the same time they're collecting money for their reelection campaigns, it may be instructive to know which members have PACs and how much they give out. The list below shows all Leadership PACs by members of Congress and other prominent party officials that made contributions to candidates in the 1990 elections.

## Members of Congress

| Sponsor | PAC Name | 1990 Contributions |
|---|---|---|
| Rep Dick Armey (R-Tex) | Policy Innovation PAC | $24,600 |
| Sen Kit Bond (R-Mo) | Heartland PAC of Missouri | $11,000 |
| Rep David Bonior (D-Mich) | Pax Americas | $24,000 |
| Rep George Brown (D-Calif) | USA Committee | $9,000 |
| Sen Robert Byrd (D-WVa) | Cmte for America's Future | $65,000 |
| Rep William Clay (D-Mo) | Congressional Black Caucus | $1,000 |
| Sen Thad Cochran (R-Miss) | Senate Victory Fund | $62,500 |
| Sen Alan Cranston (D-Calif) | Cmte for a Democratic Consensus | $103,268 |
| Sen John Danforth (R-Mo) | Fund for the Future Committee | $1,196 |
| Sen Dennis DeConcini (D-Ariz) | Arizona Leadership for America | $2,250 |
| Sen Bob Dole (R-Kans) | Campaign America | $302,497 |
| Rep Bob Dornan (R-Calif) | American Space Frontier Cmte | $300 |
| Rep Ronnie Flippo (D-Ala) | Responsible Government Fund | $1,000 |
| Rep Thomas Foley (D-Wash) | House Leadership Fund | $204,719 |
| Rep Richard Gephardt (D-Mo) | Effective Government Committee | $252,000 |
| Rep Newt Gingrich (R-Ga) | Conservative Opportunities Society | $1,175 |
| Rep William Gray III (D-Pa) | Cmte for Democratic Opportunity | $155,785 |
| Rep Bill Green (R-NY) | Modern PAC | $12,300 |
| Sen Orrin Hatch (R-Utah) | Capitol Committee | $9,000 |
| Sen Jesse Helms (R-NC) | National Congressional Club | $12,166 |
| Sen Ernest Hollings (D-SC) | Citizens for a Competitive America | $6,500 |
| Sen Daniel Inouye (D-Hawaii) | Senate Majority Fund | $45,000 |
| Sen J Bennett Johnston (D-La) | Pelican PAC | $61,886 |
| Sen Bob Kasten (R-Wisc) | Catch the Spirit PAC | $46,000 |
| Sen Edward Kennedy (D-Mass) | Fund for a Democratic Majority | $117,000 |
| Sen Frank Lautenberg (D-NJ) | Campaign for America | $4,500 |
| Sen Trent Lott (R-Miss) | New Republican Victory Fund | $5,000 |
| Sen Richard Lugar (R-Ind) | Republican Majority Fund | $59,150 |
| Rep Edward Madigan (R-Ill) | 15th District Committee | $3,000 |
| Sen Mitch McConnell (R-Ky) | Bluegrass Committee | $23,000 |
| Sen Howard Metzenbaum (D-Ohio) | Committee for Democratic Action | $13,500 |
| Rep Bob Michel (R-Ill) | Republican Leader's Fund | $163,500 |
| Rep Joe Moakley (D-Mass) | Democratic Congressional Fund | $34,500 |
| Rep David Obey (D-Wis) | Cmte for a Progressive Congress | $2,500 |
| Rep Charles Rangel (D-NY) | Cmte for the 100th Congress | $9,000 |
| Rep Dan Rostenkowski (D-Ill) | America's Leaders' Fund | $121,350 |
| Rep Neal Smith (D-Iowa) | Fund for Effective Leadership | $21,000 |
| Rep Charles Stenholm (D-Tex) | Conservative Democratic PAC | $20,000 |
| Sen Ted Stevens (R-Alaska) | Fund for a Republican Majority | $11,250 |
| Sen Steve Symms (R-Idaho) | Conservative Victory Fund | $48,493 |
| Rep Maxine Waters (D-Calif) | People Helping People | $7,000 |
| Rep Henry Waxman (D-Calif) | 24th Congressional Dist of Calif PAC | $110,000 |
| Rep Vin Weber (R-Minn) | New Majority Leadership PAC | $29,835 |

## Other Notable Officials

| Sponsor | PAC Name | 1990 Contributions |
|---|---|---|
| Art Agnos (SF Mayor) | San Franciscans Getting Things Done | $4,000 |
| Gov Richard Celeste (D-Ohio) | Participation 2000 | $14,187 |
| Former Rep Tony Coelho (D-Calif) | Valley Education Fund | $70,740 |
| Gov Mario Cuomo (D-NY) | Empire Leadership Fund | $1,500 |
| Geraldine Ferraro | Americans Concerned for Tomorrow | $1,852 |
| Jesse Jackson | Keep Hope Alive PAC | $7,025 |
| Former Sen Lee Metcalf (D-Mont) | DC Montana Committee | $1,500 |
| Former Rep Tip O'Neill (D-Mass) | Democratic Candidate Fund | $9,430 |
| Former Pres Ronald Reagan | Citizens for the Republic | $53,500 |
| Pat Robertson | Americans for the Republic | $4,241 |
| Gov Pete Wilson (R-Calif) | California for America | $1,000 |
| Former Rep Jim Wright (D-Tex) | Majority Congress Committee | $25,000 |

# A Potpourri of Issue PACs

Like metal filings drawn to a magnet, political action committees have coalesced around virtually every issue of interest — or dispute — among Americans. The amounts spent by one group versus another, and the proportions within each camp that go to Democrats versus Republicans, offer a fascinating glimpse at the political strategies of these specialized interest groups. The following mini-profiles present the highlights, combining dollars that came both from selected PACs and from individuals supporting the PACs' policies through direct contributions to candidates.

## Abortion

A total of 28 Pro-Life PACs and seven Pro-Choice PACs contributed to federal candidates in the 1990 elections. Most of the Pro-Life PACs were organized under the national Right to Life organization, and that group's national PAC gave the biggest share of the group's money.

As can be seen in the chart at right, the Pro-Choice forces were decidedly Democratic in their contributions. Pro-Life groups mainly supported Republicans.

| Leading Abortion Issue Groups | 1989-90 Total |
| --- | --- |
| **Pro-Life** | |
| Right to Life | $146,981 |
| **Pro-Choice** | |
| National Abortion Rights Action League | $385,495 |
| Voters for Choice/Friends of Family Planning | $173,263 |

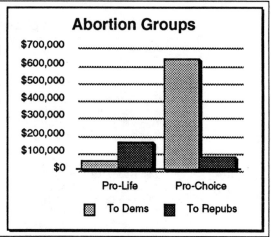

## Gun Control vs. Gun Ownership

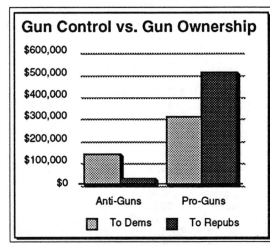

The National Rifle Association had the strongest presence by far among PACs dealing with the issue of gun control vs. gun owners' rights. Long an influential lobby on Capitol Hill, the NRA Political Victory Fund distributed nearly three-quarters of a million dollars to 221 candidates in 1989-90. PAC contributors giving directly to candidates added another $50,000 to that total. On the opposite side of the issue, the Handgun Control PAC and its supporters gave about $150,000 to 157 candidates — predominantly Democrats. But the gun control group could muster only about one fifth the total spent by the pro-gun lobby.

| Leading Pro-Gun and Anti-Gun Groups | 1989-90 Total |
| --- | --- |
| **Pro-Guns** | |
| National Rifle Assn | $749,493 |
| **Anti-Guns** | |
| Handgun Control Inc | $149,968 |

## The Left and the Right

A total of 88 ideological PACs, on both the left and right of the political spectrum, contributed to federal candidates in the 1990 elections. Most — particularly among conservative groups — were quite small, but their influence can be magnified many times over during presidential election years when they also weigh in with independent expenditures.

| Leading Liberal and Conservative PACs | 1989-90 Total |
| --- | --- |
| **Democratic/Liberal PACs** | |
| National Cmte for an Effective Congress | $598,575 |
| Independent Action | $180,490 |
| Democrats for the 80's | $117,750 |
| Hollywood Women's Political Cmte | $107,500 |
| | |
| **Conservative/Republican PACs** | |
| Conservative Victory Committee | $98,262 |
| Eagle Forum | $49,813 |

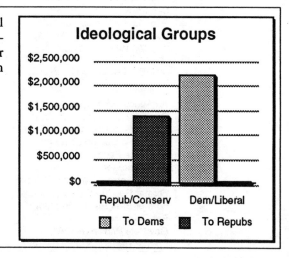

# Human Rights

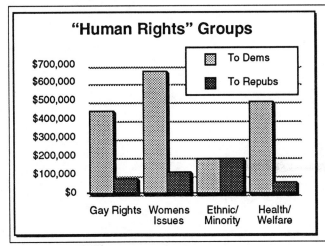

## "Human Rights" Groups

Legend: To Dems, To Repubs

Categories: Gay Rights, Womens Issues, Ethnic/Minority, Health/Welfare

Groups seeking to improve the lot of the elderly, women, children, gays and ethnic minorities were all active with political contributions in the 1990 elections. All together they gave more than $2.2 million to congressional candidates. Democrats received 81 percent of the total dollars.

| Leading Human Rights Groups | 1989-90 Total |
| --- | --- |
| **Gay/Lesbian Rights** | |
| Human Rights Campaign Fund | $479,371 |
| **Women's Issues** | |
| Emily's List | $140,313 |
| National Organization for Women | $137,920 |
| Women's Campaign Fund | $122,355 |
| **Ethnic/Minority** | $374,889 |
| **Health/Welfare** | |
| KidsPAC | $334,350 |

# War and Peace

While the end of the Cold War and the dissolution of the Soviet Union has greatly diminished the threat of global nuclear conflict, the level of debate between pro-military PACs and pro-peace PACs has simply shifted focus. The level of defense spending in the post Cold War era is a concern of both groups, though their perspectives — and the distribution of their dollars — are at opposite poles.

| Leading Pro-Military and Pro-Peace Groups | 1989-90 Total |
| --- | --- |
| **Pro-Military** | |
| Council for National Defense | $95,294 |
| Veterans of Foreign Wars | $84,250 |
| **Pro-Peace** | |
| Council for a Livable World | $171,850 |

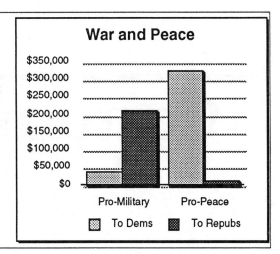

## War and Peace

Categories: Pro-Military, Pro-Peace

Legend: To Dems, To Repubs

# Other Single-Issue Groups

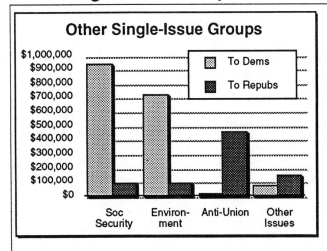

## Other Single-Issue Groups

Legend: To Dems, To Repubs

Categories: Soc Security, Environment, Anti-Union, Other Issues

Of the remaining single-issue groups, the largest are those protecting the social security and medicare systems for elderly Americans, environmental PACs and organizations seeking to reduce the influence of labor unions in the American workplace. Largest by far on the environmental front is the Sierra Club. Among the anti-union PACs, the Public Service Research Council specifically opposes unionism among public employees.

| Other Single-Issue Groups | 1989-90 Total |
| --- | --- |
| **Elderly/Social Security** | |
| National Cmte to Preserve Social Security | $914,052 |
| **Anti-Union** | |
| Public Service Research Council | $239,575 |
| Right to Work PAC | $197,904 |
| **Environmental Issues** | |
| Sierra Club | $410,210 |
| League of Conservation Voters | $159,884 |
| **Other Issues** | $201,952 |

# 3.

# Committee Profiles

# Introduction to the Committee Profiles

Most of the work that Congress does in shaping legislation takes place not on the floor of the House and Senate, but in meetings of committees and subcommittees. It is at this level that the language of bills is crafted, revised and debated, that congressional hearings are held and investigations directed. For all these reasons, much of the attention of industry and interest group lobbyists — and contributors — is focused on deliberations within the specific committees that oversee their particular industry or interest. The section which follows examines the patterns in political contributions made in 1989-90 to members of each of the 37 standing committees of the House and Senate.

## What the profiles contain

• Names of the chairman and ranking minority member of each committee and the ratio of seats between Democrats and Republicans.

• A full description of the committee's jurisdiction.

• A listing of each subcommittee, with its chairman and ranking minority member.

• A roster listing each committee member, and showing the totals they received in 1989-90 from PACs and from individual contributors giving $200 or more. The members are arranged in descending order of the amount they received. The rosters include all members who served on the committee during the 101st Congress — whether or not they ran for reelection in 1990.

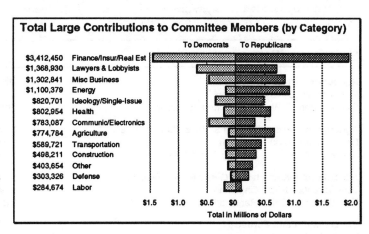

• Top 20 contributors to members of that committee, including both PACs and individual contributors of $200 and more.

• Total contributions to all members of that committee from 13 broad categories of industries and interests.

• A spotlight on the 15 largest industry and interest group sectors that contributed to committee members during 1989-90. This is a more detailed breakdown of the general categories. For example, the general chart groups all finance, insurance and real estate contributors into one broad category. The spotlight chart breaks them down further, into commercial banks, insurance companies, real estate, etc.

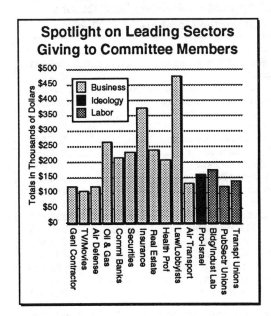

## "Generic" Committees and "Specific" Committees

The format and information shown on the committee pages varies with the jurisdictional scope of the committee. Some "generic" committees (for example, the tax-writing committees or those dealing with foreign relations, veterans' affairs, or government operations) affect a broad range of industries and interest groups more or less equally. Other committees — such as Agriculture, Armed Services, or Banking — have jurisdictions which focus on specific industries.

In generic committees, the contribution totals shown for committee members refer to the total dollars received by that member from *all* PACs and *all* individual contributors giving $200 or more. In the specific committees, the figure refers to the total received *only from those contributors whose interests coincide with the committee's jurisdiction.*

"Specific" committees also include one additional chart, highlighting those sectors most directly affected by the committee's actions.

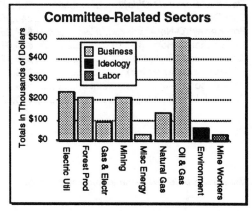

# Senate Agriculture, Nutrition, and Forestry Committee

Patrick J. Leahy (D-Vt), Chairman
Richard G. Lugar (R-Ind), Ranking Republican

**Party Ratio:** 10 Democrats
9 Republicans

> **Jurisdiction:** (1) Agricultural economics and research; (2) Agricultural extension services and experiment stations; (3) Agricultural production, marketing and stabilization of prices; (4) Agriculture and agricultural commodities; (5) Animal industry and diseases; (6) Crop insurance and soil conservation; (7) Farm credit and farm security; (8) Food from fresh waters; (9) Food stamp programs; (10) Forestry and forest reserves and wilderness areas other than those created from the public domain; (11) Home economics; (12) Home nutrition; (13) Inspection of livestock, meat, and agricultural products; (14) Pests and pesticides; (15) Plant industry, soils, and agricultural engineering; (16) Rural development, rural electrification, and watershed; (17) School nutrition programs. In addition, the committee is mandated to study and review matters relating to food, nutrition and hunger — both in the U.S. and in foreign countries — and rural areas, and to report on these matters periodically.

## Subcommittees

**Agricultural Credit**
Kent Conrad (D-ND), Chairman
Slade Gorton (R-Wash), Ranking Republican

**Agricultural Production and Stabilization of Prices**
David Pryor (D-Ark), Chairman
Jesse Helms (R-NC), Ranking Republican

**Agricultural Research and General Legislation**
Tom Daschle (D-SD), Chairman
Pete Wilson (R-Calif), Ranking Republican

**Conservation and Forestry**
Wyche Jr. Fowler (D-Ga), Chairman
Christopher S. Bond (R-Mo), Ranking Republican

**Domestic and Foreign Marketing and Product Promotion**
David L. Boren (D-Okla), Chairman
Thad Cochran (R-Miss), Ranking Republican

**Nutrition and Investigations**
Tom Harkin (D-Iowa), Chairman
Rudy Boschwitz (R-Minn), Ranking Republican

**Rural Development and Rural Electrification**
Howell Heflin (D-Ala), Chairman
Mitch McConnell (R-Ky), Ranking Republican

## Total Agriculture-Related Contributions to Committee Members

| | Total from Cmte-Related Contribs | Pct of Member's Lg Contribs |
|---|---|---|
| *Howell Heflin (D-Ala)* | $403,022 | 14% |
| *Mitch McConnell (R-Ky)* | $385,335 | 13% |
| *Rudy Boschwitz (R-Minn)* | $307,960 | 24% |
| *Jesse Helms (R-NC)* | $297,048 | 9% |
| *Thad Cochran (R-Miss)* | $293,825 | 29% |
| *Tom Harkin (D-Iowa)* | $221,424 | 7% |
| *David Pryor (D-Ark)* | $210,349 | 20% |
| *Max Baucus (D-Mont)* | $170,222 | 8% |
| Kent Conrad (D-ND) | $102,915 | 27% |
| Bob Dole (R-Kan) | $87,100 | 29% |
| Wyche Jr. Fowler (D-Ga) | $71,930 | 32% |
| *David L. Boren (D-Okla)* | $68,550 | 7% |
| Tom Daschle (D-SD) | $40,950 | 12% |
| Bob Kerrey (D-Neb) | $37,250 | 31% |
| Christopher S. Bond (R-Mo) | $30,675 | 18% |
| Slade Gorton (R-Wash) | $29,424 | 19% |
| Richard G. Lugar (R-Ind) | $26,850 | 54% |
| Pete Wilson (R-Calif) | $19,453 | 23% |
| Patrick J. Leahy (D-Vt) | $10,625 | 18% |

### Top 20 Agriculture-Related Contributors to Committee Members in 1989-90

| | | |
|---|---|---|
| 1 | Tyson Foods | $63,000 |
| 2 | Chicago Board of Trade | $55,111 |
| 3 | Philip Morris* | $54,245 |
| 4 | ACRE (Action Cmte/Rural Electrification)* | $54,200 |
| 5 | American Assn of Crop Insurers | $53,500 |
| 6 | Archer-Daniels-Midland Corp | $50,000 |
| 7 | RJR Nabisco | $49,250 |
| 8 | Chicago Mercantile Exchange | $47,500 |
| 9 | United States Tobacco Co | $45,750 |
| 10 | National Cotton Council | $44,850 |
| 11 | American Crystal Sugar Corp | $44,000 |
| 12 | Dairymen Inc* | $43,404 |
| 13 | ConAgra Inc | $43,000 |
| 14 | National Cattlemen's Assn* | $36,603 |
| 15 | Associated Milk Producers | $33,800 |
| 16 | International Paper Co | $33,000 |
| 17 | Food Marketing Institute | $31,000 |
| 18 | American Sugarbeet Growers Assn | $30,000 |
| 19 | Mid-America Dairymen | $28,500 |
| 20 | American Meat Institute | $28,000 |

\* Contributions came from more than one PAC affiliated with this sponsor.

Members in **bold italics** ran for reelection in 1990

# Summary

Dairy, sugar, tobacco and a variety of other agricultural subsidies and programs come under the jurisdiction of the Senate Agriculture Committee, making this panel crucially important to the nation's agriculture and food processing industries.

Like other Senate committees, however, the contribution patterns to committee members do not always draw a direct line between the industries and committee members. Since most Senators have four committee assignments, no one committee tends to dominate their contribution profiles. Likewise, the amount of money going to committee members varies greatly from year to year, depending on how many members are up for reelection and whether they come from big (high-budget) states, or small ones. Nevertheless, as seen in the chart at right, the agriculture industry was the second-leading source of funds for committee members in 1989-90.

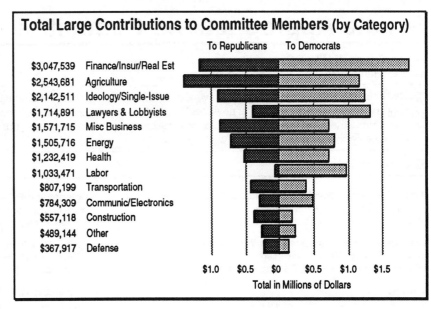

**Total Large Contributions to Committee Members (by Category)**

To Republicans    To Democrats

| | |
|---|---|
| $3,047,539 | Finance/Insur/Real Est |
| $2,543,681 | Agriculture |
| $2,142,511 | Ideology/Single-Issue |
| $1,714,891 | Lawyers & Lobbyists |
| $1,571,715 | Misc Business |
| $1,505,716 | Energy |
| $1,232,419 | Health |
| $1,033,471 | Labor |
| $807,199 | Transportation |
| $784,309 | Communic/Electronics |
| $557,118 | Construction |
| $489,144 | Other |
| $367,917 | Defense |

$1.0  $0.5  $0  $0.5  $1.0  $1.5

Total in Millions of Dollars

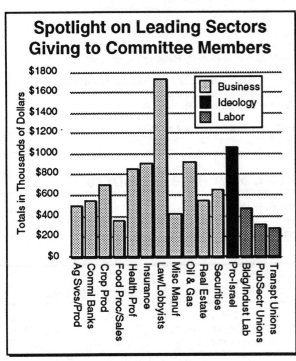

## Spotlight on Leading Sectors Giving to Committee Members

Totals in Thousands of Dollars

Legend: Business, Ideology, Labor

Categories: Ag Svcs/Prod, Comml Banks, Crop Prod, Food Proc/Sales, Health Prof, Insurance, Law/Lobbyists, Misc Manuf, Oil & Gas, Real Estate, Securities, Pro-Israel, Bldg/Indust Lab, PubSectr Unions, Transpt Unions

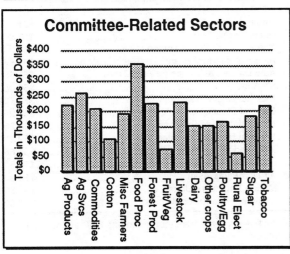

## Committee-Related Sectors

Totals in Thousands of Dollars

Categories: Ag Products, Ag Svcs, Commodities, Cotton, Misc Farmers, Food Proc, Forest Prod, Fruit/Veg, Livestock, Dairy, Other crops, Poultry/Egg, Rural Elect, Sugar, Tobacco

## Leading Committee-Related Sectors Giving to Committee Members

### Crop Production

| | |
|---|---|
| Cotton growers | $106,600 |
| Fruit & vegetable growers | $70,483 |
| Sugar growers | $179,940 |
| Other crops | $149,699 |
| Farmers, crop unspecified | $187,495 |

### Tobacco Production & Marketing

| | |
|---|---|
| Tobacco & tobacco products | $214,025 |

### Dairy

| | |
|---|---|
| Milk & dairy producers | $148,641 |

### Livestock & Poultry

| | |
|---|---|
| Livestock | $228,052 |
| Poultry & eggs | $162,750 |

### Commodities

| | |
|---|---|
| Commodity brokers/dealers | $203,651 |

### Agricultural Services & Supplies

| | |
|---|---|
| Agricultural products | $217,025 |
| Agricultural services | $255,850 |

### Food Processing & Sales

| | |
|---|---|
| Food processing & sales | $352,366 |

### Forestry

| | |
|---|---|
| Forestry & forest products | $224,360 |

### Other Committee-Related

| | |
|---|---|
| Rural electric cooperatives | $58,800 |

# Senate Appropriations Committee

Robert C. Byrd (D-WVa), Chairman
Mark O. Hatfield (R-Ore), Ranking Republican

**Party Ratio:** 16 Democrats
13 Republicans

**Jurisdiction:** (1) Appropriation of the revenue for the support of the Government; (2) Rescission of appropriations contained in appropriation acts; (3) The amount of new spending authority . . . which is to be effective for a fiscal year. Other committees of Congress may *authorize* the government to spend money on various projects and programs, but only the Appropriations committees of the House and Senate *appropriate* the funds.

## Subcommittees

**Agriculture, Rural Development, and Related Agencies**
Quentin N. Burdick (D-ND), Chairman
Thad Cochran (R-Miss), Ranking Republican

**Commerce, Justice, and State, The Judiciary, and Related Agencies**
Ernest F. Hollings (D-SC), Chairman
Warren B. Rudman (R-NH), Ranking Republican

**Defense**
Daniel K. Inouye (D-Hawaii), Chairman
Ted Stevens (R-Alaska), Ranking Republican

**District of Columbia**
Brock Adams (D-Wash), Chairman
Phil Gramm (R-Texas), Ranking Republican

**Energy and Water Development**
J. Bennett Johnston (D-La), Chairman
Mark O. Hatfield (R-Ore), Ranking Republican

**Foreign Operations**
Patrick J. Leahy (D-Vt), Chairman
Bob Kasten (R-Wis), Ranking Republican

**Interior and Related Agencies**
Robert C. Byrd (D-WVa), Chairman
James A. McClure (R-Idaho), Ranking Republican

**Labor, Health and Human Services, Education, and Related Agencies**
Tom Harkin (D-Iowa), Chairman
Arlen Specter (R-Pa), Ranking Republican

**Legislative Branch**
Harry Reid (D-Nev), Chairman
Don Nickles (R-Okla), Ranking Republican

**Military Construction**
Jim Sasser (D-Tenn), Chairman
Charles E. Grassley (R-Iowa), Ranking Republican

**Transportation and Related Agencies**
Frank Lautenberg (D-NJ), Chairman
Alfonse M. D'Amato (R-NY), Ranking Republican

**Treasury, Postal Service, and General Government**
Dennis DeConcini (D-Ariz), Chairman
Pete V. Domenici (R-NM), Ranking Republican

**VA, HUD, and Independent Agencies**
Barbara A. Mikulski (D-Md), Chairwoman
Jake Garn (R-Utah), Ranking Republican

## Total PAC & Large Individual Contributions to Committee Members

*Phil Gramm (R-Texas)* ............................................. $7,313,159
*Tom Harkin (D-Iowa)* ............................................... $3,129,211
*J. Bennett Johnston (D-La)* ..................................... $2,777,093
*Mark O. Hatfield (R-Ore)* ........................................ $1,738,163
*Pete V. Domenici (R-NM)* ....................................... $1,575,732
*Ted Stevens (R-Alaska)* .......................................... $1,167,034
*Thad Cochran (R-Miss)* ........................................... $1,024,086
Arlen Specter (R-Pa) ................................................. $473,110
Ernest F. Hollings (D-SC) .......................................... $388,860
Wyche Jr. Fowler (D-Ga) ........................................... $224,377
Frank Lautenberg (D-NJ) ........................................... $218,673
James A. McClure (R-Idaho)[1] .................................. $208,180
Alfonse M. D'Amato (R-NY) ....................................... $203,518
Barbara A. Mikulski (D-Md) ....................................... $180,575
Harry Reid (D-Nev) ................................................... $133,967
Brock Adams (D-Wash) ............................................. $127,400
Dennis DeConcini (D-Ariz) ......................................... $121,841
Bob Kerrey (D-Neb) .................................................. $119,700
Bob Kasten (R-Wis) ................................................... $106,400
Dale Bumpers (D-Ark) ............................................... $66,750
Jake Garn (R-Utah) .................................................... $58,150
Patrick J. Leahy (D-Vt) ............................................... $58,125
Charles E. Grassley (R-Iowa) ..................................... $57,254
Don Nickles (R-Okla) ................................................. $32,000
Jim Sasser (D-Tenn) .................................................. $16,326
Daniel K. Inouye (D-Hawaii) ....................................... $14,250

Members in **bold italics** ran for reelection in 1990

[1] Did not seek reelection in 1990

Warren B. Rudman (R-NH) ......................................... $5,000
Robert C. Byrd (D-WVa) ............................................ $2,500
Quentin N. Burdick (D-ND) ......................................... $250

### Top 20 Contributors to Committee Members in 1989-90

| | | |
|---|---|---|
| 1 | Salomon Brothers | $98,300 |
| 2 | Federal Express Corp | $91,500 |
| 3 | American Bankers Assn* | $75,550 |
| 4 | Teamsters Union* | $73,225 |
| 5 | AT&T | $63,880 |
| 6 | General Motors* | $61,950 |
| 7 | Union Pacific Corp | $61,600 |
| 8 | National Assn of Life Underwriters | $60,000 |
| 9 | American Medical Assn* | $57,546 |
| 10 | Auto Dealers & Drivers for Free Trade | $57,500 |
| 11 | MCA Inc | $55,050 |
| 12 | National Cable Television Assn | $53,499 |
| 13 | General Electric* | $53,259 |
| 14 | National Assn of Realtors | $53,250 |
| 15 | National Beer Wholesalers Assn | $52,200 |
| 16 | Independent Insurance Agents of America | $51,683 |
| 17 | National Assn of Letter Carriers | $50,500 |
| 18 | Air Line Pilots Assn | $50,000 |
| 19 | Marine Engineers Union* | $49,500 |
| 20 | Seafarers International Union | $49,500 |

* Contributions came from more than one PAC affiliated with this sponsor.

## Summary

The Appropriations Committee is the largest committee in the U.S. Senate; its 29 members have the job of doling out the dollars it takes to keep the government running. This makes its decisions especially important to those businesses that rely heavily on government contracts.

The unusually large level of contributions from oil & gas interests and lawyers is less a reflection of the committee's work than the fact that Texas Republican Phil Gramm, a committee member, was running a top-dollar reelection campaign. Gramm was the top recipient of oil & gas funds in the U.S. Congress and the third highest recipient of dollars from lawyers and lobbyists. Democrat Bennett Johnston of Louisiana, also a committee member, was another top oil & gas recipient.

### Total Large Contributions to Committee Members (by Category)

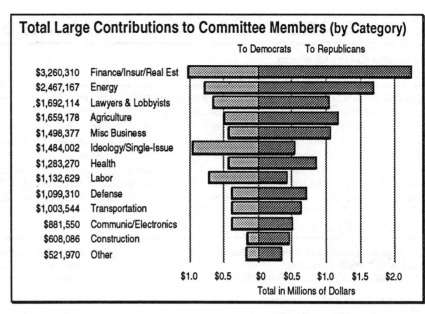

| | | |
|---|---|---|
| $3,260,310 | Finance/Insur/Real Est | |
| $2,467,167 | Energy | |
| $1,692,114 | Lawyers & Lobbyists | |
| $1,659,178 | Agriculture | |
| $1,498,377 | Misc Business | |
| $1,484,002 | Ideology/Single-Issue | |
| $1,283,270 | Health | |
| $1,132,629 | Labor | |
| $1,099,310 | Defense | |
| $1,003,544 | Transportation | |
| $881,550 | Communic/Electronics | |
| $608,086 | Construction | |
| $521,970 | Other | |

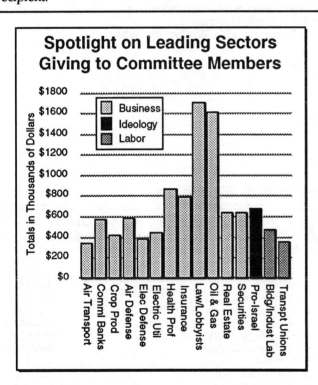

### Spotlight on Leading Sectors Giving to Committee Members

### Leading Sectors Giving to Committee Members

**Business**

| | |
|---|---|
| Air Transport | $336,033 |
| Commercial Banks | $561,153 |
| Crop Production & Basic Processing | $409,125 |
| Defense Aerospace | $579,704 |
| Defense Electronics | $369,876 |
| Environmental Svcs/Equipment | $430,200 |
| Health Professionals | $861,514 |
| Insurance | $775,980 |
| Lawyers & Lobbyists | $1,692,114 |
| Oil & Gas | $1,603,423 |
| Real Estate | $630,733 |
| Securities/Commodities Investment | $623,440 |

**Ideological/Single-Issue**

| | |
|---|---|
| Pro-Israel | $659,077 |

**Labor**

| | |
|---|---|
| Bldg Trades/Industrial/Misc Unions | $464,327 |
| Transportation Unions | $343,015 |

# Senate Armed Services Committee

Sam Nunn (D-Ga), Chairman
John W. Warner (R-Va), Ranking Republican

**Party Ratio:** 11 Democrats
9 Republicans

> **Jurisdiction:** (1) Aeronautical and space activities peculiar to or primarily associated with the development of weapons systems or military operations; (2) The common defense; (3) The Department of Defense, the Department of the Army, the Department of the Navy, and the Department of the Air Force, generally; (4) Maintenance and operation of the Panama Canal, including administration, sanitation, and government of the Canal Zone; (5) Military research and development; (6) National security aspects of nuclear energy; (7) Naval petroleum reserves, except those in Alaska; (8) Pay, promotion, retirement, and other benefits and privileges of members of the Armed Forces, including overseas education of civilian and military dependents; (9) Selective Service System; and (10) Strategic and critical materials necessary for the common defense. In addition, the committee is mandated to study and review, on a comprehensive basis, matters relating to the common defense policy of the United States and to report on them from time to time.

## Subcommittees

**Conventional Forces and Alliance Defense**
Carl Levin (D-Mich), Chairman
Pete Wilson (R-Calif), Ranking Republican

**Defense Industry and Technology**
Jeff Bingaman (D-NM), Chairman
Malcolm Wallop (R-Wyo), Ranking Republican

**Manpower and Personnel**
John Glenn (D-Ohio), Chairman
John McCain (R-Ariz), Ranking Republican

**Projection Forces and Regional Defense**
Edward M. Kennedy (D-Mass), Chairman
William S. Cohen (R-Maine), Ranking Republican

**Readiness, Sustainability and Support**
Alan J. Dixon (D-Ill), Chairman
Slade Gorton (R-Wash), Ranking Republican

**Strategic Forces and Nuclear Deterrence**
Jim Exon (D-Neb), Chairman
Strom Thurmond (R-SC), Ranking Republican

## Total Defense-Related Contributions to Committee Members

| | Total from Cmte-Related Contribs | Pct of Member's Lg Contribs |
|---|---|---|
| *John W. Warner (R-Va)* | $196,982 | 13% |
| *Daniel R. Coats (R-Ind)* | $186,239 | 7% |
| *Jim Exon (D-Neb)* | $158,337 | 8% |
| *Carl Levin (D-Mich)* | $129,201 | 3% |
| *Strom Thurmond (R-SC)* | $114,580 | 10% |
| *Sam Nunn (D-Ga)* | $112,960 | 7% |
| *Al Gore (D-Tenn)* | $100,812 | 5% |
| *William S. Cohen (R-Maine)* | $97,450 | 9% |
| Alan J. Dixon (D-Ill) | $44,750 | 12% |
| Slade Gorton (R-Wash) | $25,000 | 16% |
| Richard C. Shelby (D-Ala) | $15,000 | 7% |
| Malcolm Wallop (R-Wyo) | $12,000 | 29% |
| John McCain (R-Ariz) | $10,250 | 20% |
| Pete Wilson (R-Calif) | $8,800 | 10% |
| Tim Wirth (D-Colo) | $8,000 | 6% |
| Robert C. Byrd (D-WVa) | $3,000 | 120% |
| John Glenn (D-Ohio) | $2,000 | 4% |
| Trent Lott (R-Miss) | $1,500 | 4% |
| Edward M. Kennedy (D-Mass) | $0 | 0% |
| Jeff Bingaman (D-NM) | -$1,000 | 0% |

### Top 20 Defense-Related Contributors to Committee Members in 1989-90

| | | |
|---|---|---|
| 1 | General Motors* | $60,500 |
| 2 | Northrop Corp | $51,000 |
| 3 | AT&T | $48,300 |
| 4 | Textron Inc | $48,000 |
| 5 | Lockheed Corp | $47,000 |
| 6 | Ford Motor Co/BDM International | $46,750 |
| 7 | General Dynamics | $45,226 |
| 8 | McDonnell Douglas* | $44,500 |
| 9 | General Electric | $40,300 |
| 10 | Martin Marietta Corp | $38,250 |
| 11 | Rockwell International | $37,750 |
| 12 | LTV Corp* | $36,450 |
| 13 | Grumman Corp | $35,750 |
| 14 | Raytheon | $35,500 |
| 15 | United Technologies | $34,250 |
| 16 | Boeing Co | $32,757 |
| 17 | Allied-Signal | $25,750 |
| 18 | Westinghouse Electric | $24,500 |
| 19 | GTE Corp | $20,600 |
| 20 | Tenneco Inc | $19,250 |

\* Contributions came from more than one PAC affiliated with this sponsor.

Members in **bold italics** ran for reelection in 1990

# Summary

Defense aerospace and electronics contractors were an important source of campaign dollars to the members of the Senate Armed Services Committee, but defense interests overall ranked a surprisingly low fifth place among the 13 main categories of contributors shown in the chart at right. This is partly due to the fact that Senators routinely sit on three or four major committees, and as many as a dozen subcommittees. This tends to spread out the spectrum of interests that contribute to their campaigns.

The presence of the big three automakers on the roster of top contributors to committee members relates less to the cars and trucks they sold to the military than to their defense-related subsidiaries. In the face of declining defense budgets, however, some of the automakers are scaling back or divesting themselves of defense operations. A month before the 1990 elections, Ford Motor Co. spun off BDM International, a major defense research firm.

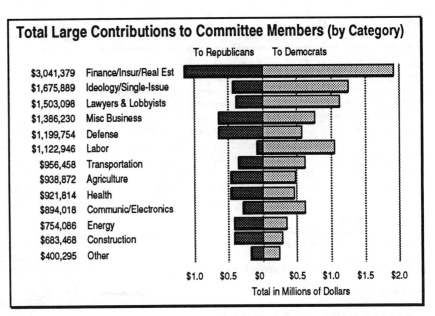

**Total Large Contributions to Committee Members (by Category)**

To Republicans    To Democrats

| | |
|---|---|
| $3,041,379 | Finance/Insur/Real Est |
| $1,675,889 | Ideology/Single-Issue |
| $1,503,098 | Lawyers & Lobbyists |
| $1,386,230 | Misc Business |
| $1,199,754 | Defense |
| $1,122,946 | Labor |
| $956,458 | Transportation |
| $938,872 | Agriculture |
| $921,814 | Health |
| $894,018 | Communic/Electronics |
| $754,086 | Energy |
| $683,468 | Construction |
| $400,295 | Other |

$1.0   $0.5   $0   $0.5   $1.0   $1.5   $2.0

Total in Millions of Dollars

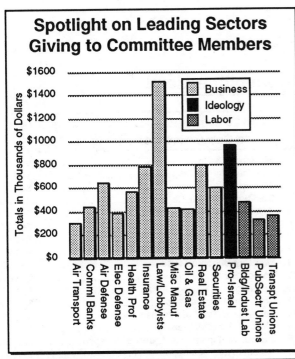

## Spotlight on Leading Sectors Giving to Committee Members

Totals in Thousands of Dollars

Legend: Business, Ideology, Labor

Categories: Air Transport, Comml Banks, Air Defense, Elec Defense, Health Prof, Insurance, Law/Lobbyists, Misc Manuf, Oil & Gas, Real Estate, Securities, Pro-Israel, Bldg/Indust Lab, PubSectr Unions, Transpt Unions

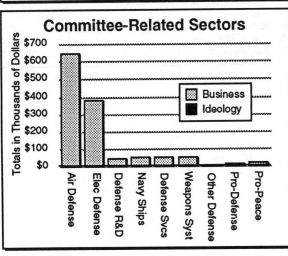

## Committee-Related Sectors

Totals in Thousands of Dollars

Legend: Business, Ideology

Categories: Air Defense, Elec Defense, Defense R&D, Navy Ships, Defense Svcs, Weapons Syst, Other Defense, Pro-Defense, Pro-Peace

## Leading Sectors Giving to Committee Members

### Business

| | |
|---|---|
| Air Transport | $288,373 |
| Commercial Banks | $434,709 |
| Defense Aerospace | $636,258 |
| Defense Electronics | $376,683 |
| Health Professionals | $551,699 |
| Insurance | $770,660 |
| Lawyers & Lobbyists | $1,503,098 |
| Misc Manufacturing & Distributing | $420,638 |
| Oil & Gas | $402,262 |
| Real Estate | $782,429 |
| Securities/Commodities Investment | $595,394 |

### Ideological/Single-Issue

| | |
|---|---|
| Pro-Israel | $953,408 |

### Labor

| | |
|---|---|
| Bldg Trades/Industrial/Misc Unions | $459,656 |
| Public Sector Unions | $316,340 |
| Transportation Unions | $346,950 |

## Leading Committee-Related Sectors Giving to Committee Members

### Business

| | |
|---|---|
| Defense aerospace contractors | $636,258 |
| Defense electronic contractors | $376,683 |
| Defense research & development | $40,950 |
| Defense shipbuilders | $45,150 |
| Defense-related services | $48,463 |
| Ground-based & other weapons systems | $49,250 |
| Other defense | $3,000 |

### Ideological/Single-Issue

| | |
|---|---|
| Pro-Defense | $9,680 |
| Pro-Peace | $16,427 |

# Senate Banking, Housing & Urban Affairs Committee

Donald W. Riegle Jr. (D-Mich), Chairman
Jake Garn (R-Utah), Ranking Republican

**Party Ratio:** 12 Democrats
9 Republicans

**Jurisdiction:** (1) Banks, banking and financial institutions; (2) Financial aid to commerce and industry; (3) Deposit insurance; (4) Public and private housing (including veterans' housing); (5) Federal monetary policy (including Federal Reserve System); (6) Money and credit, including currency and coinage; (7) Issuance and redemption of notes; (8) Control of prices of commodities, rents, and services; (9) Urban development and urban mass transit; (10) Economic stabilization and defense production; (11) Export controls; (12) Export and foreign trade promotion; (13) Nursing home construction; (14) Renegotiation of Government contracts. In addition, the committee is mandated to study and review matters relating to international economic policy as it affects U.S. monetary affairs, credit, and financial institutions, economic growth, urban affairs, and credit, and to report on these matters periodically.

## Subcommittees

**Consumer and Regulatory Affairs**
Alan J. Dixon (D-Ill), Chairman
Christopher S. Bond (R-Mo), Ranking Republican

**Housing and Urban Affairs**
Alan Cranston (D-Calif), Chairman
Alfonse M. D'Amato (R-NY), Ranking Republican

**HUD/MOD Rehab Investigation**
Bob Graham (D-Fla), Chairman
Connie Mack (R-Fla), Ranking Republican

**International Finance and Monetary Policy**
Paul S. Sarbanes (D-Md), Chairman
Phil Gramm (R-Texas), Ranking Republican

**Securities**
Christopher J. Dodd (D-Conn), Chairman
John Heinz (R-Pa), Ranking Republican

## Total Committee-Related Contributions to Committee Members

| | Total from Cmte-Related Contribs | Pct of Member's Lg Contribs |
|---|---|---|
| *Phil Gramm (R-Texas)* | $1,197,276 | 16% |
| *John Kerry (D-Mass)* | $751,417 | 21% |
| *Larry Pressler (R-SD)* | $426,057 | 26% |
| Alan J. Dixon (D-Ill) | $141,700 | 37% |
| Terry Sanford (D-NC) | $141,250 | 53% |
| Bob Graham (D-Fla) | $117,440 | 39% |
| Richard C. Shelby (D-Ala) | $111,034 | 51% |
| Christopher J. Dodd (D-Conn) | $91,212 | 58% |
| Alfonse M. D'Amato (R-NY) | $89,828 | 44% |
| *Nancy Landon Kassebaum (R-Kan)* | $86,430 | 25% |
| Christopher S. Bond (R-Mo) | $86,056 | 51% |
| Connie Mack (R-Fla) | $83,500 | 38% |
| Alan Cranston (D-Calif) | $52,500 | 26% |
| Jake Garn (R-Utah) | $49,300 | 85% |
| Tim Wirth (D-Colo) | $31,000 | 22% |
| Richard H. Bryan (D-Nev) | $29,500 | 30% |
| John Heinz (R-Pa) | $8,900 | 38% |
| William V. Roth Jr. (R-Del) | $7,000 | 54% |
| Jim Sasser (D-Tenn) | $2,250 | 14% |
| Donald W. Riegle Jr. (D-Mich) | $1,500 | 515% |
| Paul S. Sarbanes (D-Md) | $0 | 0% |

### Top 20 Committee-Related Contributors to Committee Members in 1989-90

| | | |
|---|---|---|
| 1 | JP Morgan & Co | $48,500 |
| 2 | American Family Corp | $48,000 |
| 3 | Citicorp | $47,000 |
| 4 | Goldman, Sachs & Co | $44,250 |
| 5 | American Institute of CPA's | $42,625 |
| 6 | American Bankers Assn* | $41,250 |
| 7 | American Express* | $41,150 |
| 8 | Chicago Mercantile Exchange | $40,250 |
| 9 | First City Bancorp/Texas | $37,403 |
| 10 | Barnett Banks of Florida | $35,000 |
| 11 | US League of Savings Assns* | $34,850 |
| 12 | Continental Illinois Corp | $31,000 |
| 13 | American Council of Life Insurance | $29,999 |
| 14 | Chicago Board of Trade | $29,750 |
| 15 | Independent Insurance Agents of America | $29,212 |
| 16 | National Assn of Independent Insurers | $27,356 |
| 17 | Sears* | $25,500 |
| 18 | National Assn of Realtors | $25,000 |
| 19 | Chase Manhattan | $24,446 |
| 20 | Merrill Lynch | $23,270 |

\* Contributions came from more than one PAC affiliated with this sponsor.

Members in *bold italics* ran for reelection in 1990

## Summary

The banking industry, a heavily regulated sector of American business, has become much more diversified in recent years, offering an ever-widening array of financial services. This diversification has come about as Congress (and the banking committees in particular) have gradually lifted many restrictions governing the industry. But banks are anxious for considerably more freedom — the ability to branch into stock brokerage services, for example — and the Senate Banking Committee is one of the central battlegrounds for the ongoing debate.

The issue of bank deregulation, of course, concerns not only banks but also their competitors — particularly major insurance companies who have become increasingly active in the securities field themselves. And, like many other committees in the Senate, contributions from lawyers and lobbyists (representing either their own interests or those of their clients) were substantial.

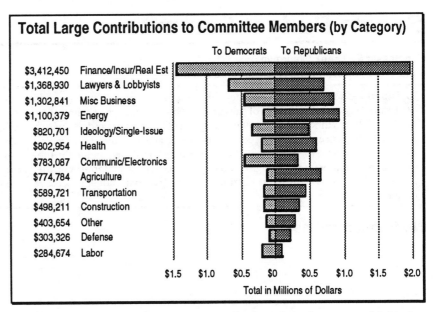

**Total Large Contributions to Committee Members (by Category)**

To Democrats    To Republicans

| | |
|---|---|
| $3,412,450 | Finance/Insur/Real Est |
| $1,368,930 | Lawyers & Lobbyists |
| $1,302,841 | Misc Business |
| $1,100,379 | Energy |
| $820,701 | Ideology/Single-Issue |
| $802,954 | Health |
| $783,087 | Communic/Electronics |
| $774,784 | Agriculture |
| $589,721 | Transportation |
| $498,211 | Construction |
| $403,654 | Other |
| $303,326 | Defense |
| $284,674 | Labor |

$1.5  $1.0  $0.5  $0  $0.5  $1.0  $1.5  $2.0

Total in Millions of Dollars

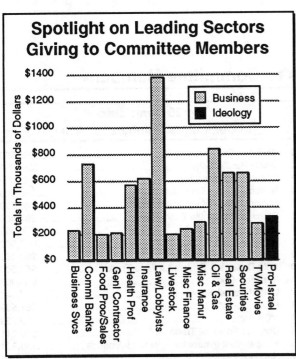

### Spotlight on Leading Sectors Giving to Committee Members

Totals in Thousands of Dollars

$1400 / $1200 / $1000 / $800 / $600 / $400 / $200 / $0

Legend: Business, Ideology

Categories: Business Svcs, Comml Banks, Food Proc/Sales, Genl Contractor, Health Prof, Insurance, Law/Lobbyists, Livestock, Misc Finance, Misc Manuf, Oil & Gas, Real Estate, Securities, TV/Movies, Pro-Israel

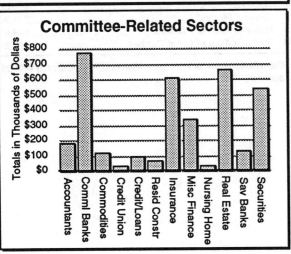

### Committee-Related Sectors

Totals in Thousands of Dollars

$800 / $700 / $600 / $500 / $400 / $300 / $200 / $100 / $0

Categories: Accountants, Comml Banks, Commodities, Credit Union, Credit/Loans, Resid Constr, Insurance, Misc Finance, Nursing Home, Real Estate, Sav Banks, Securities

### Leading Committee-Related Sectors Giving to Committee Members

**Banking**

| | |
|---|---|
| Commercial banks | $761,385 |
| Savings & loans | $123,530 |
| Credit unions | $27,678 |

**Financial Services**

| | |
|---|---|
| Finance/credit companies | $89,622 |
| Accountants | $175,257 |

**Other Financial**

| | |
|---|---|
| Insurance | $603,685 |
| Securities & investment | $531,326 |
| Commodity brokers/dealers | $117,899 |
| Misc finance | $331,516 |

**Real Estate & Construction**

| | |
|---|---|
| Real estate | $650,552 |
| Home builders | $65,500 |

**Other Committee-Related**

| | |
|---|---|
| Nursing homes | $26,750 |

# Senate Budget Committee

Jim Sasser (D-Tenn), Chairman
Pete V. Domenici (R-NM), Ranking Republican

**Party Ratio:** 13 Democrats
10 Republicans

**Jurisdiction:** (1) To report the matters needing to be reported by it under Titles III and IV of the Congressional Budget Act of 1974; (2) To make continuing studies of the effect on budget outlays of relevant existing and proposed legislation and to report the results of such studies to the Senate on a recurring basis; (3) To request and evaluate continuing studies of tax expenditures, to devise methods of coordinating tax expenditures, policies, and programs with direct budget outlays, and to report the results of such studies to the Senate on a recurring basis; (4) To review, on a continuing basis, the conduct by the Congressional Budget Office of its functions and duties; (5) To consider impoundment legislation required to be jointly referred to it, the Appropriations Committee, and other Senate Committees . . . and (6) To consider matters affecting the Congressional Budget process required to be referred to it and the Governmental Affairs Committee.

## No Subcommittees

## Total PAC & Large Individual Contributions to Committee Members

| | |
|---|---|
| *Phil Gramm (R-Texas)* | $7,313,159 |
| *Paul Simon (D-Ill)* | $4,473,338 |
| *J. Bennett Johnston (D-La)* | $2,777,093 |
| *Jim Exon (D-Neb)* | $2,024,788 |
| *Pete V. Domenici (R-NM)* | $1,575,732 |
| *Rudy Boschwitz (R-Minn)* | $1,298,047 |
| Ernest F. Hollings (D-SC) | $388,860 |
| Kent Conrad (D-ND) | $376,454 |
| Steve Symms (R-Idaho) | $278,228 |
| Terry Sanford (D-NC) | $264,550 |
| Wyche Jr. Fowler (D-Ga) | $224,377 |
| Frank Lautenberg (D-NJ) | $218,673 |
| Christopher S. Bond (R-Mo) | $167,342 |
| Christopher J. Dodd (D-Conn) | $157,261 |
| Tim Wirth (D-Colo) | $139,941 |
| Bob Kasten (R-Wis) | $106,400 |
| Charles E. Grassley (R-Iowa) | $57,254 |
| Don Nickles (R-Okla) | $32,000 |
| Charles S. Robb (D-Va) | $24,300 |
| Jim Sasser (D-Tenn) | $16,326 |
| Warren B. Rudman (R-NH) | $5,000 |
| Donald W. Riegle Jr. (D-Mich) | $291 |
| William L. Armstrong (R-Colo)[1] | -$27 |

[1] Did not seek reelection in 1990

### Top 20 Contributors to Committee Members in 1989-90

| | | |
|---|---|---|
| 1 | Salomon Brothers | $86,500 |
| 2 | Union Pacific Corp | $84,050 |
| 3 | Federal Express Corp | $82,000 |
| 4 | National Cable Television Assn | $68,000 |
| 5 | National Beer Wholesalers Assn | $66,250 |
| 6 | Chicago Mercantile Exchange | $61,800 |
| 7 | AT&T | $58,000 |
| 8 | National Assn of Life Underwriters | $57,500 |
| 9 | American Bankers Assn* | $53,550 |
| 10 | Auto Dealers & Drivers for Free Trade | $53,500 |
| 11 | Northrop Corp | $53,000 |
| 12 | United Parcel Service | $52,900 |
| 13 | Philip Morris* | $51,599 |
| 14 | MCA Inc | $50,750 |
| 15 | Chicago Board of Trade | $50,611 |
| 16 | Independent Insurance Agents of America | $50,396 |
| 17 | National PAC | $50,000 |
| 18 | General Motors* | $49,500 |
| 19 | National Assn of Realtors | $48,600 |
| 20 | National Assn of Letter Carriers | $48,500 |

\* Contributions came from more than one PAC affiliated with this sponsor.

Members in *bold italics* ran for reelection in 1990

## Summary

Perhaps no other document in the Western World is so important to so many people, yet understood by so few, as the federal government's annual budget. Weighty, befuddling, sometimes self-contradictory, and inevitably the subject of political wrangling and intense negotiation between Congress and the administration, the budget is the blueprint for federal spending and programs for the coming fiscal year. This is the committee charged with shaping that budget into something both sides can live with.

In recent years the budget deficit has been an ever-growing preoccupation of this committee. Finding ways to reduce it — at least on paper — has been a sometimes all-consuming task. Since federal spending — and the deficit in particular — affects the overall American economy, many industries have a more than casual interest in the committee's work. The financial industry was the biggest overall contributor to committee members, while lawyers and lobbyists were the single largest sector, as seen in the chart below.

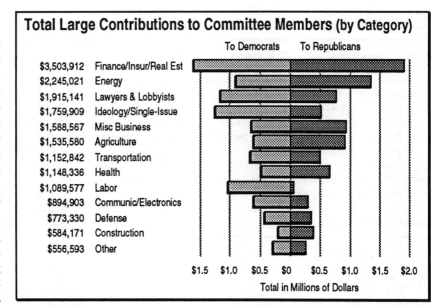

**Total Large Contributions to Committee Members (by Category)**

| | | |
|---|---|---|
| $3,503,912 | Finance/Insur/Real Est | |
| $2,245,021 | Energy | |
| $1,915,141 | Lawyers & Lobbyists | |
| $1,759,909 | Ideology/Single-Issue | |
| $1,588,567 | Misc Business | |
| $1,535,580 | Agriculture | |
| $1,152,842 | Transportation | |
| $1,148,336 | Health | |
| $1,089,577 | Labor | |
| $894,903 | Communic/Electronics | |
| $773,330 | Defense | |
| $584,171 | Construction | |
| $556,593 | Other | |

To Democrats — To Republicans

$1.5  $1.0  $0.5  $0  $0.5  $1.0  $1.5  $2.0

Total in Millions of Dollars

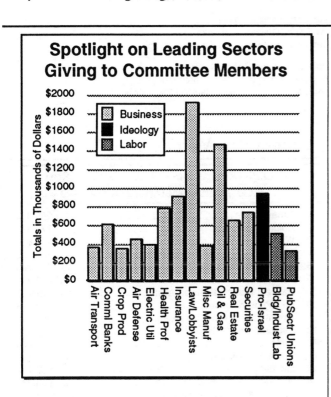

## Spotlight on Leading Sectors Giving to Committee Members

Totals in Thousands of Dollars

$2000, $1800, $1600, $1400, $1200, $1000, $800, $600, $400, $200, $0

Legend: Business, Ideology, Labor

Air Transport, Comml Banks, Crop Prod, Air Defense, Electric Util, Health Prof, Insurance, Law/Lobbyists, Misc Manuf, Oil & Gas, Real Estate, Securities, Pro-Israel, Bldg/Indust Lab, PubSectr Unions

### Leading Sectors Giving to Committee Members

**Business**

| | |
|---|---|
| Air Transport | $355,833 |
| Commercial Banks | $589,037 |
| Crop Production & Basic Processing | $342,215 |
| Defense Aerospace | $439,338 |
| Environmental Svcs/Equipment | $377,850 |
| Health Professionals | $762,498 |
| Insurance | $888,932 |
| Lawyers & Lobbyists | $1,915,141 |
| Misc Manufacturing & Distributing | $365,172 |
| Oil & Gas | $1,456,992 |
| Real Estate | $632,466 |
| Securities/Commodities Investment | $719,311 |

**Ideological/Single-Issue**

| | |
|---|---|
| Pro-Israel | $927,114 |

**Labor**

| | |
|---|---|
| Bldg Trades/Industrial/Misc Unions | $491,715 |
| Public Sector Unions | $313,645 |

# Senate Commerce, Science and Transportation Committee

Ernest F. Hollings (D-SC), Chairman
John C. Danforth (R-Mo), Ranking Republican

**Party Ratio:** 11 Democrats
9 Republicans

**Jurisdiction:** (1) Interstate commerce; (2) Transportation; (3) Regulation of interstate common carriers, including railroads, buses, trucks, vessels, pipelines, and civil aviation; (4) Merchant marine and navigation; (5) Marine and ocean navigation, safety, and transportation, including navigational aspects of deepwater ports; (6) Coast Guard; (7) Inland waterways, except construction; (8) Communications; (9) Regulation of consumer products and services, including testing related to toxic substances, other than pesticides, and except for credit, financial services, and housing; (10) The Panama Canal and interoceanic canals generally, except as referred to the Committee on Armed Services; (11) Standards and measurement; (12) Highway safety; (13) Science, engineering, and technology research and development and policy; (14) Nonmilitary aeronautical and space sciences; (15) Transportation and commerce aspects of Outer Continental Shelf lands; (16) Marine fisheries; (17) Coastal Zone Management; (18) Oceans, weather, and atmospheric activities; (19) Sports. In addition, the committee is mandated to study and review all matters relating to science and technology, oceans policy, transportation, communications and consumer affairs, and to report on these matters periodically.

## Subcommittees

**Aviation**
Wendell H. Ford (D-Ky), Chairman
John McCain (R-Ariz), Ranking Republican

**Communications**
Daniel K. Inouye (D-Hawaii), Chairman
Bob Packwood (R-Ore), Ranking Republican

**Consumer**
Richard H. Bryan (D-Nev), Chairman
Slade Gorton (R-Wash), Ranking Republican

**Foreign Commerce and Tourism**
John D. Rockefeller IV (D-WVa), Chairman
Conrad Burns (R-Mont), Ranking Republican

**Merchant Marine**
John B. Breaux (D-La), Chairman
Trent Lott (R-Miss), Ranking Republican

**Science, Technology, and Space**
Al Gore (D-Tenn), Chairman
Larry Pressler (R-SD), Ranking Republican

**Surface Transportation**
Jim Exon (D-Neb), Chairman
Bob Kasten (R-Wis), Ranking Republican

**National Ocean Policy Study**
Ernest F. Hollings (D-SC), Chairman
Ted Stevens (R-Alaska), Ranking Republican

## Total Committee-Related Contributions to Committee Members

| | Total from Cmte-Related Contribs | Pct of Member's Lg Contribs |
|---|---|---|
| *John Kerry (D-Mass)* | $868,941 | 24% |
| *Jim Exon (D-Neb)* | $765,029 | 38% |
| *John D. Rockefeller IV (D-WVa)* | $743,571 | 25% |
| *Al Gore (D-Tenn)* | $597,021 | 31% |
| *Larry Pressler (R-SD)* | $436,967 | 27% |
| *Ted Stevens (R-Alaska)* | $395,102 | 34% |
| Ernest F. Hollings (D-SC) | $222,625 | 57% |
| Slade Gorton (R-Wash) | $77,951 | 50% |
| Richard H. Bryan (D-Nev) | $47,750 | 48% |
| John B. Breaux (D-La) | $43,000 | 42% |
| Bob Kasten (R-Wis) | $36,550 | 34% |
| Conrad Burns (R-Mont) | $30,500 | 65% |
| John McCain (R-Ariz) | $18,879 | 37% |
| Trent Lott (R-Miss) | $16,250 | 45% |
| Wendell H. Ford (D-Ky) | $14,000 | 70% |
| Charles S. Robb (D-Va) | $11,750 | 48% |
| John C. Danforth (R-Mo) | $11,100 | 56% |
| Daniel K. Inouye (D-Hawaii) | $5,500 | 39% |
| Lloyd Bentsen (D-Texas) | $4,950 | 14% |
| Bob Packwood (R-Ore) | $3,126 | 81% |

### Top 20 Committee-Related Contributors to Committee Members in 1989-90

| | | |
|---|---|---|
| 1 | Time Warner | $89,000 |
| 2 | Union Pacific Corp | $71,300 |
| 3 | Walt Disney Co | $49,669 |
| 4 | American Council of Life Insurance | $48,999 |
| 5 | Air Line Pilots Assn | $42,500 |
| 6 | MCA Inc | $42,300 |
| 7 | National Cable Television Assn | $42,125 |
| 8 | Burlington Northern* | $40,598 |
| 9 | Aircraft Owners & Pilots Assn | $40,500 |
| 10 | Seafarers International Union | $39,500 |
| 11 | Mintz, Levin et al | $37,996 |
| 12 | Home Shopping Network | $37,500 |
| 13 | Independent Insurance Agents of America | $37,491 |
| 14 | National Assn of Broadcasters | $33,995 |
| 15 | National Assn of Life Underwriters | $33,500 |
| 16 | Federal Express Corp | $33,333 |
| 17 | BellSouth Corp* | $33,000 |
| 18 | Tele-Communications Inc* | $31,393 |
| 19 | Marine Engineers Union* | $31,000 |
| 20 | American Trucking Assns | $30,523 |

\* Contributions came from more than one PAC affiliated with this sponsor.

Members in **bold italics** ran for reelection in 1990

# Summary

Under the wide umbrella of the Senate Commerce Committee's jurisdiction falls a variety of industries and interests ranging from cable TV operators to telephone utilities, railroads to barge lines to interstate truckers. Disputes between competing segments within those industries contribute to a perennially heavy schedule on the committee's agenda. This is also the committee that wrestles with the issue of product liability laws, pitting lawyers on the one side against manufacturers on the other — with a host of other groups falling somewhere in between. Lawyers and lobbyists towered over all other contributors to the committee in the 1990 elections, but it is not always possible to determine what proportion of the dollars were concerned with issues such as tort reform versus lobbying efforts by lawyers on behalf of their many clients.

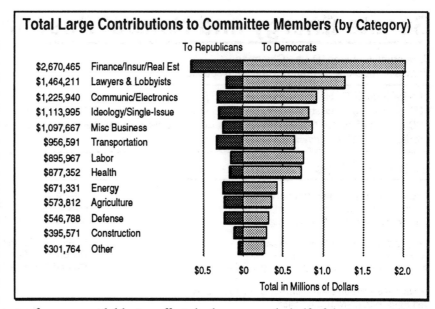

**Total Large Contributions to Committee Members (by Category)**

| Amount | Category |
|---|---|
| $2,670,465 | Finance/Insur/Real Est |
| $1,464,211 | Lawyers & Lobbyists |
| $1,225,940 | Communic/Electronics |
| $1,113,995 | Ideology/Single-Issue |
| $1,097,667 | Misc Business |
| $956,591 | Transportation |
| $895,967 | Labor |
| $877,352 | Health |
| $671,331 | Energy |
| $573,812 | Agriculture |
| $546,788 | Defense |
| $395,571 | Construction |
| $301,764 | Other |

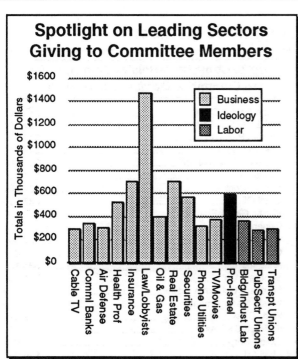

## Spotlight on Leading Sectors Giving to Committee Members

Totals in Thousands of Dollars

Business, Ideology, Labor

Cable TV, Comml Banks, Air Defense, Health Prof, Insurance, Law/Lobbyists, Oil & Gas, Real Estate, Securities, Phone Utilities, TV/Movies, Pro-Israel, Bldg/Indust Lab, PubSectr Unions, Transpt Unions

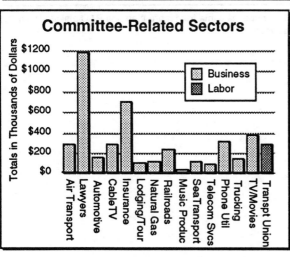

## Committee-Related Sectors

Totals in Thousands of Dollars

Business, Labor

Air Transport, Lawyers, Automotive, Cable TV, Insurance, Lodging/Tour, Natural Gas, Railroads, Music Produc, SeaTransport, Telecom Svcs, Phone Util, Trucking, TV/Movies, Transpt Union

### Leading Sectors Giving to Committee Members

#### Business

| | |
|---|---|
| Cable TV | $277,403 |
| Commercial Banks | $327,557 |
| Defense Aerospace | $295,686 |
| Health Professionals | $507,677 |
| Insurance | $690,643 |
| Lawyers & Lobbyists | $1,464,211 |
| Oil & Gas | $381,168 |
| Real Estate | $687,776 |
| Securities/Commodities Investment | $557,426 |
| Telephone Utilities | $299,595 |
| TV & Movie Production/Distribution | $363,471 |

#### Ideological/Single-Issue

| | |
|---|---|
| Pro-Israel | $580,200 |

### Leading Committee-Related Sectors Giving to Committee Members

#### Business

| | |
|---|---|
| Air transport | $270,708 |
| Attorneys & law firms | $1,179,349 |
| Automotive | $151,950 |
| Cable & satellite TV operators | $277,403 |
| Insurance | $690,643 |
| Lodging & tourism | $101,349 |
| Natural gas transmission & distribution | $114,218 |
| Railroads | $230,122 |
| Recorded music & music production | $30,150 |
| Sea transport | $103,019 |
| Telecom services & equipment | $85,842 |
| Telephone utilities | $299,595 |
| Trucking | $134,923 |
| TV & movie production/distribution | $363,471 |

#### Labor

| | |
|---|---|
| Transportation unions | $277,050 |

107

# Senate Energy and Natural Resources Committee

J. Bennett Johnston (D-La), Chairman
James A. McClure (R-Idaho), Ranking Republican

**Party Ratio:** 10 Democrats
9 Republicans

> **Jurisdiction:** Oversight and legislative responsibilities, including (1) Strategic petroleum reserves; (2) Intergovernmental Relations; (3) Outer continental shelf leasing; (4) Investigation and oversight; (5) International energy affairs; (6) Natural gas pricing and regulation; (7) Utility policy; (8) Nuclear waste and insurance programs; (9) Territorial affairs, including commonwealths; (10) Free Associated States; and (11) Antarctica.

## Subcommittees

**Energy Regulation and Conservation**
Howard M. Metzenbaum (D-Ohio), Chairman
Don Nickles (R-Okla), Ranking Republican

**Energy Research and Development**
Wendell H. Ford (D-Ky), Chairman
Pete V. Domenici (R-NM), Ranking Republican

**Mineral Resources Development and Production**
Jeff Bingaman (D-NM), Chairman
Frank H. Murkowski (R-Alaska), Ranking Republican

**Public Lands, National Parks and Forests**
Dale Bumpers (D-Ark), Chairman
Malcolm Wallop (R-Wyo), Ranking Republican

**Water and Power**
Bill Bradley (D-NJ), Chairman
Conrad Burns (R-Mont), Ranking Republican

## Total Committee-Related Contributions to Committee Members

| | Total from Cmte-Related Contribs | Pct of Member's Lg Contribs |
|---|---|---|
| *J. Bennett Johnston (D-La)* | $641,250 | 23% |
| *Mitch McConnell (R-Ky)* | $370,516 | 12% |
| *Pete V. Domenici (R-NM)* | $367,564 | 23% |
| *Howell Heflin (D-Ala)* | $261,859 | 9% |
| *John D. Rockefeller IV (D-WVa)* | $225,674 | 7% |
| *Bill Bradley (D-NJ)* | $182,589 | 3% |
| *Mark O. Hatfield (R-Ore)* | $156,807 | 9% |
| James A. McClure (R-Idaho)[1] | $81,050 | 39% |
| Kent Conrad (D-ND) | $68,700 | 18% |
| Daniel K. Akaka (D-Hawaii) | $31,876 | 2% |
| Frank H. Murkowski (R-Alaska) | $10,075 | 23% |
| Tim Wirth (D-Colo) | $9,500 | 7% |
| Dale Bumpers (D-Ark) | $7,500 | 11% |
| Conrad Burns (R-Mont) | $7,500 | 16% |
| Wendell H. Ford (D-Ky) | $4,000 | 20% |
| Don Nickles (R-Okla) | $3,250 | 10% |
| Malcolm Wallop (R-Wyo) | $2,715 | 7% |
| Jake Garn (R-Utah) | $1,500 | 3% |
| Howard M. Metzenbaum (D-Ohio) | -$20 | 0% |
| Jeff Bingaman (D-NM) | -$2,083 | 0% |

[1] Did not seek reelection in 1990

| | Top 20 Committee-Related Contributors to Committee Members in 1989-90 | |
|---|---|---|
| 1 | Union Pacific Corp | $49,999 |
| 2 | ACRE (Action Cmte/Rural Electrification)* | $47,200 |
| 3 | Atlantic Richfield | $45,900 |
| 4 | Chevron Corp | $45,000 |
| 5 | Occidental Petroleum* | $39,350 |
| 6 | Ashland Oil | $37,268 |
| 7 | Amoco Corp | $37,000 |
| 8 | Mobil Oil | $37,000 |
| 9 | Pacific Gas & Electric | $37,000 |
| 10 | General Electric | $36,450 |
| 11 | USX Corp* | $35,900 |
| 12 | Columbia Gas System* | $34,250 |
| 13 | Arkla Inc | $33,100 |
| 14 | Southern Co* | $30,500 |
| 15 | Southern California Edison | $30,400 |
| 16 | Waste Management Inc | $30,215 |
| 17 | Fluor Corp | $29,325 |
| 18 | National Coal Assn | $28,499 |
| 19 | Exxon Corp | $26,500 |
| 20 | Shell Oil | $26,000 |

\* Contributions came from more than one PAC affiliated with this sponsor.

Members in ***bold italics*** ran for reelection in 1990

## Summary

Oil & gas policies, the interstate transportation of natural gas, the ever-deepening problem of nuclear waste disposal, and a host of other energy-related issues are the primary concern of the Senate Energy and Natural Resources Committee. Its domain, and the scope of its jurisdiction, range from oilfields on the North Slope of Alaska to the ice fields of Antarctica and the oil and mineral-rich deposits beneath the seabeds of the outer continental shelf.

As the world's largest consumer of energy, and one of its largest producers, America's economic health has long been tied to the fortunes of the oil & gas industry — though the interests of the nation and the industry do not always coincide. Balancing those interests, and setting the nation's energy policy, is the charge of this committee.

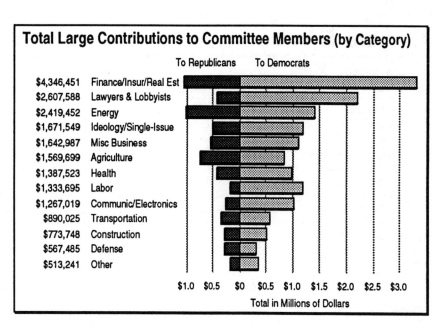

**Total Large Contributions to Committee Members (by Category)**

| | To Republicans | To Democrats |
|---|---|---|
| $4,346,451 | Finance/Insur/Real Est | |
| $2,607,588 | Lawyers & Lobbyists | |
| $2,419,452 | Energy | |
| $1,671,549 | Ideology/Single-Issue | |
| $1,642,987 | Misc Business | |
| $1,569,699 | Agriculture | |
| $1,387,523 | Health | |
| $1,333,695 | Labor | |
| $1,267,019 | Communic/Electronics | |
| $890,025 | Transportation | |
| $773,748 | Construction | |
| $567,485 | Defense | |
| $513,241 | Other | |

Total in Millions of Dollars

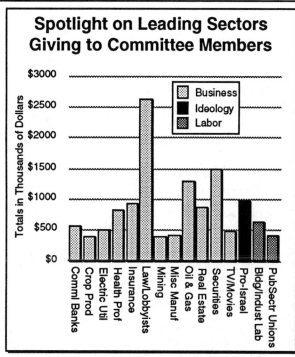

**Spotlight on Leading Sectors Giving to Committee Members**

Legend: Business, Ideology, Labor

Totals in Thousands of Dollars

Categories: Comml Banks, Crop Prod, Electric Util, Health Prof, Insurance, Law/Lobbyists, Mining, Misc Manuf, Oil & Gas, Real Estate, Securities, TV/Movies, Pro-Israel, Bldg/Indust Lab, PubSectr Unions

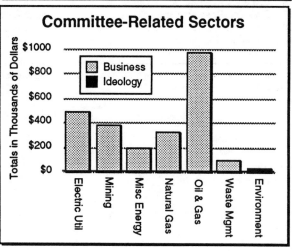

**Committee-Related Sectors**

Legend: Business, Ideology

Totals in Thousands of Dollars

Categories: Electric Util, Mining, Misc Energy, Natural Gas, Oil & Gas, Waste Mgmt, Environment

### Leading Sectors Giving to Committee Members

**Business**

| | |
|---|---|
| Commercial Banks | $541,710 |
| Crop Production & Basic Processing | $371,177 |
| Electric Utilities | $494,500 |
| Health Professionals | $813,596 |
| Insurance | $906,292 |
| Lawyers & Lobbyists | $2,607,588 |
| Mining | $373,649 |
| Misc Manufacturing & Distributing | $390,114 |
| Oil & Gas | $1,282,541 |
| Real Estate | $841,044 |
| Securities/Commodities Investment | $1,475,476 |
| TV & Movie Production/Distribution | $460,836 |

**Ideological/Single-Issue**

| | |
|---|---|
| Pro-Israel | $949,672 |

**Labor**

| | |
|---|---|
| Bldg Trades/Industrial/Misc Unions | $605,268 |
| Public Sector Unions | $399,927 |

### Leading Committee-Related Sectors Giving to Committee Members

**Business**

| | |
|---|---|
| Electric utilities | $479,350 |
| Mining | $373,649 |
| Misc energy | $186,273 |
| Natural gas transmission & distribution | $320,048 |
| Oil & gas production & marketing | $962,493 |
| Waste management | $86,939 |

**Ideological/Single-Issue**

| | |
|---|---|
| Environmental policy | $25,173 |

# Senate Environment and Public Works Committee

Quentin N. Burdick (D-ND), Chairman
John H. Chafee (R-RI), Ranking Republican

**Party Ratio:** 9 Democrats
7 Republicans

**Jurisdiction:** (1) Environmental policy; (2) Environmental research and development; (3) Ocean dumping; (4) Fisheries and wildlife; (5) Environmental aspects of Outer Continental Shelf lands; (6) Solid waste disposal and recycling; (7) Environmental effects of toxic substances, other than pesticides; (8) Water resources; (9) Flood control and improvements of rivers and harbors, including environmental aspects of deepwater ports; (10) Public works, bridges, and dams; (11) Water pollution; (12) Air pollution; (13) Noise pollution; (14) Nonmilitary environmental regulation and control of nuclear energy; (15) Regional economic development; (16) Construction and maintenance of highways; (17) Public buildings and improved grounds of the United States generally, including Federal buildings in the District of Columbia. In addition, the committee is mandated to study and review matters relating to environmental protection, resource utilization and conservation, and to report on these matters periodically.

## Subcommittees

**Environmental Protection**
Max Baucus (D-Mont), Chairman
John H. Chafee (R-RI), Ranking Republican

**Nuclear Regulation**
John B. Breaux (D-La), Chairman
Alan K. Simpson (R-Wyo), Ranking Republican

**Superfund, Ocean and Water Protection**
Frank Lautenberg (D-NJ), Chairman
Dave Durenberger (R-Minn), Ranking Republican

**Toxic Substances, Environmental Oversight, Research and Development**
Harry Reid (D-Nev), Chairman
John W. Warner (R-Va), Ranking Republican

**Water Resources, Transportation, and Infrastructure**
Daniel Patrick Moynihan (D-NY), Chairman
Steve Symms (R-Idaho), Ranking Republican

## Total Committee-Related Contributions to Committee Members

| | Total from Cmte-Related Contribs | Pct of Member's Lg Contribs |
|---|---|---|
| *Alan K. Simpson (R-Wyo)* | $282,481 | 28% |
| *John W. Warner (R-Va)* | $250,125 | 17% |
| *Max Baucus (D-Mont)* | $240,682 | 11% |
| Steve Symms (R-Idaho) | $64,600 | 23% |
| Bob Graham (D-Fla) | $44,600 | 15% |
| Frank Lautenberg (D-NJ) | $34,738 | 16% |
| Dave Durenberger (R-Minn) | $32,963 | 22% |
| Harry Reid (D-Nev) | $26,817 | 20% |
| John B. Breaux (D-La) | $26,500 | 26% |
| Joseph Lieberman I. (D-Conn) | $7,754 | 7% |
| John H. Chafee (R-RI) | $3,724 | 18% |
| James M. Jeffords (R-Vt) | $2,000 | 67% |
| Daniel Patrick Moynihan (D-NY) | $1,700 | 28% |
| Quentin N. Burdick (D-ND) | $1,000 | 400% |
| George J. Mitchell (D-Maine) | $500 | 4% |
| Howard M. Metzenbaum (D-Ohio) | $0 | 0% |
| Gordon J. Humphrey (R-NH)[1] | $0 | 0% |

---

[1] Did not seek reelection in 1990

| | Top 20 Committee-Related Contributors to Committee Members in 1989-90 | |
|---|---|---|
| 1 | Fluor Corp | $27,125 |
| 2 | Waste Management Inc | $26,457 |
| 3 | Auto Dealers & Drivers for Free Trade | $23,000 |
| 4 | Teamsters Union* | $22,700 |
| 5 | National Auto Dealers Assn | $20,000 |
| 6 | Marine Engineers Union* | $17,000 |
| 7 | ACRE (Action Cmte/Rural Electrification) | $14,000 |
| 8 | National Utility Contractors Assn | $14,000 |
| 9 | Browning-Ferris Industries | $13,799 |
| 10 | United Transportation Union | $13,500 |
| 11 | Amoco Corp | $13,000 |
| 12 | Joseph E Seagram & Sons | $13,000 |
| 13 | Mobil Oil | $13,000 |
| 14 | American Trucking Assns | $12,317 |
| 15 | Consolidated Freightways | $12,000 |
| 16 | Seafarers International Union | $12,000 |
| 17 | Dominion Resources Inc | $11,000 |
| 18 | FMC Corp | $11,000 |
| 19 | Occidental Petroleum* | $10,500 |
| 20 | Columbia Gas System* | $10,250 |

\* Contributions came from more than one PAC affiliated with this sponsor.

Members in ***bold italics*** ran for reelection in 1990

# Summary

"Infrastructure" is not a glamorous word or a particularly inspiring political cause, but it is crucial to the health of the nation. The building and maintenance of the nation's highways, waterways and other public facilities is a central concern of this committee — and of many of the industries that supply campaign dollars to committee members.

But there is another side to development, one that often *does* inspire political action — the effect that our modern industrial infrastructure has on the environment of the planet. That too is a major preoccupation of this committee. Often, these dual responsibilities come together in a single issue, as in the continuing debate over nuclear power. Environmental groups, which showed more of a financial presence in the 1988 elections, gave very little to committee members in 1990 — though that was likely reflective of the fact that only three committee members had reelection races, and two of them were conservative Republicans.

## Total Large Contributions to Committee Members (by Category)

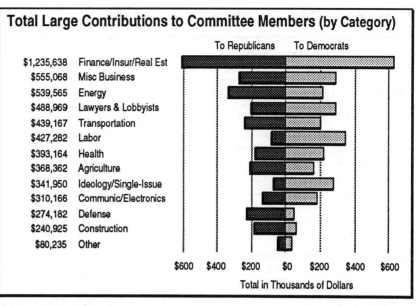

| | To Republicans | To Democrats |
| --- | --- | --- |
| $1,235,638 | Finance/Insur/Real Est | |
| $555,068 | Misc Business | |
| $539,565 | Energy | |
| $488,969 | Lawyers & Lobbyists | |
| $439,167 | Transportation | |
| $427,282 | Labor | |
| $393,164 | Health | |
| $368,362 | Agriculture | |
| $341,950 | Ideology/Single-Issue | |
| $310,166 | Communic/Electronics | |
| $274,182 | Defense | |
| $240,925 | Construction | |
| $80,235 | Other | |

Total in Thousands of Dollars

## Spotlight on Leading Sectors Giving to Committee Members

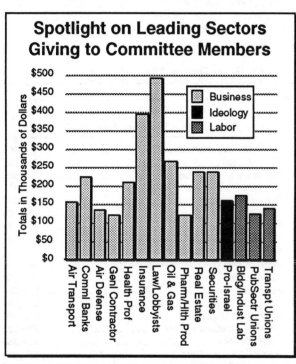

## Committee-Related Sectors

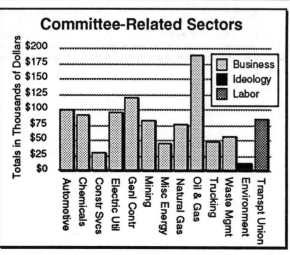

## Leading Sectors Giving to Committee Members

### Business

| | |
| --- | --- |
| Air Transport | $153,200 |
| Commercial Banks | $221,340 |
| Defense Aerospace | $130,682 |
| General Contractors | $118,075 |
| Health Professionals | $206,531 |
| Insurance | $393,147 |
| Lawyers & Lobbyists | $488,969 |
| Oil & Gas | $262,578 |
| Pharmaceuticals/Health Products | $115,933 |
| Real Estate | $236,425 |
| Securities/Commodities Investment | $233,101 |

### Ideological/Single-Issue

| | |
| --- | --- |
| Pro-Israel | $155,516 |

### Labor

| | |
| --- | --- |
| Bldg Trades/Industrial/Misc Unions | $170,982 |
| Public Sector Unions | $120,150 |
| Transportation Unions | $136,150 |

## Leading Committee-Related Sectors Giving to Committee Members

### Business

| | |
| --- | --- |
| Automotive | $99,350 |
| Chemical & related manufacturing | $90,000 |
| Construction services | $28,600 |
| Electric power utilities | $92,700 |
| General contractors | $118,075 |
| Mining | $80,200 |
| Misc energy | $44,081 |
| Natural gas transmission & distribution | $74,936 |
| Oil & gas production & marketing | $187,642 |
| Trucking | $46,167 |
| Waste management | $54,506 |

### Labor

| | |
| --- | --- |
| Transportation unions | $81,950 |

### Ideological/Single-Issue

| | |
| --- | --- |
| Environmental policy | $10,977 |

# Senate Finance Committee

Lloyd Bentsen (D-Texas), Chairman
Bob Packwood (R-Ore), Ranking Republican

**Party Ratio:** 11 Democrats
9 Republicans

> **Jurisdiction:** (1) Except as provided in the Congressional Budget Act of 1974, revenue measures generally; (2) Except as provided in the Congressional Budget Act of 1974, the bonded debt of the United States; (3) The deposit of public moneys; (4) Customs, collection districts, and ports of entry and delivery; (5) Reciprocal trade agreements; (6) Transportation of dutiable goods; (7) Revenue measures relating to the insular possessions; (8) Tariffs and import quotas, and matters related thereto; (9) National social security; (10) General revenue sharing; (11) Health programs under the Social Security Act and health programs financed by a specific tax or trust fund.

## Subcommittees

**Energy and Agricultural Taxation**
David L. Boren (D-Okla), Chairman
William L. Armstrong (R-Colo), Ranking Republican

**Health for Families and the Uninsured**
Donald W. Riegle Jr. (D-Mich), Chairman
John H. Chafee (R-RI), Ranking Republican

**International Debt**
Bill Bradley (D-NJ), Chairman
Bob Dole (R-Kan), Ranking Republican

**International Trade**
Max Baucus (D-Mont), Chairman
John C. Danforth (R-Mo), Ranking Republican

**Medicare and Long-Term Care**
John D. Rockefeller IV (D-WVa), Chairman
Dave Durenberger (R-Minn), Ranking Republican

**Private Retirement Plans and Oversight of the Internal Revenue Service**
David Pryor (D-Ark), Chairman
John Heinz (R-Pa), Ranking Republican

**Social Security and Family Policy**
Daniel Patrick Moynihan (D-NY), Chairman
Bob Dole (R-Kan), Ranking Republican

**Taxation and Debt Management**
Spark M. Matsunaga (D-Hawaii), Chairman
William V. Roth Jr. (R-Del), Ranking Republican

## Total PAC & Large Individual Contributions to Committee Members

*Bill Bradley (D-NJ)* .............................................. $6,684,141
*John D. Rockefeller IV (D-WVa)* ..................... $3,027,432
*Max Baucus (D-Mont)* ...................................... $2,193,526
*David Pryor (D-Ark)* .......................................... $1,048,118
*David L. Boren (D-Okla)* ................................... $1,039,939
Tom Daschle (D-SD) ............................................ $341,304
Bob Dole (R-Kan) ................................................. $304,050
Steve Symms (R-Idaho) ....................................... $278,228
Dave Durenberger (R-Minn) ................................ $147,801
John B. Breaux (D-La) .......................................... $102,350
Lloyd Bentsen (D-Texas) ....................................... $35,480
John Heinz (R-Pa) .................................................. $23,550
John H. Chafee (R-RI) ............................................ $21,174
John C. Danforth (R-Mo) ........................................ $19,850
William V. Roth Jr. (R-Del) ...................................... $13,080
George J. Mitchell (D-Maine) ................................. $13,000
Daniel Patrick Moynihan (D-NY) ............................. $6,094
Bob Packwood (R-Ore) ............................................ $3,876
Donald W. Riegle Jr. (D-Mich) ..................................... $291
William L. Armstrong (R-Colo)[1] ..................................... $0
Spark M. Matsunaga (D-Hawaii)[2] .......................... -$2,000

[1] Did not seek reelection in 1990
[2] Died Apr 15, 1990

| # | Top 20 Contributors to Committee Members in 1989-90 | |
|---|---|---|
| 1 | American Express* | $102,590 |
| 2 | Time Warner | $93,525 |
| 3 | Goldman, Sachs & Co | $77,900 |
| 4 | Prudential Insurance* | $67,876 |
| 5 | Salomon Brothers | $67,550 |
| 6 | Bear Stearns & Co | $57,225 |
| 7 | Walt Disney Co | $55,115 |
| 8 | Skadden, Arps et al | $54,900 |
| 9 | Willkie, Farr & Gallagher | $52,000 |
| 10 | Assn of Trial Lawyers of America | $44,000 |
| 11 | Merrill Lynch | $42,550 |
| 12 | Morgan Stanley & Co | $41,675 |
| 13 | Operating Engineers Union* | $41,200 |
| 14 | Teamsters Union* | $40,700 |
| 15 | American Institute of CPA's | $39,500 |
| 16 | Smith Barney | $39,350 |
| 17 | Federal Express Corp | $39,242 |
| 18 | American Council of Life Insurance | $39,000 |
| 19 | National Assn of Letter Carriers | $36,500 |
| 20 | American Hospital Assn* | $36,000 |

* Contributions came from more than one PAC affiliated with this sponsor.

Members in **bold italics** ran for reelection in 1990

## Summary

The contributions going to members of the Senate Finance Committee were more heavily skewed to Democratic candidates than any other committee in Congress in 1990. This was not reflective of the committee's jurisdiction, however, but rather of the fact that five committee Democrats (and no Republicans) waged reelection campaigns that year. Leading the list was Bill Bradley of New Jersey, who was far and away Congress's leading recipient of campaign dollars from lawyers and the securities industry. That fact can be seen clearly in the sector chart below.

Quite apart from the reelection campaigns of its Democratic members, this committee is one of the most important in Congress to virtually every business interest in the nation. Along with the House Ways and Means Committee, this is the panel that debates and defines the nation's tax laws. As such, it is the scene of some of the most intensive lobbying on Capitol Hill whenever tax changes are being considered.

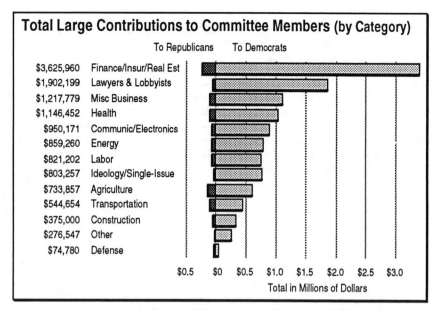

**Total Large Contributions to Committee Members (by Category)**

To Republicans    To Democrats

| | |
|---|---|
| $3,625,960 | Finance/Insur/Real Est |
| $1,902,199 | Lawyers & Lobbyists |
| $1,217,779 | Misc Business |
| $1,146,452 | Health |
| $950,171 | Communic/Electronics |
| $859,260 | Energy |
| $821,202 | Labor |
| $803,257 | Ideology/Single-Issue |
| $733,857 | Agriculture |
| $544,654 | Transportation |
| $375,000 | Construction |
| $276,547 | Other |
| $74,780 | Defense |

Total in Millions of Dollars

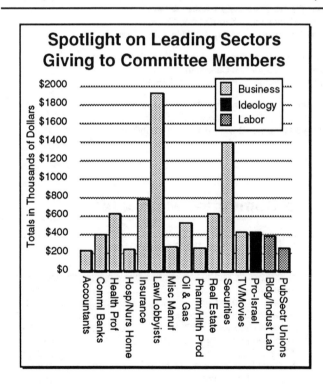

**Spotlight on Leading Sectors Giving to Committee Members**

Business
Ideology
Labor

Totals in Thousands of Dollars

Accountants, Comml Banks, Health Prof, Hosp/Nurs Home, Insurance, Law/Lobbyists, Misc Manuf, Oil & Gas, Pharm/Hlth Prod, Real Estate, Securities, TV/Movies, Pro-Israel, Bldg/Indust Lab, PubSectr Unions

**Leading Sectors
Giving to Committee Members**

### Business

| | |
|---|---|
| Accountants | $214,160 |
| Commercial Banks | $385,938 |
| Health Professionals | $615,642 |
| Hospitals/Nursing Homes | $228,867 |
| Insurance | $764,291 |
| Lawyers & Lobbyists | $1,902,199 |
| Misc Manufacturing & Distributing | $256,514 |
| Oil & Gas | $516,330 |
| Pharmaceuticals/Health Products | $234,693 |
| Real Estate | $614,133 |
| Securities/Commodities Investment | $1,375,554 |
| TV & Movie Production/Distribution | $405,976 |

### Ideological/Single-Issue

| | |
|---|---|
| Pro-Israel | $415,184 |

### Labor

| | |
|---|---|
| Bldg Trades/Industrial/Misc Unions | $370,752 |
| Public Sector Unions | $241,800 |

113

# Senate Foreign Relations Committee

Claiborne Pell (D-RI), Chairman
Jesse Helms (R-NC), Ranking Republican

**Party Ratio:** 10 Democrats
9 Republicans

**Jurisdiction:** (1) Relations of the United States with foreign nations generally; (2) Treaties and executive agreements, except reciprocal trade agreements; (3) Boundaries of the United States; (4) Protection of United States citizens abroad and expatriation; (5) Intervention abroad and declarations of war; (6) Foreign economic, military, technical, and humanitarian assistance;(7) United Nations and its affiliated organizations; (8) International conferences and congresses; (9) Diplomatic service; (10) International law as it relates to foreign policy; (11) Oceans and international environmental and scientific affairs as they relate to foreign policy; (12) International activities of the American National Red Cross and the International Committee of the Red Cross; (13) International aspects of nuclear energy, including nuclear transfer policy; (14) Foreign loans; (15) Measures to foster commercial intercourse with foreign nations and to safeguard American business interests abroad; (16) The World Bank group, the regional development banks, and other international organizations established primarily for development assistance purposes; (17) The International Monetary Fund and other international organizations established primarily for international monetary purposes (except that, at the request of the Committee on Banking, Housing, and Urban Affairs, any proposed legislation relating to such subjects reported by the Committee on Foreign Relations shall be referred to the Committee on Banking, Housing, and Urban Affairs); (18) Acquisition of land and buildings for embassies and legations in foreign countries; (19) National security and international aspects of trusteeships of the United States. In addition, the committee is mandated to study and review matters relating to the national security policy, foreign policy, and international economic policy as it relates to foreign policy of the U.S., and matters relating to food, hunger, and nutrition in foreign countries, and to report on these matters periodically.

## Subcommittees

**African Affairs**
Paul Simon (D-Ill), Chairman
Nancy Landon Kassebaum (R-Kan), Ranking Republican

**East Asian and Pacific Affairs**
Alan Cranston (D-Calif), Chairman
Frank H. Murkowski (R-Alaska), Ranking Republican

**European Affairs**
Joseph R. Biden Jr. (D-Del), Chairman
Larry Pressler (R-SD), Ranking Republican

**International Economic Policy, Trade, Oceans and Environment**
Paul S. Sarbanes (D-Md), Chairman
Gordon J. Humphrey (R-NH), Ranking Republican

**Near Eastern and South Asian Affairs**
Daniel Patrick Moynihan (D-NY), Chairman
Rudy Boschwitz (R-Minn), Ranking Republican

**Terrorism, Narcotics and International Operations**
John Kerry (D-Mass), Chairman
Mitch McConnell (R-Ky), Ranking Republican

**Western Hemisphere and Peace Corps Affairs**
Christopher J. Dodd (D-Conn), Chairman
Richard G. Lugar (R-Ind), Ranking Republican

## Total PAC & Large Individual Contributions to Committee Members

*Paul Simon (D-Ill)* .................................................$4,473,338
*John Kerry (D-Mass)* ...........................................$3,626,799
*Jesse Helms (R-NC)* ............................................$3,442,351
*Mitch McConnell (R-Ky)* ......................................$3,057,489
*Claiborne Pell (D-RI)* ..........................................$1,823,207
*Larry Pressler (R-SD)* ..........................................$1,609,209
*Joseph R. Biden Jr. (D-Del)* ................................$1,456,158
*Rudy Boschwitz (R-Minn)* ....................................$1,298,047
*Nancy Landon Kassebaum (R-Kan)* ....................$346,087
Terry Sanford (D-NC) ............................................$264,550
Connie Mack (R-Fla) ..............................................$218,100
Alan Cranston (D-Calif) .........................................$203,440
Christopher J. Dodd (D-Conn) ..............................$157,261
Richard G. Lugar (R-Ind) .......................................$49,900
Frank H. Murkowski (R-Alaska) .............................$43,715
Charles S. Robb (D-Va) .........................................$24,300
Daniel Patrick Moynihan (D-NY) ...........................$6,094
Gordon J. Humphrey (R-NH)[1] .............................$1,000
Paul S. Sarbanes (D-Md) .......................................$0

---

[1] Did not seek reelection in 1990

Members in **bold italics** ran for reelection in 1990

| Top 20 Contributors to Committee Members in 1989-90 | |
|---|---|
| 1  Time Warner | $78,650 |
| 2  Federal Express Corp | $65,833 |
| 3  American Bankers Assn* | $63,000 |
| 4  Citizens Organized PAC | $60,000 |
| 5  American Family Corp | $58,000 |
| 6  AT&T | $56,000 |
| 7  National Beer Wholesalers Assn | $54,750 |
| 8  American Institute of CPA's | $54,375 |
| 9  Delaware Valley PAC | $50,000 |
| 10  Auto Dealers & Drivers for Free Trade | $49,500 |
| 11  Desert Caucus | $49,000 |
| 12  Waste Management Inc | $48,000 |
| 13  American Medical Assn* | $47,650 |
| 14  National PAC | $47,000 |
| 15  National Assn of Home Builders* | $47,000 |
| 16  Washington PAC | $46,500 |
| 17  Chicago Mercantile Exchange | $46,050 |
| 18  National Assn of Life Underwriters | $46,000 |
| 19  Walt Disney Co | $44,169 |
| 20  Chicago Board of Trade | $43,361 |

\* Contributions came from more than one PAC affiliated with this sponsor.

## Summary

The Senate Foreign Relations Committee may be the one committee in Congress that is more important to the world at large than to the community of PACs and other high-level contributors here at home. Since foreign nationals and their governments are prohibited from making direct contributions to U.S. candidates, they must find other means to make their voices heard when the committee debates such issues as the level and focus of American foreign aid.

Many lobbyists in Washington *are* engaged by foreign governments and corporations, however. That could be one reason that lawyers and lobbyists were the largest sector giving to committee members in 1990. Pro-Israel groups are another major source of campaign funds. Six members of the committee — Paul Simon, Claiborne Pell, Mitch McConnell, Larry Pressler, John Kerry and Rudy Boschwitz — each drew $100,000 or more from pro-Israel contributors. (Joseph Biden collected $99,900). Leading the list of pro-Israel recipients was Paul Simon, with $453,000.

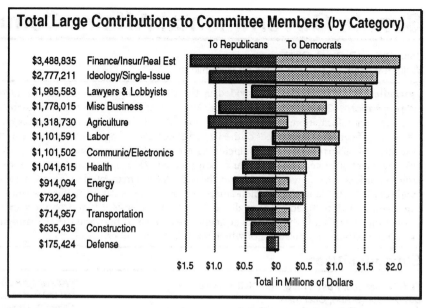

**Total Large Contributions to Committee Members (by Category)**

| | To Republicans | To Democrats |
| --- | --- | --- |
| $3,488,835 | Finance/Insur/Real Est | |
| $2,777,211 | Ideology/Single-Issue | |
| $1,985,583 | Lawyers & Lobbyists | |
| $1,778,015 | Misc Business | |
| $1,318,730 | Agriculture | |
| $1,101,591 | Labor | |
| $1,101,502 | Communic/Electronics | |
| $1,041,615 | Health | |
| $914,094 | Energy | |
| $732,482 | Other | |
| $714,957 | Transportation | |
| $635,435 | Construction | |
| $175,424 | Defense | |

$1.5  $1.0  $0.5  $0  $0.5  $1.0  $1.5  $2.0
Total in Millions of Dollars

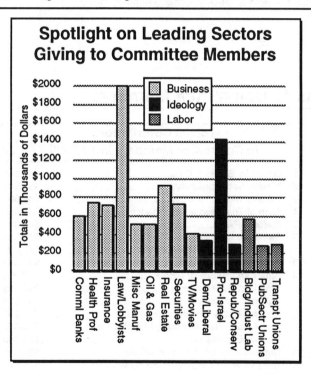

## Spotlight on Leading Sectors Giving to Committee Members

Totals in Thousands of Dollars

Legend: Business, Ideology, Labor

Categories: Comml Banks, Health Prof, Insurance, Law/Lobbyists, Misc Manuf, Oil & Gas, Real Estate, Securities, TV/Movies, Dem/Liberal, Pro-Israel, Repub/Conserv, Bldg/Indust Lab, PubSectr Unions, Transpt Unions

### Leading Sectors Giving to Committee Members

**Business**

| | |
| --- | --- |
| Commercial Banks | $579,662 |
| Health Professionals | $722,515 |
| Insurance | $695,958 |
| Lawyers & Lobbyists | $1,985,583 |
| Misc Manufacturing & Distributing | $500,782 |
| Oil & Gas | $496,790 |
| Real Estate | $902,370 |
| Securities/Commodities Investment | $714,376 |
| TV & Movie Production/Distribution | $387,976 |

**Ideological/Single-Issue**

| | |
| --- | --- |
| Democratic/Liberal | $320,684 |
| Pro-Israel | $1,405,733 |
| Republican/Conservative | $286,578 |

**Labor**

| | |
| --- | --- |
| Bldg Trades/Industrial/Misc Unions | $557,549 |
| Public Sector Unions | $268,750 |
| Transportation Unions | $275,292 |

# Senate Governmental Affairs Committee

John Glenn (D-Ohio), Chairman
William V. Roth Jr. (R-Del), Ranking Republican

**Party Ratio:** 8 Democrats
6 Republicans

**Jurisdiction:** (1) Except as provided in the Congressional Budget Act of 1974, budget and accounting measures, other than appropriations; (2) Organization and reorganization of the executive branch of the Government; (3) Intergovernmental relations; (4) Government information; (5) Municipal affairs of the District of Columbia, except appropriations therefor; (6) Federal Civil Service; (7) Status of officers and employees of the United States, including their classification, compensation, and benefits; (8) Postal Service; (9) Census and collection of statistics, including economic and social statistics; (10) Archives of the United States; (11) Organization and management of United States nuclear export policy; (12) Congressional organization, except for any part of the matter that amends the rules or orders of the Senate. In addition, the committee is mandated to (a) receive and examine reports of the U.S. Comptroller General and submit to the Senate recommendations relating thereto; (b) study the efficiency, economy, and effectiveness of the Government's agencies and departments; (c) evaluate the effects of laws enacted to reorganize the legislative and executive branches of the Government; (d) study the intergovernmental relationships between the U.S. and the states and municipalities, and between the U.S. and international organizations of which the U.S. is a member.

## Subcommittees

**Federal Service, Post Office, and Civil Service**
David Pryor (D-Ark), Chairman
Ted Stevens (R-Alaska), Ranking Republican

**General Service, Federalism, and the District of Columbia**
Jim Sasser (D-Tenn), Chairman
John Heinz (R-Pa), Ranking Republican

**Government Information and Regulation**
Jeff Bingaman (D-NM), Chairman
Warren B. Rudman (R-NH), Ranking Republican

**Oversight of Government Management**
Carl Levin (D-Mich), Chairman
William S. Cohen (R-Maine), Ranking Republican

**Permanent Subcommittee on Investigations**
Sam Nunn (D-Ga), Chairman
William V. Roth Jr. (R-Del), Ranking Republican

## Total PAC & Large Individual Contributions to Committee Members

*Carl Levin (D-Mich)* .......................................$4,281,016
*Sam Nunn (D-Ga)* ...........................................$1,694,369
*Daniel K. Akaka (D-Hawaii)* ..........................$1,450,054
*Ted Stevens (R-Alaska)* ..................................$1,167,034
*William S. Cohen (R-Maine)* ..........................$1,082,039
*David Pryor (D-Ark)* .......................................$1,048,118
Joseph Lieberman I. (D-Conn) .........................$108,920
Pete Wilson (R-Calif) ..........................................$84,871
John Glenn (D-Ohio) ...........................................$49,200
John Heinz (R-Pa) ...............................................$23,550
Jim Sasser (D-Tenn) ...........................................$16,326
William V. Roth Jr. (R-Del) ..................................$13,080
Warren B. Rudman (R-NH) .....................................$5,000
Herb Kohl (D-Wis) .....................................................$0

| Top 20 Contributors to Committee Members in 1989-90 | | |
|---|---|---|
| 1 | Goldman, Sachs & Co | $59,350 |
| 2 | Warner Communications | $52,500 |
| 3 | General Motors* | $46,500 |
| 4 | Assn of Trial Lawyers of America | $46,000 |
| 5 | National PAC | $45,000 |
| 6 | Seafarers International Union* | $43,000 |
| 7 | National Assn of Letter Carriers | $42,000 |
| 8 | National Assn of Realtors | $41,550 |
| 9 | American Institute of CPA's | $40,625 |
| 10 | American Bankers Assn | $40,500 |
| 11 | Salomon Brothers | $40,500 |
| 12 | National Cable Television Assn | $40,249 |
| 13 | Natl Assn of Retired Federal Employees | $40,000 |
| 14 | Federal Express Corp | $39,500 |
| 15 | National Assn of Life Underwriters | $38,500 |
| 16 | National Rural Letter Carriers Assn | $38,500 |
| 17 | AT&T | $38,000 |
| 18 | Air Line Pilots Assn | $37,500 |
| 19 | American Postal Workers Union | $36,500 |
| 20 | Marine Engineers Union* | $35,500 |

\* Contributions came from more than one PAC affiliated with this sponsor.

Members in ***bold italics*** ran for reelection in 1990

## Summary

Other committees of Congress have more direct relevance to particular industries or interest groups than Senate Governmental Affairs, which focuses more on the government itself. The federal civil service and postal system do fall within its purview, as does reorganization of executive branch agencies. Affairs relating to the District of Columbia are also debated here.

The breakdown of contributions by industry and sector among Government Affairs members is more likely affected by the members' other committee assignments than by work specifically done on this committee.

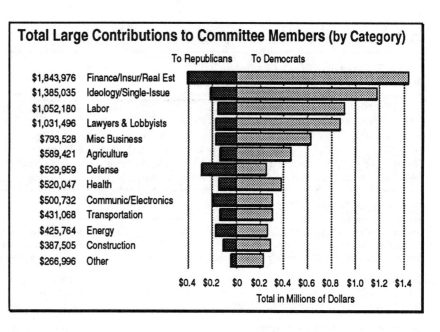

### Total Large Contributions to Committee Members (by Category)

| | |
|---|---|
| $1,843,976 | Finance/Insur/Real Est |
| $1,385,035 | Ideology/Single-Issue |
| $1,052,180 | Labor |
| $1,031,496 | Lawyers & Lobbyists |
| $793,528 | Misc Business |
| $589,421 | Agriculture |
| $529,959 | Defense |
| $520,047 | Health |
| $500,732 | Communic/Electronics |
| $431,068 | Transportation |
| $425,764 | Energy |
| $387,505 | Construction |
| $266,996 | Other |

Total in Millions of Dollars

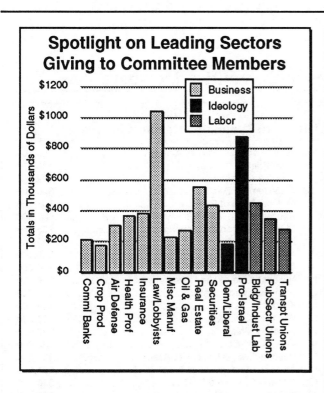

## Spotlight on Leading Sectors Giving to Committee Members

Totals in Thousands of Dollars

Business / Ideology / Labor

Comml Banks, Crop Prod, Air Defense, Health Prof, Insurance, Law/Lobbyists, Misc Manuf, Oil & Gas, Real Estate, Securities, Dem/Liberal, Pro-Israel, Bldg/Indust Lab, PubSectr Unions, Transpt Unions

### Leading Sectors Giving to Committee Members

#### Business

| | |
|---|---|
| Commercial Banks | $204,935 |
| Crop Production & Basic Processing | $169,491 |
| Defense Aerospace | $293,925 |
| Health Professionals | $360,302 |
| Insurance | $372,801 |
| Lawyers & Lobbyists | $1,031,496 |
| Misc Manufacturing & Distributing | $223,838 |
| Oil & Gas | $265,794 |
| Real Estate | $544,475 |
| Securities/Commodities Investment | $426,340 |

#### Ideological/Single-Issue

| | |
|---|---|
| Democratic/Liberal | $177,880 |
| Pro-Israel | $869,164 |

#### Labor

| | |
|---|---|
| Bldg Trades/Industrial/Misc Unions | $441,640 |
| Public Sector Unions | $335,640 |
| Transportation Unions | $274,900 |

# Senate Judiciary Committee

Joseph R. Biden Jr. (D-Del), Chairman
Strom Thurmond (R-SC), Ranking Republican

**Party Ratio:** 8 Democrats
6 Republicans

> **Jurisdiction:** All areas not delegated to the subcommittees, including but not limited to: (1) Nominations; (2) Holidays, commemorations, Federal charters and celebrations; (3) Department of Justice oversight, authorization and budget; (4) Revision and codification of the statutes of the United States; (5) Criminal justice, including (a) criminal laws, (b) criminal judicial proceedings, (c) Rules of Criminal Procedure, (d) national penitentiaries, (e) Bureau of Prisons, (f) U.S. Parole Commission, (g) oversight of the Criminal Division of the U.S. Department of Justice, (h) juvenile justice, (i) Youthful Offenders Act, (j) oversight of the Office of Justice Programs. (Excluded from (5) above is criminal legislation delegated to the Subcommittee on the Constitution.)

## Subcommittees

**Antitrust, Monopolies and Business Rights**
Howard M. Metzenbaum (D-Ohio), Chairman
Strom Thurmond (R-SC), Ranking Republican

**Constitution**
Paul Simon (D-Ill), Chairman
Arlen Specter (R-Pa), Ranking Republican

**Courts and Administrative Practice**
Howell Heflin (D-Ala), Chairman
Charles E. Grassley (R-Iowa), Ranking Republican

**Immigration and Refugee Affairs**
Edward M. Kennedy (D-Mass), Chairman
Alan K. Simpson (R-Wyo), Ranking Republican

**Patents, Copyrights and Trademarks**
Dennis DeConcini (D-Ariz), Chairman
Orrin G. Hatch (R-Utah), Ranking Republican

**Technology and the Law**
Patrick J. Leahy (D-Vt), Chairman
Gordon J. Humphrey (R-NH), Ranking Republican

## Total PAC & Large Individual Contributions to Committee Members

*Paul Simon (D-Ill)* ............................................. $4,473,338
*Howell Heflin (D-Ala)* ......................................... $2,794,792
*Joseph R. Biden Jr. (D-Del)* ................................. $1,456,158
*Strom Thurmond (R-SC)* ..................................... $1,188,675
*Alan K. Simpson (R-Wyo)* ................................... $1,012,602
Arlen Specter (R-Pa) ............................................. $473,110
Dennis DeConcini (D-Ariz) ..................................... $121,841
Patrick J. Leahy (D-Vt) ............................................ $58,125
Charles E. Grassley (R-Iowa) ................................... $57,254
Orrin G. Hatch (R-Utah) ........................................... $26,051
Gordon J. Humphrey (R-NH)[1] .................................. $1,000
Herb Kohl (D-Wis) ........................................................... $0
Howard M. Metzenbaum (D-Ohio) ................................... -$20
Edward M. Kennedy (D-Mass) ............................... -$4,850

[1] Did not seek reelection in 1990

| | Top 20 Contributors to Committee Members in 1989-90 | |
|---|---|---|
| 1 | Assn of Trial Lawyers of America | $55,500 |
| 2 | Time Warner | $46,950 |
| 3 | American Institute of CPA's | $42,000 |
| 4 | American Bankers Assn | $40,000 |
| 5 | National Assn of Realtors | $38,125 |
| 6 | National Cable Television Assn | $37,000 |
| 7 | Chicago Mercantile Exchange | $35,550 |
| 8 | AT&T | $35,500 |
| 9 | Air Line Pilots Assn | $35,000 |
| 10 | Chicago Board of Trade | $34,950 |
| 11 | National Assn of Life Underwriters | $34,500 |
| 12 | American Medical Assn* | $33,750 |
| 13 | KidsPAC | $33,000 |
| 14 | West Publishing | $33,000 |
| 15 | Laborers Union* | $32,950 |
| 16 | JMB Realty Corp | $32,600 |
| 17 | National Beer Wholesalers Assn | $32,250 |
| 18 | American Federation of Teachers | $31,000 |
| 19 | Citizens Organized PAC | $30,000 |
| 20 | National Assn of Letter Carriers | $30,000 |

\* Contributions came from more than one PAC affiliated with this sponsor.

Members in **_bold italics_** ran for reelection in 1990

## Summary

Though it is most known to the public for its sometimes dramatic hearings on the confirmation of presidential appointments to the Supreme Court, cabinet positions and other top government posts, the Senate Judiciary Committee is also important to a wide range of businesses and industries — none more so than lawyers. From the criminal justice system to antitrust legislation to copyright and patent law, to new areas of the law arising from the birth of new high-tech industries, the committee plays a major role in defining the system of laws that governs the nation. Its jurisdiction over immigration matters also has important repercussions to those segments of the business community that rely on immigrant labor.

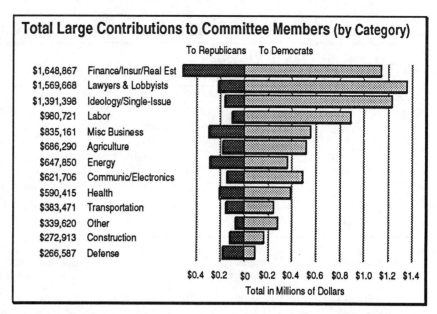

**Total Large Contributions to Committee Members (by Category)**

| | |
|---|---|
| $1,648,867 | Finance/Insur/Real Est |
| $1,569,668 | Lawyers & Lobbyists |
| $1,391,398 | Ideology/Single-Issue |
| $980,721 | Labor |
| $835,161 | Misc Business |
| $686,290 | Agriculture |
| $647,850 | Energy |
| $621,706 | Communic/Electronics |
| $590,415 | Health |
| $383,471 | Transportation |
| $339,620 | Other |
| $272,913 | Construction |
| $266,587 | Defense |

Total in Millions of Dollars

Lawyers and lobbyists were by far the leading sector contributing to committee members in 1989-90, as seen in the chart below. The extent of their giving may have been well known to committee members (and to lawyers), but was largely invisible to the public, since three-quarters of the dollars came not from political action committees but from individual contributions from attorneys, lobbyists and their families.

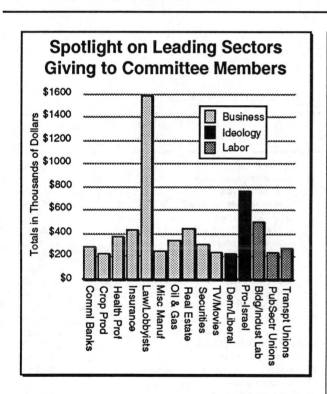

**Spotlight on Leading Sectors Giving to Committee Members**

Legend: Business, Ideology, Labor

### Leading Sectors Giving to Committee Members

**Business**

| | |
|---|---|
| Commercial Banks | $267,895 |
| Crop Production & Basic Processing | $213,711 |
| Health Professionals | $357,039 |
| Insurance | $418,947 |
| Lawyers & Lobbyists | $1,569,668 |
| Misc Manufacturing & Distributing | $235,787 |
| Oil & Gas | $329,090 |
| Real Estate | $429,158 |
| Securities/Commodities Investment | $296,888 |
| TV & Movie Production/Distribution | $221,298 |

**Ideological/Single-Issue**

| | |
|---|---|
| Democratic/Liberal | $216,509 |
| Pro-Israel | $750,703 |

**Labor**

| | |
|---|---|
| Bldg Trades/Industrial/Misc Unions | $491,529 |
| Public Sector Unions | $229,950 |
| Transportation Unions | $259,242 |

# Senate Labor and Human Resources Committee

Edward M. Kennedy (D-Mass), Chairman
Orrin G. Hatch (R-Utah), Ranking Republican

**Party Ratio:** 9 Democrats
7 Republicans

**Jurisdiction:** (1) Education, labor, health and public welfare; (2) Labor standards and labor statistics; (3) Wages and hours of labor; (4) Child labor; (5) Mediation and arbitration of labor disputes; (6) Convict labor and the entry of goods made by convicts into interstate commerce; (7) Regulation of foreign laborers; (8) Handicapped individuals; (9) Equal employment opportunity; (10) Occupational safety and health, including the welfare of miners; (11) Private pension plans; (12) Aging; (13) Railway labor and retirement; (14) Public health; (15) Arts and humanities; (16) Gallaudet College, Howard University, and Saint Elizabeths Hospital; (17) Biomedical research and development; (18) Student loans; (19) Agricultural colleges; (20) Domestic activities of the American Red Cross. The committee is also mandated to study and review matters relating to health, education and training, and public welfare, and to report thereon from time to time.

## Subcommittees

**Aging**
Spark M. Matsunaga (D-Hawaii), Chairman
Thad Cochran (R-Miss), Ranking Republican

**Children, Family, Drugs and Alcoholism**
Christopher J. Dodd (D-Conn), Chairman
Daniel R. Coats (R-Ind), Ranking Republican

**Education, Arts and Humanities**
Claiborne Pell (D-RI), Chairman
Nancy Landon Kassebaum (R-Kan), Ranking Republican

**Employment and Productivity**
Paul Simon (D-Ill), Chairman
Strom Thurmond (R-SC), Ranking Republican

**Handicapped**
Tom Harkin (D-Iowa), Chairman
Dave Durenberger (R-Minn), Ranking Republican

**Labor**
Howard M. Metzenbaum (D-Ohio), Chairman
James M. Jeffords (R-Vt), Ranking Republican

## Total PAC & Large Individual Contributions to Committee Members

| | |
|---|---|
| *Paul Simon (D-Ill)* | $4,473,338 |
| *Tom Harkin (D-Iowa)* | $3,129,211 |
| *Daniel R. Coats (R-Ind)* | $2,692,428 |
| *Claiborne Pell (D-RI)* | $1,823,207 |
| *Strom Thurmond (R-SC)* | $1,188,675 |
| *Thad Cochran (R-Miss)* | $1,024,086 |
| *Nancy Landon Kassebaum (R-Kan)* | $346,087 |
| Barbara A. Mikulski (D-Md) | $180,575 |
| Christopher J. Dodd (D-Conn) | $157,261 |
| Dave Durenberger (R-Minn) | $147,801 |
| Brock Adams (D-Wash) | $127,400 |
| Orrin G. Hatch (R-Utah) | $26,051 |
| James M. Jeffords (R-Vt) | $3,000 |
| Howard M. Metzenbaum (D-Ohio) | -$20 |
| Spark M. Matsunaga (D-Hawaii)[1] | -$2,000 |
| Jeff Bingaman (D-NM) | -$2,083 |
| Edward M. Kennedy (D-Mass) | -$4,850 |

[1] Died Apr 15, 1990

| Top 20 Contributors to Committee Members in 1989-90 | |
|---|---|
| 1  Eli Lilly & Co | $55,700 |
| 2  Federal Express Corp | $53,000 |
| 3  JMB Realty Corp | $51,740 |
| 4  American Hospital Assn* | $51,250 |
| 5  Salomon Brothers | $50,425 |
| 6  Occidental Petroleum* | $50,000 |
| 7  American Bankers Assn* | $48,250 |
| 8  National PAC | $47,000 |
| 9  National Assn of Life Underwriters | $46,000 |
| 10  Seafarers International Union | $43,500 |
| 11  American Podiatry Assn | $41,500 |
| 12  Auto Dealers & Drivers for Free Trade | $41,500 |
| 13  American Institute of CPA's | $40,750 |
| 14  Assn of Trial Lawyers of America | $39,000 |
| 15  National Assn of Realtors | $39,000 |
| 16  General Motors* | $38,950 |
| 17  American Federation of Teachers | $38,200 |
| 18  Teamsters Union* | $38,000 |
| 19  Laborers Union* | $37,950 |
| 20  American Medical Assn* | $36,900 |

* Contributions came from more than one PAC affiliated with this sponsor.

Members in **bold italics** ran for reelection in 1990

## Summary

The Senate Labor Committee is the birthplace for many of the standards and rules that govern the American workplace. As such, it is of natural interest to the nation's labor unions, which provided more than $1.2 million in contributions to its members in 1989-90. But decisions about labor conditions affect not only workers, but also their employers, who must live by the rules. Consequently, many of the issues discussed and debated by the committee are closely followed by a wide cross-section of business interests. And those businesses delivered substantial campaign contributions to committee members.

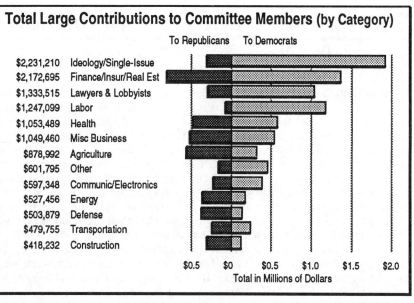

**Total Large Contributions to Committee Members (by Category)**

To Republicans  To Democrats

| Amount | Category |
|---|---|
| $2,231,210 | Ideology/Single-Issue |
| $2,172,695 | Finance/Insur/Real Est |
| $1,333,515 | Lawyers & Lobbyists |
| $1,247,099 | Labor |
| $1,053,489 | Health |
| $1,049,460 | Misc Business |
| $878,992 | Agriculture |
| $601,795 | Other |
| $597,348 | Communic/Electronics |
| $527,456 | Energy |
| $503,879 | Defense |
| $479,755 | Transportation |
| $418,232 | Construction |

Total in Millions of Dollars

The Labor committee's cash profile reveals another important fact about the relationship between business and labor contributors: if PACs alone are counted, organized labor ranks as the single largest industry group giving to committee members (followed closely by ideological PACs). But if *all* contributors are included — PACs *and* individuals giving $200 or more — labor falls to fourth place. This illustrates the fact that business contributors give heavily both through PACs and individuals, while labor gives almost all its contributions through PACs. Because of that, looking at PAC contributions alone substantially overstates the cash clout of organized labor in American politics and understates the clout of business interests.

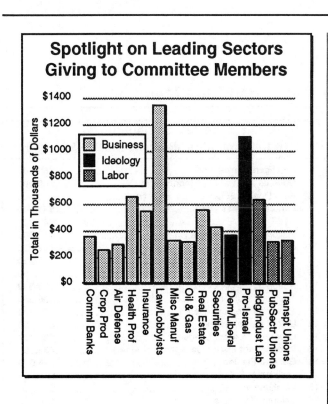

**Spotlight on Leading Sectors Giving to Committee Members**

Totals in Thousands of Dollars

Legend:
- Business
- Ideology
- Labor

Categories: Comml Banks, Crop Prod, Air Defense, Health Prof, Insurance, Law/Lobbyists, Misc Manuf, Oil & Gas, Real Estate, Securities, Dem/Liberal, Pro-Israel, Bldg/Indust Lab, PubSectr Unions, Transpt Unions

### Leading Sectors Giving to Committee Members

**Business**

| | |
|---|---|
| Commercial Banks | $342,858 |
| Crop Production & Basic Processing | $248,314 |
| Defense Aerospace | $283,865 |
| Health Professionals | $649,844 |
| Insurance | $533,518 |
| Lawyers & Lobbyists | $1,333,515 |
| Misc Manufacturing & Distributing | $320,905 |
| Oil & Gas | $305,121 |
| Real Estate | $550,100 |
| Securities/Commodities Investment | $419,750 |

**Ideological/Single-Issue**

| | |
|---|---|
| Democratic/Liberal | $352,475 |
| Pro-Israel | $1,093,528 |

**Labor**

| | |
|---|---|
| Bldg Trades/Industrial/Misc Unions | $630,002 |
| Public Sector Unions | $305,115 |
| Transportation Unions | $311,982 |

# Senate Rules and Administration Committee

Wendell H. Ford (D-Ky), Chairman
Ted Stevens (R-Alaska), Ranking Republican

**Party Ratio:** 9 Democrats
7 Republicans

**Jurisdiction:** (1) Administration of the Senate Office Buildings and the Senate wing of the Capitol, including the assignment of office space. (2) Congressional organization relative to rules and procedures, and Senate rules and regulations, including floor and gallery rules. (3) Corrupt practices. (4) Credentials and qualifications of Members of the Senate, contested elections, and acceptance of incompatible offices. (5) Federal elections generally, including the election of the President, Vice President, and Members of the Congress. (6) Government Printing Office, and the printing and correction of the *Congressional Record*, as well as those matters provided for under rule XI. (7) Meetings of the Congress and attendance of Members. (8) Payment of money out of the contingent fund of the Senate or creating a charge upon the same (except that any resolution relating to substantive matter within the jurisdiction of any other standing committee of the Senate shall be first referred to such committee). (9) Presidential succession. (10) Purchase of books and manuscripts and erection of monuments to the memory of individuals. (11) Senate Library and statuary, art, and pictures in the Capitol and Senate Office Buildings. (12) Services to the Senate, including the Senate restaurant. (13) United States Capitol and congressional office buildings, the Library of Congress, the Smithsonian Institution (and the incorporation of similar institutions), and the Botanic Garden. The committee is also mandated to (A) make a continuing study of the organization and operation of the Congress of the United States and recommend improvements in such organization and operation with a view toward strengthening the Congress, simplifying its operations, improving its relationships with other branches of the U.S. Government, and enabling it to better meet its responsibilities under the Constitution of the United States; and (B) identify any court proceeding or action which, in its opinion, is of vital interest to the Congress as a constitutionally established institution of the Federal Government and call such proceeding or action to the attention of the Senate.

## No Subcommittees

## Total PAC & Large Individual Contributions to Committee Members

*Jesse Helms (R-NC)* ..................................... $3,442,351
*Mitch McConnell (R-Ky)* ............................... $3,057,489
*Al Gore (D-Tenn)* ......................................... $1,944,865
*Claiborne Pell (D-RI)* ................................... $1,823,207
*Mark O. Hatfield (R-Ore)* ............................. $1,738,163
*Ted Stevens (R-Alaska)* ............................... $1,167,034
Bob Dole (R-Kan) ............................................. $304,050
James A. McClure (R-Idaho)[1] ......................... $208,180
Christopher J. Dodd (D-Conn) ......................... $157,261
Brock Adams (D-Wash) ................................... $127,400
Dennis DeConcini (D-Ariz) ............................... $121,841
Jake Garn (R-Utah) ........................................... $58,150
Wendell H. Ford (D-Ky) ...................................... $19,876
Daniel K. Inouye (D-Hawaii) .............................. $14,250
Daniel Patrick Moynihan (D-NY) .......................... $6,094
Robert C. Byrd (D-WVa) ...................................... $2,500

---

[1] Did not seek reelection in 1990

### Top 20 Contributors to Committee Members in 1989-90

| | | |
|---|---|---|
| 1 | American Bankers Assn | $63,500 |
| 2 | National Assn of Life Underwriters | $50,000 |
| 3 | Auto Dealers & Drivers for Free Trade | $46,500 |
| 4 | Federal Express Corp | $41,500 |
| 5 | AT&T | $40,900 |
| 6 | National Assn of Home Builders* | $40,500 |
| 7 | BellSouth Corp* | $40,050 |
| 8 | National Assn of Realtors | $39,250 |
| 9 | Textron Inc | $38,750 |
| 10 | National Assn of Letter Carriers | $38,500 |
| 11 | Teamsters Union | $38,250 |
| 12 | American Medical Assn* | $37,200 |
| 13 | United Parcel Service | $37,100 |
| 14 | Laborers' Political League | $36,000 |
| 15 | Independent Insurance Agents of America | $35,703 |
| 16 | General Electric | $35,600 |
| 17 | Occidental Petroleum* | $35,550 |
| 18 | Washington PAC | $34,250 |
| 19 | Salomon Brothers | $34,000 |
| 20 | Associated General Contractors* | $33,500 |

\* Contributions came from more than one PAC affiliated with this sponsor.

Members in **bold italics** ran for reelection in 1990

## Summary

In any legislative body, the key to success often lies in a mastery of the body's rules and procedures. Those rules — from the assignment of office space to the conducting of business on the Senate floor and even the rules governing federal elections — are debated within this committee.

As part of its role in setting election procedures, the committee is also at center stage in revising the laws governing campaign financing. The rules governing PACs, the spending limits and reporting requirements of contributors to federal campaigns, the oversight of the process by the Federal Election Commission — all these elements of American elections fall within the jurisdiction of the Senate Rules Committee.

### Total Large Contributions to Committee Members (by Category)

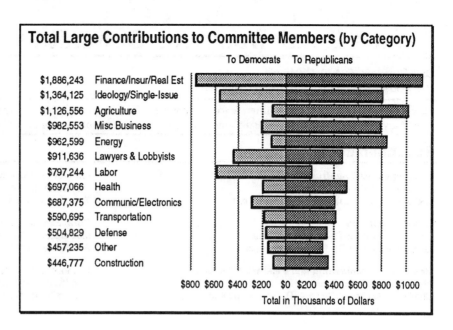

| | |
|---|---|
| $1,886,243 | Finance/Insur/Real Est |
| $1,364,125 | Ideology/Single-Issue |
| $1,126,556 | Agriculture |
| $982,553 | Misc Business |
| $962,599 | Energy |
| $911,636 | Lawyers & Lobbyists |
| $797,244 | Labor |
| $697,066 | Health |
| $687,375 | Communic/Electronics |
| $590,695 | Transportation |
| $504,829 | Defense |
| $457,235 | Other |
| $446,777 | Construction |

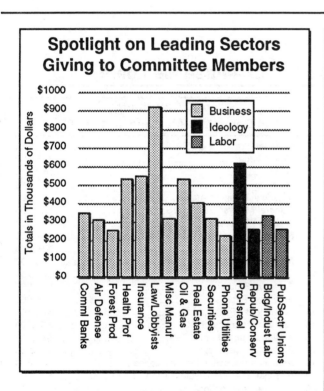

### Spotlight on Leading Sectors Giving to Committee Members

### Leading Sectors Giving to Committee Members

**Business**

| | |
|---|---|
| Commercial Banks | $340,339 |
| Defense Aerospace | $303,167 |
| Forestry & Forest Products | $247,950 |
| Health Professionals | $523,416 |
| Insurance | $542,622 |
| Lawyers & Lobbyists | $911,636 |
| Misc Manufacturing & Distributing | $309,762 |
| Oil & Gas | $528,816 |
| Real Estate | $395,744 |
| Securities/Commodities Investment | $309,794 |
| Telephone Utilities | $217,255 |

**Ideological/Single-Issue**

| | |
|---|---|
| Pro-Israel | $609,466 |
| Republican/Conservative | $254,766 |

**Labor**

| | |
|---|---|
| Bldg Trades/Industrial/Misc Unions | $327,917 |
| Public Sector Unions | $258,227 |

# Senate Small Business Committee

Dale Bumpers (D-Ark), Chairman
Rudy Boschwitz (R-Minn), Ranking Republican

**Party Ratio:** 10 Democrats
9 Republicans

**Jurisdiction:** (1) All legislation referred to the committee; (2) Jurisdiction over all matters related to the Small Business Administration; (3) Study and survey, through research and investigation, of all problems of American small business enterprises.

## Subcommittees

**Competition and Antitrust Enforcement**
Tom Harkin (D-Iowa), Chairman
Ted Stevens (R-Alaska), Ranking Republican

**Export Expansion**
Barbara A. Mikulski (D-Md), Chairwoman
Larry Pressler (R-SD), Ranking Republican

**Government Contracting and Paperwork Reduction**
Alan J. Dixon (D-Ill), Chairman
Charles E. Grassley (R-Iowa), Ranking Republican

**Innovation, Technology and Productivity**
Carl Levin (D-Mich), Chairman
Trent Lott (R-Miss), Ranking Republican

**Rural Economy and Family Farming**
Max Baucus (D-Mont), Chairman
Bob Kasten (R-Wis), Ranking Republican

**Urban and Minority-Owned Business Development**
John Kerry (D-Mass), Chairman
Conrad Burns (R-Mont), Ranking Republican

## Total PAC & Large Individual Contributions to Committee Members

*Carl Levin (D-Mich)* .......................................... $4,281,016
*John Kerry (D-Mass)* .......................................... $3,626,799
*Tom Harkin (D-Iowa)* .......................................... $3,129,211
*Max Baucus (D-Mont)* .......................................... $2,193,526
*Sam Nunn (D-Ga)* .......................................... $1,694,369
*Larry Pressler (R-SD)* .......................................... $1,609,209
*Rudy Boschwitz (R-Minn)* .......................................... $1,298,047
*Ted Stevens (R-Alaska)* .......................................... $1,167,034
*David L. Boren (D-Okla)* .......................................... $1,039,939
Alan J. Dixon (D-Ill) .......................................... $383,850
Barbara A. Mikulski (D-Md) .......................................... $180,575
Christopher S. Bond (R-Mo) .......................................... $167,342
Joseph Lieberman I. (D-Conn) .......................................... $108,920
Bob Kasten (R-Wis) .......................................... $106,400
Dale Bumpers (D-Ark) .......................................... $66,750
Charles E. Grassley (R-Iowa) .......................................... $57,254
Conrad Burns (R-Mont) .......................................... $47,236
Malcolm Wallop (R-Wyo) .......................................... $40,715
Trent Lott (R-Miss) .......................................... $35,950

| Top 20 Contributors to Committee Members in 1989-90 | |
|---|---|
| 1 Goldman, Sachs & Co | $91,150 |
| 2 Time Warner | $85,500 |
| 3 AT&T | $67,680 |
| 4 MCA Inc | $63,250 |
| 5 American Bankers Assn* | $61,300 |
| 6 General Motors* | $60,250 |
| 7 Air Line Pilots Assn | $59,000 |
| 8 National Assn of Life Underwriters | $57,000 |
| 9 Archer-Daniels-Midland Corp | $56,000 |
| 10 National Assn of Letter Carriers | $55,000 |
| 11 National PAC | $55,000 |
| 12 Salomon Brothers | $52,250 |
| 13 American Express* | $52,050 |
| 14 Washington PAC | $51,750 |
| 15 Citizens Organized PAC | $50,000 |
| 16 American Institute of CPA's | $48,875 |
| 17 Federal Express Corp | $47,333 |
| 18 American Council of Life Insurance | $46,499 |
| 19 National Beer Wholesalers Assn | $46,000 |
| 20 Seafarers International Union | $46,000 |

\* Contributions came from more than one PAC affiliated with this sponsor.

Members in **bold Italics** ran for reelection in 1990

## Summary

Its statement of jurisdiction is the shortest of all Senate committees, but the expanse of that jurisdiction reaches into every city and town across America. Overseeing the concerns of small business — from the corner grocery to the family farm — is the committee's charge, and considering the fact that both the corner grocery and the family farm are endangered species in America today, the concerns of small business are large indeed.

As with most committees in the Senate, the single biggest source of campaign funds to committee members came from the financial industry, while lawyers and lobbyists were the leading group in the interest group sectors shown below. Pro-Israel groups were another major source of funds, though their dollars had less to do with the concerns of the committee than with the reelection campaigns of several of the committee members. Among them, Michigan Democrat Carl Levin was the top congressional recipient of pro-Israel contributions in the 1990 elections.

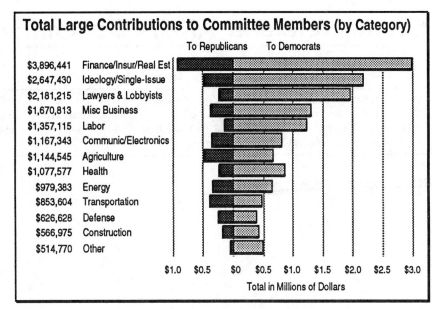

**Total Large Contributions to Committee Members (by Category)**

| | |
|---|---|
| $3,896,441 | Finance/Insur/Real Est |
| $2,647,430 | Ideology/Single-Issue |
| $2,181,215 | Lawyers & Lobbyists |
| $1,670,813 | Misc Business |
| $1,357,115 | Labor |
| $1,167,343 | Communic/Electronics |
| $1,144,545 | Agriculture |
| $1,077,577 | Health |
| $979,383 | Energy |
| $853,604 | Transportation |
| $626,628 | Defense |
| $566,975 | Construction |
| $514,770 | Other |

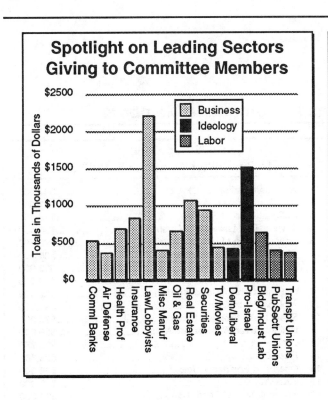

**Spotlight on Leading Sectors Giving to Committee Members**

## Leading Sectors Giving to Committee Members

### Business

| | |
|---|---|
| Commercial Banks | $517,899 |
| Defense Aerospace | $352,820 |
| Health Professionals | $664,657 |
| Insurance | $807,309 |
| Lawyers & Lobbyists | $2,181,215 |
| Misc Manufacturing & Distributing | $384,621 |
| Oil & Gas | $634,642 |
| Real Estate | $1,043,397 |
| Securities/Commodities Investment | $920,904 |
| TV & Movie Production/Distribution | $420,717 |

### Ideological/Single-Issue

| | |
|---|---|
| Democratic/Liberal | $405,316 |
| Pro-Israel | $1,500,169 |

### Labor

| | |
|---|---|
| Bldg Trades/Industrial/Misc Unions | $617,070 |
| Public Sector Unions | $384,205 |
| Transportation Unions | $355,840 |

# Senate Veterans' Affairs Committee

Alan Cranston (D-Calif), Chairman
Frank H. Murkowski (R-Alaska), Ranking Republican

**Party Ratio:** 6 Democrats
5 Republicans

**Jurisdiction:** Veterans' measures generally; (2) Pensions of all wars of the U.S., general and special; (3) Life insurance issued by the Government on account of service in the Armed Forces; (4) Compensation of veterans; (5) Vocational rehabilitation and education of veterans; (6) Veterans' hospitals, medical care and treatment of veterans; (7) Soldiers' and sailors' civil relief; (8) Readjustment of servicemen to civil life; (9) National cemeteries.

## No Subcommittees

## Total PAC & Large Individual Contributions to Committee Members

| | |
|---|---|
| *John D. Rockefeller IV (D-WVa)* | $3,027,432 |
| *Daniel K. Akaka (D-Hawaii)* | $1,450,054 |
| *Strom Thurmond (R-SC)* | $1,188,675 |
| *Alan K. Simpson (R-Wyo)* | $1,012,602 |
| Arlen Specter (R-Pa) | $473,110 |
| Bob Graham (D-Fla) | $304,522 |
| Alan Cranston (D-Calif) | $203,440 |
| Dennis DeConcini (D-Ariz) | $121,841 |
| Frank H. Murkowski (R-Alaska) | $43,715 |
| George J. Mitchell (D-Maine) | $13,000 |
| James M. Jeffords (R-Vt) | $3,000 |
| Spark M. Matsunaga (D-Hawaii)[1] | -$2,000 |

---

[1] Died Apr 15, 1990

### Top 20 Contributors to Committee Members in 1989-90

| | | |
|---|---|---|
| 1 | American Institute of CPA's | $42,000 |
| 2 | American Bankers Assn | $37,000 |
| 3 | National Assn of Realtors | $36,500 |
| 4 | Assn of Trial Lawyers of America | $36,000 |
| 5 | National Assn of Life Underwriters | $35,500 |
| 6 | Chicago Mercantile Exchange | $33,500 |
| 7 | Federal Express Corp | $33,000 |
| 8 | Teamsters Union | $33,000 |
| 9 | National Cable Television Assn | $32,000 |
| 10 | Air Line Pilots Assn | $30,000 |
| 11 | Sheet Metal Workers Union | $30,000 |
| 12 | National Beer Wholesalers Assn | $29,000 |
| 13 | Laborers Union* | $28,750 |
| 14 | Fluor Corp | $28,500 |
| 15 | Operating Engineers Union* | $28,000 |
| 16 | KidsPAC | $27,000 |
| 17 | National Assn of Letter Carriers | $26,000 |
| 18 | American Medical Assn* | $25,500 |
| 19 | American Federation of Teachers | $25,000 |
| 20 | National Education Assn | $24,500 |

\* Contributions came from more than one PAC affiliated with this sponsor.

Members in **bold italics** ran for reelection in 1990

## Summary

Insurance companies and health professionals were major contributors to the Senate Veterans Affairs Committee in 1990, ranking only behind lawyers and lobbyists as the leading sectors giving to committee members. While government life insurance to veterans does fall within its jurisdiction, as does the VA hospital system, most of the committee's work does not directly affect any particular segments of American business in a major way. Perhaps because of this, the Veterans Affairs Committee has never been a central focus of political fundraising on Capitol Hill.

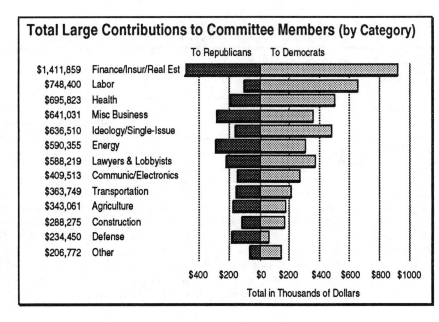

**Total Large Contributions to Committee Members (by Category)**

| Amount | Category |
|---|---|
| $1,411,859 | Finance/Insur/Real Est |
| $748,400 | Labor |
| $695,823 | Health |
| $641,031 | Misc Business |
| $636,510 | Ideology/Single-Issue |
| $590,355 | Energy |
| $588,219 | Lawyers & Lobbyists |
| $409,513 | Communic/Electronics |
| $363,749 | Transportation |
| $343,061 | Agriculture |
| $288,275 | Construction |
| $234,450 | Defense |
| $206,772 | Other |

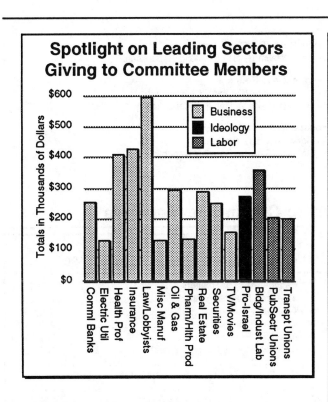

**Spotlight on Leading Sectors Giving to Committee Members**

Legend: Business, Ideology, Labor

Categories: Comml Banks, Electric Util, Health Prof, Insurance, Law/Lobbyists, Misc Manuf, Oil & Gas, Pharm/Hlth Prod, Real Estate, Securities, TV/Movies, Pro-Israel, Bldg/Indust Lab, PubSectr Unions, Transpt Unions

### Leading Sectors Giving to Committee Members

**Business**

| | |
|---|---|
| Commercial Banks | $251,408 |
| Environmental Svcs/Equipment | $127,550 |
| Health Professionals | $406,472 |
| Insurance | $421,516 |
| Lawyers & Lobbyists | $588,219 |
| Misc Manufacturing & Distributing | $126,850 |
| Oil & Gas | $289,075 |
| Pharmaceuticals/Health Products | $129,876 |
| Real Estate | $284,225 |
| Securities/Commodities Investment | $248,435 |
| TV & Movie Production/Distribution | $150,650 |

**Ideological/Single-Issue**

| | |
|---|---|
| Pro-Israel | $267,450 |

**Labor**

| | |
|---|---|
| Bldg Trades/Industrial/Misc Unions | $354,250 |
| Public Sector Unions | $198,150 |
| Transportation Unions | $196,000 |

# House Administration Committee

Frank Annunzio (D-Ill), Chairman
Bill Thomas (R-Calif), Ranking Republican

**Party Ratio:** 13 Democrats
8 Republicans

**Jurisdiction:** (1) Appropriations from the contingent fund; (2) Auditing and settling of all accounts which may be charged to the contingent fund; (3) Employment of persons by the House, including clerks for Members and committees, and reporters of debates; (4) Matters relating to the Library of Congress and the House Library; statuary and pictures; acceptance or purchase of works of art for the Capitol; the Botanic Gardens; management of the Library of Congress, purchase of books and manuscripts; erection of monuments to the memory of individuals; (5) Matters relating to the Smithsonian Institution and the incorporation of similar institutions; (6) Expenditure of contingent fund of the House; (7) Matters relating to printing and correction of the Congressional Record; (8) Measures relating to accounts of the House generally; (9) Measures relating to assignment of office space for Members and committees; (10) measures relating to the disposition of useless executive papers; (11) Measures relating to the election of the President, Vice President, or Members of Congress; corrupt practices; contested elections; credentials and qualifications; and Federal elections generally; (12) Measures relating to services to the House, including the House Restaurant, parking facilities and administration of the House office Buildings and of the House wing of the Capitol; (13) Measures relating to the travel of Members of the House; (14) Measures relating to the raising, reporting and use of campaign contributions for candidates for office of Representative in the House of Representatives and of Resident Commissioner to the United States from Puerto Rico; (15) Measures relating to the compensation, retirement and other benefits of the Members, officers, and employees of the Congress.

## Subcommittees

**Accounts**
Joseph M. Gaydos (D-Pa), Chairman
Barbara F. Vucanovich (R-Nev), Ranking Republican

**Elections**
Al Swift (D-Wash), Chairman
Bill Thomas (R-Calif), Ranking Republican

**Libraries and Memorials**
William L. Clay (D-Mo), Chairman
Paul E. Gillmor (R-Ohio), Ranking Republican

**Office Systems**
Charlie Rose (D-NC), Chairman
James T. Walsh (R-NY), Ranking Republican

**Personnel and Police**
Mary Rose Oakar (D-Ohio), Chairwoman
Pat Roberts (R-Kan), Ranking Republican

**Procurement and Printing**
Jim Bates (D-Calif), Chairman
Pat Roberts (R-Kan), Ranking Republican

## Total PAC & Large Individual Contributions to Committee Members

Newt Gingrich (R-Ga) .......... $996,023
Frank Annunzio (D-Ill) .......... $593,998
Martin Frost (D-Texas) .......... $580,230
Thomas J. Manton (D-NY) .......... $548,757
Al Swift (D-Wash) .......... $409,307
Jim Bates (D-Calif) .......... $353,388
Mary Rose Oakar (D-Ohio) .......... $311,591
Bill Thomas (R-Calif) .......... $306,621
Sam Gejdenson (D-Conn) .......... $301,442
Bill Dickinson (R-Ala) .......... $299,958
Barbara F. Vucanovich (R-Nev) .......... $275,796
Paul E. Gillmor (R-Ohio) .......... $264,607
Ronnie G. Flippo (D-Ala)[1] .......... $258,050
John P. Hiler (R-Ind) .......... $247,837
James T. Walsh (R-NY) .......... $244,095
Charlie Rose (D-NC) .......... $236,036
William L. Clay (D-Mo) .......... $182,600
Leon E. Panetta (D-Calif) .......... $176,850
Joe Kolter (D-Pa) .......... $173,736
Joseph M. Gaydos (D-Pa) .......... $171,216
Pat Roberts (R-Kan) .......... $150,250
Tony Coelho (D-Calif)[2] .......... $32,688

| Top 20 Contributors to Committee Members in 1989-90 | |
|---|---|
| 1 National Assn of Realtors | $142,850 |
| 2 American Medical Assn* | $113,400 |
| 3 Teamsters Union* | $80,950 |
| 4 National Education Assn | $72,950 |
| 5 American Bankers Assn* | $69,750 |
| 6 National Assn of Letter Carriers* | $68,850 |
| 7 AT&T | $65,625 |
| 8 Natl Assn of Retired Federal Employees | $61,000 |
| 9 Laborers Union* | $60,150 |
| 10 National Assn of Life Underwriters | $59,350 |
| 11 Carpenters & Joiners Union | $55,800 |
| 12 United Auto Workers | $53,450 |
| 13 American Institute of CPA's | $50,000 |
| 14 Machinists/Aerospace Workers Union* | $49,800 |
| 15 Amer Fedn of State/County/Munic Employees | $48,550 |
| 16 Assn of Trial Lawyers of America | $45,500 |
| 17 National Auto Dealers Assn | $44,850 |
| 18 Intl Brotherhood of Electrical Workers* | $42,900 |
| 19 Air Line Pilots Assn | $41,500 |
| 20 National Assn of Home Builders | $40,100 |

[1] Did not seek reelection in 1990
[2] Resigned June 15, 1989

* Contributions came from more than one PAC affiliated with this sponsor.

## Summary

Since the Committee on House Administration is more concerned with matters internal to the House than the world of industry and commerce beyond it, the pattern of contributions to its members closely parallels that of the rest of Congress. The parallel is so close, in fact, that every one of the Top 20 contributors to committee members also ranks among the Top 20 contributors to Congress as a whole.

In one respect, the committee does figure prominently in the world of money and politics on Capitol Hill, however. Its Subcommittee on Elections is the panel that oversees the drafting of changes in the nation's campaign finance laws.

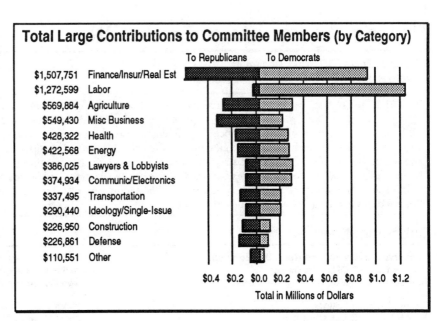

### Total Large Contributions to Committee Members (by Category)

| | |
|---|---|
| $1,507,751 | Finance/Insur/Real Est |
| $1,272,599 | Labor |
| $569,884 | Agriculture |
| $549,430 | Misc Business |
| $428,322 | Health |
| $422,568 | Energy |
| $386,025 | Lawyers & Lobbyists |
| $374,934 | Communic/Electronics |
| $337,495 | Transportation |
| $290,440 | Ideology/Single-Issue |
| $226,950 | Construction |
| $226,861 | Defense |
| $110,551 | Other |

Total in Millions of Dollars

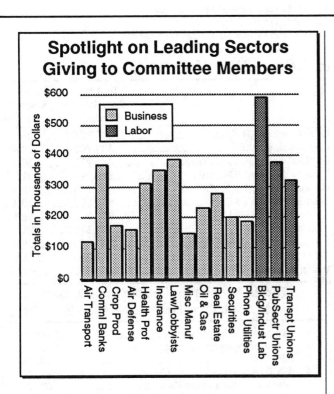

### Spotlight on Leading Sectors Giving to Committee Members

### Leading Sectors Giving to Committee Members

**Business**

| | |
|---|---|
| Air Transport | $118,805 |
| Commercial Banks | $367,320 |
| Crop Production & Basic Processing | $167,905 |
| Defense Aerospace | $158,340 |
| Health Professionals | $308,622 |
| Insurance | $350,441 |
| Lawyers & Lobbyists | $386,025 |
| Misc Manufacturing & Distributing | $143,190 |
| Oil & Gas | $223,793 |
| Real Estate | $272,772 |
| Securities/Commodities Investment | $196,750 |
| Telephone Utilities | $183,134 |

**Labor**

| | |
|---|---|
| Bldg Trades/Industrial/Misc Unions | $583,694 |
| Public Sector Unions | $373,905 |
| Transportation Unions | $315,000 |

# House Agriculture Committee

Kika de la Garza (D-Texas), Chairman
Edward R. Madigan (R-Ill) Ranking Republican

**Party Ratio:** 27 Democrats
18 Republicans

> **Jurisdiction:** (1) Adulteration of seeds, insect pests, and protection of birds and animals in forest reserves; (2) Agriculture generally; (3) Agricultural and industrial chemistry; (4) Agricultural colleges and experimental stations; (5) Agricultural economics and research; (6) Agricultural education extension services; (7) Agricultural production and marketing and stabilization of prices of agricultural products and commodities (not including distribution outside the United States); (8) Animal industry and diseases of animals; (9) Crop insurance and soil conservation; (10) Dairy industry; (11) Entomology and plant quarantine; (12) Extension of farm credit and farm security; (13) Forestry in general, and forest reserves other than those created from the public domain; (14) Human nutrition and home economics; (15) Inspection of livestock and meat products; (16) Plant industry, soils, and agricultural engineering; (17) Rural electrification; (18) Commodities exchanges; (19) Rural development.

## Subcommittees

**Conservation, Credit, and Rural Development**
Glenn English (D-Okla), Chairman
Tom Coleman (R-Mo), Ranking Republican

**Cotton, Rice, and Sugar**
Jerry Huckaby (D-La), Chairman
Arlan Stangeland (R-Minn), Ranking Republican

**Department Operations, Research, and Foreign Agriculture**
George E. Brown Jr. (D-Calif), Chairman
Pat Roberts (R-Kan), Ranking Republican

**Livestock, Dairy, and Poultry**
Charles W. Stenholm (D-Texas), Chairman
Steve Gunderson (R-Wis), Ranking Republican

**Tobacco and Peanuts**
Charlie Rose (D-NC), Chairman
Larry J. Hopkins (R-Ky), Ranking Republican

**Wheat, Soybeans, and Feed Grains**
Dan Glickman (D-Kan), Chairman
Ron Marlenee (R-Mont), Ranking Republican

## Total Agriculture-Related Contributions to Committee Members

| | Total from Cmte-Related Contribs | Pct of Member's Lg Contribs |
|---|---|---|
| Bill Schuette (R-Mich)[1] | $245,986 | 31% |
| Bill Emerson (R-Mo) | $151,331 | 33% |
| Wally Herger (R-Calif) | $133,609 | 35% |
| Gary Condit (D-Calif) | $127,695 | 40% |
| Arlan Stangeland (R-Minn) | $114,851 | 40% |
| Bill Sarpalius (D-Texas) | $105,430 | 21% |
| Clyde C. Holloway (R-La) | $104,250 | 39% |
| Mike Espy (D-Miss) | $103,065 | 25% |
| Charles Hatcher (D-Ga) | $99,155 | 38% |
| Fred Grandy (R-Iowa) | $99,150 | 29% |
| Charlie Rose (D-NC) | $96,200 | 41% |
| Steve Gunderson (R-Wis) | $96,105 | 34% |
| Bob Smith (R-Ore) | $93,202 | 41% |
| Jerry Huckaby (D-La) | $89,325 | 56% |
| Bill Grant (R-Fla) | $83,472 | 28% |
| Jill L. Long (D-Ind) | $78,452 | 12% |
| Jim Jontz (D-Ind) | $75,538 | 17% |
| Ron Marlenee (R-Mont) | $73,950 | 38% |
| Dan Glickman (D-Kan) | $73,050 | 17% |
| Charles W. Stenholm (D-Texas) | $71,525 | 47% |
| George E. Brown Jr. (D-Calif) | $70,900 | 13% |
| Pat Roberts (R-Kan) | $70,050 | 47% |
| Edward Madigan (R-Ill) | $69,818 | 23% |
| Harold L. Volkmer (D-Mo) | $69,400 | 29% |
| Richard Stallings (D-Idaho) | $68,030 | 23% |
| Tom Lewis (R-Fla) | $66,350 | 37% |
| Tom Coleman (R-Mo) | $63,176 | 29% |
| Tim Johnson (D-SD) | $61,000 | 20% |
| Glenn English (D-Okla) | $60,980 | 36% |
| Robin Tallon (D-SC) | $60,900 | 34% |
| H. Martin Lancaster (D-NC) | $56,930 | 19% |
| Ben Nighthorse Campbell (D-Colo) | $51,965 | 21% |
| Jim Olin (D-Va) | $50,850 | 28% |
| Dave Nagle (D-Iowa) | $50,525 | 19% |
| Larry Combest (R-Texas) | $48,825 | 34% |
| Roy Dyson (D-Md) | $43,700 | 9% |
| E. "Kika" de la Garza (D-Texas) | $42,775 | 56% |
| Timothy J. Penny (D-Minn) | $42,750 | 37% |
| Harley O. Staggers Jr. (D-WVa) | $42,700 | 13% |
| Leon E. Panetta (D-Calif) | $40,550 | 23% |
| James T. Walsh (R-NY) | $39,950 | 16% |
| Claude Harris (D-Ala) | $39,582 | 21% |
| Larry J. Hopkins (R-Ky) | $33,850 | 39% |
| Sid Morrison (R-Wash) | $17,250 | 35% |
| Walter B. Jones (D-NC) | $13,800 | 19% |

> ### Top 20 Agriculture-Related Contributors to Committee Members in 1989-90
>
> | | | |
> |---|---|---|
> | 1 | Associated Milk Producers | $146,800 |
> | 2 | Mid-America Dairymen | $109,500 |
> | 3 | RJR Nabisco | $89,900 |
> | 4 | ACRE (Action Cmte/Rural Electrification)* | $77,100 |
> | 5 | American Crystal Sugar Corp | $76,750 |
> | 6 | American Assn of Crop Insurers | $74,050 |
> | 7 | National Cattlemen's Assn* | $72,134 |
> | 8 | Chicago Board of Trade | $69,700 |
> | 9 | Philip Morris* | $65,800 |
> | 10 | Food Marketing Institute | $61,990 |
> | 11 | Dairymen Inc* | $59,697 |
> | 12 | American Sugarbeet Growers Assn | $54,826 |
> | 13 | Southern Minnesota Beet Sugar Co-op | $53,150 |
> | 14 | Chicago Mercantile Exchange | $52,200 |
> | 15 | American Veterinary Medical Assn | $52,000 |
> | 16 | American Meat Institute | $49,105 |
> | 17 | National Cotton Council | $46,150 |
> | 18 | National Broiler Council | $45,550 |
> | 19 | ConAgra Inc | $40,300 |
> | 20 | National Council of Farmer Co-ops | $35,850 |

[1] Ran for U.S. Senate in 1990

\* Contributions came from more than one PAC affiliated with this sponsor.

# Summary

Farmers, co-ops and corporations involved in the production of crops were the leading source of campaign funds for members of the House Agriculture committee, but committee members also drew contributions from many other agriculture-related industries. Dairy farmers, agricultural chemical manufacturers, and a wide variety of agricultural service companies were also major sources of cash, as were livestock and poultry producers, commodities brokers, tobacco companies and timber and paper producers. Within the crop production sector, sugar growers led all other groups by a wide margin — a reflection of the importance of sugar in the American diet and also of the role of federal subsidies in sweetening the growers' profits.

## Total Large Contributions to Committee Members (by Category)

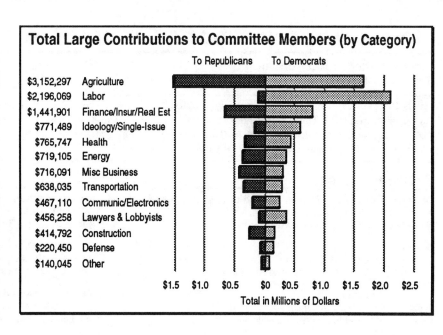

| | | To Republicans | To Democrats |
|---|---|---|---|
| $3,152,297 | Agriculture | | |
| $2,196,069 | Labor | | |
| $1,441,901 | Finance/Insur/Real Est | | |
| $771,489 | Ideology/Single-Issue | | |
| $765,747 | Health | | |
| $719,105 | Energy | | |
| $716,091 | Misc Business | | |
| $638,035 | Transportation | | |
| $467,110 | Communic/Electronics | | |
| $456,258 | Lawyers & Lobbyists | | |
| $414,792 | Construction | | |
| $220,450 | Defense | | |
| $140,045 | Other | | |

$1.5  $1.0  $0.5  $0  $0.5  $1.0  $1.5  $2.0  $2.5

Total in Millions of Dollars

## Spotlight on Leading Sectors Giving to Committee Members

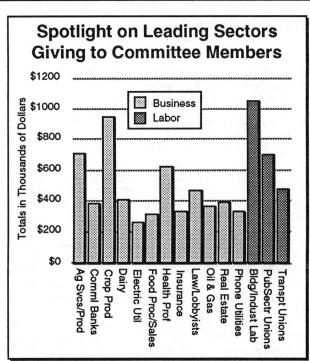

Business
Labor

Totals in Thousands of Dollars

Ag Svcs/Prod, Comml Banks, Crop Prod, Dairy, Electric Util, Food Proc/Sales, Health Prof, Insurance, Law/Lobbyists, Oil & Gas, Real Estate, Phone Utilities, Bldg/Indust Lab, PubSectr Unions, Transpt Unions

## Committee-Related Sectors

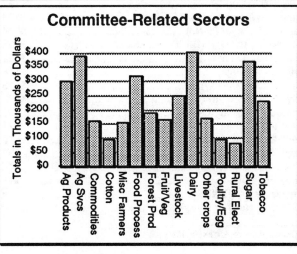

Totals in Thousands of Dollars

Ag Products, Ag Svcs, Commodities, Cotton, Misc Farmers, Food Process, Forest Prod, Fruit/Veg, Livestock, Dairy, Other crops, Poultry/Egg, Rural Elect, Sugar, Tobacco

## Leading Committee-Related Sectors Giving to Committee Members

### Crop Production

| | |
|---|---|
| Cotton growers | $88,608 |
| Fruit & vegetable growers | $161,791 |
| Sugar growers | $367,833 |
| Other crops | $167,917 |
| Farmers, crop unspecified | $153,904 |

### Tobacco Production & Marketing

| | |
|---|---|
| Tobacco & tobacco products | $225,975 |

### Dairy

| | |
|---|---|
| Milk & dairy producers | $399,326 |

### Livestock & Poultry

| | |
|---|---|
| Livestock | $246,112 |
| Poultry & eggs | $91,675 |

### Commodities

| | |
|---|---|
| Commodity brokers/dealers | $155,950 |

### Agricultural Services & Supplies

| | |
|---|---|
| Agricultural products | $296,450 |
| Agricultural services | $383,834 |

### Food Processing & Sales

| | |
|---|---|
| Food processing & sales | $313,150 |

### Forestry

| | |
|---|---|
| Forestry & forest products | $186,122 |

### Other Committee-Related

| | |
|---|---|
| Rural electric cooperatives | $78,600 |

131

# House Appropriations Committee

Jamie L. Whitten (D-Miss), Chairman
Silvio O. Conte (R-Mass), Ranking Republican

**Party Ratio:** 35 Democrats
22 Republicans

**Jurisdiction:** (1) Appropriation of the revenue for the support of the Government; (2) Rescissions of appropriations contained in appropriation acts; (3) Transfers of unexpended balances, and a variety of other duties involving the appropriation of government funds. Other committees of Congress may *authorize* the government to spend money on various projects and programs, but only the Appropriations committee *appropriates* the funds.

## Subcommittees

**Commerce, Justice, and State, The Judiciary and Related Agencies**
Neal Smith (D-Iowa), Chairman
Harold Rogers (R-Ky), Ranking Republican

**Defense**
John P. Murtha (D-Pa), Chairman
Joseph M. McDade (R-Pa), Ranking Republican

**District of Columbia**
Julian C. Dixon (D-Calif), Chairman
Dean A. Gallo (R-NJ), Ranking Republican

**Energy and Water Development**
Tom Bevill (D-Ala), Chairman
John T. Myers (R-Ind), Ranking Republican

**Foreign Operations, Export Financing and Related Programs**
David R. Obey (D-Wis), Chairman
Mickey Edwards (R-Okla), Ranking Republican

**Interior and Related Agencies**
Sidney R. Yates (D-Ill), Chairman
Ralph Regula (R-Ohio), Ranking Republican

**Labor, Health and Human Services, Education, and Related Agencies**
William H. Natcher (D-Ky), Chairman
Silvio O. Conte (R-Mass), Ranking Republican

**Legislative Branch**
Vic Fazio (D-Calif), Chairman
Jerry Lewis (R-Calif), Ranking Republican

**Military Construction**
W. G. "Bill" Hefner (D-NC), Chairman
Bill Lowery (R-Calif), Ranking Republican

**Rural Development, Agriculture, and Related Agencies**
Jamie L. Whitten (D-Miss), Chairman
Virginia Smith (R-Neb), Ranking Republican

**Transportation and Related Agencies**
William Lehman (D-Fla), Chairman
Lawrence Coughlin (R-Pa), Ranking Republican

**Treasury, Postal Service, and General Government**
Edward R. Roybal (D-Calif), Chairman
Joe Skeen (R-NM), Ranking Republican

**VA, HUD, and Independent Agencies**
Bob Traxler (D-Mich), Chairman
Bill Green (R-NY), Ranking Republican

## Total PAC & Large Individual Contributions to Committee Members

| | |
|---|---|
| John P. Murtha (D-Pa) | $755,407 |
| Vic Fazio (D-Calif) | $679,446 |
| William H. Gray III (D-Pa) | $661,705 |
| Sidney R. Yates (D-Ill) | $614,423 |
| Steny H. Hoyer (D-Md) | $593,945 |
| Bill Alexander (D-Ark) | $578,000 |
| Chester G. Atkins (D-Mass) | $568,300 |
| Charles Wilson (D-Texas) | $557,689 |
| W. G. "Bill" Hefner (D-NC) | $542,256 |
| Bill Green (R-NY) | $528,775 |
| Dean A. Gallo (R-NJ) | $525,325 |
| Les AuCoin (D-Ore) | $504,900 |
| Jim Chapman (D-Texas) | $441,488 |
| David R. Obey (D-Wis) | $440,441 |
| Bill Lowery (R-Calif) | $440,346 |
| Jerry Lewis (R-Calif) | $418,551 |
| Robert J. Mrazek (D-NY) | $414,804 |
| William Lehman (D-Fla) | $377,903 |
| Vin Weber (R-Minn) | $368,222 |
| Frank R. Wolf (R-Va) | $352,898 |
| Norm Dicks (D-Wash) | $327,052 |
| Joseph M. McDade (R-Pa) | $312,903 |
| Bob Carr (D-Mich) | $301,083 |
| Tom DeLay (R-Texas) | $275,342 |
| Martin Olav Sabo (D-Minn) | $264,290 |
| Lawrence Coughlin (R-Pa) | $260,353 |
| Mickey Edwards (R-Okla) | $254,522 |
| Ronald D. Coleman (D-Texas) | $244,609 |
| Richard J. Durbin (D-Ill) | $228,353 |
| Jim Kolbe (R-Ariz) | $223,611 |
| Lindsay Thomas (D-Ga) | $221,546 |
| Bob Livingston (R-La) | $217,474 |
| Bob Traxler (D-Mich) | $208,394 |
| Joseph D. Early (D-Mass) | $203,516 |
| John Porter (R-Ill) | $181,920 |
| Louis Stokes (D-Ohio) | $181,850 |
| Alan B. Mollohan (D-WVa) | $173,281 |
| Marcy Kaptur (D-Ohio) | $168,855 |
| Julian C. Dixon (D-Calif) | $157,150 |
| Carl D. Pursell (R-Mich) | $141,585 |
| Joe Skeen (R-NM) | $139,689 |
| C. W. Bill Young (R-Fla) | $137,750 |
| Jamie L. Whitten (D-Miss) | $134,450 |
| Bernard J. Dwyer (D-NJ) | $134,361 |
| Matthew F. McHugh (D-NY) | $133,970 |
| Neal Smith (D-Iowa) | $122,820 |
| Tom Bevill (D-Ala) | $116,300 |
| Harold Rogers (R-Ky) | $115,006 |
| John T. Myers (R-Ind) | $106,556 |
| Edward R. Roybal (D-Calif) | $97,777 |
| Clarence E. Miller (R-Ohio) | $71,928 |
| Silvio O. Conte (R-Mass) | $70,316 |
| Ralph Regula (R-Ohio) | $30,930 |
| Wes Watkins (D-Okla)[1] | $17,800 |
| Lindy Boggs (D-La)[1] | $16,000 |
| Virginia Smith (R-Neb)[1] | $150 |
| William H. Natcher (D-Ky) | -$734 |

[1] Did not seek reelection in 1990

## Summary

Businesses and industries that rely heavily on government contracts keep a sharp eye on the activities of the congressional appropriations committees — particularly defense contractors, whose fortunes may rise or fall depending on decisions reached by these panels. John Murtha, the Pennsylvania Democrat who chairs the Defense Appropriations subcommittee, collected over $212,000 from defense contractors in 1989-90, leading all other House recipients in defense dollars. Three other committee members — Charles Wilson (D-Texas), Bill Hefner (D-NC) and Joseph McDade (R-Pa) — drew $100,000 or more from defense contributors.

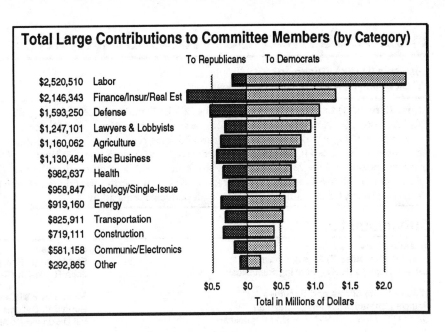

**Total Large Contributions to Committee Members (by Category)**

To Republicans    To Democrats

| | |
|---|---|
| $2,520,510 | Labor |
| $2,146,343 | Finance/Insur/Real Est |
| $1,593,250 | Defense |
| $1,247,101 | Lawyers & Lobbyists |
| $1,160,062 | Agriculture |
| $1,130,484 | Misc Business |
| $982,637 | Health |
| $958,847 | Ideology/Single-Issue |
| $919,160 | Energy |
| $825,911 | Transportation |
| $719,111 | Construction |
| $581,158 | Communic/Electronics |
| $292,865 | Other |

$0.5   $0   $0.5   $1.0   $1.5   $2.0

Total in Millions of Dollars

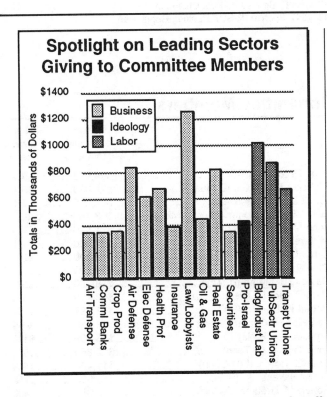

## Spotlight on Leading Sectors Giving to Committee Members

Totals in Thousands of Dollars

$1400, $1200, $1000, $800, $600, $400, $200, $0

- Business
- Ideology
- Labor

Air Transport, Comml Banks, Crop Prod, Air Defense, Elec Defense, Health Prof, Insurance, Law/Lobbyists, Oil & Gas, Real Estate, Securities, Pro-Israel, Bldg/Indust Lab, PubSectr Unions, Transpt Unions

### Top 20 Contributors to Committee Members in 1989-90

| | | |
|---|---|---|
| 1 | National Assn of Realtors | $327,893 |
| 2 | American Medical Assn* | $235,107 |
| 3 | National Education Assn* | $228,905 |
| 4 | Teamsters Union* | $199,250 |
| 5 | AT&T | $156,655 |
| 6 | National Assn of Letter Carriers* | $128,550 |
| 7 | Natl Assn of Retired Federal Employees | $128,200 |
| 8 | United Auto Workers | $126,900 |
| 9 | National Assn of Home Builders | $119,850 |
| 10 | National PAC | $115,500 |
| 11 | Carpenters & Joiners Union* | $110,640 |
| 12 | Laborers Union* | $106,400 |
| 13 | Amer Fedn of State/County/Munic Employees | $105,500 |
| 14 | American Dental Assn | $99,900 |
| 15 | National Auto Dealers Assn | $99,000 |
| 16 | Marine Engineers Union* | $95,850 |
| 17 | Air Line Pilots Assn | $95,500 |
| 18 | Associated Milk Producers | $94,200 |
| 19 | General Motors* | $86,790 |
| 20 | Operating Engineers Union* | $85,265 |

\* Contributions came from more than one PAC affiliated with this sponsor.

## Leading Sectors
## Giving to Committee Members

### Business

| | |
|---|---|
| Air Transport | $339,860 |
| Commercial Banks | $333,090 |
| Crop Production & Basic Processing | $342,786 |
| Defense Aerospace | $823,691 |
| Defense Electronics | $605,259 |
| Health Professionals | $668,322 |
| Insurance | $377,133 |
| Lawyers & Lobbyists | $1,247,101 |
| Oil & Gas | $434,061 |
| Real Estate | $808,894 |
| Securities/Commodities Investment | $333,772 |

### Ideological/Single-Issue

| | |
|---|---|
| Pro-Israel | $419,289 |

### Labor

| | |
|---|---|
| Bldg Trades/Industrial/Misc Unions | $1,006,670 |
| Public Sector Unions | $856,240 |
| Transportation Unions | $657,600 |

# House Armed Services Committee

Les Aspin (D-Wis), Chairman
Bill Dickinson (R-Ala), Ranking Republican

**Party Ratio:** 32 Democrats
21 Republicans

**Jurisdiction:** (1) Common defense generally; (2) The Department of Defense generally, including the Department of the Army, Navy, and Air Force; (3) Ammunition depots; forts; arsenals; Army, Navy, and Air Force reservations and establishments; (4) Conservation, development, and use of naval petroleum and oil shale reserves; (5) Pay, promotion, retirement, and other benefits and privileges of members of the armed forces; (6) Scientific research and development in support of the armed services; (7) Selective service; (8) Size and composition of the Army, Navy and Air Force; (9) Soldiers' and sailors' homes; (10) Strategic and critical materials necessary for the common defense; (11) Military applications of nuclear energy. The committee also has oversight duties with respect to international arms control and disarmament, and military dependents' education.

## Subcommittees

### Investigations
Nicholas Mavroules (D-Mass), Chairman
Larry J. Hopkins (R-Ky), Ranking Republican

### Military Installations and Facilities
Patricia Schroeder (D-Colo), Chairman
David O'B. Martin (R-NY), Ranking Republican

### Military Personnel and Compensation
Beverly B. Byron (D-Md), Chairman
Herbert H. Bateman (R-Va), Ranking Republican

### Procurement and Military Nuclear Systems
Les Aspin (D-Wis), Chairman
Jim Courter (R-NJ), Ranking Republican

### Readiness
Earl Hutto (D-Fla), Chairman
John R. Kasich (R-Ohio), Ranking Republican

### Research and Development
Ronald V. Dellums (D-Calif), Chairman
Bill Dickinson (R-Ala), Ranking Republican

### Seapower and Strategic and Critical Materials
Charles E. Bennett (D-Fla), Chairman
Floyd D. Spence (R-SC), Ranking Republican

## Total Defense-Related Contributions to Committee Members

| | Total from Cmte-Related Contribs | Pct of Member's Lg Contribs |
|---|---|---|
| Bill Dickinson (R-Ala) | $124,640 | 42% |
| Les Aspin (D-Wis) | $115,985 | 21% |
| Herbert H. Bateman (R-Va) | $95,100 | 25% |
| Robert C. Smith (R-NH)[1] | $94,350 | 9% |
| Robert W. Davis (R-Mich) | $75,525 | 27% |
| Ike Skelton (D-Mo) | $67,815 | 22% |
| Dave McCurdy (D-Okla) | $66,450 | 27% |
| Roy Dyson (D-Md) | $62,100 | 12% |
| Beverly B. Byron (D-Md) | $56,380 | 30% |
| James V. Hansen (R-Utah) | $55,213 | 25% |
| George J. Hochbrueckner (D-NY) | $53,876 | 11% |
| Ronald K. Machtley (R-RI) | $53,550 | 10% |
| Richard Ray (D-Ga) | $50,000 | 23% |
| Duncan Hunter (R-Calif) | $46,340 | 16% |
| Curt Weldon (R-Pa) | $46,050 | 13% |
| Marilyn Lloyd (D-Tenn) | $44,250 | 14% |
| George "Buddy" Darden (D-Ga) | $43,600 | 15% |
| Jon Kyl (R-Ariz) | $42,400 | 9% |
| Bob Stump (R-Ariz) | $40,265 | 22% |
| Dennis M. Hertel (D-Mich) | $37,945 | 17% |
| Jim McCrery (R-La) | $37,250 | 10% |
| Norman Sisisky (D-Va) | $36,350 | 20% |
| Albert G. Bustamante (D-Texas) | $35,200 | 11% |
| Earl Hutto (D-Fla) | $31,100 | 23% |
| H. Martin Lancaster (D-NC) | $30,050 | 10% |
| Andy Ireland (R-Fla) | $29,600 | 12% |
| Floyd D. Spence (R-SC) | $29,225 | 23% |
| Owen B. Pickett (D-Va) | $27,350 | 12% |
| Joel Hefley (R-Colo) | $26,750 | 22% |
| Thomas M. Foglietta (D-Pa) | $25,300 | 6% |
| James Bilbray (D-Nev) | $25,050 | 6% |
| Solomon P. Ortiz (D-Texas) | $25,000 | 14% |
| John R. Kasich (R-Ohio) | $24,900 | 9% |
| Nicholas Mavroules (D-Mass) | $24,850 | 13% |
| Frank McCloskey (D-Ind) | $24,200 | 7% |
| G. V. "Sonny" Montgomery (D-Miss) | $23,750 | 29% |
| John M. Spratt Jr. (D-SC) | $21,500 | 25% |
| Michael R. McNulty (D-NY) | $21,000 | 11% |
| Larry J. Hopkins (R-Ky) | $19,500 | 22% |
| Glen Browder (D-Ala) | $19,200 | 8% |
| David O'B. Martin (R-NY) | $18,750 | 33% |
| Gene Taylor (D-Miss) | $18,400 | 8% |
| Robert K. Dornan (R-Calif) | $17,087 | 6% |
| Ben Blaz (R-Guam)[2] | $14,250 | 86% |
| Jim Courter (R-NJ)[3] | $13,800 | 61% |
| John Tanner (D-Tenn) | $12,350 | 5% |
| John G. Rowland (R-Conn)[3] | $11,400 | 14% |
| Arthur Ravenel Jr. (R-SC) | $10,800 | 7% |
| Ronald V. Dellums (D-Calif) | $8,050 | 4% |
| Patricia Schroeder (D-Colo) | $7,409 | 5% |
| Joseph E. Brennan (D-Maine)[3] | $7,250 | 14% |
| Lane Evans (D-Ill) | $5,250 | 2% |
| Charles E. Bennett (D-Fla) | $4,050 | 12% |
| Marvin Leath (D-Texas)[3] | $0 | 0% |

[1] Ran for U.S. Senate in 1990
[2] Non-voting Delegate
[3] Did not seek reelection in 1990

## Summary

The demise of the Soviet Union and a general warming in international relations may be welcome news to most Americans, but it also signals hard times for the nation's defense industry. The House and Senate Armed Services and Appropriations committees are the key congressional panels wrestling with the problem of downsizing the military without crippling the American defense industry.

The patterns of contributions within the committee reflects the industry's concern. Defense contractors delivered nearly $2 million in contributions to House Armed Services members in the 1990 elections, and the Top 20 list of contributors bears a close resemblance to the Pentagon's list of top contractors. The downturn in defense spending is causing many large corporations to cut back their defense operations. A recent example was Ford Motor Co., which sold BDM International, a major defense research company, in October 1990.

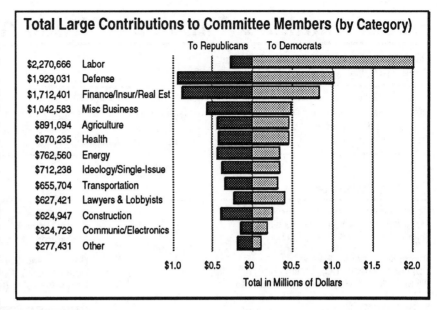

**Total Large Contributions to Committee Members (by Category)**

| | |
|---|---|
| $2,270,666 | Labor |
| $1,929,031 | Defense |
| $1,712,401 | Finance/Insur/Real Est |
| $1,042,583 | Misc Business |
| $891,094 | Agriculture |
| $870,235 | Health |
| $762,560 | Energy |
| $712,238 | Ideology/Single-Issue |
| $655,704 | Transportation |
| $627,421 | Lawyers & Lobbyists |
| $624,947 | Construction |
| $324,729 | Communic/Electronics |
| $277,431 | Other |

Total in Millions of Dollars

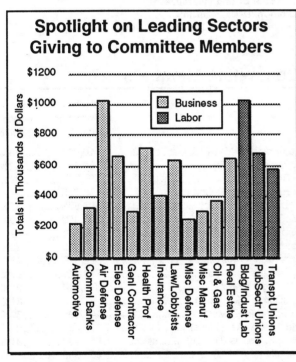

## Spotlight on Leading Sectors Giving to Committee Members

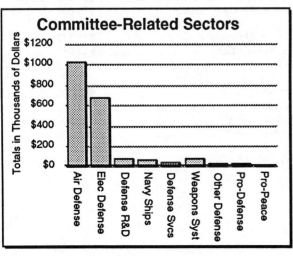

## Committee-Related Sectors

### Top 20 Defense-Related Contributors to Committee Members in 1989-90

| | | |
|---|---|---|
| 1 | AT&T | $145,075 |
| 2 | McDonnell Douglas* | $115,825 |
| 3 | Lockheed Corp | $86,400 |
| 4 | General Motors* | $79,120 |
| 5 | General Dynamics | $78,250 |
| 6 | Raytheon* | $76,450 |
| 7 | Northrop Corp | $75,027 |
| 8 | Textron Inc | $70,600 |
| 9 | Grumman Corp | $69,300 |
| 10 | Rockwell International | $66,640 |
| 11 | United Technologies | $64,600 |
| 12 | Martin Marietta Corp | $63,100 |
| 13 | Ford Motor Co/BDM International | $52,025 |
| 14 | Boeing Co | $51,200 |
| 15 | LTV Aerospace & Defense Co | $49,050 |
| 16 | Litton Industries | $41,900 |
| 17 | General Electric | $34,050 |
| 18 | Tenneco Inc | $33,050 |
| 19 | FMC Corp | $30,550 |
| 20 | E-Systems* | $30,150 |

* Contributions came from more than one PAC affiliated with this sponsor.

### Leading Committee-Related Sectors Giving to Committee Members

**Business**

| | |
|---|---|
| Defense aerospace contractors | $1,019,468 |
| Defense electronic contractors | $660,913 |
| Defense research & development | $72,500 |
| Defense shipbuilders | $60,150 |
| Defense-related services | $30,750 |
| Ground-based & other weapons systems | $73,750 |
| Other defense | $11,500 |

**Ideological/Single-Issue**

| | |
|---|---|
| Pro-defense | $22,285 |
| Pro-peace | $6,489 |

# House Banking, Finance & Urban Affairs Committee

Henry B. Gonzalez (D-Texas), Chairman
Chalmers P. Wylie (R-Ohio), Ranking Republican

**Party Ratio:** 30 Democrats
20 Republicans

> **Jurisdiction:** (1) Banks and banking, including deposit insurance and Federal monetary policy; (2) money and credit, including currency and the issuance of notes and redemption thereof; gold and silver, including the coinage thereof; valuation and revaluation of the dollar; (3) Urban development; (4) Public and private housing; (5) Economic stabilization, defense production, renegotiation, and control of the price of commodities, rents, and services; (6) International finance; (7) Financial and Monetary organizations.

## Subcommittees

**Consumer Affairs and Coinage**
Richard H. Lehman (D-Calif), Chairman
John P. Hiler (R-Ind), Ranking Republican

**Domestic Monetary Policy**
Stephen L. Neal (D-NC), Chairman
Bill McCollum (R-Fla), Ranking Republican

**Economic Stabilization**
Mary Rose Oakar (D-Ohio), Chairwoman
Norman D. Shumway (R-Calif), Ranking Republican

**Financial Institutions Supervision, Regulation and Insurance**
Frank Annunzio (D-Ill), Chairman
Chalmers P. Wylie (R-Ohio), Ranking Republican

**General Oversight and Investigations**
Carroll Hubbard Jr. (D-Ky), Chairman
Stan Parris (R-Va), Ranking Republican

**Housing and Community Development**
Henry B. Gonzalez (D-Texas), Chairman
Marge Roukema (R-NJ), Ranking Republican

**International Development, Finance, Trade and Monetary Policy**
Walter E. Fauntroy (D- DC), Chairman
Jim Leach (R-Iowa), Ranking Republican

**Policy Research and Insurance**
Ben Erdreich (D-Ala), Chairman
Doug Bereuter (R-Neb), Ranking Republican

## Total Committee-Related Contributions to Committee Members

| | Total from Cmte-Related Contribs | Pct of Member's Lg Contribs |
|---|---|---|
| Charles E. Schumer (D-NY) | $349,902 | 56% |
| Frank Annunzio (D-Ill) | $248,724 | 42% |
| Patricia Saiki (R-Hawaii)[1] | $231,142 | 24% |
| Stephen L. Neal (D-NC) | $222,100 | 43% |
| Steve Bartlett (R-Texas) | $214,210 | 35% |
| Peter Hoagland (D-Neb) | $212,641 | 28% |
| Doug Barnard Jr. (D-Ga) | $209,362 | 65% |
| Bill Paxon (R-NY) | $167,517 | 33% |
| Thomas R. Carper (D-Del) | $159,615 | 37% |
| Joseph P. Kennedy II (D-Mass) | $158,425 | 25% |
| David E. Price (D-NC) | $155,350 | 32% |
| Marge Roukema (R-NJ) | $145,398 | 42% |
| Carroll Hubbard Jr. (D-Ky) | $144,977 | 48% |
| H. James Saxton (R-NJ) | $143,897 | 36% |
| John P. Hiler (R-Ind) | $136,726 | 55% |
| Tom Ridge (R-Pa) | $136,675 | 39% |
| Chalmers P. Wylie (R-Ohio) | $133,455 | 65% |
| Al McCandless (R-Calif) | $131,250 | 32% |
| John J. LaFalce (D-NY) | $128,950 | 56% |
| Jim Bunning (R-Ky) | $120,325 | 33% |
| Liz J. Patterson (D-SC) | $118,177 | 32% |
| Cliff Stearns (R-Fla) | $116,988 | 33% |
| Paul E. Kanjorski (D-Pa) | $116,552 | 42% |
| Stan Parris (R-Va) | $116,050 | 37% |
| Nancy Pelosi (D-Calif) | $112,950 | 25% |
| Richard H. Lehman (D-Calif) | $110,330 | 45% |

| | Total from Cmte-Related Contribs | Pct of Member's Lg Contribs |
|---|---|---|
| Barney Frank (D-Mass) | $110,292 | 28% |
| David Dreier (R-Calif) | $103,356 | 32% |
| Toby Roth (R-Wis) | $99,789 | 39% |
| Mary Rose Oakar (D-Ohio) | $97,725 | 31% |
| Paul E. Gillmor (R-Ohio) | $97,575 | 37% |
| Bill McCollum (R-Fla) | $96,850 | 30% |
| Richard E. Neal (D-Mass) | $91,719 | 29% |
| Richard H. Baker (R-La) | $89,648 | 32% |
| Ben Erdreich (D-Ala) | $82,610 | 40% |
| Doug Bereuter (R-Neb) | $78,521 | 47% |
| Eliot L. Engel (D-NY) | $73,210 | 21% |
| Jim McDermott (D-Wash) | $67,200 | 31% |
| Bruce F. Vento (D-Minn) | $63,600 | 32% |
| Gerald D. Kleczka (D-Wis) | $62,233 | 29% |
| Esteban E. Torres (D-Calif) | $61,900 | 31% |
| Kweisi Mfume (D-Md) | $57,353 | 31% |
| Bruce A. Morrison (D-Conn)[2] | $56,634 | 51% |
| Henry B. Gonzalez (D-Texas) | $54,900 | 43% |
| Norman D. Shumway (R-Calif)[2] | $47,772 | 61% |
| Tom Lantos (D-Calif) | $43,983 | 16% |
| Floyd H. Flake (D-NY) | $39,183 | 27% |
| Walter E. Fauntroy (D-DC)[3] | $11,050 | 70% |
| Robert Garcia (D-NY)[4] | $10,300 | 16% |
| Ted Weiss (D-NY) | $9,950 | 9% |
| Bill Nelson (D-Fla)[2] | $9,500 | 23% |
| Jim Leach (R-Iowa) | $1,300 | 8% |

[1] Ran for U.S. Senate in 1990
[2] Did not seek reelection in 1990
[3] Non-voting Delegate/Did not seek reelection in 1990
[4] Resigned Jan 7, 1990

## Summary

Commercial banks were the leading (but hardly the only) major contributor to members of the House Banking Committee in 1989-90, since no committee in the House is as important to the heavily-regulated banking industry. The issue of bank deregulation has been high on the committee's agenda in recent years, as Congress tries to shore up the sagging fortunes of many of the nation's leading financial institutions. This is the same committee that in the early 1980s loosened the rules governing savings & loans — thereby setting the stage for what became the most expensive political scandal (and subsequent bailout) in American history.

Aside from banking and financial interests, the committee also deals with housing issues — a fact that helped attract nearly $1.3 million dollars in contributions from the real estate and homebuilding industries.

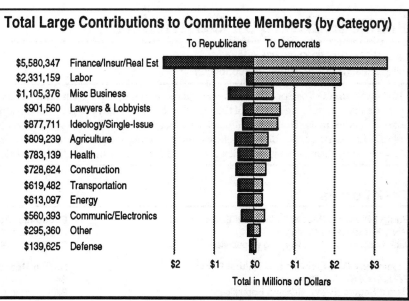

**Total Large Contributions to Committee Members (by Category)**

To Republicans — To Democrats

| | | |
|---|---|---|
| $5,580,347 | Finance/Insur/Real Est | |
| $2,331,159 | Labor | |
| $1,105,376 | Misc Business | |
| $901,560 | Lawyers & Lobbyists | |
| $877,711 | Ideology/Single-Issue | |
| $809,239 | Agriculture | |
| $783,139 | Health | |
| $728,624 | Construction | |
| $619,482 | Transportation | |
| $613,097 | Energy | |
| $560,393 | Communic/Electronics | |
| $295,360 | Other | |
| $139,625 | Defense | |

Total in Millions of Dollars

## Spotlight on Leading Sectors Giving to Committee Members

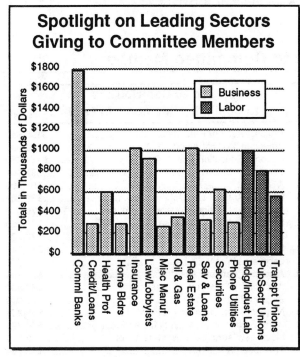

Legend: Business, Labor

Totals in Thousands of Dollars

Sectors: Comml Banks, Credit/Loans, Health Prof, Home Bldrs, Insurance, Law/Lobbyists, Misc Manuf, Oil & Gas, Real Estate, Sav & Loans, Securities, Phone Utilities, Bldg/Indust Lab, PubSectr Unions, Transpt Unions

## Committee-Related Sectors

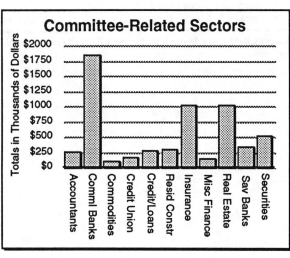

Totals in Thousands of Dollars

Sectors: Accountants, Comml Banks, Commodities, Credit Union, Credit/Loans, Resid Constr, Insurance, Misc Finance, Real Estate, Sav Banks, Securities

### Top 20 Committee-Related Contributors to Committee Members in 1989-90

| | | |
|---|---|---|
| 1 | National Assn of Realtors | $361,065 |
| 2 | American Bankers Assn* | $326,584 |
| 3 | JP Morgan & Co | $180,750 |
| 4 | National Assn of Home Builders* | $174,296 |
| 5 | American Institute of CPA's | $151,750 |
| 6 | Barnett Banks of Florida | $137,500 |
| 7 | National Assn of Life Underwriters | $134,450 |
| 8 | Credit Union National Assn* | $116,900 |
| 9 | Citicorp | $106,600 |
| 10 | American Council of Life Insurance | $98,147 |
| 11 | Independent Insurance Agents of America | $96,385 |
| 12 | US League of Savings Assns* | $91,111 |
| 13 | Bankers Trust | $77,050 |
| 14 | Chase Manhattan* | $69,828 |
| 15 | Mortgage Bankers Assn of America | $63,125 |
| 16 | Independent Bankers Assn | $52,300 |
| 17 | Goldman, Sachs & Co | $52,050 |
| 18 | BankAmerica* | $48,750 |
| 19 | First Chicago Corp | $48,350 |
| 20 | Chemical Bank* | $48,250 |

\* Contributions came from more than one PAC affiliated with this sponsor.

### Leading Committee-Related Sectors Giving to Committee Members

**Banking**

| | |
|---|---|
| Commercial banks | $1,825,916 |
| Savings & loans | $320,843 |
| Credit unions | $153,450 |

**Financial Services**

| | |
|---|---|
| Finance/credit companies | $274,859 |
| Accountants | $245,728 |

**Other Financial**

| | |
|---|---|
| Insurance | $1,012,998 |
| Securities & investment | $512,627 |
| Commodity brokers/dealers | $95,600 |
| Misc finance | $129,213 |

**Real Estate & Construction**

| | |
|---|---|
| Real estate | $1,009,113 |
| Home builders | $279,494 |

# House Budget Committee

Leon E. Panetta (D-Calif), Chairman
Bill Frenzel (R-Minn), Ranking Republican

**Party Ratio:** 21 Democrats
14 Republicans

> **Jurisdiction:** (1) To report the matters required to be reported by it under titles III and IV of the Congressional Budget Act of 1974; (2) To make continuing studies of the effect on budget outlays of relevant existing and proposed legislation and to report the results of such studies to the House on a recurring basis; (3) To request and evaluate continuing studies of tax expenditures, to devise methods of coordinating tax expenditures, policies, and programs with direct budget outlays, and to report the results of such studies to the House on a recurring basis; and (4) To review, on a continuing basis, the conduct by the Congressional Budget Office of its functions and duties.

## Task Forces

**Budget Process, Reconciliation and Enforcement**
Marty Russo (D-Ill), Chairman
Jack Buechner (R-Mo), Ranking Republican

**Community Development and Natural Resources**
Ed Jenkins (D-Ga), Chairman
Harold Rogers (R-Ky), Ranking Republican

**Defense, Foreign Policy and Space**
Marvin Leath (D-), Chairman
Denny Smith (R-Ore), Ranking Republican)

**Economic Policy, Projections and Revenues**
Jim Slattery (D-Kan), Chairman
Bill Thomas (R-Calif), Ranking Republican

**Human Resources**
Barbara Boxer (D-Calif), Chairwoman
Bill Goodling (R-Pa), Ranking Republican

**Urgent Fiscal Issues**
Charles E. Schumer, D-NY), Chairman
Dick Armey (R-Texas), Ranking Republican

## Total PAC & Large Individual Contributions to Committee Members

Richard A. Gephardt (D-Mo) ............................................. $1,659,584
Bill Schuette (R-Mich)[1] ................................................ $790,924
Barbara Boxer (D-Calif) ................................................. $700,811
John Bryant (D-Texas) ................................................... $656,586
Charles E. Schumer (D-NY) .............................................. $626,952
Dean A. Gallo (R-NJ) .................................................... $525,325
Helen Delich Bentley (R-Md) ............................................ $522,883
Marty Russo (D-Ill) ..................................................... $486,574
Frank J. Guarini (D-NJ) ................................................. $451,038
Howard L. Berman (D-Calif) ............................................. $448,460
Mike Espy (D-Miss) ...................................................... $404,873
Dick Armey (R-Texas) .................................................... $393,200
Jim Slattery (D-Kan) .................................................... $391,077
Jim McCrery (R-La) ...................................................... $381,382
Denny Smith (R-Ore) ..................................................... $353,015
Bill Thomas (R-Calif) ................................................... $306,621
James L. Oberstar (D-Minn) ............................................. $292,199
Amo Houghton (R-NY) ..................................................... $279,400
John R. Kasich (R-Ohio) ................................................. $266,590
Martin Olav Sabo (D-Minn) .............................................. $264,290
Jack Buechner (R-Mo) .................................................... $259,796
Richard J. Durbin (D-Ill) ............................................... $228,353
Ed Jenkins (D-Ga) ....................................................... $224,450
Dale E. Kildee (D-Mich) ................................................. $196,164
Anthony C. Beilenson (D-Calif) ......................................... $179,200
Leon E. Panetta (D-Calif) ............................................... $176,850
Jerry Huckaby (D-La) .................................................... $158,895
Bob Wise (D-WVa) ........................................................ $144,700
Bernard J. Dwyer (D-NJ) ................................................. $134,361
Harold Rogers (R-Ky) .................................................... $115,006
John M. Spratt Jr. (D-SC) ............................................... $85,113
Bill Gradison (R-Ohio) .................................................. $50,157
Bill Goodling (R-Pa) .................................................... $13,853
Bill Frenzel (R-Minn)[2] ................................................ $5,824
Marvin Leath (D-Texas)[2] ............................................... $4,268

| | Top 20 Contributors to Committee Members in 1989-90 | |
|---|---|---|
| 1 | National Assn of Realtors | $196,550 |
| 2 | American Medical Assn* | $142,300 |
| 3 | National Education Assn* | $111,250 |
| 4 | Teamsters Union | $97,000 |
| 5 | AT&T | $91,900 |
| 6 | National Assn of Life Underwriters | $88,300 |
| 7 | Natl Assn of Retired Federal Employees | $79,000 |
| 8 | National Auto Dealers Assn | $78,450 |
| 9 | National Assn of Home Builders | $77,600 |
| 10 | United Auto Workers | $74,847 |
| 11 | Laborers Union* | $73,750 |
| 12 | American Bankers Assn* | $73,150 |
| 13 | Assn of Trial Lawyers of America | $70,800 |
| 14 | Air Line Pilots Assn | $68,000 |
| 15 | National Assn of Letter Carriers* | $66,950 |
| 16 | Amer Fedn of State/County/Munic Employees | $66,499 |
| 17 | Machinists/Aerospace Workers Union* | $62,850 |
| 18 | Thompson & Mitchell | $62,760 |
| 19 | Operating Engineers Union* | $61,210 |
| 20 | Carpenters & Joiners Union* | $59,900 |

\* Contributions came from more than one PAC affiliated with this sponsor.

---

[1] Ran for U.S. Senate in 1990
[2] Did not seek reelection in 1990

## Summary

Along with its counterpart in the Senate, the House Budget Committee is the panel in Congress chiefly responsible for putting together the federal government's annual budget. That assignment, though important to the nation as a whole, is not focused directly on any one industry or interest group — so the patterns in campaign contributions are typical of Congress as a whole. The financial sector was the biggest funder of committee members' 1990 campaigns. Organized labor was second, delivering its dollars overwhelmingly to Democrats.

### Total Large Contributions to Committee Members (by Category)

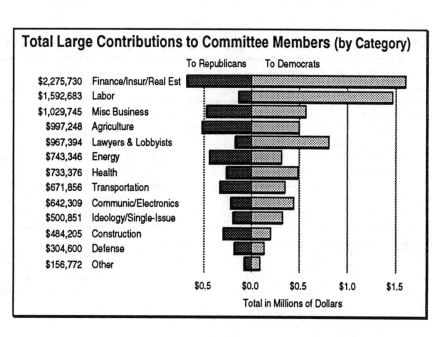

| | To Republicans | To Democrats |
|---|---|---|
| $2,275,730 | Finance/Insur/Real Est | |
| $1,592,683 | Labor | |
| $1,029,745 | Misc Business | |
| $997,248 | Agriculture | |
| $967,394 | Lawyers & Lobbyists | |
| $743,346 | Energy | |
| $733,376 | Health | |
| $671,856 | Transportation | |
| $642,309 | Communic/Electronics | |
| $500,851 | Ideology/Single-Issue | |
| $484,205 | Construction | |
| $304,600 | Defense | |
| $156,772 | Other | |

Total in Millions of Dollars

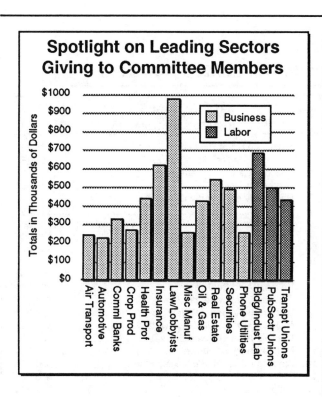

### Spotlight on Leading Sectors Giving to Committee Members

Totals in Thousands of Dollars

Business
Labor

Air Transport, Automotive, Comml Banks, Crop Prod, Health Prof, Insurance, Law/Lobbyists, Misc Manuf, Oil & Gas, Real Estate, Securities, Phone Utilities, Bldg/Indust Lab, PubSctr Unions, Transpt Unions

### Leading Sectors Giving to Committee Members

#### Business

| | |
|---|---|
| Air Transport | $232,310 |
| Automotive | $222,411 |
| Commercial Banks | $317,266 |
| Crop Production & Basic Processing | $259,822 |
| Health Professionals | $435,101 |
| Insurance | $609,824 |
| Lawyers & Lobbyists | $967,394 |
| Misc Manufacturing & Distributing | $243,843 |
| Oil & Gas | $415,703 |
| Real Estate | $531,326 |
| Securities/Commodities Investment | $483,214 |
| Telephone Utilities | $245,955 |

#### Labor

| | |
|---|---|
| Bldg Trades/Industrial/Misc Unions | $673,312 |
| Public Sector Unions | $491,621 |
| Transportation Unions | $427,750 |

# House District of Columbia Committee

Ronald V. Dellums (D-Calif), Chairman
Stan Parris (R-Va), Ranking Republican

**Party Ratio:** 7 Democrats
4 Republicans

**Jurisdiction:** (1) Local government, delegated authority, form, finances, operations and programs, of local government bodies, as authorized by . . . the U.S. Constitution—"Congress shall have the power to exercise exclusive legislation in all cases whatsoever over such District . . ."; (2) Political status, jurisdiction and boundaries of the District of Columbia; (3) The annual federal payment — pension fund financing for police, firefighters and teachers; (4) Delegate to the House of Representatives; courts: organization, operations; appointment and removal mechanisms and term of judges; (5) Organizations chartered by Congress: determination of tax-exempt status; (6) Planning and design of the national capital: (a) building height limitation, National Capital Planning Commission, protection of Old Georgetown, the Commission of Fine Arts; (7) Metropolitan regional affairs: (a) Washington Metropolitan Area Transit Authority, (b) emergency planning and procedures, Potomac River shoreline and water quality improvement; (8) The International Community.

## Subcommittees

**Fiscal Affairs and Health**
Walter E. Fauntroy (D-DC), Chairman
Thomas J. Bliley Jr. (R-Va), Ranking Republican

**Government Operations and Metropolitan Affairs**
Alan Wheat (D-Mo), Chairman
Larry Combest (R-Texas), Ranking Republican

**Judiciary and Education**
Mervyn M. Dymally (D-Calif), Chairman
Dana Rohrabacher (R-Calif), Ranking Republican

## Total PAC & Large Individual Contributions to Committee Members

William H. Gray III (D-Pa) .................................... $661,705
Thomas J. Bliley Jr. (R-Va) ................................. $487,470
Pete Stark (D-Calif) ............................................ $411,146
Dana Rohrabacher (R-Calif) ............................... $380,066
Mervyn M. Dymally (D-Calif) ............................... $365,450
Stan Parris (R-Va) .............................................. $315,768
Alan Wheat (D-Mo) ............................................. $268,254
Jim McDermott (D-Wash) .................................... $214,530
Ronald V. Dellums (D-Calif) ................................ $192,750
Larry Combest (R-Texas) .................................... $144,126
Bruce A. Morrison (D-Conn)[1] ............................ $111,034
Walter E. Fauntroy (D-DC)[2] ............................... $15,800

| | Top 20 Contributors to Committee Members in 1989-90 | |
|---|---|---|
| 1 | National Assn of Realtors | $58,050 |
| 2 | American Medical Assn* | $51,350 |
| 3 | National Education Assn | $50,300 |
| 4 | Teamsters Union | $48,500 |
| 5 | National Assn of Letter Carriers* | $33,740 |
| 6 | AT&T | $32,350 |
| 7 | Amer Fedn of State/County/Munic Employees | $32,000 |
| 8 | Carpenters & Joiners Union* | $31,600 |
| 9 | American Bankers Assn* | $31,000 |
| 10 | American Institute of CPA's | $31,000 |
| 11 | United Auto Workers | $27,900 |
| 12 | National Auto Dealers Assn | $24,900 |
| 13 | Assn of Trial Lawyers of America | $24,050 |
| 14 | Machinists/Aerospace Workers Union | $24,000 |
| 15 | National Assn of Life Underwriters | $24,000 |
| 16 | National Assn of Home Builders | $23,650 |
| 17 | Marine Engineers Union* | $21,000 |
| 18 | American Council of Life Insurance | $20,550 |
| 19 | Philip Morris* | $20,499 |
| 20 | Laborers Union* | $19,850 |

\* Contributions came from more than one PAC affiliated with this sponsor.

[1] Did not seek reelection in 1990
[2] Non-voting Delegate/Did not seek reelection in 1990

## Summary

Unlike every other city in America, the nation's capital is governed only partly by its own elected officials, and partly by the U.S. Congress, which has overseen the city's affairs since the District of Columbia was created in 1790. The degree of congressional control has lessened over the years and the city now enjoys most benefits of home rule. But the Congress still controls a major part of the city's purse strings, and decisions made in this committee affect the lives of every resident of Washington.

Since D.C. is not a state, its residents do not elect their own representative, but rather a "delegate," like those who represent Puerto Rico, the Virgin Islands, Guam and American Samoa. Delegates may not vote for bills on the House floor, but they are entitled to debate and vote on issues within the committees on which they serve.

This second-class status has long rankled D.C. residents. In 1990, in addition to electing their delegate to Congress, the district's voters also elected two "shadow Senators" — one of them the Rev. Jesse Jackson — to lobby for statehood. Unlike the D.C. delegate, the shadow Senators enjoy no official status in Congress, formal or otherwise.

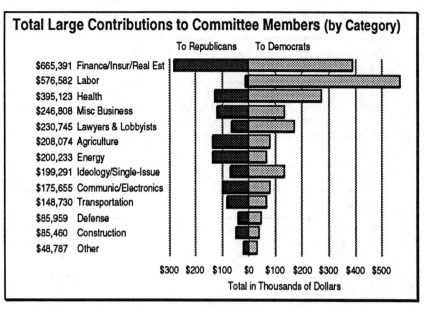

**Total Large Contributions to Committee Members (by Category)**

| | To Republicans | To Democrats |
|---|---|---|
| $665,391 | Finance/Insur/Real Est | |
| $576,582 | Labor | |
| $395,123 | Health | |
| $246,808 | Misc Business | |
| $230,745 | Lawyers & Lobbyists | |
| $208,074 | Agriculture | |
| $200,233 | Energy | |
| $199,291 | Ideology/Single-Issue | |
| $175,655 | Communic/Electronics | |
| $148,730 | Transportation | |
| $85,959 | Defense | |
| $85,460 | Construction | |
| $48,787 | Other | |

Total in Thousands of Dollars

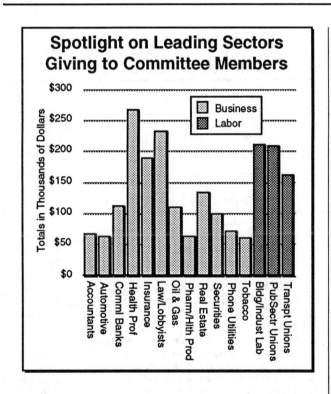

**Spotlight on Leading Sectors Giving to Committee Members**

Totals in Thousands of Dollars

- Business
- Labor

**Leading Sectors Giving to Committee Members**

**Business**

| | |
|---|---|
| Accountants | $64,572 |
| Automotive | $61,100 |
| Commercial Banks | $110,925 |
| Health Professionals | $264,070 |
| Insurance | $187,434 |
| Lawyers & Lobbyists | $230,745 |
| Oil & Gas | $108,433 |
| Pharmaceuticals/Health Products | $61,203 |
| Real Estate | $132,700 |
| Securities/Commodities Investment | $96,500 |
| Telephone Utilities | $71,405 |
| Tobacco | $59,199 |

**Labor**

| | |
|---|---|
| Bldg Trades/Industrial/Misc Unions | $209,522 |
| Public Sector Unions | $207,560 |
| Transportation Unions | $159,500 |

# House Education and Labor Committee

Augustus F. Hawkins (D-Calif), Chairman
Bill Goodling (R-Pa), Ranking Republican

**Party Ratio:** 22 Democrats
14 Republicans

**Jurisdiction:** (1) Measures relating to education or labor generally; (2) Child labor; (3) Columbia Institution for the Deaf, Dumb, and Blind; Howard University; Freedman's Hospital; (4) Convict labor and the entry of goods made by convicts into interstate commerce; (5) Labor standards; (6) Labor statistics; (7) Mediation and arbitration of labor disputes; (8) Regulation or prevention of importation of foreign laborers under contract; (9) Food programs for children in schools; (10) United States Employees' Compensation Commission; (11) Vocational rehabilitation; (12) Wages and hours of labor; (13) Welfare of miners; (14) Work incentives programs. The committee also has a special oversight function with respect to domestic educational programs and institutions, and programs of student assistance, which are within the jurisdiction of other committees.

## Subcommittees

**Elementary, Secondary, and Vocational Education**
Augustus F. Hawkins (D-Calif), Chairman
Bill Goodling (R-Pa), Ranking Republican

**Employment Opportunities**
Matthew G. Martinez (D-Calif), Chairman
Steve Gunderson (R-Wis), Ranking Republican

**Health and Safety**
Joseph M. Gaydos (D-Pa), Chairman
Paul B. Henry (R-Mich), Ranking Republican

**Human Resources**
Dale E. Kildee (D-Mich), Chairman
Thomas J. Tauke (R-Iowa), Ranking Republican

**Labor-Management Relations**
William L. Clay (D-Mo), Chairman
Harris W. Fawell (R-Ill), Ranking Republican

**Labor Standards**
Austin J. Murphy (D-Pa), Chairman
Thomas E. Petri (R-Wis), Ranking Republican

**Postsecondary Education**
Pat Williams (D-Mont), Chairman
Tom Coleman (R-Mo), Ranking Republican

## Total PAC & Large Individual Contributions to Committee Members

| | |
|---|---|
| Tom Tauke (R-Iowa)[1] | $1,371,078 |
| Nita M. Lowey (D-NY) | $971,719 |
| Jolene Unsoeld (D-Wash) | $784,386 |
| Steve Bartlett (R-Texas) | $605,786 |
| Jim Jontz (D-Ind) | $454,392 |
| Marge Roukema (R-NJ) | $344,139 |
| Pat Williams (D-Mont) | $341,945 |
| Fred Grandy (R-Iowa) | $336,797 |
| George Miller (D-Calif) | $332,363 |
| Carl C. Perkins (D-Ky) | $321,926 |
| Peter Smith (R-Vt) | $308,674 |
| William D. Ford (D-Mich) | $304,473 |
| Steve Gunderson (R-Wis) | $280,780 |
| Harris W. Fawell (R-Ill) | $277,777 |
| Cass Ballenger (R-NC) | $253,934 |
| Donald M. Payne (D-NJ) | $225,667 |
| Tom Coleman (R-Mo) | $219,190 |
| Paul B. Henry (R-Mich) | $212,425 |
| Thomas C. Sawyer (D-Ohio) | $211,699 |
| Matthew G. Martinez (D-Calif) | $201,514 |
| Dale E. Kildee (D-Mich) | $196,164 |
| Kweisi Mfume (D-Md) | $187,089 |
| William L. Clay (D-Mo) | $182,600 |
| Joseph M. Gaydos (D-Pa) | $171,216 |
| Austin J. Murphy (D-Pa) | $155,270 |
| Craig Washington (D-Texas) | $116,232 |
| Major R. Owens (D-NY) | $115,675 |
| Jose E. Serrano (D-NY) | $107,666 |
| Thomas E. Petri (R-Wis) | $106,265 |
| Charles A. Hayes (D-Ill) | $98,950 |

| | |
|---|---|
| Bill Goodling (R-Pa) | $13,853 |
| Glenn Poshard (D-Ill) | $12,347 |
| Tommy F. Robinson (R-Ark)[2] | $8,750 |
| Jaime B. Fuster (D-Puerto Rico)[3] | $1,000 |
| Augustus F. Hawkins (D-Calif)[2] | -$250 |

### Top 20 Contributors to Committee Members in 1989-90

| | | |
|---|---|---|
| 1 | Teamsters Union* | $150,650 |
| 2 | National Assn of Realtors | $143,725 |
| 3 | National Education Assn | $140,470 |
| 4 | United Auto Workers | $135,747 |
| 5 | American Medical Assn* | $130,700 |
| 6 | Amer Fedn of State/County/Munic Employees | $129,499 |
| 7 | National Assn of Letter Carriers* | $119,300 |
| 8 | Air Line Pilots Assn | $99,000 |
| 9 | Laborers Union* | $97,375 |
| 10 | Machinists/Aerospace Workers Union* | $95,100 |
| 11 | American Federation of Teachers* | $94,931 |
| 12 | Natl Assn of Retired Federal Employees | $94,500 |
| 13 | Assn of Trial Lawyers of America* | $83,900 |
| 14 | Carpenters & Joiners Union | $82,700 |
| 15 | American Postal Workers Union* | $72,200 |
| 16 | National Assn of Home Builders | $70,573 |
| 17 | Intl Brotherhood of Electrical Workers* | $70,550 |
| 18 | AFL-CIO* | $68,910 |
| 19 | Food & Commercial Workers Union* | $68,850 |
| 20 | Operating Engineers Union* | $67,775 |

\* Contributions came from more than one PAC affiliated with this sponsor.

[1] Ran for U.S. Senate in 1990
[2] Did not seek reelection in 1990
[3] Non-voting Delegate

# Summary

Not surprisingly, labor unions dominate the political contributions to members of the Education and Labor Committee. But decisions made by this panel affect virtually every American business, whether or not they employ union workers. Minimum wage laws, safety rules, and dozens of other labor-related standards and regulations fall within the purview of this committee.

Organized unions do have an enormous stake in the issues debated here, however, and they accounted for 17 of the top 20 contributors to the committee and nearly $2 million in contributions overall to committee members. By contrast, educational interests (with the exception of the two main teachers unions, the National Education Association

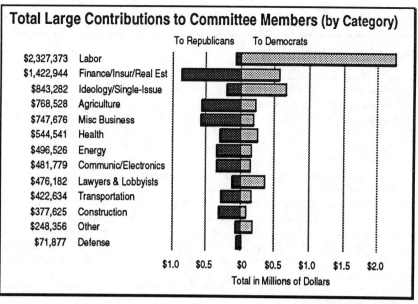

**Total Large Contributions to Committee Members (by Category)**

|  | To Republicans | To Democrats |
| --- | --- | --- |
| $2,327,373 | Labor | |
| $1,422,944 | Finance/Insur/Real Est | |
| $843,282 | Ideology/Single-Issue | |
| $768,528 | Agriculture | |
| $747,676 | Misc Business | |
| $544,541 | Health | |
| $496,526 | Energy | |
| $481,779 | Communic/Electronics | |
| $476,182 | Lawyers & Lobbyists | |
| $422,634 | Transportation | |
| $377,625 | Construction | |
| $248,356 | Other | |
| $71,877 | Defense | |

$1.0   $0.5   $0   $0.5   $1.0   $1.5   $2.0
Total in Millions of Dollars

and the American Federation of Teachers) were relatively minor players in the world of political finance. Education-related contributors gave just $128,000 to committee members in the 1990 elections, and about $1.3 million to members of Congress as a whole. Labor unions, by comparison, gave $36.6 million during the 1989-90 election cycle.

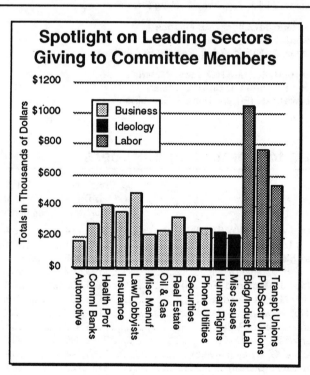

# Spotlight on Leading Sectors Giving to Committee Members

Totals in Thousands of Dollars

$1200
$1000
$800
$600
$400
$200
$0

Legend: Business, Ideology, Labor

Automotive, Comml Banks, Health Prof, Insurance, Law/Lobbyists, Misc Manuf, Oil & Gas, Real Estate, Securities, Phone Utilities, Human Rights, Misc Issues, Bldg/Indust Lab, PubSectr Unions, Transpt Unions

### Leading Sectors Giving to Committee Members

**Business**

| | |
| --- | --- |
| Automotive | $171,790 |
| Commercial Banks | $279,935 |
| Health Professionals | $395,926 |
| Insurance | $360,493 |
| Lawyers & Lobbyists | $476,182 |
| Misc Manufacturing & Distributing | $210,109 |
| Oil & Gas | $235,943 |
| Real Estate | $318,710 |
| Securities/Commodities Investment | $228,450 |
| Telephone Utilities | $252,540 |

**Ideological/Single-Issue**

| | |
| --- | --- |
| Human Rights | $231,605 |
| Misc Issues | $207,606 |

**Labor**

| | |
| --- | --- |
| Bldg Trades/Industrial/Misc Unions | $1,040,140 |
| Public Sector Unions | $759,003 |
| Transportation Unions | $528,230 |

# House Energy and Commerce Committee

John D. Dingell (D-Mich), Chairman
Norman F. Lent (R-NY), Ranking Republican

**Party Ratio:** 26 Democrats
17 Republicans

**Jurisdiction:** (1) Interstate and foreign commerce generally; (2) National energy policy generally; (3) Measures relating to the exploration, production, storage, supply, marketing, pricing, and regulation of energy resources, including all fossil fuels, solar energy, and other unconventional or renewable energy resources; (4) Measures relating to the conservation of energy resources; (5) Measures relating to the commercial application of energy technology; (6) Measures relating to energy information generally; (7) Measures relating to (A) the generation and marketing of power (except by federally chartered or Federal regional power marketing authorities), (B) the reliability and interstate transmission of, and rate making for, all power, and (C) the siting of generation facilities; except the installation of interconnections between Government waterpower projects. (The committee's jurisdiction extends both to nuclear and nonnuclear facilities and energy). (8) Interstate energy compacts; (9) Measures relating to general management of the Department of Energy, and the management and all functions of the Federal Energy Regulatory Commission; (10) Inland waterways; (11) Railroads, including railroad labor, railroad retirement and unemployment, except revenue measures related thereto; (12) Regulation of interstate and foreign communication; (13) Securities and exchanges; (14) Consumer affairs and consumer protection; (15) Travel and tourism; (16) Public health and quarantine; (17) Health and health facilities, except health care supported by payroll deductions; (18) Biomedical research and development. The committee also has special oversight functions with respect to all laws, programs, and Government activities affecting nuclear and other energy.

## Subcommittees

**Commerce, Consumer Protection, and Competitiveness**
James J. Florio (D-NJ), Chairman
Don Ritter (R-Pa), Ranking Republican

**Energy and Power**
Philip R. Sharp (D-Ind), Chairman
Carlos J. Moorhead (R-Calif), Ranking Republican

**Health and the Environment**
Henry A. Waxman (D-Calif), Chairman
Edward Madigan (R-Ill), Ranking Republican

**Oversight and Investigations**
John D. Dingell (D-Mich), Chairman
Thomas J. Bliley Jr. (R-Va), Ranking Republican

**Telecommunications and Finance**
Edward J. Markey (D-Mass), Chairman
Matthew J. Rinaldo (R-NJ), Ranking Republican

**Transportation and Hazardous Materials**
Thomas A. Luken (D-Ohio), Chairman
Bob Whittaker (R-Kan), Ranking Republican

## Total Committee-Related PAC Contributions to Committee Members

| | Total from Cmte-Related Contribs | Pct of Member's Lg Contribs | | Total from Cmte-Related Contribs | Pct of Member's Lg Contribs |
|---|---|---|---|---|---|
| Tom Tauke (R-Iowa)[1] | $771,536 | 56% | Matthew J. Rinaldo (R-NJ) | $206,754 | 48% |
| John D. Dingell (D-Mich) | $461,480 | 61% | Terry L. Bruce (D-Ill) | $196,131 | 58% |
| John Bryant (D-Texas) | $347,371 | 53% | Alex McMillan (R-NC) | $193,965 | 57% |
| Norman F. Lent (R-NY) | $310,000 | 68% | Edward Madigan (R-Ill) | $190,597 | 63% |
| Philip R. Sharp (D-Ind) | $301,342 | 52% | Carlos J. Moorhead (R-Calif) | $174,630 | 66% |
| W. J. "Billy" Tauzin (D-La) | $288,275 | 65% | Ralph M. Hall (D-Texas) | $172,991 | 78% |
| Joe L. Barton (R-Texas) | $286,745 | 54% | J. Roy Rowland (D-Ga) | $170,265 | 66% |
| Henry A. Waxman (D-Calif) | $282,050 | 66% | Dan Schaefer (R-Colo) | $165,983 | 58% |
| Thomas J. Manton (D-NY) | $280,866 | 51% | Gerry Sikorski (D-Minn) | $159,296 | 43% |
| Thomas J. Bliley Jr. (R-Va) | $275,268 | 56% | Michael G. Oxley (R-Ohio) | $151,544 | 70% |
| Tom McMillen (D-Md) | $273,450 | 44% | Jim Bates (D-Calif) | $131,723 | 37% |
| Ron Wyden (D-Ore) | $259,805 | 48% | Edward J. Markey (D-Mass) | $123,400 | 59% |
| Bill Richardson (D-NM) | $242,805 | 56% | Cardiss Collins (D-Ill) | $122,962 | 49% |
| Don Ritter (R-Pa) | $238,659 | 53% | William E. Dannemeyer (R-Calif) | $121,675 | 44% |
| Jim Slattery (D-Kan) | $232,250 | 59% | Sonny Callahan (R-Ala) | $120,750 | 45% |
| Dennis E. Eckart (D-Ohio) | $231,615 | 52% | Edolphus Towns (D-NY) | $100,604 | 46% |
| Rick Boucher (D-Va) | $229,950 | 53% | Jim Cooper (D-Tenn) | $91,850 | 64% |
| Mike Synar (D-Okla) | $227,800 | 56% | James H. Scheuer (D-NY) | $86,600 | 54% |
| Al Swift (D-Wash) | $220,685 | 54% | Thomas A. Luken (D-Ohio)[2] | $58,550 | 58% |
| Michael Bilirakis (R-Fla) | $216,779 | 56% | Bob Whittaker (R-Kan)[2] | $48,500 | 75% |
| Doug Walgren (D-Pa) | $214,250 | 51% | James J. Florio (D-NJ)[3] | $44,700 | 59% |
| Jack Fields (R-Texas) | $208,150 | 59% | Mickey Leland (D-Texas)[4] | $28,900 | 54% |
| | | | Howard C. Nielson (R-Utah)[2] | -$500 | 0% |

[1] Ran for U.S. Senate in 1990
[2] Did not seek reelection in 1990
[3] Resigned Jan 1, 1990 to assume office as Governor of New Jersey
[4] Died Aug 7, 1989

## Summary

One glance at the volume of campaign dollars flowing into the reelection campaigns of Energy and Commerce Committee members is enough to see why a seat on this committee is considered a plum assignment on Capitol Hill. Its jurisdiction gives it important influence over some of the most politically active industries in America: oil & gas, health care, telecommunications, finance, and a host of smaller industries and interests.

The committee is perennially the scene of fierce infighting between competing industries — such as the ongoing tug of war between the cable TV industry and the regional Bell telephone systems over which group will be able to provide emerging new information technologies to millions of American homes. The battles over national health care and energy policies are two more examples of issues debated on this committee that will translate into billions of dollars won or lost by specific American industries.

### Total Large Contributions to Committee Members (by Category)

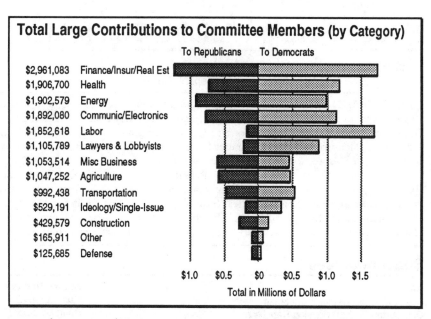

| Amount | Category |
|---|---|
| $2,961,083 | Finance/Insur/Real Est |
| $1,906,700 | Health |
| $1,902,579 | Energy |
| $1,892,080 | Communic/Electronics |
| $1,852,618 | Labor |
| $1,105,789 | Lawyers & Lobbyists |
| $1,053,514 | Misc Business |
| $1,047,252 | Agriculture |
| $992,438 | Transportation |
| $529,191 | Ideology/Single-Issue |
| $429,579 | Construction |
| $165,911 | Other |
| $125,685 | Defense |

Total in Millions of Dollars

### Spotlight on Leading Sectors Giving to Committee Members

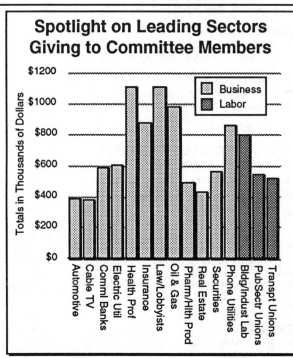

### Committee-Related Sectors

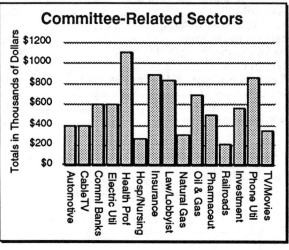

### Top 20 Committee-Related Contributors to Committee Members in 1989-90

| | | |
|---|---|---|
| 1 | American Medical Assn* | $238,930 |
| 2 | National Cable Television Assn | $184,650 |
| 3 | American Bankers Assn* | $148,450 |
| 4 | AT&T | $148,075 |
| 5 | American Dental Assn | $123,500 |
| 6 | Assn of Trial Lawyers of America | $113,350 |
| 7 | National Auto Dealers Assn | $110,950 |
| 8 | National Assn of Life Underwriters | $104,600 |
| 9 | BellSouth Corp* | $93,050 |
| 10 | United Transportation Union | $92,350 |
| 11 | American Academy of Ophthalmology | $90,781 |
| 12 | American Council of Life Insurance | $83,961 |
| 13 | National Assn of Broadcasters | $75,148 |
| 14 | Pacific Telesis Group | $72,675 |
| 15 | American Family Corp | $70,450 |
| 16 | American Health Care Assn | $69,100 |
| 17 | JP Morgan & Co | $68,600 |
| 18 | American Hospital Assn | $63,205 |
| 19 | Columbia Gas System* | $62,950 |
| 20 | Bell Atlantic* | $62,800 |

\* Contributions came from more than one PAC affiliated with this sponsor.

### Leading Committee-Related Sectors Giving to Committee Members

| | |
|---|---|
| Automotive | $383,445 |
| Cable & satellite TV operators | $376,908 |
| Commercial banks | $589,033 |
| Electric power utilities | $589,849 |
| Health professionals | $1,102,191 |
| Hospitals/nursing homes | $246,662 |
| Insurance | $872,821 |
| Lawyers & lobbyists | $816,909 |
| Natural gas transmission & distribution | $289,473 |
| Oil & gas production & marketing | $680,031 |
| Pharmaceuticals/health products | $482,532 |
| Railroads | $203,866 |
| Securities & commodities investment | $553,891 |
| Telephone utilities | $853,147 |
| TV & movie production/distribution | $330,248 |

# House Foreign Affairs Committee

Dante B. Fascell (D-Fla), Chairman
William S. Broomfield (R-Mich), Ranking Republican

**Party Ratio:** 26 Democrats
17 Republicans

**Jurisdiction:** (1) Relations of the United States with foreign nations generally; (2) Acquisition of land and buildings for embassies and legations in foreign countries; (3) Establishment of boundary lines between the United States and foreign nations; (4) Foreign loans; (5) International conferences and congresses; (6) Intervention abroad and declarations of war; (7) Measures relating to the diplomatic service; (8) Measures to foster commercial intercourse with foreign nations and to safeguard American business interests abroad; (9) Neutrality; (10) Protection of American citizens abroad and expatriation; (11) The American National Red Cross; (12) United Nations Organizations; (13) Measures relating to international economic policy; (14) Export controls, including non-proliferation of nuclear technology and nuclear hardware; (15) International commodity agreements (other than those involving sugar), including all agreements for cooperation in the export of nuclear technology and nuclear hardware; (16) Trading with the enemy; (17) International education. The committee also has special oversight functions with respect to customs administration, intelligence activities relating to foreign policy, international financial and monetary organizations, and international fishing agreements.

## Subcommittees

**Africa**
Howard Wolpe (D-Mich), Chairman
Dan Burton (R-Ind), Ranking Republican

**Arms Control, International Security and Science**
Dante B. Fascell (D-Fla), Chairman
William S. Broomfield (R-Mich), Ranking Republican

**Asian and Pacific Affairs**
Stephen J. Solarz (D-NY), Chairman
Jim Leach (R-Iowa), Ranking Republican

**Europe and the Middle East**
Lee H. Hamilton (D-Ind), Chairman
Benjamin A. Gilman (R-NY), Ranking Republican

**Human Rights and International Organizations**
Gus Yatron (D-Pa), Chairman
Doug Bereuter (R-Neb), Ranking Republican

**International Economic Policy and Trade**
Sam Gejdenson (D-Conn), Chairman
Toby Roth (R-Wis), Ranking Republican

**International Operations**
Mervyn M. Dymally (D-Calif), Chairman
Olympia J. Snowe (R-Maine), Ranking Republican

**Western Hemisphere Affairs**
George W. Crockett Jr. (D-Mich), Chairman
Robert J. Lagomarsino (R-Calif), Ranking Republican

## Total PAC & Large Individual Contributions to Committee Members

| | |
|---|---|
| Mel Levine (D-Calif) | $1,233,445 |
| Wayne Owens (D-Utah) | $827,672 |
| Robert G. Torricelli (D-NJ) | $590,107 |
| Howard Wolpe (D-Mich) | $524,117 |
| Peter H. Kostmayer (D-Pa) | $517,270 |
| John Miller (R-Wash) | $510,984 |
| Ileana Ros-Lehtinen (R-Fla) | $502,375 |
| Lawrence J. Smith (D-Fla) | $456,277 |
| Howard L. Berman (D-Calif) | $448,460 |
| Elton Gallegly (R-Calif) | $447,135 |
| Dan Burton (R-Ind) | $386,568 |
| Harry A. Johnston (D-Fla) | $381,495 |
| Robert J. Lagomarsino (R-Calif) | $365,506 |
| Mervyn M. Dymally (D-Calif) | $365,450 |
| Stephen J. Solarz (D-NY) | $363,962 |
| Eliot L. Engel (D-NY) | $355,347 |
| Frank McCloskey (D-Ind) | $334,928 |
| Gerry E. Studds (D-Mass) | $322,270 |
| Benjamin A. Gilman (R-NY) | $311,640 |
| Dante B. Fascell (D-Fla) | $309,786 |
| Sam Gejdenson (D-Conn) | $301,442 |
| Amo Houghton (R-NY) | $279,400 |
| Tom Lantos (D-Calif) | $274,498 |
| Edward F. Feighan (D-Ohio) | $274,061 |

| | |
|---|---|
| Gary L. Ackerman (D-NY) | $265,901 |
| James McClure Clarke (D-NC) | $260,709 |
| Lee H. Hamilton (D-Ind) | $256,104 |
| Toby Roth (R-Wis) | $256,028 |
| Porter J. Goss (R-Fla) | $233,507 |
| Donald M. Payne (D-NJ) | $225,667 |
| Henry J. Hyde (R-Ill) | $216,411 |
| Douglas H. Bosco (D-Calif) | $191,811 |
| Christopher H. Smith (R-NJ) | $170,627 |
| Doug Bereuter (R-Neb) | $165,356 |
| Olympia J. Snowe (R-Maine) | $165,072 |
| Gus Yatron (D-Pa) | $164,401 |
| Jan Meyers (R-Kan) | $152,096 |
| Morris K. Udall (D-Ariz) | $140,050 |
| Ted Weiss (D-NY) | $109,730 |
| William S. Broomfield (R-Mich) | $96,400 |
| Michael DeWine (R-Ohio)[1] | $33,725 |
| George W. Crockett Jr. (D-Calif)[1] | $17,020 |
| Ben Blaz (R-Guam)[2] | $16,575 |
| Eni F. H. Faleomavaega (D-American Samoa)[2] | $15,850 |
| Jim Leach (R-Iowa) | $15,649 |
| Donald E. "Buz" Lukens (R-Ohio) | $4,300 |
| Jaime B. Fuster (D-Puerto Rico)[2] | $1,000 |

[1] Did not seek reelection in 1990
[2] Non-voting Delegate

## Summary

Though its agenda spans foreign policy issues around the world, the House Foreign Affairs Committee is not a center of great interest for a majority of the PAC community or among other major political contributors. There is one important exception, however —ideological and single-issue groups whose main focus is foreign policy. Within that group, none is more formidable on Capitol Hill than supporters of strong U.S. ties to Israel. Pro-Israel PACs and their members are heavy contributors to Congress as a whole (giving more than $6.7 million in the 1990 elections), and to this committee in particular. Foreign Affairs members received a combined $642,000 from pro-Israel contributors in the last election cycle — an average of

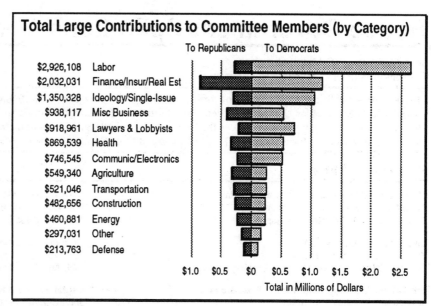

### Total Large Contributions to Committee Members (by Category)

| | Category | |
|---|---|---|
| $2,926,108 | Labor | |
| $2,032,031 | Finance/Insur/Real Est | |
| $1,350,328 | Ideology/Single-Issue | |
| $938,117 | Misc Business | |
| $918,961 | Lawyers & Lobbyists | |
| $869,539 | Health | |
| $746,545 | Communic/Electronics | |
| $549,340 | Agriculture | |
| $521,046 | Transportation | |
| $482,656 | Construction | |
| $460,881 | Energy | |
| $297,031 | Other | |
| $213,763 | Defense | |

Total in Millions of Dollars

more than $13,000 per member. Overall, however, most of the pro-Israel dollars went not to House members, but to Senators — particularly those who sit on the Senate Foreign Relations Committee.

### Spotlight on Leading Sectors Giving to Committee Members

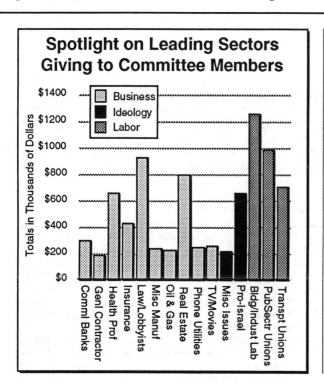

### Top 20 Contributors to Committee Members in 1989-90

| | | |
|---|---|---|
| 1 | National Assn of Realtors | $279,421 |
| 2 | American Medical Assn* | $192,427 |
| 3 | Teamsters Union* | $190,160 |
| 4 | National Education Assn* | $186,545 |
| 5 | Natl Assn of Retired Federal Employees | $165,200 |
| 6 | National Assn of Letter Carriers* | $162,750 |
| 7 | Amer Fedn of State/County/Munic Employees | $150,552 |
| 8 | United Auto Workers | $150,275 |
| 9 | National PAC | $135,000 |
| 10 | Machinists/Aerospace Workers Union | $130,400 |
| 11 | Marine Engineers Union* | $120,750 |
| 12 | Laborers Union* | $119,300 |
| 13 | Carpenters & Joiners Union* | $108,724 |
| 14 | Assn of Trial Lawyers of America* | $100,550 |
| 15 | Air Line Pilots Assn | $98,500 |
| 16 | American Federation of Teachers | $94,500 |
| 17 | National Assn of Home Builders | $93,650 |
| 18 | AT&T | $89,960 |
| 19 | Seafarers International Union | $88,200 |
| 20 | American Postal Workers Union | $87,450 |

\* Contributions came from more than one PAC affiliated with this sponsor.

### Leading Sectors Giving to Committee Members

#### Business

| | |
|---|---|
| Commercial Banks | $286,606 |
| General Contractors | $177,265 |
| Health Professionals | $643,648 |
| Insurance | $414,231 |
| Lawyers & Lobbyists | $918,961 |
| Misc Manufacturing & Distributing | $226,720 |
| Oil & Gas | $212,472 |
| Real Estate | $788,772 |
| Telephone Utilities | $239,778 |
| TV & Movie Production/Distribution | $243,950 |

#### Ideological/Single-Issue

| | |
|---|---|
| Misc Issues | $211,306 |
| Pro-Israel | $642,763 |

#### Labor

| | |
|---|---|
| Bldg Trades/Industrial/Misc Unions | $1,246,486 |
| Public Sector Unions | $979,752 |
| Transportation Unions | $699,870 |

# House Government Operations Committee

John Conyers Jr. (D-Mich), Chairman
Frank Horton (R-NY), Ranking Republican

**Party Ratio:** 24 Democrats
15 Republicans

> **Jurisdiction:** (1) Budget and accounting measures, other than appropriations; (2) The overall economy and efficiency of Government operations and activities, including Federal procurement; (3) Reorganizations in the executive branch of the Government; (4) Intergovernmental relationships between the United States and the States and municipalities, and general revenue sharing; (5) National archives; (6) Measures providing for off-budget treatment of Federal agencies or programs.

## Subcommittees

**Commerce, Consumer and Monetary Affairs**
Doug Barnard Jr. (D-Ga), Chairman
Dennis Hastert (R-Ill), Ranking Republican

**Employment and Housing**
Tom Lantos (D-Calif), Chairman
Donald E. "Buz" Lukens (R-Ohio), Ranking Republican

**Environment, Energy and Natural Resources**
Mike Synar (D-Okla), Chairman
William F. Clinger Jr. (R-Pa), Ranking Republican

**Government Activities and Transportation**
Cardiss Collins (D-Ill), Chairwoman
Howard C. Nielson (R-Utah), Ranking Republican

**Government Information, Justice, and Agriculture**
Bob Wise (D-WVa), Chairman
Al McCandless (R-Calif), Ranking Republican

**Human Resources and Intergovernmental Relations**
Ted Weiss (D-NY), Chairman
Dick Armey (R-Texas), Ranking Republican

**Legislation and National Security**
John Conyers Jr. (D-Mich), Chairman
Frank Horton (R-NY), Ranking Republican

## Total PAC & Large Individual Contributions to Committee Members

| | |
|---|---|
| Barbara Boxer (D-Calif) | $700,811 |
| C. Christopher Cox (R-Calif) | $654,079 |
| Stephen L. Neal (D-NC) | $516,062 |
| Ileana Ros-Lehtinen (R-Fla) | $502,375 |
| Jon Kyl (R-Ariz) | $454,989 |
| Nancy Pelosi (D-Calif) | $450,650 |
| Dennis E. Eckart (D-Ohio) | $442,764 |
| Henry A. Waxman (D-Calif) | $427,760 |
| Al McCandless (R-Calif) | $411,974 |
| Mike Synar (D-Okla) | $403,459 |
| Dick Armey (R-Texas) | $393,200 |
| Barney Frank (D-Mass) | $387,496 |
| Jim Bates (D-Calif) | $353,388 |
| Doug Barnard Jr. (D-Ga) | $322,842 |
| Gary Condit (D-Calif) | $321,600 |
| Steven H. Schiff (R-NM) | $316,411 |
| Albert G. Bustamante (D-Texas) | $310,784 |
| Peter Smith (R-Vt) | $308,674 |
| Dennis Hastert (R-Ill) | $281,777 |
| Tom Lantos (D-Calif) | $274,498 |
| John Conyers Jr. (D-Mich) | $266,652 |
| Craig Thomas (R-Wyo) | $263,800 |
| Cardiss Collins (D-Ill) | $252,212 |
| Christopher Shays (R-Conn) | $249,483 |
| Chuck Douglas (R-NH) | $247,611 |
| William F. Clinger Jr. (R-Pa) | $231,679 |
| Donald M. Payne (D-NJ) | $225,667 |
| Edolphus Towns (D-NY) | $216,549 |
| Gerald D. Kleczka (D-Wis) | $212,183 |
| Ben Erdreich (D-Ala) | $207,169 |
| Matthew G. Martinez (D-Calif) | $201,514 |
| Frank Horton (R-NY) | $170,140 |
| Glenn English (D-Okla) | $167,767 |
| Bob Wise (D-WVa) | $144,700 |
| Major R. Owens (D-NY) | $115,675 |
| Ted Weiss (D-NY) | $109,730 |
| Larkin Smith (R-Miss)[1] | $25,650 |
| Donald E. "Buz" Lukens (R-Ohio) | $4,300 |
| Howard C. Nielson (R-Utah)[2] | -$400 |

[1] Died Aug 13, 1989
[2] Did not seek reelection in 1990

### Top 20 Contributors to Committee Members in 1989-90

| | | |
|---|---|---|
| 1 | National Assn of Realtors | $187,830 |
| 2 | American Medical Assn* | $173,950 |
| 3 | National Education Assn | $160,080 |
| 4 | Teamsters Union | $142,250 |
| 5 | National Assn of Letter Carriers* | $103,700 |
| 6 | United Auto Workers | $95,700 |
| 7 | Natl Assn of Retired Federal Employees | $93,550 |
| 8 | AT&T | $93,080 |
| 9 | American Bankers Assn* | $92,150 |
| 10 | American Institute of CPA's | $90,100 |
| 11 | Amer Fedn of State/County/Munic Employees | $87,500 |
| 12 | Laborers Union* | $85,350 |
| 13 | Air Line Pilots Assn | $79,000 |
| 14 | Assn of Trial Lawyers of America* | $78,550 |
| 15 | Machinists/Aerospace Workers Union | $75,200 |
| 16 | Carpenters & Joiners Union* | $73,750 |
| 17 | National Assn of Home Builders | $69,600 |
| 18 | National Auto Dealers Assn | $66,100 |
| 19 | American Academy of Ophthalmology | $55,300 |
| 20 | National PAC | $55,000 |

\* Contributions came from more than one PAC affiliated with this sponsor.

## Summary

Despite a name which might make it seem preoccupied with affairs inside the federal bureaucracy, the Government Operations Committee has a wide-ranging jurisdiction that touches upon large segments of American business. Among other things, this committee has an important say in the reorganization of executive branch agencies—something that can have important repercussions on heavily-regulated industries.

Banking and other financial interests were an important element in the members' contribution profile. The panel's Commerce, Consumer and Monetary Affairs subcommittee is of particular interest to that industry.

### Total Large Contributions to Committee Members (by Category)

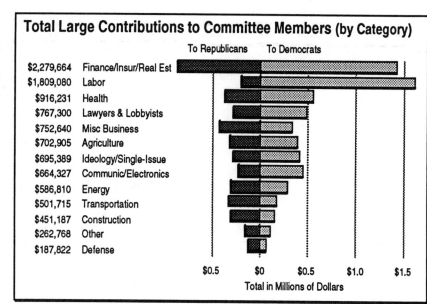

| | |
|---|---|
| $2,279,664 | Finance/Insur/Real Est |
| $1,809,080 | Labor |
| $916,231 | Health |
| $767,300 | Lawyers & Lobbyists |
| $752,640 | Misc Business |
| $702,905 | Agriculture |
| $695,389 | Ideology/Single-Issue |
| $664,327 | Communic/Electronics |
| $586,810 | Energy |
| $501,715 | Transportation |
| $451,187 | Construction |
| $262,768 | Other |
| $187,822 | Defense |

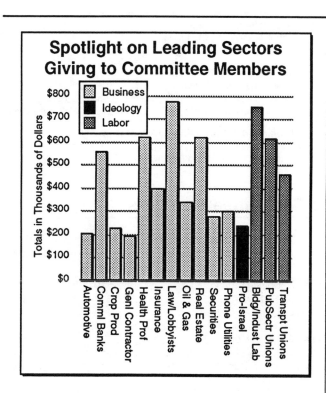

### Spotlight on Leading Sectors Giving to Committee Members

### Leading Sectors Giving to Committee Members

#### Business

| | |
|---|---|
| Automotive | $196,450 |
| Commercial Banks | $550,890 |
| Crop Production & Basic Processing | $219,055 |
| General Contractors | $184,827 |
| Health Professionals | $616,704 |
| Insurance | $393,366 |
| Lawyers & Lobbyists | $767,300 |
| Oil & Gas | $332,696 |
| Real Estate | $613,749 |
| Securities/Commodities Investment | $271,578 |
| Telephone Utilities | $297,179 |

#### Ideological/Single-Issue

| | |
|---|---|
| Pro-Israel | $231,010 |

#### Labor

| | |
|---|---|
| Bldg Trades/Industrial/Misc Unions | $743,769 |
| Public Sector Unions | $610,496 |
| Transportation Unions | $454,815 |

# House Interior and Insular Affairs Committee

Morris K. Udall (D-Ariz), Chairman
Don Young (R-Alaska), Ranking Republican

**Party Ratio:** 23 Democrats
14 Republicans

**Jurisdiction:** (1) Forest reserves and national parks created from the public domain; (2) Forfeiture of land grants and alien ownership, including alien ownership of mineral lands; (3) Geological survey; (4) Interstate compacts relating to apportionment of waters for irrigation purposes; (5) Irrigation and reclamation, including water supply for reclamation projects, and easements of public lands for irrigation projects, and acquisition of private lands when necessary to complete irrigation project; (6) Measures relating to the care and management of Indians, including the care and allotment of Indian lands and general and special measures relating to claims which are paid out of Indian funds; (7) Measures relating generally to the insular possessions of the United States, except those affecting the revenue and appropriations; (8) Military parks and battlefields; national cemeteries administered by the Secretary of the Interior, and parks within the District of Columbia; (9) Mineral land laws and claims and entries thereunder; (10) Mineral resources of the public lands; (11) Mining interest generally; (12) Mining schools and experimental stations; (13) Petroleum conservation on the public lands and conservation of the radium supply in the United States; (14) Preservation of prehistoric ruins and objects of interest on the public domain; (15) Public lands generally, including entry, easements, and grazing thereon; (16) Relations of the United States with the Indians and the Indian tribes; (17) Regulation of the domestic nuclear energy industry, including regulation of research and development reactors and nuclear regulatory research. The committee also has special oversight functions with respect to all programs affecting Indians and nonmilitary nuclear energy and research and development including the disposal of nuclear waste.

## Subcommittees

**Energy and The Environment**
Morris K. Udall (D-Ariz), Chairman
James V. Hansen (R-Utah), Ranking Republican

**General Oversight and Investigations**
Peter H. Kostmayer (D-Pa), Chairman
Barbara F. Vucanovich (R-Nev), Ranking Republican

**Insular and International Affairs**
Ron de Lugo (D-Virgin Islands), Chairman
Robert J. Lagomarsino (R-Calif), Ranking Republican

**Mining and Natural Resources**
Nick J. Rahall II (D-WVa), Chairman
Larry E. Craig (R-Idaho), Ranking Republican

**National Parks and Public Lands**
Bruce F. Vento (D-Minn), Chairman
Ron Marlenee (R-Mont), Ranking Republican (Public Lands)
Robert J. Lagomarsino (R-Calif), Ranking Republican (National Parks)

**Water, Power and Offshore Energy Resources**
George Miller (D-Calif), Chairman
Denny Smith (R-Ore), Ranking Republican

## Total Committee-Related Contributions to Committee Members

| | Total from Cmte-Related Contribs | Pct of Member's Lg Contribs | | Total from Cmte-Related Contribs | Pct of Member's Lg Contribs |
|---|---|---|---|---|---|
| Larry E. Craig (R-Idaho)[1] | $303,534 | 26% | Morris K. Udall (D-Ariz) | $19,600 | 14% |
| Philip R. Sharp (D-Ind) | $137,772 | 24% | Mel Levine (D-Calif) | $18,350 | 1% |
| Don Young (R-Alaska) | $111,925 | 24% | Jim Ross Lightfoot (R-Iowa) | $16,950 | 8% |
| Denny Smith (R-Ore) | $90,489 | 26% | Peter H. Kostmayer (D-Pa) | $16,464 | 3% |
| Craig Thomas (R-Wyo) | $72,570 | 28% | Pat Williams (D-Mont) | $13,950 | 4% |
| Bob Smith (R-Ore) | $55,097 | 24% | Austin J. Murphy (D-Pa) | $13,490 | 9% |
| Nick J. Rahall II (D-WVa) | $47,550 | 13% | John J. "Jimmy" Duncan Jr. (R-Tenn) | $11,867 | 5% |
| George Miller (D-Calif) | $45,723 | 14% | Sam Gejdenson (D-Conn) | $10,450 | 3% |
| Bill Richardson (D-NM) | $43,905 | 10% | Peter A. DeFazio (D-Ore) | $9,600 | 5% |
| Barbara F. Vucanovich (R-Nev) | $43,150 | 16% | Jim McDermott (D-Wash) | $9,434 | 4% |
| John J. Rhodes III (R-Ariz) | $42,800 | 15% | John Lewis (D-Ga) | $8,650 | 3% |
| Ron Marlenee (R-Mont) | $41,258 | 21% | Richard H. Lehman (D-Calif) | $8,180 | 3% |
| Wayne Owens (D-Utah) | $38,990 | 5% | Peter J. Visclosky (D-Ind) | $7,950 | 4% |
| Robert J. Lagomarsino (R-Calif) | $38,400 | 11% | Tony Coelho (D-Calif)[2] | $7,000 | 21% |
| Stan Parris (R-Va) | $32,050 | 10% | Tim Johnson (D-SD) | $6,800 | 2% |
| James V. Hansen (R-Utah) | $30,500 | 14% | Bruce F. Vento (D-Minn) | $4,450 | 2% |
| Elton Gallegly (R-Calif) | $29,687 | 7% | Edward J. Markey (D-Mass) | $1,050 | 1% |
| George "Buddy" Darden (D-Ga) | $28,875 | 10% | Ben Blaz (R-Guam)[3] | $500 | 3% |
| Beverly B. Byron (D-Md) | $24,200 | 13% | Eni F. H. Faleomavaega (D-Amer Samoa)[3] | $250 | 2% |
| James McClure Clarke (D-NC) | $21,367 | 8% | Ron de Lugo (D-Virgin Islands)[3] | $250 | 3% |
| Ben Nighthorse Campbell (D-Colo) | $21,150 | 8% | Jaime B. Fuster (D-Puerto Rico)[3] | $0 | 0% |

[1] Ran for U.S. Senate in 1990
[2] Resigned June 15, 1989
[3] Non-voting Delegate

# Summary

Debates over the use and disposal of public lands are a central focus of the House Interior Committee — a focus that makes it vitally important to states in the Western U.S., where much of the land is still federally owned. The committee is also vital to mining, oil & gas and other industries that extract natural resources from public lands through federal leases. In recent years the committee has been a battleground for issues — like preserving the spotted owl in northwest forests or drilling for oil in Alaska's Arctic Wildlife Refuge — that pit the interests of industry versus those of environmentalists.

The committee is also important to American territories and possessions, from Puerto Rico to American Samoa. Delegates from U.S. possessions may debate and vote on committee actions, but they may not vote for final passage of bills on the House floor.

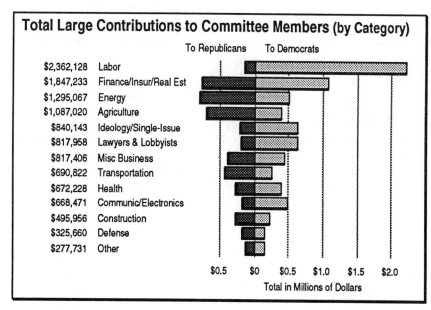

### Total Large Contributions to Committee Members (by Category)

| | | To Republicans | To Democrats |
|---|---|---|---|
| $2,362,128 | Labor | | |
| $1,847,233 | Finance/Insur/Real Est | | |
| $1,295,067 | Energy | | |
| $1,087,020 | Agriculture | | |
| $840,143 | Ideology/Single-Issue | | |
| $817,958 | Lawyers & Lobbyists | | |
| $817,406 | Misc Business | | |
| $690,822 | Transportation | | |
| $672,228 | Health | | |
| $668,471 | Communic/Electronics | | |
| $495,956 | Construction | | |
| $325,660 | Defense | | |
| $277,731 | Other | | |

Total in Millions of Dollars

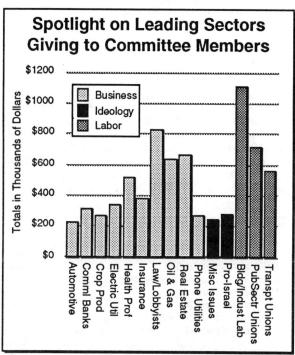

## Spotlight on Leading Sectors Giving to Committee Members

Business
Ideology
Labor

(Automotive, Comml Banks, Crop Prod, Electric Util, Health Prof, Insurance, Law/Lobbyists, Oil & Gas, Real Estate, Phone Utilities, Misc Issues, Pro-Israel, Bldg/Indust Lab, PubSectr Unions, Transpt Unions)

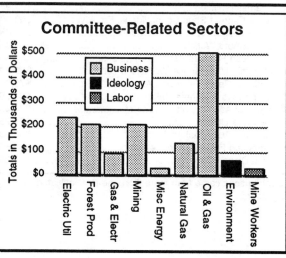

## Committee-Related Sectors

Business
Ideology
Labor

(Electric Util, Forest Prod, Gas & Electr, Mining, Misc Energy, Natural Gas, Oil & Gas, Environment, Mine Workers)

### Top 20 Committee-Related Contributors to Committee Members in 1989-90

| | | |
|---|---|---|
| 1 | ACRE (Action Cmte/Rural Electrification)* | $50,100 |
| 2 | Sierra Club | $37,192 |
| 3 | Atlantic Richfield | $32,134 |
| 4 | Chevron Corp | $31,908 |
| 5 | United Mine Workers | $30,990 |
| 6 | Amoco Corp | $28,150 |
| 7 | Southern Co* | $27,300 |
| 8 | Pacific Gas & Electric | $27,190 |
| 9 | Exxon Corp | $25,950 |
| 10 | Southern California Edison | $25,700 |
| 11 | Litton Industries | $20,100 |
| 12 | FMC Corp | $20,050 |
| 13 | Coastal Corp | $20,000 |
| 14 | Union Pacific Corp | $19,600 |
| 15 | Cyprus Minerals Co | $19,050 |
| 16 | Pacific Enterprises | $18,350 |
| 17 | Texas Utilities Electric Co | $18,150 |
| 18 | National Coal Assn | $17,950 |
| 19 | BP America | $16,500 |
| 20 | Union Oil | $15,553 |

\* Contributions came from more than one PAC affiliated with this sponsor.

### Leading Committee-Related Sectors Giving to Committee Members

**Business**

| | |
|---|---|
| Electric power utilities | $233,234 |
| Forestry & forest products | $205,692 |
| Gas & electric utilities | $88,540 |
| Mining | $205,109 |
| Misc energy | $30,900 |
| Natural gas transmission & distribution | $128,918 |
| Oil & gas production & marketing | $500,240 |

**Labor**

| | |
|---|---|
| Mining unions | $30,990 |

**Ideological/Single-Issue**

| | |
|---|---|
| Environmental policy | $62,604 |

# House Judiciary Committee

Peter W. Rodino Jr. (D-NJ), Chairman
Hamilton Fish Jr. (R-NY), Ranking Republican

**Party Ratio:** 22 Democrats
14 Republicans

**Jurisdiction:** (1) Judicial proceedings, civil and criminal generally; (2) Apportionment of Representatives; (3) Bankruptcy, mutiny, espionage, and counterfeiting; (4) Civil liberties; (5) Constitutional amendments; (6) Federal courts and judges; (7) Immigration and naturalization; (8) Interstate compacts generally; (9) Local courts in the Territories and possessions; (10) Measures relating to claims against the United States; (11) Meetings of Congress, attendance of Members and their acceptance of incompatible offices; ((12) National penitentiaries; (13) Patent Office; (14) Patents, copyrights, and trademarks; (15) Presidential succession; (16) Protection of trade and commerce against unlawful restraints and monopolies; (17) Revision and codification of the Statutes of the United States; (18) State and territorial boundary lines; (19) Communist and other subversive activities affecting the internal security of the United States.

## Subcommittees

**Administrative Law and Governmental Relations**
Barney Frank (D-Mass), Chairman
Craig T. James (R-Fla), Ranking Republican

**Civil and Constitutional Rights**
Don Edwards (D-Calif), Chairman
F. James Sensenbrenner Jr. (R-Wis), Ranking Republican

**Courts, Intellectual Property, and the Administration of Justice**
Robert W. Kastenmeier (D-Wis), Chairman
Carlos J. Moorhead (R-Calif), Ranking Republican

**Crime**
William J. Hughes (D-NJ), Chairman
Bill McCollum (R-Fla), Ranking Republican

**Criminal Justice**
Charles E. Schumer (D-NY), Chairman
George W. Gekas (R-Pa), Ranking Republican

**Economic and Commercial Law**
Jack Brooks (D-Texas), Chairman
Hamilton Fish Jr. (R-NY), Ranking Republican

**Immigration, Refugees, and International Law**
Bruce A. Morrison (D-Conn), Chairman
Lamar Smith (R-Texas), Ranking Republican

## Total PAC & Large Individual Contributions to Committee Members

| | |
|---|---|
| Mel Levine (D-Calif) | $1,233,445 |
| Tom Campbell (R-Calif) | $1,086,318 |
| John Bryant (D-Texas) | $656,586 |
| Jack Brooks (D-Texas) | $647,821 |
| Charles E. Schumer (D-NY) | $626,952 |
| Lawrence J. Smith (D-Fla) | $456,277 |
| Howard L. Berman (D-Calif) | $448,460 |
| Rick Boucher (D-Va) | $435,585 |
| Dan Glickman (D-Kan) | $432,735 |
| Mike Synar (D-Okla) | $403,459 |
| Lamar Smith (R-Texas) | $389,623 |
| Barney Frank (D-Mass) | $387,496 |
| Craig T. James (R-Fla) | $380,606 |
| George E. Sangmeister (D-Ill) | $378,649 |
| Howard Coble (R-NC) | $340,880 |
| Harley O. Staggers Jr. (D-WVa) | $327,582 |
| Bill McCollum (R-Fla) | $317,648 |
| Hamilton Fish Jr. (R-NY) | $302,889 |
| D. French Slaughter Jr. (R-Va) | $302,888 |
| William E. Dannemeyer (R-Calif) | $277,713 |
| Edward F. Feighan (D-Ohio) | $274,061 |
| John Conyers Jr. (D-Mich) | $266,652 |
| Carlos J. Moorhead (R-Calif) | $265,609 |
| Chuck Douglas (R-NH) | $247,611 |
| Henry J. Hyde (R-Ill) | $216,411 |
| Don Edwards (D-Calif) | $198,975 |
| Robert W. Kastenmeier (D-Wis) | $181,400 |
| William J. Hughes (D-NJ) | $173,776 |
| Patricia Schroeder (D-Colo) | $158,927 |
| F. James Sensenbrenner Jr. (R-Wis) | $141,130 |
| Craig Washington (D-Texas) | $116,232 |

| | |
|---|---|
| Bruce A. Morrison (D-Conn)[1] | $111,034 |
| Romano L. Mazzoli (D-Ky) | $109,456 |
| George W. Gekas (R-Pa) | $80,320 |
| Michael DeWine (R-Ohio)[1] | $33,725 |
| Larkin Smith (R-Miss)[2] | $25,650 |
| George W. Crockett Jr. (D-Calif)[1] | $17,020 |

### Top 20 Contributors to Committee Members in 1989-90

| | | |
|---|---|---|
| 1 | National Assn of Realtors | $199,263 |
| 2 | Assn of Trial Lawyers of America* | $141,900 |
| 3 | National Education Assn* | $137,510 |
| 4 | American Medical Assn* | $131,984 |
| 5 | American Institute of CPA's | $121,000 |
| 6 | Natl Assn of Retired Federal Employees | $114,550 |
| 7 | AT&T | $102,125 |
| 8 | Teamsters Union | $99,950 |
| 9 | Amer Fedn of State/County/Munic Employees | $93,000 |
| 10 | National Assn of Life Underwriters | $81,650 |
| 11 | United Auto Workers | $80,550 |
| 12 | American Bankers Assn* | $80,400 |
| 13 | Machinists/Aerospace Workers Union | $80,300 |
| 14 | National Cable Television Assn | $79,700 |
| 15 | Carpenters & Joiners Union* | $74,950 |
| 16 | National Assn of Letter Carriers* | $74,460 |
| 17 | Laborers Union* | $71,250 |
| 18 | National Auto Dealers Assn | $66,000 |
| 19 | American Federation of Teachers | $58,500 |
| 20 | Walt Disney Co | $57,850 |

\* Contributions came from more than one PAC affiliated with this sponsor.

---

[1] Did not seek reelection in 1990
[2] Died Aug 13, 1989

## Summary

The shape of the American judicial and criminal justice system is the central focus of the House Judiciary Committee. It is a role that makes it important not only to lawyers, but to every sector of the American business community as well. As is true in most committees of Congress, the financial industry provided the biggest level of support to committee members—nearly $2.6 million in 1989-90. But attorneys and lobbyists were particularly active in this committee, delivering a combined $1.1 million, mostly through individual contributions as opposed to PACs. The average committee member received more than $31,000 from lawyers and lobbyists in the 1990 elections — the highest average from the legal community to any House committee.

### Total Large Contributions to Committee Members (by Category)

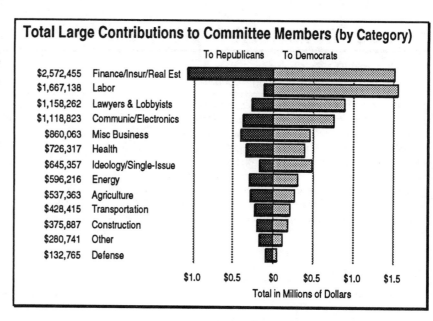

| | | |
|---|---|---|
| $2,572,455 | Finance/Insur/Real Est | |
| $1,667,138 | Labor | |
| $1,158,262 | Lawyers & Lobbyists | |
| $1,118,823 | Communic/Electronics | |
| $860,063 | Misc Business | |
| $726,317 | Health | |
| $645,357 | Ideology/Single-Issue | |
| $596,216 | Energy | |
| $537,363 | Agriculture | |
| $428,415 | Transportation | |
| $375,887 | Construction | |
| $280,741 | Other | |
| $132,765 | Defense | |

### Spotlight on Leading Sectors Giving to Committee Members

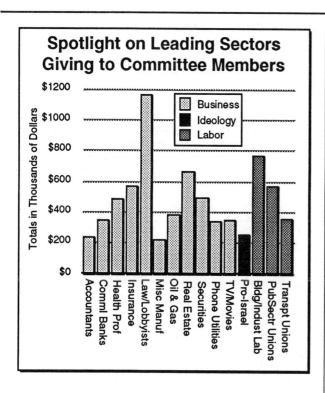

### Leading Sectors Giving to Committee Members

**Business**

| | |
|---|---|
| Accountants | $230,385 |
| Commercial Banks | $341,308 |
| Health Professionals | $478,387 |
| Insurance | $566,257 |
| Lawyers & Lobbyists | $1,158,262 |
| Misc Manufacturing & Distributing | $207,799 |
| Oil & Gas | $370,071 |
| Real Estate | $656,134 |
| Securities/Commodities Investment | $487,252 |
| Telephone Utilities | $327,398 |
| TV & Movie Production/Distribution | $337,391 |

**Ideological/Single-Issue**

| | |
|---|---|
| Pro-Israel | $243,046 |

**Labor**

| | |
|---|---|
| Bldg Trades/Industrial/Misc Unions | $756,330 |
| Public Sector Unions | $558,933 |
| Transportation Unions | $351,875 |

# House Merchant Marine and Fisheries Committee

Walter B. Jones (D-NC), Chairman
Robert W. Davis (R-Mich), Ranking Republican

**Party Ratio:** 27 Democrats
18 Republicans

**Jurisdiction:** (1) Merchant marine generally; (2) Oceanography and marine affairs, including coastal zone management; (3) Coast Guard, including lifesaving service, lighthouses, lightships and ocean derelicts; (4) Fisheries and wildlife, including research, restoration, refuges and conservation; (5) Measures relating to the regulation of common carriers by water (except matters subject to the jurisdiction of the Interstate Commerce Commission) and to the inspection of merchant marine vessels, lights and signals, lifesaving equipment and fire protection on such vessels; (6) Merchant marine officers and seamen; (7) Navigation and the laws relating thereto, including pilotage; (8) Panama Canal and the maintenance and operation of the Panama Canal, including the administration, sanitation and government of the Canal Zone; and interoceanic canals generally; (9) Registering and licensing of vessels and small boats; (10) Rules and international arrangements to prevent collisions at sea; (11) United States Coast Guard and Merchant Marine Academies, and State maritime academies; (12) International fishing agreements. The committee also oversees offshore oil and gas matters on the U.S. Outer Continental Shelf.

## Subcommittees

**Coast Guard and Navigation**
W. J. "Billy" Tauzin (D-La), Chairman
Robert W. Davis (R-Mich), Ranking Republican

**Fisheries and Wildlife Conservation and Environment**
Gerry E. Studds (D-Mass), Chairman
Don Young (R-Alaska), Ranking Republican

**Merchant Marine**
Walter B. Jones (D-NC), Chairman
Norman F. Lent (R-NY), Ranking Republican

**Oceanography and Great Lakes**
Dennis M. Hertel (D-Mich), Chairman
Norman D. Shumway (R-Calif), Ranking Republican

**Oversight and Investigations**
Thomas M. Foglietta (D-Pa), Chairman
Claudine Schneider (R-RI), Ranking Republican

**Panama Canal/Outer Continental Shelf**
Roy P. Dyson (D-Md), Chairman
Jack Fields (R-Texas), Ranking Republican

## Total Committee-Related Contributions to Committee Members

| | Total from Cmte-Related Contribs | Pct of Member's Lg Contribs |
|---|---|---|
| Don Young (R-Alaska) | $127,575 | 27% |
| Patricia Saiki (R-Hawaii)[1] | $102,999 | 11% |
| Helen Delich Bentley (R-Md) | $86,400 | 17% |
| Jolene Unsoeld (D-Wash) | $84,539 | 11% |
| James M. Inhofe (R-Okla) | $82,999 | 19% |
| Greg Laughlin (D-Texas) | $71,874 | 11% |
| John Miller (R-Wash) | $70,806 | 14% |
| W. J. "Billy" Tauzin (D-La) | $63,150 | 14% |
| Jack Fields (R-Texas) | $62,325 | 18% |
| Claudine Schneider (R-RI)[1] | $56,356 | 8% |
| Frank Pallone Jr. (D-NJ) | $50,153 | 10% |
| Gerry E. Studds (D-Mass) | $48,711 | 15% |
| Roy Dyson (D-Md) | $42,900 | 8% |
| Robert W. Davis (R-Mich) | $42,200 | 15% |
| H. James Saxton (R-NJ) | $38,944 | 10% |
| George J. Hochbrueckner (D-NY) | $36,000 | 7% |
| Norman F. Lent (R-NY) | $32,600 | 7% |
| Thomas J. Manton (D-NY) | $32,269 | 6% |
| Nita M. Lowey (D-NY) | $31,450 | 3% |
| Herbert H. Bateman (R-Va) | $30,800 | 8% |
| Thomas M. Foglietta (D-Pa) | $30,700 | 7% |
| Walter B. Jones (D-NC) | $29,550 | 40% |

| | Total from Cmte-Related Contribs | Pct of Member's Lg Contribs |
|---|---|---|
| Carroll Hubbard Jr. (D-Ky) | $29,500 | 10% |
| Wally Herger (R-Calif) | $25,925 | 7% |
| Gene Taylor (D-Miss) | $23,650 | 10% |
| Douglas H. Bosco (D-Calif) | $23,000 | 12% |
| Jim Bunning (R-Ky) | $20,350 | 6% |
| Owen B. Pickett (D-Va) | $19,400 | 8% |
| Curt Weldon (R-Pa) | $18,550 | 5% |
| Thomas R. Carper (D-Del) | $18,450 | 4% |
| Porter J. Goss (R-Fla) | $17,450 | 7% |
| Solomon P. Ortiz (D-Texas) | $16,400 | 9% |
| Robert A. Borski (D-Pa) | $16,000 | 6% |
| Bob Clement (D-Tenn) | $15,650 | 4% |
| Robin Tallon (D-SC) | $15,300 | 9% |
| Howard Coble (R-NC) | $14,500 | 4% |
| Stephen J. Solarz (D-NY) | $14,100 | 4% |
| Dennis M. Hertel (D-Mich) | $13,650 | 6% |
| William O. Lipinski (D-Ill) | $12,825 | 8% |
| Arthur Ravenel Jr. (R-SC) | $11,764 | 8% |
| William J. Hughes (D-NJ) | $11,250 | 6% |
| Norman D. Shumway (R-Calif)[2] | $8,400 | 11% |
| Earl Hutto (D-Fla) | $8,100 | 6% |
| Joseph E. Brennan (D-Maine)[2] | $5,000 | 9% |
| Charles E. Bennett (D-Fla) | $2,500 | 7% |

[1] Ran for U.S. Senate in 1990
[2] Did not seek reelection in 1990

# Summary

The House Merchant Marine and Fisheries Committee presents an interesting example of one of the often-overlooked realities of PAC giving in Congress — that the interests of labor unions and businesses are not always in conflict. Foreign competition and a dwindling American presence on the open seas have put labor and business together in trying to preserve what is left of the increasingly imperiled U.S. merchant marine. While the two sides do have their differences, they often work to achieve consensus on issues of basic interest to the survival of the industry.

Oil & gas producers and exploration companies also pay close attention to this committee's deliberations, as this is the panel that wrangles over the economic and environmental repercussions of offshore oil drilling.

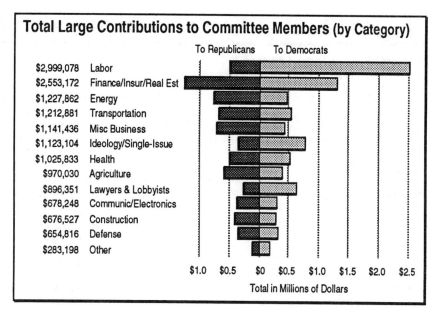

Total Large Contributions to Committee Members (by Category)

| | To Republicans / To Democrats |
|---|---|
| $2,999,078 | Labor |
| $2,553,172 | Finance/Insur/Real Est |
| $1,227,862 | Energy |
| $1,212,881 | Transportation |
| $1,141,436 | Misc Business |
| $1,123,104 | Ideology/Single-Issue |
| $1,025,833 | Health |
| $970,030 | Agriculture |
| $896,351 | Lawyers & Lobbyists |
| $678,248 | Communic/Electronics |
| $676,527 | Construction |
| $654,816 | Defense |
| $283,198 | Other |

Total in Millions of Dollars

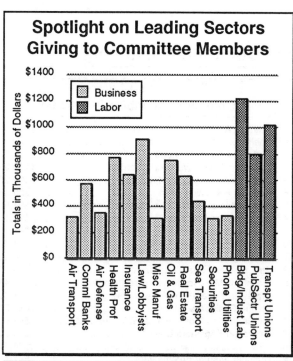

## Spotlight on Leading Sectors Giving to Committee Members

Totals in Thousands of Dollars

Business / Labor

Air Transport, Comml Banks, Air Defense, Health Prof, Insurance, Law/Lobbyists, Misc Manuf, Oil & Gas, Real Estate, Sea Transport, Securities, Phone Utilities, Bldg/Indust Lab, PubSectr Unions, Transpt Unions

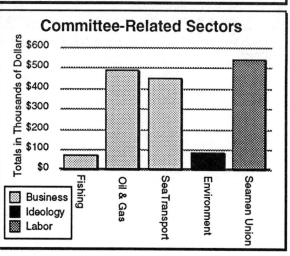

## Committee-Related Sectors

Totals in Thousands of Dollars

Business / Ideology / Labor

Fishing, Oil & Gas, Sea Transport, Environment, Seamen Union

## Top 20 Committee-Related Contributors to Committee Members in 1989-90

| | | |
|---|---|---|
| 1 | Marine Engineers Union* | $247,425 |
| 2 | Seafarers International Union | $157,796 |
| 3 | Masters, Mates & Pilots Union | $59,800 |
| 4 | CSX Corp* | $54,500 |
| 5 | Sierra Club | $49,993 |
| 6 | American President Lines | $38,850 |
| 7 | American Pilots Assn | $38,550 |
| 8 | Chevron Corp | $33,649 |
| 9 | Atlantic Richfield | $33,450 |
| 10 | Alexander & Baldwin Inc* | $33,300 |
| 11 | International Longshoremen Assn* | $33,000 |
| 12 | Amoco Corp | $30,675 |
| 13 | Boilermakers Union | $29,000 |
| 14 | Exxon Corp | $27,650 |
| 15 | Tenneco Inc | $27,000 |
| 16 | Occidental Petroleum* | $24,550 |
| 17 | Phillips Petroleum | $23,997 |
| 18 | Cooper Industries | $21,800 |
| 19 | Mobil Oil | $21,000 |
| 20 | BP America | $20,000 |

\* Contributions came from more than one PAC affiliated with this sponsor.

## Leading Committee-Related Sectors Giving to Committee Members

**Business**

| Commercial fishing | $68,192 |
|---|---|
| Oil & gas | $485,625 |
| Sea transport | $443,703 |

**Labor**

| Sea transport unions | $537,171 |
|---|---|

**Ideological/Single-Issue**

| Environmental policy | $82,323 |
|---|---|

# House Post Office and Civil Service Committee

William D. Ford (D-Mich), Chairman
Benjamin A. Gilman (R-NY), Ranking Republican

**Party Ratio:** 14 Democrats
9 Republicans

**Jurisdiction:** (1) Census and the collection of statistics generally; (2) All Federal Civil Service, including intergovernmental personnel; (3) Postal-savings banks; (4) Postal Service generally, including the railway mail service, and measures relating to ocean mail and pneumatic-tube service; but excluding post roads; (5) Status of officers and employees of the United States, including their compensation, classification, and retirement; (6) Hatch Act; (7) Holidays and celebrations; (8) Population and demography.

## Subcommittees

**Census and Population**
Thomas C. Sawyer (D-Ohio), Chairman
Tom Ridge (R-Pa), Ranking Republican

**Civil Service**
Gerry Sikorski (D-Minn), Chairman
Constance A. Morella (R-Md), Ranking Republican

**Compensation and Employee Benefits**
Gary L. Ackerman (D-NY), Chairman
John T. Myers (R-Ind), Ranking Republican

**Human Resources**
Paul E. Kanjorski (D-Pa), Chairman
Dan Burton (R-Ind), Ranking Republican

**Investigations**
William D. Ford (D-Mich), Chairman
Rod Chandler (R-Wash), Ranking Republican

**Postal Operations and Services**
Frank McCloskey (D-Ind), Chairman
Frank Horton (R-NY), Ranking Republican

**Postal Personnel and Modernization**
Charles A. Hayes (D-Ill), Chairman
Don Young (R-Alaska), Ranking Republican

## Total PAC & Large Individual Contributions to Committee Members

Don Young (R-Alaska) ............................................ $465,663
Dan Burton (R-Ind) ................................................ $386,568
Gerry Sikorski (D-Minn) ......................................... $371,891
Mervyn M. Dymally (D-Calif) ................................... $365,450
Rod Chandler (R-Wash) ......................................... $364,410
Constance A. Morella (R-Md) .................................. $363,049
Tom Ridge (R-Pa) .................................................. $349,646
Frank McCloskey (D-Ind) ........................................ $334,928
Benjamin A. Gilman (R-NY) ..................................... $311,640
Mary Rose Oakar (D-Ohio) ..................................... $311,591
William D. Ford (D-Mich) ......................................... $304,473
Paul E. Kanjorski (D-Pa) ......................................... $275,748
Gary L. Ackerman (D-NY) ....................................... $265,901
Thomas C. Sawyer (D-Ohio) ................................... $211,699
Michael R. McNulty (D-NY) ..................................... $185,229
William L. Clay (D-Mo) ........................................... $182,600
Frank Horton (R-NY) .............................................. $170,140
Gus Yatron (D-Pa) ................................................ $164,401
Patricia Schroeder (D-Colo) .................................... $158,927
Morris K. Udall (D-Ariz) .......................................... $140,050
John T. Myers (R-Ind) ............................................ $106,556
Charles A. Hayes (D-Ill) .......................................... $98,950
Robert Garcia (D-NY)[1] .......................................... $65,500
Mickey Leland (D-Texas)[2] ...................................... $53,027
Tommy F. Robinson (R-Ark)[3] ................................. $8,750
Ron de Lugo (D-Virgin Islands)[4] ............................. $7,650

### Top 20 Contributors to Committee Members in 1989-90

| | | |
|---|---|---|
| 1 | National Assn of Letter Carriers* | $182,800 |
| 2 | Teamsters Union* | $129,094 |
| 3 | National Assn of Realtors | $113,525 |
| 4 | American Postal Workers Union* | $110,950 |
| 5 | Natl Assn of Retired Federal Employees | $105,200 |
| 6 | National Education Assn | $98,475 |
| 7 | Amer Fedn of State/County/Munic Employees | $94,500 |
| 8 | American Medical Assn* | $94,165 |
| 9 | Laborers Union* | $84,200 |
| 10 | Carpenters & Joiners Union* | $74,724 |
| 11 | United Auto Workers | $70,225 |
| 12 | Air Line Pilots Assn | $58,000 |
| 13 | Machinists/Aerospace Workers Union* | $55,450 |
| 14 | American Federation of Teachers | $51,825 |
| 15 | Marine Engineers Union* | $51,500 |
| 16 | Intl Brotherhood of Electrical Workers* | $49,800 |
| 17 | Operating Engineers Union* | $49,204 |
| 18 | AT&T | $48,900 |
| 19 | National Assn of Postmasters | $47,436 |
| 20 | Natl Cmte to Preserve Social Security | $46,300 |

\* Contributions came from more than one PAC affiliated with this sponsor.

[1] Resigned Jan 7, 1990
[2] Died Aug 7, 1989
[3] Did not seek reelection in 1990
[4] Non-voting Delegate

## Summary

Steelworkers, teamsters and assembly line operators may be popularly thought of as the mainstream of organized labor, but government employees and postal workers are an increasingly powerful segment of the labor community — and one which has weighed in heavily with PAC contributions to members of Congress. The Post Office and Civil Service Committee is of particular interest to government and postal PACs, since it debates crucial issues ranging from salaries to government workers' participation in political activities.

Public sector unions (which includes postal workers, government unions and teacher unions) gave an average of over $33,000 to committee members — far more than to any other House committee. Non-government unions were also generous to committee members. In all, committee members received an average $75,525 from labor unions, more than any other committee in the House.

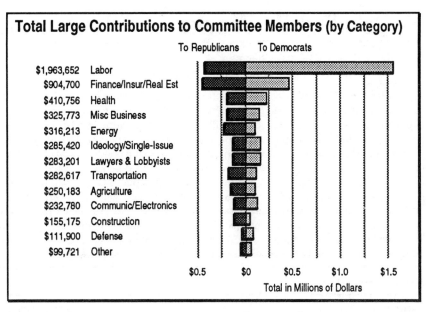

Total Large Contributions to Committee Members (by Category)

| | To Republicans / To Democrats |
|---|---|
| $1,963,652 | Labor |
| $904,700 | Finance/Insur/Real Est |
| $410,756 | Health |
| $325,773 | Misc Business |
| $316,213 | Energy |
| $285,420 | Ideology/Single-Issue |
| $283,201 | Lawyers & Lobbyists |
| $282,617 | Transportation |
| $250,183 | Agriculture |
| $232,780 | Communic/Electronics |
| $155,175 | Construction |
| $111,900 | Defense |
| $99,721 | Other |

Total in Millions of Dollars

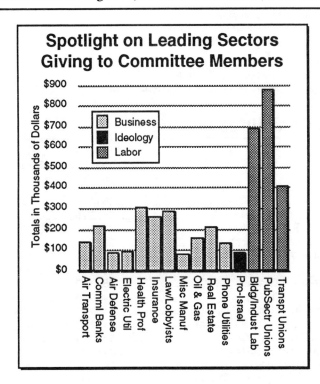

## Spotlight on Leading Sectors Giving to Committee Members

Totals in Thousands of Dollars

- Business
- Ideology
- Labor

(Air Transport, Comml Banks, Air Defense, Electric Util, Health Prof, Insurance, Law/Lobbyists, Misc Manuf, Oil & Gas, Real Estate, Phone Utilities, Pro-Israel, Bldg/Indust Lab, PubSectr Unions, Transpt Unions)

### Leading Sectors
### Giving to Committee Members

**Business**

| | |
|---|---|
| Air Transport | $131,687 |
| Commercial Banks | $207,555 |
| Defense Aerospace | $81,200 |
| Environmental Svcs/Equipment | $84,900 |
| Health Professionals | $300,790 |
| Insurance | $255,695 |
| Lawyers & Lobbyists | $283,201 |
| Misc Manufacturing & Distributing | $76,676 |
| Oil & Gas | $154,913 |
| Real Estate | $203,755 |
| Telephone Utilities | $127,530 |

**Ideological/Single-Issue**

| | |
|---|---|
| Pro-Israel | $84,381 |

**Labor**

| | |
|---|---|
| Bldg Trades/Industrial/Misc Unions | $686,115 |
| Public Sector Unions | $872,733 |
| Transportation Unions | $404,804 |

# House Public Works and Transportation Committee

Glenn M. Anderson (D-Calif), Chairman
John Paul Hammerschmidt (R-Ark), Ranking Republican

**Party Ratio:** 30 Democrats
20 Republicans

> **Jurisdiction:** (1) Flood control and improvement of rivers and harbors; (2) Measures relating to the Capitol Building and the Senate and the House Office Buildings; (3) Measures relating to the construction or maintenance of roads and post roads, other than appropriations therefor; but no bill providing general legislation in relation to roads may contain any provision for any specific road, nor may any bill in relation to a specific road embrace a provision in relation to any other specific road; (4) Measures relating to the construction or reconstruction, maintenance and care of the buildings and grounds of the Botanic Garden, the Library of Congress, and the Smithsonian Institution; (5) Measures relating to the purchase of sites and construction of post offices, customhouses, Federal courthouses, and Government buildings within the District of Columbia; (6) Oil and other pollution of navigable waters; (7) Public buildings and occupied or improved grounds of the United States generally; (8) Public works for the benefit of navigation, including bridges and dams (other than international bridges and dams); (9) Water power; (10) Transportation, including civil aviation except railroads, railroad labor, and pensions; (11) Roads and the safety thereof; (12) Water transportation subject to the jurisdiction of the Interstate Commerce Commission; (13) Related transportation regulatory agencies, except (A) the Interstate Commerce Commission as it relates to railroads, (B) Federal Railroad Administration, and (C) Amtrak.

## Subcommittees

**Aviation**
James L. Oberstar (D-Minn), Chairman
William F. Clinger Jr. (R-Pa), Ranking Republican

**Economic Development**
Gus Savage (D-Ill), Chairman
Bob McEwen (R-Ohio), Ranking Republican

**Investigations and Oversight**
Glenn M. Anderson (D-Calif), Chairman
Guy V. Molinari (R-NY), Ranking Republican

**Public Buildings and Grounds**
Douglas H. Bosco (D-Calif), Chairman
Thomas E. Petri (R-Wis), Ranking Republican

**Surface Transportation**
Norman Y. Mineta (D-Calif), Chairman
Bud Shuster (R-Pa), Ranking Republican

**Water Resources**
Henry J. Nowak (D-NY), Chairman
Arlan Stangeland (R-Minn), Ranking Republican

## Total Committee-Related Contributions to Committee Members

| | Total from Cmte-Related Contribss | Pct of Member's Lg Contribs | | Total from Cmte-Related Contribs | Pct of Member's Lg Contribs |
|---|---|---|---|---|---|
| Norman Y. Mineta (D-Calif) | $200,480 | 39% | Bob McEwen (R-Ohio) | $59,000 | 30% |
| Robert A. Roe (D-NJ) | $181,057 | 38% | William O. Lipinski (D-Ill) | $58,775 | 37% |
| Bud Shuster (R-Pa) | $177,069 | 44% | David E. Skaggs (D-Colo) | $58,050 | 17% |
| Glenn M. Anderson (D-Calif) | $171,766 | 47% | Fred Upton (R-Mich) | $56,373 | 19% |
| Greg Laughlin (D-Texas) | $145,677 | 22% | Robert A. Borski (D-Pa) | $53,800 | 21% |
| Larry E. Craig (R-Idaho)[1] | $130,715 | 11% | Mel Hancock (R-Mo) | $52,550 | 26% |
| James L. Oberstar (D-Minn) | $118,850 | 41% | Sherwood Boehlert (R-NY) | $52,150 | 26% |
| James M. Inhofe (R-Okla) | $114,250 | 26% | Joe Kolter (D-Pa) | $48,750 | 28% |
| Jerry F. Costello (D-Ill) | $102,492 | 20% | Peter A. DeFazio (D-Ore) | $47,750 | 26% |
| Frank Pallone Jr. (D-NJ) | $102,450 | 21% | Jim Ross Lightfoot (R-Iowa) | $47,550 | 24% |
| William F. Clinger Jr. (R-Pa) | $97,577 | 42% | Ron Packard (R-Calif) | $46,110 | 38% |
| Bob Clement (D-Tenn) | $97,150 | 25% | Tim Valentine (D-NC) | $46,100 | 23% |
| Nick J. Rahall II (D-WVa) | $86,500 | 23% | John Lewis (D-Ga) | $42,750 | 16% |
| John Paul Hammerschmidt (R-Ark) | $84,550 | 42% | Cass Ballenger (R-NC) | $41,600 | 16% |
| Pete Geren (D-Texas) | $83,504 | 18% | Henry J. Nowak (D-NY) | $41,050 | 40% |
| Arlan Stangeland (R-Minn) | $77,600 | 27% | Peter J. Visclosky (D-Ind) | $39,650 | 20% |
| C. Christopher Cox (R-Calif) | $76,125 | 12% | George E. Sangmeister (D-Ill) | $38,500 | 10% |
| Douglas H. Bosco (D-Calif) | $72,025 | 38% | Gus Savage (D-Ill) | $38,350 | 28% |
| Carl C. Perkins (D-Ky) | $67,300 | 21% | Bill Grant (R-Fla) | $36,800 | 12% |
| Ben Jones (D-Ga) | $65,050 | 12% | Edolphus Towns (D-NY) | $36,170 | 17% |
| Mike Parker (D-Miss) | $64,835 | 15% | Susan Molinari (R-NY) | $32,150 | 15% |
| Lewis F. Payne Jr. (D-Va) | $64,400 | 22% | Gary L. Ackerman (D-NY) | $31,850 | 12% |
| John J. "Jimmy" Duncan Jr. (R-Tenn) | $63,600 | 26% | Douglas Applegate (D-Ohio) | $30,670 | 36% |
| Bill Emerson (R-Mo) | $62,700 | 14% | Thomas E. Petri (R-Wis) | $28,690 | 27% |
| Jimmy Hayes (D-La) | $62,500 | 22% | James A. Traficant Jr. (D-Ohio) | $13,725 | 20% |
| Dennis Hastert (R-Ill) | $61,720 | 22% | Guy V. Molinari (R-NY)[2] | $5,550 | 47% |
| | | | Ron de Lugo (D-Virgin Islands)[3] | $3,750 | 49% |

[1] Ran for U.S. Senate in 1990
[2] Resigned Jan 1, 1990 to assume office as Staten Island Borough President
[3] Non-voting Delegate

## Summary

The biggest contributors on this committee are related to the transportation industry — and those interests are represented not only by the airlines, trucking companies, railroads and freight services, but by the labor unions representing the people who drive the trucks, pilot the planes and ride the rails across America. Together, transportation companies and transport unions gave more than $2.9 million to the committee's members during the 1989-90 election cycle.

The committee also earmarks billions of dollars in federally-funded public works projects that are built each year in every congressional district in the nation — projects that employ thousands of construction workers and supply important revenues to the nation's builders and other construction-related businesses. Here too the contributions came both from the business and labor sectors, though most businesses gave more to Republicans and the labor PACs heavily favored Democrats.

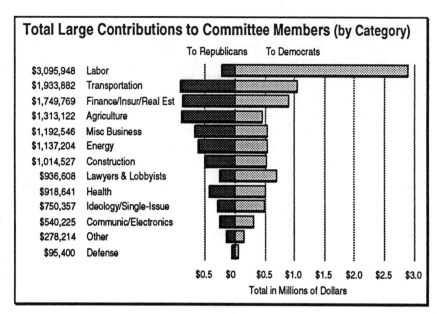

### Total Large Contributions to Committee Members (by Category)

| Amount | Category |
|---|---|
| $3,095,948 | Labor |
| $1,933,882 | Transportation |
| $1,749,769 | Finance/Insur/Real Est |
| $1,313,122 | Agriculture |
| $1,192,546 | Misc Business |
| $1,137,204 | Energy |
| $1,014,527 | Construction |
| $936,608 | Lawyers & Lobbyists |
| $918,641 | Health |
| $750,357 | Ideology/Single-Issue |
| $540,225 | Communic/Electronics |
| $278,214 | Other |
| $95,400 | Defense |

Total in Millions of Dollars

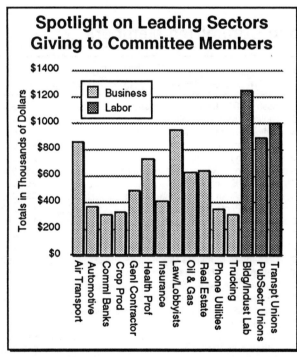

### Spotlight on Leading Sectors Giving to Committee Members

Totals in Thousands of Dollars

Business / Labor

Air Transport, Automotive, Comml Banks, Crop Prod, Genl Contractor, Health Prof, Insurance, Law/Lobbyists, Oil & Gas, Real Estate, Phone Utilities, Trucking, Bldg/Indust Lab, PubSectr Unions, Transpt Unions

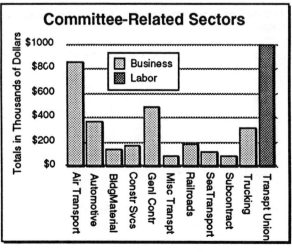

### Committee-Related Sectors

Totals in Thousands of Dollars

Business / Labor

Air Transport, Automotive, BldgMaterial, Constr Svcs, Genl Contr, Misc Transport, Railroads, SeaTransport, Subcontract, Trucking, Transpt Union

### Top 20 Committee-Related Contributors to Committee Members in 1989-90

| | | |
|---|---|---|
| 1 | Teamsters Union | $242,500 |
| 2 | Air Line Pilots Assn | $220,500 |
| 3 | Aircraft Owners & Pilots Assn | $152,950 |
| 4 | National Auto Dealers Assn | $133,400 |
| 5 | Federal Express Corp | $130,600 |
| 6 | United Parcel Service | $110,660 |
| 7 | Marine Engineers Union* | $94,175 |
| 8 | National Utility Contractors Assn | $93,068 |
| 9 | United Transportation Union | $86,050 |
| 10 | Associated General Contractors* | $84,719 |
| 11 | Seafarers International Union* | $82,846 |
| 12 | Amalgamated Transit Union | $76,500 |
| 13 | American Trucking Assns* | $65,573 |
| 14 | Auto Dealers & Drivers for Free Trade | $58,200 |
| 15 | Norfolk Southern Corp* | $47,950 |
| 16 | American Airlines | $44,904 |
| 17 | United Airlines | $43,900 |
| 18 | Union Pacific Corp | $40,069 |
| 19 | Transport Workers Union | $38,625 |
| 20 | CSX Corp* | $37,100 |

\* Contributions came from more than one PAC affiliated with this sponsor.

### Leading Committee-Related Sectors Giving to Committee Members

**Business**

| | |
|---|---|
| Air transport | $845,189 |
| Automotive | $360,895 |
| Building materials & equipment | $137,750 |
| Construction services | $161,361 |
| General contractors | $480,637 |
| Misc transport | $79,242 |
| Railroads | $179,614 |
| Sea transport | $113,280 |
| Special trade contractors | $75,524 |
| Trucking | $301,297 |

**Labor**

| | |
|---|---|
| Transportation unions | $985,366 |

# House Rules Committee

Joe Moakley (D-Mass), Chairman
James H. Quillen (R-Tenn), Ranking Republican

**Party Ratio:** 9 Democrats
4 Republicans

**Jurisdiction:** (1) The rules and joint rules (other than rules or joint rules relating to the Code of Official Conduct), and order of business of the House; (2) Emergency waivers (under the Congressional Budget Act of 1974) of the required reporting date for bills and resolutions authorizing new budget authority; (3) Recesses and final adjournments of Congress.

## Subcommittees

**Rules of the House**
Joe Moakley (D-Mass), Chairman
Gerald B. H. Solomon (R-NY), Ranking Republican

**The Legislative Process**
Butler Derrick (D-SC), Chairman
Lynn M. Martin (R-Ill), Ranking Republican

## Total PAC & Large Individual Contributions to Committee Members

| | |
|---|---|
| Lynn Martin (R-Ill)[1] | $1,288,144 |
| David E. Bonior (D-Mich) | $890,430 |
| Butler Derrick (D-SC) | $679,142 |
| Martin Frost (D-Texas) | $580,230 |
| James H. Quillen (R-Tenn) | $445,029 |
| Louise M. Slaughter (D-NY) | $377,754 |
| Bart Gordon (D-Tenn) | $371,125 |
| Joe Moakley (D-Mass) | $355,703 |
| Alan Wheat (D-Mo) | $268,254 |
| Charles Pashayan Jr. (R-Calif) | $242,677 |
| Gerald B. H. Solomon (R-NY) | $197,624 |
| Anthony C. Beilenson (D-Calif) | $179,200 |
| Tony P. Hall (D-Ohio) | $132,715 |
| Claude Pepper (D-Fla) | $3,500 |

### Top 20 Contributors to Committee Members in 1989-90

| | | |
|---|---|---|
| 1 | Assn of Trial Lawyers of America | $67,500 |
| 2 | National Assn of Realtors | $67,450 |
| 3 | National Assn of Letter Carriers | $65,015 |
| 4 | Teamsters Union* | $64,950 |
| 5 | American Medical Assn* | $64,200 |
| 6 | Natl Assn of Retired Federal Employees | $64,200 |
| 7 | National Education Assn | $57,000 |
| 8 | National Assn of Life Underwriters | $52,000 |
| 9 | Air Line Pilots Assn | $44,797 |
| 10 | National Rifle Assn | $44,550 |
| 11 | Federal Express Corp | $44,000 |
| 12 | American Bankers Assn* | $43,200 |
| 13 | Carpenters & Joiners Union | $43,097 |
| 14 | National Auto Dealers Assn | $42,950 |
| 15 | Marine Engineers Union* | $42,500 |
| 16 | National Cable Television Assn | $42,500 |
| 17 | Amer Fedn of State/County/Munic Employees | $41,921 |
| 18 | American Institute of CPA's | $40,900 |
| 19 | AT&T | $40,100 |
| 20 | United Auto Workers | $40,005 |

\* Contributions came from more than one PAC affiliated with this sponsor.

[1] Ran for U.S. Senate in 1990

## Summary

On the floor of the U.S. Senate, any Senator can offer an amendment to a bill under discussion, whether or not the amendment is germane to the bill itself. In the House, with its 435 members, such a policy could lead to a nightmare of legislative gridlock. To prevent that, the House is far more structured in its legislative procedures. Before any bill is brought to the House floor, specific rules are determined over whether amendments can be offered, and if so what type. Those rules — and a variety of other important legislative guidelines — are determined by the House Rules Committee.

While the shape of those rules can be important to a bill's passage, they do not specifically affect any particular industry or interest group more than any other. Correspondingly, PAC contributions to the committee came from a diversity of sources and were reflective of the overall patterns of PAC giving to members of Congress in general.

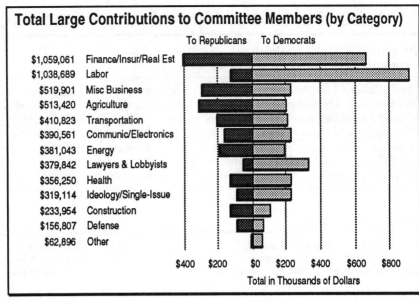

**Total Large Contributions to Committee Members (by Category)**

| | |
|---|---|
| $1,059,061 | Finance/Insur/Real Est |
| $1,038,689 | Labor |
| $519,901 | Misc Business |
| $513,420 | Agriculture |
| $410,823 | Transportation |
| $390,561 | Communic/Electronics |
| $381,043 | Energy |
| $379,842 | Lawyers & Lobbyists |
| $356,250 | Health |
| $319,114 | Ideology/Single-Issue |
| $233,954 | Construction |
| $156,807 | Defense |
| $62,896 | Other |

Total in Thousands of Dollars

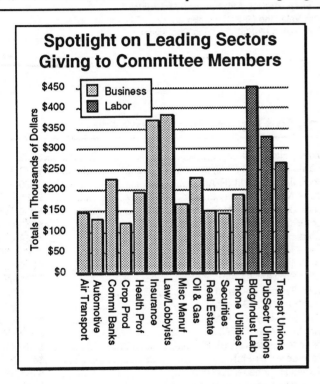

**Spotlight on Leading Sectors Giving to Committee Members**

### Leading Sectors Giving to Committee Members

**Business**

| | |
|---|---|
| Air Transport | $144,073 |
| Automotive | $128,346 |
| Commercial Banks | $223,929 |
| Crop Production & Basic Processing | $117,316 |
| Health Professionals | $190,854 |
| Insurance | $366,874 |
| Lawyers & Lobbyists | $379,842 |
| Misc Manufacturing & Distributing | $162,142 |
| Oil & Gas | $225,794 |
| Real Estate | $147,093 |
| Securities/Commodities Investment | $138,785 |
| Telephone Utilities | $185,420 |

**Labor**

| | |
|---|---|
| Bldg Trades/Industrial/Misc Unions | $448,587 |
| Public Sector Unions | $328,330 |
| Transportation Unions | $261,772 |

# House Science, Space and Technology Committee

Robert A. Roe (D-NJ), Chairman
Robert S. Walker (R-Pa), Ranking Republican

**Party Ratio:** 30 Democrats
19 Republicans

**Jurisdiction:** (1) Astronautical research and development, including resources, personnel, equipment and facilities; (2) Bureau of Standards, standardization of weights and measures and the metric system; (3) National Aeronautics and Space Administration; (4) National Aeronautics and Space Council; (5) National Science Foundation; (6) Outer space, including exploration and control thereof; (7) Science scholarships; (8) Scientific research, development, and demonstration, and projects therefor, and all federally owned or operated nonmilitary energy laboratories; (9) Civil aviation research and development; (10) Environmental research and development; (11) All energy research, development, and demonstration, and projects therefor, and all federally owned or operated nonmilitary energy laboratories; (12) National Weather Service. The committee also has oversight with respect to all nonmilitary research and development.

## Subcommittees

**Energy Research and Development**
Marilyn Lloyd (D-Tenn), Chairwoman
Sid Morrison (R-Wash), Ranking Republican

**Environment**
James H. Scheuer (D-NY), Chairman
Claudine Schneider (R-RI), Ranking Republican

**International Scientific Cooperation**
Ralph M. Hall (D-Texas), Chairman
Ron Packard (R-Calif), Ranking Republican

**Investigations and Oversight**
Robert A. Roe (D-NJ), Chairman
Don Ritter (R-Pa), Ranking Republican

**Science, Research and Technology**
Doug Walgren (D-Pa), Chairman
Sherwood Boehlert (R-NY), Ranking Republican

**Space Science and Applications**
Bill Nelson (D-Fla), Chairman
F. James Sensenbrenner Jr. (R-Wis), Ranking Republican

**Transportation, Aviation and Materials**
Tim Valentine (D-NC), Chairman
Tom Lewis (R-Fla), Ranking Republican

## Total PAC & Large Individual Contributions to Committee Members

| | |
|---|---|
| Tom Campbell (R-Calif) | $1,086,318 |
| Claudine Schneider (R-RI)[1] | $723,227 |
| Tom McMillen (D-Md) | $625,875 |
| Robert G. Torricelli (D-NJ) | $590,107 |
| George E. Brown Jr. (D-Calif) | $535,402 |
| Howard Wolpe (D-Mich) | $524,117 |
| Norman Y. Mineta (D-Calif) | $516,191 |
| Jerry F. Costello (D-Ill) | $515,114 |
| David E. Price (D-NC) | $478,939 |
| Robert A. Roe (D-NJ) | $476,222 |
| Don Ritter (R-Pa) | $454,080 |
| Rick Boucher (D-Va) | $435,585 |
| Dan Glickman (D-Kan) | $432,735 |
| Doug Walgren (D-Pa) | $423,220 |
| Lamar Smith (R-Texas) | $389,623 |
| Harry A. Johnston (D-Fla) | $381,495 |
| Dana Rohrabacher (R-Calif) | $380,066 |
| Constance A. Morella (R-Md) | $363,049 |
| David E. Skaggs (D-Colo) | $340,572 |
| Terry L. Bruce (D-Ill) | $336,057 |
| Carl C. Perkins (D-Ky) | $321,926 |
| Steven H. Schiff (R-NM) | $316,411 |
| Marilyn Lloyd (D-Tenn) | $313,337 |
| D. French Slaughter Jr. (R-Va) | $302,888 |
| Richard Stallings (D-Idaho) | $293,400 |
| Jimmy Hayes (D-La) | $278,719 |
| Harris W. Fawell (R-Ill) | $277,777 |
| John J. Rhodes III (R-Ariz) | $276,858 |
| Dave Nagle (D-Iowa) | $264,484 |
| Jack Buechner (R-Mo) | $259,796 |
| Lee H. Hamilton (D-Ind) | $256,104 |
| Christopher Shays (R-Conn) | $249,483 |
| Dave McCurdy (D-Okla) | $242,300 |
| Harold L. Volkmer (D-Mo) | $239,181 |
| Glen Browder (D-Ala) | $231,429 |
| John Tanner (D-Tenn) | $230,260 |
| Ralph M. Hall (D-Texas) | $221,876 |
| Paul B. Henry (R-Mich) | $212,425 |
| Tim Valentine (D-NC) | $199,851 |
| Sherwood Boehlert (R-NY) | $199,446 |
| Tom Lewis (R-Fla) | $181,258 |
| James H. Scheuer (D-NY) | $160,590 |
| F. James Sensenbrenner Jr. (R-Wis) | $141,130 |
| Ron Packard (R-Calif) | $120,445 |
| Henry J. Nowak (D-NY) | $101,524 |
| James A. Traficant Jr. (D-Ohio) | $69,680 |
| Robert S. Walker (R-Pa) | $68,810 |
| Sid Morrison (R-Wash) | $49,280 |
| Bill Nelson (D-Fla)[2] | $41,500 |

[1] Ran for U.S. Senate in 1990
[2] Did not seek reelection in 1990

## Summary

As the mainstream of the American economy has shifted away from the old heavy industrial base and into new high-tech and information industries, the attention of Congress has come to focus more and more on the legal and political ramifications of emerging technologies and the post-industrial economy. Much of the legislative debate on these new industries — and the unique new problems and legal challenges they present — has fallen under the jurisdiction of the Science, Space and Technology Committee. Formed in 1959, a year after the Russians launched Sputnik, the committee has also been deeply involved with the U.S. space program and NASA. Accordingly, the aerospace industry was one of the leading contributors to committee members in the 1990 elections.

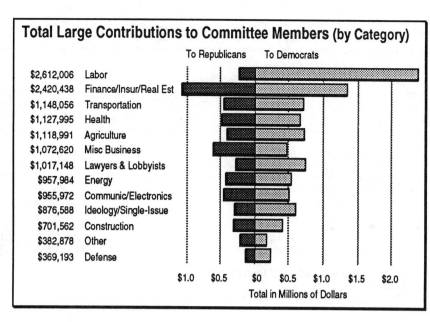

**Total Large Contributions to Committee Members (by Category)**

| | | To Republicans | To Democrats |
|---|---|---|---|
| $2,612,006 | Labor | | |
| $2,420,438 | Finance/Insur/Real Est | | |
| $1,148,056 | Transportation | | |
| $1,127,995 | Health | | |
| $1,118,991 | Agriculture | | |
| $1,072,620 | Misc Business | | |
| $1,017,148 | Lawyers & Lobbyists | | |
| $957,984 | Energy | | |
| $955,972 | Communic/Electronics | | |
| $876,588 | Ideology/Single-Issue | | |
| $701,562 | Construction | | |
| $382,878 | Other | | |
| $369,193 | Defense | | |

Total in Millions of Dollars

---

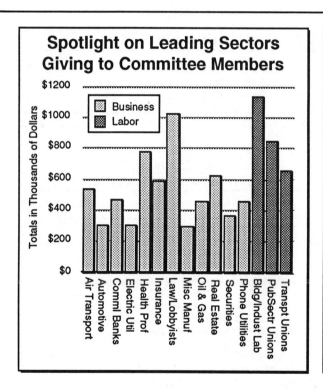

## Spotlight on Leading Sectors Giving to Committee Members

Totals in Thousands of Dollars

Business / Labor

Air Transport, Automotive, Comml Banks, Electric Util, Health Prof, Insurance, Law/Lobbyists, Misc Manuf, Oil & Gas, Real Estate, Securities, Phone Utilities, Bldg/Indust Lab, PubSectr Unions, Transpt Unions

### Top 20 Contributors to Committee Members in 1989-90

| | | |
|---|---|---|
| 1 | National Assn of Realtors | $261,629 |
| 2 | American Medical Assn* | $245,960 |
| 3 | National Education Assn* | $190,600 |
| 4 | Teamsters Union | $170,500 |
| 5 | Natl Assn of Retired Federal Employees | $158,000 |
| 6 | Assn of Trial Lawyers of America* | $154,300 |
| 7 | National Assn of Letter Carriers* | $148,280 |
| 8 | United Auto Workers | $138,450 |
| 9 | AT&T | $135,850 |
| 10 | Machinists/Aerospace Workers Union* | $118,600 |
| 11 | Air Line Pilots Assn | $116,000 |
| 12 | Amer Fedn of State/County/Munic Employees | $112,240 |
| 13 | American Bankers Assn* | $112,000 |
| 14 | Carpenters & Joiners Union* | $108,600 |
| 15 | National Auto Dealers Assn | $97,500 |
| 16 | National Assn of Life Underwriters | $95,500 |
| 17 | Intl Brotherhood of Electrical Workers* | $90,210 |
| 18 | Marine Engineers Union* | $88,700 |
| 19 | Laborers Union* | $86,225 |
| 20 | National Assn of Home Builders | $81,400 |

\* Contributions came from more than one PAC affiliated with this sponsor.

## Leading Sectors
## Giving to Committee Members

### Business

| | |
|---|---|
| Air Transport | $524,615 |
| Automotive | $295,935 |
| Commercial Banks | $460,737 |
| Environmental Svcs/Equipment | $295,188 |
| Health Professionals | $772,351 |
| Insurance | $579,822 |
| Lawyers & Lobbyists | $1,017,148 |
| Misc Manufacturing & Distributing | $287,755 |
| Oil & Gas | $454,451 |
| Real Estate | $611,757 |
| Securities/Commodities Investment | $359,431 |
| Telephone Utilities | $451,163 |

### Labor

| | |
|---|---|
| Bldg Trades/Industrial/Misc Unions | $1,126,850 |
| Public Sector Unions | $833,781 |
| Transportation Unions | $651,375 |

# House Small Business Committee

John J. LaFalce (D-NY), Chairman
Joseph M. McDade (R-Pa), Ranking Republican

**Party Ratio:** 27 Democrats
17 Republicans

> **Jurisdiction:** (1) Assistance to and protection of small business, including financial aid; (2) Participation of small-business enterprises in Federal procurement and Government contracts. The committee also has oversight with respect to the problems of small business.

## Subcommittees

**Antitrust, Impact of Deregulation and Privatization**
Dennis E. Eckart (D-Ohio), Chairman
David Dreier (R-Calif), Ranking Republican

**Environment and Labor**
Esteban E. Torres (D-Calif), Chairman
John P. Hiler (R-Ind), Ranking Republican

**Procurement, Tourism and Rural Development**
Ike Skelton (D-Mo), Chairman
Silvio O. Conte (R-Mass), Ranking Republican

**Regulation, Business Opportunities, and Energy**
Ron Wyden (D-Ore), Chairman
William S. Broomfield (R-Mich), Ranking Republican

**SBA, The General Economy, and Minority Enterprise Development**
John J. LaFalce (D-NY), Chairman
Joseph M. McDade (R-Pa), Ranking Republican

## Total PAC & Large Individual Contributions to Committee Members

Peter Hoagland (D-Neb) ......................................$764,993
Ronald K. Machtley (R-RI) ...................................$560,854
Ron Wyden (D-Ore) .............................................$546,896
Bill Sarpalius (D-Texas) ......................................$493,455
Dennis E. Eckart (D-Ohio) ..................................$442,764
James Bilbray (D-Nev) ........................................$421,631
Eliot L. Engel (D-NY)...........................................$355,347
David Dreier (R-Calif) .........................................$327,373
Richard E. Neal (D-Mass) ...................................$320,363
Joseph M. McDade (R-Pa) ..................................$312,903
Ike Skelton (D-Mo) .............................................$311,698
Fred Upton (R-Mich) ...........................................$304,426
D. French Slaughter Jr. (R-Va) ...........................$302,888
H. Martin Lancaster (D-NC) ................................$302,430
Richard H. Baker (R-La).......................................$280,510
John J. Rhodes III (R-Ariz)...................................$276,858
Clyde C. Holloway (R-La) ....................................$267,099
John Conyers Jr. (D-Mich)....................................$266,652
Charles Hatcher (D-Ga) ......................................$259,652
John P. Hiler (R-Ind) ...........................................$247,837
Andy Ireland (R-Fla) ...........................................$247,621
John J. LaFalce (D-NY) .......................................$231,168
Richard Ray (D-Ga) ............................................$214,054
Susan Molinari (R-NY) ........................................$208,885
Mel Hancock (R-Mo) ...........................................$199,843
Esteban E. Torres (D-Calif) .................................$197,603
Nicholas Mavroules (D-Mass) .............................$196,884
Kweisi Mfume (D-Md) ..........................................$187,089
Jim Olin (D-Va)....................................................$183,056
Norman Sisisky (D-Va) ........................................$178,600
Jan Meyers (R-Kan) ............................................$152,096
Floyd H. Flake (D-NY)..........................................$146,358
Larry Combest (R-Texas) .....................................$144,126
Jim Cooper (D-Tenn) ..........................................$142,625
Gus Savage (D-Ill)...............................................$135,750
Neal Smith (D-Iowa)............................................$122,820
Joel Hefley (R-Colo) ...........................................$120,005
Romano L. Mazzoli (D-Ky)...................................$109,456

Jose E. Serrano (D-NY) .......................................$107,666
Thomas A. Luken (D-Ohio)[1] ..............................$100,750
William S. Broomfield (R-Mich) ...........................$96,400
Silvio O. Conte (R-Mass) ....................................$70,316
Glenn Poshard (D-Ill) ..........................................$12,347

| | Top 20 Contributors to Committee Members in 1989-90 | |
|---|---|---|
| 1 | National Assn of Realtors | $242,039 |
| 2 | American Medical Assn* | $175,162 |
| 3 | National Education Assn* | $128,610 |
| 4 | Teamsters Union | $122,650 |
| 5 | American Bankers Assn* | $121,600 |
| 6 | AT&T | $118,850 |
| 7 | Natl Assn of Retired Federal Employees | $106,300 |
| 8 | National Assn of Home Builders | $99,100 |
| 9 | National Assn of Letter Carriers | $88,600 |
| 10 | National Auto Dealers Assn | $88,450 |
| 11 | Assn of Trial Lawyers of America | $87,850 |
| 12 | United Auto Workers | $80,450 |
| 13 | National PAC | $75,000 |
| 14 | American Academy of Ophthalmology | $74,930 |
| 15 | National Assn of Life Underwriters | $74,000 |
| 16 | Machinists/Aerospace Workers Union* | $73,000 |
| 17 | Carpenters & Joiners Union | $62,350 |
| 18 | Natl Cmte to Preserve Social Security | $62,250 |
| 19 | Laborers Union* | $59,025 |
| 20 | American Institute of CPA's | $57,900 |

\* Contributions came from more than one PAC affiliated with this sponsor.

---

[1] Did not seek reelection in 1990

## Summary

Small businesses have always been an important constituency of Congress. Every congressional district in the land has its local chamber of commerce, with its bankers, lawyers, doctors, insurance agents and real estate brokers — many of whom take a keen interest in those items of federal government policy that affect their businesses.

Judging by the patterns in contributions to committee members, those doctors, lawyers, bankers and Realtors paid the closest attention of all. Financial industry contributors led all others overall, just as they did in contributions to Congress as a whole. And as on most committees, organized labor PACs were a major source of funds for Democrats.

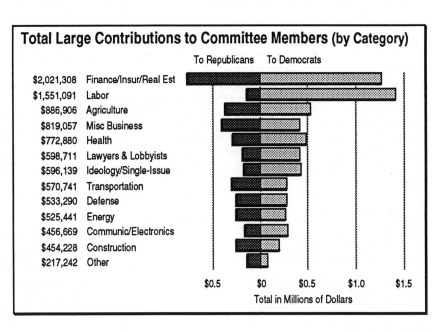

**Total Large Contributions to Committee Members (by Category)**

| | Category |
|---|---|
| $2,021,308 | Finance/Insur/Real Est |
| $1,551,091 | Labor |
| $886,906 | Agriculture |
| $819,057 | Misc Business |
| $772,880 | Health |
| $598,711 | Lawyers & Lobbyists |
| $596,139 | Ideology/Single-Issue |
| $570,741 | Transportation |
| $533,290 | Defense |
| $525,441 | Energy |
| $456,669 | Communic/Electronics |
| $454,228 | Construction |
| $217,242 | Other |

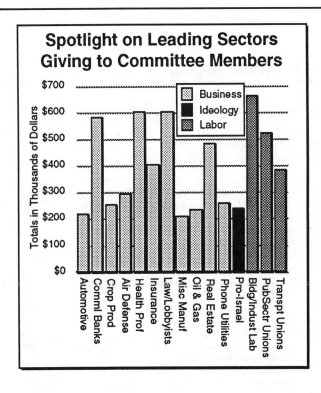

**Spotlight on Leading Sectors Giving to Committee Members**

### Leading Sectors Giving to Committee Members

**Business**

| | |
|---|---|
| Automotive | $215,289 |
| Commercial Banks | $577,762 |
| Crop Production & Basic Processing | $249,310 |
| Defense Aerospace | $286,440 |
| Health Professionals | $599,617 |
| Insurance | $397,746 |
| Lawyers & Lobbyists | $598,711 |
| Misc Manufacturing & Distributing | $203,139 |
| Oil & Gas | $230,304 |
| Real Estate | $479,668 |
| Telephone Utilities | $254,955 |

**Ideological/Single-Issue**

| | |
|---|---|
| Pro-Israel | $233,573 |

**Labor**

| | |
|---|---|
| Bldg Trades/Industrial/Misc Unions | $656,843 |
| Public Sector Unions | $518,498 |
| Transportation Unions | $375,750 |

# House Veterans' Affairs Committee

G. V. "Sonny" Montgomery (D-Miss), Chairman
Bob Stump (R-Ariz), Ranking Republican

**Party Ratio:** 21 Democrats
13 Republicans

**Jurisdiction:** (1) Veterans' measures generally; (2) Cemeteries of the United States in which veterans of any war or conflict are or may be buried, whether in the United States or abroad, except cemeteries administered by the Secretary of the Interior; (3) Compensation, vocational rehabilitation and education of veterans; (4) Life insurance issued by the Government on account of service in the Armed Forces; (5) Pensions of all the wars of the United States, general and special; (6) Compensation for service-related disability; (7) Readjustment of servicemen to civil life; (8) Soldiers' and sailors' civil relief; (9) Veterans' hospitals, medical care, and treatment of veterans.

## Subcommittees

**Compensation, Pension and Insurance**
Douglas Applegate (D-Ohio), Chairman
Bob McEwen (R-Ohio), Ranking Republican

**Education, Training and Employment**
Timothy J. Penny (D-Minn), Chairman
Christopher H. Smith (R-NJ), Ranking Republican

**Hospitals and Health Care**
G. V. "Sonny" Montgomery (D-Miss), Chairman
John Paul Hammerschmidt (R-Ark), Ranking Republican

**Housing and Memorial Affairs**
Harley O. Staggers Jr. (D-WVa), Chairman
Dan Burton (R-Ind), Ranking Republican

**Oversight and Investigations**
Lane Evans (D-Ill), Chairman
Bob Stump (R-Ariz), Ranking Republican

## Total PAC & Large Individual Contributions to Committee Members

Robert C. Smith (R-NH)[1] .......................... $1,108,068
Jill L. Long (D-Ind) .................................... $643,702
Joseph P. Kennedy II (D-Mass) ................... $633,593
Ben Jones (D-Ga) ..................................... $525,414
Bill Paxon (R-NY) ..................................... $509,253
George J. Hochbrueckner (D-NY) ................ $485,728
Pete Geren (D-Texas) ................................ $456,239
Jim Jontz (D-Ind) ..................................... $454,392
Mike Parker (D-Miss) ................................ $425,190
Michael Bilirakis (R-Fla) ............................ $387,817
Dan Burton (R-Ind) ................................... $386,568
Craig T. James (R-Fla) ............................... $380,606
George E. Sangmeister (D-Ill) ..................... $378,649
Liz J. Patterson (D-SC) .............................. $366,840
Cliff Stearns (R-Fla) .................................. $355,087
Tom Ridge (R-Pa) ..................................... $349,646
Harley O. Staggers Jr. (D-WVa) ................... $327,582
Tim Johnson (D-SD) .................................. $311,330
Lewis F. Payne Jr. (D-Va) ........................... $293,762
Lane Evans (D-Ill) ..................................... $262,257
J. Roy Rowland (D-Ga) .............................. $258,665
Chalmers P. Wylie (R-Ohio) ........................ $206,045
John Paul Hammerschmidt (R-Ark) .............. $203,150
Don Edwards (D-Calif) ............................... $198,975
Bob McEwen (R-Ohio) ............................... $195,656
Claude Harris (D-Ala) ................................ $188,282
Bob Stump (R-Ariz) ................................... $182,315
Christopher H. Smith (R-NJ) ....................... $170,627
Charles W. Stenholm (D-Texas) .................. $153,275
Timothy J. Penny (D-Minn) ........................ $116,870
Bruce A. Morrison (D-Conn)[2] ..................... $111,034

Douglas Applegate (D-Ohio) ....................... $85,350
G. V. "Sonny" Montgomery (D-Miss) ............ $82,550
John G. Rowland (R-Conn) ......................... $80,725
James J. Florio (D-NJ)[3] ............................. $75,400
Tommy F. Robinson (R-Ark)[2] ....................... $8,750

### Top 20 Contributors to Committee Members in 1989-90

| | | |
|---|---|---|
| 1 | National Assn of Realtors | $230,428 |
| 2 | American Medical Assn* | $195,244 |
| 3 | Teamsters Union | $153,000 |
| 4 | National Assn of Letter Carriers* | $141,300 |
| 5 | National Assn of Home Builders | $119,096 |
| 6 | National Education Assn | $112,350 |
| 7 | Assn of Trial Lawyers of America | $108,550 |
| 8 | Natl Assn of Retired Federal Employees | $107,500 |
| 9 | American Bankers Assn* | $105,209 |
| 10 | United Auto Workers | $102,650 |
| 11 | National Auto Dealers Assn | $95,000 |
| 12 | Machinists/Aerospace Workers Union* | $90,750 |
| 13 | Carpenters & Joiners Union* | $88,550 |
| 14 | National Assn of Life Underwriters | $87,500 |
| 15 | AT&T | $86,825 |
| 16 | American Academy of Ophthalmology | $83,309 |
| 17 | Intl Brotherhood of Electrical Workers | $81,625 |
| 18 | Independent Insurance Agents of America | $77,089 |
| 19 | Air Line Pilots Assn | $76,000 |
| 20 | AFL-CIO* | $68,350 |

* Contributions came from more than one PAC affiliated with this sponsor.

---

[1] Ran for U.S. Senate in 1990
[2] Did not seek reelection in 1990
[3] Resigned Jan 1, 1990 to assume office as Governor of New Jersey

## Summary

The profile—and problems—of America's veterans have changed considerably over the past generation. The postwar boom of the late 1940s and early 50s, when veterans of World War II and Korea came home to raise new families, build new suburbs and go on to college with the G.I. Bill has been replaced by the postwar trauma of Vietnam era vets, many of whom have still not been able to shake off the war's lingering effects.

The Gulf War added a new class of combat veterans, many of whom came not from the regular ranks of active services but from reserve units all around the nation. They have since been joined by yet another group of veterans — those whose military careers are ending prematurely due to the post-Cold War downsizing of the active military. The Veterans Affairs committee pays close attention to the needs of all these ex-servicemen and women, but the scope of its political contributions reflect no special patterns apart from Congress as a whole.

### Total Large Contributions to Committee Members (by Category)

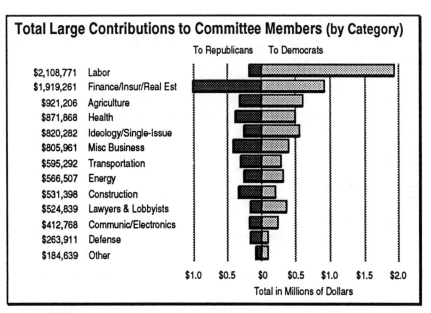

| | |
|---|---|
| $2,108,771 | Labor |
| $1,919,261 | Finance/Insur/Real Est |
| $921,206 | Agriculture |
| $871,868 | Health |
| $820,282 | Ideology/Single-Issue |
| $805,961 | Misc Business |
| $595,292 | Transportation |
| $566,507 | Energy |
| $531,398 | Construction |
| $524,839 | Lawyers & Lobbyists |
| $412,768 | Communic/Electronics |
| $263,911 | Defense |
| $184,639 | Other |

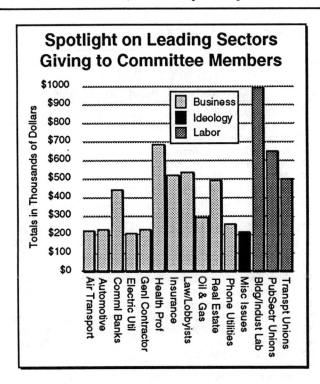

## Spotlight on Leading Sectors Giving to Committee Members

### Leading Sectors Giving to Committee Members

#### Business

| | |
|---|---|
| Air Transport | $213,879 |
| Automotive | $217,510 |
| Commercial Banks | $430,242 |
| Environmental Svcs/Equipment | $196,225 |
| General Contractors | $221,685 |
| Health Professionals | $673,198 |
| Insurance | $509,025 |
| Lawyers & Lobbyists | $524,839 |
| Oil & Gas | $283,066 |
| Real Estate | $485,034 |
| Telephone Utilities | $249,949 |

#### Ideological/Single-Issue

| | |
|---|---|
| Misc Issues | $207,902 |

#### Labor

| | |
|---|---|
| Bldg Trades/Industrial/Misc Unions | $983,582 |
| Public Sector Unions | $636,969 |
| Transportation Unions | $488,220 |

# House Ways and Means Committee

Dan Rostenkowski (D-Ill), Chairman
Bill Archer (R-Texas), Ranking Republican

**Party Ratio:** 23 Democrats
13 Republicans

**Jurisdiction:** (1) Customs, collection districts, and ports of entry and delivery; (2) Reciprocal trade agreements; (3) Revenue measures generally; (4) Revenue measures relating to the insular possessions; (5) The bonded debt of the United States; (6) The deposit of public moneys; (7) Transportation of dutiable goods; (8) Tax-exempt foundations and charitable trusts; (9) National social security, except (a) health care and facilities programs that are supported form general revenues as opposed to payroll deductions, and (b) work incentive programs.

## Subcommittees

**Health**
Pete Stark (D-Calif), Chairman
Bill Gradison (R-Ohio), Ranking Republican

**Human Resources**
Thomas J. Downey (D-NY), Chairman
E. Clay Shaw Jr. (R-Fla), Ranking Republican

**Oversight**
J. J. Pickle (D-Texas), Chairman
Dick Schulze (R-Pa), Ranking Republican

**Select Revenue Measures**
Charles B. Rangel (D-NY), Chairman
Guy Vander Jagt (R-Mich), Ranking Republican

**Social Security**
Andrew Jacobs Jr. (D-Ind), Chairman
Hank Brown (R-Colo), Ranking Republican

**Trade**
Sam M. Gibbons (D-Fla), Chairman
Philip M. Crane (R-Ill), Ranking Republican

## Total PAC & Large Individual Contributions to Committee Members

| | |
|---|---|
| Hank Brown (R-Colo)[1] | $2,812,468 |
| Robert T. Matsui (D-Calif) | $894,962 |
| Jim Moody (D-Wis) | $605,323 |
| Don Sundquist (R-Tenn) | $496,357 |
| Charles B. Rangel (D-NY) | $487,520 |
| Marty Russo (D-Ill) | $486,574 |
| Dick Schulze (R-Pa) | $481,753 |
| Byron L. Dorgan (D-ND) | $476,805 |
| Thomas J. Downey (D-NY) | $459,931 |
| Benjamin L. Cardin (D-Md) | $458,618 |
| Frank J. Guarini (D-NJ) | $451,038 |
| Barbara B. Kennelly (D-Conn) | $428,589 |
| Beryl Anthony Jr. (D-Ark) | $427,420 |
| Raymond J. McGrath (R-NY) | $420,167 |
| Pete Stark (D-Calif) | $411,146 |
| J. J. Pickle (D-Texas) | $402,874 |
| Michael A. Andrews (D-Texas) | $394,712 |
| Nancy L. Johnson (R-Conn) | $391,901 |
| Sam M. Gibbons (D-Fla) | $373,631 |
| Rod Chandler (R-Wash) | $364,410 |
| E. Clay Shaw Jr. (R-Fla) | $353,103 |
| Bill Thomas (R-Calif) | $306,621 |
| Guy Vander Jagt (R-Mich) | $297,836 |
| Sander M. Levin (D-Mich) | $295,626 |
| Ronnie G. Flippo (D-Ala) | $258,050 |
| Dan Rostenkowski (D-Ill) | $249,066 |
| Harold E. Ford (D-Tenn) | $248,840 |
| Ed Jenkins (D-Ga) | $224,450 |
| Don J. Pease (D-Ohio) | $221,612 |
| Brian Donnelly (D-Mass) | $191,566 |
| William J. Coyne (D-Pa) | $147,025 |
| Bill Archer (R-Texas) | $85,564 |
| Bill Gradison (R-Ohio) | $50,157 |
| Philip M. Crane (R-Ill) | $41,460 |
| Bill Frenzel (R-Minn) | $5,824 |
| Andrew Jacobs Jr. (D-Ind) | $4,200 |

### Top 20 Contributors to Committee Members in 1989-90

| | | |
|---|---|---|
| 1 | National Assn of Realtors | $200,700 |
| 2 | National Assn of Life Underwriters | $186,500 |
| 3 | American Medical Assn* | $144,122 |
| 4 | National Education Assn | $137,650 |
| 5 | American Institute of CPA's | $137,000 |
| 6 | American Dental Assn | $117,250 |
| 7 | American Bankers Assn* | $115,000 |
| 8 | Metropolitan Life* | $114,408 |
| 9 | American Council of Life Insurance | $111,999 |
| 10 | Assn of Trial Lawyers of America | $111,000 |
| 11 | AT&T | $91,550 |
| 12 | National Beer Wholesalers Assn | $84,350 |
| 13 | Teamsters Union | $79,750 |
| 14 | Amer Fedn of State/County/Munic Employees | $77,150 |
| 15 | Federal Express Corp | $76,650 |
| 16 | National Assn of Home Builders | $71,381 |
| 17 | National Venture Capital Assn | $70,000 |
| 18 | National Assn of Letter Carriers* | $68,975 |
| 19 | RJR Nabisco | $67,000 |
| 20 | American Hospital Assn | $66,943 |

* Contributions came from more than one PAC affiliated with this sponsor.

[1] Ran for U.S. Senate in 1990
[2] Did not seek reelection in 1990
[3] Did not seek reelection in 1990

## Summary

No committee in the House of Representatives — and possibly in all of Congress — is more important to as wide a breath of industries, interests and political contributors as Ways and Means. Along with its counterpart, the Senate Finance Committee, this is where the first drafts of the nation's tax laws are written and where the final chapters (along with footnotes, abridgments and special exceptions) are hammered into shape. Ways and Means operates in an arcane world of lawyers and tax accountants, where every comma, semicolon and parenthetical addendum can mean millions or billions of dollars to individual companies and industries.

Towering above all other industries in its contributions to committee members is the

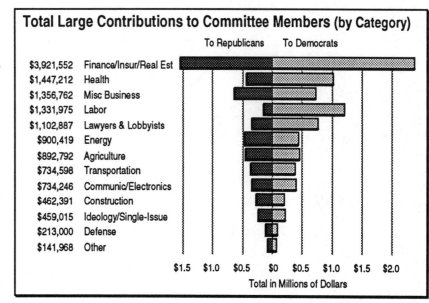

nation's financial community — particularly the insurance industry, which delivered $1.7 million to committee members in the 1990 elections, an average of nearly $48,000 per member. The top recipient of all was Colorado Republican Hank Brown, who drew over $182,000 in insurance industry contributions during his successful campaign for the U.S. Senate.

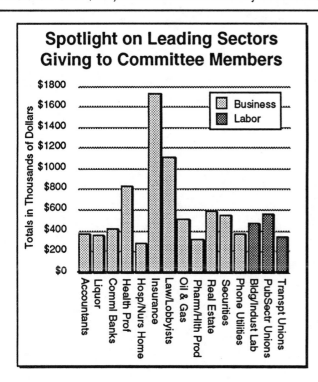

### Leading Sectors
### Giving to Committee Members

**Business**

| | |
|---|---|
| Accountants | $354,436 |
| Beer, Wine & Liquor | $338,568 |
| Commercial Banks | $408,596 |
| Health Professionals | $818,616 |
| Hospitals/Nursing Homes | $258,646 |
| Insurance | $1,722,945 |
| Lawyers & Lobbyists | $1,102,887 |
| Oil & Gas | $495,762 |
| Pharmaceuticals/Health Products | $307,350 |
| Real Estate | $570,335 |
| Securities/Commodities Investment | $539,951 |
| Telephone Utilities | $357,431 |

**Labor**

| | |
|---|---|
| Bldg Trades/Industrial/Misc Unions | $455,293 |
| Public Sector Unions | $548,082 |
| Transportation Unions | $328,600 |

# 4.

# Member Profiles

# What's included in the Member Profiles...

These mini-profiles aim to convey a sense of each member's financial supporters. Readers may particularly note the correlation (or lack of it) between a member's "cash constituents" and his or her committee assigments.

For senators, this shows the period of the fundraising shown below and in the category chart at right. For House members, the fundraising period is 1989-90 and the dates are not shown. *For senators who did not run in 1990, the totals refer only to receipts from political action committees.* In those cases, the notation "PACs only" is included next to the year.

District number (or office, in the case of senators)

*Totals in Thousands of Dollars*

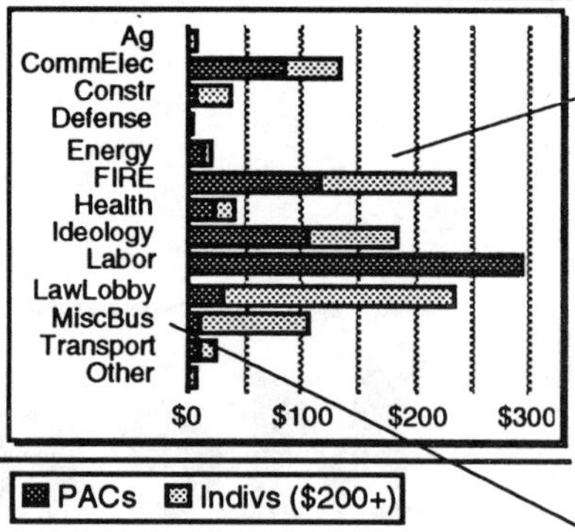

## Sen. Joseph R. Biden Jr. (D)

**1990 Committees: Foreign Relations  Judiciary**
**First elected: 1972**

1985-90 Total Rcpts: ............$2,819,280
1990 Year-end cash: ..............$190,151

**Source of Funds**
- ■ PACs.............................................24%
- ▨ Lg Individuals ($200+) .............46%
- □ Individuals under $200 ............19%
- ▨ Other..........................................11%

**1985-90**

**Top Industries & Interest Groups**

Insurance .....................................$104,800
Securities & Investment ...............$58,750
Commercial Banks .......................$55,450
Oil & Gas ......................................$51,950
Health Professionals ....................$40,500

Unidentified.................................$178,205

Ag
CommElec
Constr
Defense
Energy
FIRE
Health
Ideology
Labor
LawLobby
MiscBus
Transport
Other

$0    $100    $200    $300

■ PACs  ▨ Indivs ($200+)

## Sources of Campaign Revenues

This box and pie chart gives the broad breakdown of where each member's campaign funds came from. In the case of House members, the percentages cover funds raised in the 1989-90 election cycle. For senators, the figures cover the past six years (less if they were elected more recently). The sources include:

**PACs.** Contributions from political action committees.

**Indivs $200+.** These are contributions of $200 or more made by individuals. Under federal law, each of these contributions must be itemized and the contributor identified by name, address, employer and occupation.

**Indivs under $200.** Contributions from individuals who gave $200 or less. The FEC does not require that these contributions be itemized, but only reported in the aggregate. This figure was derived by subtracting the itemized contributions from the total individual contributions reported by the member.

**Other.** This covers funds from all other sources including, but not limited to, party contributions and funds from the candidate's own pocket. This figure was calculated by subtracting the member's total contributions from the total they received from PACs and individuals.

This is a more detailed breakdown of the industries and interest groups that contributed the most money to the member's campaign. Each member's five leading contributor groups are listed.

This is the total of contributions from PACs and large individual donations that the center was not able to identify or classify into any of the other categories.

172

## Committee Abbreviations

**Senate Committees**

| | |
|---|---|
| Agric | Senate Agriculture, Nutrition & Forestry Committee |
| Approp | Senate Appropriations Committee |
| ArmServ | Senate Armed Services Committee |
| Banking | Senate Banking, Housing & Urban Affairs Committee |
| Budget | Senate Budget Committee |
| Commerce | Senate Commerce, Science & Transportation Committee |
| Energy | Senate Energy & Natural Resources Committee |
| Envir | Senate Environment & Public Works Committee |
| Finance | Senate Finance Committee |
| ForRel | Senate Foreign Relations Committee |
| GovAff | Senate Governmental Affairs Committee |
| Judiciary | Senate Judiciary Committee |
| Labor | Senate Labor & Human Resources Committee |
| Rules | Senate Rules & Administration Committee |
| SmBus | Senate Small Business Committee |
| Vet Affairs | Senate Veterans' Affairs Committee |

**House Committees**

| | |
|---|---|
| Admin | House Administration Committee |
| Agric | House Agriculture Committee |
| Approp | House Appropriations Committee |
| ArmServ | House Armed Services Committee |
| Banking | House Banking, Finance & Urban Affairs Committee |
| Budget | House Budget Committee |
| DC | House District of Columbia Committee |
| Educ/Labor | House Education & Labor Committee |
| Energy & Commerce | House Energy & Commerce Committee |
| ForAff | House Foreign Affairs Committee |
| Govt Ops | House Government Operations Committee |
| Interior | House Interior & Insular Affairs Committee |
| Judiciary | House Judiciary Committee |
| Merchand Marine | House Merchant Marine & Fisheries Committee |
| Post Office | House Post Office & Civil Service Committee |
| PubWorks | House Public Works & Transportation Committee |
| Rules | House Rules Committee |
| Science | House Science, Space & Technology Committee |
| SmBus | House Small Business Committee |
| Vet Affairs | House Veterans' Affairs Committee |
| Ways & Means | House Ways & Means Committee |

## Contribution Totals by Category

To allow for easy comparison of the sources of campaign funds among different candidates, each contribution was grouped into one of 13 broad categories. This chart shows how much the member got from each, as well as the proportion of funds from PACs and individuals within each group. The categories are described below.

## Categories

**Agriculture (Ag)**. Includes farmers and all other segments of the agriculture industry, including food processors and supermarkets. Also covers timber companies and paper manufacturers.

**Communications/Electronics (Comm Elec)**. This includes telecommunications, broadcasting, TV & movie production, printing and publishing, and the computer and electronics industries.

**Construction (Const)** and related services, materials and equipment.

**Defense**. Defense contractors (like Boeing and General Motors) that earn most of their revenues from non-defense activities are *not* classified as defense unless the member sits on a defense related committee.

**Energy & Natural Resources (Energy)**. Besides the oil & gas industry, this includes electric utilities, mining companies, waste management and related industries.

**Finance, Insurance & Real Estate (FIRE)**. Includes banks, stock brokerage and investment firms, insurance and real estate companies, accountants, commodities brokers and all other financial services.

**Health**. Includes health professionals, hospitals, nursing homes, pharmaceutical companies and others providing health services or products.

**Ideology/Single Issue (Ideology)**. Also includes "leadership" PACs.

**Labor**. Includes all varieties of labor union PACs.

**Lawyers & Lobbyists (LawLobby)**. Includes law firms and lawyers' professional associations, as well as other firms specializing in lobbying and public relations counseling.

**Miscellaneous Businesses (Misc Bus)**. This includes a variety of manufacturing, sales and service-related companies not classified elsewhere.

**Transportation (Transport)**. Also includes non-defense aerospace manufacturers.

**Other**. Includes companies that do not fit easily into the other categories, as well as groups (such as retirees) who have no specific financial interest.

# Alabama

## Senate Spending

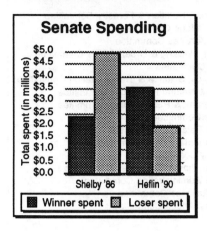

Total spent (in millions)

Winner spent  Loser spent

## Spending in 1990 House Races

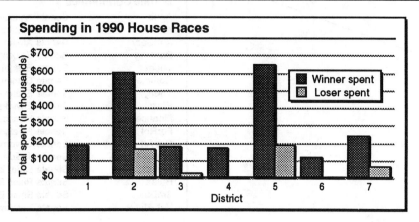

Total spent (in thousands)

Winner spent
Loser spent

District

## 1990 Elections at a Glance

| Dist | Name | Party | Vote Pct | Race Type |
|------|------|-------|----------|-----------|
| Sen | Howell Heflin (1990) | Dem | 61% | Reelected |
| Sen | Richard C. Shelby (1986) | Dem | 50% | Beat Incumb |
| 1 | Sonny Callahan | Rep | 100% | Reelected |
| 2 | Bill Dickinson | Rep | 51% | Reelected |
| 3 | Glen Browder | Dem | 74% | Reelected |
| 4 | Tom Bevill | Dem | 100% | Reelected |
| 5 | Bud Cramer | Dem | 67% | Open Seat |
| 6 | Ben Erdreich | Dem | 93% | Reelected |
| 7 | Claude Harris | Dem | 70% | Reelected |

*Totals in Thousands of Dollars*

## Sen. Howell Heflin (D)

**1990 Committees: Agriculture Energy Judiciary**
**First elected: 1978**

1985-90 Total Rcpts: ..........$4,005,473
1990 Year-end cash: ...........$1,036,023

**Source of Funds**
- PACs ................................. 36%
- Lg Individuals ($200+) ........ 41%
- Individuals under $200 ......... 9%
- Other ............................... 14%

### 1985-90

**Top Industries & Interest Groups**

| | |
|---|---|
| Lawyers & Lobbyists | $495,064 |
| Pro-Israel | $168,986 |
| Crop Production/Processing | $161,861 |
| Oil & Gas | $149,115 |
| Insurance | $123,031 |
| Unidentified | $227,323 |

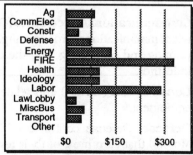

## Sen. Richard C. Shelby (D)

**1990 Committees: Armed Services  Banking**
**First elected: 1986**

1985-90 Total Rcpts: ...........$3,362,292
1990 Year-end cash: ..............$746,551

**Source of Funds**
- PACs ................................. 36%
- Lg Individuals ($200+) ........ 19%
- Individuals under $200 ......... 10%
- Other ............................... 35%

### 1985-90 (PACs only)

**Top Industries & Interest Groups**

| | |
|---|---|
| Bldg/Indust/Misc Unions | $152,574 |
| Commercial Banks | $105,046 |
| Insurance | $76,250 |
| Transportation Unions | $73,000 |
| Pro-Israel | $64,025 |

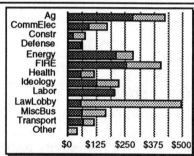

## 1. Sonny Callahan (R)

**1990 Committees: Energy & Commerce**
**First elected: 1984**

1989-90 Total receipts: ...........$318,680
1990 Year-end cash: ..............$236,511

**Source of Funds**
- PACs ................................. 53%
- Lg Individuals ($200+) ........ 31%
- Individuals under $200 ......... 10%
- Other ................................. 6%

**Top Industries & Interest Groups**

| | |
|---|---|
| Oil & Gas | $21,300 |
| Health Professionals | $19,850 |
| Forestry & Forest Products | $13,500 |
| Telephone Utilities | $12,450 |
| Insurance | $10,500 |
| Unidentified | $30,330 |

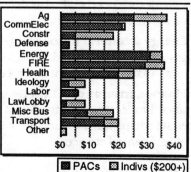

PACs  Indivs ($200+)

Key to committee & category abbreviations is on page 173

## 2. Bill Dickinson (R)

**1990 Committees:** Admin  Armed Services
**First elected:** 1964

1989-90 Total receipts: ............$425,127
1990 Year-end cash: ...............$250,325

**Source of Funds**

- PACs .................................................. 50%
- Lg Individuals ($200+) .................... 21%
- Individuals under $200 ..................... 19%
- Other ................................................ 10%

**Top Industries & Interest Groups**

Defense Aerospace ..................$74,840
Defense Electronics ..................$33,300
Misc Defense ...........................$16,500
General Contractors ..................$14,750
Real Estate ..............................$14,250

Unidentified ................................$9,250

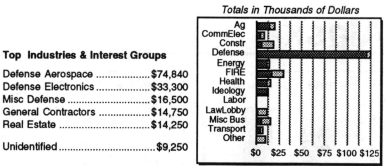
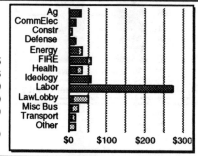

## 3. Glen Browder (D)

**1990 Committees:** Armed Services  Science
**First elected:** 1989

1989-90 Total receipts: ............$874,518
1990 Year-end cash: ...............$119,913

**Source of Funds**

- PACs .................................................. 57%
- Lg Individuals ($200+) .................... 17%
- Individuals under $200 ..................... 12%
- Other ................................................ 14%

**Top Industries & Interest Groups**

Bldg/Indust/Misc Unions ..........$160,175
Public Sector Unions ................$67,516
Lawyers & Lobbyists .................$51,450
Transportation Unions ..............$45,950
Leadership PACs ......................$25,000

Unidentified ..............................$16,110

## 4. Tom Bevill (D)

**1990 Committees:** Appropriations
**First elected:** 1966

1989-90 Total receipts: ............$220,907
1990 Year-end cash: ...............$566,499

**Source of Funds**

- PACs .................................................. 46%
- Lg Individuals ($200+) ...................... 6%
- Individuals under $200 ....................... 2%
- Other ................................................ 46%

**Top Industries & Interest Groups**

Bldg/Indust/Misc Unions ..............$9,500
Oil & Gas ...................................$9,000
Electric Utilities ..........................$8,750
Lawyers & Lobbyists ...................$7,500
Health Professionals ...................$7,050

Unidentified ................................$1,500

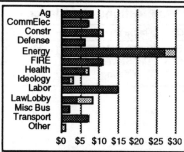

## 5. Bud Cramer (D)

**1991-92 Committees:** Public Works  Science
**First elected:** 1990

1989-90 Total receipts: ............$662,457
1990 Year-end cash: .................$20,771

**Source of Funds**

- PACs .................................................. 34%
- Lg Individuals ($200+) .................... 34%
- Individuals under $200 ..................... 14%
- Other ................................................ 18%

**Top Industries & Interest Groups**

Health Professionals ..................$52,000
Lawyers & Lobbyists .................$33,962
Bldg/Indust/Misc Unions ...........$32,000
Public Sector Unions ................$23,500
Real Estate ..............................$18,950

Unidentified ..............................$51,360

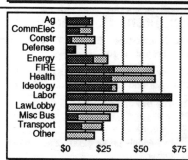

## 6. Ben Erdreich (D)

**1990 Committees:** Banking  Govt Ops
**First elected:** 1982

1989-90 Total receipts: ............$237,722
1990 Year-end cash: ...............$364,025

**Source of Funds**
- PACs .................................................. 74%
- Lg Individuals ($200+) .................... 13%
- Individuals under $200 ....................... 1%
- Other ................................................ 12%

**Top Industries & Interest Groups**

Commercial Banks ....................$41,610
Public Sector Unions ................$14,750
Bldg/Indust/Misc Unions ...........$12,150
Real Estate ..............................$10,600
Health Professionals ..................$10,250

Unidentified ................................$8,650

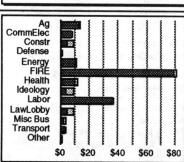

## 7. Claude Harris (D)

**1990 Committees:** Agriculture  Vet Affairs
**First elected:** 1986

1989-90 Total receipts: ............$237,577
1990 Year-end cash: .................$77,742

**Source of Funds**

- PACs .................................................. 59%
- Lg Individuals ($200+) .................... 16%
- Individuals under $200 ..................... 13%
- Other ................................................ 12%

**Top Industries & Interest Groups**

Bldg/Indust/Misc Unions ...........$19,800
Transportation Unions ..............$12,550
Telephone Utilities ....................$10,900
Health Professionals ..................$10,250
Crop Production/Processing ......$10,002

Unidentified ..............................$11,600

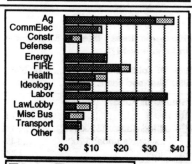

■ PACs  ⊠ Indivs ($200+)    **175**

# Alaska

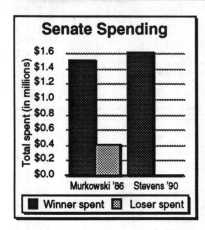

Senate Spending

Murkowski '86    Stevens '90

■ Winner spent    ▨ Loser spent

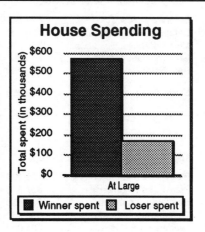

House Spending

At Large

■ Winner spent    ▨ Loser spent

## 1990 Elections at a Glance

| Dist | Name | Party | Vote Pct | Race Type |
|------|------|-------|----------|-----------|
| Sen | Frank H. Murkowski (1986) | Rep | 54% | Reelected |
| Sen | Ted Stevens (1990) | Rep | 66% | Reelected |
| 1 | Don Young | Rep | 52% | Reelected |

*Totals in Thousands of Dollars*

## Sen. Frank H. Murkowski (R)

**1990 Committees:  Energy  Foreign Relations  VetAffairs**
**First elected: 1980**

1985-90 Total Rcpts: ............$1,640,320
1990 Year-end cash: ................$22,014

**Source of Funds**
■ PACs ........................................... 40%
▨ Lg Individuals ($200+) ............... 22%
□ Individuals under $200 ............... 24%
▨ Other ........................................... 14%

**1985-90 (PACs only)**
**Top  Industries & Interest Groups**

Oil & Gas ....................................$86,971
Defense Aerospace ..................$37,225
Air Transport ............................$34,575
Health Professionals ................$30,000
Electric Utilities ........................$29,200

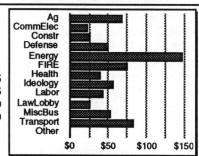

## Sen. Ted Stevens (R)

**1990 Committees:  Approp  Comm  GovAff  Rules  SmBus**
**First elected: 1970 (Appointed 1968)**

1985-90 Total Rcpts: ............$1,676,916
1990 Year-end cash: ..............$237,125

**Source of Funds**
■ PACs ........................................... 54%
▨ Lg Individuals ($200+) ............... 24%
□ Individuals under $200 ............... 5%
▨ Other ........................................... 17%

**1985-90**
**Top  Industries & Interest Groups**

Defense Aerospace ................$110,275
Lawyers & Lobbyists...............$103,000
Oil & Gas ................................$101,100
Public Sector Unions ................$65,300
Insurance ..................................$61,617

Unidentified ..............................$70,149

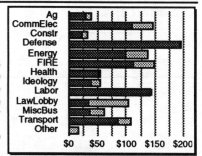

## 1.  Don Young (R)

**1990 Committees:  Interior  Merchant Marine  Post Office**
**First elected: 1973**

1989-90 Total receipts: ...........$560,908
1990 Year-end cash: ..................$5,543

**Source of Funds**
■ PACs ........................................... 47%
▨ Lg Individuals ($200+) ............... 31%
□ Individuals under $200 ............... 14%
▨ Other ........................................... 8%

**Top  Industries & Interest Groups**

Oil & Gas ....................................$78,000
Lawyers & Lobbyists .................$44,350
Sea Transport ...........................$36,575
Transportation Unions .............$31,300
Public Sector Unions ................$26,900

Unidentified ..............................$21,300

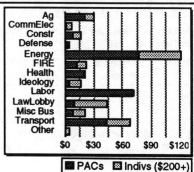

■ PACs  ▨ Indivs ($200+)

Key to committee & category abbreviations is on page 173

# Arizona

## Senate Spending

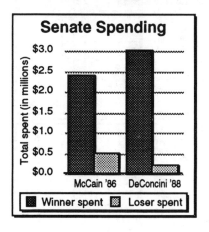

Total spent (in millions)

$3.0 / $2.5 / $2.0 / $1.5 / $1.0 / $0.5 / $0.0

McCain '86    DeConcini '88

■ Winner spent   ▨ Loser spent

## Spending in 1990 House Races

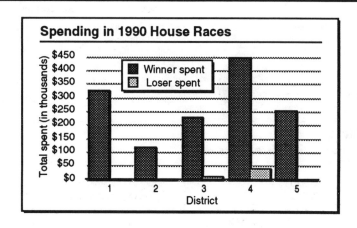

Total spent (in thousands)

$450 / $400 / $350 / $300 / $250 / $200 / $150 / $100 / $50 / $0

■ Winner spent
▨ Loser spent

District    1    2    3    4    5

## 1990 Elections at a Glance

| Dist | Name | Party | Vote Pct | Race Type |
|------|------|-------|----------|-----------|
| Sen | Dennis DeConcini (1988) | Dem | 57% | Reelected |
| Sen | John McCain (1986) | Rep | 61% | Open Seat |
| 1 | John J. Rhodes III | Rep | 100% | Reelected |
| 2 | Morris K. Udall | Dem | 66% | Reelected |
| 3 | Bob Stump | Rep | 57% | Reelected |
| 4 | Jon Kyl | Rep | 61% | Reelected |
| 5 | Jim Kolbe | Rep | 65% | Reelected |

*Totals in Thousands of Dollars*

## Sen. Dennis DeConcini (D)

**1990 Committees: Approp  Judiciary  Rules  Vet Affairs**
**First elected: 1976**

1985-90 Total Rcpts: ............$3,650,019
1990 Year-end cash: ................$34,401

**Source of Funds**
■ PACs ....................................34%
▨ Lg Individuals ($200+) ..............36%
□ Individuals under $200 ..............20%
▨ Other ....................................10%

### 1985-90 (PACs only)

**Top Industries & Interest Groups**

| | |
|---|---|
| Insurance ................................. | $79,150 |
| Defense Aerospace .................. | $69,550 |
| Bldg/Indust/Misc Unions ........... | $60,550 |
| Public Sector Unions ................ | $60,350 |
| Defense Electronics .................. | $48,269 |

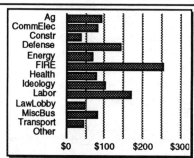

Ag / CommElec / Constr / Defense / Energy / FIRE / Health / Ideology / Labor / LawLobby / MiscBus / Transport / Other

$0   $100   $200   $300

## Sen. John McCain (R)

**1990 Committees: Armed Services  Commerce**
**First elected: 1986**

1985-90 Total Rcpts: ............$2,870,336
1990 Year-end cash: ..............$143,531

**Source of Funds**
■ PACs ....................................28%
▨ Lg Individuals ($200+) ..............31%
□ Individuals under $200 ..............20%
▨ Other ....................................22%

### 1985-90 (PACs only)

**Top Industries & Interest Groups**

| | |
|---|---|
| Oil & Gas .................................. | $61,000 |
| Defense Aerospace .................. | $55,840 |
| Insurance ................................. | $42,850 |
| Defense Electronics .................. | $38,620 |
| Pro-Israel ................................. | $38,500 |
| | |
| Unidentified ................................. | $7,650 |

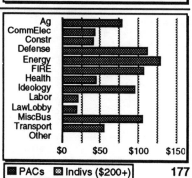

Ag / CommElec / Constr / Defense / Energy / FIRE / Health / Ideology / Labor / LawLobby / MiscBus / Transport / Other

$0   $50   $100   $150

■ PACs   ▨ Indivs ($200+)

177

## 1. John J. Rhodes III (R)

**1990 Committees:** Interior  Science  Sm Business
**First elected:** 1986

1989-90 Total receipts: ........... $326,640
1990 Year-end cash: ................. $9,621

**Source of Funds**
- ■ PACs ........................... 51%
- ▨ Lg Individuals ($200+) ........ 34%
- □ Individuals under $200 ......... 14%
- ⊠ Other ............................ 2%

**Top Industries & Interest Groups**

Lawyers & Lobbyists ................. $22,070
Real Estate ......................... $19,800
Telephone Utilities ................. $16,350
Electric Utilities .................. $16,250
Oil & Gas ........................... $13,200

Unidentified ........................ $23,862

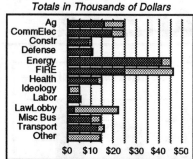

## 2. Morris K. Udall (D)

**1990 Committees:** Foreign Affairs  Interior  Post Office
**First elected:** 1961

1989-90 Total receipts: ........... $153,320
1990 Year-end cash: ................. $73,749

**Source of Funds**
- ■ PACs ........................... 85%
- ▨ Lg Individuals ($200+) ......... 6%
- □ Individuals under $200 .......... 1%
- ⊠ Other ............................ 8%

**Top Industries & Interest Groups**

Bldg/Indust/Misc Unions ............ $29,500
Public Sector Unions ............... $28,500
Lawyers & Lobbyists ................. $16,000
Electric Utilities .................. $9,500
Transportation Unions ............... $7,500

Unidentified ........................ $3,250

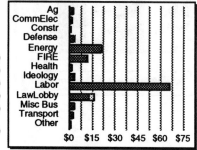

## 3. Bob Stump (R)

**1990 Committees:** Armed Services  Vet Affairs
**First elected:** 1976

1989-90 Total receipts: ........... $231,127
1990 Year-end cash: ............... $113,651

**Source of Funds**
- ■ PACs ........................... 56%
- ▨ Lg Individuals ($200+) ........ 24%
- □ Individuals under $200 ......... 11%
- ⊠ Other ............................ 9%

**Top Industries & Interest Groups**

Defense Aerospace ................... $20,715
Defense Electronics ................. $17,050
Crop Production/Processing ....... $16,050
Health Professionals ................ $11,750
Real Estate ......................... $8,550

Unidentified ........................ $7,650

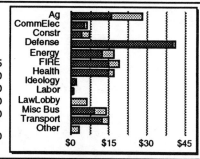

## 4. Jon Kyl (R)

**1990 Committees:** Armed Services  Govt Ops
**First elected:** 1986

1989-90 Total receipts: ........... $588,180
1990 Year-end cash: ............... $335,702

**Source of Funds**
- ■ PACs ........................... 29%
- ▨ Lg Individuals ($200+) ........ 49%
- □ Individuals under $200 ......... 15%
- ⊠ Other ............................ 8%

**Top Industries & Interest Groups**

Lawyers & Lobbyists ................. $45,374
Real Estate ......................... $39,578
Health Professionals ................ $37,800
Defense Aerospace ................... $23,950
Retired ............................. $22,520

Unidentified ........................ $49,450

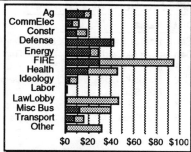

## 5. Jim Kolbe (R)

**1990 Committees:** Appropriations
**First elected:** 1984

1989-90 Total receipts: ........... $325,457
1990 Year-end cash: ................. $81,087

**Source of Funds**
- ■ PACs ........................... 41%
- ▨ Lg Individuals ($200+) ........ 27%
- □ Individuals under $200 ......... 30%
- ⊠ Other ............................ 2%

**Top Industries & Interest Groups**

Real Estate ......................... $13,150
Automotive .......................... $12,200
Lawyers & Lobbyists ................. $11,350
Oil & Gas ........................... $11,250
Defense Electronics ................. $10,055

Unidentified ........................ $14,850

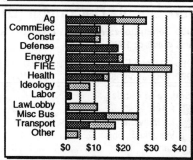

■ PACs  ⊠ Indivs ($200+)

# Arkansas

## Senate Spending

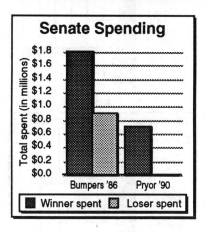

Total spent (in millions)

Winner spent  Loser spent

Bumpers '86   Pryor '90

## Spending in 1990 House Races

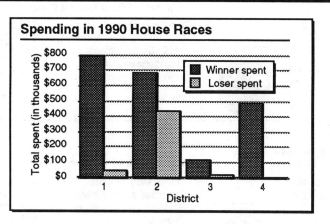

Total spent (in thousands)

Winner spent
Loser spent

District

## 1990 Elections at a Glance

| Dist | Name | Party | Vote Pct | Race Type |
|------|------|-------|----------|-----------|
| Sen | Dale Bumpers (1986) | Dem | 62% | Reelected |
| Sen | David Pryor (1990) | Dem | 100% | Reelected |
| 1 | Bill Alexander | Dem | 64% | Reelected |
| 2 | Ray Thornton | Dem | 60% | Open Seat |
| 3 | John Paul Hammerschmidt | Rep | 70% | Reelected |
| 4 | Beryl Anthony Jr. | Dem | 72% | Reelected |

*Totals in Thousands of Dollars*

## Sen. Dale Bumpers (D)

**1990 Committees: Appropriations  Energy  Sm Business**
**First elected: 1974**

1985-90 Total Rcpts: ............$1,849,409
1990 Year-end cash: ..............$110,363

**Source of Funds**
- PACs............................................31%
- Lg Individuals ($200+)..............38%
- Individuals under $200 .............24%
- Other ...........................................7%

### 1985-90 (PACs only)

**Top  Industries & Interest Groups**

| | |
|---|---|
| Public Sector Unions ................ | $62,500 |
| Bldg/Indust/Misc Unions ........... | $30,000 |
| Insurance .................................. | $27,956 |
| Commercial Banks ................... | $25,050 |
| Transportation Unions .............. | $22,900 |

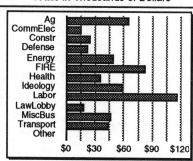

## Sen. David Pryor (D)

**1990 Committees: Agriculture  Finance  Govt Affairs**
**First elected: 1978**

1985-90 Total Rcpts: ...........$1,498,368
1990 Year-end cash: ...........$1,005,464

**Source of Funds**
- PACs............................................39%
- Lg Individuals ($200+) .............44%
- Individuals under $200 .............3%
- Other ...........................................14%

### 1985-90

**Top  Industries & Interest Groups**

| | |
|---|---|
| Lawyers & Lobbyists ............... | $116,817 |
| Crop Production/Processing ...... | $86,383 |
| Insurance .................................. | $83,562 |
| Securities & Investment ........... | $68,890 |
| Health Professionals ................ | $60,000 |
| | |
| Unidentified ............................... | $95,499 |

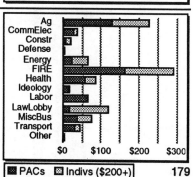

PACs   Indivs ($200+)

179

# 1. Bill Alexander (D)

**1990 Committees: Appropriations**
**First elected: 1968**

1989-90 Total receipts: ............$773,016
1990 Year-end cash: ...................$4,763

**Source of Funds**

- ■ PACs.................................................53%
- ▨ Lg Individuals ($200+) ...............22%
- □ Individuals under $200 ..............15%
- ▧ Other...............................................11%

**Top Industries & Interest Groups**

Bldg/Indust/Misc Unions ............$88,300
Crop Production/Processing......$47,325
Public Sector Unions .................$44,400
Transportation Unions ...............$42,000
Lawyers & Lobbyists ..................$34,500

Unidentified ...............................$28,150

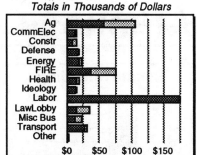

# 2. Ray Thornton (D)

**1991-92 Committees: Govt Ops Science**
**First elected: 1990 (also served 1973-79)**

1989-90 Total receipts: ............$697,067
1990 Year-end cash: .................$18,638

**Source of Funds**

- ■ PACs.................................................35%
- ▨ Lg Individuals ($200+) ...............50%
- □ Individuals under $200 ................4%
- ▧ Other...............................................11%

**Top Industries & Interest Groups**

Lawyers & Lobbyists ..................$65,695
Securities & Investment ............$61,200
Bldg/Indust/Misc Unions ...........$46,500
Public Sector Unions .................$29,750
Commercial Banks ....................$28,850

Unidentified ...............................$47,024

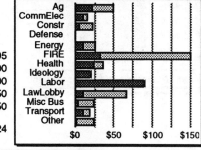

# 3. John Paul Hammerschmidt (R)

**1990 Committees: Public Works Vet Affairs**
**First elected: 1966**

1989-90 Total receipts: ............$266,438
1990 Year-end cash: ..............$500,684

**Source of Funds**

- ■ PACs.................................................63%
- ▨ Lg Individuals ($200+) ...............13%
- □ Individuals under $200 ................3%
- ▧ Other...............................................21%

**Top Industries & Interest Groups**

Air Transport ..............................$33,500
Misc Manufacturing & Distrib .....$18,500
Transportation Unions ...............$11,500
Trucking .....................................$11,300
Health Professionals ...................$9,500

Unidentified .................................$4,500

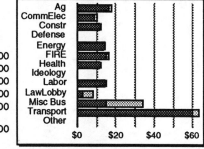

# 4. Beryl Anthony Jr. (D)

**1990 Committees: Ways & Means**
**First elected: 1978**

1989-90 Total receipts: ............$530,662
1990 Year-end cash: ..............$364,662

**Source of Funds**

- ■ PACs.................................................71%
- ▨ Lg Individuals ($200+) .................9%
- □ Individuals under $200 ................4%
- ▧ Other...............................................16%

**Top Industries & Interest Groups**

Insurance ...................................$67,300
Health Professionals .................$25,950
Oil & Gas ...................................$22,900
Securities & Investment ............$21,750
Lawyers & Lobbyists ..................$21,750

Unidentified .................................$2,850

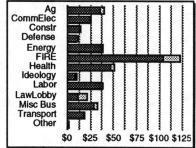

▨ PACs  ▧ Indivs ($200+)

# California

## Spending in 1990 House Races

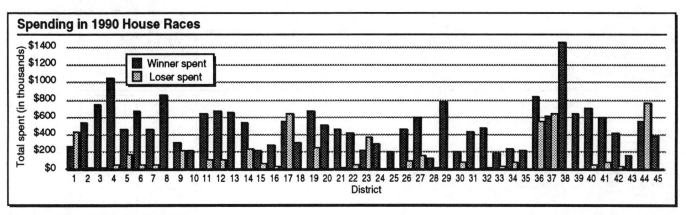

Total spent (in thousands) vs District

- Winner spent
- Loser spent

## Senate Spending

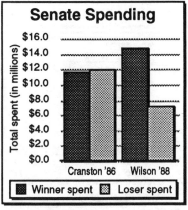

Total spent (in millions)

- Winner spent
- Loser spent

Cranston '86    Wilson '88

NOTE: Sen. Pete Wilson resigned his Senate seat after winning election as governor in 1990.

## 1990 Elections at a Glance

| Dist | Name | Party | Vote Pct | Race Type | Dist | Name | Party | Vote Pct | Race Type |
|------|------|-------|----------|-----------|------|------|-------|----------|-----------|
| Sen | Alan Cranston (1986) | Dem | 49% | Reelected | 23 | Anthony C. Beilenson | Dem | 62% | Reelected |
| Sen | John Seymour | Rep | N/A | Appt'd 1991 | 24 | Henry A. Waxman | Dem | 69% | Reelected |
| 1 | Frank Riggs | Rep | 43% | Beat Incumb | 25 | Edward R. Roybal | Dem | 70% | Reelected |
| 2 | Wally Herger | Rep | 64% | Reelected | 26 | Howard L. Berman | Dem | 61% | Reelected |
| 3 | Robert T. Matsui | Dem | 60% | Reelected | 27 | Mel Levine | Dem | 58% | Reelected |
| 4 | Vic Fazio | Dem | 55% | Reelected | 28 | Julian C. Dixon | Dem | 73% | Reelected |
| 5 | Nancy Pelosi | Dem | 77% | Reelected | 29 | Maxine Waters | Dem | 79% | Open Seat |
| 6 | Barbara Boxer | Dem | 68% | Reelected | 30 | Matthew G. Martinez | Dem | 58% | Reelected |
| 7 | George Miller | Dem | 60% | Reelected | 31 | Mervyn M. Dymally | Dem | 67% | Reelected |
| 8 | Ronald V. Dellums | Dem | 61% | Reelected | 32 | Glenn M. Anderson | Dem | 62% | Reelected |
| 9 | Pete Stark | Dem | 58% | Reelected | 33 | David Dreier | Rep | 64% | Reelected |
| 10 | Don Edwards | Dem | 63% | Reelected | 34 | Esteban E. Torres | Dem | 61% | Reelected |
| 11 | Tom Lantos | Dem | 66% | Reelected | 35 | Jerry Lewis | Rep | 61% | Reelected |
| 12 | Tom Campbell | Rep | 61% | Reelected | 36 | George E. Brown Jr. | Dem | 53% | Reelected |
| 13 | Norman Y. Mineta | Dem | 58% | Reelected | 37 | Al McCandless | Rep | 50% | Reelected |
| 14 | John T. Doolittle | Rep | 52% | Open Seat | 38 | Robert K. Dornan | Rep | 58% | Reelected |
| 15 | Gary Condit | Dem | 66% | Reelected | 39 | William E. Dannemeyer | Rep | 65% | Reelected |
| 16 | Leon E. Panetta | Dem | 74% | Reelected | 40 | C. Christopher Cox | Rep | 68% | Reelected |
| 17 | Calvin Dooley | Dem | 54% | Beat Incumb | 41 | Bill Lowery | Rep | 49% | Reelected |
| 18 | Richard H. Lehman | Dem | 100% | Reelected | 42 | Dana Rohrabacher | Rep | 59% | Reelected |
| 19 | Robert J. Lagomarsino | Rep | 55% | Reelected | 43 | Ron Packard | Rep | 68% | Reelected |
| 20 | Bill Thomas | Rep | 60% | Reelected | 44 | Randy "Duke" Cunningham | Rep | 46% | Beat Incumb |
| 21 | Elton Gallegly | Rep | 58% | Reelected | 45 | Duncan Hunter | Rep | 73% | Reelected |
| 22 | Carlos J. Moorhead | Rep | 60% | Reelected | | | | | |

## Sen. Alan Cranston (D)

**1990 Committees: Banking  Foreign Relations  VetAff**
**First elected: 1968**

1985-90 Total Rcpts: .........$13,076,997
1990 Year-end cash: ..............$406,090

### Source of Funds
- ■ PACs....................................11%
- ▨ Lg Individuals ($200+)...............19%
- ☐ Individuals under $200.............53%
- ▧ Other...................................17%

**1985-90 (PACs only)**
**Top Industries & Interest Groups**

| | |
|---|---|
| Pro-Israel ................................. | $209,607 |
| Bldg/Indust/Misc Unions .......... | $152,550 |
| Securities & Investment ........... | $101,050 |
| Transportation Unions .............. | $99,800 |
| Insurance ................................... | $84,100 |

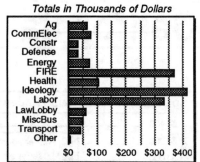

*Totals in Thousands of Dollars*

## Sen. John Seymour (R)

**1991-92 Committees: Agric  Energy  GovAff  SmBus**
**First elected: 1991 (Appointed)**

1989-90 Total receipts: ........................$0
1990 Year-end cash: ...........................$0

### Source of Funds
- ■ PACs.....................................0%
- ▨ Lg Individuals ($200+)................0%
- ☐ Individuals under $200..............0%
- ▧ Other....................................0%

**Top Industries & Interest Groups**

No funds collected in 1989-90

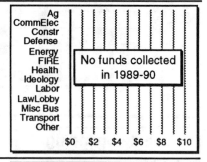

No funds collected in 1989-90

## 1. Frank Riggs (R)

**1991-92 Committees: Banking  Public Works**
**First elected: 1990**

1989-90 Total receipts: ...........$253,481
1990 Year-end cash: .....................$-595

### Source of Funds
- ■ PACs.......................................3%
- ▨ Lg Individuals ($200+)...............22%
- ☐ Individuals under $200.............14%
- ▧ Other...................................61%

**Top Industries & Interest Groups**

| | |
|---|---|
| Automotive ................................. | $10,950 |
| Real Estate ................................. | $8,980 |
| General Contractors .................... | $6,480 |
| Lawyers & Lobbyists ................... | $4,279 |
| Business Services ....................... | $2,750 |
| Unidentified ...............................:.. | $7,810 |

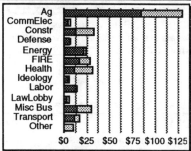

## 2. Wally Herger (R)

**1990 Committees: Agriculture  Merchant Marine**
**First elected: 1986**

1989-90 Total receipts: ...........$616,075
1990 Year-end cash: ..............$114,862

### Source of Funds
- ■ PACs.....................................34%
- ▨ Lg Individuals ($200+)...............29%
- ☐ Individuals under $200.............33%
- ▧ Other....................................4%

**Top Industries & Interest Groups**

| | |
|---|---|
| Crop Production/Processing ...... | $43,454 |
| Health Professionals ................. | $26,801 |
| Misc Agriculture ......................... | $19,150 |
| Agric Services/Products ............ | $17,920 |
| Oil & Gas .................................... | $14,875 |
| Unidentified ................................ | $41,612 |

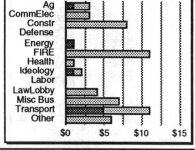

## 3. Robert T. Matsui (D)

**1990 Committees: Ways & Means**
**First elected: 1978**

1989-90 Total receipts: .........$1,207,843
1990 Year-end cash: ...........$1,128,637

### Source of Funds
- ■ PACs.....................................47%
- ▨ Lg Individuals ($200+)...............27%
- ☐ Individuals under $200.............13%
- ▧ Other...................................13%

**Top Industries & Interest Groups**

| | |
|---|---|
| Health Professionals ................. | $87,175 |
| Lawyers & Lobbyists ................... | $84,475 |
| Insurance ................................... | $67,300 |
| Real Estate ................................. | $52,775 |
| Beer, Wine & Liquor .................. | $42,250 |
| Unidentified ................................ | $47,475 |

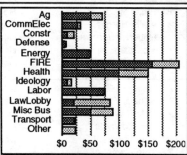

## 4. Vic Fazio (D)

**1990 Committees: Appropriations**
**First elected: 1978**

1989-90 Total receipts: .........$1,217,430
1990 Year-end cash: ..............$194,935

### Source of Funds
- ■ PACs.....................................54%
- ▨ Lg Individuals ($200+)...............27%
- ☐ Individuals under $200.............11%
- ▧ Other....................................8%

**Top Industries & Interest Groups**

| | |
|---|---|
| Lawyers & Lobbyists ................. | $64,500 |
| Bldg/Indust/Misc Unions ........... | $54,225 |
| Public Sector Unions ................ | $49,550 |
| Crop Production/Processing ...... | $48,750 |
| Real Estate ................................. | $41,950 |
| Unidentified ................................ | $57,350 |

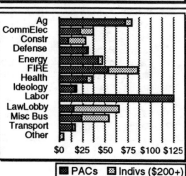

**■ PACs  ▨ Indivs ($200+)**

182    Key to committee & category abbreviations is on page 173

# 5. Nancy Pelosi (D)

**1990 Committees:** Banking  Govt Ops
**First elected:** 1987

1989-90 Total receipts: ...........$462,664
1990 Year-end cash: ...............$97,689

### Source of Funds
| | |
|---|---|
| ■ PACs | 55% |
| ▦ Lg Individuals ($200+) | 42% |
| □ Individuals under $200 | 1% |
| ▨ Other | 1% |

**Top Industries & Interest Groups**

Lawyers & Lobbyists .................$52,700
Bldg/Indust/Misc Unions ...........$51,750
Transportation Unions ..............$26,650
Public Sector Unions .................$26,000
Real Estate ............................$25,450

Unidentified ..............................$29,300

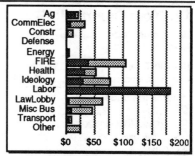

# 6. Barbara Boxer (D)

**1990 Committees:** Budget  Govt Ops
**First elected:** 1982

1989-90 Total receipts: ...........$929,732
1990 Year-end cash: ...............$499,349

### Source of Funds
| | |
|---|---|
| ■ PACs | 35% |
| ▦ Lg Individuals ($200+) | 40% |
| □ Individuals under $200 | 18% |
| ▨ Other | 7% |

**Top Industries & Interest Groups**

Bldg/Indust/Misc Unions ...........$69,900
Public Sector Unions .................$69,197
Lawyers & Lobbyists .................$63,575
Transportation Unions ..............$42,600
Real Estate ............................$36,825

Unidentified ..............................$73,195

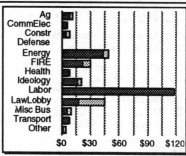

# 7. George Miller (D)

**1990 Committees:** Educ/Labor  Interior
**First elected:** 1974

1989-90 Total receipts: ...........$469,400
1990 Year-end cash: ...............$438,229

### Source of Funds
| | |
|---|---|
| ■ PACs | 56% |
| ▦ Lg Individuals ($200+) | 15% |
| □ Individuals under $200 | 12% |
| ▨ Other | 17% |

**Top Industries & Interest Groups**

Bldg/Indust/Misc Unions ...........$62,150
Lawyers & Lobbyists .................$45,350
Public Sector Unions .................$29,050
Transportation Unions ..............$27,750
Electric Utilities .........................$23,400

Unidentified ..............................$11,800

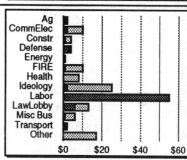

# 8. Ronald V. Dellums (D)

**1990 Committees:** Armed Services  DC
**First elected:** 1970

1989-90 Total receipts: ...........$779,275
1990 Year-end cash: ...............$82,629

### Source of Funds
| | |
|---|---|
| ■ PACs | 10% |
| ▦ Lg Individuals ($200+) | 15% |
| □ Individuals under $200 | 54% |
| ▨ Other | 21% |

**Top Industries & Interest Groups**

Public Sector Unions .................$19,600
Bldg/Indust/Misc Unions ...........$18,300
Transportation Unions ..............$17,100
Democratic/Liberal ....................$14,250
Lawyers & Lobbyists .................$12,500

Unidentified ..............................$36,050

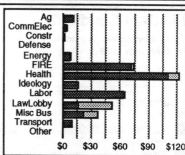

# 9. Pete Stark (D)

**1990 Committees:** DC  Ways & Means
**First elected:** 1972

1989-90 Total receipts: ...........$525,271
1990 Year-end cash: ...............$356,004

### Source of Funds
| | |
|---|---|
| ■ PACs | 64% |
| ▦ Lg Individuals ($200+) | 14% |
| □ Individuals under $200 | 12% |
| ▨ Other | 9% |

**Top Industries & Interest Groups**

Health Professionals .................$75,300
Lawyers & Lobbyists .................$52,180
Insurance ................................$39,000
Public Sector Unions .................$29,150
Bldg/Indust/Misc Unions ...........$22,150

Unidentified ................................$8,500

# 10. Don Edwards (D)

**1990 Committees:** Judiciary  Vet Affairs
**First elected:** 1962

1989-90 Total receipts: ...........$224,999
1990 Year-end cash: .................$55,464

### Source of Funds
| | |
|---|---|
| ■ PACs | 75% |
| ▦ Lg Individuals ($200+) | 13% |
| □ Individuals under $200 | 8% |
| ▨ Other | 4% |

**Top Industries & Interest Groups**

Bldg/Indust/Misc Unions ...........$36,500
Public Sector Unions .................$31,075
Transportation Unions ..............$23,625
Lawyers & Lobbyists .................$17,650
Real Estate ............................$12,500

Unidentified ................................$2,250

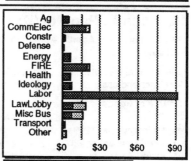

■ PACs  ▨ Indivs ($200+)

183

## 11. Tom Lantos (D)

**1990 Committees: Banking Foreign Affairs Govt Ops**
**First elected: 1980**

1989-90 Total receipts: ............$788,298
1990 Year-end cash: ..............$637,734

**Source of Funds**
- PACs .................................15%
- Lg Individuals ($200+) .............20%
- Individuals under $200 .............56%
- Other ................................9%

**Top Industries & Interest Groups**

Pro-Israel ...................................$28,865
Real Estate ................................$27,550
Transportation Unions ...............$26,500
Public Sector Unions .................$21,000
Bldg/Indust/Misc Unions ...........$20,000

Unidentified ...............................$32,100

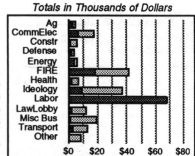

## 12. Tom Campbell (R)

**1990 Committees: Judiciary Science**
**First elected: 1988**

1989-90 Total receipts: .........$1,286,200
1990 Year-end cash: ..............$633,197

**Source of Funds**
- PACs .................................19%
- Lg Individuals ($200+) .............66%
- Individuals under $200 .............11%
- Other ................................4%

**Top Industries & Interest Groups**

Securities & Investment ...........$128,950
Lawyers & Lobbyists .................$78,501
Real Estate ................................$77,665
Computer Equipment & Svcs ....$50,685
Retired ......................................$39,850

Unidentified ..............................$267,082

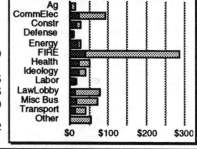

## 13. Norman Y. Mineta (D)

**1990 Committees: Public Works Science**
**First elected: 1974**

1989-90 Total receipts: ............$666,915
1990 Year-end cash: ..............$342,701

**Source of Funds**
- PACs .................................56%
- Lg Individuals ($200+) .............22%
- Individuals under $200 .............17%
- Other ................................6%

**Top Industries & Interest Groups**

Air Transport .............................$52,000
Bldg/Indust/Misc Unions ...........$46,235
Transportation Unions ...............$43,200
Lawyers & Lobbyists .................$36,400
Trucking ....................................$30,970

Unidentified ...............................$38,311

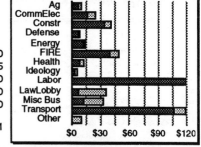

## 14. John T. Doolittle (R)

**1991-92 Committees: Interior Merchant Marine**
**First elected: 1990**

1989-90 Total receipts: ............$537,313
1990 Year-end cash: .................$12,142

**Source of Funds**
- PACs .................................39%
- Lg Individuals ($200+) .............29%
- Individuals under $200 .............21%
- Other ................................11%

**Top Industries & Interest Groups**

Real Estate ................................$24,400
Commercial Banks ....................$24,150
Lawyers & Lobbyists .................$21,250
Health Professionals .................$21,175
General Contractors .................$18,600

Unidentified ...............................$57,817

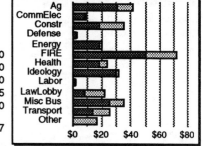

## 15. Gary Condit (D)

**1990 Committees: Agriculture Govt Ops**
**First elected: 1989**

1989-90 Total receipts: .........$1,394,470
1990 Year-end cash: .................$12,061

**Source of Funds**
- PACs .................................31%
- Lg Individuals ($200+) .............21%
- Individuals under $200 .............17%
- Other ................................31%

**Top Industries & Interest Groups**

Crop Production/Processing....$108,819
Bldg/Indust/Misc Unions ...........$90,850
Public Sector Unions .................$52,350
Real Estate ................................$40,321
Beer, Wine & Liquor .................$28,876

Unidentified ...............................$78,820

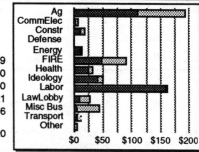

## 16. Leon E. Panetta (D)

**1990 Committees: Admin Agriculture Budget**
**First elected: 1976**

1989-90 Total receipts: ............$295,399
1990 Year-end cash: ..............$204,599

**Source of Funds**
- PACs .................................44%
- Lg Individuals ($200+) .............16%
- Individuals under $200 .............31%
- Other ................................10%

**Top Industries & Interest Groups**

Public Sector Unions .................$18,550
Bldg/Indust/Misc Unions ...........$14,750
Health Professionals .................$13,350
Crop Production/Processing......$13,300
Beer, Wine & Liquor .................$13,200

Unidentified .................................$2,650

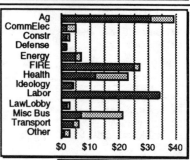

Key to committee & category abbreviations is on page 173

■ PACs ▨ Indivs ($200+)

## 17. Calvin Dooley (D)

**1991-92 Committees: Agriculture  Sm Business**
**First elected: 1990**

1989-90 Total receipts: ............ $547,763
1990 Year-end cash: ................... $9,409

**Source of Funds**
- ■ PACs ............................................. 29%
- ▨ Lg Individuals ($200+) ............... 20%
- □ Individuals under $200 ............. 31%
- ▨ Other ........................................... 21%

**Top Industries & Interest Groups**

Crop Production/Processing ...... $50,550
Bldg/Indust/Misc Unions ........... $43,500
Public Sector Unions ................. $20,500
Dairy ............................................ $15,178
Leadership PACs ....................... $13,500

Unidentified ............................... $19,779

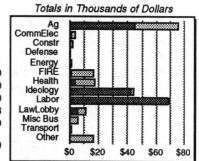

## 18. Richard H. Lehman (D)

**1990 Committees: Banking  Interior**
**First elected: 1982**

1989-90 Total receipts: ............ $302,473
1990 Year-end cash: ................. $96,145

**Source of Funds**
- ■ PACs ............................................. 66%
- ▨ Lg Individuals ($200+) ............... 16%
- □ Individuals under $200 ............. 12%
- ▨ Other ............................................. 6%

**Top Industries & Interest Groups**

Bldg/Indust/Misc Unions ........... $31,600
Real Estate ................................ $25,100
Commercial Banks .................... $22,550
Public Sector Unions ................ $17,210
Crop Production/Processing ...... $15,530

Unidentified ............................... $8,780

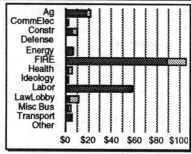

## 19. Robert J. Lagomarsino (R)

**1990 Committees: Foreign Affairs  Interior**
**First elected: 1974**

1989-90 Total receipts: ............ $643,444
1990 Year-end cash: ................. $13,120

**Source of Funds**
- ■ PACs ............................................. 21%
- ▨ Lg Individuals ($200+) ............... 36%
- □ Individuals under $200 ............. 36%
- ▨ Other ............................................. 7%

**Top Industries & Interest Groups**

Real Estate ................................ $30,580
Crop Production/Processing ...... $25,168
Oil & Gas ................................... $23,350
Retired ....................................... $21,748
Lawyers & Lobbyists ................. $20,065

Unidentified ............................... $48,750

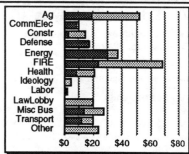

## 20. Bill Thomas (R)

**1990 Committees: Admin  Budget  Ways & Means**
**First elected: 1978**

1989-90 Total receipts: ............ $430,525
1990 Year-end cash: .............. $157,392

**Source of Funds**
- ■ PACs ............................................. 59%
- ▨ Lg Individuals ($200+) ............... 12%
- □ Individuals under $200 ............. 24%
- ▨ Other ............................................. 5%

**Top Industries & Interest Groups**

Insurance ................................... $34,000
Crop Production/Processing ...... $31,525
Oil & Gas ................................... $25,199
Real Estate ................................ $23,347
Lawyers & Lobbyists ................. $20,700

Unidentified ............................... $14,825

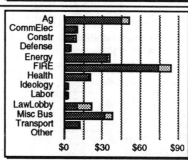

## 21. Elton Gallegly (R)

**1990 Committees: Foreign Affairs  Interior**
**First elected: 1986**

1989-90 Total receipts: ............ $599,454
1990 Year-end cash: .............. $231,271

**Source of Funds**
- ■ PACs ............................................. 26%
- ▨ Lg Individuals ($200+) ............... 49%
- □ Individuals under $200 ............. 20%
- ▨ Other ............................................. 6%

**Top Industries & Interest Groups**

Real Estate ................................ $74,445
Oil & Gas ................................... $22,137
Health Professionals ................. $20,510
Lawyers & Lobbyists ................. $20,115
Home Builders .......................... $14,052

Unidentified ............................... $88,809

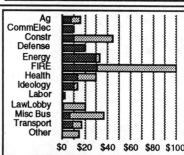

## 22. Carlos J. Moorhead (R)

**1990 Committees: Energy & Commerce  Judiciary**
**First elected: 1972**

1989-90 Total receipts: ............ $444,157
1990 Year-end cash: .............. $666,684

**Source of Funds**
- ■ PACs ............................................. 52%
- ▨ Lg Individuals ($200+) ............... 8%
- □ Individuals under $200 ............. 15%
- ▨ Other ........................................... 26%

**Top Industries & Interest Groups**

Oil & Gas ................................... $24,530
Electric Utilities ......................... $23,300
Insurance ................................... $20,650
Health Professionals ................. $18,050
Pharmaceuticals/Health Prod .... $15,850

Unidentified ............................... $10,100

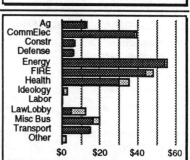

*Totals in Thousands of Dollars*

■ PACs    ▨ Indivs ($200+)

185

## 23. Anthony C. Beilenson (D)

**1990 Committees: Budget Rules**
First elected: 1976

1989-90 Total receipts: ............$231,386
1990 Year-end cash: ................$45,449

**Source of Funds**
- ■ PACs ..................................................0%
- ▓ Lg Individuals ($200+) ................77%
- ☐ Individuals under $200 ..............20%
- ▨ Other ................................................3%

**Top Industries & Interest Groups**

Lawyers & Lobbyists ..................$39,550
Retired ........................................$17,100
TV & Movies ................................$12,050
Real Estate ..................................$11,450
Misc Finance ................................$7,400

Unidentified ................................$44,400

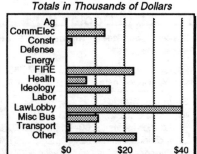

## 24. Henry A. Waxman (D)

**1990 Committees: Energy & Commerce Govt Ops**
First elected: 1974

1989-90 Total receipts: ............$500,847
1990 Year-end cash: ..............$468,893

**Source of Funds**
- ■ PACs ................................................64%
- ▓ Lg Individuals ($200+) ................22%
- ☐ Individuals under $200 ................5%
- ▨ Other ................................................9%

**Top Industries & Interest Groups**

Health Professionals ..................$95,500
Hospitals/Nursing Homes ..........$31,000
Lawyers & Lobbyists ..................$28,150
Bldg/Indust/Misc Unions ............$27,250
Pharmaceuticals/Health Prod ....$26,500

Unidentified ................................$13,490

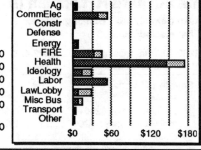

## 25. Edward R. Roybal (D)

**1990 Committees: Appropriations**
First elected: 1962

1989-90 Total receipts: ............$144,260
1990 Year-end cash: ..............$196,852

**Source of Funds**
- ■ PACs ................................................55%
- ▓ Lg Individuals ($200+) ................13%
- ☐ Individuals under $200 ..............12%
- ▨ Other ..............................................21%

**Top Industries & Interest Groups**

Public Sector Unions ..................$17,350
Bldg/Indust/Misc Unions ..........$10,700
Health Professionals ....................$9,700
Beer, Wine & Liquor ....................$7,700
Lawyers & Lobbyists ....................$5,300
Transportation Unions ................$5,300

Unidentified ................................$5,650

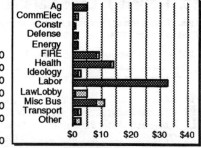

## 26. Howard L. Berman (D)

**1990 Committees: Budget Foreign Affairs Judiciary**
First elected: 1982

1989-90 Total receipts: ............$510,538
1990 Year-end cash: ..............$200,471

**Source of Funds**
- ■ PACs ................................................35%
- ▓ Lg Individuals ($200+) ................53%
- ☐ Individuals under $200 ................6%
- ▨ Other ................................................7%

**Top Industries & Interest Groups**

Lawyers & Lobbyists ..................$56,150
TV & Movies ................................$46,150
Bldg/Indust/Misc Unions ............$38,350
Real Estate ..................................$31,760
Pro-Israel ....................................$27,150

Unidentified ................................$52,150

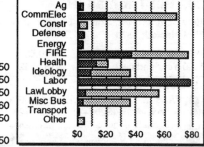

## 27. Mel Levine (D)

**1990 Committees: Foreign Affairs Interior Judiciary**
First elected: 1982

1989-90 Total receipts: .........$1,496,790
1990 Year-end cash: ...........$1,714,807

**Source of Funds**
- ■ PACs ................................................15%
- ▓ Lg Individuals ($200+) ................67%
- ☐ Individuals under $200 ................3%
- ▨ Other ..............................................14%

**Top Industries & Interest Groups**

Lawyers & Lobbyists ................$145,600
TV & Movies ..............................$143,800
Real Estate ..............................$118,550
Pro-Israel ....................................$86,529
Public Sector Unions ................$33,050

Unidentified ..............................$252,366

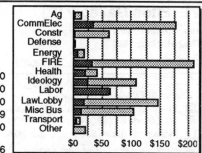

## 28. Julian C. Dixon (D)

**1990 Committees: Appropriations**
First elected: 1978

1989-90 Total receipts: ............$161,900
1990 Year-end cash: ..............$136,981

**Source of Funds**
- ■ PACs ................................................77%
- ▓ Lg Individuals ($200+) ................20%
- ☐ Individuals under $200 ................3%
- ▨ Other ................................................0%

**Top Industries & Interest Groups**

Public Sector Unions ................$22,500
Bldg/Indust/Misc Unions ............$21,800
Defense Aerospace ......................$7,800
Transportation Unions ................$7,700
Real Estate ..................................$7,550

Unidentified ................................$5,400

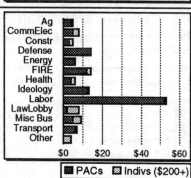

Key to committee & category abbreviations is on page 173

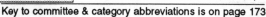
■ PACs  ▨ Indivs ($200+)

## 29. Maxine Waters (D)

**1991-92 Committees: Banking  Vet Affairs**
**First elected: 1990**

1989-90 Total receipts: ...........$740,793
1990 Year-end cash: ...............$27,717

**Source of Funds**

■ PACs ...........................................27%
▨ Lg Individuals ($200+) ...............34%
□ Individuals under $200 .............20%
▨ Other ........................................20%

**Top  Industries & Interest Groups**

Bldg/Indust/Misc Unions ...........$45,850
Lawyers & Lobbyists .................$28,150
Public Sector Unions ................$26,750
Human Rights ...........................$22,385
Health Professionals ................$22,030

Unidentified ............................$101,753

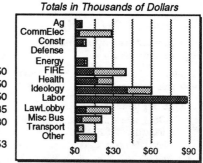

Ag
CommElec
Constr
Defense
Energy
FIRE
Health
Ideology
Labor
LawLobby
Misc Bus
Transport
Other
$0    $30    $60    $90

## 30. Matthew G. Martinez (D)

**1990 Committees: Educ/Labor  Govt Ops**
**First elected: 1982**

1989-90 Total receipts: ...........$209,495
1990 Year-end cash: ...............$43,205

**Source of Funds**

■ PACs ...........................................47%
▨ Lg Individuals ($200+) ...............49%
□ Individuals under $200 ...............4%
▨ Other ..........................................0%

**Top  Industries & Interest Groups**

Bldg/Indust/Misc Unions ...........$21,950
Public Sector Unions ................$20,631
Real Estate ...............................$19,600
Transportation Unions ...............$19,000
Food & Beverage .......................$6,500

Unidentified ..............................$46,430

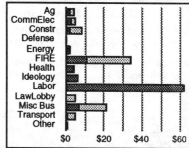

Ag
CommElec
Constr
Defense
Energy
FIRE
Health
Ideology
Labor
LawLobby
Misc Bus
Transport
Other
$0    $20    $40    $60

## 31. Mervyn M. Dymally (D)

**1990 Committees: DC  Foreign Affairs  Post Office**
**First elected: 1980**

1989-90 Total receipts: ...........$436,143
1990 Year-end cash: ...............$25,418

**Source of Funds**

■ PACs ...........................................38%
▨ Lg Individuals ($200+) ...............46%
□ Individuals under $200 ...............9%
▨ Other ..........................................7%

**Top  Industries & Interest Groups**

Public Sector Unions ................$44,400
Health Professionals ................$33,950
Bldg/Indust/Misc Unions ...........$32,100
Oil & Gas ..................................$18,050
Transportation Unions ...............$18,000

Unidentified ..............................$71,800

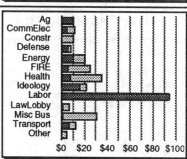

Ag
CommElec
Constr
Defense
Energy
FIRE
Health
Ideology
Labor
LawLobby
Misc Bus
Transport
Other
$0   $20   $40   $60   $80  $100

## 32. Glenn M. Anderson (D)

**1990 Committees: Public Works**
**First elected: 1968**

1989-90 Total receipts: ...........$411,845
1990 Year-end cash: ...............$31,783

**Source of Funds**

■ PACs ...........................................61%
▨ Lg Individuals ($200+) ...............26%
□ Individuals under $200 ...............4%
▨ Other ..........................................8%

**Top  Industries & Interest Groups**

Transportation Unions ...............$44,650
Air Transport ............................$38,450
Trucking ...................................$26,000
Lawyers & Lobbyists .................$22,600
Bldg/Indust/Misc Unions ...........$22,100

Unidentified ..............................$21,350

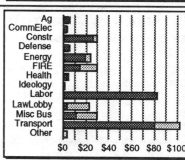

Ag
CommElec
Constr
Defense
Energy
FIRE
Health
Ideology
Labor
LawLobby
Misc Bus
Transport
Other
$0   $20   $40   $60   $80  $100

## 33. David Dreier (R)

**1990 Committees: Banking  Sm Business**
**First elected: 1980**

1989-90 Total receipts: ...........$591,313
1990 Year-end cash: ...........$1,669,915

**Source of Funds**

■ PACs ...........................................17%
▨ Lg Individuals ($200+) ...............38%
□ Individuals under $200 ...............4%
▨ Other ........................................41%

**Top  Industries & Interest Groups**

Commercial Banks ....................$33,850
Real Estate ...............................$20,806
Automotive ...............................$17,250
Savings & Loans .......................$16,250
Health Professionals ................$14,800

Unidentified ..............................$50,576

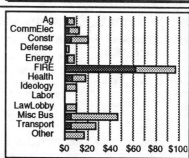

Ag
CommElec
Constr
Defense
Energy
FIRE
Health
Ideology
Labor
LawLobby
Misc Bus
Transport
Other
$0   $20   $40   $60   $80  $100

## 34. Esteban E. Torres (D)

**1990 Committees: Banking  Sm Business**
**First elected: 1982**

1989-90 Total receipts: ...........$241,635
1990 Year-end cash: ...............$148,388

**Source of Funds**

■ PACs ...........................................48%
▨ Lg Individuals ($200+) ...............34%
□ Individuals under $200 ...............8%
▨ Other ........................................10%

**Top  Industries & Interest Groups**

Bldg/Indust/Misc Unions ...........$28,800
Real Estate ...............................$21,100
Public Sector Unions ................$16,500
Savings & Loans .......................$16,250
Transportation Unions ...............$11,000

Unidentified ..............................$26,120

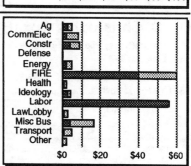

Ag
CommElec
Constr
Defense
Energy
FIRE
Health
Ideology
Labor
LawLobby
Misc Bus
Transport
Other
$0    $20    $40    $60

■ PACs  ▨ Indivs ($200+)

## 35. Jerry Lewis (R)

**1990 Committees: Appropriations**
**First elected: 1978**

1989-90 Total receipts: ............ $452,381
1990 Year-end cash: .............. $338,797

**Source of Funds**
- PACs .................................... 64%
- Lg Individuals ($200+) ............ 29%
- Individuals under $200 ........ 4%
- Other .................................. 3%

**Top Industries & Interest Groups**

Insurance ................................ $38,040
Real Estate ............................. $29,000
Health Professionals ............... $21,000
Crop Production/Processing ...... $19,650
Defense Aerospace ................. $19,599

Unidentified ........................... $24,375

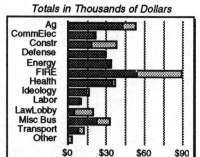

## 36. George E. Brown Jr. (D)

**1990 Committees: Agriculture Science**
**First elected: 1962 (did not serve 1971-73)**

1989-90 Total receipts: ............ $818,181
1990 Year-end cash: .................. $4,345

**Source of Funds**
- PACs .................................... 53%
- Lg Individuals ($200+) ............ 10%
- Individuals under $200 ........ 29%
- Other .................................. 7%

**Top Industries & Interest Groups**

Bldg/Indust/Misc Unions .......... $107,070
Public Sector Unions ............... $63,025
Leadership PACs .................... $39,370
Transportation Unions .............. $30,200
Agric Services/Products ........... $28,850

Unidentified ........................... $15,500

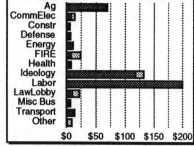

## 37. Al McCandless (R)

**1990 Committees: Banking Govt Ops**
**First elected: 1982**

1989-90 Total receipts: ............ $549,789
1990 Year-end cash: .................. $5,600

**Source of Funds**
- PACs .................................... 30%
- Lg Individuals ($200+) ............ 39%
- Individuals under $200 ........ 9%
- Other .................................. 22%

**Top Industries & Interest Groups**

Real Estate ............................. $46,000
Commercial Banks ................... $39,000
Crop Production/Processing ...... $26,750
Retired .................................. $22,150
Automotive ............................. $17,600

Unidentified ........................... $56,649

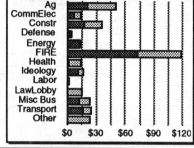

## 38. Robert K. Dornan (R)

**1990 Committees: Armed Services**
**First elected: 1976**

1989-90 Total receipts: ......... $1,665,723
1990 Year-end cash: .............. $185,200

**Source of Funds**
- PACs .................................... 2%
- Lg Individuals ($200+) ............ 15%
- Individuals under $200 ........ 83%
- Other .................................. 0%

**Top Industries & Interest Groups**

Republican/Conservative .......... $77,460
Retired .................................. $25,864
Oil & Gas ............................... $10,550
Real Estate ............................. $9,000
General Contractors ................. $7,525

Unidentified ........................... $59,742

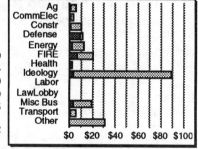

## 39. William E. Dannemeyer (R)

**1990 Committees: Energy & Commerce Judiciary**
**First elected: 1978**

1989-90 Total receipts: ............ $594,692
1990 Year-end cash: ................ $97,744

**Source of Funds**
- PACs .................................... 22%
- Lg Individuals ($200+) ............ 25%
- Individuals under $200 ........ 52%
- Other .................................. 2%

**Top Industries & Interest Groups**

Oil & Gas ............................... $22,400
Health Professionals ................ $21,950
Insurance ............................... $21,100
Republican/Conservative .......... $18,700
Real Estate ............................. $13,550

Unidentified ........................... $39,530

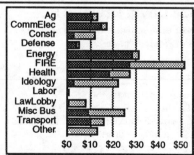

## 40. C. Christopher Cox (R)

**1990 Committees: Govt Ops Public Works**
**First elected: 1988**

1989-90 Total receipts: ............ $688,836
1990 Year-end cash: .................. $5,113

**Source of Funds**
- PACs .................................... 26%
- Lg Individuals ($200+) ............ 69%
- Individuals under $200 ........ 4%
- Other .................................. 1%

**Top Industries & Interest Groups**

Lawyers & Lobbyists ................ $84,750
Real Estate ............................. $71,146
General Contractors ................. $34,525
Securities & Investment ............ $34,057
Republican/Conservative .......... $22,275

Unidentified ........................... $130,317

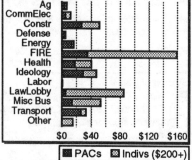

*Totals in Thousands of Dollars*

188          Key to committee & category abbreviations is on page 173

■ PACs   ⊠ Indivs ($200+)

## 41. Bill Lowery (R)

**1990 Committees: Appropriations**
**First elected: 1980**

1989-90 Total receipts: ...........$485,964
1990 Year-end cash: .................$28,497

**Source of Funds**

- PACs..........................................43%
- Lg Individuals ($200+)...............50%
- Individuals under $200 ................5%
- Other........................................2%

**Top Industries & Interest Groups**

Real Estate ..................................$35,476
Defense Aerospace ....................$30,920
General Contractors ...................$25,800
Health Professionals ...................$22,425
Defense Electronics ...................$16,450

Unidentified ...............................$50,890

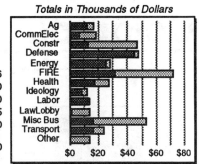

## 42. Dana Rohrabacher (R)

**1990 Committees: DC Science**
**First elected: 1988**

1989-90 Total receipts: ...........$423,924
1990 Year-end cash: .................$50,587

**Source of Funds**

- PACs..........................................29%
- Lg Individuals ($200+)...............61%
- Individuals under $200 ................9%
- Other........................................1%

**Top Industries & Interest Groups**

Health Professionals .................$28,400
Lawyers & Lobbyists .................$28,050
Real Estate ...............................$22,250
Oil & Gas .................................$21,819
Automotive ...............................$15,250

Unidentified ...............................$89,601

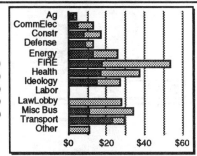

## 43. Ron Packard (R)

**1990 Committees: Public Works Science**
**First elected: 1982**

1989-90 Total receipts: ...........$167,017
1990 Year-end cash: ...............$174,589

**Source of Funds**

- PACs..........................................63%
- Lg Individuals ($200+)...............10%
- Individuals under $200 ..............15%
- Other........................................12%

**Top Industries & Interest Groups**

Air Transport ..............................$21,110
Health Professionals .................$12,750
Real Estate ..................................$9,680
Electric Utilities ............................$6,100
General Contractors ...................$5,850

Unidentified .................................$4,550

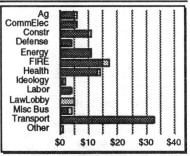

## 44. Randy "Duke" Cunningham (R)

**1991-92 Committees: Armed Services Merchant Marine**
**First elected: 1990**

1989-90 Total receipts: ...........$539,721
1990 Year-end cash: ...................$5,553

**Source of Funds**

- PACs..........................................32%
- Lg Individuals ($200+)...............35%
- Individuals under $200 ..............14%
- Other........................................20%

**Top Industries & Interest Groups**

Sea Transport ...........................$23,750
Misc Manufacturing & Distrib .....$18,700
Misc Issues ...............................$18,700
Real Estate ...............................$17,333
Defense Aerospace ..................$15,550

Unidentified ...............................$50,595

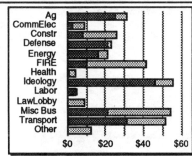

## 45. Duncan Hunter (R)

**1990 Committees: Armed Services**
**First elected: 1980**

1989-90 Total receipts: ...........$368,560
1990 Year-end cash: ...................$6,229

**Source of Funds**
- PACs..........................................30%
- Lg Individuals ($200+)...............47%
- Individuals under $200 ..............20%
- Other........................................3%

**Top Industries & Interest Groups**

Defense Aerospace ..................$24,740
General Contractors .................$22,649
Real Estate ...............................$20,854
Sea Transport ...........................$16,271
Defense Electronics ..................$14,700

Unidentified ...............................$36,170

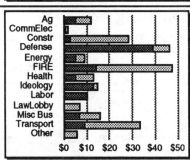

PACs    Indivs ($200+)

# Colorado

## Senate Spending

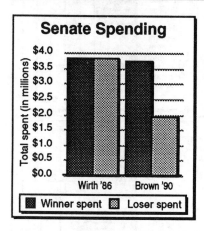

Total spent (in millions)

Winner spent | Loser spent

Wirth '86 | Brown '90

## Spending in 1990 House Races

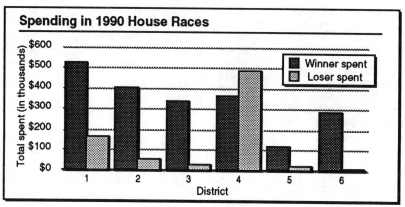

Total spent (in thousands)

Winner spent | Loser spent

District

## 1990 Elections at a Glance

| Dist | Name | Party | Vote Pct | Race Type |
|------|------|-------|----------|-----------|
| Sen | Hank Brown (1990) | Rep | 56% | Open Seat |
| Sen | Tim Wirth (1986) | Dem | 50% | Open Seat |
| 1 | Patricia Schroeder | Dem | 64% | Reelected |
| 2 | David E. Skaggs | Dem | 61% | Reelected |
| 3 | Ben Nighthorse Campbell | Dem | 70% | Reelected |
| 4 | Wayne Allard | Rep | 54% | Open Seat |
| 5 | Joel Hefley | Rep | 66% | Reelected |
| 6 | Dan Schaefer | Rep | 64% | Reelected |

*Totals in Thousands of Dollars*

## Sen. Hank Brown (R)

**1990 House Committees:** Ways & Means
**First elected:** 1990

1989-90 Total Rcpts: ...........$4,179,746
1990 Year-end cash: ...............$455,834

**Source of Funds**
- PACs .................................................31%
- Lg Individuals ($200+) ..............32%
- Individuals under $200 ..............13%
- Other ...............................................23%

### 1989-90

**Top Industries & Interest Groups**

Insurance ...................................$185,589
Lawyers & Lobbyists ...............$167,010
Oil & Gas ...................................$154,091
Securities & Investment ..........$116,601
Real Estate ...............................$102,625

Unidentified ..............................$459,893

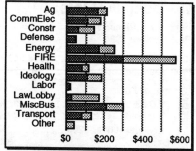

## Sen. Tim Wirth (D)

**1990 Committees:** ArmServ Banking Budget Energy
**First elected:** 1986

1985-90 Total Rcpts: ...........$5,107,183
1990 Year-end cash: ...............$152,088

**Source of Funds**
- PACs .................................................21%
- Lg Individuals ($200+) ..............27%
- Individuals under $200 ..............39%
- Other ...............................................12%

### 1985-90 (PACs only)

**Top Industries & Interest Groups**

Bldg/Indust/Misc Unions ..........$137,699
Pro-Israel ....................................$94,250
Securities & Investment ............$89,550
Public Sector Unions ................$71,950
Democratic/Liberal ....................$68,285

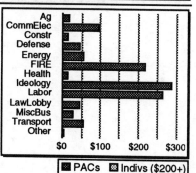

Key to committee & category abbreviations is on page 173

## 1. Patricia Schroeder (D)

**1990 Committees: Armed Services  Judiciary  Post Office**
**First elected: 1972**

1989-90 Total receipts: ...........$441,609
1990 Year-end cash: ...............$182,156

**Source of Funds**
- PACs ............................................26%
- Lg Individuals ($200+) ..............9%
- Individuals under $200 ..............56%
- Other .........................................9%

**Top Industries & Interest Groups**

Public Sector Unions ................$23,750
Bldg/Indust/Misc Unions ...........$21,750
Lawyers & Lobbyists ..................$12,400
Health Professionals ...................$7,850
Transportation Unions ................$7,250

Unidentified ..................................$5,300

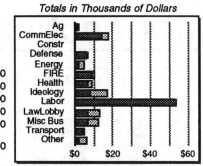

## 2. David E. Skaggs (D)

**1990 Committees: Public Works  Science**
**First elected: 1986**

1989-90 Total receipts: ...........$415,235
1990 Year-end cash: .................$31,628

**Source of Funds**
- PACs ............................................59%
- Lg Individuals ($200+) ..............22%
- Individuals under $200 ..............18%
- Other .........................................1%

**Top Industries & Interest Groups**

Bldg/Indust/Misc Unions ...........$43,750
Public Sector Unions ................$43,250
Lawyers & Lobbyists ..................$34,800
Transportation Unions ................$24,650
Air Transport .............................$19,900

Unidentified ................................$21,686

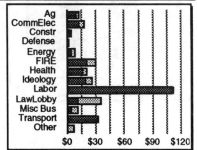

## 3. Ben Nighthorse Campbell (D)

**1990 Committees: Agriculture  Interior**
**First elected: 1986**

1989-90 Total receipts: ...........$311,716
1990 Year-end cash: .................$13,513

**Source of Funds**
- PACs ............................................65%
- Lg Individuals ($200+) ..............15%
- Individuals under $200 ..............14%
- Other .........................................5%

**Top Industries & Interest Groups**

Bldg/Indust/Misc Unions ...........$45,000
Transportation Unions ..............$20,300
Public Sector Unions ................$16,600
Dairy ...........................................$14,250
Oil & Gas ....................................$12,950

Unidentified ................................$11,655

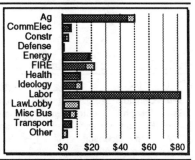

## 4. Wayne Allard (R)

**1991-92 Committees: Agriculture  Interior  Sm Business**
**First elected: 1990**

1989-90 Total receipts: ...........$363,633
1990 Year-end cash: ...................$3,428

**Source of Funds**
- PACs ............................................39%
- Lg Individuals ($200+) ..............18%
- Individuals under $200 ..............18%
- Other .........................................25%

**Top Industries & Interest Groups**

Oil & Gas ....................................$19,150
Real Estate .................................$17,000
Dairy ...........................................$13,400
Agric Services/Products ............$11,850
Business Associations ................$9,647

Unidentified ................................$10,260

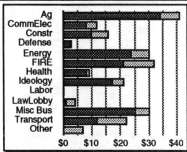

## 5. Joel Hefley (R)

**1990 Committees: Armed Services  Sm Business**
**First elected: 1986**

1989-90 Total receipts: ...........$135,707
1990 Year-end cash: .................$85,219

**Source of Funds**
- PACs ............................................83%
- Lg Individuals ($200+) ..............5%
- Individuals under $200 ..............4%
- Other .........................................8%

**Top Industries & Interest Groups**

Defense Aerospace ....................$13,650
Defense Electronics ...................$10,550
Health Professionals ...................$6,850
Real Estate ...................................$6,650
Oil & Gas .....................................$6,400

Unidentified ...................................$400

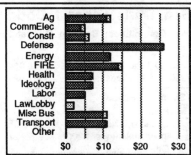

## 6. Dan Schaefer (R)

**1990 Committees: Energy & Commerce**
**First elected: 1983**

1989-90 Total receipts: ...........$375,683
1990 Year-end cash: ...............$122,410

**Source of Funds**
- PACs ............................................60%
- Lg Individuals ($200+) ..............16%
- Individuals under $200 ..............19%
- Other .........................................5%

**Top Industries & Interest Groups**

Cable TV .....................................$24,283
Oil & Gas ....................................$22,200
Health Professionals .................$21,750
Insurance ...................................$18,450
Telephone Utilities ....................$12,875

Unidentified ..................................$7,490

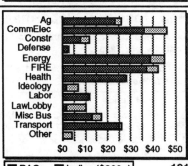

■ PACs  ☒ Indivs ($200+)

191

# Connecticut

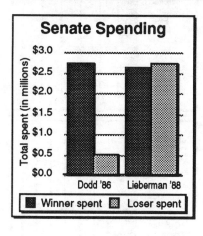

## Senate Spending

Total spent (in millions)

$3.0
$2.5
$2.0
$1.5
$1.0
$0.5
$0.0

Dodd '86    Lieberman '88

■ Winner spent    ▨ Loser spent

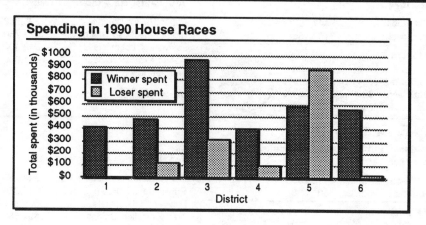

## Spending in 1990 House Races

Total spent (in thousands)

$1000
$900
$800
$700
$600
$500
$400
$300
$200
$100
$0

■ Winner spent
▨ Loser spent

1    2    3    4    5    6

District

## 1990 Elections at a Glance

| Dist | Name | Party | Vote Pct | Race Type |
|------|------|-------|----------|-----------|
| Sen | Christopher J. Dodd (1986) | Dem | 65% | Reelected |
| Sen | Joseph I. Lieberman (1988) | Dem | 50% | Beat Incumb |
| 1 | Barbara B. Kennelly | Dem | 71% | Reelected |
| 2 | Sam Gejdenson | Dem | 60% | Reelected |
| 3 | Rosa DeLauro | Dem | 52% | Open Seat |
| 4 | Christopher Shays | Rep | 76% | Reelected |
| 5 | Gary Franks (1990) | Rep | 52% | Open Seat |
| 6 | Nancy L. Johnson | Rep | 74% | Reelected |

*Totals in Thousands of Dollars*

## Sen. Christopher J. Dodd (D)

**1990 Committees: Banking Budget ForRel Labor Rules**
**First elected: 1980**

1985-90 Total Rcpts: ........... $2,918,064
1990 Year-end cash: .............. $357,521

**Source of Funds**
| | |
|---|---|
| ■ PACs .......... | 31% |
| ▨ Lg Individuals ($200+) .......... | 34% |
| □ Individuals under $200 .......... | 27% |
| ▨ Other .......... | 8% |

### 1985-90 (PACs only)

**Top Industries & Interest Groups**

Insurance ................................. $144,705
Bldg/Indust/Misc Unions ......... $103,700
Securities & Investment ............ $75,479
Transportation Unions .............. $54,800
Public Sector Unions ................ $46,300

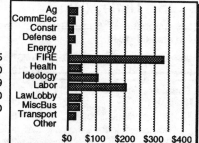

Ag
CommElec
Constr
Defense
Energy
FIRE
Health
Ideology
Labor
LawLobby
MiscBus
Transport
Other

$0    $100    $200    $300    $400

## Sen. Joseph I. Lieberman (D)

**1990 Committees: Envir/Public Works GovAff SmBus**
**First elected: 1988**

1987-90 Total Rcpts: ........... $3,051,426
1990 Year-end cash: ................. $87,721

**Source of Funds**
| | |
|---|---|
| ■ PACs .......... | 11% |
| ▨ Lg Individuals ($200+) .......... | 48% |
| □ Individuals under $200 .......... | 30% |
| ▨ Other .......... | 11% |

### 1987-90 (PACs only)

**Top Industries & Interest Groups**

Leadership PACs ...................... $41,067
Public Sector Unions ................ $36,200
Pro-Israel ................................. $30,216
Public Sector Unions ................ $26,700
Insurance ................................. $24,650

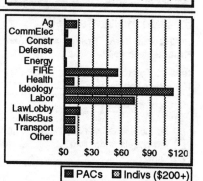

Ag
CommElec
Constr
Defense
Energy
FIRE
Health
Ideology
Labor
LawLobby
MiscBus
Transport
Other

$0    $30    $60    $90    $120

■ PACs   ▨ Indivs ($200+)

Key to committee & category abbreviations is on page 173

## 1. Barbara B. Kennelly (D)

**1990 Committees:** Ways & Means
**First elected:** 1982

1989-90 Total receipts: ............$483,041
1990 Year-end cash: ..............$176,983

**Source of Funds**
- ■ PACs ....................................61%
- ▨ Lg Individuals ($200+) ..........27%
- □ Individuals under $200 ...........5%
- ⊠ Other .................................6%

**Top Industries & Interest Groups**

Insurance ..................................$103,825
Lawyers & Lobbyists ..................$33,100
Bldg/Indust/Misc Unions ...........$24,950
Public Sector Unions ................$20,000
Health Professionals ..................$15,950

Unidentified ..............................$31,250

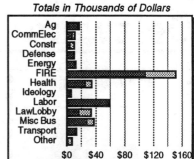

## 2. Sam Gejdenson (D)

**1990 Committees:** Admin  Foreign Affairs  Interior
**First elected:** 1980

1989-90 Total receipts: ............$460,980
1990 Year-end cash: ..................$6,658

**Source of Funds**
- ■ PACs ....................................40%
- ▨ Lg Individuals ($200+) ..........25%
- □ Individuals under $200 ..........28%
- ⊠ Other .................................8%

**Top Industries & Interest Groups**

Bldg/Indust/Misc Unions ...........$38,900
Pro-Israel ..................................$27,250
Public Sector Unions ................$27,150
Transportation Unions ..............$22,550
Lawyers & Lobbyists ..................$20,000

Unidentified ..............................$31,250

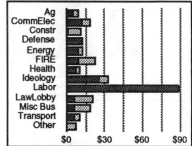

## 3. Rosa DeLauro (D)

**1991-92 Committees:** Govt Ops  Public Works
**First elected:** 1990

1989-90 Total receipts: ............$981,758
1990 Year-end cash: ..................$15,642

**Source of Funds**
- ■ PACs ....................................38%
- ▨ Lg Individuals ($200+) ..........32%
- □ Individuals under $200 ..........22%
- ⊠ Other .................................7%

**Top Industries & Interest Groups**

Bldg/Indust/Misc Unions ...........$99,050
Human Rights ............................$79,384
Public Sector Unions ................$55,750
Lawyers & Lobbyists ..................$54,100
Transportation Unions ..............$33,600

Unidentified ..............................$80,022

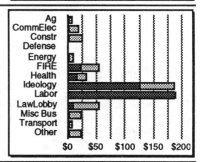

## 4. Christopher Shays (R)

**1990 Committees:** Govt Ops  Science
**First elected:** 1987

1989-90 Total receipts: ............$447,327
1990 Year-end cash: ..................$74,546

**Source of Funds**
- ■ PACs ....................................12%
- ▨ Lg Individuals ($200+) ..........44%
- □ Individuals under $200 ..........40%
- ⊠ Other .................................4%

**Top Industries & Interest Groups**

Securities & Investment .............$18,325
Bldg/Indust/Misc Unions ...........$12,650
Retired ......................................$11,650
Misc Manufacturing & Distrib .....$10,500
Real Estate ...............................$10,075

Unidentified ..............................$63,758

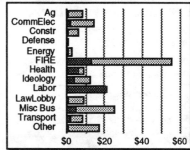

## 5. Gary Franks (R)

**1991-92 Committees:** Armed Services  Sm Business
**First elected:** 1990

1989-90 Total receipts: ............$587,045
1990 Year-end cash: ..................$5,430

**Source of Funds**
- ■ PACs ....................................33%
- ▨ Lg Individuals ($200+) ..........22%
- □ Individuals under $200 ..........17%
- ⊠ Other .................................29%

**Top Industries & Interest Groups**

Oil & Gas ..................................$17,250
Food & Beverage ......................$14,800
Health Professionals ..................$14,700
Food Processing & Sales .........$12,350
Real Estate ...............................$12,250

Unidentified ..............................$83,620

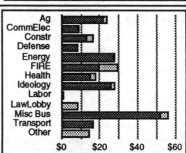

## 6. Nancy L. Johnson (R)

**1990 Committees:** Ways & Means
**First elected:** 1982

1989-90 Total receipts: ............$517,724
1990 Year-end cash: ..............$117,662

**Source of Funds**
- ■ PACs ....................................50%
- ▨ Lg Individuals ($200+) ..........26%
- □ Individuals under $200 ..........20%
- ⊠ Other .................................4%

**Top Industries & Interest Groups**

Insurance ..................................$61,524
Health Professionals ..................$31,800
General Contractors ..................$14,300
Real Estate ...............................$14,150
Hospitals/Nursing Homes .........$11,843

Unidentified ..............................$39,200

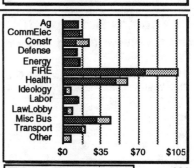

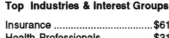
■ PACs  ▨ Indivs ($200+)

193

# Delaware

## Senate Spending

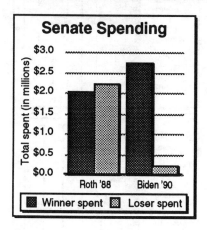

Total spent (in millions)

Roth '88 — Biden '90

■ Winner spent  ▨ Loser spent

## House Spending

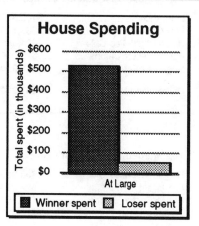

Total spent (in thousands)

At Large

■ Winner spent  ▨ Loser spent

## 1990 Elections at a Glance

| Dist | Name | Party | Vote Pct | Race Type |
|------|------|-------|----------|-----------|
| Sen | Joseph R. Biden Jr. (1990) | Dem | 63% | Reelected |
| Sen | William V. Roth Jr. (1988) | Rep | 62% | Reelected |
| 1 | Thomas R. Carper | Dem | 66% | Reelected |

*Totals in Thousands of Dollars*

## Sen. Joseph R. Biden Jr. (D)

**1990 Committees: Foreign Relations  Judiciary**
**First elected: 1972**

1985-90 Total Rcpts: ............$2,819,280
1990 Year-end cash: ..............$190,151

**Source of Funds**
- ■ PACs .................................................. 24%
- ▨ Lg Individuals ($200+) ............. 46%
- □ Individuals under $200 ............. 19%
- ▨ Other ............................................... 11%

### 1985-90

**Top  Industries & Interest Groups**

Lawyers & Lobbyists ................$232,275
Bldg/Indust/Misc Unions .........$143,149
Pro-Israel ...................................$101,900
Transportation Unions ..............$89,500
Real Estate ................................$74,175

Unidentified ..............................$178,205

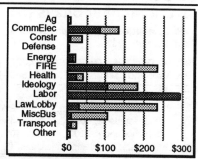

## Sen. William V. Roth Jr. (R)

**1990 Committees: Banking  Finance  Govt Affairs**
**First elected: 1970**

1985-90 Total Rcpts: ............$2,026,860
1990 Year-end cash: .................$68,566

**Source of Funds**
- ■ PACs .................................................. 41%
- ▨ Lg Individuals ($200+) ............. 31%
- □ Individuals under $200 ............. 19%
- ▨ Other ................................................. 9%

### 1985-90 (PACs only)

**Top  Industries & Interest Groups**

Insurance ..................................$104,800
Securities & Investment ............$58,750
Commercial Banks ....................$55,450
Oil & Gas ....................................$51,950
Health Professionals .................$40,500

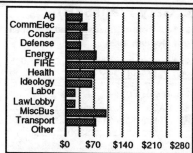

## 1. Thomas R. Carper (D)

**1990 Committees: Banking  Merchant Marine**
**First elected: 1982**

1989-90 Total receipts: ............$548,682
1990 Year-end cash: .................$53,814

**Source of Funds**
- ■ PACs .................................................. 37%
- ▨ Lg Individuals ($200+) ............. 42%
- □ Individuals under $200 ............. 19%
- ▨ Other ................................................. 2%

**Top  Industries & Interest Groups**

Commercial Banks .....................$71,865
Lawyers & Lobbyists ..................$59,156
Bldg/Indust/Misc Unions ............$24,950
Real Estate .................................$24,650
Public Sector Unions .................$17,500

Unidentified ................................$30,340

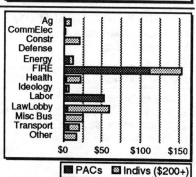

■ PACs  ▨ Indivs ($200+)

Key to committee & category abbreviations is on page 173

# Florida

## Senate Spending

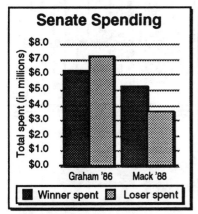

Total spent (in millions)

$8.0
$7.0
$6.0
$5.0
$4.0
$3.0
$2.0
$1.0
$0.0

Graham '86    Mack '88

■ Winner spent    ▨ Loser spent

## Spending in 1990 House Races

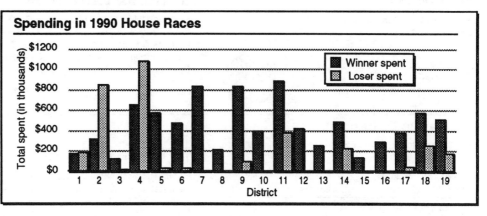

Total spent (in thousands)

$1200
$1000
$800
$600
$400
$200
$0

1  2  3  4  5  6  7  8  9  10  11  12  13  14  15  16  17  18  19
District

■ Winner spent
▨ Loser spent

## 1990 Elections at a Glance

| Dist | Name | Party | Vote Pct | Race Type | Dist | Name | Party | Vote Pct | Race Type |
|------|------|-------|----------|-----------|------|------|-------|----------|-----------|
| Sen | Bob Graham (1986) | Dem | 55% | Beat Incumb | 10 | Andy Ireland | Rep | 100% | Reelected |
| Sen | Connie Mack (1988) | Rep | 50% | Open Seat | 11 | Jim Bacchus | Dem | 52% | Open Seat |
| 1 | Earl Hutto | Dem | 52% | Reelected | 12 | Tom Lewis | Rep | 100% | Reelected |
| 2 | Pete Peterson | Dem | 57% | Beat Incumb | 13 | Porter J. Goss | Rep | 100% | Reelected |
| 3 | Charles E. Bennett | Dem | 73% | Reelected | 14 | Harry A. Johnston | Dem | 66% | Reelected |
| 4 | Craig T. James | Rep | 56% | Reelected | 15 | E. Clay Shaw Jr. | Rep | 98% | Reelected |
| 5 | Bill McCollum | Rep | 60% | Reelected | 16 | Lawrence J. Smith | Dem | 100% | Reelected |
| 6 | Cliff Stearns | Rep | 59% | Reelected | 17 | William Lehman | Dem | 78% | Reelected |
| 7 | Sam M. Gibbons | Dem | 68% | Reelected | 18 | Ileana Ros-Lehtinen | Rep | 60% | Reelected |
| 8 | C. W. Bill Young | Rep | 100% | Reelected | 19 | Dante B. Fascell | Dem | 62% | Reelected |
| 9 | Michael Bilirakis | Rep | 58% | Reelected | | | | | |

*Totals in Thousands of Dollars*

## Sen. Bob Graham (D)

**1990 Committees:** Banking  Envir/Pub Works  VetAff
**First elected:** 1986

1985-90 Total Rcpts: ............$6,886,607
1990 Year-end cash: ..............$308,177

**Source of Funds**
- ■ PACs ............................................17%
- ▨ Lg Individuals ($200+) ..............52%
- □ Individuals under $200 ..............20%
- ▨ Other ..........................................12%

### 1985-90 (PACs only)

**Top Industries & Interest Groups**

| | |
|---|---|
| Bldg/Indust/Misc Unions | $166,200 |
| Commercial Banks | $101,119 |
| Public Sector Unions | $95,537 |
| Transportation Unions | $83,250 |
| Securities & Investment | $57,000 |

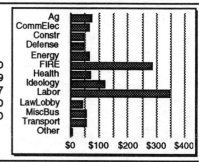

Ag, CommElec, Constr, Defense, Energy, FIRE, Health, Ideology, Labor, LawLobby, MiscBus, Transport, Other

$0  $100  $200  $300  $400

## Sen. Connie Mack (R)

**1990 Committees:** Banking  Foreign Relations
**First elected:** 1988

1987-90 Total Rcpts: ............$6,352,241
1990 Year-end cash: ................$11,499

**Source of Funds**
- ■ PACs ............................................18%
- ▨ Lg Individuals ($200+) ..............27%
- □ Individuals under $200 ..............38%
- ▨ Other ..........................................17%

### 1987-90 (PACs only)

**Top Industries & Interest Groups**

| | |
|---|---|
| Oil & Gas | $89,150 |
| Commercial Banks | $72,000 |
| Leadership PACs | $57,457 |
| Insurance | $55,400 |
| Health Professionals | $42,950 |

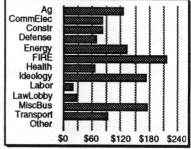

Ag, CommElec, Constr, Defense, Energy, FIRE, Health, Ideology, Labor, LawLobby, MiscBus, Transport, Other

$0  $60  $120  $180  $240

## 1.  Earl Hutto (D)

**1990 Committees:** Armed Services  Merchant Marine
**First elected:** 1978

1989-90 Total receipts: ...........$177,546
1990 Year-end cash: ..............$109,103

**Source of Funds**
- ■ PACs ............................................49%
- ▨ Lg Individuals ($200+) ..............19%
- □ Individuals under $200 ..............13%
- ▨ Other ..........................................19%

**Top Industries & Interest Groups**

| | |
|---|---|
| Defense Aerospace | $17,750 |
| Real Estate | $11,700 |
| Health Professionals | $8,600 |
| Commercial Banks | $8,450 |
| Defense Electronics | $8,350 |
| | |
| Unidentified | $9,250 |

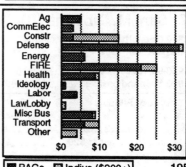

Ag, CommElec, Constr, Defense, Energy, FIRE, Health, Ideology, Labor, LawLobby, Misc Bus, Transport, Other

$0  $10  $20  $30

■ PACs    ▨ Indivs ($200+)

## 2. Pete Peterson (D)

**1991-92 Committees: Public Works  Vet Affairs**
**First elected: 1990**

1989-90 Total receipts: ............$306,429
1990 Year-end cash: ......................$323

**Source of Funds**

- PACs............................................38%
- Lg Individuals ($200+) ..............19%
- Individuals under $200 ..............13%
- Other .........................................29%

**Top  Industries & Interest Groups**

Bldg/Indust/Misc Unions ............$55,500
Public Sector Unions .................$23,300
Lawyers & Lobbyists ..................$20,574
Transportation Unions ...............$19,850
Crop Production/Processing ........$8,650

Unidentified ...................................$6,109

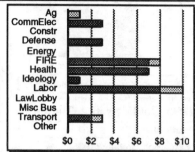

## 3. Charles E. Bennett (D)

**1990 Committees: Armed Services  Merchant Marine**
**First elected: 1948**

1989-90 Total receipts: ..............$87,580
1990 Year-end cash: ...............$280,990

**Source of Funds**

- PACs............................................36%
- Lg Individuals ($200+) .................4%
- Individuals under $200 .................7%
- Other ...........................................53%

**Top  Industries & Interest Groups**

Health Professionals ...................$7,000
Real Estate ..................................$6,000
Bldg/Indust/Misc Unions ..............$5,000
Transportation Unions ................$4,500
Telephone Utilities ......................$3,000

Unidentified ....................................$200

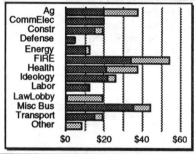

## 4. Craig T. James (R)

**1990 Committees: Judiciary  Vet Affairs**
**First elected: 1988**

1989-90 Total receipts: ............$643,579
1990 Year-end cash: .................$11,526

**Source of Funds**
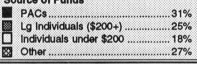
- PACs............................................31%
- Lg Individuals ($200+) ..............25%
- Individuals under $200 ..............18%
- Other ...........................................27%

**Top  Industries & Interest Groups**

Health Professionals ..................$31,875
Lawyers & Lobbyists ..................$18,800
Insurance .....................................$17,900
Real Estate ..................................$15,731
Telephone Utilities .....................$15,000

Unidentified ...............................$69,349

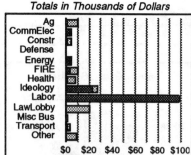

## 5. Bill McCollum (R)

**1990 Committees: Banking  Judiciary**
**First elected: 1980**

1989-90 Total receipts: ............$427,325
1990 Year-end cash: ...............$101,264

**Source of Funds**

- PACs............................................36%
- Lg Individuals ($200+) ..............39%
- Individuals under $200 ..............10%
- Other ...........................................15%

**Top  Industries & Interest Groups**

Lawyers & Lobbyists .................$28,750
Commercial Banks ....................$27,800
Real Estate ..................................$22,550
Insurance .....................................$21,200
Health Professionals .................$19,900

Unidentified ...............................$42,701

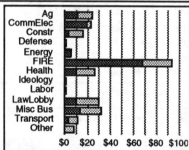

## 6. Cliff Stearns (R)

**1990 Committees: Banking  Vet Affairs**
**First elected: 1988**

1989-90 Total receipts: ............$497,703
1990 Year-end cash: .................$47,634

**Source of Funds**

- PACs............................................37%
- Lg Individuals ($200+) ..............30%
- Individuals under $200 ..............20%
- Other ...........................................13%

**Top  Industries & Interest Groups**

Commercial Banks ....................$41,800
Health Professionals .................$38,900
Real Estate ..................................$24,869
Insurance .....................................$18,331
Lawyers & Lobbyists .................$11,350

Unidentified ...............................$43,597

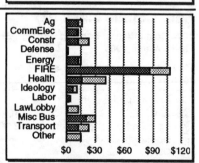

## 7. Sam M. Gibbons (D)

**1990 Committees: Ways & Means**
**First elected: 1962**

1989-90 Total receipts: ............$492,517
1990 Year-end cash: ...............$278,960

**Source of Funds**

- PACs............................................64%
- Lg Individuals ($200+) ..............12%
- Individuals under $200 .................6%
- Other ...........................................18%

**Top  Industries & Interest Groups**

Lawyers & Lobbyists .................$51,815
Insurance .....................................$47,000
Oil & Gas ......................................$18,850
Pharmaceuticals/Health Prod ....$18,600
Telephone Utilities .....................$14,750

Unidentified ...................................$6,350

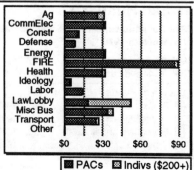

Key to committee & category abbreviations is on page 173

■ PACs  ▩ Indivs ($200+)

## 8. C. W. Bill Young (R)

**1990 Committees:** Appropriations
**First elected:** 1970

1989-90 Total receipts: ...........$231,400
1990 Year-end cash: ...............$341,773

**Source of Funds**
- ■ PACs ..................................55%
- ▨ Lg Individuals ($200+) .........6%
- ☐ Individuals under $200 .......14%
- ⊠ Other .............................24%

**Top Industries & Interest Groups**

| | |
|---|---|
| Defense Aerospace | $36,500 |
| Defense Electronics | $24,000 |
| Health Professionals | $16,100 |
| Real Estate | $8,000 |
| Misc Defense | $7,500 |

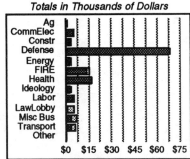

## 9. Michael Bilirakis (R)

**1990 Committees:** Energy & Commerce  Vet Affairs
**First elected:** 1982

1989-90 Total receipts: ...........$600,670
1990 Year-end cash: ...................$2,617

**Source of Funds**
- ■ PACs ..................................39%
- ▨ Lg Individuals ($200+) .......25%
- ☐ Individuals under $200 .......25%
- ⊠ Other .............................11%

**Top Industries & Interest Groups**

| | |
|---|---|
| Health Professionals | $58,049 |
| Electric Utilities | $21,925 |
| Telephone Utilities | $20,500 |
| Real Estate | $16,775 |
| Insurance | $14,650 |
| | |
| Unidentified | $37,625 |

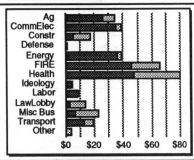

## 10. Andy Ireland (R)

**1990 Committees:** Armed Services  Sm Business
**First elected:** 1976

1989-90 Total receipts: ...........$410,468
1990 Year-end cash: .................$98,267

**Source of Funds**
- ■ PACs ..................................41%
- ▨ Lg Individuals ($200+) .......20%
- ☐ Individuals under $200 .......36%
- ⊠ Other ...............................3%

**Top Industries & Interest Groups**

| | |
|---|---|
| Real Estate | $14,550 |
| Defense Aerospace | $13,800 |
| Commercial Banks | $12,950 |
| Lawyers & Lobbyists | $12,670 |
| Defense Electronics | $11,200 |
| Health Professionals | $11,200 |
| | |
| Unidentified | $24,400 |

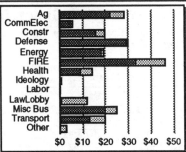

## 11. Jim Bacchus (D)

**1991-92 Committees:** Banking  Science
**First elected:** 1990

1989-90 Total receipts: ...........$877,500
1990 Year-end cash: ...................$2,112

**Source of Funds**
- ■ PACs ..................................42%
- ▨ Lg Individuals ($200+) .......33%
- ☐ Individuals under $200 .......11%
- ⊠ Other .............................14%

**Top Industries & Interest Groups**

| | |
|---|---|
| Lawyers & Lobbyists | $98,599 |
| Bldg/Indust/Misc Unions | $87,850 |
| Public Sector Unions | $52,500 |
| Real Estate | $37,532 |
| Health Professionals | $35,278 |
| | |
| Unidentified | $66,780 |

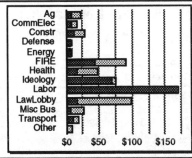

## 12. Tom Lewis (R)

**1990 Committees:** Agriculture  Science
**First elected:** 1982

1989-90 Total receipts: ...........$336,333
1990 Year-end cash: ...............$121,358

**Source of Funds**
- ■ PACs ..................................22%
- ▨ Lg Individuals ($200+) .......32%
- ☐ Individuals under $200 .......36%
- ⊠ Other .............................10%

**Top Industries & Interest Groups**

| | |
|---|---|
| Crop Production/Processing | $43,100 |
| Lawyers & Lobbyists | $10,150 |
| Real Estate | $9,150 |
| Telephone Utilities | $6,750 |
| Air Transport | $6,750 |
| | |
| Unidentified | $33,608 |

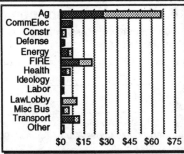

## 13. Porter J. Goss (R)

**1990 Committees:** Foreign Affairs  Merchant Marine
**First elected:** 1988

1989-90 Total receipts: ...........$303,600
1990 Year-end cash: ...............$101,074

**Source of Funds**
- ■ PACs ..................................39%
- ▨ Lg Individuals ($200+) .......39%
- ☐ Individuals under $200 .......19%
- ⊠ Other ...............................4%

**Top Industries & Interest Groups**

| | |
|---|---|
| Real Estate | $21,150 |
| Health Professionals | $17,000 |
| Transportation Unions | $10,100 |
| Lawyers & Lobbyists | $9,500 |
| Public Sector Unions | $8,500 |
| | |
| Unidentified | $37,245 |

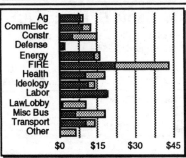

*Totals in Thousands of Dollars*

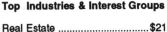

■ PACs  ⊠ Indivs ($200+)

197

## 14. Harry A. Johnston (D)

**1990 Committees: Foreign Affairs  Science**
**First elected: 1988**

1989-90 Total receipts: ............ $510,490
1990 Year-end cash: ................ $42,284

**Source of Funds**
- ■ PACs .................................................. 48%
- ▨ Lg Individuals ($200+) .............. 27%
- □ Individuals under $200 .............. 19%
- ▩ Other ............................................... 6%

**Top  Industries & Interest Groups**

Public Sector Unions ............... $40,750
Transportation Unions ............. $32,150
Lawyers & Lobbyists .................. $31,000
Bldg/Indust/Misc Unions .......... $30,500
Real Estate ................................ $28,775

Unidentified ............................... $28,850

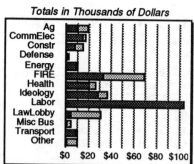

## 15. E. Clay Shaw Jr. (R)

**1990 Committees:  Ways & Means**
**First elected: 1980**

1989-90 Total receipts: ............ $413,387
1990 Year-end cash: .............. $306,224

**Source of Funds**
- ■ PACs .................................................. 57%
- ▨ Lg Individuals ($200+) .............. 28%
- □ Individuals under $200 .............. 9%
- ▩ Other ............................................... 6%

**Top  Industries & Interest Groups**

Insurance ..................................... $40,050
Accountants ............................... $27,444
Health Professionals ................. $24,600
Real Estate ................................ $21,800
Lawyers & Lobbyists .................. $18,910

Unidentified ............................... $31,050

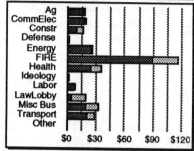

## 16. Lawrence J. Smith (D)

**1990 Committees: Foreign Affairs  Judiciary**
**First elected: 1982**

1989-90 Total receipts: ............ $527,994
1990 Year-end cash: .............. $413,843

**Source of Funds**
- ■ PACs .................................................. 47%
- ▨ Lg Individuals ($200+) .............. 40%
- □ Individuals under $200 .............. 4%
- ▩ Other ............................................... 9%

**Top  Industries & Interest Groups**

Lawyers & Lobbyists .................. $49,530
Health Professionals ................. $45,400
Public Sector Unions ................. $37,150
Pro-Israel ................................... $35,067
Transportation Unions .............. $33,000

Unidentified ............................... $21,700

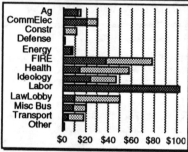

## 17. William Lehman (D)

**1990 Committees:  Appropriations**
**First elected: 1972**

1989-90 Total receipts: ............ $425,117
1990 Year-end cash: .............. $275,781

**Source of Funds**
- ■ PACs .................................................. 50%
- ▨ Lg Individuals ($200+) .............. 38%
- □ Individuals under $200 .............. 4%
- ▩ Other ............................................... 8%

**Top  Industries & Interest Groups**

Lawyers & Lobbyists .................. $53,750
Air Transport ............................. $36,150
Transportation Unions .............. $23,500
Pro-Israel ................................... $20,600
Bldg/Indust/Misc Unions ........... $16,800

Unidentified ............................... $32,453

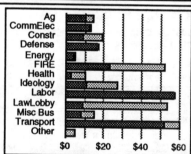

## 18. Ileana Ros-Lehtinen (R)

**1990 Committees: Foreign Affairs  Govt Ops**
**First elected: 1989**

1989-90 Total receipts: ......... $1,634,518
1990 Year-end cash: ................ $14,387

**Source of Funds**
- ■ PACs .................................................. 24%
- ▨ Lg Individuals ($200+) .............. 56%
- □ Individuals under $200 .............. 9%
- ▩ Other ............................................... 11%

**Top  Industries & Interest Groups**

Health Professionals ............... $143,220
Lawyers & Lobbyists .................. $87,624
Real Estate ................................ $81,662
Insurance ..................................... $63,150
General Contractors ................. $50,095

Unidentified ............................... $244,886

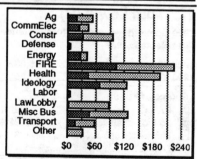

## 19. Dante B. Fascell (D)

**1990 Committees:  Foreign Affairs**
**First elected: 1954**

1989-90 Total receipts: ............ $459,789
1990 Year-end cash: .............. $546,593

**Source of Funds**
- ■ PACs .................................................. 36%
- ▨ Lg Individuals ($200+) .............. 31%
- □ Individuals under $200 .............. 9%
- ▩ Other ............................................... 24%

**Top  Industries & Interest Groups**

Lawyers & Lobbyists .................. $47,796
Bldg/Indust/Misc Unions ........... $25,000
Pro-Israel ................................... $18,000
Real Estate ................................ $17,625
Public Sector Unions ................. $16,500

Unidentified ............................... $21,150

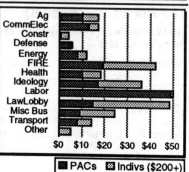

Key to committee & category abbreviations is on page 173

# Georgia

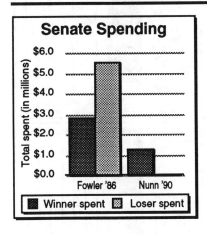

## Senate Spending

Total spent (in millions)

Winner spent  Loser spent

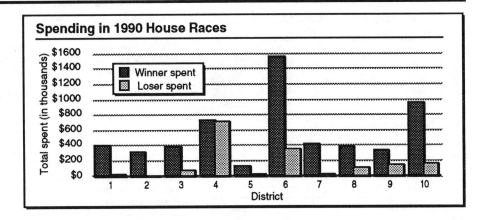

## Spending in 1990 House Races

Total spent (in thousands)

- Winner spent
- Loser spent

District

## 1990 Elections at a Glance

| Dist | Name | Party | Vote Pct | Race Type |
|------|------|-------|----------|-----------|
| Sen | Wyche Fowler Jr. (1986) | Dem | 51% | Beat Incumb |
| Sen | Sam Nunn (1990) | Dem | 100% | Reelected |
| 1 | Lindsay Thomas | Dem | 71% | Reelected |
| 2 | Charles Hatcher | Dem | 73% | Reelected |
| 3 | Richard Ray | Dem | 63% | Reelected |
| 4 | Ben Jones | Dem | 52% | Reelected |
| 5 | John Lewis | Dem | 76% | Reelected |
| 6 | Newt Gingrich | Rep | 50% | Reelected |
| 7 | George "Buddy" Darden | Dem | 60% | Reelected |
| 8 | J. Roy Rowland | Dem | 69% | Reelected |
| 9 | Ed Jenkins | Dem | 56% | Reelected |
| 10 | Doug Barnard Jr. | Dem | 58% | Reelected |

*Totals in Thousands of Dollars*

## Sen. Wyche Fowler Jr. (D)

**1990 Committees: Agriculture Appropriations Budget**
**First elected: 1986**

1985-90 Total Rcpts: ............$4,173,758
1990 Year-end cash: ..............$751,373

**Source of Funds**
- PACs .................................... 23%
- Lg Individuals ($200+) .............. 18%
- Individuals under $200 .............. 27%
- Other ................................... 32%

### 1985-90 (PACs only)
**Top Industries & Interest Groups**

| | |
|---|---|
| Bldg/Indust/Misc Unions | $155,959 |
| Pro-Israel | $94,850 |
| Insurance | $78,101 |
| Public Sector Unions | $71,245 |
| Lawyers & Lobbyists | $43,600 |

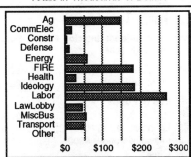

## Sen. Sam Nunn (D)

**1990 Committees: Armed Services Govt Affairs SmBus**
**First elected: 1972**

1985-90 Total Rcpts: ............$2,118,911
1990 Year-end cash: ............$1,550,058

**Source of Funds**
- PACs ....................................... 30%
- Lg Individuals ($200+) ............... 52%
- Individuals under $200 ............. 4%
- Other ...................................... 15%

### 1985-90
**Top Industries & Interest Groups**

| | |
|---|---|
| Lawyers & Lobbyists | $182,520 |
| Securities & Investment | $125,650 |
| Real Estate | $107,500 |
| Defense Aerospace | $68,804 |
| Commercial Banks | $68,295 |
| Unidentified | $191,303 |

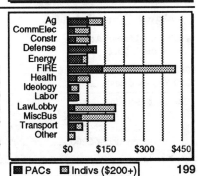

PACs  Indivs ($200+)

## 1. Lindsay Thomas (D)

**1990 Committees: Appropriations**
**First elected: 1982**

1989-90 Total receipts: ............$378,206
1990 Year-end cash: ................$67,690

**Source of Funds**
- ■ PACs .......................................42%
- ▨ Lg Individuals ($200+) ...........16%
- ☐ Individuals under $200 ..........35%
- ⊠ Other ....................................8%

**Top Industries & Interest Groups**

Forestry & Forest Products .......$17,400
Lawyers & Lobbyists ..................$14,200
Health Professionals .................$13,800
Real Estate .............................$11,500
Commercial Banks ....................$11,400

Unidentified .............................$12,081

## 2. Charles Hatcher (D)

**1990 Committees: Agriculture  Sm Business**
**First elected: 1980**

1989-90 Total receipts: ............$328,506
1990 Year-end cash: ................$38,709

**Source of Funds**
- ■ PACs .......................................62%
- ▨ Lg Individuals ($200+) ...........15%
- ☐ Individuals under $200 ..........18%
- ⊠ Other ....................................5%

**Top Industries & Interest Groups**

Crop Production/Processing ......$38,525
Public Sector Unions ................$18,450
Agric Services/Products ...........$18,180
Health Professionals .................$16,750
Commercial Banks ....................$11,550

Unidentified .............................$12,200

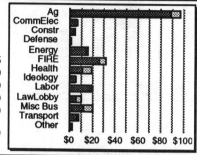

## 3. Richard Ray (D)

**1990 Committees: Armed Services  Sm Business**
**First elected: 1982**

1989-90 Total receipts: ............$370,858
1990 Year-end cash: ................$180,654

**Source of Funds**
- ■ PACs .......................................41%
- ▨ Lg Individuals ($200+) ...........17%
- ☐ Individuals under $200 ..........18%
- ⊠ Other ....................................24%

**Top Industries & Interest Groups**

Defense Aerospace ..................$27,200
Defense Electronics ..................$19,600
Health Professionals .................$13,050
Real Estate .............................$12,700
Commercial Banks ....................$11,802

Unidentified .............................$7,295

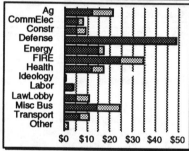

## 4. Ben Jones (D)

**1990 Committees: Public Works  Vet Affairs**
**First elected: 1988**

1989-90 Total receipts: ............$707,046
1990 Year-end cash: ..................$1,959

**Source of Funds**
- ■ PACs .......................................56%
- ▨ Lg Individuals ($200+) ...........16%
- ☐ Individuals under $200 ..........19%
- ⊠ Other ....................................8%

**Top Industries & Interest Groups**

Bldg/Indust/Misc Unions ...........$92,000
Public Sector Unions ................$45,700
Lawyers & Lobbyists .................$35,980
Transportation Unions ..............$34,150
Health Professionals .................$32,000

Unidentified .............................$22,150

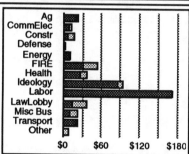

## 5. John Lewis (D)

**1990 Committees: Interior  Public Works**
**First elected: 1986**

1989-90 Total receipts: ............$276,450
1990 Year-end cash: ..............$260,822

**Source of Funds**
- ■ PACs .......................................67%
- ▨ Lg Individuals ($200+) ...........25%
- ☐ Individuals under $200 ............8%
- ⊠ Other ....................................0%

**Top Industries & Interest Groups**

Bldg/Indust/Misc Unions ...........$49,150
Transportation Unions ..............$30,150
Lawyers & Lobbyists .................$22,300
Public Sector Unions ................$21,200
Health Professionals .................$15,700

Unidentified .............................$13,600

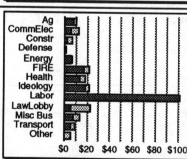

## 6. Newt Gingrich (R)

**1990 Committees: Admin**
**First elected: 1978**

1989-90 Total receipts: ........$1,558,934
1990 Year-end cash: ................$24,739

**Source of Funds**
- ■ PACs .......................................28%
- ▨ Lg Individuals ($200+) ...........36%
- ☐ Individuals under $200 ..........34%
- ⊠ Other ....................................2%

**Top Industries & Interest Groups**

Health Professionals .................$62,208
Misc Manufacturing & Distrib .....$52,815
Lawyers & Lobbyists .................$43,050
Insurance ...............................$39,250
Food & Beverage .....................$35,849

Unidentified .............................$181,866

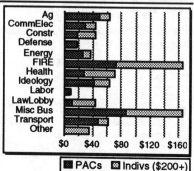

Key to committee & category abbreviations is on page 173

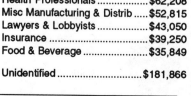

# 7. George "Buddy" Darden (D)

**1990 Committees: Armed Services  Interior**
**First elected: 1983**

1989-90 Total receipts: ...........$389,231
1990 Year-end cash: ..............$100,237

**Source of Funds**
- ■ PACs ....................................51%
- ▨ Lg Individuals ($200+) ............26%
- □ Individuals under $200 .............16%
- ▧ Other ..................................7%

**Top Industries & Interest Groups**

Defense Aerospace ..................$26,900
Health Professionals ................$24,050
Lawyers & Lobbyists .................$19,625
Misc Manufacturing & Distrib .....$18,800
Real Estate .............................$15,350

Unidentified .............................$16,762

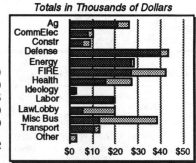

# 8. J. Roy Rowland (D)

**1990 Committees: Energy & Commerce  Vet Affairs**
**First elected: 1982**

1989-90 Total receipts: ...........$368,200
1990 Year-end cash: ..............$210,642

**Source of Funds**
- ■ PACs ....................................61%
- ▨ Lg Individuals ($200+) ............10%
- □ Individuals under $200 .............16%
- ▧ Other ..................................14%

**Top Industries & Interest Groups**

Health Professionals ................$47,850
Telephone Utilities ....................$18,150
Pharmaceuticals/Health Prod ....$15,200
Insurance ................................$13,450
Electric Utilities ........................$12,100

Unidentified .............................$3,050

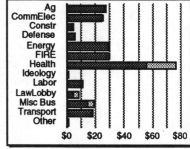

# 9. Ed Jenkins (D)

**1990 Committees: Budget  Ways & Means**
**First elected: 1976**

1989-90 Total receipts: ...........$302,029
1990 Year-end cash: ..............$448,273

**Source of Funds**
- ■ PACs ....................................61%
- ▨ Lg Individuals ($200+) ............10%
- □ Individuals under $200 .............3%
- ▧ Other ..................................26%

**Top Industries & Interest Groups**

Insurance ................................$32,900
Misc Manufacturing & Distrib .....$18,000
Health Professionals .................$16,750
Real Estate .............................$13,500
Telephone Utilities ....................$12,200

Unidentified .............................$3,200

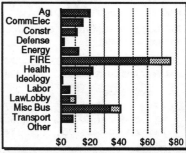

# 10. Doug Barnard Jr. (D)

**1990 Committees: Banking  Govt Ops**
**First elected: 1976**

1989-90 Total receipts: ...........$778,139
1990 Year-end cash: ..............$359,869

**Source of Funds**
- ■ PACs ....................................33%
- ▨ Lg Individuals ($200+) ............8%
- □ Individuals under $200 .............7%
- ▧ Other ..................................52%

**Top Industries & Interest Groups**

Commercial Banks ...................$96,300
Real Estate .............................$31,750
Lawyers & Lobbyists .................$21,690
Securities & Investment ............$14,000
Savings & Loans ......................$13,712

Unidentified .............................$4,839

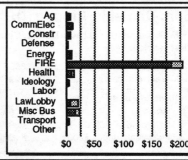

■ PACs  ▨ Indivs ($200+)

201

# Hawaii

## 1990 Elections at a Glance

| Dist | Name | Party | Vote Pct | Race Type |
|------|------|-------|----------|-----------|
| Sen | Daniel K. Akaka (1990) | Dem | 54% | Reelected |
| Sen | Daniel K. Inouye (1986) | Dem | 74% | Reelected |
| 1 | Neil Abercrombie | Dem | 60% | Open Seat |
| 2 | Patsy T. Mink | Dem | 66% | Reelected |

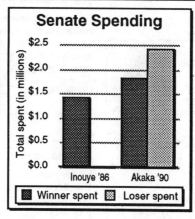

**Senate Spending**

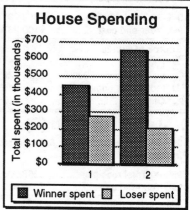

**House Spending**

*Totals in Thousands of Dollars*

## Sen. Daniel K. Akaka (D)

**1990 Committees:** Energy  Govt Affairs  Vet Affairs
**First elected:** 1990

1989-90 Total Rcpts: ............$1,714,374
1990 Year-end cash: ..............$160,134

**Source of Funds**
- PACs.................................47%
- Lg Individuals ($200+)...........33%
- Individuals under $200 ..........14%
- Other.................................7%

**1989-90**

**Top Industries & Interest Groups**

Bldg/Indust/Misc Unions ..........$170,800
Pro-Israel ............................$106,900
Public Sector Unions ................$94,150
Transportation Unions ..............$89,500
Construction Services...............$77,375

Unidentified ...........................$218,050

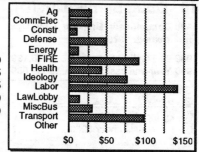

## Sen. Daniel K. Inouye (D)

**1990 Committees:** Appropriations  Commerce  Rules
**First elected:** 1962

1985-90 Total Rcpts: ...........$1,370,655
1990 Year-end cash: ..............$250,229

**Source of Funds**
- PACs.................................45%
- Lg Individuals ($200+)...........28%
- Individuals under $200 ...........8%
- Other................................19%

**1985-90 (PACs only)**

**Top Industries & Interest Groups**

Transportation Unions ..............$65,500
Bldg/Indust/Misc Unions ...........$60,385
Pro-Israel .............................$49,175
Defense Aerospace ..................$32,500
Health Professionals.................$32,500

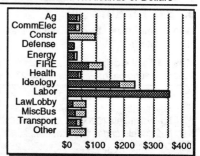

## 1. Neil Abercrombie (D)

**1991-92 Committees:** Armed Services  Merchant Marine
**First elected:** 1990 (also served 1986-87)

1989-90 Total receipts: ...........$574,714
1990 Year-end cash: ................$34,017

**Source of Funds**
- PACs.................................29%
- Lg Individuals ($200+)...........15%
- Individuals under $200 ..........47%
- Other.................................9%

**Top Industries & Interest Groups**

Bldg/Indust/Misc Unions ...........$49,500
Public Sector Unions ................$29,250
Transportation Unions ..............$18,500
Lawyers & Lobbyists ..................$9,225
Leadership PACs .......................$7,000

Unidentified ...........................$46,975

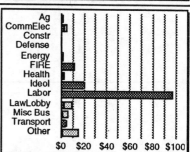

## 2. Patsy T. Mink (D)

**1991-92 Committees:** Educ/Labor  Govt Ops
**First elected:** 1990 (also served 1965-77)

1989-90 Total receipts: ...........$641,324
1990 Year-end cash: .....................$288

**Source of Funds**
- PACs.................................23%
- Lg Individuals ($200+)...........14%
- Individuals under $200 ..........28%
- Other................................35%

**Top Industries & Interest Groups**

Public Sector Unions ................$40,250
Bldg/Indust/Misc Unions ...........$36,000
Retired ................................$17,560
Transportation Unions ..............$15,500
Human Rights .........................$15,455

Unidentified ...........................$22,859

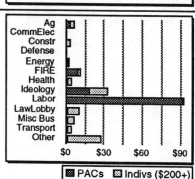

Key to committee & category abbreviations is on page 173

# Idaho

## Senate Spending

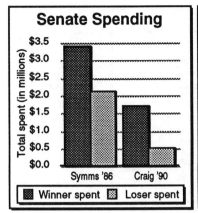

Total spent (in millions)

$3.5 / $3.0 / $2.5 / $2.0 / $1.5 / $1.0 / $0.5 / $0.0

Symms '86    Craig '90

■ Winner spent    ▨ Loser spent

## House Spending

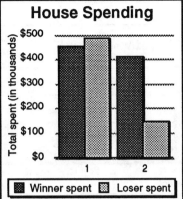

Total spent (in thousands)

$500 / $400 / $300 / $200 / $100 / $0

1    2

■ Winner spent    ▨ Loser spent

### 1990 Elections at a Glance

| Dist | Name | Party | Vote Pct | Race Type |
|------|------|-------|----------|-----------|
| Sen | Larry E. Craig (1990) | Rep | 61% | Open Seat |
| Sen | Steve Symms (1986) | Rep | 52% | Reelected |
| 1 | Larry LaRocco | Dem | 53% | Open Seat |
| 2 | Richard Stallings | Dem | 64% | Reelected |

*Totals in Thousands of Dollars*

## Sen. Larry E. Craig (R)

**1990 House Committees: Interior  Public Works**
**First elected: 1990**

1989-90 Total Rcpts: ............$1,734,617
1990 Year-end cash: .................$91,834

**Source of Funds**
■ PACs .................................................43%
▨ Lg Individuals ($200+) ..............20%
□ Individuals under $200 ...............21%
▨ Other .................................................16%

### 1989-90

**Top  Industries & Interest Groups**

Oil & Gas ..................................$119,308
Forestry & Forest Products........$79,820
Mining ...........................................$62,756
Insurance ....................................$52,800
Food Processing & Sales ..........$49,809

Unidentified ................................$75,355

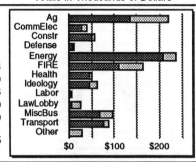

## Sen. Steve Symms (R)

**1990 Committees: Budget  Envir/Public Works  Finance**
**First elected: 1980**

1985-90 Total Rcpts: ............$3,929,597
1990 Year-end cash: ..............$487,698

**Source of Funds**
■ PACs.................................................41%
▨ Lg Individuals ($200+) ..............28%
□ Individuals under $200 ...............21%
▨ Other.................................................9%

### 1985-90 (PACs only)
**Top  Industries & Interest Groups**

Insurance .....................................$196,550
Oil & Gas .....................................$133,782
Securities & Investment.............$73,550
Leadership PACs ........................$62,600
Food Processing & Sales ..........$62,150

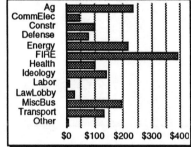

## 1.  Larry LaRocco (D)

**1991-92 Committees: Banking  Interior**
**First elected: 1990**

1989-90 Total receipts: ............$449,419
1990 Year-end cash: ...................$1,522

**Source of Funds**
■ PACs.................................................47%
▨ Lg Individuals ($200+) ...............15%
□ Individuals under $200 ...............16%
▨ Other .................................................22%

**Top  Industries & Interest Groups**

Bldg/Indust/Misc Unions ............$71,500
Public Sector Unions ................$36,750
Transportation Unions ..............$24,850
Misc Issues ..................................$19,366
Lawyers & Lobbyists .................$17,271

Unidentified ................................$13,724

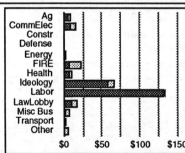

## 2.  Richard Stallings (D)

**1990 Committees: Agriculture  Science**
**First elected: 1984**

1989-90 Total receipts: ............$405,115
1990 Year-end cash: ......................$583

**Source of Funds**
■ PACs.................................................64%
▨ Lg Individuals ($200+) .................6%
□ Individuals under $200 ...............25%
▨ Other .................................................5%

**Top  Industries & Interest Groups**

Public Sector Unions ................$27,300
Bldg/Indust/Misc Unions ...........$24,700
Crop Production/Processing......$22,980
Health Professionals .................$16,650
Transportation Unions ..............$15,900

Unidentified ..................................$3,100

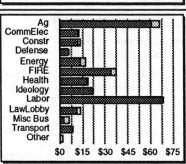

■ PACs  ▨ Indivs ($200+)

203

# Illinois

## Spending in 1990 House Races

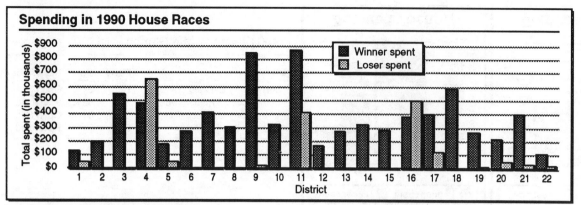

Winner spent
Loser spent

Total spent (in thousands)

District

## Senate Spending

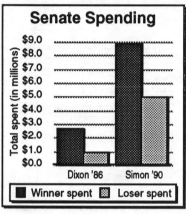

Winner spent | Loser spent

## 1990 Elections at a Glance

| Dist | Name | Party | Vote Pct | Race Type |
|------|------|-------|----------|-----------|
| Sen | Alan J. Dixon (1986) | Dem | 65% | Reelected |
| Sen | Paul Simon (1990) | Dem | 65% | Reelected |
| 1 | Charles A. Hayes | Dem | 94% | Reelected |
| 2 | Gus Savage | Dem | 78% | Reelected |
| 3 | Marty Russo | Dem | 71% | Reelected |
| 4 | George E. Sangmeister | Dem | 59% | Reelected |
| 5 | William O. Lipinski | Dem | 66% | Reelected |
| 6 | Henry J. Hyde | Rep | 67% | Reelected |
| 7 | Cardiss Collins | Dem | 80% | Reelected |
| 8 | Dan Rostenkowski | Dem | 79% | Reelected |
| 9 | Sidney R. Yates | Dem | 71% | Reelected |
| 10 | John Porter | Rep | 68% | Reelected |
| 11 | Frank Annunzio | Dem | 54% | Reelected |
| 12 | Philip M. Crane | Rep | 82% | Reelected |
| 13 | Harris W. Fawell | Rep | 66% | Reelected |
| 14 | Dennis Hastert | Rep | 67% | Reelected |
| 15 | Edward Madigan | Rep | 100% | Reelected |
| 16 | John W. Cox Jr. | Dem | 55% | Open Seat |
| 17 | Lane Evans | Dem | 66% | Reelected |
| 18 | Robert H. Michel | Rep | 98% | Reelected |
| 19 | Terry L. Bruce | Dem | 66% | Reelected |
| 20 | Richard J. Durbin | Dem | 66% | Reelected |
| 21 | Jerry F. Costello | Dem | 66% | Reelected |
| 22 | Glenn Poshard | Dem | 84% | Reelected |

*Totals in Thousands of Dollars*

## Sen. Alan J. Dixon (D)

**1990 Committees: Armed Services Banking SmBus**
**First elected: 1978**

1985-90 Total Rcpts: ............$3,505,255
1990 Year-end cash: ............$1,223,259

**Source of Funds**
- PACs............................................43%
- Lg Individuals ($200+)................23%
- Individuals under $200 ..............28%
- Other............................................6%

### 1985-90 (PACs only)
**Top Industries & Interest Groups**

Commercial Banks ..................$141,740
Insurance ..................................$112,025
Bldg/Indust/Misc Unions ..........$108,325
Defense Aerospace ..................$89,500
Transportation Unions ..............$86,500

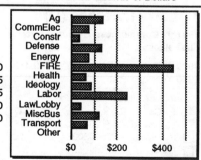

## Sen. Paul Simon (D)

**1990 Committees: Budget ForRel Judiciary Labor**
**First elected: 1984**

1985-90 Total Rcpts: ............$9,643,884
1990 Year-end cash: ..............$843,731

**Source of Funds**
- PACs............................................16%
- Lg Individuals ($200+)................31%
- Individuals under $200 ..............41%
- Other............................................12%

### 1985-90
**Top Industries & Interest Groups**

Lawyers & Lobbyists................$647,030
Pro-Israel ..................................$446,017
Bldg/Indust/Misc Unions ..........$346,997
Real Estate ..............................$220,800
Democratic/Liberal..................$172,434

Unidentified..............................$832,351

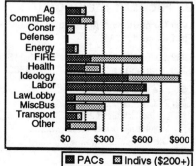

PACs | Indivs ($200+)

Key to committee & category abbreviations is on page 173

## 1. Charles A. Hayes (D)

**1990 Committees:** Educ/Labor Post Office
**First elected:** 1983

1989-90 Total receipts: ............$114,165
1990 Year-end cash: .................$25,702

**Source of Funds**
- ■ PACs ...............................................76%
- ▨ Lg Individuals ($200+) .............13%
- ☐ Individuals under $200 ...............7%
- ⊠ Other ...............................................4%

**Top Industries & Interest Groups**

Bldg/Indust/Misc Unions ............$34,100
Public Sector Unions ..............$27,300
Transportation Unions ..............$12,200
Waste Management ...................$4,000
Real Estate ...........................$3,000

Unidentified..................................$1,400

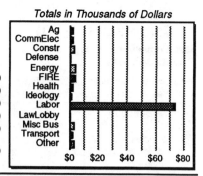

## 2. Gus Savage (D)

**1990 Committees:** Public Works Sm Business
**First elected:** 1980

1989-90 Total receipts: ............$196,636
1990 Year-end cash: ..................$5,941

**Source of Funds**
- ■ PACs...............................................32%
- ▨ Lg Individuals ($200+) .............37%
- ☐ Individuals under $200 .............22%
- ⊠ Other ...............................................9%

**Top Industries & Interest Groups**

Bldg/Indust/Misc Unions ...........$24,550
Transportation Unions ..............$18,600
Public Sector Unions ...............$13,500
Food Processing & Sales ............$8,800
Retail Sales..............................$6,800

Unidentified..................................$12,850

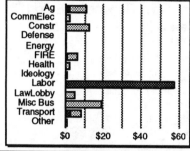

## 3. Marty Russo (D)

**1990 Committees:** Budget Ways & Means
**First elected:** 1974

1989-90 Total receipts: ............$547,782
1990 Year-end cash: ....................$8,789

**Source of Funds**
- ■ PACs...............................................70%
- ▨ Lg Individuals ($200+) .............19%
- ☐ Individuals under $200 .............11%
- ⊠ Other...................................................0%

**Top Industries & Interest Groups**

Insurance .........................$80,700
Lawyers & Lobbyists .................$43,300
Securities & Investment ............$37,792
Bldg/Indust/Misc Unions ...........$31,700
Transportation Unions ..............$24,100

Unidentified..................................$14,700

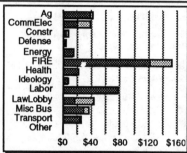

## 4. George E. Sangmeister (D)

**1990 Committees:** Judiciary Public Works Vet Affairs
**First elected:** 1988

1989-90 Total receipts: ............$481,112
1990 Year-end cash: .................$23,142

**Source of Funds**
- ■ PACs...............................................66%
- ▨ Lg Individuals ($200+) ...............8%
- ☐ Individuals under $200 .............12%
- ⊠ Other.............................................14%

**Top Industries & Interest Groups**

Bldg/Indust/Misc Unions .........$110,450
Public Sector Unions ...............$60,500
Transportation Unions ..............$29,600
Leadership PACs .......................$27,350
Lawyers & Lobbyists ..................$17,500

Unidentified..................................$7,790

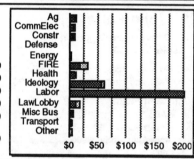

## 5. William O. Lipinski (D)

**1990 Committees:** Merchant Marine Public Works
**First elected:** 1982

1989-90 Total receipts: ............$183,213
1990 Year-end cash: .................$19,110

**Source of Funds**
- ■ PACs...............................................73%
- ▨ Lg Individuals ($200+) .............15%
- ☐ Individuals under $200 ...............9%
- ⊠ Other...............................................3%

**Top Industries & Interest Groups**

Transportation Unions ..............$31,525
Bldg/Indust/Misc Unions ...........$28,575
Public Sector Unions ...............$15,750
Lawyers & Lobbyists ..................$10,010
Civil Servants/Officials ................$9,875

Unidentified..................................$4,150

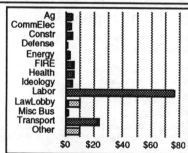

## 6. Henry J. Hyde (R)

**1990 Committees:** Foreign Affairs Judiciary
**First elected:** 1974

1989-90 Total receipts: ............$302,541
1990 Year-end cash: ...............$187,768

**Source of Funds**
- ■ PACs...............................................43%
- ▨ Lg Individuals ($200+) .............29%
- ☐ Individuals under $200 .............18%
- ⊠ Other.............................................11%

**Top Industries & Interest Groups**

Lawyers & Lobbyists .................$15,295
Insurance ...........................$13,740
Real Estate ...........................$13,640
Health Professionals .................$13,510
Commercial Banks ....................$12,330

Unidentified..................................$25,850

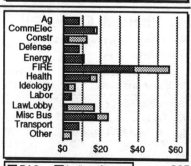

■ PACs ⊠ Indivs ($200+)

205

## 7. Cardiss Collins (D)

**1990 Committees:** Energy & Commerce  Govt Ops
**First elected:** 1973

1989-90 Total receipts: ............$338,392
1990 Year-end cash: ................$90,094

**Source of Funds**
- PACs .............................................77%
- Lg Individuals ($200+) ..............9%
- Individuals under $200 ...........2%
- Other ..........................................12%

**Top Industries & Interest Groups**

Bldg/Indust/Misc Unions ............$31,950
Insurance ....................................$29,662
Transportation Unions ...............$22,700
Public Sector Unions ..................$22,550
Securities & Investment .............$18,750

Unidentified ..................................$2,950

## 8. Dan Rostenkowski (D)

**1990 Committees:** Ways & Means
**First elected:** 1958

1989-90 Total receipts: ............$378,282
1990 Year-end cash: ............$1,114,068

**Source of Funds**
- PACs .............................................58%
- Lg Individuals ($200+) ................8%
- Individuals under $200 ...........0%
- Other ..........................................34%

**Top Industries & Interest Groups**

Securities & Investment .............$17,500
Lawyers & Lobbyists ..................$17,300
Automotive ...................................$16,500
Health Professionals ..................$14,500
Beer, Wine & Liquor ...................$13,000
Retail Sales .................................$13,000

Unidentified ..................................$4,000

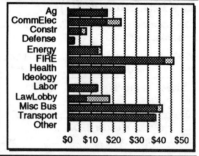

## 9. Sidney R. Yates (D)

**1990 Committees:** Appropriations
**First elected:** 1948

1989-90 Total receipts: ............$779,125
1990 Year-end cash: ................$53,828

**Source of Funds**
- PACs .............................................29%
- Lg Individuals ($200+) ..............50%
- Individuals under $200 ...........13%
- Other ............................................8%

**Top Industries & Interest Groups**

Pro-Israel ....................................$75,750
Bldg/Indust/Misc Unions ...........$59,500
Lawyers & Lobbyists .................$46,700
Real Estate .................................$40,850
Public Sector Unions ................$30,000

Unidentified ................................$68,278

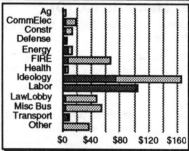

## 10. John Porter (R)

**1990 Committees:** Appropriations
**First elected:** 1980

1989-90 Total receipts: ............$255,970
1990 Year-end cash: ................$71,996

**Source of Funds**
- PACs .............................................41%
- Lg Individuals ($200+) ..............30%
- Individuals under $200 ...........18%
- Other ..........................................11%

**Top Industries & Interest Groups**

Real Estate .................................$14,750
Health Professionals .................$13,125
Pharmaceuticals/Health Prod ....$10,350
Insurance ......................................$8,700
Human Rights ...............................$8,150

Unidentified ................................$23,025

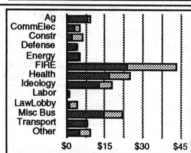

## 11. Frank Annunzio (D)

**1990 Committees:** Admin  Banking
**First elected:** 1964

1989-90 Total receipts: ............$723,159
1990 Year-end cash: ................$35,719

**Source of Funds**
- PACs .............................................60%
- Lg Individuals ($200+) ..............21%
- Individuals under $200 ...........7%
- Other ..........................................12%

**Top Industries & Interest Groups**

Bldg/Indust/Misc Unions ...........$98,400
Insurance ....................................$58,774
Lawyers & Lobbyists .................$56,600
Securities & Investment .............$40,300
Finance/Credit Companies ........$35,750

Unidentified ................................$23,700

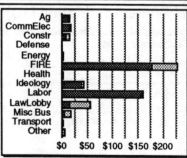

## 12. Philip M. Crane (R)

**1990 Committees:** Ways & Means
**First elected:** 1969

1989-90 Total receipts: ............$178,141
1990 Year-end cash: ..............$115,919

**Source of Funds**
- PACs ...............................................0%
- Lg Individuals ($200+) ..............23%
- Individuals under $200 ...........62%
- Other ..........................................15%

**Top Industries & Interest Groups**

Republican/Conservative ............$5,750
Pharmaceuticals/Health Prod ......$4,200
Health Professionals ...................$3,000
Real Estate ...................................$2,000
Insurance ......................................$1,900

Unidentified ................................$17,850

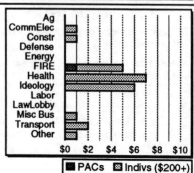

Key to committee & category abbreviations is on page 173

**Totals in Thousands of Dollars**

■ PACs   ▨ Indivs ($200+)

## 13. Harris W. Fawell (R)

**1990 Committees: Educ/Labor Science**
**First elected: 1984**

1989-90 Total receipts: ........... $336,789
1990 Year-end cash: .............. $103,808

**Source of Funds**
■ PACs .......................................... 35%
▨ Lg Individuals ($200+) ............. 48%
☐ Individuals under $200 ............ 14%
▩ Other ........................................ 3%

**Top Industries & Interest Groups**

Insurance ....................................... $17,925
Health Professionals ................... $15,375
General Contractors .................... $12,250
Misc Manufacturing & Distrib ..... $11,081
Commercial Banks ....................... $9,525

Unidentified ................................. $52,494

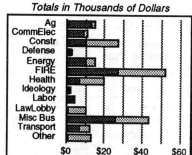

## 14. Dennis Hastert (R)

**1990 Committees: Govt Ops Public Works**
**First elected: 1986**

1989-90 Total receipts: ........... $460,270
1990 Year-end cash: .............. $191,061

**Source of Funds**
■ PACs .......................................... 38%
▨ Lg Individuals ($200+) ............. 23%
☐ Individuals under $200 ............ 33%
▩ Other ........................................ 6%

**Top Industries & Interest Groups**

Telephone Utilities ..................... $21,460
Health Professionals ................... $20,150
Commercial Banks ....................... $14,850
Automotive ................................... $13,300
General Contractors .................... $13,150

Unidentified ................................. $30,050

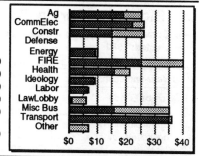

## 15. Edward Madigan (R)

**1990 Committees: Agriculture Energy & Commerce**
**First elected: 1972**

1989-90 Total receipts: ........... $432,247
1990 Year-end cash: .............. $542,570

**Source of Funds**
■ PACs .......................................... 64%
▨ Lg Individuals ($200+) ............. 6%
☐ Individuals under $200 ............ 11%
▩ Other ........................................ 19%

**Top Industries & Interest Groups**

Health Professionals ................... $38,940
Pharmaceuticals/Health Prod .... $28,414
Insurance ...................................... $21,150
Agric Services/Products ............. $20,036
Telephone Utilities ..................... $20,000

Unidentified ................................. $5,200

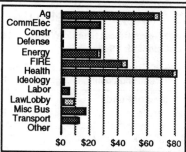

## 16. John W. Cox Jr. (D)

**1991-92 Committees: Banking Govt Ops**
**First elected: 1990**

1989-90 Total receipts: ........... $377,421
1990 Year-end cash: .................. $6,306

**Source of Funds**
■ PACs .......................................... 46%
▨ Lg Individuals ($200+) ............. 15%
☐ Individuals under $200 ............ 26%
▩ Other ........................................ 13%

**Top Industries & Interest Groups**

Bldg/Indust/Misc Unions ........... $77,350
Public Sector Unions ................. $30,700
Democratic/Liberal ..................... $20,115
Misc Issues ................................. $16,096
Lawyers & Lobbyists ................. $12,766

Unidentified ................................. $10,329

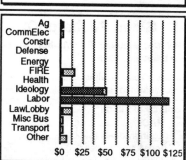

## 17. Lane Evans (D)

**1990 Committees: Armed Services Vet Affairs**
**First elected: 1982**

1989-90 Total receipts: ........... $417,626
1990 Year-end cash: ................ $30,911

**Source of Funds**
■ PACs .......................................... 53%
▨ Lg Individuals ($200+) ............. 10%
☐ Individuals under $200 ............ 34%
▩ Other ........................................ 4%

**Top Industries & Interest Groups**

Bldg/Indust/Misc Unions ........... $89,865
Public Sector Unions ................. $36,700
Transportation Unions ............... $34,150
Lawyers & Lobbyists ................. $16,750
Real Estate ................................. $9,000

Unidentified ................................. $5,662

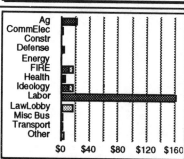

## 18. Robert H. Michel (R)

**1990 Committees: Minority Leader**
**First elected: 1956**

1989-90 Total receipts: ........... $705,878
1990 Year-end cash: .............. $241,996

**Source of Funds**
■ PACs .......................................... 71%
▨ Lg Individuals ($200+) ............. 11%
☐ Individuals under $200 ............ 12%
▩ Other ........................................ 6%

**Top Industries & Interest Groups**

Insurance ...................................... $52,200
Health Professionals ................... $30,100
Telephone Utilities ..................... $26,000
Agric Services/Products ............. $24,631
Defense Aerospace .................... $21,500

Unidentified ................................. $7,760

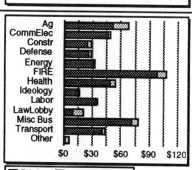

■ PACs  ▨ Indivs ($200+)

207

*Totals in Thousands of Dollars*

## 19. Terry L. Bruce (D)

**1990 Committees:** Energy & Commerce  Science
**First elected:** 1984

1989-90 Total receipts: ............$471,745
1990 Year-end cash: ..............$574,423

**Source of Funds**
- ■ PACs...........................................67%
- ▨ Lg Individuals ($200+) ...............4%
- □ Individuals under $200 ..............9%
- ▩ Other.........................................20%

**Top Industries & Interest Groups**

Health Professionals .................$31,131
Telephone Utilities ....................$23,700
Oil & Gas ...................................$22,600
Public Sector Unions ................$22,300
Insurance ..................................$19,750

Unidentified ................................$5,250

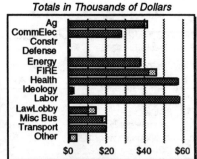

## 20. Richard J. Durbin (D)

**1990 Committees:** Appropriations  Budget
**First elected:** 1982

1989-90 Total receipts: ............$338,066
1990 Year-end cash: ..............$307,371

**Source of Funds**
- ■ PACs...........................................60%
- ▨ Lg Individuals ($200+) ...............6%
- □ Individuals under $200 ............22%
- ▩ Other.........................................12%

**Top Industries & Interest Groups**

Public Sector Unions ................$28,400
Bldg/Indust/Misc Unions ...........$26,050
Transportation Unions ..............$21,700
Lawyers & Lobbyists .................$13,000
Air Transport .............................$10,830

Unidentified ................................$2,768

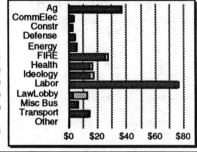

## 21. Jerry F. Costello (D)

**1990 Committees:** Public Works  Science
**First elected:** 1988

1989-90 Total receipts: ............$719,747
1990 Year-end cash: ..............$273,831

**Source of Funds**
- ■ PACs...........................................34%
- ▨ Lg Individuals ($200+) .............43%
- □ Individuals under $200 ............14%
- ▩ Other...........................................8%

**Top Industries & Interest Groups**

Lawyers & Lobbyists ...............$105,725
Bldg/Indust/Misc Unions ...........$55,300
Health Professionals .................$31,350
Public Sector Unions ................$30,750
Transportation Unions ..............$29,350

Unidentified ..............................$52,350

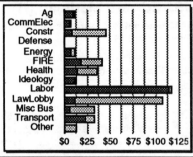

## 22. Glenn Poshard (D)

**1990 Committees:** Educ/Labor  Sm Business
**First elected:** 1988

1989-90 Total receipts: ..............$68,178
1990 Year-end cash: ..................$2,136

**Source of Funds**
- ■ PACs.............................................4%
- ▨ Lg Individuals ($200+) .............13%
- □ Individuals under $200 ............72%
- ▩ Other.........................................10%

**Top Industries & Interest Groups**

Leadership PACs ........................$3,000
Lawyers & Lobbyists ...................$1,800
Misc Finance ..............................$1,000
Securities & Investment ..............$1,000
Education ......................................$750

Unidentified ................................$2,750

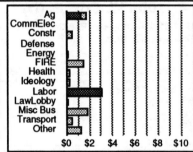

■ PACs ▨ Indivs ($200+)

Key to committee & category abbreviations is on page 173

# Indiana

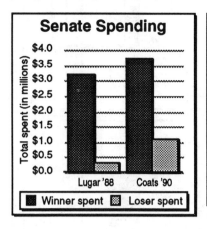
## Spending in 1990 House Races

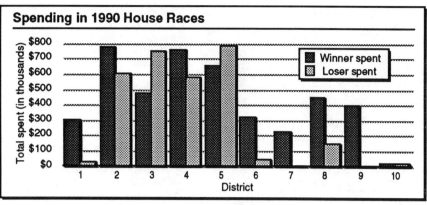

Total spent (in thousands)

$800
$700
$600
$500
$400
$300
$200
$100
$0

1  2  3  4  5  6  7  8  9  10

District

■ Winner spent
▨ Loser spent

## 1990 Elections at a Glance

| Dist | Name | Party | Vote Pct | Race Type |
|------|------|-------|----------|-----------|
| Sen | Daniel R. Coats (1990) | Rep | 54% | Reelected |
| Sen | Richard G. Lugar (1988) | Rep | 68% | Reelected |
| 1 | Peter J. Visclosky | Dem | 66% | Reelected |
| 2 | Philip R. Sharp | Dem | 59% | Reelected |
| 3 | Tim Roemer | Dem | 51% | Beat Incumb |
| 4 | Jill L. Long | Dem | 61% | Reelected |
| 5 | Jim Jontz | Dem | 53% | Reelected |
| 6 | Dan Burton | Rep | 64% | Reelected |
| 7 | John T. Myers | Rep | 58% | Reelected |
| 8 | Frank McCloskey | Dem | 55% | Reelected |
| 9 | Lee H. Hamilton | Dem | 69% | Reelected |
| 10 | Andrew Jacobs Jr. | Dem | 66% | Reelected |

*Totals in Thousands of Dollars*

## Sen. Daniel R. Coats (R)

**1990 Committees: Armed Services Labor**
**First elected: 1990 (Appointed 1988)**

1989-90 Total Rcpts: ............$4,085,244
1990 Year-end cash: ..............$343,559

**Source of Funds**
| | |
|---|---|
| ■ PACs .................................................27% | |
| ▨ Lg Individuals ($200+) ...............33% | |
| ☐ Individuals under $200 .............20% | |
| ▨ Other .................................................19% | |

### 1988-90

**Top Industries & Interest Groups**

| | |
|---|---|
| Insurance ................................. | $141,709 |
| Defense Aerospace ................. | $111,215 |
| Pharmaceuticals/Health Prod .. | $106,970 |
| Health Professionals ................. | $106,672 |
| Oil & Gas .................................... | $99,800 |
| Unidentified ............................... | $568,578 |

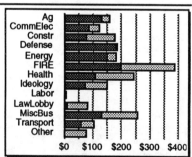

Ag, CommElec, Constr, Defense, Energy, FIRE, Health, Ideology, Labor, LawLobby, MiscBus, Transport, Other

$0  $100  $200  $300  $400

## Sen. Richard G. Lugar (R)

**1990 Committees: Agriculture Foreign Relations**
**First elected: 1976**

1985-90 Total Rcpts: ............$4,020,016
1990 Year-end cash: ..............$842,595

**Source of Funds**
| | |
|---|---|
| ■ PACs .................................................21% | |
| ▨ Lg Individuals ($200+) ...............19% | |
| ☐ Individuals under $200 .............50% | |
| ▨ Other .................................................11% | |

### 1985-90 (PACs only)

**Top Industries & Interest Groups**

| | |
|---|---|
| Agric Services/Products ............ | $74,380 |
| Food Processing & Sales ......... | $71,485 |
| Insurance ................................... | $53,665 |
| Securities & Investment ............ | $52,850 |
| Oil & Gas .................................... | $45,975 |

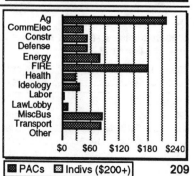

Ag, CommElec, Constr, Defense, Energy, FIRE, Health, Ideology, Labor, LawLobby, MiscBus, Transport, Other

$0  $60  $120  $180  $240

■ PACs  ▨ Indivs ($200+)

209

## 1. Peter J. Visclosky (D)

**1990 Committees: Interior  Public Works**
**First elected: 1984**

1989-90 Total receipts: ............$248,272
1990 Year-end cash: ................$43,701

**Source of Funds**
- PACs..................................68%
- Lg Individuals ($200+) ..............10%
- Individuals under $200 ............16%
- Other....................................7%

**Top Industries & Interest Groups**

Bldg/Indust/Misc Unions ............$61,050
Transportation Unions ..............$25,700
Public Sector Unions ................$23,000
Health Professionals ..................$10,650
Real Estate ..............................$8,700

Unidentified ..............................$5,120

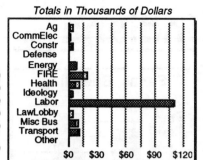

## 2. Philip R. Sharp (D)

**1990 Committees: Energy & Commerce  Interior**
**First elected: 1974**

1989-90 Total receipts: ............$714,491
1990 Year-end cash: ................$29,944

**Source of Funds**
- PACs..................................70%
- Lg Individuals ($200+) ..............10%
- Individuals under $200 ............15%
- Other....................................5%

**Top Industries & Interest Groups**

Bldg/Indust/Misc Unions ............$83,250
Electric Utilities ........................$62,299
Oil & Gas ................................$51,773
Public Sector Unions ................$41,100
Lawyers & Lobbyists ................$34,450

Unidentified ..............................$11,497

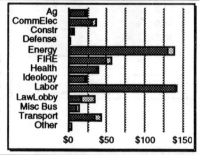

## 3. Tim Roemer (D)

**1991-92 Committees: Educ/Labor  Science**
**First elected: 1990**

1989-90 Total receipts: ............$504,884
1990 Year-end cash: ................$31,826

**Source of Funds**
- PACs..................................51%
- Lg Individuals ($200+) ..............28%
- Individuals under $200 ............12%
- Other....................................9%

**Top Industries & Interest Groups**

Bldg/Indust/Misc Unions ............$74,300
Lawyers & Lobbyists ..................$54,733
Public Sector Unions ................$35,800
Transportation Unions ..............$31,250
Leadership PACs ......................$25,500

Unidentified ..............................$36,400

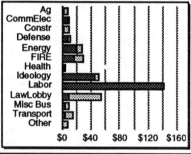

## 4. Jill L. Long (D)

**1990 Committees: Agriculture  Vet Affairs**
**First elected: 1980**

1989-90 Total receipts: .........$1,159,045
1990 Year-end cash: ....................$1,369

**Source of Funds**
- PACs..................................54%
- Lg Individuals ($200+) ..............16%
- Individuals under $200 ............17%
- Other....................................13%

**Top Industries & Interest Groups**

Bldg/Indust/Misc Unions ..........$211,700
Public Sector Unions ..............$100,704
Human Rights ............................$71,282
Health Professionals ..................$56,810
Transportation Unions ..............$48,200

Unidentified ..............................$39,850

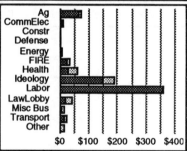

## 5. Jim Jontz (D)

**1990 Committees: Agriculture  Educ/Labor  Vet Affairs**
**First elected: 1986**

1989-90 Total receipts: ............$620,713
1990 Year-end cash: ....................$1,746

**Source of Funds**
- PACs..................................63%
- Lg Individuals ($200+) ..............9%
- Individuals under $200 ............21%
- Other....................................7%

**Top Industries & Interest Groups**

Bldg/Indust/Misc Unions ..........$107,617
Public Sector Unions ................$58,650
Transportation Unions ..............$32,550
Misc Issues ..............................$31,450
Health Professionals ..................$27,567

Unidentified ..............................$12,882

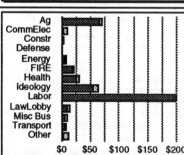

## 6. Dan Burton (R)

**1990 Committees: Foreign Affairs  Post Office  Vet Affairs**
**First elected: 1982**

1989-90 Total receipts: ............$526,451
1990 Year-end cash: ..............$400,894

**Source of Funds**
- PACs..................................38%
- Lg Individuals ($200+) ..............36%
- Individuals under $200 ............16%
- Other....................................10%

**Top Industries & Interest Groups**

Insurance ................................$27,947
Health Professionals ..................$26,250
Public Sector Unions ................$18,150
Pro-Israel ................................$16,850
Real Estate ..............................$16,620

Unidentified ..............................$75,439

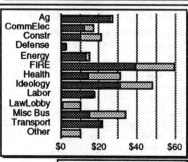

Key to committee & category abbreviations is on page 173

■ PACs  ▨ Indivs ($200+)

## 7. John T. Myers (R)

**1990 Committees: Appropriations  Post Office**
**First elected: 1966**

1989-90 Total receipts: ...........$189,646
1990 Year-end cash: ..............$102,885

**Source of Funds**

- ■ PACs ...........................................53%
- ▨ Lg Individuals ($200+) ................4%
- ☐ Individuals under $200 .............20%
- ⊠ Other .........................................24%

**Top Industries & Interest Groups**

Public Sector Unions ................$10,600
Automotive ...............................$7,000
Agric Services/Products .............$6,900
Real Estate ..............................$6,600
Air Transport ............................$6,300

Unidentified.................................$1,050

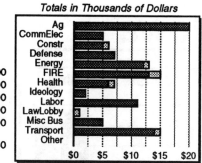

## 8. Frank McCloskey (D)

**1990 Committees: Armed Serv  Foreign Aff  Post Office**
**First elected: 1982**

1989-90 Total receipts: ...........$467,981
1990 Year-end cash: ................$23,382

**Source of Funds**

- ■ PACs ...........................................64%
- ▨ Lg Individuals ($200+) ................4%
- ☐ Individuals under $200 .............22%
- ⊠ Other ...........................................9%

**Top Industries & Interest Groups**

Bldg/Indust/Misc Unions ...........$96,700
Public Sector Unions ................$73,100
Transportation Unions ..............$26,700
Defense Aerospace ...................$16,400
Pro-Israel .................................$12,750

Unidentified.................................$5,158

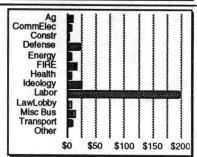

## 9. Lee H. Hamilton (D)

**1990 Committees: Foreign Affairs  Science**
**First elected: 1964**

1989-90 Total receipts: ...........$399,758
1990 Year-end cash: ................$58,592

**Source of Funds**

- ■ PACs ...........................................46%
- ▨ Lg Individuals ($200+) ..............18%
- ☐ Individuals under $200 .............28%
- ⊠ Other ...........................................8%

**Top Industries & Interest Groups**

Bldg/Indust/Misc Unions ...........$30,300
Pro-Israel ..................................$27,500
Real Estate ...............................$20,000
Lawyers & Lobbyists .................$16,992
Public Sector Unions ................$12,050

Unidentified.................................$17,822

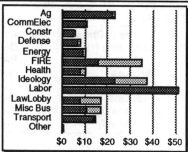

## 10. Andrew Jacobs Jr. (D)

**1990 Committees: Ways & Means**
**First elected: 1964**

1989-90 Total receipts: .............$28,712
1990 Year-end cash: ................$32,188

**Source of Funds**

- ■ PACs ............................................0%
- ▨ Lg Individuals ($200+) ..............15%
- ☐ Individuals under $200 .............74%
- ⊠ Other .........................................11%

**Top Industries & Interest Groups**

Lawyers & Lobbyists ...................$1,800
Cable TV .......................................$400
Retired ..........................................$300
Human Rights ................................$250

Unidentified.....................................$50

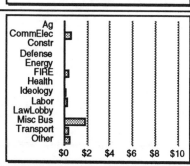

■ PACs  ⊠ Indivs ($200+)

211

# Iowa

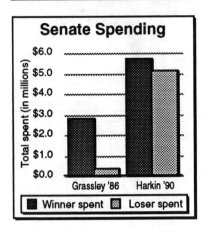

## Senate Spending

Total spent (in millions)

$6.0
$5.0
$4.0
$3.0
$2.0
$1.0
$0.0

Grassley '86    Harkin '90

■ Winner spent    ▨ Loser spent

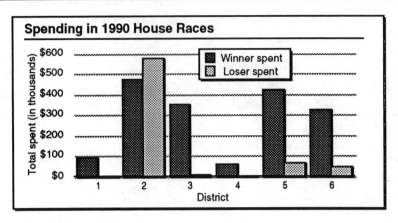

## Spending in 1990 House Races

Total spent (in thousands)

$600
$500
$400
$300
$200
$100
$0

■ Winner spent
▨ Loser spent

1    2    3    4    5    6

District

## 1990 Elections at a Glance

| Dist | Name | Party | Vote Pct | Race Type |
|------|------|-------|----------|-----------|
| Sen | Charles E. Grassley (1986) | Rep | 66% | Reelected |
| Sen | Tom Harkin (1990) | Dem | 54% | Reelected |
| 1 | Jim Leach | Rep | 100% | Reelected |
| 2 | Jim Nussle | Rep | 50% | Open Seat |
| 3 | Dave Nagle | Dem | 99% | Reelected |
| 4 | Neal Smith | Dem | 98% | Reelected |
| 5 | Jim Ross Lightfoot | Rep | 68% | Reelected |
| 6 | Fred Grandy | Rep | 72% | Reelected |

*Totals in Thousands of Dollars*

## Sen. Charles E. Grassley (R)

**1990 Committees: Approp Budget Judiciary SmBus**
**First elected: 1980**

1985-90 Total Rcpts: ............$3,080,000
1990 Year-end cash: ...............$653,101

### Source of Funds

■ PACs .............................................33%
▨ Lg Individuals ($200+) ................13%
□ Individuals under $200 ..............39%
▨ Other .............................................16%

### 1985-90 (PACs only)
**Top Industries & Interest Groups**

Insurance ...................................$134,744
Oil & Gas ....................................$49,750
Securities & Investment .............$42,924
Pharmaceuticals/Health Prod ....$39,600
Food Processing & Sales ..........$36,800

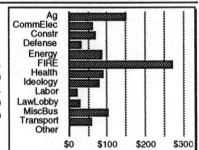

Ag
CommElec
Constr
Defense
Energy
FIRE
Health
Ideology
Labor
LawLobby
MiscBus
Transport
Other

$0    $100    $200    $300

## Sen. Tom Harkin (D)

**1990 Committees: Agriculture Approp Labor SmBus**
**First elected: 1984**

1985-90 Total Rcpts: ............$5,715,839
1990 Year-end cash: ................$59,737

### Source of Funds

■ PACs .............................................29%
▨ Lg Individuals ($200+) ................29%
□ Individuals under $200 ..............33%
▨ Other ...............................................9%

### 1985-90
**Top Industries & Interest Groups**

Pro-Israel ...................................$338,400
Lawyers & Lobbyists ...............$269,536
Bldg/Indust/Misc Unions ..........$240,875
Health Professionals ...............$172,015
Real Estate ...............................$169,275

Unidentified ...............................$390,444

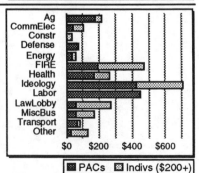

Ag
CommElec
Constr
Defense
Energy
FIRE
Health
Ideology
Labor
LawLobby
MiscBus
Transport
Other

$0    $200    $400    $600

■ PACs    ▨ Indivs ($200+)

Key to committee & category abbreviations is on page 173

# 1. Jim Leach (R)

**1990 Committees:** Banking  Foreign Affairs
**First elected:** 1976

1989-90 Total receipts: ...........$115,051
1990 Year-end cash: ..............$46,917

**Source of Funds**
- ■ PACs..................................0%
- ▨ Lg Individuals ($200+) ........15%
- □ Individuals under $200 ..........80%
- ▧ Other................................5%

### Top Industries & Interest Groups

Sea Transport ..............................$2,510
Retired .......................................$1,620
Health Professionals ...................$1,430
Crop Production/Processing.......$1,000
Building Materials & Equip..........$1,000

Unidentified ................................$6,140

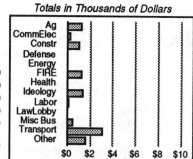

# 2. Jim Nussle (R)

**1991-92 Committees:** Agriculture  Banking
**First elected:** 1990

1989-90 Total receipts: ...........$469,933
1990 Year-end cash: ..................$3,673

**Source of Funds**
- ■ PACs..................................27%
- ▨ Lg Individuals ($200+) ........32%
- □ Individuals under $200 ..........17%
- ▧ Other................................23%

### Top Industries & Interest Groups

Automotive ................................$19,435
Health Professionals .................$18,550
Insurance .................................$17,250
Misc Manufacturing & Distrib ...$14,200
Commercial Banks ...................$13,470

Unidentified ..............................$40,000

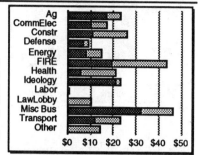

# 3. Dave Nagle (D)

**1990 Committees:** Agriculture  Science
**First elected:** 1986

1989-90 Total receipts: ...........$366,251
1990 Year-end cash: ................$30,045

**Source of Funds**
- ■ PACs..................................72%
- ▨ Lg Individuals ($200+) ..........1%
- □ Individuals under $200 ..........23%
- ▧ Other................................4%

### Top Industries & Interest Groups

Bldg/Indust/Misc Unions ...........$65,900
Public Sector Unions ................$34,150
Transportation Unions ..............$27,450
Commercial Banks ...................$18,080
Dairy .........................................$15,900

Unidentified ................................$1,150

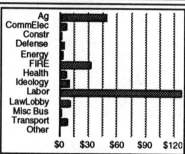

# 4. Neal Smith (D)

**1990 Committees:** Appropriations  Sm Business
**First elected:** 1958

1989-90 Total receipts: ...........$167,829
1990 Year-end cash: ...............$375,509

**Source of Funds**
- ■ PACs..................................69%
- ▨ Lg Individuals ($200+) ..........4%
- □ Individuals under $200 ...........2%
- ▧ Other................................25%

### Top Industries & Interest Groups

Public Sector Unions ................$19,000
Health Professionals .................$14,850
Bldg/Indust/Misc Unions ...........$10,000
Lawyers & Lobbyists ...................$7,600
Commercial Banks .......................$6,000

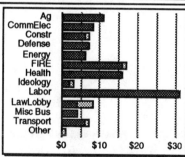

# 5. Jim Ross Lightfoot (R)

**1990 Committees:** Interior  Public Works
**First elected:** 1984

1989-90 Total receipts: ...........$497,363
1990 Year-end cash: ...............$140,810

**Source of Funds**
- ■ PACs..................................29%
- ▨ Lg Individuals ($200+) ........11%
- □ Individuals under $200 ..........55%
- ▧ Other................................5%

### Top Industries & Interest Groups

Air Transport ............................$21,000
Crop Production/Processing......$16,250
Health Professionals .................$10,100
Oil & Gas ...................................$9,800
Commercial Banks .......................$8,250

Unidentified ..............................$13,241

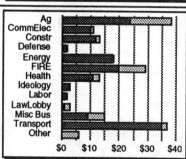

# 6. Fred Grandy (R)

**1990 Committees:** Agriculture  Educ/Labor
**First elected:** 1986

1989-90 Total receipts: ...........$409,067
1990 Year-end cash: ................$85,951

**Source of Funds**
- ■ PACs..................................62%
- ▨ Lg Individuals ($200+) ........20%
- □ Individuals under $200 ..........15%
- ▧ Other................................2%

### Top Industries & Interest Groups

Agric Services/Products ...........$35,800
Insurance .................................$25,059
Crop Production/Processing......$16,600
Commercial Banks ...................$15,895
Food Processing & Sales .........$15,300

Unidentified ..............................$29,372

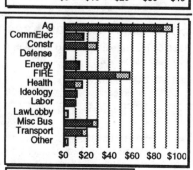

*Totals in Thousands of Dollars*

■ PACs   ▨ Indivs ($200+)

213

# Kansas

## Senate Spending

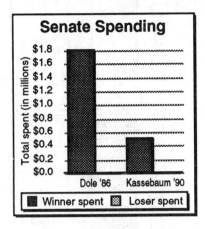

Total spent (in millions)

Dole '86  Kassebaum '90

■ Winner spent  ▨ Loser spent

## Spending in 1990 House Races

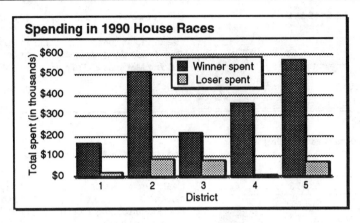

Total spent (in thousands)

■ Winner spent
▨ Loser spent

District

## 1990 Elections at a Glance

| Dist | Name | Party | Vote Pct | Race Type |
|------|------|-------|----------|-----------|
| Sen | Bob Dole (1986) | Rep | 70% | Reelected |
| Sen | Nancy Kassebaum (1990) | Rep | 74% | Reelected |
| 1 | Pat Roberts | Rep | 63% | Reelected |
| 2 | Jim Slattery | Dem | 63% | Reelected |
| 3 | Jan Meyers | Rep | 60% | Reelected |
| 4 | Dan Glickman | Dem | 71% | Reelected |
| 5 | Dick Nichols | Rep | 59% | Open Seat |

*Totals in Thousands of Dollars*

## Sen. Bob Dole (R)

**1990 Committees: Agriculture Finance Rules**
**First elected: 1968**

1985-90 Total Rcpts: ............ $3,420,229
1990 Year-end cash: ............ $1,383,644

**Source of Funds**
■ PACs .................................... 41%
▨ Lg Individuals ($200+) ............. 34%
□ Individuals under $200 .............. 7%
▨ Other .................................. 18%

### 1985-90 (PACs only)
**Top Industries & Interest Groups**

Insurance ................................. $182,583
Oil & Gas ................................. $130,750
Crop Production/Processing .... $115,532
Securities & Investment .......... $107,050
Commercial Banks ................... $92,540

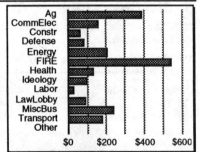

## Sen. Nancy Landon Kassebaum (R)

**1990 Committees: Banking Foreign Relations Labor**
**First elected: 1978**

1985-90 Total Rcpts: .............. $532,964
1990 Year-end cash: ................ $21,135

**Source of Funds**
■ PACs .................................... 31%
▨ Lg Individuals ($200+) ............. 28%
□ Individuals under $200 ............. 13%
▨ Other .................................. 28%

### 1985-90
**Top Industries & Interest Groups**

Commercial Banks ................... $33,200
Oil & Gas ................................. $18,208
Insurance ................................. $13,430
Air Transport ............................ $13,300
Health Professionals ................. $13,200

Unidentified .............................. $40,449

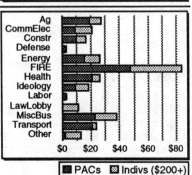

■ PACs  ▨ Indivs ($200+)

Key to committee & category abbreviations is on page 173

# 1. Pat Roberts (R)

**1990 Committees: Admin Agriculture**
**First elected: 1980**

1989-90 Total receipts: ...........$225,572
1990 Year-end cash: ..............$399,529

**Source of Funds**
- PACs ..............................................58%
- Lg Individuals ($200+) ..............8%
- Individuals under $200 ..............8%
- Other ............................................26%

**Top Industries & Interest Groups**

Agric Services/Products ............$25,000
Crop Production/Processing ......$15,300
Commercial Banks ....................$12,500
Food Processing & Sales .........$12,100
Real Estate ................................$8,000
Health Professionals ..................$8,000

Unidentified ................................$1,750

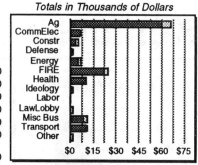

# 2. Jim Slattery (D)

**1990 Committees: Budget Energy & Commerce**
**First elected: 1982**

1989-90 Total receipts: ...........$467,018
1990 Year-end cash: ................$52,999

**Source of Funds**
- PACs ..............................................69%
- Lg Individuals ($200+) ............15%
- Individuals under $200 ............11%
- Other ..............................................5%

**Top Industries & Interest Groups**

Bldg/Indust/Misc Unions ............$29,100
Insurance ..................................$28,550
Lawyers & Lobbyists ................$25,050
Health Professionals ..................$24,450
Telephone Utilities ....................$23,750

Unidentified ................................$20,217

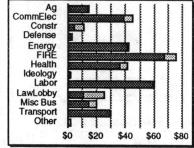

# 3. Jan Meyers (R)

**1990 Committees: Foreign Affairs Sm Business**
**First elected: 1984**

1989-90 Total receipts: ...........$211,505
1990 Year-end cash: ...................$2,081

**Source of Funds**
- PACs ..............................................52%
- Lg Individuals ($200+) ............20%
- Individuals under $200 ............24%
- Other ..............................................4%

**Top Industries & Interest Groups**

Insurance ..................................$13,350
Health Professionals ..................$12,450
Telephone Utilities ......................$8,200
Real Estate ................................$7,950
Automotive ................................$7,950

Unidentified ..............................$16,675

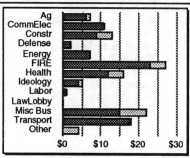

# 4. Dan Glickman (D)

**1990 Committees: Agriculture Judiciary Science**
**First elected: 1976**

1989-90 Total receipts: ...........$520,945
1990 Year-end cash: ..............$192,262

**Source of Funds**
- PACs ..............................................56%
- Lg Individuals ($200+) ............27%
- Individuals under $200 ............12%
- Other ..............................................5%

**Top Industries & Interest Groups**

Lawyers & Lobbyists .................$45,600
Insurance ..................................$29,315
Air Transport .............................$27,650
Bldg/Indust/Misc Unions ............$26,050
Health Professionals .................$23,810

Unidentified ..............................$27,000

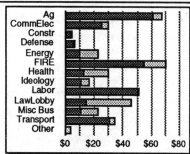

# 5. Dick Nichols (R)

**1991-92 Committees: Public Works Vet Affairs**
**First elected: 1990**

1989-90 Total receipts: ...........$573,188
1990 Year-end cash: ...................$7,776

**Source of Funds**
- PACs ..............................................18%
- Lg Individuals ($200+) ............16%
- Individuals under $200 ............11%
- Other ..............................................55%

**Top Industries & Interest Groups**

Commercial Banks ....................$30,675
Oil & Gas ...................................$15,800
Health Professionals .................$15,425
Food & Beverage ......................$11,700
Retired .......................................$10,900

Unidentified ..............................$23,905

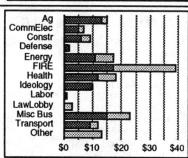

PACs ▨ Indivs ($200+)

# Kentucky

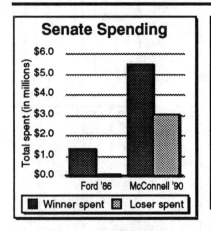

## Senate Spending

Total spent (in millions)

Ford '86   McConnell '90

■ Winner spent   ▨ Loser spent

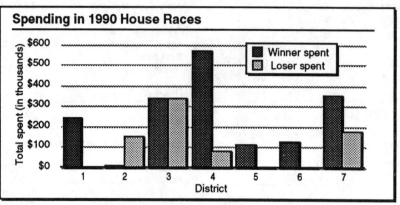

## Spending in 1990 House Races

Total spent (in thousands)

■ Winner spent
▨ Loser spent

District

### 1990 Elections at a Glance

| Dist | Name | Party | Vote Pct | Race Type |
|------|------|-------|----------|-----------|
| Sen | Wendell H. Ford (1986) | Dem | 74% | Reelected |
| Sen | Mitch McConnell (1990) | Rep | 52% | Reelected |
| 1 | Carroll Hubbard Jr. | Dem | 87% | Reelected |
| 2 | William H. Natcher | Dem | 66% | Reelected |
| 3 | Romano L. Mazzoli | Dem | 61% | Reelected |
| 4 | Jim Bunning | Rep | 69% | Reelected |
| 5 | Harold Rogers | Rep | 100% | Reelected |
| 6 | Larry J. Hopkins | Rep | 100% | Reelected |
| 7 | Carl C. Perkins | Dem | 51% | Reelected |

*Totals in Thousands of Dollars*

## Sen. Wendell H. Ford (D)

**1990 Committees: Commerce Energy Rules**
**First elected: 1974**

1985-90 Total Rcpts: ............$1,608,575
1990 Year-end cash: ...............$197,145

**Source of Funds**

■ PACs ............................................54%
▨ Lg Individuals ($200+) ...............20%
□ Individuals under $200 ...............17%
▨ Other ...........................................9%

**1985-90 (PACs only)**
**Top Industries & Interest Groups**

Bldg/Indust/Misc Unions ...........$85,367
Insurance ..................................$80,150
Oil & Gas ..................................$58,183
Transportation Unions ..............$56,650
Public Sector Unions ................$42,550

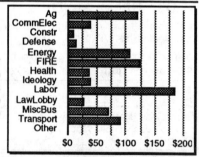

## Sen. Mitch McConnell (R)

**1990 Committees: Agriculture Energy ForRel Rules**
**First elected: 1984**

1985-90 Total Rcpts: ............$5,707,726
1990 Year-end cash: ...............$190,373

**Source of Funds**

■ PACs ............................................22%
▨ Lg Individuals ($200+) ...............43%
□ Individuals under $200 ...............18%
▨ Other ..........................................17%

**1985-90**
**Top Industries & Interest Groups**

Pro-Israel ..................................$232,400
Oil & Gas ..................................$214,522
Health Professionals ...............$182,625
Lawyers & Lobbyists ...............$179,343
Insurance .................................$122,906

Unidentified ............................$538,291

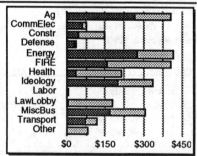

## 1. Carroll Hubbard Jr. (D)

**1990 Committees: Banking Merchant Marine**
**First elected: 1974**

1989-90 Total receipts: ...........$351,966
1990 Year-end cash: ...............$335,477

**Source of Funds**

■ PACs ............................................78%
▨ Lg Individuals ($200+) ...............8%
□ Individuals under $200 ...............3%
▨ Other ..........................................11%

**Top Industries & Interest Groups**

Commercial Banks ....................$52,850
Insurance ..................................$28,000
Savings & Loans ........................$21,077
Transportation Unions ..............$20,000
Bldg/Indust/Misc Unions ...........$12,500

Unidentified ...............................$4,200

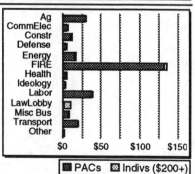

■ PACs  ▨ Indivs ($200+)

Key to committee & category abbreviations is on page 173

## 2. William H. Natcher (D)

**1990 Committees: Appropriations**
**First elected: 1953**

1989-90 Total receipts: ................$6,768
1990 Year-end cash: ...........................$0

**Source of Funds**
■ PACs.................................................0%
▨ Lg Individuals ($200+) .................0%
□ Individuals under $200 ................0%
⊠ Other................................................100%

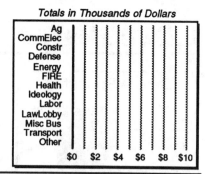

**Top Industries & Interest Groups**

NOTE: Natcher financed his own campaign in 1990, as is his custom. It was the least expensive winning campaign of the year, by far.

## 3. Romano L. Mazzoli (D)

**1990 Committees: Judiciary  Sm Business**
**First elected: 1970**

1989-90 Total receipts: ............$303,488
1990 Year-end cash: ......................$290

**Source of Funds**
■ PACs.................................................0%
▨ Lg Individuals ($200+) .............35%
□ Individuals under $200 ..............49%
⊠ Other.................................................15%

**Top Industries & Interest Groups**

Health Professionals .................$17,100
Lawyers & Lobbyists .................$15,900
Retired .........................................$5,200
Insurance ......................................$4,350
Food & Beverage .........................$4,000

Unidentified ..................................$19,240

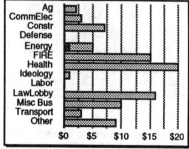

## 4. Jim Bunning (R)

**1990 Committees: Banking  Merchant Marine**
**First elected: 1986**

1989-90 Total receipts: ............$532,775
1990 Year-end cash: .................$97,018

**Source of Funds**
■ PACs...............................................42%
▨ Lg Individuals ($200+) .............27%
□ Individuals under $200 ..............23%
⊠ Other...................................................8%

**Top Industries & Interest Groups**

Commercial Banks ....................$36,650
Insurance .....................................$28,125
Health Professionals .................$26,150
Telephone Utilities .....................$13,500
Lawyers & Lobbyists .................$12,150

Unidentified ..................................$34,650

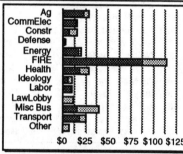

## 5. Harold Rogers (R)

**1990 Committees: Appropriations  Budget**
**First elected: 1980**

1989-90 Total receipts: ............$185,130
1990 Year-end cash: ...............$267,078

**Source of Funds**
■ PACs...............................................35%
▨ Lg Individuals ($200+) .............27%
□ Individuals under $200 ..............16%
⊠ Other.................................................22%

**Top Industries & Interest Groups**

Oil & Gas .....................................$11,800
Mining ...........................................$9,500
Lawyers & Lobbyists ....................$7,000
Tobacco ........................................$6,000
Real Estate ...................................$5,500

Unidentified ....................................$9,156

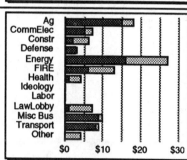

## 6. Larry J. Hopkins (R)

**1990 Committees: Agriculture  Armed Services**
**First elected: 1978**

1989-90 Total receipts: ............$203,286
1990 Year-end cash: ...............$691,433

**Source of Funds**
■ PACs...............................................43%
▨ Lg Individuals ($200+) ...............0%
□ Individuals under $200 ................0%
⊠ Other.................................................56%

**Top Industries & Interest Groups**

Tobacco ........................................$13,500
Defense Electronics.....................$9,000
Defense Aerospace ......................$8,500
Insurance ......................................$5,500
Health Professionals ...................$5,000

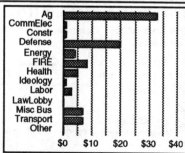

## 7. Carl C. Perkins (D)

**1990 Committees: Educ/Labor  Public Works  Science**
**First elected: 1984**

1989-90 Total receipts: ............$340,047
1990 Year-end cash: ...................$3,640

**Source of Funds**
■ PACs...............................................78%
▨ Lg Individuals ($200+) .............15%
□ Individuals under $200 ................5%
⊠ Other...................................................2%

**Top Industries & Interest Groups**

Bldg/Indust/Misc Unions ............$73,950
Public Sector Unions .................$53,000
Transportation Unions ..............$40,650
Lawyers & Lobbyists .................$15,950
Education .....................................$13,350

Unidentified ..................................$18,650

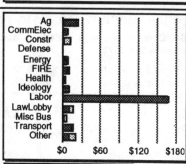

■ PACs  ⊠ Indivs ($200+)

217

# Louisiana

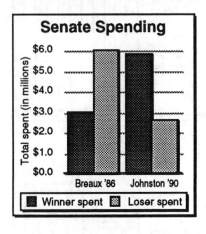

## Senate Spending

Total spent (in millions)

Breaux '86    Johnston '90

■ Winner spent  ▨ Loser spent

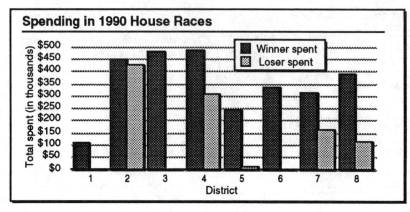

## Spending in 1990 House Races

Total spent (in thousands)

■ Winner spent
▨ Loser spent

District

## 1990 Elections at a Glance

| Dist | Name | Party | Vote Pct | Race Type |
|------|------|-------|----------|-----------|
| Sen | John B. Breaux (1986) | Dem | 53% | Open Seat |
| Sen | J. Bennett Johnston (1990) | Dem | 54% | Reelected |
| 1 | Bob Livingston | Rep | 84% | Reelected |
| 2 | William J. Jefferson | Dem | 52% | Open Seat |
| 3 | W. J. "Billy" Tauzin | Dem | 88% | Reelected |
| 4 | Jim McCrery | Rep | 55% | Reelected |
| 5 | Jerry Huckaby | Dem | 74% | Reelected |
| 6 | Richard H. Baker | Rep | 100% | Reelected |
| 7 | Jimmy Hayes | Dem | 58% | Reelected |
| 8 | Clyde C. Holloway | Rep | 56% | Reelected |

*Totals in Thousands of Dollars*

## Sen. John B. Breaux (D)

**1990 Committees: Commerce Envir/Pub Works Finance**
**First elected: 1986**

1985-90 Total Rcpts: ............$4,032,305
1990 Year-end cash: ..............$518,739

**Source of Funds**
■ PACs ...........................................29%
▨ Lg Individuals ($200+) .............33%
□ Individuals under $200 .............21%
▨ Other .........................................18%

### 1985-90 (PACs only)
**Top Industries & Interest Groups**

Oil & Gas ...................................$115,091
Bldg/Indust/Misc Unions .........$109,568
Public Sector Unions ................$81,450
Transportation Unions .............$64,000
Lawyers & Lobbyists .................$45,479

Unidentified ...............................$12,100

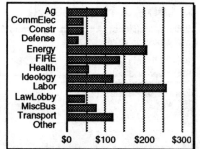

## Sen. J. Bennett Johnston (D)

**1990 Committees: Appropriations Budget Energy**
**First elected: 1972**

1985-90 Total Rcpts: ............$4,816,299
1990 Year-end cash: ..............$945,371

**Source of Funds**
■ PACs ...........................................30%
▨ Lg Individuals ($200+) .............28%
□ Individuals under $200 .............19%
▨ Other .........................................24%

### 1985-90
**Top Industries & Interest Groups**

Oil & Gas ...................................$341,900
Lawyers & Lobbyists ...............$303,150
Electric Utilities .........................$175,650
Pro-Israel ..................................$128,002
Defense Aerospace .................$101,750

Unidentified ..............................$254,545

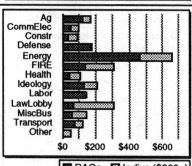

■ PACs  ▨ Indivs ($200+)

218          Key to committee & category abbreviations is on page 173

## 1. Bob Livingston (R)

**1990 Committees: Appropriations**
**First elected: 1977**

1989-90 Total receipts: ........... $279,603
1990 Year-end cash: .............. $282,513

**Source of Funds**
- PACs ........................................... 53%
- Lg Individuals ($200+) ............... 25%
- Individuals under $200 ................ 16%
- Other .......................................... 6%

**Top Industries & Interest Groups**

Defense Aerospace ................. $27,800
Defense Electronics .................. $25,400
Lawyers & Lobbyists ................. $23,100
Oil & Gas ................................ $18,150
Health Professionals ................ $13,200

Unidentified ............................ $14,495

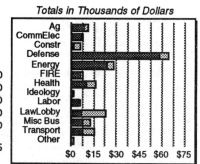

## 2. William J. Jefferson (D)

**1991-92 Committees: Educ/Labor  Merchant Marine**
**First elected: 1990**

1989-90 Total receipts: ........... $448,100
1990 Year-end cash: ................... $1,355

**Source of Funds**
- PACs ........................................... 22%
- Lg Individuals ($200+) ............... 49%
- Individuals under $200 ................ 4%
- Other .......................................... 24%

**Top Industries & Interest Groups**

Lawyers & Lobbyists ................. $47,236
Bldg/Indust/Misc Unions ........... $27,500
Construction Services ............... $24,000
Public Sector Unions ................ $11,000
Transportation Unions ................ $8,000

Unidentified ............................ $127,200

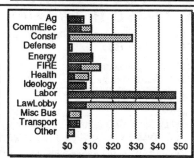

## 3. W. J. "Billy" Tauzin (D)

**1990 Committees: Energy & Commerce  Merch Marine**
**First elected: 1980**

1989-90 Total receipts: ........... $460,418
1990 Year-end cash: ................. $48,411

**Source of Funds**
- PACs ........................................... 74%
- Lg Individuals ($200+) ............... 19%
- Individuals under $200 ................ 7%
- Other .......................................... 0%

**Top Industries & Interest Groups**

Oil & Gas ................................ $54,800
Lawyers & Lobbyists ................. $33,500
Electric Utilities .......................... $30,600
Insurance ................................ $28,200
Commercial Banks .................... $22,400

Unidentified ............................. $24,700

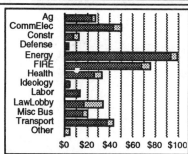

## 4. Jim McCrery (R)

**1990 Committees: Armed Services  Budget**
**First elected: 1988**

1989-90 Total receipts: ........... $469,766
1990 Year-end cash: ................. $37,690

**Source of Funds**
- PACs ........................................... 36%
- Lg Individuals ($200+) ............... 38%
- Individuals under $200 ................ 9%
- Other .......................................... 18%

**Top Industries & Interest Groups**

Oil & Gas ................................ $39,200
Health Professionals ................. $23,675
Forestry & Forest Products ....... $22,450
Defense Aerospace .................. $17,450
Defense Electronics .................. $17,300

Unidentified ............................. $69,450

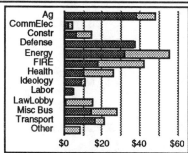

## 5. Jerry Huckaby (D)

**1990 Committees: Agriculture  Budget**
**First elected: 1976**

1989-90 Total receipts: ........... $218,774
1990 Year-end cash: .............. $273,331

**Source of Funds**
- PACs ........................................... 49%
- Lg Individuals ($200+) ............... 24%
- Individuals under $200 ................ 6%
- Other .......................................... 21%

**Top Industries & Interest Groups**

Crop Production/Processing ...... $53,225
Agric Services/Products ............ $15,550
Oil & Gas .................................. $9,400
Telephone Utilities ...................... $7,000
Dairy ......................................... $6,800

Unidentified ............................... $4,850

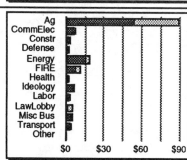

## 6. Richard H. Baker (R)

**1990 Committees: Banking  Sm Business**
**First elected: 1986**

1989-90 Total receipts: ........... $382,622
1990 Year-end cash: ................. $67,056

**Source of Funds**
- PACs ........................................... 40%
- Lg Individuals ($200+) ............... 33%
- Individuals under $200 ................ 24%
- Other .......................................... 3%

**Top Industries & Interest Groups**

Commercial Banks .................... $36,600
Lawyers & Lobbyists ................. $25,400
Insurance ................................ $17,529
Oil & Gas ................................ $13,300
Health Professionals ................. $13,000

Unidentified ............................. $25,500

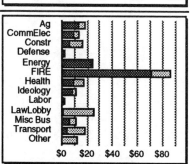

PACs  Indivs ($200+)

## 7. Jimmy Hayes (D)

**1990 Committees: Public Works  Science**
**First elected: 1986**

1989-90 Total receipts: ............$458,945
1990 Year-end cash: ................$48,849

**Source of Funds**
| | | |
|---|---|---|
| ■ PACs | ............... | 65% |
| ▨ Lg Individuals ($200+) | .............. | 26% |
| ☐ Individuals under $200 | ............... | 9% |
| ▨ Other | ............................. | 0% |

**Top  Industries & Interest Groups**

Lawyers & Lobbyists .................$36,050
Oil & Gas .................................$32,050
Air Transport ............................$19,450
Transportation Unions ..............$18,100
Bldg/Indust/Misc Unions ...........$17,950

Unidentified ...............................$16,300

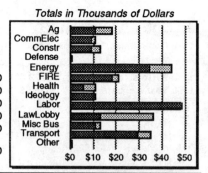

## 8. Clyde C. Holloway (R)

**1990 Committees: Agriculture  Sm Business**
**First elected: 1986**

1989-90 Total receipts: ............$383,701
1990 Year-end cash: ................$62,110

**Source of Funds**
| | | |
|---|---|---|
| ■ PACs | ............................. | 38% |
| ▨ Lg Individuals ($200+) | .............. | 32% |
| ☐ Individuals under $200 | .............. | 28% |
| ▨ Other | ............................. | 3% |

**Top  Industries & Interest Groups**

Crop Production/Processing ......$58,300
Oil & Gas .................................$18,350
Health Professionals .................$17,512
Agric Services/Products ...........$17,200
Lawyers & Lobbyists .................$10,275

Unidentified ...............................$13,475

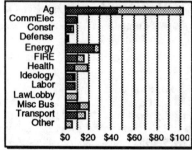

▨ PACs  ▨ Indivs ($200+)

Key to committee & category abbreviations is on page 173

# Maine

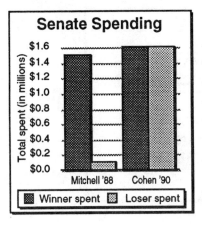

## Senate Spending

Total spent (in millions)

$1.6
$1.4
$1.2
$1.0
$0.8
$0.6
$0.4
$0.2
$0.0

Mitchell '88    Cohen '90

■ Winner spent    ▨ Loser spent

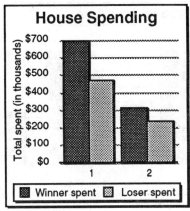

## House Spending

Total spent (in thousands)

$700
$600
$500
$400
$300
$200
$100
$0

1    2

■ Winner spent    ▨ Loser spent

### 1990 Elections at a Glance

| Dist | Name | Party | Vote Pct | Race Type |
|------|------|-------|----------|-----------|
| Sen | William S. Cohen (1990) | Rep | 61% | Reelected |
| Sen | George J. Mitchell (1988) | Dem | 81% | Reelected |
| 1 | Thomas H. Andrews | Dem | 60% | Open Seat |
| 2 | Olympia J. Snowe | Rep | 51% | Reelected |

*Totals in Thousands of Dollars*

## Sen. William S. Cohen (R)

**1990 Committees: Armed Services  Govt Affairs**
**First elected: 1978**

1985-90 Total Rcpts: ............$1,511,559
1990 Year-end cash: .................$30,738

**Source of Funds**
■ PACs .........................................34%
▨ Lg Individuals ($200+) ...............33%
□ Individuals under $200 ...............15%
▨ Other .........................................17%

### 1985-90
**Top Industries & Interest Groups**

Pro-Israel ...................................$114,950
Securities & Investment .............$72,900
Lawyers & Lobbyists ...................$61,200
Real Estate ................................$58,600
Health Professionals ..................$52,950

Unidentified ...............................$86,991

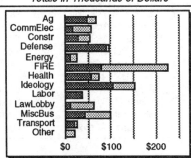

## Sen. George J. Mitchell (D)

**1990 Committees: Envir  Finance  VetAff/Majority Leader**
**First elected: 1982 (Appointed 1980)**

1985-90 Total Rcpts: ............$1,931,588
1990 Year-end cash: ...............$493,401

**Source of Funds**
■ PACs .........................................39%
▨ Lg Individuals ($200+) ...............31%
□ Individuals under $200 ...............20%
▨ Other .........................................11%

### 1985-90 (PACs only)
**Top Industries & Interest Groups**

Insurance ...................................$98,124
Bldg/Indust/Misc Unions ...........$65,500
Pro-Israel ...................................$61,000
Health Professionals ..................$54,009
Transportation Unions ...............$41,000

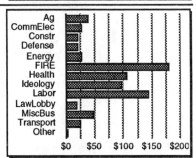

## 1.  Thomas H. Andrews (D)

**1991-92 Committees: Armed Services  Sm Business**
**First elected: 1990**

1989-90 Total receipts: ............$697,604
1990 Year-end cash: ...................$4,437

**Source of Funds**
■ PACs .........................................31%
▨ Lg Individuals ($200+) ...............34%
□ Individuals under $200 ...............21%
▨ Other .........................................14%

**Top Industries & Interest Groups**

Bldg/Indust/Misc Unions ...........$65,700
Public Sector Unions .................$40,950
Lawyers & Lobbyists ...................$35,700
Democratic/Liberal ....................$24,215
Misc Issues ...............................$22,811

Unidentified ...............................$67,638

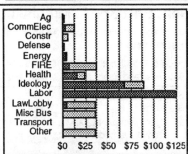

## 2.  Olympia J. Snowe (R)

**1990 Committees:  Foreign Affairs**
**First elected: 1978**

1989-90 Total receipts: ............$278,223
1990 Year-end cash: ...................$3,335

**Source of Funds**
■ PACs .........................................35%
▨ Lg Individuals ($200+) ...............24%
□ Individuals under $200 ...............33%
▨ Other ...........................................8%

**Top Industries & Interest Groups**

Forestry & Forest Products ........$13,000
Transportation Unions ...............$11,750
Insurance ...................................$10,850
Misc Manufacturing & Distrib .....$10,450
Lawyers & Lobbyists ....................$9,550

Unidentified ...............................$19,222

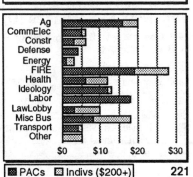

■ PACs    ▨ Indivs ($200+)

221

# Maryland

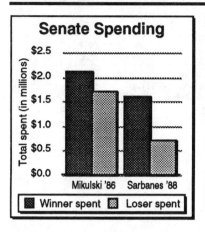

## Senate Spending

Total spent (in millions)

Mikulski '86    Sarbanes '88

■ Winner spent    ▨ Loser spent

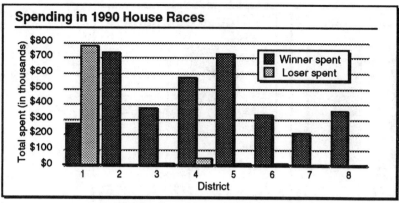

## Spending in 1990 House Races

Total spent (in thousands)

■ Winner spent
▨ Loser spent

District

### 1990 Elections at a Glance

| Dist | Name | Party | Vote Pct | Race Type |
|------|------|-------|----------|-----------|
| Sen | Barbara A. Mikulski (1986) | Dem | 61% | Open Seat |
| Sen | Paul S. Sarbanes (1988) | Dem | 62% | Reelected |
| 1 | Wayne T. Gilchrest | Rep | 57% | Beat Incumb |
| 2 | Helen Delich Bentley | Rep | 74% | Reelected |
| 3 | Benjamin L. Cardin | Dem | 70% | Reelected |
| 4 | Tom McMillen | Dem | 59% | Reelected |
| 5 | Steny H. Hoyer | Dem | 81% | Reelected |
| 6 | Beverly B. Byron | Dem | 65% | Reelected |
| 7 | Kweisi Mfume | Dem | 85% | Reelected |
| 8 | Constance A. Morella | Rep | 74% | Reelected |

*Totals in Thousands of Dollars*

## Sen. Barbara A. Mikulski (D)

**1990 Committees: Appropriations Labor SmBus**
**First elected: 1986**

1985-90 Total Rcpts: ............$3,010,494
1990 Year-end cash: ..............$490,202

**Source of Funds**
| | |
|---|---|
| ■ PACs | 27% |
| ▨ Lg Individuals ($200+) | 16% |
| □ Individuals under $200 | 41% |
| ▨ Other | 16% |

**1985-90 (PACs only)**
**Top Industries & Interest Groups**

Bldg/Indust/Misc Unions ..........$182,229
Transportation Unions ...............$90,403
Public Sector Unions .................$73,780
Health Professionals ..................$44,970
Human Rights ............................$40,007

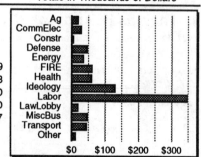

## Sen. Paul S. Sarbanes (D)

**1990 Committees: Banking Foreign Relations**
**First elected: 1976**

1985-90 Total Rcpts: ............$1,544,409
1990 Year-end cash: ..................$2,283

**Source of Funds**
| | |
|---|---|
| ■ PACs | 39% |
| ▨ Lg Individuals ($200+) | 32% |
| □ Individuals under $200 | 23% |
| ▨ Other | 6% |

**1985-90 (PACs only)**
**Top Industries & Interest Groups**

Bldg/Indust/Misc Unions ..........$126,825
Transportation Unions ...............$84,000
Public Sector Unions .................$74,950
Pro-Israel .................................$37,000
Securities & Investment ............$30,500

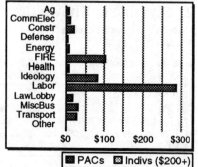

■ PACs    ▨ Indivs ($200+)

Key to committee & category abbreviations is on page 173

# 1. Wayne T. Gilchrest (R)

**1991-92 Committees:** Merchant Marine  Science
**First elected:** 1990

1989-90 Total receipts: ............$266,930
1990 Year-end cash: ..................$2,856

### Source of Funds

- ■ PACs ........................................ 24%
- ▨ Lg Individuals ($200+) .............. 24%
- □ Individuals under $200 ............. 24%
- ▨ Other ..................................... 29%

**Top Industries & Interest Groups**

Retired ..............................................$28,777
Leadership PACs ........................$12,350
Health Professionals ...................$8,850
Misc Manufacturing & Distrib .......$8,700
Insurance ....................................$7,000

Unidentified ................................$9,966

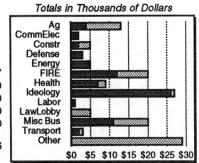

# 2. Helen Delich Bentley (R)

**1990 Committees:** Budget  Merchant Marine
**First elected:** 1984

1989-90 Total receipts: ............$834,214
1990 Year-end cash: ..............$131,837

### Source of Funds

- ■ PACs............................................ 27%
- ▨ Lg Individuals ($200+) .............. 40%
- □ Individuals under $200 ............. 29%
- ▨ Other ........................................ 4%

**Top Industries & Interest Groups**

Transportation Unions ...............$41,300
Sea Transport ............................$38,000
Oil & Gas ..................................$28,800
Lawyers & Lobbyists ..................$23,725
Real Estate ...............................$22,990

Unidentified .............................$129,232

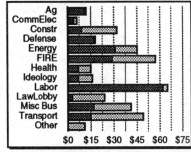

# 3. Benjamin L. Cardin (D)

**1990 Committees:** Ways & Means
**First elected:** 1986

1989-90 Total receipts: ............$532,752
1990 Year-end cash: ..............$250,724

### Source of Funds

- ■ PACs............................................ 57%
- ▨ Lg Individuals ($200+) .............. 28%
- □ Individuals under $200 ...............7%
- ▨ Other ........................................ 8%

**Top Industries & Interest Groups**

Insurance ....................................$43,200
Health Professionals ..................$37,150
Pro-Israel ..................................$29,550
Lawyers & Lobbyists ..................$28,210
Bldg/Indust/Misc Unions ...........$27,018

Unidentified ...............................$38,450

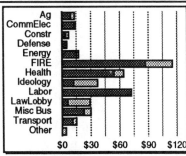

# 4. Tom McMillen (D)

**1990 Committees:** Energy & Commerce  Science
**First elected:** 1986

1989-90 Total receipts: ............$757,145
1990 Year-end cash: ..............$328,285

### Source of Funds

- ■ PACs............................................ 52%
- ▨ Lg Individuals ($200+) .............. 28%
- □ Individuals under $200 ............. 11%
- ▨ Other ...................................... 10%

**Top Industries & Interest Groups**

Lawyers & Lobbyists ..................$55,650
Commercial Banks ....................$37,700
Real Estate ...............................$36,500
Bldg/Indust/Misc Unions ...........$35,025
Transportation Unions ...............$32,100

Unidentified ...............................$61,925

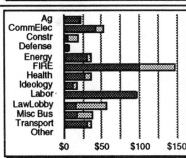

# 5. Steny H. Hoyer (D)

**1990 Committees:** Appropriations
**First elected:** 1981

1989-90 Total receipts: ............$725,418
1990 Year-end cash: ..............$321,405

### Source of Funds

- ■ PACs............................................ 57%
- ▨ Lg Individuals ($200+) .............. 26%
- □ Individuals under $200 ...............9%
- ▨ Other ........................................ 8%

**Top Industries & Interest Groups**

Lawyers & Lobbyists ..................$63,090
Public Sector Unions ................$52,605
Health Professionals ..................$46,750
Bldg/Indust/Misc Unions ...........$35,440
Real Estate ...............................$29,700

Unidentified ................................$43,715

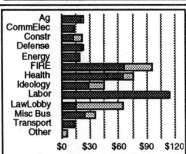

# 6. Beverly B. Byron (D)

**1990 Committees:** Armed Services  Interior
**First elected:** 1978

1989-90 Total receipts: ............$282,677
1990 Year-end cash: ................$33,737

### Source of Funds
- ■ PACs............................................ 59%
- ▨ Lg Individuals ($200+) ...............9%
- □ Individuals under $200 ............. 29%
- ▨ Other ........................................ 3%

**Top Industries & Interest Groups**

Defense Aerospace ...................$33,380
Defense Electronics ..................$15,500
Health Professionals ..................$15,250
Lawyers & Lobbyists ...................$7,900
Real Estate ..................................$7,750

Unidentified ..................................$4,200

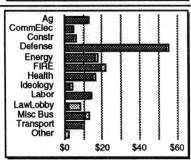

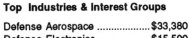
■ PACs  ▨ Indivs ($200+)

223

# 7. Kweisi Mfume (D)

**1990 Committees: Banking Educ/Labor Sm Business**
**First elected: 1986**

1989-90 Total receipts: ...........$224,826
1990 Year-end cash: ................$84,387

**Source of Funds**
- PACs .......................................56%
- Lg Individuals ($200+) .............27%
- Individuals under $200 ..............11%
- Other .......................................6%

**Top Industries & Interest Groups**

Bldg/Indust/Misc Unions ...........$19,280
Commercial Banks ....................$18,570
Real Estate .................................$15,800
Public Sector Unions .................$15,300
Pro-Israel ..................................$14,733

Unidentified ...............................$15,293

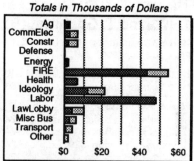

# 8. Constance A. Morella (R)

**1990 Committees: Post Office Science**
**First elected: 1986**

1989-90 Total receipts: ............$542,961
1990 Year-end cash: ...............$201,384

**Source of Funds**
- PACs ........................................43%
- Lg Individuals ($200+) ..............24%
- Individuals under $200 ..............29%
- Other .........................................4%

**Top Industries & Interest Groups**

Public Sector Unions .................$51,200
Health Professionals ..................$26,975
Real Estate .................................$20,750
Lawyers & Lobbyists .................$20,315
Human Rights ............................$14,073

Unidentified ...............................$33,235

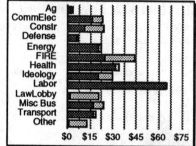

■ PACs ▨ Indivs ($200+)

Key to committee & category abbreviations is on page 173

# Massachusetts

## Senate Spending

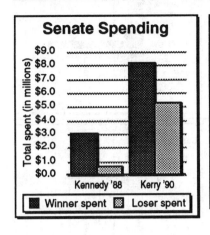

Total spent (in millions)

- Winner spent
- Loser spent

## Spending in 1990 House Races

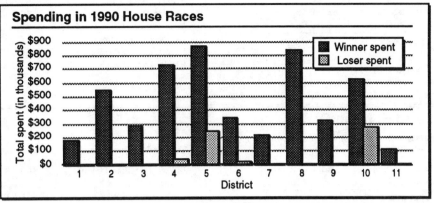

Total spent (in thousands)

- Winner spent
- Loser spent

District

## 1990 Elections at a Glance

| Dist | Name | Party | Vote Pct | Race Type |
|------|------|-------|----------|-----------|
| Sen | Edward M. Kennedy (1988) | Dem | 65% | Reelected |
| Sen | John Kerry (1990) | Dem | 57% | Reelected |
| 1 | Silvio O. Conte | Rep | 78% | Reelected |
| 2 | Richard E. Neal | Dem | 100% | Reelected |
| 3 | Joseph D. Early | Dem | 99% | Reelected |
| 4 | Barney Frank | Dem | 66% | Reelected |
| 5 | Chester G. Atkins | Dem | 52% | Reelected |
| 6 | Nicholas Mavroules | Dem | 65% | Reelected |
| 7 | Edward J. Markey | Dem | 100% | Reelected |
| 8 | Joseph P. Kennedy II | Dem | 72% | Reelected |
| 9 | Joe Moakley | Dem | 70% | Reelected |
| 10 | Gerry E. Studds | Dem | 53% | Reelected |
| 11 | Brian Donnelly | Dem | 100% | Reelected |

*Totals in Thousands of Dollars*

## Sen. Edward M. Kennedy (D)

**1990 Committees: Armed Services Judiciary Labor**
**First elected: 1962**

1985-90 Total Rcpts: ............$3,624,800
1990 Year-end cash: ..............$453,288

**Source of Funds**
- PACs.........................................10%
- Lg Individuals ($200+) ...............59%
- Individuals under $200 ..............26%
- Other .........................................5%

### 1985-90 (PACs only)
**Top Industries & Interest Groups**

Bldg/Indust/Misc Unions ............$76,000
Transportation Unions ...............$28,000
Public Sector Unions .................$27,500
Pro-Israel ...................................$22,000
Health Professionals ..................$19,500

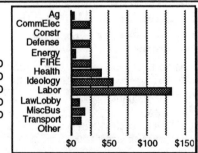

## Sen. John Kerry (D)

**1990 Committees: Banking Commerce ForRel SmBus**
**First elected: 1984**

1985-90 Total Rcpts: ............$8,041,413
1990 Year-end cash: .................$12,055

**Source of Funds**
- PACs...........................................0%
- Lg Individuals ($200+) ...............53%
- Individuals under $200 ..............35%
- Other .........................................12%

### 1985-90
**Top Industries & Interest Groups**

Lawyers & Lobbyists................$573,732
Real Estate ..............................$295,072
Securities & Investment...........$190,742
TV & Movies ............................$153,450
Pro-Israel ................................$110,295

Unidentified ..............................$865,766

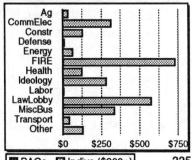

- PACs
- Indivs ($200+)

225

# 1. Silvio O. Conte (R)

**1990 Committees: Appropriations  Sm Business**
**First elected: 1958**

1989-90 Total receipts: ............$146,537
1990 Year-end cash: ...............$258,037

**Source of Funds**
- ■ PACs.............................................44%
- ▨ Lg Individuals ($200+) ...............4%
- ☐ Individuals under $200 ...........17%
- ▧ Other...........................................35%

### Top  Industries & Interest Groups

Transportation Unions ................$8,500
Public Sector Unions ...................$7,500
Human Rights .............................$6,000
Misc Issues ................................$5,100
General Contractors ...................$5,000
Lawyers & Lobbyists ..................$5,000
Pro-Israel ...................................$5,000

Unidentified.................................$2,500

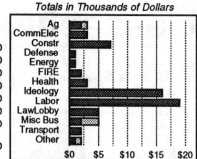

# 2. Richard E. Neal (D)

**1990 Committees: Banking  Sm Business**
**First elected: 1988**

1989-90 Total receipts: ............$462,672
1990 Year-end cash: .................$12,496

**Source of Funds**
- ■ PACs.............................................52%
- ▨ Lg Individuals ($200+) .............17%
- ☐ Individuals under $200 ...........15%
- ▧ Other...........................................15%

### Top  Industries & Interest Groups

Bldg/Indust/Misc Unions ............$68,150
Insurance ...................................$38,099
Commercial Banks ....................$25,550
Public Sector Unions ................$23,000
Lawyers & Lobbyists .................$18,100

Unidentified.................................$29,520

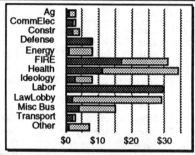

# 3. Joseph D. Early (D)

**1990 Committees: Appropriations**
**First elected: 1974**

1989-90 Total receipts: ............$281,707
1990 Year-end cash: ...............$111,190

**Source of Funds**
- ■ PACs.............................................29%
- ▨ Lg Individuals ($200+) .............43%
- ☐ Individuals under $200 ...........26%
- ▧ Other.............................................2%

### Top  Industries & Interest Groups

Lawyers & Lobbyists ..................$29,100
Health Professionals .................$15,750
Insurance ...................................$14,750
Hospitals/Nursing Homes .........$12,300
Bldg/Indust/Misc Unions ...........$11,400

Unidentified.................................$25,200

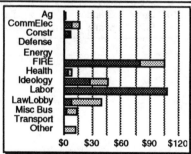

# 4. Barney Frank (D)

**1990 Committees: Banking  Govt Ops  Judiciary**
**First elected: 1980**

1989-90 Total receipts: ............$643,920
1990 Year-end cash: .................$53,329

**Source of Funds**
- ■ PACs.............................................38%
- ▨ Lg Individuals ($200+) .............22%
- ☐ Individuals under $200 ...........40%
- ▧ Other...............................................0%

### Top  Industries & Interest Groups

Bldg/Indust/Misc Unions ............$58,650
Commercial Banks ....................$50,250
Lawyers & Lobbyists ..................$38,700
Public Sector Unions ................$34,100
Real Estate ................................$26,392

Unidentified.................................$28,215

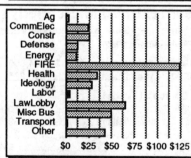

# 5. Chester G. Atkins (D)

**1990 Committees: Appropriations**
**First elected: 1984**

1989-90 Total receipts: ............$843,893
1990 Year-end cash: ...................$2,449

**Source of Funds**
- ■ PACs...............................................1%
- ▨ Lg Individuals ($200+) .............67%
- ☐ Individuals under $200 ...........31%
- ▧ Other...............................................1%

### Top  Industries & Interest Groups

Real Estate ................................$70,136
Lawyers & Lobbyists ..................$65,271
Securities & Investment ............$29,950
Education ....................................$23,075
Business Services ....................$18,075

Unidentified...............................$142,078

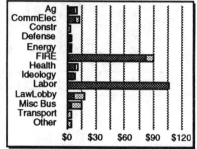

# 6. Nicholas Mavroules (D)

**1990 Committees: Armed Services  Sm Business**
**First elected: 1978**

1989-90 Total receipts: ............$289,794
1990 Year-end cash: .................$61,574

**Source of Funds**
- ■ PACs.............................................43%
- ▨ Lg Individuals ($200+) .............25%
- ☐ Individuals under $200 ...........32%
- ▧ Other...............................................0%

### Top  Industries & Interest Groups

Bldg/Indust/Misc Unions ...........$24,324
Transportation Unions ...............$19,440
Public Sector Unions .................$15,650
Defense Electronics...................$11,900
Lawyers & Lobbyists ...................$8,550

Unidentified.................................$19,700

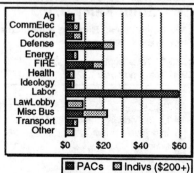

Key to committee & category abbreviations is on page 173

**■ PACs   ▨ Indivs ($200+)**

## 7. Edward J. Markey (D)

**1990 Committees:** Energy & Commerce  Interior
**First elected:** 1976

1989-90 Total receipts: ............$336,209
1990 Year-end cash: ..............$579,994

**Source of Funds**
■ PACs ................................................2%
▨ Lg Individuals ($200+) ............61%
□ Individuals under $200 .............16%
▨ Other .............................................22%

**Top Industries & Interest Groups**

Lawyers & Lobbyists ..................$64,100
TV & Movies ...............................$28,250
Cable TV .....................................$19,750
Telephone Utilities .....................$13,600
Securities & Investment ............$10,000

Unidentified ................................$21,950

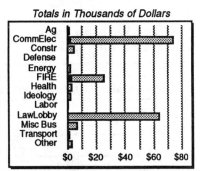

## 8. Joseph P. Kennedy II (D)

**1990 Committees:** Banking  Vet Affairs
**First elected:** 1986

1989-90 Total receipts: ............$805,013
1990 Year-end cash: ...............$227,284

**Source of Funds**
■ PACs ..............................................16%
▨ Lg Individuals ($200+) .............62%
□ Individuals under $200 ..............16%
▨ Other ...............................................6%

**Top Industries & Interest Groups**

Securities & Investment .............$54,075
Real Estate .................................$48,200
Lawyers & Lobbyists ..................$47,997
Bldg/Indust/Misc Unions ............$29,850
Business Services .....................$22,300

Unidentified .............................$126,339

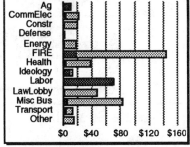

## 9. Joe Moakley (D)

**1990 Committees:** Rules
**First elected:** 1972

1989-90 Total receipts: ............$517,858
1990 Year-end cash: ...............$489,816

**Source of Funds**
■ PACs .............................................54%
▨ Lg Individuals ($200+) ..............15%
□ Individuals under $200 ..............21%
▨ Other .............................................11%

**Top Industries & Interest Groups**

Lawyers & Lobbyists .................$34,799
Bldg/Indust/Misc Unions ...........$34,458
Insurance ...................................$32,900
Transportation Unions ..............$26,800
Commercial Banks ....................$18,850
Public Sector Unions ................$18,850

Unidentified ................................$9,000

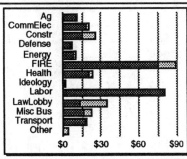

## 10. Gerry E. Studds (D)

**1990 Committees:** Foreign Affairs  Merchant Marine
**First elected:** 1972

1989-90 Total receipts: ............$600,325
1990 Year-end cash: .................$21,912

**Source of Funds**
■ PACs .............................................34%
▨ Lg Individuals ($200+) ..............16%
□ Individuals under $200 ..............36%
▨ Other .............................................14%

**Top Industries & Interest Groups**

Bldg/Indust/Misc Unions ............$64,400
Public Sector Unions .................$36,300
Transportation Unions ..............$31,750
Lawyers & Lobbyists ..................$19,860
Human Rights ............................$19,400

Unidentified .............................$26,500

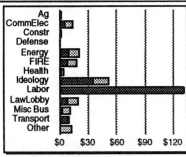

## 11. Brian Donnelly (D)

**1990 Committees:** Ways & Means
**First elected:** 1978

1989-90 Total receipts: ............$303,943
1990 Year-end cash: ..............$669,414

**Source of Funds**
■ PACs .............................................56%
▨ Lg Individuals ($200+) ................7%
□ Individuals under $200 ................8%
▨ Other .............................................29%

**Top Industries & Interest Groups**

Insurance ...................................$37,500
Public Sector Unions .................$16,250
Bldg/Indust/Misc Unions ...........$15,450
Transportation Unions ..............$13,000
Lawyers & Lobbyists ..................$11,550

Unidentified ................................$3,500

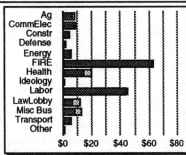

▨ PACs  ▨ Indivs ($200+)

227

# Michigan

## Spending in 1990 House Races

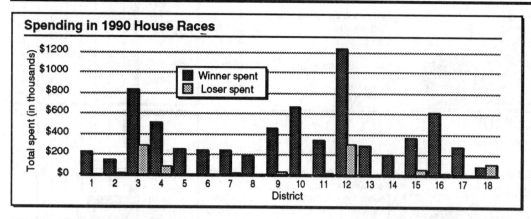

Total spent (in thousands)

$1200
$1000
$800
$600
$400
$200
$0

■ Winner spent
▨ Loser spent

District: 1 2 3 4 5 6 7 8 9 10 11 12 13 14 15 16 17 18

## Senate Spending

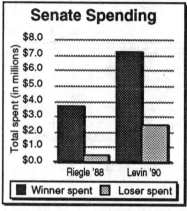

Total spent (in millions)

$8.0
$7.0
$6.0
$5.0
$4.0
$3.0
$2.0
$1.0
$0.0

Riegle '88    Levin '90

■ Winner spent    ▨ Loser spent

## 1990 Elections at a Glance

| Dist | Name | Party | Vote Pct | Race Type |
|------|------|-------|----------|-----------|
| Sen | Carl Levin (1990) | Dem | 58% | Reelected |
| Sen | Donald W. Riegle Jr. (1988) | Dem | 60% | Reelected |
| 1 | John Conyers Jr. | Dem | 89% | Reelected |
| 2 | Carl D. Pursell | Rep | 64% | Reelected |
| 3 | Howard Wolpe | Dem | 58% | Reelected |
| 4 | Fred Upton | Rep | 58% | Reelected |
| 5 | Paul B. Henry | Rep | 75% | Reelected |
| 6 | Bob Carr | Dem | 100% | Reelected |
| 7 | Dale E. Kildee | Dem | 68% | Reelected |
| 8 | Bob Traxler | Dem | 69% | Reelected |
| 9 | Guy Vander Jagt | Rep | 55% | Reelected |
| 10 | Dave Camp | Rep | 65% | Open Seat |
| 11 | Robert W. Davis | Rep | 61% | Reelected |
| 12 | David E. Bonior | Dem | 65% | Reelected |
| 13 | Barbara-Rose Collins | Dem | 80% | Open Seat |
| 14 | Dennis M. Hertel | Dem | 64% | Reelected |
| 15 | William D. Ford | Dem | 61% | Reelected |
| 16 | John D. Dingell | Dem | 67% | Reelected |
| 17 | Sander M. Levin | Dem | 70% | Reelected |
| 18 | William S. Broomfield | Rep | 66% | Reelected |

*Totals in Thousands of Dollars*

## Sen. Carl Levin (D)

**1990 Committees: Armed Services Gov Affairs SmBus**
**First elected: 1978**

1985-90 Total Rcpts: ............$7,228,954
1990 Year-end cash: ..............$201,966

**Source of Funds**
■ PACs ..........................................18%
▨ Lg Individuals ($200+) ..............40%
□ Individuals under $200 ..............30%
▨ Other ........................................12%

### 1985-90
**Top Industries & Interest Groups**

Pro-Israel ................................$570,103
Lawyers & Lobbyists ...............$509,808
Real Estate ...............................$295,800
Bldg/Indust/Misc Unions .........$209,740
Democratic/Liberal ..................$127,580

Unidentified ............................$606,038

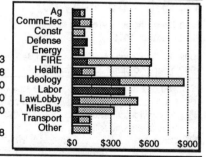

Ag
CommElec
Constr
Defense
Energy
FIRE
Health
Ideology
Labor
LawLobby
MiscBus
Transport
Other

$0    $300    $600    $900

## Sen. Donald W. Riegle Jr. (D)

**1990 Committees: Banking Budget Finance**
**First elected: 1976**

1985-90 Total Rcpts: ............$4,196,439
1990 Year-end cash: ..............$626,188

**Source of Funds**
■ PACs ..........................................37%
▨ Lg Individuals ($200+) ..............34%
□ Individuals under $200 ..............15%
▨ Other ........................................14%

### 1985-90 (PACs only)
**Top Industries & Interest Groups**

Securities & Investment ..........$148,462
Bldg/Indust/Misc Unions .........$143,800
Insurance .................................$138,700
Commercial Banks ..................$113,975
Transportation Unions ..............$69,500

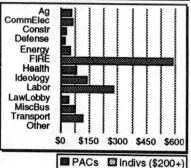

Ag
CommElec
Constr
Defense
Energy
FIRE
Health
Ideology
Labor
LawLobby
MiscBus
Transport
Other

$0    $150    $300    $450    $600

■ PACs    ▨ Indivs ($200+)

Key to committee & category abbreviations is on page 173

# 1. John Conyers Jr. (D)

**1990 Committees:** Govt Ops  Judiciary  Sm Business
**First elected:** 1964

1989-90 Total receipts: ............$385,337
1990 Year-end cash: .................$38,192

**Source of Funds**
- ■ PACs ...........................................62%
- ▨ Lg Individuals ($200+) ............24%
- □ Individuals under $200 ............12%
- ⊠ Other ...........................................2%

**Top Industries & Interest Groups**

Bldg/Indust/Misc Unions ............$34,730
Transportation Unions ...............$32,050
Public Sector Unions .................$30,638
Lawyers & Lobbyists ..................$26,964
Defense Aerospace ...................$12,500

Unidentified ...............................$37,650

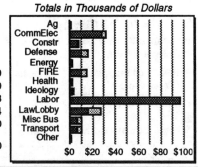

# 2. Carl D. Pursell (R)

**1990 Committees:** Appropriations
**First elected:** 1976

1989-90 Total receipts: ............$285,808
1990 Year-end cash: ..............$240,044

**Source of Funds**
- ■ PACs ...........................................34%
- ▨ Lg Individuals ($200+) .............16%
- □ Individuals under $200 ............41%
- ⊠ Other ...........................................9%

**Top Industries & Interest Groups**

Health Professionals .................$22,450
Electric Utilities ...........................$9,565
Misc Manufacturing & Distrib .......$7,350
Real Estate ..................................$5,600
Oil & Gas .....................................$4,850

Unidentified ...............................$11,450

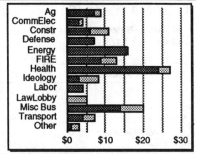

# 3. Howard Wolpe (D)

**1990 Committees:** Foreign Affairs  Science
**First elected:** 1978

1989-90 Total receipts: ............$791,685
1990 Year-end cash: .................$59,327

**Source of Funds**
- ■ PACs ...........................................49%
- ▨ Lg Individuals ($200+) .............14%
- □ Individuals under $200 ............24%
- ⊠ Other .........................................13%

**Top Industries & Interest Groups**

Bldg/Indust/Misc Unions ...........$119,325
Public Sector Unions .................$52,000
Pro-Israel ....................................$49,050
Transportation Unions ...............$41,450
Leadership PACs .......................$29,750

Unidentified ...............................$21,050

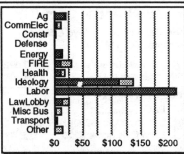

# 4. Fred Upton (R)

**1990 Committees:** Public Works  Sm Business
**First elected:** 1986

1989-90 Total receipts: ............$445,881
1990 Year-end cash: .................$42,144

**Source of Funds**
- ■ PACs ...........................................34%
- ▨ Lg Individuals ($200+) .............34%
- □ Individuals under $200 ............28%
- ⊠ Other ...........................................4%

**Top Industries & Interest Groups**

Health Professionals .................$22,500
Misc Manufacturing & Distrib .....$18,490
Automotive .................................$13,850
Air Transport .............................$12,950
Retired ........................................$12,700

Unidentified ...............................$45,675

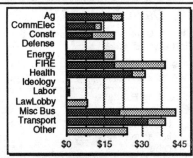

# 5. Paul B. Henry (R)

**1990 Committees:** Educ/Labor  Science
**First elected:** 1984

1989-90 Total receipts: ............$398,627
1990 Year-end cash: ..............$275,521

**Source of Funds**
- ■ PACs ...........................................22%
- ▨ Lg Individuals ($200+) .............31%
- □ Individuals under $200 ............39%
- ⊠ Other ...........................................7%

**Top Industries & Interest Groups**

Health Professionals .................$18,875
Insurance ...................................$17,775
Misc Manufacturing & Distrib .....$17,550
Lawyers & Lobbyists ..................$12,334
General Contractors ..................$11,100

Unidentified ...............................$27,700

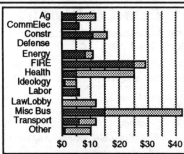

# 6. Bob Carr (D)

**1990 Committees:** Appropriations
**First elected:** 1974

1989-90 Total receipts: ............$397,155
1990 Year-end cash: ..............$256,626

**Source of Funds**
- ■ PACs ...........................................52%
- ▨ Lg Individuals ($200+) .............23%
- □ Individuals under $200 ............15%
- ⊠ Other .........................................10%

**Top Industries & Interest Groups**

Air Transport .............................$28,450
Lawyers & Lobbyists ..................$20,825
Transportation Unions ...............$16,900
Defense Aerospace ...................$15,300
Health Professionals .................$15,300

Unidentified ...............................$26,133

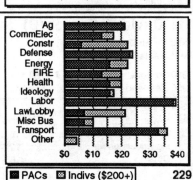

■ PACs  ⊠ Indivs ($200+)

229

## 7. Dale E. Kildee (D)

**1990 Committees:** Budget  Educ/Labor
**First elected:** 1976

1989-90 Total receipts: ............$259,480
1990 Year-end cash: ................$39,580

**Source of Funds**
PACs ...............................................71%
Lg Individuals ($200+) ...............4%
Individuals under $200 ..............21%
Other .................................................3%

**Top Industries & Interest Groups**

Bldg/Indust/Misc Unions ............$50,747
Public Sector Unions ................$48,399
Transportation Unions .............$23,050
Human Rights .........................$13,500
Lawyers & Lobbyists ...................$7,552

Unidentified .................................$4,100

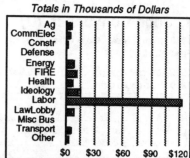

## 8. Bob Traxler (D)

**1990 Committees:** Appropriations
**First elected:** 1974

1989-90 Total receipts: ............$297,221
1990 Year-end cash: ...............$360,148

**Source of Funds**
PACs ...............................................62%
Lg Individuals ($200+) ................8%
Individuals under $200 ..............17%
Other ..............................................13%

**Top Industries & Interest Groups**

Bldg/Indust/Misc Unions ............$22,640
Defense Aerospace ...................$20,950
Public Sector Unions ................$20,930
Transportation Unions ..............$15,500
Dairy ....................................$13,720

Unidentified .................................$4,960

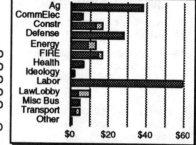

## 9. Guy Vander Jagt (R)

**1990 Committees:** Ways & Means
**First elected:** 1966

1989-90 Total receipts: ............$448,892
1990 Year-end cash: ...............$104,106

**Source of Funds**
PACs ...............................................61%
Lg Individuals ($200+) ................6%
Individuals under $200 ..............33%
Other .................................................0%

**Top Industries & Interest Groups**

Insurance .....................................$31,490
Health Professionals .................$22,150
Transportation Unions ..............$17,900
Beer, Wine & Liquor .................$15,400
Automotive ................................$14,950

Unidentified .................................$3,220

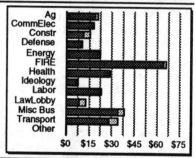

## 10. Dave Camp (R)

**1991-92 Committees:** Agriculture  Sm Business
**First elected:** 1990

1989-90 Total receipts: ............$667,713
1990 Year-end cash: .................$10,483

**Source of Funds**
PACs ...............................................26%
Lg Individuals ($200+) ..............38%
Individuals under $200 ..............16%
Other ..............................................20%

**Top Industries & Interest Groups**

Chemicals ..................................$102,050
Retired ........................................$37,930
Health Professionals .................$25,350
Oil & Gas ....................................$14,150
Lawyers & Lobbyists .................$13,600

Unidentified .................................$46,634

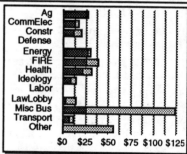

## 11. Robert W. Davis (R)

**1990 Committees:** Armed Services  Merchant Marine
**First elected:** 1978

1989-90 Total receipts: ............$340,079
1990 Year-end cash: ...............$114,637

**Source of Funds**
PACs ...............................................72%
Lg Individuals ($200+) ................9%
Individuals under $200 ..............14%
Other .................................................5%

**Top Industries & Interest Groups**

Defense Aerospace ...................$39,850
Transportation Unions ..............$35,200
Bldg/Indust/Misc Unions ...........$27,700
Defense Electronics ..................$27,675
Public Sector Unions ................$19,900

Unidentified .................................$5,600

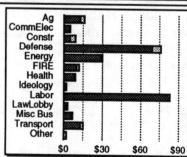

## 12. David E. Bonior (D)

**1990 Committees:** Rules
**First elected:** 1976

1989-90 Total receipts: .........$1,189,127
1990 Year-end cash: .................$89,849

**Source of Funds**
PACs ...............................................56%
Lg Individuals ($200+) ..............16%
Individuals under $200 ..............12%
Other ..............................................16%

**Top Industries & Interest Groups**

Bldg/Indust/Misc Unions .........$131,355
Public Sector Unions ................$68,020
Lawyers & Lobbyists ................$63,900
Transportation Unions ............$58,255
Insurance ...................................$45,363

Unidentified ...............................$27,740

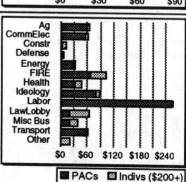

230

 PACs   Indivs ($200+)

## 13. Barbara-Rose Collins (D)

**1991-92 Committees:** Public Works  Science
**First elected:** 1990

1989-90 Total receipts: ............\$335,736
1990 Year-end cash: ...............\$61,044

**Source of Funds**
- ■ PACs ....................................... 19%
- ▨ Lg Individuals (\$200+) .............. 24%
- □ Individuals under \$200 ............. 16%
- ▩ Other ..................................... 41%

**Top Industries & Interest Groups**

Bldg/Indust/Misc Unions ............\$19,500
Public Sector Unions ..................\$12,000
General Contractors ....................\$6,050
Waste Management ....................\$5,900
Business Services ........................\$4,250
Automotive ................................\$4,250
Pro-Israel ..................................\$4,250

Unidentified ..............................\$28,385

*Totals in Thousands of Dollars*

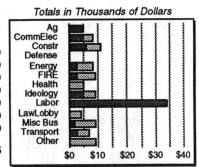

## 14. Dennis M. Hertel (D)

**1990 Committees:** Armed Services  Merchant Marine
**First elected:** 1980

1989-90 Total receipts: ............\$306,850
1990 Year-end cash: ...............\$281,310

**Source of Funds**
- ■ PACs ....................................... 60%
- ▨ Lg Individuals (\$200+) .............. 12%
- □ Individuals under \$200 ............. 18%
- ▩ Other ..................................... 10%

**Top Industries & Interest Groups**

Bldg/Indust/Misc Unions ............\$47,260
Public Sector Unions ................\$29,435
Transportation Unions ..............\$29,400
Defense Aerospace ..................\$23,495
Lawyers & Lobbyists ..................\$19,460

Unidentified ................................\$8,160

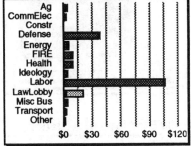

## 15. William D. Ford (D)

**1990 Committees:** Educ/Labor  Post Office
**First elected:** 1964

1989-90 Total receipts: ............\$390,216
1990 Year-end cash: ...............\$186,613

**Source of Funds**
- ■ PACs ....................................... 68%
- ▨ Lg Individuals (\$200+) .............. 8%
- □ Individuals under \$200 ............. 9%
- ▩ Other ..................................... 15%

**Top Industries & Interest Groups**

Public Sector Unions ................\$79,698
Bldg/Indust/Misc Unions ..........\$54,450
Transportation Unions ..............\$29,700
Lawyers & Lobbyists ..................\$20,450
Education ................................\$15,250

Unidentified ................................\$3,950

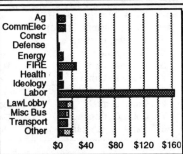

## 16. John D. Dingell (D)

**1990 Committees:** Energy & Commerce
**First elected:** 1955

1989-90 Total receipts: ............\$843,579
1990 Year-end cash: ...............\$491,371

**Source of Funds**
- ■ PACs ....................................... 74%
- ▨ Lg Individuals (\$200+) .............. 16%
- □ Individuals under \$200 ............. 5%
- ▩ Other ..................................... 6%

**Top Industries & Interest Groups**

Lawyers & Lobbyists ................\$73,163
Securities & Investment ............\$54,200
Oil & Gas ................................\$51,600
Insurance ................................\$39,000
TV & Movies ............................\$36,800

Unidentified ..............................\$18,200

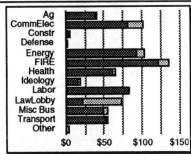

## 17. Sander M. Levin (D)

**1990 Committees:** Ways & Means
**First elected:** 1982

1989-90 Total receipts: ............\$356,280
1990 Year-end cash: ...............\$255,205

**Source of Funds**
- ■ PACs ....................................... 70%
- ▨ Lg Individuals (\$200+) .............. 12%
- □ Individuals under \$200 ............. 12%
- ▩ Other ..................................... 5%

**Top Industries & Interest Groups**

Bldg/Indust/Misc Unions ............\$39,050
Public Sector Unions ................\$36,025
Lawyers & Lobbyists ................\$24,471
Health Professionals ................\$21,000
Insurance ................................\$19,305

Unidentified ................................\$7,675

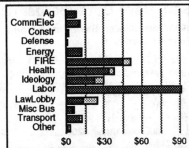

## 18. William S. Broomfield (R)

**1990 Committees:** Foreign Affairs  Sm Business
**First elected:** 1956

1989-90 Total receipts: ............\$243,762
1990 Year-end cash: ...............\$754,678

**Source of Funds**
- ■ PACs ....................................... 23%
- ▨ Lg Individuals (\$200+) .............. 17%
- □ Individuals under \$200 ............. 16%
- ▩ Other ..................................... 45%

**Top Industries & Interest Groups**

Pro-Israel ..................................\$7,750
Health Professionals ..................\$7,450
Food & Beverage ........................\$6,500
Telephone Utilities ......................\$6,000
Real Estate ................................\$5,750

Unidentified ..............................\$9,950

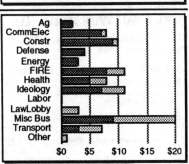

■ PACs  ▨ Indivs (\$200+)

# Minnesota

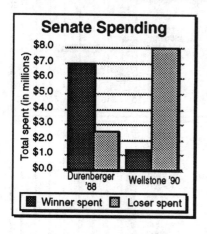

### Senate Spending

Total spent (in millions)

Durenberger '88   Wellstone '90

■ Winner spent   ▨ Loser spent

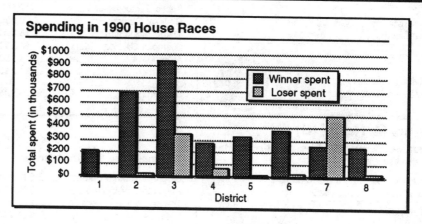

### Spending in 1990 House Races

Total spent (in thousands)

■ Winner spent
▨ Loser spent

District

## 1990 Elections at a Glance

| Dist | Name | Party | Vote Pct | Race Type |
|------|------|-------|----------|-----------|
| Sen | Dave Durenberger (1988) | Rep | 56% | Reelected |
| Sen | Paul Wellstone (1990) | Dem | 50% | Beat Incumb |
| 1 | Timothy J. Penny | Dem | 78% | Reelected |
| 2 | Vin Weber | Rep | 62% | Reelected |
| 3 | Jim Ramstad | Rep | 67% | Open Seat |
| 4 | Bruce F. Vento | Dem | 65% | Reelected |
| 5 | Martin Olav Sabo | Dem | 73% | Reelected |
| 6 | Gerry Sikorski | Dem | 65% | Reelected |
| 7 | Collin C. Peterson | Dem | 54% | Beat Incumb |
| 8 | James L. Oberstar | Dem | 73% | Reelected |

*Totals in Thousands of Dollars*

## Sen. Dave Durenberger (R)

**1990 Committees: Envir/Public Works  Finance  Labor**
**First elected: 1978**

1985-90 Total Rcpts: ............ $6,761,094
1990 Year-end cash: ................ $17,669

**Source of Funds**
■ PACs .................................................. 27%
▨ Lg Individuals ($200+) ................. 14%
□ Individuals under $200 .............. 51%
▨ Other ................................................. 8%

### 1985-90 (PACs only)
**Top  Industries & Interest Groups**

Pro-Israel ..................................... $169,750
Insurance ..................................... $156,892
Health Professionals ................ $119,096
Securities & Investment .......... $102,655
Pharmaceuticals/Health Prod .... $75,050

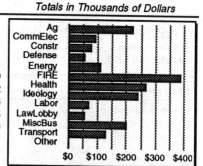

Ag, CommElec, Constr, Defense, Energy, FIRE, Health, Ideology, Labor, LawLobby, MiscBus, Transport, Other

$0   $100   $200   $300   $400

## Sen. Paul Wellstone (D)

**1991-92 Committees: Energy  Labor  Sm Business**
**First elected: 1990**

1989-90 Total Rcpts: ............ $1,401,706
1990 Year-end cash: ................ $21,146

**Source of Funds**
■ PACs .................................................. 19%
▨ Lg Individuals ($200+) ................. 17%
□ Individuals under $200 .............. 53%
▨ Other ................................................. 12%

### 1989-90
**Top  Industries & Interest Groups**

Bldg/Indust/Misc Unions ......... $111,950
Public Sector Unions ................ $63,736
Democratic/Liberal..................... $33,842
Lawyers & Lobbyists .................. $29,106
Misc Issues ................................. $25,937

Unidentified ............................. $108,540

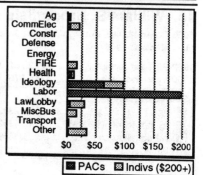

Ag, CommElec, Constr, Defense, Energy, FIRE, Health, Ideology, Labor, LawLobby, MiscBus, Transport, Other

$0   $50   $100   $150   $200

■ PACs   ▨ Indivs ($200+)

Key to committee & category abbreviations is on page 173

## 1. Timothy J. Penny (D)

**1990 Committees: Agriculture  Vet Affairs**
**First elected: 1982**

1989-90 Total receipts: ............ $230,040
1990 Year-end cash: .............. $256,193

**Source of Funds**
- ■ PACs .......................................... 50%
- ▨ Lg Individuals ($200+) .................. 1%
- ☐ Individuals under $200 .............. 36%
- ⊠ Other ........................................ 13%

**Top  Industries & Interest Groups**

Agric Services/Products ............ $11,850
Health Professionals .................. $11,570
Food Processing & Sales ............ $7,950
Crop Production/Processing ........ $7,900
Real Estate .................................. $7,350

Unidentified ................................ $450

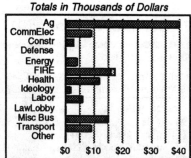

## 2. Vin Weber (R)

**1990 Committees:  Appropriations**
**First elected: 1980**

1989-90 Total receipts: ............ $614,423
1990 Year-end cash: .............. $214,356

**Source of Funds**
- ■ PACs .......................................... 39%
- ▨ Lg Individuals ($200+) ................ 21%
- ☐ Individuals under $200 .............. 32%
- ⊠ Other .......................................... 8%

**Top  Industries & Interest Groups**

Pro-Israel .................................... $47,000
Securities & Investment ............. $21,600
Crop Production/Processing ...... $20,650
Health Professionals .................. $15,600
Agric Services/Products ............ $11,550

Unidentified ................................ $27,030

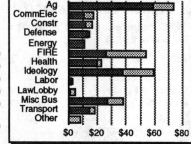

## 3. Jim Ramstad (R)

**1991-92 Committees:  Judiciary  Sm Business**
**First elected: 1990**

1989-90 Total receipts: ............ $938,222
1990 Year-end cash: ................... $2,448

**Source of Funds**
- ■ PACs .......................................... 25%
- ▨ Lg Individuals ($200+) ................ 47%
- ☐ Individuals under $200 .............. 25%
- ⊠ Other .......................................... 3%

**Top  Industries & Interest Groups**

Lawyers & Lobbyists .................. $48,125
Misc Manufacturing & Distrib ..... $31,065
Securities & Investment ............. $29,800
Health Professionals .................. $24,249
Retired ........................................ $23,400

Unidentified .............................. $133,128

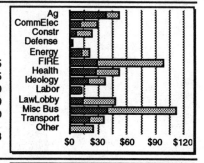

## 4. Bruce F. Vento (D)

**1990 Committees: Banking  Interior**
**First elected: 1976**

1989-90 Total receipts: ............ $259,456
1990 Year-end cash: .............. $155,180

**Source of Funds**
- ■ PACs .......................................... 73%
- ▨ Lg Individuals ($200+) .................. 4%
- ☐ Individuals under $200 .............. 12%
- ⊠ Other ........................................ 12%

**Top  Industries & Interest Groups**

Public Sector Unions ................. $37,188
Bldg/Indust/Misc Unions ............ $35,682
Real Estate ................................ $18,000
Securities & Investment ............. $12,200
Commercial Banks .................... $11,125

Unidentified .................................... $470

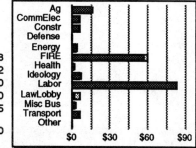

## 5. Martin Olav Sabo (D)

**1990 Committees: Appropriations  Budget**
**First elected: 1978**

1989-90 Total receipts: ............ $355,684
1990 Year-end cash: .............. $216,221

**Source of Funds**
- ■ PACs .......................................... 66%
- ▨ Lg Individuals ($200+) .................. 8%
- ☐ Individuals under $200 .............. 13%
- ⊠ Other ........................................ 13%

**Top  Industries & Interest Groups**

Public Sector Unions ................. $28,350
Bldg/Indust/Misc Unions ............ $27,150
Lawyers & Lobbyists .................. $26,300
Defense Electronics .................. $23,500
Defense Aerospace .................... $22,300

Unidentified ................................ $5,500

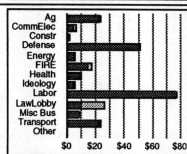

## 6. Gerry Sikorski (D)

**1990 Committees: Energy & Commerce  Post Office**
**First elected: 1982**

1989-90 Total receipts: ............ $443,381
1990 Year-end cash: .............. $306,294

**Source of Funds**
- ■ PACs .......................................... 75%
- ▨ Lg Individuals ($200+) .................. 8%
- ☐ Individuals under $200 ................ 5%
- ⊠ Other ........................................ 12%

**Top  Industries & Interest Groups**

Public Sector Unions ................. $55,850
Bldg/Indust/Misc Unions ............ $47,900
Lawyers & Lobbyists .................. $36,571
Health Professionals .................. $32,850
Transportation Unions .............. $32,019

Unidentified ................................ $6,490

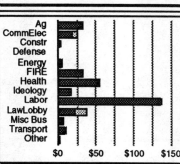

■ PACs  ⊠ Indivs ($200+)

## 7. Collin C. Peterson (D)

**1991-92 Committees: Agriculture Govt Ops**
**First elected: 1990**

1989-90 Total receipts: ............$356,546
1990 Year-end cash: ...................$9,233

| Source of Funds | |
|---|---|
| ■ PACs..............................................58% | |
| ▨ Lg Individuals ($200+).................9% | |
| □ Individuals under $200 ............11% | |
| ▨ Other..........................................22% | |

**Top Industries & Interest Groups**

Bldg/Indust/Misc Unions ............$75,179
Public Sector Unions .................$60,036
Crop Production/Processing ......$18,825
Transportation Unions ..............$17,800
Misc Issues ................................$16,910

Unidentified .................................$5,700

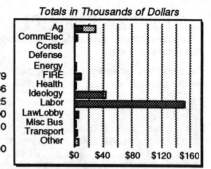

## 8. James L. Oberstar (D)

**1990 Committees: Budget Public Works**
**First elected: 1974**

1989-90 Total receipts: ............$364,577
1990 Year-end cash: ..............$393,551

| Source of Funds | |
|---|---|
| ■ PACs..............................................67% | |
| ▨ Lg Individuals ($200+).................11% | |
| □ Individuals under $200 ................8% | |
| ▨ Other..........................................14% | |

**Top Industries & Interest Groups**

Air Transport ..............................$45,400
Transportation Unions ..............$45,350
Public Sector Unions .................$34,250
Bldg/Indust/Misc Unions ...........$30,900
Lawyers & Lobbyists .................$14,650

Unidentified .................................$5,600

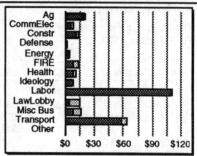

■ PACs  ▨ Indivs ($200+)

Key to committee & category abbreviations is on page 173

# Mississippi

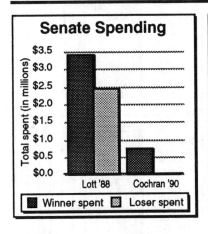

## Senate Spending

Total spent (in millions)

- Lott '88
- Cochran '90

Winner spent / Loser spent

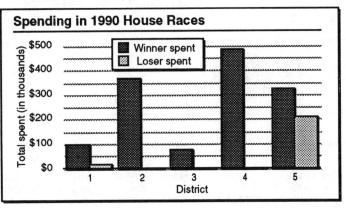

## Spending in 1990 House Races

Total spent (in thousands)

Winner spent
Loser spent

District: 1 2 3 4 5

## 1990 Elections at a Glance

| Dist | Name | Party | Vote Pct | Race Type |
|------|------|-------|----------|-----------|
| Sen | Thad Cochran (1990) | Rep | 100% | Reelected |
| Sen | Trent Lott (1988) | Rep | 54% | Open Seat |
| 1 | Jamie L. Whitten | Dem | 65% | Reelected |
| 2 | Mike Espy | Dem | 84% | Reelected |
| 3 | G. V. "Sonny" Montgomery | Dem | 100% | Reelected |
| 4 | Mike Parker | Dem | 81% | Reelected |
| 5 | Gene Taylor | Dem | 81% | Reelected |

*Totals in Thousands of Dollars*

## Sen. Thad Cochran (R)

**1990 Committees: Agriculture Appropriations Labor**
**First elected: 1978**

1985-90 Total Rcpts: ............$1,462,865
1990 Year-end cash: ..............$908,834

### Source of Funds
- PACs ....................................46%
- Lg Individuals ($200+) ............27%
- Individuals under $200 .............10%
- Other ...................................17%

### 1985-90

**Top Industries & Interest Groups**

Crop Production/Processing ....$134,875
Lawyers & Lobbyists .................$71,950
Oil & Gas ................................$59,150
Health Professionals ...............$56,350
Insurance ...............................$53,732

Unidentified .............................$61,084

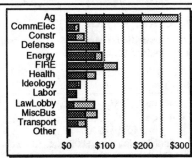

Ag, CommElec, Constr, Defense, Energy, FIRE, Health, Ideology, Labor, LawLobby, MiscBus, Transport, Other

$0  $100  $200  $300

## Sen. Trent Lott (R)

**1990 Committees: Armed Services Commerce SmBus**
**First elected: 1988**

1987-90 Total Rcpts: ............$3,708,751
1990 Year-end cash: ..............$109,867

### Source of Funds
- PACs ....................................27%
- Lg Individuals ($200+) ............31%
- Individuals under $200 .............21%
- Other ...................................21%

### 1987-90 (PACs only)

**Top Industries & Interest Groups**

Oil & Gas ................................$82,000
Food Processing & Sales ..........$53,200
Insurance ...............................$50,250
Leadership PACs ......................$49,627
Misc Manufacturing & Distrib ....$48,700

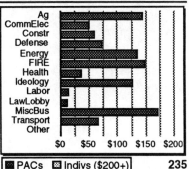

Ag, CommElec, Constr, Defense, Energy, FIRE, Health, Ideology, Labor, LawLobby, MiscBus, Transport, Other

$0  $50  $100  $150  $200

PACs  Indivs ($200+)

235

# 1. Jamie L. Whitten (D)

**1990 Committees: Appropriations**
**First elected: 1941**

1989-90 Total receipts: ............$183,612
1990 Year-end cash: ..............$435,724

**Source of Funds**

- ■ PACs.............................................69%
- ▨ Lg Individuals ($200+) .........4%
- □ Individuals under $200 .........1%
- ▧ Other...........................................26%

### Top Industries & Interest Groups

Public Sector Unions .................$15,000
Lawyers & Lobbyists ..................$13,500
Health Professionals ...................$8,500
Defense Aerospace .......................$8,000
Air Transport ..................................$8,000

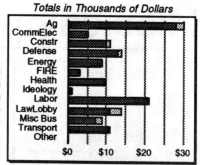

# 2. Mike Espy (D)

**1990 Committees: Agriculture  Budget**
**First elected: 1986**

1989-90 Total receipts: ............$448,212
1990 Year-end cash: .................$85,449

**Source of Funds**

- ■ PACs.............................................66%
- ▨ Lg Individuals ($200+) .......25%
- □ Individuals under $200 .........8%
- ▧ Other.............................................1%

### Top Industries & Interest Groups

Bldg/Indust/Misc Unions ............$41,650
Crop Production/Processing ......$40,965
Public Sector Unions .................$30,350
Lawyers & Lobbyists ..................$22,650
Health Professionals ..................$21,150

Unidentified .................................$10,525

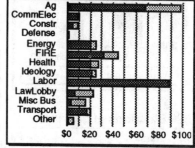

# 3. G. V. "Sonny" Montgomery (D)

**1990 Committees: Armed Services  Vet Affairs**
**First elected: 1966**

1989-90 Total receipts: ............$112,779
1990 Year-end cash: ..............$171,908

**Source of Funds**

- ■ PACs.............................................49%
- ▨ Lg Individuals ($200+) .......24%
- □ Individuals under $200 .......11%
- ▧ Other...........................................16%

### Top Industries & Interest Groups

Defense Aerospace ...................$12,000
Defense Electronics....................$8,750
Health Professionals ...................$6,450
Oil & Gas .......................................$6,150
Retired ...........................................$3,150

Unidentified ..................................$4,550

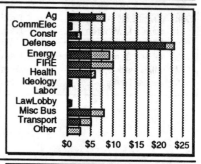

# 4. Mike Parker (D)

**1990 Committees: Public Works  Vet Affairs**
**First elected: 1988**

1989-90 Total receipts: ............$526,715
1990 Year-end cash: .................$48,162

**Source of Funds**

- ■ PACs.............................................53%
- ▨ Lg Individuals ($200+) .......27%
- □ Individuals under $200 .......15%
- ▧ Other.............................................4%

### Top Industries & Interest Groups

Oil & Gas .....................................$41,169
Insurance ....................................$32,644
Health Professionals .................$27,159
Air Transport ..............................$20,550
Pro-Israel ....................................$16,100

Unidentified .................................$16,270

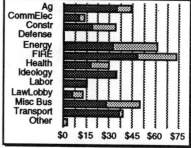

# 5. Gene Taylor (D)

**1990 Committees: Armed Services  Merchant Marine**
**First elected: 1988**

1989-90 Total receipts: ............$652,912
1990 Year-end cash: ...................$2,874

**Source of Funds**

- ■ PACs.............................................33%
- ▨ Lg Individuals ($200+) .......26%
- □ Individuals under $200 .......27%
- ▧ Other...........................................14%

### Top Industries & Interest Groups

Lawyers & Lobbyists .................$47,650
Health Professionals .................$43,333
Leadership PACs .......................$20,000
Public Sector Unions .................$18,000
Insurance ....................................$17,215

Unidentified .................................$35,775

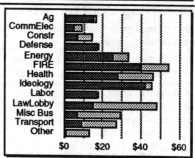

■ PACs  ▧ Indivs ($200+)

# Missouri

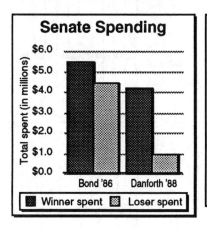

## Senate Spending

Total spent (in millions)

Bond '86 — Danforth '88

Winner spent / Loser spent

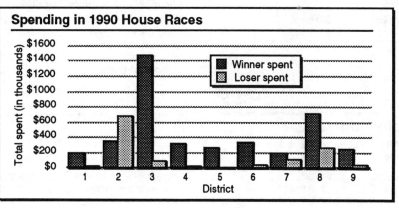

## Spending in 1990 House Races

Total spent (in thousands)

Winner spent / Loser spent

District 1-9

## 1990 Elections at a Glance

| Dist | Name | Party | Vote Pct | Race Type |
|------|------|-------|----------|-----------|
| Sen | Christopher S. Bond (1986) | Rep | 53% | Open Seat |
| Sen | John C. Danforth (1988) | Rep | 68% | Reelected |
| 1 | William L. Clay | Dem | 61% | Reelected |
| 2 | Joan Kelly Horn | Dem | 50% | Beat Incumb |
| 3 | Richard A. Gephardt | Dem | 57% | Reelected |
| 4 | Ike Skelton | Dem | 62% | Reelected |
| 5 | Alan Wheat | Dem | 62% | Reelected |
| 6 | Tom Coleman | Rep | 52% | Reelected |
| 7 | Mel Hancock | Rep | 52% | Reelected |
| 8 | Bill Emerson | Rep | 57% | Reelected |
| 9 | Harold L. Volkmer | Dem | 58% | Reelected |

*Totals in Thousands of Dollars*

## Sen. Christopher S. Bond (R)

**1990 Committees: Agriculture  Banking  Budget  SmBus**
**First elected: 1986**

1985-90 Total Rcpts: ............ $6,481,497
1990 Year-end cash: .............. $614,801

### Source of Funds
- PACs ........................... 24%
- Lg Individuals ($200+) ............. 31%
- Individuals under $200 ............. 37%
- Other ........................... 8%

### 1985-90 (PACs only)
**Top Industries & Interest Groups**

Insurance ................................. $151,700
Commercial Banks ................. $103,308
Oil & Gas .............................. $93,850
Leadership PACs ..................... $75,419
Food Processing & Sales ......... $66,975

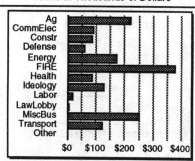

## Sen. John C. Danforth (R)

**1990 Committees: Commerce  Finance**
**First elected: 1976**

1985-90 Total Rcpts: ............ $4,777,164
1990 Year-end cash: .............. $564,695

### Source of Funds
- PACs ........................... 27%
- Lg Individuals ($200+) ............. 38%
- Individuals under $200 ............. 23%
- Other ........................... 12%

### 1985-90 (PACs only)
**Top Industries & Interest Groups**

Insurance ................................. $158,125
Telephone Utilities ..................... $57,971
Air Transport ............................ $56,000
Defense Aerospace .................. $50,861
Oil & Gas ................................ $50,655

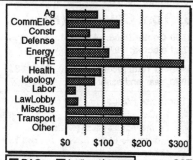

PACs  Indivs ($200+)

**237**

## 1. William L. Clay (D)

**1990 Committees:** Admin Educ/Labor Post Office
**First elected:** 1968

1989-90 Total receipts: .......... $216,480
1990 Year-end cash: ............. $119,666

**Source of Funds**
- PACs ......................................... 80%
- Lg Individuals ($200+) ................. 5%
- Individuals under $200 ................ 6%
- Other ........................................... 9%

**Top Industries & Interest Groups**

Bldg/Indust/Misc Unions ............. $48,950
Public Sector Unions ................. $48,400
Transportation Unions ............... $27,350
Air Transport ............................... $9,000
Commercial Banks ...................... $8,500

Unidentified ................................. $4,400

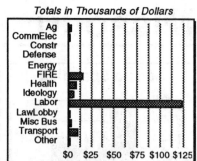

*Totals in Thousands of Dollars*

## 2. Joan Kelly Horn (D)

**1991-92 Committees:** Public Works Science
**First elected:** 1990

1989-90 Total receipts: .......... $356,766
1990 Year-end cash: ................ $15,676

**Source of Funds**
- PACs ......................................... 45%
- Lg Individuals ($200+) ............... 30%
- Individuals under $200 .............. 18%
- Other ........................................... 7%

**Top Industries & Interest Groups**

Bldg/Indust/Misc Unions ............. $90,150
Transportation Unions ............... $23,000
Public Sector Unions ................. $20,200
Human Rights ............................ $16,950
Education ................................... $12,650

Unidentified ................................. $43,500

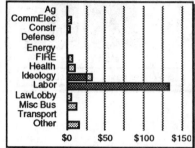

## 3. Richard A. Gephardt (D)

**1990 Committees:** Budget/Majority Leader
**First elected:** 1976

1989-90 Total receipts: ......... $1,647,415
1990 Year-end cash: ............... $193,485

**Source of Funds**
- PACs ......................................... 51%
- Lg Individuals ($200+) ............... 44%
- Individuals under $200 ................ 5%
- Other ........................................... 0%

**Top Industries & Interest Groups**

Lawyers & Lobbyists ................ $222,003
Bldg/Indust/Misc Unions .......... $117,525
Insurance .................................. $96,800
Beer, Wine & Liquor .................. $75,250
Securities & Investment ............. $68,000

Unidentified ............................... $123,241

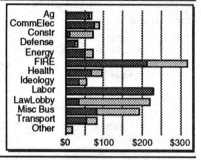

## 4. Ike Skelton (D)

**1990 Committees:** Armed Services Sm Business
**First elected:** 1976

1989-90 Total receipts: .......... $390,115
1990 Year-end cash: ............... $311,648

**Source of Funds**
- PACs ......................................... 62%
- Lg Individuals ($200+) ............... 18%
- Individuals under $200 .............. 19%
- Other ........................................... 1%

**Top Industries & Interest Groups**

Defense Aerospace ................... $43,065
Bldg/Indust/Misc Unions ............ $30,250
Defense Electronics ................... $16,000
Health Professionals ................. $12,100
Automotive ................................ $11,250

Unidentified ................................. $8,750

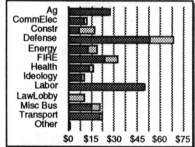

## 5. Alan Wheat (D)

**1990 Committees:** DC Rules
**First elected:** 1982

1989-90 Total receipts: .......... $312,016
1990 Year-end cash: ............... $264,999

**Source of Funds**
- PACs ......................................... 72%
- Lg Individuals ($200+) ............... 13%
- Individuals under $200 ................ 6%
- Other ......................................... 10%

**Top Industries & Interest Groups**

Bldg/Indust/Misc Unions ............ $44,777
Public Sector Unions ................. $31,010
Transportation Unions ............... $23,200
Lawyers & Lobbyists .................. $19,640
Telephone Utilities ..................... $11,880

Unidentified ................................. $13,110

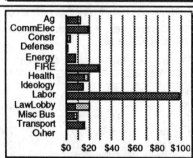

## 6. Tom Coleman (R)

**1990 Committees:** Agriculture Educ/Labor
**First elected:** 1976

1989-90 Total receipts: .......... $281,837
1990 Year-end cash: ................ $33,407

**Source of Funds**
- PACs ......................................... 64%
- Lg Individuals ($200+) ............... 13%
- Individuals under $200 .............. 13%
- Other ......................................... 10%

**Top Industries & Interest Groups**

Agric Services/Products ............. $17,850
Food Processing & Sales .......... $13,450
Lawyers & Lobbyists .................. $13,096
Commercial Banks ..................... $12,250
Crop Production/Processing ...... $10,792

Unidentified ................................. $5,942

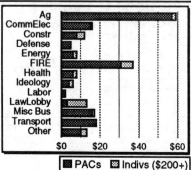

238    Key to committee & category abbreviations is on page 173

■ PACs  ▨ Indivs ($200+)

## 7. Mel Hancock (R)

**1990 Committees: Public Works  Sm Business**
**First elected: 1988**

1989-90 Total receipts: ........... $280,787
1990 Year-end cash: .............. $129,033

**Source of Funds**
- ■ PACs .................................... 44%
- ▨ Lg Individuals ($200+) ............. 28%
- ☐ Individuals under $200 ............. 20%
- ⊠ Other .................................. 8%

**Top  Industries & Interest Groups**

Automotive ................................. $15,750
Health Professionals ................. $14,255
Air Transport ............................ $11,300
Real Estate .............................. $11,200
Insurance ................................. $6,985

Unidentified ............................. $15,560

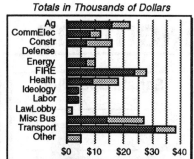

## 8. Bill Emerson (R)

**1990 Committees: Agriculture  Public Works**
**First elected: 1980**

1989-90 Total receipts: ........... $625,060
1990 Year-end cash: ................. $7,761

**Source of Funds**
- ■ PACs .................................... 51%
- ▨ Lg Individuals ($200+) ............. 21%
- ☐ Individuals under $200 ............. 23%
- ⊠ Other .................................. 6%

**Top  Industries & Interest Groups**

Crop Production/Processing ...... $43,531
Agric Services/Products ........... $33,250
Health Professionals ................. $26,945
Food Processing & Sales ......... $24,850
Insurance ................................. $19,250

Unidentified ............................. $33,106

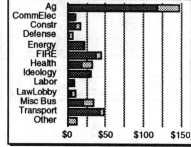

## 9. Harold L. Volkmer (D)

**1990 Committees: Agriculture  Science**
**First elected: 1976**

1989-90 Total receipts: ........... $308,533
1990 Year-end cash: .............. $159,821

**Source of Funds**
- ■ PACs .................................... 71%
- ▨ Lg Individuals ($200+) ............... 6%
- ☐ Individuals under $200 ............. 19%
- ⊠ Other .................................. 4%

**Top  Industries & Interest Groups**

Bldg/Indust/Misc Unions ........... $40,200
Public Sector Unions ................ $20,700
Dairy ....................................... $20,000
Transportation Unions .............. $14,250
Agric Services/Products ........... $13,000

Unidentified ............................... $1,050

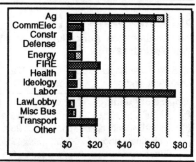

■ PACs  ⊠ Indivs ($200+)

239

# Montana

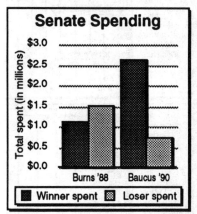

## Senate Spending

Total spent (in millions)

$3.0
$2.5
$2.0
$1.5
$1.0
$0.5
$0.0

Burns '88    Baucus '90

■ Winner spent    ▨ Loser spent

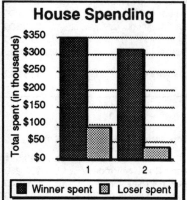

## House Spending

Total spent (in thousands)

$350
$300
$250
$200
$150
$100
$50
$0

1         2

■ Winner spent    ▨ Loser spent

## 1990 Elections at a Glance

| DistName | | Party | Vote Pct | Race Type |
|------|------|------|------|------|
| Sen | Max Baucus (1990) | Dem | 68% | Reelected |
| Sen | Conrad Burns (1988) | Rep | 52% | Beat Incumb |
| 1 | Pat Williams | Dem | 61% | Reelected |
| 2 | Ron Marlenee | Rep | 63% | Reelected |

*Totals in Thousands of Dollars*

## Sen. Max Baucus (D)

**1990 Committees: Agriculture Envir Finance SmBus**
**First elected: 1978**

1985-90 Total Rcpts: ............$3,075,422
1990 Year-end cash: ..............$514,678

**Source of Funds**
■ PACs ............................................52%
▨ Lg Individuals ($200+) ..............28%
□ Individuals under $200 ..............12%
▨ Other .............................................9%

### 1985-90
**Top Industries & Interest Groups**

Lawyers & Lobbyists ...............$266,745
Insurance ...................................$180,774
Securities & Investment ..........$145,366
Bldg/Indust/Misc Unions .........$119,330
Pro-Israel ..................................$117,100

Unidentified ..............................$105,959

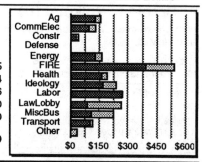

## Sen. Conrad Burns (R)

**1990 Committees: Commerce Energy SmBusiness**
**First elected: 1988**

1987-90 Total Rcpts: ............$1,332,260
1990 Year-end cash: ................$79,369

**Source of Funds**
■ PACs ............................................34%
▨ Lg Individuals ($200+) ..............22%
□ Individuals under $200 ..............21%
▨ Other ...........................................22%

### 1987-90 (PACs only)
**Top Industries & Interest Groups**

Leadership PACs .......................$56,000
Insurance ...................................$32,061
Pro-Israel ..................................$30,800
Oil & Gas ...................................$24,200
Automotive ................................$22,500

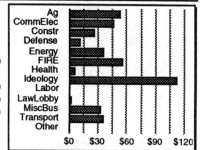

## 1. Pat Williams (D)

**1990 Committees: Educ/Labor Interior**
**First elected: 1978**

1989-90 Total receipts: ...........$557,328
1990 Year-end cash: ..............$214,350

**Source of Funds**
■ PACs ............................................63%
▨ Lg Individuals ($200+) ..............11%
□ Individuals under $200 ..............20%
▨ Other .............................................6%

**Top Industries & Interest Groups**

Bldg/Indust/Misc Unions ...........$93,500
Public Sector Unions .................$49,850
Transportation Unions ...............$37,250
Education ...................................$17,600
Human Rights ...........................$14,000

Unidentified ..............................$10,060

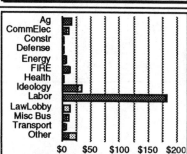

## 2. Ron Marlenee (R)

**1990 Committees: Agriculture Interior**
**First elected: 1976**

1989-90 Total receipts: ...........$297,771
1990 Year-end cash: ................$76,486

**Source of Funds**
■ PACs ............................................46%
▨ Lg Individuals ($200+) ..............20%
□ Individuals under $200 ..............26%
▨ Other .............................................8%

**Top Industries & Interest Groups**

Oil & Gas ...................................$20,600
Crop Production/Processing ......$19,150
Agric Services/Products ............$11,250
Real Estate ................................$10,700
Livestock ...................................$10,400

Unidentified ..............................$11,500

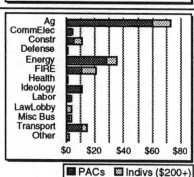

■ PACs    ▨ Indivs ($200+)

Key to committee & category abbreviations is on page 173

# Nebraska

## Senate Spending

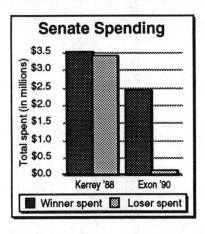

Total spent (in millions)

Kerrey '88    Exon '90

■ Winner spent    ▨ Loser spent

## Spending in 1990 House Races

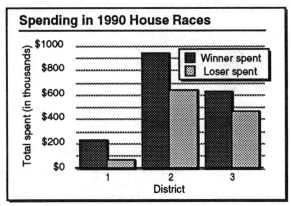

Total spent (in thousands)

■ Winner spent
▨ Loser spent

District

## 1990 Elections at a Glance

| Dist | Name | Party | Vote Pct | Race Type |
|------|------|-------|----------|-----------|
| Sen | Jim Exon (1990) | Dem | 59% | Reelected |
| Sen | Bob Kerrey (1988) | Dem | 57% | Beat Incumb |
| 1 | Doug Bereuter | Rep | 65% | Reelected |
| 2 | Peter Hoagland | Dem | 58% | Reelected |
| 3 | Bill Barrett | Rep | 51% | Open Seat |

*Totals in Thousands of Dollars*

## Sen. Jim Exon (D)

**1990 Committees: ArmServ Budget Commerce**
**First elected: 1978**

1985-90 Total Rcpts: ............$2,637,149
1990 Year-end cash: ..............$270,574

**Source of Funds**
- ■ PACs ............................................55%
- ▨ Lg Individuals ($200+) ..............20%
- ☐ Individuals under $200 ..............17%
- ▨ Other ............................................8%

### 1985-90
**Top Industries & Interest Groups**

Insurance .................................$145,973
Lawyers & Lobbyists ...............$137,604
Transportation Unions ............$109,300
Bldg/Indust/Misc Unions ..........$106,800
Railroads ...................................$99,815

Unidentified ...............................$94,074

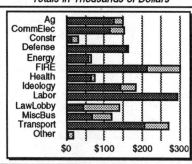

## Sen. Bob Kerrey (D)

**1990 Committees: Agriculture Appropriations**
**First elected: 1988**

1987-90 Total Rcpts: ............$3,820,627
1990 Year-end cash: ................$87,160

**Source of Funds**
- ■ PACs ............................................24%
- ▨ Lg Individuals ($200+) ..............28%
- ☐ Individuals under $200 ..............41%
- ▨ Other ............................................7%

### 1987-90 (PACs only)
**Top Industries & Interest Groups**

Bldg/Indust/Misc Unions ..........$145,950
Transportation Unions ..............$86,250
Pro-Israel ..................................$85,000
Public Sector Unions .................$72,800
Leadership PACs ......................$54,471

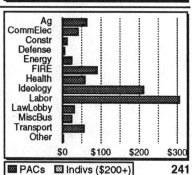

■ PACs  ▨ Indivs ($200+)

241

## 1. Doug Bereuter (R)

**1990 Committees: Banking  Foreign Affairs**
**First elected: 1978**

1989-90 Total receipts: ............$254,654
1990 Year-end cash: .................$54,730

### Source of Funds
| | |
|---|---|
| ■ PACs ...............................................58% |
| ▨ Lg Individuals ($200+) .................7% |
| ☐ Individuals under $200 ..............31% |
| ▩ Other ..............................................4% |

**Top Industries & Interest Groups**

Commercial Banks ....................$33,900
Insurance ................................$16,259
Health Professionals ....................$8,850
Securities & Investment ..............$8,250
Real Estate ..............................$7,412

Unidentified ................................$1,350

## 2. Peter Hoagland (D)

**1990 Committees: Banking  Sm Business**
**First elected: 1988**

1989-90 Total receipts: ............$945,952
1990 Year-end cash: .................$11,430

### Source of Funds
| | |
|---|---|
| ■ PACs ...............................................63% |
| ▨ Lg Individuals ($200+) ...............15% |
| ☐ Individuals under $200 ..............12% |
| ▩ Other ............................................10% |

**Top Industries & Interest Groups**

Bldg/Indust/Misc Unions ..........$117,644
Commercial Banks ....................$72,850
Public Sector Unions .................$62,100
Lawyers & Lobbyists .................$60,425
Insurance ..................................$57,941

Unidentified ................................$17,775

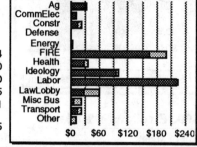

## 3. Bill Barrett (R)

**1991-92 Committees: Agriculture  Educ/Labor  Admin**
**First elected: 1990**

1989-90 Total receipts: ............$644,559
1990 Year-end cash: .................$19,982

### Source of Funds
| | |
|---|---|
| ■ PACs ...............................................25% |
| ▨ Lg Individuals ($200+) ...............25% |
| ☐ Individuals under $200 ..............28% |
| ▩ Other ............................................22% |

**Top Industries & Interest Groups**

Insurance ..................................$34,770
Commercial Banks ....................$26,925
Food Processing & Sales ..........$21,200
Health Professionals ..................$16,200
Oil & Gas ..................................$16,100

Unidentified ................................$35,692

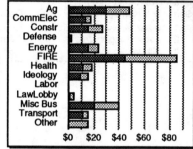

■ PACs  ▩ Indivs ($200+)

# Nevada

## Senate Spending

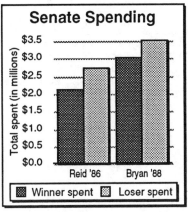

Total spent (in millions)

$3.5 $3.0 $2.5 $2.0 $1.5 $1.0 $0.5 $0.0

Reid '86    Bryan '88

▨ Winner spent    ▨ Loser spent

## House Spending

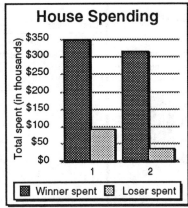

Total spent (in thousands)

$350 $300 $250 $200 $150 $100 $50 $0

1    2

▨ Winner spent    ▨ Loser spent

## 1990 Elections at a Glance

| Dist | Name | Party | Vote Pct | Race Type |
|------|------|-------|----------|-----------|
| Sen | Richard H. Bryan (1988) | Dem | 50% | Beat Incumb |
| Sen | Harry Reid (1986) | Dem | 50% | Open Seat |
| 1 | James Bilbray | Dem | 61% | Reelected |
| 2 | Barbara F. Vucanovich | Rep | 59% | Reelected |

## Sen. Richard H. Bryan (D)

**1990 Committees: Banking  Commerce**
**First elected: 1988**

1987-90 Total Rcpts: ............$3,174,777
1990 Year-end cash: ...................$6,336

**Source of Funds**
- PACs...............................................27%
- Lg Individuals ($200+) ...............51%
- Individuals under $200 .............13%
- Other ...............................................9%

### 1987-90 (PACs only)
**Top Industries & Interest Groups**

Bldg/Indust/Misc Unions .........$152,800
Transportation Unions ..............$83,250
Pro-Israel ....................................$80,250
Public Sector Unions ................$70,750
Insurance ...................................$52,499

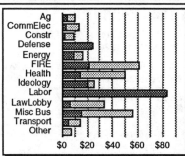

## Sen. Harry Reid (D)

**1990 Committees: Appropriations  Envir/Public Works**
**First elected: 1986**

1985-90 Total Rcpts: ............$3,318,240
1990 Year-end cash: ..............$728,395

**Source of Funds**
- PACs...............................................30%
- Lg Individuals ($200+) ...............29%
- Individuals under $200 .............28%
- Other .............................................13%

### 1985-90 (PACs only)
**Top Industries & Interest Groups**

Bldg/Indust/Misc Unions .........$158,000
Pro-Israel ..................................$157,590
Public Sector Unions ................$80,750
Transportation Unions ..............$66,750
Recreation/Live Entertainment ..$55,500

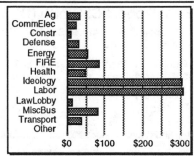

## 1.  James Bilbray (D)

**1990 Committees: Armed Services  Sm Business**
**First elected: 1986**

1989-90 Total receipts: ............$686,010
1990 Year-end cash: ...................$1,107

**Source of Funds**
- PACs...............................................30%
- Lg Individuals ($200+) ...............31%
- Individuals under $200 .............3%
- Other .............................................36%

### Top Industries & Interest Groups

Health Professionals .................$43,410
Bldg/Indust/Misc Unions ...........$43,400
Real Estate .................................$39,320
Recreation/Live Entertainment ..$34,000
Lawyers & Lobbyists .................$33,973

Unidentified ...............................$18,450

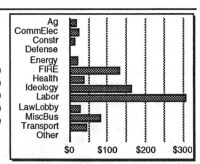

## 2.  Barbara F. Vucanovich (R)

**1990 Committees: Admin  Interior**
**First elected: 1982**

1989-90 Total receipts: ...........$445,465
1990 Year-end cash: ...................$5,705

**Source of Funds**
- PACs...............................................35%
- Lg Individuals ($200+) ...............27%
- Individuals under $200 .............31%
- Other ...............................................7%

### Top Industries & Interest Groups

Recreation/Live Entertainment ..$27,400
Real Estate .................................$20,000
Mining .........................................$16,900
Oil & Gas ....................................$16,450
Retired ........................................$16,200

Unidentified ...............................$18,950

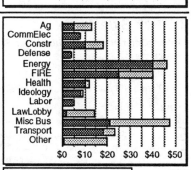

▨ PACs   ▨ Indivs ($200+)

243

# New Hampshire

## Senate Spending

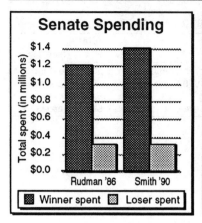

Total spent (in millions)

- ■ Winner spent
- ▨ Loser spent

## House Spending

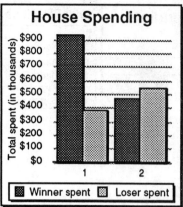

Total spent (in thousands)

- ■ Winner spent
- ▨ Loser spent

| Dist | Name | Party | Vote Pct | Race Type |
|------|------|-------|----------|-----------|
| Sen | Warren B. Rudman (1986) | Rep | 63% | Reelected |
| Sen | Robert C. Smith (1990) | Rep | 65% | Open Seat |
| 1 | Bill Zeliff | Rep | 55% | Open Seat |
| 2 | Dick Swett | Dem | 53% | Beat Incumb |

*Totals in Thousands of Dollars*

## Sen. Warren B. Rudman (R)

**1990 Committees: Appropriations Budget Govt Affairs**
**First elected: 1980**

1985-90 Total Rcpts: ...........$1,015,538
1990 Year-end cash: ................$60,969

**Source of Funds**
- ■ PACs .................................................. 2%
- ▨ Lg Individuals ($200+) ................. 52%
- □ Individuals under $200 .............. 34%
- ▨ Other ............................................. 13%

**1985-90 (PACs only)**
**Top Industries & Interest Groups**

Commercial Banks ......................$5,300
Defense Aerospace ....................$5,000
Food & Beverage ........................$3,000
Real Estate .................................$2,000
Savings & Loans .........................$1,500

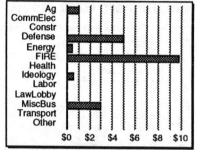

## Sen. Robert C. Smith (R)

**1990 Committees: Armed Services Vet Affairs**
**First elected: 1990**

1989-90 Total Rcpts: ...........$1,509,288
1990 Year-end cash: ................$89,118

**Source of Funds**
- ■ PACs ................................................ 41%
- ▨ Lg Individuals ($200+) ................. 28%
- □ Individuals under $200 .............. 13%
- ▨ Other ............................................. 19%

**1989-90**
**Top Industries & Interest Groups**

Insurance ...................................$73,675
Defense Aerospace ..................$55,000
General Contractors .................$46,600
Real Estate ................................$44,725
Oil & Gas ...................................$42,800

Unidentified ...............................$96,680

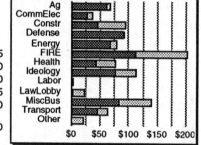

## 1. Bill Zeliff (R)

**1991-92 Committees: Govt Ops Public Works**
**First elected: 1990**

1989-90 Total receipts: ...........$950,621
1990 Year-end cash: ..................$4,826

**Source of Funds**
- ■ PACs ................................................ 16%
- ▨ Lg Individuals ($200+) ................. 22%
- □ Individuals under $200 .............. 8%
- ▨ Other ............................................. 54%

**Top Industries & Interest Groups**

Real Estate ................................$39,200
Food & Beverage ......................$37,350
Insurance ...................................$27,600
Health Professionals .................$16,550
Pharmaceuticals/Health Prod ....$12,000

Unidentified ...............................$60,829

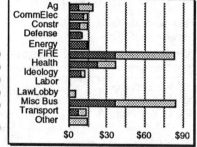

## 2. Dick Swett (D)

**1991-92 Committees: Public Works Science**
**First elected: 1990**

1989-90 Total receipts: ...........$470,252
1990 Year-end cash: ..................$5,090

**Source of Funds**
- ■ PACs ................................................ 34%
- ▨ Lg Individuals ($200+) ................. 50%
- □ Individuals under $200 .............. 8%
- ▨ Other ............................................. 8%

**Top Industries & Interest Groups**

Bldg/Indust/Misc Unions ...........$63,448
Public Sector Unions ................$25,000
Human Rights ...........................$24,000
Transportation Unions ..............$23,800
Real Estate ...............................$23,450

Unidentified ...............................$62,050

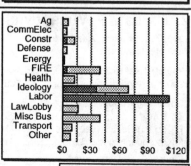

244    Key to committee & category abbreviations is on page 173

- ■ PACs
- ▨ Indivs ($200+)

# New Jersey

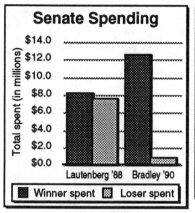

### Senate Spending

Total spent (in millions)

- $14.0
- $12.0
- $10.0
- $8.0
- $6.0
- $4.0
- $2.0
- $0.0

Lautenberg '88    Bradley '90

■ Winner spent   ▨ Loser spent

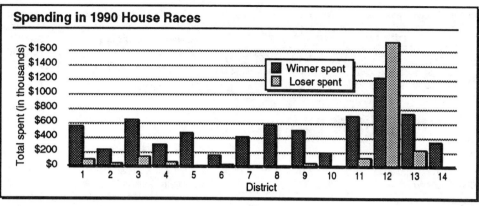

### Spending in 1990 House Races

Total spent (in thousands)

- $1600
- $1400
- $1200
- $1000
- $800
- $600
- $400
- $200
- $0

■ Winner spent
▨ Loser spent

District  1  2  3  4  5  6  7  8  9  10  11  12  13  14

## 1990 Elections at a Glance

| Dist | Name | Party | Vote Pct | Race Type |
|------|------|-------|----------|-----------|
| Sen | Bill Bradley (1990) | Dem | 50% | Reelected |
| Sen | Frank Lautenberg (1988) | Dem | 54% | Reelected |
| 1 | Robert E. Andrews | Dem | 54% | Open Seat |
| 2 | William J. Hughes | Dem | 88% | Reelected |
| 3 | Frank Pallone Jr. | Dem | 49% | Reelected |
| 4 | Christopher H. Smith | Rep | 63% | Reelected |
| 5 | Marge Roukema | Rep | 76% | Reelected |
| 6 | Bernard J. Dwyer | Dem | 50% | Reelected |
| 7 | Matthew J. Rinaldo | Rep | 75% | Reelected |
| 8 | Robert A. Roe | Dem | 77% | Reelected |
| 9 | Robert G. Torricelli | Dem | 57% | Reelected |
| 10 | Donald M. Payne | Dem | 82% | Reelected |
| 11 | Dean A. Gallo | Rep | 65% | Reelected |
| 12 | Dick Zimmer | Rep | 64% | Open Seat |
| 13 | H. James Saxton | Rep | 58% | Reelected |
| 14 | Frank J. Guarini | Dem | 66% | Reelected |

*Totals in Thousands of Dollars*

## Sen. Bill Bradley (D)

**1990 Committees: Energy Finance**
**First elected: 1978**

1985-90 Total Rcpts: .......... $12,874,229
1990 Year-end cash: .............. $775,770

**Source of Funds**

- ■ PACs ................................ 11%
- ▨ Lg Individuals ($200+) .............. 67%
- □ Individuals under $200 .............. 14%
- ▨ Other ................................ 9%

### 1985-90

**Top Industries & Interest Groups**

| | |
|---|---|
| Lawyers & Lobbyists | $1,064,213 |
| Securities & Investment | $986,548 |
| Real Estate | $312,008 |
| TV & Movies | $288,150 |
| Insurance | $269,484 |
| | |
| Unidentified | $1,309,601 |

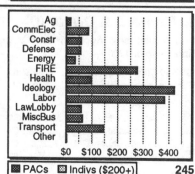

Ag, CommElec, Constr, Defense, Energy, FIRE, Health, Ideology, Labor, LawLobby, MiscBus, Transport, Other

$0   $500  $1000 $1500 $2000

## Sen. Frank Lautenberg (D)

**1990 Committees: Appropriations Budget Envir**
**First elected: 1982**

1985-90 Total Rcpts: ........... $8,337,711
1990 Year-end cash: ................. $35,424

**Source of Funds**
- ■ PACs ................................ 19%
- ▨ Lg Individuals ($200+) .............. 43%
- □ Individuals under $200 .............. 24%
- ▨ Other ................................ 14%

### 1985-90 (PACs only)

**Top Industries & Interest Groups**

| | |
|---|---|
| Pro-Israel | $240,000 |
| Bldg/Indust/Misc Unions | $188,500 |
| Transportation Unions | $108,802 |
| Insurance | $102,000 |
| Public Sector Unions | $85,000 |

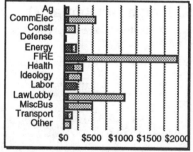

Ag, CommElec, Constr, Defense, Energy, FIRE, Health, Ideology, Labor, LawLobby, MiscBus, Transport, Other

$0   $100   $200   $300   $400

■ PACs   ▨ Indivs ($200+)

245

## 1. Robert E. Andrews (D)

**1991-92 Committees: Educ/Labor  Sm Business**
**First elected: 1990**

1989-90 Total receipts: ............$542,535
1990 Year-end cash: ......................$574

**Source of Funds**
PACs.................................................41%
Lg Individuals ($200+) ..............34%
Individuals under $200 .............13%
Other................................................12%

**Top Industries & Interest Groups**

Bldg/Indust/Misc Unions ..........$114,850
Construction Services................$32,600
Lawyers & Lobbyists ..................$30,830
Public Sector Unions .................$27,000
General Contractors ...................$18,450

Unidentified ..................................$47,841

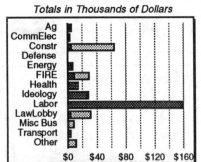

## 2. William J. Hughes (D)

**1990 Committees:  Judiciary  Merchant Marine**
**First elected: 1974**

1989-90 Total receipts: ............$282,731
1990 Year-end cash: ...............$208,172

**Source of Funds**
PACs.................................................45%
Lg Individuals ($200+) ...............16%
Individuals under $200 .............24%
Other................................................15%

**Top Industries & Interest Groups**

Lawyers & Lobbyists ..................$17,500
Bldg/Indust/Misc Unions ...........$15,600
Commercial Banks ....................$10,950
Transportation Unions ................$9,050
Real Estate .................................$8,700

Unidentified ..................................$16,150

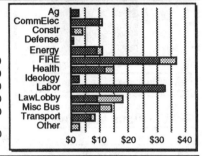

## 3. Frank Pallone Jr. (D)

**1990 Committees:  Merchant Marine  Public Works**
**First elected: 1988**

1989-90 Total receipts: ............$632,450
1990 Year-end cash: ......................$761

**Source of Funds**
PACs.................................................58%
Lg Individuals ($200+) ...............19%
Individuals under $200 .............14%
Other................................................10%

**Top Industries & Interest Groups**

Bldg/Indust/Misc Unions ...........$89,800
Transportation Unions ...............$59,150
Public Sector Unions .................$49,150
Misc Issues .................................$30,581
Health Professionals .................$25,286

Unidentified ..................................$39,282

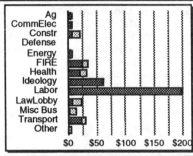

## 4. Christopher H. Smith (R)

**1990 Committees:  Foreign Affairs  Vet Affairs**
**First elected: 1980**

1989-90 Total receipts: ............$280,579
1990 Year-end cash: .................$65,394

**Source of Funds**
PACs.................................................43%
Lg Individuals ($200+) ...............18%
Individuals under $200 .............35%
Other..................................................4%

**Top Industries & Interest Groups**

Transportation Unions ...............$16,755
Bldg/Indust/Misc Unions ...........$16,600
Pro-Life ........................................$12,652
Real Estate .................................$11,700
Health Professionals .................$10,050

Unidentified ..................................$18,565

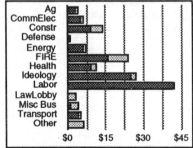

## 5. Marge Roukema (R)

**1990 Committees:  Banking  Educ/Labor**
**First elected: 1980**

1989-90 Total receipts: ............$446,589
1990 Year-end cash: .................$98,290

**Source of Funds**
PACs.................................................48%
Lg Individuals ($200+) ...............29%
Individuals under $200 .............16%
Other..................................................7%

**Top Industries & Interest Groups**

Commercial Banks ....................$33,350
Real Estate .................................$23,500
Insurance ....................................$20,148
Securities & Investment ............$17,950
Health Professionals .................$17,150

Unidentified ..................................$34,450

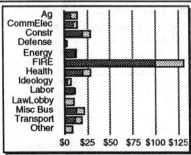

## 6. Bernard J. Dwyer (D)

**1990 Committees:  Appropriations  Budget**
**First elected: 1980**

1989-90 Total receipts: ............$146,908
1990 Year-end cash: .................$70,432

**Source of Funds**
PACs.................................................86%
Lg Individuals ($200+) .................5%
Individuals under $200 ...............0%
Other..................................................8%

**Top Industries & Interest Groups**

Bldg/Indust/Misc Unions ...........$22,250
Public Sector Unions .................$17,000
Transportation Unions ...............$15,550
Insurance ....................................$14,761
Pharmaceuticals/Health Prod ....$11,500

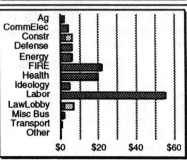

Key to committee & category abbreviations is on page 173

■ PACs  ☒ Indivs ($200+)

## 7. Matthew J. Rinaldo (R)

**1990 Committees: Energy & Commerce**
**First elected: 1972**

1989-90 Total receipts: ...........$626,502
1990 Year-end cash: ..............$967,326

### Source of Funds
- PACs ..................................39%
- Lg Individuals ($200+) ...........30%
- Individuals under $200 ...........11%
- Other ................................21%

**Top Industries & Interest Groups**

Securities & Investment ...........$28,500
Bldg/Indust/Misc Unions ...........$28,500
Health Professionals ..................$26,200
Insurance ................................$22,900
Commercial Banks ....................$22,200

Unidentified ..............................$48,550

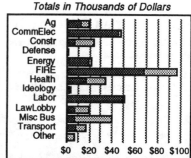

## 8. Robert A. Roe (D)

**1990 Committees: Public Works  Science**
**First elected: 1969**

1989-90 Total receipts: ...........$651,952
1990 Year-end cash: ..............$577,940

### Source of Funds
- PACs ..................................49%
- Lg Individuals ($200+) ...........25%
- Individuals under $200 ............6%
- Other ................................21%

**Top Industries & Interest Groups**

Air Transport ..............................$55,800
Bldg/Indust/Misc Unions ...........$45,550
Lawyers & Lobbyists ..................$34,000
Construction Services ...............$32,307
General Contractors .................$28,800

Unidentified ..............................$34,400

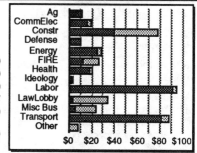

## 9. Robert G. Torricelli (D)

**1990 Committees: Foreign Affairs  Science**
**First elected: 1982**

1989-90 Total receipts: ...........$923,467
1990 Year-end cash: ..............$846,461

### Source of Funds
- PACs ..................................25%
- Lg Individuals ($200+) ...........38%
- Individuals under $200 ...........13%
- Other ................................24%

**Top Industries & Interest Groups**

Lawyers & Lobbyists ..................$68,475
Health Professionals ..................$53,488
Bldg/Indust/Misc Unions ...........$48,960
Transportation Unions ...............$41,650
Real Estate ..............................$28,550

Unidentified ..............................$83,475

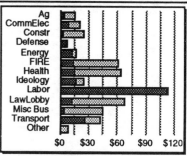

## 10. Donald M. Payne (D)

**1990 Committees: Educ/Labor  Foreign Affairs  Govt Op**
**First elected: 1988**

1989-90 Total receipts: ...........$303,436
1990 Year-end cash: ..............$266,605

### Source of Funds
- PACs ..................................58%
- Lg Individuals ($200+) ...........16%
- Individuals under $200 ...........13%
- Other ................................12%

**Top Industries & Interest Groups**

Bldg/Indust/Misc Unions ...........$46,450
Transportation Unions ...............$24,130
Lawyers & Lobbyists ..................$22,100
Public Sector Unions ................$21,320
Insurance ................................$12,192

Unidentified ..............................$8,260

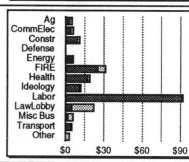

## 11. Dean A. Gallo (R)

**1990 Committees: Appropriations  Budget**
**First elected: 1984**

1989-90 Total receipts: ...........$652,386
1990 Year-end cash: ................$71,891

### Source of Funds
- PACs ..................................29%
- Lg Individuals ($200+) ...........53%
- Individuals under $200 ...........14%
- Other ..................................5%

**Top Industries & Interest Groups**

Lawyers & Lobbyists ..................$34,475
Real Estate ..............................$30,625
General Contractors .................$26,400
Pharmaceuticals/Health Prod ....$22,850
Home Builders ..........................$21,800

Unidentified ..............................$137,375

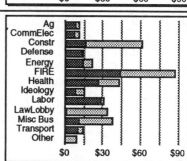

## 12. Dick Zimmer (R)

**1991-92 Committees: Govt Ops  Science**
**First elected: 1990**

1989-90 Total receipts: .........$1,326,818
1990 Year-end cash: ...................$3,115

### Source of Funds
- PACs ..................................15%
- Lg Individuals ($200+) ...........54%
- Individuals under $200 ...........17%
- Other ................................14%

**Top Industries & Interest Groups**

Lawyers & Lobbyists ..................$97,833
Securities & Investment .............$53,431
Pharmaceuticals/Health Prod ....$34,600
Real Estate ..............................$29,850
Retired ....................................$27,125

Unidentified ..............................$198,238

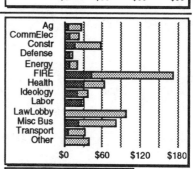

247

## 13. H. James Saxton (R)

**1990 Committees: Banking  Merchant Marine**
**First elected: 1984**

1989-90 Total receipts: ...........$628,142
1990 Year-end cash: ................$48,861

**Source of Funds**

■ PACs.........................................40%
▨ Lg Individuals ($200+) ..............24%
□ Individuals under $200 ..............30%
▨ Other.........................................6%

**Top  Industries & Interest Groups**

Insurance ...................................$49,637
Real Estate ................................$27,532
Sea Transport ...........................$17,250
Lawyers & Lobbyists .................$16,954
Commercial Banks ...................$15,285

Unidentified ...............................$48,933

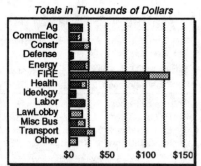

## 14. Frank J. Guarini (D)

**1990 Committees:  Budget  Ways & Means**
**First elected: 1978**

1989-90 Total receipts: ...........$465,248
1990 Year-end cash: ..............$330,515

**Source of Funds**

■ PACs.........................................62%
▨ Lg Individuals ($200+) ..............31%
□ Individuals under $200 ................1%
▨ Other.........................................6%

**Top  Industries & Interest Groups**

Insurance ...................................$54,000
Lawyers & Lobbyists .................$46,100
Bldg/Indust/Misc Unions ...........$28,650
Health Professionals .................$26,000
Transportation Unions ..............$22,250

Unidentified ...............................$27,750

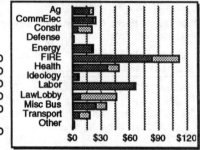

▨ PACs  ▨ Indivs ($200+)

Key to committee & category abbreviations is on page 173

# New Mexico

## Senate Spending

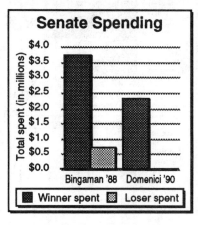

Total spent (in millions)

- Winner spent
- Loser spent

Bingaman '88    Domenici '90

## Spending in 1990 House Races

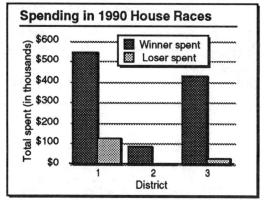

Total spent (in thousands)

- Winner spent
- Loser spent

District

## 1990 Elections at a Glance

| Dist | Name | Party | Vote Pct | Race Type |
|------|------|-------|----------|-----------|
| Sen | Jeff Bingaman (1988) | Dem | 63% | Reelected |
| Sen | Pete V. Domenici (1990) | Rep | 73% | Reelected |
| 1 | Steven H. Schiff | Rep | 70% | Reelected |
| 2 | Joe Skeen | Rep | 100% | Reelected |
| 3 | Bill Richardson | Dem | 74% | Reelected |

## Sen. Jeff Bingaman (D)

**1990 Committees: Armed Services  Energy  Labor**
**First elected: 1982**

1985-90 Total Rcpts: ............$3,795,542
1990 Year-end cash: ..............$318,865

**Source of Funds**
- PACs.............................................31%
- Lg Individuals ($200+) ..............18%
- Individuals under $200 ..............41%
- Other.............................................9%

### 1985-90 (PACs only)

**Top Industries & Interest Groups**

| | |
|---|---|
| Pro-Israel .................................. | $144,100 |
| Bldg/Indust/Misc Unions .......... | $133,589 |
| Oil & Gas .................................. | $90,243 |
| Public Sector Unions ................ | $82,700 |
| Transportation Unions .............. | $81,750 |

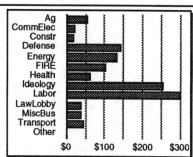

## Sen. Pete V. Domenici (R)

**1990 Committees: Appropriations  Budget  Energy**
**First elected: 1972**

1985-90 Total Rcpts: ............$2,434,289
1990 Year-end cash: ..............$218,513

**Source of Funds**
- PACs.............................................35%
- Lg Individuals ($200+) ..............29%
- Individuals under $200 ..............19%
- Other.............................................17%

### 1985-90

**Top Industries & Interest Groups**

| | |
|---|---|
| Oil & Gas .................................. | $249,248 |
| Lawyers & Lobbyists................ | $107,573 |
| Securities & Investment .......... | $100,935 |
| Electric Utilities ......................... | $66,350 |
| Defense Aerospace .................. | $64,400 |
| Unidentified .............................. | $122,130 |

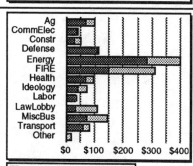

249

## 1. Steven H. Schiff (R)

**1990 Committees: Govt Ops  Science**
**First elected: 1988**

1989-90 Total receipts: ............$554,676
1990 Year-end cash: ................$20,540

### Source of Funds

| | |
|---|---|
| ■ PACs | 38% |
| ▨ Lg Individuals ($200+) | 19% |
| □ Individuals under $200 | 40% |
| ▨ Other | 3% |

### Top Industries & Interest Groups

| | |
|---|---|
| Health Professionals | $42,650 |
| Pro-Israel | $31,950 |
| Real Estate | $16,650 |
| Lawyers & Lobbyists | $16,375 |
| Oil & Gas | $15,100 |
| | |
| Unidentified | $13,750 |

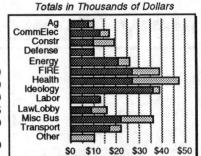

## 2. Joe Skeen (R)

**1990 Committees: Appropriations**
**First elected: 1980**

1989-90 Total receipts: ............$197,830
1990 Year-end cash: ..............$196,902

### Source of Funds

| | |
|---|---|
| ■ PACs | 54% |
| ▨ Lg Individuals ($200+) | 16% |
| □ Individuals under $200 | 21% |
| ▨ Other | 9% |

### Top Industries & Interest Groups

| | |
|---|---|
| Oil & Gas | $15,756 |
| Crop Production/Processing | $12,710 |
| Agric Services/Products | $9,850 |
| Automotive | $6,850 |
| Defense Electronics | $6,050 |
| | |
| Unidentified | $5,601 |

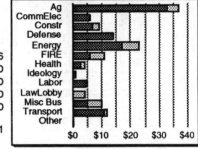

## 3. Bill Richardson (D)

**1990 Committees: Energy & Commerce  Interior**
**First elected: 1982**

1989-90 Total receipts: ............$531,096
1990 Year-end cash: ..............$329,903

### Source of Funds

| | |
|---|---|
| ■ PACs | 64% |
| ▨ Lg Individuals ($200+) | 19% |
| □ Individuals under $200 | 8% |
| ▨ Other | 10% |

### Top Industries & Interest Groups

| | |
|---|---|
| Health Professionals | $36,250 |
| Lawyers & Lobbyists | $33,323 |
| Bldg/Indust/Misc Unions | $27,650 |
| Insurance | $27,350 |
| Oil & Gas | $24,505 |
| | |
| Unidentified | $14,850 |

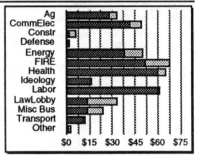

■ PACs  ▨ Indivs ($200+)

Key to committee & category abbreviations is on page 173

# New York

## Spending in 1990 House Races

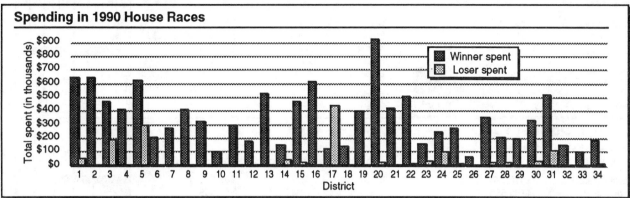

## 1990 Elections at a Glance

| Dist | Name | Party | Vote Pct | Race Type |
|------|------|-------|----------|-----------|
| Sen | Alfonse M. D'Amato (1986) | Rep | 57% | Reelected |
| Sen | Daniel P. Moynihan (1988) | Dem | 67% | Reelected |
| 1 | George J. Hochbrueckner | Dem | 56% | Reelected |
| 2 | Thomas J. Downey | Dem | 56% | Reelected |
| 3 | Robert J. Mrazek | Dem | 53% | Reelected |
| 4 | Norman F. Lent | Rep | 61% | Reelected |
| 5 | Raymond J. McGrath | Rep | 55% | Reelected |
| 6 | Floyd H. Flake | Dem | 73% | Reelected |
| 7 | Gary L. Ackerman | Dem | 100% | Reelected |
| 8 | James H. Scheuer | Dem | 72% | Reelected |
| 9 | Thomas J. Manton | Dem | 64% | Reelected |
| 10 | Charles E. Schumer | Dem | 80% | Reelected |
| 11 | Edolphus Towns | Dem | 93% | Reelected |
| 12 | Major R. Owens | Dem | 95% | Reelected |
| 13 | Stephen J. Solarz | Dem | 80% | Reelected |
| 14 | Susan Molinari | Rep | 60% | Reelected |
| 15 | Bill Green | Rep | 59% | Reelected |
| 16 | Charles B. Rangel | Dem | 97% | Reelected |
| 17 | Ted Weiss | Dem | 80% | Reelected |
| 18 | Jose E. Serrano | Dem | 93% | Reelected |
| 19 | Eliot L. Engel | Dem | 61% | Reelected |
| 20 | Nita M. Lowey | Dem | 63% | Reelected |
| 21 | Hamilton Fish Jr. | Rep | 71% | Reelected |
| 22 | Benjamin A. Gilman | Rep | 69% | Reelected |
| 23 | Michael R. McNulty | Dem | 64% | Reelected |
| 24 | Gerald B. H. Solomon | Rep | 68% | Reelected |

## Senate Spending

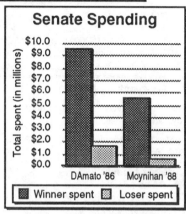

| Dist | Name | Party | Vote Pct | Race Type |
|------|------|-------|----------|-----------|
| 25 | Sherwood Boehlert | Rep | 84% | Reelected |
| 26 | David O'B Martin | Rep | 100% | Reelected |
| 27 | James T. Walsh | Rep | 63% | Reelected |
| 28 | Matthew F. McHugh | Dem | 65% | Reelected |
| 29 | Frank Horton | Rep | 63% | Reelected |
| 30 | Louise M. Slaughter | Dem | 59% | Reelected |
| 31 | Bill Paxon | Rep | 57% | Reelected |
| 32 | John J. LaFalce | Dem | 55% | Reelected |
| 33 | Henry J. Nowak | Dem | 78% | Reelected |
| 34 | Amo Houghton | Rep | 70% | Reelected |

*Totals in Thousands of Dollars*

## Sen. Alfonse M. D'Amato (R)

**1990 Committees: Appropriations Banking**
**First elected: 1980**

1985-90 Total Rcpts: .......... $11,174,367
1990 Year-end cash: ........... $2,787,012

### Source of Funds
- ■ PACs ................................... 11%
- ▨ Lg Individuals ($200+) .............. 37%
- □ Individuals under $200 ............. 33%
- ▧ Other ................................. 20%

### 1985-90 (PACs only)
**Top Industries & Interest Groups**

Securities & Investment .......... $175,900
Transportation Unions .............. $96,600
Insurance ................................. $94,698
Savings & Loans ....................... $74,355
Bldg/Indust/Misc Unions ........... $11,450

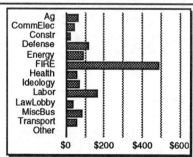

## Sen. Daniel Patrick Moynihan (D)

**1990 Committees: Envir Finance ForRel Rules**
**First elected: 1976**

1985-90 Total Rcpts: ........... $5,910,222
1990 Year-end cash: .............. $446,436

### Source of Funds
- ■ PACs ................................... 21%
- ▨ Lg Individuals ($200+) .............. 32%
- □ Individuals under $200 ............. 42%
- ▧ Other ................................. 5%

### 1985-90 (PACs only)
**Top Industries & Interest Groups**

Securities & Investment .......... $123,178
Bldg/Indust/Misc Unions ......... $121,004
Commercial Banks ................... $100,155
Insurance ................................. $80,227
Health Professionals ................. $66,680

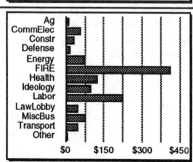

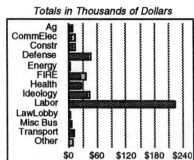

# 1. George J. Hochbrueckner (D)

**1990 Committees: Armed Serv  Merch Marine  Vet Affairs**
**First elected: 1986**

1989-90 Total receipts: ............$655,297
1990 Year-end cash: ................$15,836

**Source of Funds**

- PACs.............................................59%
- Lg Individuals ($200+) ..............14%
- Individuals under $200 ..............18%
- Other..............................................9%

**Top Industries & Interest Groups**

Bldg/Indust/Misc Unions ..........$107,100
Public Sector Unions .................$65,800
Transportation Unions ...............$51,050
Health Professionals ..................$27,442
Defense Electronics ...................$26,000

Unidentified ...............................$31,105

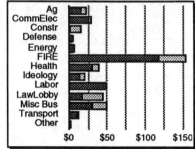

# 2. Thomas J. Downey (D)

**1990 Committees: Ways & Means**
**First elected: 1974**

1989-90 Total receipts: ............$612,878
1990 Year-end cash: ...............$486,556

**Source of Funds**

- PACs.............................................53%
- Lg Individuals ($200+) ..............22%
- Individuals under $200 ..............11%
- Other............................................14%

**Top Industries & Interest Groups**

Insurance ....................................$69,350
Lawyers & Lobbyists .................$43,859
Securities & Investment ............$39,800
Public Sector Unions .................$21,000
Bldg/Indust/Misc Unions ...........$18,900

Unidentified ...............................$13,185

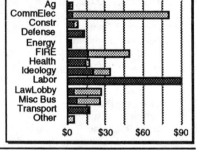

# 3. Robert J. Mrazek (D)

**1990 Committees: Appropriations**
**First elected: 1982**

1989-90 Total receipts: ............$602,613
1990 Year-end cash: ...............$351,185

**Source of Funds**

- PACs.............................................31%
- Lg Individuals ($200+) ..............37%
- Individuals under $200 ..............19%
- Other............................................13%

**Top Industries & Interest Groups**

TV & Movies ...............................$68,250
Public Sector Unions ................$35,150
Transportation Unions ...............$30,100
Lawyers & Lobbyists .................$27,050
Bldg/Indust/Misc Unions ...........$24,740

Unidentified ...............................$43,575

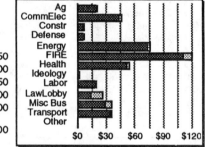

# 4. Norman F. Lent (R)

**1990 Committees: Energy & Commerce  Merch Marine**
**First elected: 1970**

1989-90 Total receipts: ...........$596,305
1990 Year-end cash: ...............$687,015

**Source of Funds**

- PACs.............................................69%
- Lg Individuals ($200+) ................8%
- Individuals under $200 ..............13%
- Other............................................11%

**Top Industries & Interest Groups**

Insurance ....................................$43,650
Oil & Gas ....................................$33,700
Securities & Investment ............$29,050
Electric Utilities .........................$26,900
Lawyers & Lobbyists .................$26,700

Unidentified ...............................$6,700

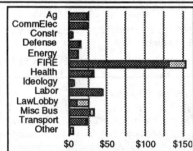

# 5. Raymond J. McGrath (R)

**1990 Committees: Ways & Means**
**First elected: 1980**

1989-90 Total receipts: ............$537,366
1990 Year-end cash: ...............$245,216

**Source of Funds**

- PACs.............................................65%
- Lg Individuals ($200+) ..............12%
- Individuals under $200 ..............14%
- Other..............................................8%

**Top Industries & Interest Groups**

Insurance ....................................$72,420
Lawyers & Lobbyists .................$25,755
Health Professionals ..................$20,950
Securities & Investment ............$19,250
Transportation Unions ..............$18,600

Unidentified ...............................$13,695

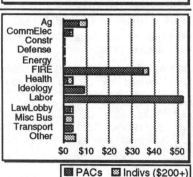

# 6. Floyd H. Flake (D)

**1990 Committees: Banking  Sm Business**
**First elected: 1986**

1989-90 Total receipts: ...........$240,869
1990 Year-end cash: .................$48,396

**Source of Funds**

- PACs.............................................49%
- Lg Individuals ($200+) ..............12%
- Individuals under $200 ..............32%
- Other..............................................8%

**Top Industries & Interest Groups**

Public Sector Unions .................$22,600
Bldg/Indust/Misc Unions ............$19,800
Commercial Banks ....................$12,300
Transportation Unions ...............$9,900
Savings & Loans ........................$6,500

Unidentified ...............................$9,288

252                    Key to committee & category abbreviations is on page 173

■ PACs   ▨ Indivs ($200+)

## 7. Gary L. Ackerman (D)

**1990 Committees:** Foreign Affairs  Post Off  Public Works
**First elected:** 1983

1989-90 Total receipts: ............$305,414
1990 Year-end cash: ..............$285,362

**Source of Funds**
- ■ PACs ..................................62%
- ▨ Lg Individuals ($200+) ............26%
- ☐ Individuals under $200 .............5%
- ▧ Other ................................8%

**Top Industries & Interest Groups**

Public Sector Unions ................$56,200
Bldg/Indust/Misc Unions ..........$29,437
Transportation Unions .............$23,200
Health Professionals ...............$17,300
Insurance ...............................$16,200

Unidentified ............................$18,700

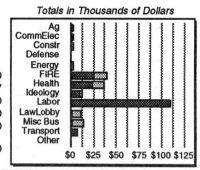

## 8. James H. Scheuer (D)

**1990 Committees:** Energy & Commerce  Science
**First elected:** 1964

1989-90 Total receipts: ............$414,085
1990 Year-end cash: ................$15,215

**Source of Funds**
- ■ PACs ..................................23%
- ▨ Lg Individuals ($200+) ............16%
- ☐ Individuals under $200 .............1%
- ▧ Other ...............................60%

**Top Industries & Interest Groups**

Lawyers & Lobbyists .................$17,850
TV & Movies ...........................$12,500
Health Professionals ..................$9,750
Public Sector Unions ..................$9,240
Pharmaceuticals/Health Prod ......$8,150

Unidentified ............................$14,100

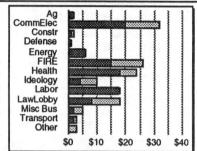

## 9. Thomas J. Manton (D)

**1990 Committees:** Admin  Energy & Comm  Merch Marine
**First elected:** 1984

1989-90 Total receipts: ............$620,609
1990 Year-end cash: ..............$478,772

**Source of Funds**
- ■ PACs ..................................73%
- ▨ Lg Individuals ($200+) ............17%
- ☐ Individuals under $200 .............4%
- ▧ Other ................................7%

**Top Industries & Interest Groups**

Bldg/Indust/Misc Unions ...........$54,150
Transportation Unions ..............$51,025
Insurance ...............................$42,797
Lawyers & Lobbyists .................$36,150
Commercial Banks ...................$27,200

Unidentified ............................$19,450

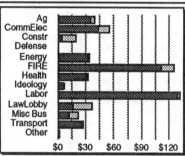

## 10. Charles E. Schumer (D)

**1990 Committees:** Banking  Budget  Judiciary
**First elected:** 1980

1989-90 Total receipts: ............$819,952
1990 Year-end cash: ...........$1,580,475

**Source of Funds**
- ■ PACs ..................................20%
- ▨ Lg Individuals ($200+) ............57%
- ☐ Individuals under $200 .............1%
- ▧ Other ................................23%

**Top Industries & Interest Groups**

Securities & Investment...........$170,602
Real Estate ..............................$80,050
Insurance ...............................$51,000
Lawyers & Lobbyists .................$47,300
Pro-Israel ...............................$23,000

Unidentified ............................$106,850

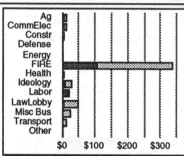

## 11. Edolphus Towns (D)

**1990 Committees:** Energy & Comm  Govt Ops  Pub Works
**First elected:** 1982

1989-90 Total receipts: ............$335,807
1990 Year-end cash: ..............$140,918

**Source of Funds**
- ■ PACs ..................................55%
- ▨ Lg Individuals ($200+) .............9%
- ☐ Individuals under $200 ............28%
- ▧ Other ................................8%

**Top Industries & Interest Groups**

Transportation Unions .............$19,220
Public Sector Unions ................$16,050
Health Professionals ...............$14,150
Bldg/Indust/Misc Unions ...........$13,800
Pharmaceuticals/Health Prod ....$12,450

Unidentified ..............................$9,375

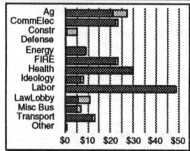

## 12. Major R. Owens (D)

**1990 Committees:** Educ/Labor  Govt Ops
**First elected:** 1982

1989-90 Total receipts: ............$168,086
1990 Year-end cash: ..................$6,451

**Source of Funds**
- ■ PACs ..................................61%
- ▨ Lg Individuals ($200+) .............8%
- ☐ Individuals under $200 ............17%
- ▧ Other ................................13%

**Top Industries & Interest Groups**

Bldg/Indust/Misc Unions ...........$29,050
Public Sector Unions ................$23,300
Transportation Unions .............$21,700
Health Professionals ..................$5,800
Pro-Israel ................................$5,000

Unidentified ..............................$9,750

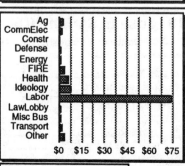

■ PACs   ▧ Indivs ($200+)

## 13. Stephen J. Solarz (D)

**1990 Committees:** Foreign Affairs  Merchant Marine
**First elected:** 1974

1989-90 Total receipts: ......... $1,223,447
1990 Year-end cash: ........... $1,859,603

**Source of Funds**
- ■ PACs ............................................ 4%
- ▨ Lg Individuals ($200+) ............... 25%
- □ Individuals under $200 ............. 50%
- ▩ Other ........................................ 20%

**Top Industries & Interest Groups**

| | |
|---|---|
| Health Professionals ................. | $60,800 |
| Misc Manufacturing & Distrib ..... | $24,700 |
| Public Sector Unions ................. | $15,500 |
| Pro-Israel ................................. | $13,300 |
| Real Estate ............................... | $10,750 |
| Unidentified ............................... | $91,751 |

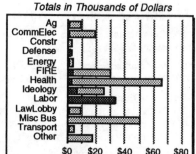

## 14. Susan Molinari (R)

**1990 Committees:** Public Works  Sm Business
**First elected:** 1980

1989-90 Total receipts: ............ $627,426
1990 Year-end cash: ................ $16,012

**Source of Funds**
- ■ PACs .......................................... 31%
- ▨ Lg Individuals ($200+) ............... 44%
- □ Individuals under $200 ............. 10%
- ▩ Other ........................................ 15%

**Top Industries & Interest Groups**

| | |
|---|---|
| Health Professionals ................. | $50,201 |
| Lawyers & Lobbyists ................. | $38,873 |
| Real Estate .............................. | $30,050 |
| Human Rights ........................... | $17,700 |
| Insurance ................................. | $17,100 |
| Unidentified ............................. | $116,110 |

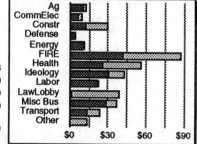

## 15. Bill Green (R)

**1990 Committees:** Appropriations
**First elected:** 1978

1989-90 Total receipts: ............ $705,383
1990 Year-end cash: .............. $310,107

**Source of Funds**
- ■ PACs .......................................... 22%
- ▨ Lg Individuals ($200+) ............... 53%
- □ Individuals under $200 ............. 17%
- ▩ Other .......................................... 8%

**Top Industries & Interest Groups**

| | |
|---|---|
| Lawyers & Lobbyists ................. | $89,084 |
| Securities & Investment ............ | $84,900 |
| Real Estate .............................. | $46,916 |
| Commercial Banks ................... | $25,000 |
| Pro-Israel ................................. | $20,200 |
| Unidentified .............................. | $58,260 |

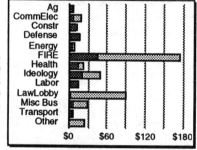

## 16. Charles B. Rangel (D)

**1990 Committees:** Ways & Means
**First elected:** 1970

1989-90 Total receipts: ........... $541,762
1990 Year-end cash: .............. $304,007

**Source of Funds**
- ■ PACs .......................................... 66%
- ▨ Lg Individuals ($200+) ............... 24%
- □ Individuals under $200 ............... 9%
- ▩ Other .......................................... 1%

**Top Industries & Interest Groups**

| | |
|---|---|
| Insurance ................................. | $63,795 |
| Lawyers & Lobbyists ................. | $36,550 |
| Securities & Investment ............ | $35,225 |
| Bldg/Indust/Misc Unions ........... | $30,100 |
| Public Sector Unions ................ | $28,500 |
| Unidentified ............................. | $19,900 |

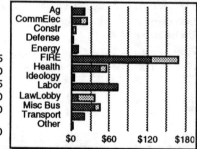

## 17. Ted Weiss (D)

**1990 Committees:** Banking  Foreign Affairs  Govt Ops
**First elected:** 1976

1989-90 Total receipts: ............ $144,408
1990 Year-end cash: ................ $80,492

**Source of Funds**
- ■ PACs .......................................... 52%
- ▨ Lg Individuals ($200+) ............... 22%
- □ Individuals under $200 ............. 26%
- ▩ Other .......................................... 0%

**Top Industries & Interest Groups**

| | |
|---|---|
| Bldg/Indust/Misc Unions ........... | $22,500 |
| Public Sector Unions ................ | $20,550 |
| Human Rights ........................... | $7,750 |
| Transportation Unions ............... | $7,000 |
| Health Professionals ................. | $6,400 |
| Unidentified ............................. | $7,750 |

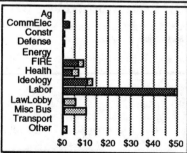

## 18. Jose E. Serrano (D)

**1990 Committees:** Educ/Labor  Sm Business
**First elected:** 1990

1989-90 Total receipts: ........... $354,385
1990 Year-end cash: ................ $69,641

**Source of Funds**
- ■ PACs .......................................... 58%
- ▨ Lg Individuals ($200+) ............... 24%
- □ Individuals under $200 ............... 8%
- ▩ Other ........................................ 10%

**Top Industries & Interest Groups**

| | |
|---|---|
| Bldg/Indust/Misc Unions ........... | $53,625 |
| Public Sector Unions ................ | $37,550 |
| Health Professionals ................. | $25,250 |
| Transportation Unions .............. | $24,400 |
| Lawyers & Lobbyists ................. | $18,999 |
| Unidentified ............................. | $20,900 |

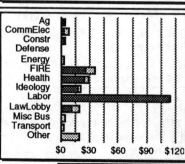

Key to committee & category abbreviations is on page 173

■ PACs  ▨ Indivs ($200+)

## 19. Eliot L. Engel (D)

**1990 Committees:** Banking  Foreign Affairs  Sm Business
**First elected:** 1988

1989-90 Total receipts: ...........$469,119
1990 Year-end cash: ................$11,899

**Source of Funds**
- ■ PACs ...........................................78%
- ▨ Lg Individuals ($200+) ...............9%
- □ Individuals under $200 ...............9%
- ▨ Other ..........................................5%

### Top Industries & Interest Groups

Bldg/Indust/Misc Unions ...........$59,050
Public Sector Unions ................$45,350
Pro-Israel .................................$27,750
Transportation Unions ..............$27,000
Health Professionals .................$23,087

Unidentified ..................................$8,650

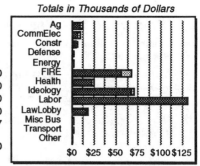

## 20. Nita M. Lowey (D)

**1990 Committees:** Educ/Labor  Merchant Marine
**First elected:** 1988

1989-90 Total receipts: .........$1,223,045
1990 Year-end cash: ...............$339,552

**Source of Funds**
- ■ PACs ...........................................36%
- ▨ Lg Individuals ($200+) .............44%
- □ Individuals under $200 .............17%
- ▨ Other ..........................................4%

### Top Industries & Interest Groups

Lawyers & Lobbyists ................$129,200
Bldg/Indust/Misc Unions ...........$94,085
Securities & Investment .............$88,550
Public Sector Unions .................$61,850
Transportation Unions ...............$46,250

Unidentified ..............................$129,339

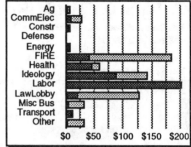

## 21. Hamilton Fish Jr. (R)

**1990 Committees:** Judiciary
**First elected:** 1968

1989-90 Total receipts: ...........$348,209
1990 Year-end cash: ...............$134,830

**Source of Funds**
- ■ PACs ...........................................57%
- ▨ Lg Individuals ($200+) .............28%
- □ Individuals under $200 .............15%
- ▨ Other ..........................................0%

### Top Industries & Interest Groups

Insurance ...................................$34,759
Lawyers & Lobbyists .................$21,264
Commercial Banks ....................$18,950
Bldg/Indust/Misc Unions ...........$17,900
Securities & Investment .............$14,800

Unidentified ................................$25,228

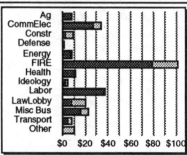

## 22. Benjamin A. Gilman (R)

**1990 Committees:** Foreign Affairs  Post Office
**First elected:** 1972

1989-90 Total receipts: ...........$445,481
1990 Year-end cash: .................$68,257

**Source of Funds**
- ■ PACs ...........................................43%
- ▨ Lg Individuals ($200+) .............27%
- □ Individuals under $200 .............23%
- ▨ Other ..........................................7%

### Top Industries & Interest Groups

Public Sector Unions .................$45,170
Bldg/Indust/Misc Unions ...........$29,904
Transportation Unions ...............$24,435
Real Estate ...............................$13,760
Pro-Israel .................................$11,650

Unidentified ................................$41,096

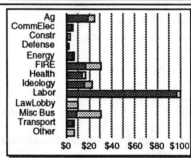

## 23. Michael R. McNulty (D)

**1990 Committees:** Armed Services  Post Office
**First elected:** 1988

1989-90 Total receipts: ...........$240,736
1990 Year-end cash: ...............$100,394

**Source of Funds**
- ■ PACs ...........................................64%
- ▨ Lg Individuals ($200+) .............10%
- □ Individuals under $200 .............24%
- ▨ Other ..........................................2%

### Top Industries & Interest Groups

Bldg/Indust/Misc Unions ...........$36,474
Public Sector Unions .................$33,825
Transportation Unions ...............$17,500
Defense Aerospace ...................$15,550
Health Professionals .................$13,000

Unidentified ..................................$7,350

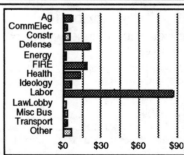

## 24. Gerald B. H. Solomon (R)

**1990 Committees:** Rules
**First elected:** 1978

1989-90 Total receipts: ...........$255,758
1990 Year-end cash: ...............$112,820

**Source of Funds**
- ■ PACs ...........................................63%
- ▨ Lg Individuals ($200+) .............13%
- □ Individuals under $200 .............24%
- ▨ Other ..........................................0%

### Top Industries & Interest Groups

Insurance ...................................$19,300
Health Professionals .................$18,650
Transportation Unions ...............$12,570
Automotive ................................$10,950
Real Estate ...............................$10,270

Unidentified ................................$12,320

*Totals in Thousands of Dollars*

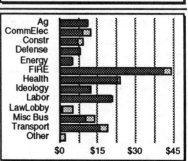

■ PACs  ▨ Indivs ($200+)

255

## 25. Sherwood Boehlert (R)

**1990 Committees: Public Works  Science**
**First elected: 1982**

1989-90 Total receipts: ............ $303,746
1990 Year-end cash: .............. $189,652

**Source of Funds**
- PACs ................................ 44%
- Lg Individuals ($200+) ........ 22%
- Individuals under $200 ......... 17%
- Other ............................... 18%

**Top Industries & Interest Groups**

Transportation Unions .............. $20,150
Air Transport ........................... $15,650
Public Sector Unions ................ $14,500
Dairy ...................................... $11,500
Health Professionals ................. $9,350

Unidentified ............................. $18,250

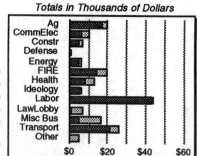

## 26. David O'B Martin (R)

**1990 Committees: Armed Services**
**First elected: 1980**

1989-90 Total receipts: .............. $74,891
1990 Year-end cash: ................. $84,339

**Source of Funds**
- PACs ................................ 61%
- Lg Individuals ($200+) ........ 13%
- Individuals under $200 ......... 9%
- Other ............................... 17%

**Top Industries & Interest Groups**

Defense Aerospace ................... $11,500
Health Professionals .................. $6,000
Defense Electronics .................... $4,500
Food Processing & Sales ........... $2,500
Transportation Unions ............... $2,500

Unidentified ............................. $2,750

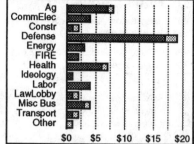

## 27. James T. Walsh (R)

**1990 Committees: Admin  Agriculture**
**First elected: 1988**

1989-90 Total receipts: ............ $365,536
1990 Year-end cash: ................. $40,952

**Source of Funds**
- PACs ................................ 37%
- Lg Individuals ($200+) ........ 29%
- Individuals under $200 ......... 31%
- Other ............................... 2%

**Top Industries & Interest Groups**

Health Professionals ................. $20,901
Real Estate .............................. $14,850
Bldg/Indust/Misc Unions ........... $13,200
Insurance ................................ $12,700
Agric Services/Products ............ $11,200

Unidentified ............................. $39,150

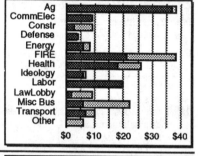

## 28. Matthew F. McHugh (D)

**1990 Committees: Appropriations**
**First elected: 1974**

1989-90 Total receipts: ............ $227,716
1990 Year-end cash: .............. $137,521

**Source of Funds**
- PACs ................................ 52%
- Lg Individuals ($200+) ......... 7%
- Individuals under $200 ......... 30%
- Other ............................... 12%

**Top Industries & Interest Groups**

Bldg/Indust/Misc Unions ........... $23,540
Public Sector Unions ................ $21,950
Transportation Unions ............... $13,250
Lawyers & Lobbyists .................. $9,750
Commercial Banks ..................... $7,600

Unidentified ............................. $3,050

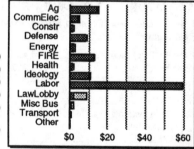

## 29. Frank Horton (R)

**1990 Committees: Govt Ops  Post Office**
**First elected: 1962**

1989-90 Total receipts: ............ $207,092
1990 Year-end cash: .............. $162,845

**Source of Funds**
- PACs ................................ 77%
- Lg Individuals ($200+) ......... 5%
- Individuals under $200 ......... 11%
- Other ............................... 7%

**Top Industries & Interest Groups**

Public Sector Unions ................ $40,150
Bldg/Indust/Misc Unions ........... $25,650
Transportation Unions ............... $11,850
Misc Manufacturing & Distrib ....... $9,650
Accountants ............................. $7,300

Unidentified ............................. $850

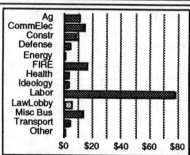

## 30. Louise M. Slaughter (D)

**1990 Committees: Rules**
**First elected: 1986**

1989-90 Total receipts: ............ $449,184
1990 Year-end cash: .............. $129,299

**Source of Funds**
- PACs ................................ 65%
- Lg Individuals ($200+) ........ 18%
- Individuals under $200 ......... 14%
- Other ............................... 3%

**Top Industries & Interest Groups**

Bldg/Indust/Misc Unions ........... $79,100
Public Sector Unions ................ $57,570
Transportation Unions ............... $24,200
Lawyers & Lobbyists ................. $22,650
Health Professionals ................. $20,550

Unidentified ............................. $17,516

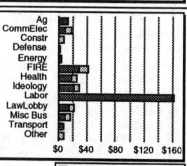

Key to committee & category abbreviations is on page 173

■ PACs  ▨ Indivs ($200+)

# 31. Bill Paxon (R)

**1990 Committees: Banking  Vet Affairs**
**First elected: 1988**

1989-90 Total receipts: ............$686,209
1990 Year-end cash: ..............$177,950

**Source of Funds**
■ PACs.............................................36%
▨ Lg Individuals ($200+) ...............38%
☐ Individuals under $200 ..............24%
▨ Other................................................1%

**Top Industries & Interest Groups**

Insurance ....................$45,385
Commercial Banks ....................$44,972
General Contractors .................$35,535
Real Estate ...............................$29,815
Health Professionals ..................$21,835

Unidentified ................................$62,821

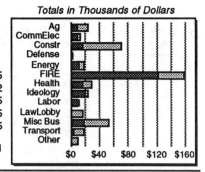

# 32. John J. LaFalce (D)

**1990 Committees: Banking  Sm Business**
**First elected: 1974**

1989-90 Total receipts: ...........$339,919
1990 Year-end cash: ...............$645,138

**Source of Funds**
■ PACs.............................................60%
▨ Lg Individuals ($200+) ................8%
☐ Individuals under $200 ...............7%
▨ Other..............................................25%

**Top Industries & Interest Groups**

Commercial Banks ....................$62,250
Bldg/Indust/Misc Unions ...........$14,000
Real Estate ..............................$12,500
Lawyers & Lobbyists .................$12,200
Public Sector Unions .................$11,250

Unidentified .................................$4,529

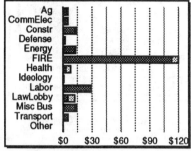

# 33. Henry J. Nowak (D)

**1990 Committees: Public Works  Science**
**First elected: 1974**

1989-90 Total receipts: ............$150,832
1990 Year-end cash: ...............$238,450

**Source of Funds**
■ PACs.............................................65%
▨ Lg Individuals ($200+) ................2%
☐ Individuals under $200 ..............10%
▨ Other..............................................23%

**Top Industries & Interest Groups**

Bldg/Indust/Misc Unions ............$15,350
Transportation Unions ...............$13,800
Public Sector Unions .................$10,500
General Contractors ....................$8,000
Air Transport ..............................$7,250

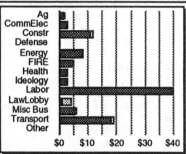

# 34. Amo Houghton (R)

**1990 Committees: Budget  Foreign Affairs**
**First elected: 1986**

1989-90 Total receipts: ...........$333,962
1990 Year-end cash: ...............$306,780

**Source of Funds**
■ PACs.............................................32%
▨ Lg Individuals ($200+) ...............53%
☐ Individuals under $200 ..............11%
▨ Other..............................................5%

**Top Industries & Interest Groups**

Telecom Services & Equip ........$33,500
Securities & Investment .............$31,200
Retired .......................................$15,900
Commercial Banks ....................$13,250
Oil & Gas ...................................$12,300

Unidentified ................................$38,450

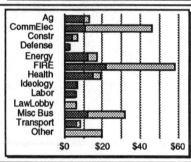

▨ PACs  ▨ Indivs ($200+)

257

# North Carolina

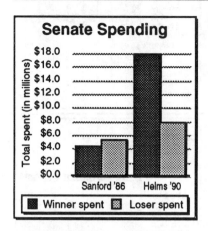

## Senate Spending

Total spent (in millions)

Winner spent | Loser spent

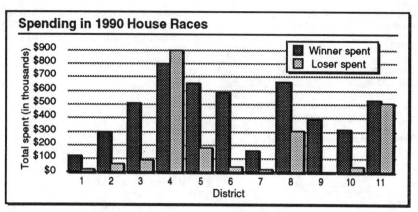

## Spending in 1990 House Races

Total spent (in thousands)

Winner spent | Loser spent

District

## 1990 Elections at a Glance

| Dist | Name | Party | Vote Pct | Race Type |
|------|------|-------|----------|-----------|
| Sen | Jesse Helms (1990) | Rep | 53% | Reelected |
| Sen | Terry Sanford (1986) | Dem | 52% | Open Seat |
| 1 | Walter B. Jones | Dem | 65% | Reelected |
| 2 | Tim Valentine | Dem | 75% | Reelected |
| 3 | H. Martin Lancaster | Dem | 59% | Reelected |
| 4 | David E. Price | Dem | 58% | Reelected |
| 5 | Stephen L. Neal | Dem | 59% | Reelected |
| 6 | Howard Coble | Rep | 67% | Reelected |
| 7 | Charlie Rose | Dem | 66% | Reelected |
| 8 | W. G. "Bill" Hefner | Dem | 55% | Reelected |
| 9 | Alex McMillan | Rep | 62% | Reelected |
| 10 | Cass Ballenger | Rep | 62% | Reelected |
| 11 | Charles H. Taylor | Rep | 51% | Beat Incumb |

*Totals in Thousands of Dollars*

## Sen. Jesse Helms (R)

**1990 Committees: Agriculture  Foreign Relations  Rules**
**First elected: 1972**

1985-90 Total Rcpts: ..........$17,773,414
1990 Year-end cash: ................$12,326

**Source of Funds**
- PACs.................................................5%
- Lg Individuals ($200+) ...............16%
- Individuals under $200 .............64%
- Other ..............................................15%

### 1985-90
**Top  Industries & Interest Groups**

Republican/Conservative ........$173,520
Misc Manufacturing & Distrib... $157,044
Retired .................................$122,389
Health Professionals................$119,054
Lawyers & Lobbyists .................$81,750

Unidentified..........................$1,524,697

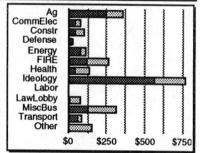

Ag, CommElec, Constr, Defense, Energy, FIRE, Health, Ideology, Labor, LawLobby, MiscBus, Transport, Other

$0   $250   $500   $750

## Sen. Terry Sanford (D)

**1990 Committees: Banking  Budget  Foreign Relations**
**First elected: 1986**

1985-90 Total Rcpts: ............$6,425,529
1990 Year-end cash: ................$80,200

**Source of Funds**
- PACs..............................................22%
- Lg Individuals ($200+) ...............25%
- Individuals under $200 .............30%
- Other ..............................................23%

### 1985-90 (PACs only)
**Top  Industries & Interest Groups**

Commercial Banks ..................$194,000
Bldg/Indust/Misc Unions ..........$181,750
Public Sector Unions ...............$130,700
Insurance ..............................$103,249
Securities & Investment ............$84,750

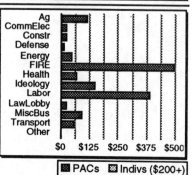

Ag, CommElec, Constr, Defense, Energy, FIRE, Health, Ideology, Labor, LawLobby, MiscBus, Transport, Other

$0   $125   $250   $375   $500

PACs   Indivs ($200+)

Key to committee & category abbreviations is on page 173

Totals in Thousands of Dollars

# 1. Walter B. Jones (D)

**1990 Committees: Agriculture Merchant Marine**
**First elected: 1966**

1989-90 Total receipts: ............$127,710
1990 Year-end cash: ..............$328,428

**Source of Funds**

- PACs .................................................52%
- Lg Individuals ($200+) ..............4%
- Individuals under $200 ..............1%
- Other ..............................................44%

**Top Industries & Interest Groups**

Sea Transport ............................$10,250
Oil & Gas ...................................$10,000
Transportation Unions ................$8,500
Lawyers & Lobbyists ...................$7,000
Public Sector Unions ..................$4,500

Unidentified ................................$1,000

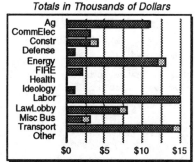

# 2. Tim Valentine (D)

**1990 Committees: Public Works Science**
**First elected: 1982**

1989-90 Total receipts: ............$261,712
1990 Year-end cash: ................$20,314

**Source of Funds**

- PACs.................................................58%
- Lg Individuals ($200+) .............16%
- Individuals under $200 ............18%
- Other ..................................................8%

**Top Industries & Interest Groups**

Air Transport ..............................$15,250
Tobacco ......................................$14,725
Lawyers & Lobbyists ..................$12,150
Public Sector Unions ..................$9,250
Telephone Utilities ......................$9,200

Unidentified ................................$15,650

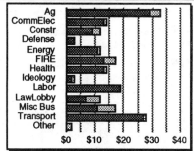

# 3. H. Martin Lancaster (D)

**1990 Committees: Agriculture Arm Serv Sm Business**
**First elected: 1986**

1989-90 Total receipts: ............$421,283
1990 Year-end cash: ................$20,581

**Source of Funds**

- PACs.................................................47%
- Lg Individuals ($200+) .............23%
- Individuals under $200 ............22%
- Other ..................................................8%

**Top Industries & Interest Groups**

Health Professionals ..................$25,330
Tobacco ......................................$18,950
Defense Aerospace ....................$15,800
Lawyers & Lobbyists ..................$13,650
Real Estate ................................$11,005

Unidentified ................................$51,365

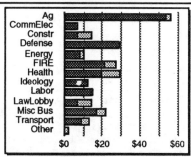

# 4. David E. Price (D)

**1990 Committees: Banking Science**
**First elected: 1986**

1989-90 Total receipts: ............$771,624
1990 Year-end cash: ................$11,899

**Source of Funds**

- PACs.................................................47%
- Lg Individuals ($200+) .............14%
- Individuals under $200 ............30%
- Other ..................................................9%

**Top Industries & Interest Groups**

Commercial Banks ....................$63,600
Public Sector Unions ................$40,350
Bldg/Indust/Misc Unions ............$38,310
Lawyers & Lobbyists ..................$28,350
Insurance ...................................$25,000

Unidentified ................................$23,300

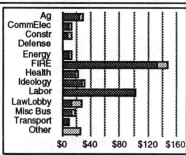

# 5. Stephen L. Neal (D)

**1990 Committees: Banking Govt Ops**
**First elected: 1974**

1989-90 Total receipts: ............$671,884
1990 Year-end cash: ................$27,665

**Source of Funds**

- PACs.................................................56%
- Lg Individuals ($200+) .............18%
- Individuals under $200 ............11%
- Other ................................................15%

**Top Industries & Interest Groups**

Commercial Banks ....................$104,400
Public Sector Unions ................$37,800
Tobacco ......................................$29,387
Real Estate ................................$25,250
Lawyers & Lobbyists .................$24,925

Unidentified ................................$21,525

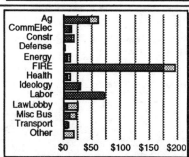

# 6. Howard Coble (R)

**1990 Committees: Judiciary Merchant Marine**
**First elected: 1984**

1989-90 Total receipts: ............$572,043
1990 Year-end cash: ................$15,846

**Source of Funds**

- PACs.................................................39%
- Lg Individuals ($200+) ..............21%
- Individuals under $200 ............37%
- Other ..................................................3%

**Top Industries & Interest Groups**

Misc Manufacturing & Distrib .....$51,279
Insurance ...................................$25,457
Telephone Utilities .....................$17,200
Lawyers & Lobbyists ..................$17,100
Real Estate ................................$15,534

Unidentified ................................$24,135

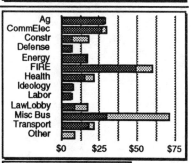

■ PACs ☒ Indivs ($200+)

## 7. Charlie Rose (D)

**1990 Committees: Admin  Agriculture**
**First elected: 1972**

1989-90 Total receipts: ............$328,232
1990 Year-end cash: ..............$540,833

**Source of Funds**
- ■ PACs..............................................55%
- ▨ Lg Individuals ($200+) ...............12%
- □ Individuals under $200 ...............3%
- ⊠ Other...........................................30%

**Top  Industries & Interest Groups**

Crop Production/Processing ......$31,850
Tobacco .....................................$23,000
Dairy ..........................................$15,250
Agric Services/Products ............$14,600
Public Sector Unions .................$14,000

Unidentified ................................$7,250

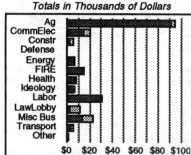

## 8. W. G. "Bill" Hefner (D)

**1990 Committees:  Appropriations**
**First elected: 1974**

1989-90 Total receipts: ............$660,311
1990 Year-end cash: ..............$111,471

**Source of Funds**
- ■ PACs..............................................61%
- ▨ Lg Individuals ($200+) ...............19%
- □ Individuals under $200 ...............8%
- ⊠ Other...........................................12%

**Top  Industries & Interest Groups**

Defense Aerospace ...................$47,650
Defense Electronics ...................$47,150
Public Sector Unions .................$35,300
Bldg/Indust/Misc Unions ...........$33,000
Lawyers & Lobbyists .................$29,900

Unidentified ................................$18,700

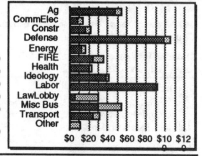

## 9. Alex McMillan (R)

**1990 Committees:  Energy & Commerce**
**First elected: 1984**

1989-90 Total receipts: ............$399,007
1990 Year-end cash: ...............$103,331

**Source of Funds**
- ■ PACs..............................................70%
- ▨ Lg Individuals ($200+) ...............14%
- □ Individuals under $200 ............11%
- ⊠ Other...............................................4%

**Top  Industries & Interest Groups**

Commercial Banks ...................$43,500
Electric Utilities ..........................$24,550
Insurance ..................................$20,800
Misc Manufacturing & Distrib .....$16,950
Pharmaceuticals/Health Prod ....$14,600

Unidentified ...............................$18,750

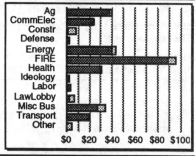

## 10. Cass Ballenger (R)

**1990 Committees:  Educ/Labor  Public Works**
**First elected: 1986**

1989-90 Total receipts: ............$297,417
1990 Year-end cash: .................$21,544

**Source of Funds**
- ■ PACs..............................................62%
- ▨ Lg Individuals ($200+) ...............23%
- □ Individuals under $200 ............15%
- ⊠ Other...............................................0%

**Top  Industries & Interest Groups**

Misc Manufacturing & Distrib .....$45,917
Health Professionals .................$14,800
Air Transport .............................$14,600
Chemicals ..................................$11,075
Real Estate ...............................$11,000

Unidentified ...............................$14,342

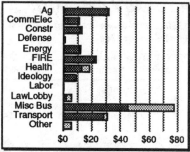

## 11. Charles H. Taylor (R)

**1991-92 Committees:  Interior  Public Works**
**First elected: 1990**

1989-90 Total receipts: ............$523,580
1990 Year-end cash: ......................$543

**Source of Funds**
- ■ PACs..............................................20%
- ▨ Lg Individuals ($200+) ...............16%
- □ Individuals under $200 ............17%
- ⊠ Other...........................................48%

**Top  Industries & Interest Groups**

Automotive .................................$17,500
Misc Manufacturing & Distrib .....$14,000
Health Professionals .................$12,000
Retired ......................................$11,832
Oil & Gas ..................................$11,700

Unidentified ...............................$18,670

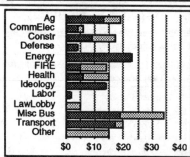

⊠ PACs  ⊠ Indivs ($200+)

Key to committee & category abbreviations is on page 173

# North Dakota

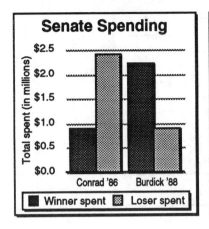

## Senate Spending

Total spent (in millions)

$2.5
$2.0
$1.5
$1.0
$0.5
$0.0

Conrad '86    Burdick '88

■ Winner spent    ▨ Loser spent

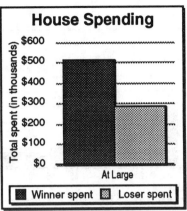

## House Spending

Total spent (in thousands)

$600
$500
$400
$300
$200
$100
$0

At Large

■ Winner spent    ▨ Loser spent

### 1990 Elections at a Glance

| Dist | Name | Party | Vote Pct | Race Type |
|------|------|-------|----------|-----------|
| Sen | Quentin N. Burdick (1988) | Dem | 59% | Reelected |
| Sen | Kent Conrad (1986) | Dem | 50% | Beat Incumb |
| 1 | Byron L. Dorgan | Dem | 65% | Reelected |

## Sen. Quentin N. Burdick (D)

**1990 Committees: Appropriations  Envir/Public Works**
**First elected: 1960**

1985-90 Total Rcpts: ............$1,983,997
1990 Year-end cash: .................$13,829

**Source of Funds**
■ PACs ...........................................57%
▨ Lg Individuals ($200+) ...........25%
□ Individuals under $200 ............8%
▨ Other ........................................10%

### 1985-90 (PACs only)

**Top  Industries & Interest Groups**

Bldg/Indust/Misc Unions ..........$139,800
Transportation Unions .............$100,350
Public Sector Unions .................$88,450
Pro-Israel ...................................$69,050
Oil & Gas ...................................$49,150

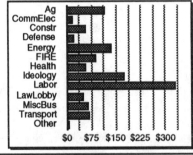

Ag, CommElec, Constr, Defense, Energy, FIRE, Health, Ideology, Labor, LawLobby, MiscBus, Transport, Other

$0   $75   $150   $225   $300

## Sen. Kent Conrad (D)

**1990 Committees: Agriculture  Budget  Energy**
**First elected: 1986**

1985-90 Total Rcpts: ............$1,784,773
1990 Year-end cash: ..............$510,092

**Source of Funds**
■ PACs ...........................................54%
▨ Lg Individuals ($200+) ..............10%
□ Individuals under $200 ............26%
▨ Other ........................................10%

### 1985-90 (PACs only)

**Top  Industries & Interest Groups**

Bldg/Indust/Misc Unions ..........$187,389
Public Sector Unions .................$93,700
Crop Production/Processing ......$63,165
Transportation Unions ..............$51,350
Insurance ...................................$46,138

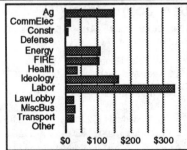

Ag, CommElec, Constr, Defense, Energy, FIRE, Health, Ideology, Labor, LawLobby, MiscBus, Transport, Other

$0   $100   $200   $300

## 1. Byron L. Dorgan (D)

**1990 Committees: Ways & Means**
**First elected: 1980**

1989-90 Total receipts: ............$598,471
1990 Year-end cash: ..............$237,008

**Source of Funds**
■ PACs ...........................................67%
▨ Lg Individuals ($200+) ..............5%
□ Individuals under $200 ............11%
▨ Other ........................................16%

### Top  Industries & Interest Groups

Insurance ...................................$85,256
Public Sector Unions ................$37,807
Lawyers & Lobbyists .................$35,500
Bldg/Indust/Misc Unions ...........$29,300
Health Professionals .................$22,250

Unidentified ..................................$4,400

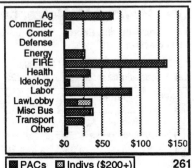

Ag, CommElec, Constr, Defense, Energy, FIRE, Health, Ideology, Labor, LawLobby, Misc Bus, Transport, Other

$0   $50   $100   $150

■ PACs    ▨ Indivs ($200+)

261

# Ohio

## Spending in 1990 House Races

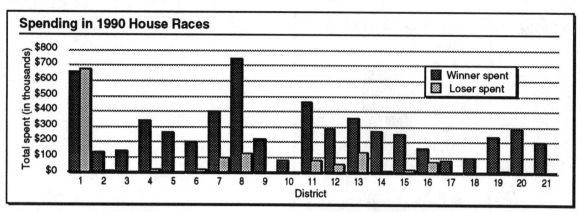

Total spent (in thousands)

$800, $700, $600, $500, $400, $300, $200, $100, $0

Districts 1–21

■ Winner spent  ▨ Loser spent

## Senate Spending

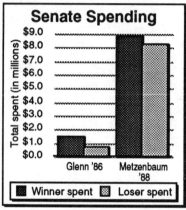

Total spent (in millions)

$9.0, $8.0, $7.0, $6.0, $5.0, $4.0, $3.0, $2.0, $1.0, $0.0

Glenn '86    Metzenbaum '88

■ Winner spent  ▨ Loser spent

## 1990 Elections at a Glance

| Dist | Name | Party | Vote Pct | Race Type |
|------|------|-------|----------|-----------|
| Sen | John Glenn (1986) | Dem | 62% | Reelected |
| Sen | Howard Metzenbaum (1988) | Dem | 57% | Reelected |
| 1 | Charles Luken | Dem | 51% | Open Seat |
| 2 | Bill Gradison | Rep | 64% | Reelected |
| 3 | Tony P. Hall | Dem | 100% | Reelected |
| 4 | Michael G. Oxley | Rep | 62% | Reelected |
| 5 | Paul E. Gillmor | Rep | 68% | Reelected |
| 6 | Bob McEwen | Rep | 71% | Reelected |
| 7 | David L. Hobson | Rep | 62% | Open Seat |
| 8 | John A. Boehner | Rep | 61% | Beat Incumb |
| 9 | Marcy Kaptur | Dem | 78% | Reelected |
| 10 | Clarence E. Miller | Rep | 63% | Reelected |
| 11 | Dennis E. Eckart | Dem | 66% | Reelected |
| 12 | John R. Kasich | Rep | 72% | Reelected |
| 13 | Don J. Pease | Dem | 57% | Reelected |
| 14 | Thomas C. Sawyer | Dem | 60% | Reelected |
| 15 | Chalmers P. Wylie | Rep | 59% | Reelected |
| 16 | Ralph Regula | Rep | 59% | Reelected |
| 17 | James A. Traficant Jr. | Dem | 78% | Reelected |
| 18 | Douglas Applegate | Dem | 74% | Reelected |
| 19 | Edward F. Feighan | Dem | 65% | Reelected |
| 20 | Mary Rose Oakar | Dem | 73% | Reelected |
| 21 | Louis Stokes | Dem | 80% | Reelected |

*Totals in Thousands of Dollars*

## Sen. John Glenn (D)

**1990 Committees: Armed Services   Govt Affairs**
**First elected: 1974**

1985-90 Total Rcpts: ............$2,386,616
1990 Year-end cash: ..............$142,497

**Source of Funds**
- ■ PACs ...................................... 28%
- ▨ Lg Individuals ($200+) .............. 16%
- □ Individuals under $200 .............. 45%
- ▨ Other ..................................... 11%

### 1985-90 (PACs only)

**Top  Industries & Interest Groups**

Bldg/Indust/Misc Unions .......... $150,600
Defense Aerospace .................. $62,400
Public Sector Unions ................ $61,400
Transportation Unions .............. $59,250
Defense Electronics .................. $48,350

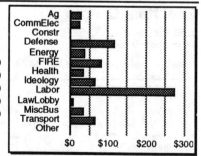

Ag, CommElec, Constr, Defense, Energy, FIRE, Health, Ideology, Labor, LawLobby, MiscBus, Transport, Other

$0   $100   $200   $300

## Sen. Howard M. Metzenbaum (D)

**1990 Committees: Energy  Envir  Judiciary  Labor**
**First elected: 1976**

1985-90 Total Rcpts: ............$7,869,812
1990 Year-end cash: ..............$164,029

**Source of Funds**
- ■ PACs ...................................... 13%
- ▨ Lg Individuals ($200+) ............. 37%
- □ Individuals under $200 ............. 34%
- ▨ Other ..................................... 16%

### 1985-90 (PACs only)

**Top  Industries & Interest Groups**

Pro-Israel ................................. $245,085
Bldg/Indust/Misc Unions .......... $239,930
Transportation Unions ............. $110,800
Public Sector Unions ................ $81,000
Leadership PACs ...................... $51,500

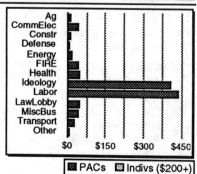

Ag, CommElec, Constr, Defense, Energy, FIRE, Health, Ideology, Labor, LawLobby, MiscBus, Transport, Other

$0   $150   $300   $450

■ PACs  ▨ Indivs ($200+)

Key to committee & category abbreviations is on page 173

# 1. Charles Luken (D)

**1991-92 Committees:** Banking  Govt Ops
**First elected:** 1990

1989-90 Total receipts: ............$688,414
1990 Year-end cash: ................$29,243

**Source of Funds**
- ■ PACs ............................... 48%
- ▨ Lg Individuals ($200+) ............. 24%
- □ Individuals under $200 ............. 12%
- ▧ Other ............................. 15%

**Top Industries & Interest Groups**

Bldg/Indust/Misc Unions ...........$96,350
Lawyers & Lobbyists .................$39,390
Public Sector Unions ................$34,250
Transportation Unions ..............$28,800
Insurance ...........................$28,040

Unidentified ........................$42,625

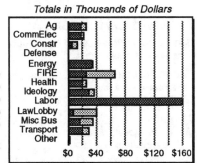

# 2. Bill Gradison (R)

**1990 Committees:** Budget  Ways & Means
**First elected:** 1974

1989-90 Total receipts: ............$202,809
1990 Year-end cash: ...............$443,301

**Source of Funds**
- ■ PACs .............................. 2%
- ▨ Lg Individuals ($200+) ............. 23%
- □ Individuals under $200 ............. 33%
- ▧ Other ............................. 43%

**Top Industries & Interest Groups**

Insurance ...........................$15,050
Lawyers & Lobbyists ....................$8,157
Misc Manufacturing & Distrib .......$3,100
Real Estate ..........................$3,000
Health Professionals ....................$2,250

Unidentified .........................$6,500

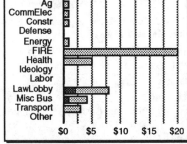

# 3. Tony P. Hall (D)

**1990 Committees:** Rules
**First elected:** 1978

1989-90 Total receipts: ............$173,805
1990 Year-end cash: ...............$312,635

**Source of Funds**
- ■ PACs .............................. 73%
- ▨ Lg Individuals ($200+) ............. 3%
- □ Individuals under $200 ............. 2%
- ▧ Other ............................. 22%

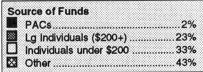

**Top Industries & Interest Groups**

Bldg/Indust/Misc Unions ...........$23,300
Public Sector Unions ................$17,900
Transportation Unions ..............$12,550
Lawyers & Lobbyists ..................$10,550
Insurance ............................$8,550

Unidentified .........................$1,100

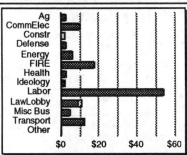

# 4. Michael G. Oxley (R)

**1990 Committees:** Energy & Commerce
**First elected:** 1981

1989-90 Total receipts: ............$298,581
1990 Year-end cash: ...............$188,791

**Source of Funds**
- ■ PACs ............................. 69%
- ▨ Lg Individuals ($200+) ............. 3%
- □ Individuals under $200 ............. 10%
- ▧ Other ............................. 19%

**Top Industries & Interest Groups**

Telephone Utilities .....................$26,950
Electric Utilities .........................$19,275
Oil & Gas .................................$18,850
Insurance .................................$16,519
Commercial Banks .....................$9,700

Unidentified ................................$2,150

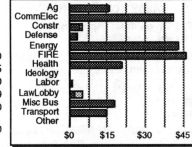

# 5. Paul E. Gillmor (R)

**1990 Committees:** Admin  Banking
**First elected:** 1988

1989-90 Total receipts: ............$325,743
1990 Year-end cash: ................$83,139

**Source of Funds**
- ■ PACs ............................. 66%
- ▨ Lg Individuals ($200+) .............. 12%
- □ Individuals under $200 ............. 14%
- ▧ Other .............................. 8%

**Top Industries & Interest Groups**

Commercial Banks .....................$41,725
Insurance .................................$25,700
Health Professionals .................$17,550
Misc Manufacturing & Distrib .....$17,500
Real Estate .............................$12,500

Unidentified ..............................$12,150

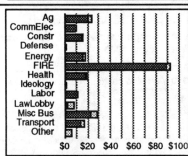

# 6. Bob McEwen (R)

**1990 Committees:** Public Works  Vet Affairs
**First elected:** 1980

1989-90 Total receipts: ............$292,650
1990 Year-end cash: ...............$118,666

**Source of Funds**
- ■ PACs ............................. 51%
- ▨ Lg Individuals ($200+) .............. 16%
- □ Individuals under $200 ............. 31%
- ▧ Other .............................. 2%

**Top Industries & Interest Groups**

Air Transport ...............................$21,150
Health Professionals .................$10,740
General Contractors ....................$9,950
Automotive ................................$9,900
Real Estate ...............................$8,800

Unidentified ..............................$20,006

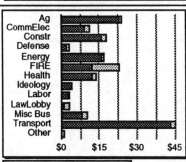

■ PACs  ▨ Indivs ($200+)

263

**Totals in Thousands of Dollars**

## 7. David L. Hobson (R)

**1991-92 Committees:** Govt Ops  Public Works
**First elected:** 1990

1989-90 Total receipts: ...........$389,738
1990 Year-end cash: .......................$602

**Source of Funds**
- PACs .................................................. 50%
- Lg Individuals ($200+) ...... 17%
- Individuals under $200 .......... 27%
- Other .................................................. 6%

**Top  Industries & Interest Groups**

Health Professionals ...................$27,700
Automotive .....................................$17,700
Insurance .........................................$16,800
Real Estate ......................................$14,600
Telephone Utilities ........................$9,926

Unidentified .....................................$16,350

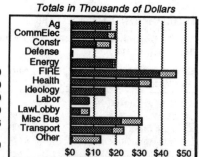

## 8. John A. Boehner (R)

**1991-92 Committees:** Agriculture  Educ/Labor  Sm Bus
**First elected:** 1990

1989-90 Total receipts: ...........$737,441
1990 Year-end cash: ....................$4,674

**Source of Funds**
- PACs .................................................. 29%
- Lg Individuals ($200+) ...... 24%
- Individuals under $200 .......... 21%
- Other .................................................. 26%

**Top  Industries & Interest Groups**

Health Professionals ...................$27,800
Automotive .....................................$21,250
Misc Manufacturing & Distrib .....$20,200
General Contractors ....................$20,050
Business Services ........................$19,300

Unidentified .....................................$58,990

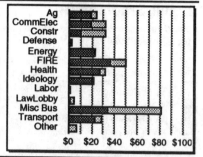

## 9. Marcy Kaptur (D)

**1990 Committees:** Appropriations
**First elected:** 1982

1989-90 Total receipts: ...........$227,820
1990 Year-end cash: ..................$58,129

**Source of Funds**
- PACs .................................................. 68%
- Lg Individuals ($200+) ........ 5%
- Individuals under $200 .......... 22%
- Other .................................................. 5%

**Top  Industries & Interest Groups**

Bldg/Indust/Misc Unions ...........$52,300
Public Sector Unions ..................$20,600
Transportation Unions ...............$18,750
Insurance .........................................$14,400
Real Estate ........................................$6,900

Unidentified .......................................$3,000

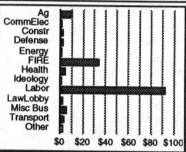

## 10. Clarence E. Miller (R)

**1990 Committees:** Appropriations
**First elected:** 1966

1989-90 Total receipts: ..............$99,589
1990 Year-end cash: ...............$126,334

**Source of Funds**
- PACs .................................................. 68%
- Lg Individuals ($200+) ........ 5%
- Individuals under $200 ............ 6%
- Other .................................................. 21%

**Top  Industries & Interest Groups**

Defense Aerospace ......................$8,750
Defense Electronics.....................$8,100
Real Estate ......................................$7,000
Dairy ..................................................$4,650
Automotive .......................................$4,500

Unidentified .......................................$1,200

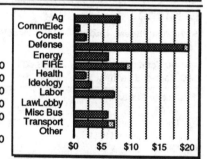

## 11. Dennis E. Eckart (D)

**1990 Committees:** Energy & Commerce  Govt Op  Sm Bus
**First elected:** 1980

1989-90 Total receipts: ...........$510,699
1990 Year-end cash: ...............$159,440

**Source of Funds**
- PACs .................................................. 73%
- Lg Individuals ($200+) ...... 12%
- Individuals under $200 ............ 7%
- Other .................................................. 9%

**Top  Industries & Interest Groups**

Bldg/Indust/Misc Unions ...........$39,265
Lawyers & Lobbyists ..................$32,800
Telephone Utilities ......................$28,275
Accountants ...................................$20,375
Public Sector Unions ................$19,760

Unidentified .....................................$22,360

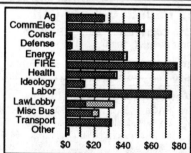

## 12. John R. Kasich (R)

**1990 Committees:** Armed Services  Budget
**First elected:** 1982

1989-90 Total receipts: ...........$328,624
1990 Year-end cash: ..................$93,542

**Source of Funds**
- PACs .................................................. 40%
- Lg Individuals ($200+) ...... 42%
- Individuals under $200 .......... 10%
- Other .................................................. 8%

**Top  Industries & Interest Groups**

Real Estate ......................................$18,550
Health Professionals ...................$18,300
Lawyers & Lobbyists .................$16,675
Misc Manufacturing & Distrib .....$14,425
Defense Electronics ..................$13,200

Unidentified .....................................$44,350

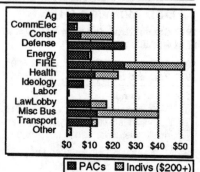

264  Key to committee & category abbreviations is on page 173

**█ PACs  ▧ Indivs ($200+)**

## 13. Don J. Pease (D)

**1990 Committees:** Ways & Means
**First elected:** 1976

1989-90 Total receipts: ............$311,899
1990 Year-end cash: ...............$221,677

**Source of Funds**
- ■ PACs ..................................... 59%
- ▨ Lg Individuals ($200+) ........... 11%
- ☐ Individuals under $200 ........... 16%
- ⊠ Other ................................... 15%

**Top Industries & Interest Groups**

Bldg/Indust/Misc Unions ............$38,300
Public Sector Unions ................$22,975
Transportation Unions ...............$14,500
Insurance ................................$12,750
Health Professionals .................$12,050

Unidentified ..............................$8,845

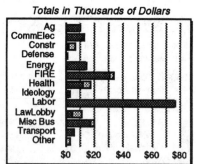

## 14. Thomas C. Sawyer (D)

**1990 Committees:** Educ/Labor  Post Office
**First elected:** 1986

1989-90 Total receipts: ............$262,812
1990 Year-end cash: .................$48,321

**Source of Funds**
- ■ PACs ..................................... 69%
- ▨ Lg Individuals ($200+) ........... 11%
- ☐ Individuals under $200 ........... 14%
- ⊠ Other ..................................... 6%

**Top Industries & Interest Groups**

Bldg/Indust/Misc Unions ............$46,800
Public Sector Unions ................$42,550
Transportation Unions ...............$21,850
Health Professionals .................$13,300
Automotive ................................$8,450

Unidentified ..............................$9,299

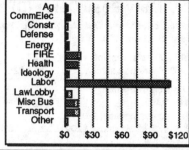

## 15. Chalmers P. Wylie (R)

**1990 Committees:** Banking  Vet Affairs
**First elected:** 1966

1989-90 Total receipts: ............$227,878
1990 Year-end cash: .................$18,194

**Source of Funds**
- ■ PACs ..................................... 75%
- ▨ Lg Individuals ($200+) ........... 15%
- ☐ Individuals under $200 ........... 9%
- ⊠ Other ..................................... 0%

**Top Industries & Interest Groups**

Insurance ................................$41,599
Commercial Banks ....................$25,125
Lawyers & Lobbyists .................$20,800
Real Estate ..............................$18,250
Home Builders ..........................$15,731

Unidentified ..............................$4,950

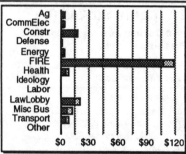

## 16. Ralph Regula (R)

**1990 Committees:** Appropriations
**First elected:** 1972

1989-90 Total receipts: ............$110,331
1990 Year-end cash: .................$52,654

**Source of Funds**
- ■ PACs ..................................... 0%
- ▨ Lg Individuals ($200+) ........... 29%
- ☐ Individuals under $200 ........... 61%
- ⊠ Other ................................... 10%

**Top Industries & Interest Groups**

Food Processing & Sales ............$4,500
Health Professionals ..................$4,150
Real Estate ................................$2,000
Automotive ................................$2,000
Retired ......................................$1,700

Unidentified ..............................$9,680

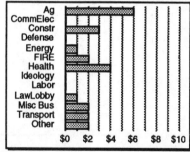

## 17. James A. Traficant Jr. (D)

**1990 Committees:** Public Works  Science
**First elected:** 1984

1989-90 Total receipts: ..............$99,644
1990 Year-end cash: .................$76,169

**Source of Funds**
- ■ PACs ..................................... 55%
- ▨ Lg Individuals ($200+) ........... 16%
- ☐ Individuals under $200 ........... 24%
- ⊠ Other ..................................... 5%

**Top Industries & Interest Groups**

Bldg/Indust/Misc Unions ............$29,000
Transportation Unions ...............$10,775
Public Sector Unions ...................$4,250
Real Estate ................................$4,200
Dairy ........................................$2,000

Unidentified ..............................$4,000

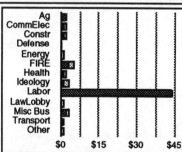

## 18. Douglas Applegate (D)

**1990 Committees:** Public Works  Vet Affairs
**First elected:** 1976

1989-90 Total receipts: ............$125,772
1990 Year-end cash: ...............$161,523

**Source of Funds**
- ■ PACs ..................................... 62%
- ▨ Lg Individuals ($200+) ........... 6%
- ☐ Individuals under $200 ........... 17%
- ⊠ Other ................................... 15%

**Top Industries & Interest Groups**

Transportation Unions ...............$16,000
Bldg/Indust/Misc Unions ............$11,500
Real Estate ................................$6,000
Public Sector Unions ...................$6,000
Telephone Utilities .....................$5,000

Unidentified ..............................$1,800

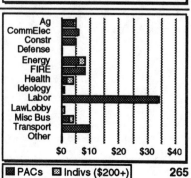

■ PACs  ⊠ Indivs ($200+)

265

## 19.  Edward F. Feighan (D)

**1990 Committees:  Foreign Affairs  Judiciary**
**First elected: 1982**

1989-90 Total receipts: ........... $323,072
1990 Year-end cash: .............. $290,445

**Source of Funds**
- ■ PACs ............................................. 68%
- ▨ Lg Individuals ($200+) ............... 16%
- □ Individuals under $200 .............. 9%
- ▧ Other ........................................... 7%

**Top  Industries & Interest Groups**

Bldg/Indust/Misc Unions ........... $54,400
Insurance .................................... $26,000
Public Sector Unions ................. $23,250
Transportation Unions ................ $22,550
Lawyers & Lobbyists .................. $21,800

Unidentified ............................... $19,725

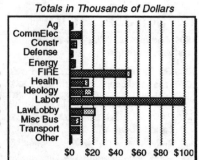

## 20.  Mary Rose Oakar (D)

**1990 Committees:  Admin  Banking  Post Office**
**First elected: 1976**

1989-90 Total receipts: ........... $337,442
1990 Year-end cash: ................. $57,025

**Source of Funds**
- ■ PACs ............................................. 85%
- ▨ Lg Individuals ($200+) ................. 7%
- □ Individuals under $200 .............. 8%
- ▧ Other ............................................. 0%

**Top  Industries & Interest Groups**

Public Sector Unions ................. $46,800
Bldg/Indust/Misc Unions ........... $43,900
Commercial Banks .................... $42,200
Transportation Unions .............. $22,800
Health Professionals ................. $17,500

Unidentified ................................. $8,950

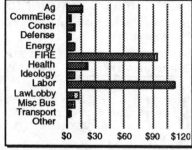

## 21.  Louis Stokes (D)

**1990 Committees:  Appropriations**
**First elected: 1968**

1989-90 Total receipts: ........... $250,022
1990 Year-end cash: .............. $241,864

**Source of Funds**
- ■ PACs ............................................. 55%
- ▨ Lg Individuals ($200+) ............... 17%
- □ Individuals under $200 .............. 5%
- ▧ Other ........................................... 23%

**Top  Industries & Interest Groups**

Bldg/Indust/Misc Unions ........... $28,600
Public Sector Unions ................. $25,450
Transportation Unions .............. $14,500
Health Professionals ................. $12,350
Real Estate ................................ $10,500

Unidentified ................................. $4,900

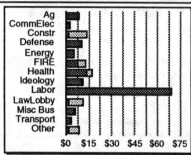

▨ PACs  ▧ Indivs ($200+)

Key to committee & category abbreviations is on page 173

# Oklahoma

## Senate Spending

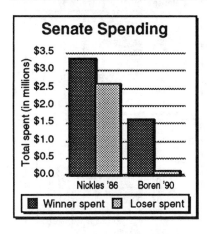

Total spent (in millions)

$3.5
$3.0
$2.5
$2.0
$1.5
$1.0
$0.5
$0.0

Nickles '86    Boren '90

■ Winner spent    ▨ Loser spent

## Spending in 1990 House Races

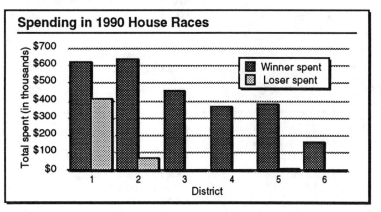

Total spent (in thousands)

$700
$600
$500
$400
$300
$200
$100
$0

1    2    3    4    5    6
District

■ Winner spent
▨ Loser spent

## 1990 Elections at a Glance

| Dist | Name | Party | Vote Pct | Race Type |
|------|------|-------|----------|-----------|
| Sen | David L. Boren (1990) | Dem | 83% | Reelected |
| Sen | Don Nickles (1986) | Rep | 55% | Reelected |
| 1 | James M. Inhofe | Rep | 56% | Reelected |
| 2 | Mike Synar | Dem | 61% | Reelected |
| 3 | Bill Brewster | Dem | 80% | Open Seat |
| 4 | Dave McCurdy | Dem | 74% | Reelected |
| 5 | Mickey Edwards | Rep | 70% | Reelected |
| 6 | Glenn English | Dem | 80% | Reelected |

*Totals in Thousands of Dollars*

## Sen. David L. Boren (D)

**1990 Committees: Agriculture  Finance  SmBus**
**First elected: 1978**

1985-90 Total Rcpts: ...........$1,716,590
1990 Year-end cash: ..............$158,133

**Source of Funds**
- ■ PACs............................................0%
- ▨ Lg Individuals ($200+)..............81%
- □ Individuals under $200.............12%
- ▨ Other.........................................7%

### 1985-90

**Top  Industries & Interest Groups**

Oil & Gas ...............................$177,260
Lawyers & Lobbyists................$164,450
Securities & Investment...........$57,350
Real Estate ...............................$43,500
Commercial Banks ...................$36,830

Unidentified.............................$165,929

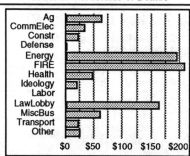

Ag
CommElec
Constr
Defense
Energy
FIRE
Health
Ideology
Labor
LawLobby
MiscBus
Transport
Other

$0    $50    $100    $150    $200

## Sen. Don Nickles (R)

**1990 Committees: Appropriations  Budget  Energy**
**First elected: 1980**

1985-90 Total Rcpts: ...........$3,447,516
1990 Year-end cash: ..............$651,214

**Source of Funds**
- ■ PACs..........................................25%
- ▨ Lg Individuals ($200+)..............31%
- □ Individuals under $200.............27%
- ▨ Other.........................................18%

### 1985-90 (PACs only)

**Top  Industries & Interest Groups**

Oil & Gas ................................$149,622
Insurance ................................$100,916
General Contractors .................$35,750
Leadership PACs .......................$34,058
Misc Manufacturing & Distrib .....$33,300

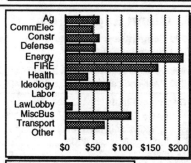

Ag
CommElec
Constr
Defense
Energy
FIRE
Health
Ideology
Labor
LawLobby
MiscBus
Transport
Other

$0    $50    $100    $150    $200

■ PACs    ▨ Indivs ($200+)    **267**

## 1. James M. Inhofe (R)

**1990 Committees:  Merchant Marine  Public Works**
**First elected: 1986**

1989-90 Total receipts: ............$609,786
1990 Year-end cash: ..................$1,120

**Source of Funds**
- PACs ............................................46%
- Lg Individuals ($200+) ..............21%
- Individuals under $200 ..............11%
- Other ...........................................22%

**Top Industries & Interest Groups**

Oil & Gas ....................................$78,699
Air Transport .............................$35,800
Automotive ..................................$25,850
Health Professionals .................$22,300
Insurance ...................................$17,000

Unidentified ...............................$27,149

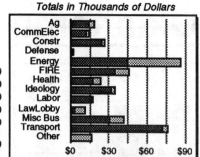

## 2. Mike Synar (D)

**1990 Committees:  Energy & Comm  Govt Ops  Judiciary**
**First elected: 1978**

1989-90 Total receipts: ............$622,454
1990 Year-end cash: ................$24,882

**Source of Funds**
- PACs ..............................................0%
- Lg Individuals ($200+) ..............65%
- Individuals under $200 ..............33%
- Other ..............................................2%

**Top Industries & Interest Groups**

Oil & Gas ....................................$66,075
Lawyers & Lobbyists ..................$60,500
TV & Movies ................................$24,850
Securities & Investment ............$24,450
Cable TV .....................................$21,200

Unidentified ...............................$51,375

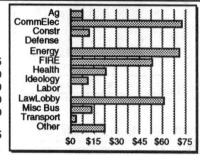

## 3. Bill Brewster (D)

**1991-92 Committees:  Public Works  Vet Affairs**
**First elected: 1990**

1989-90 Total receipts: ............$448,824
1990 Year-end cash: ..................$2,055

**Source of Funds**
- PACs ............................................37%
- Lg Individuals ($200+) ..............28%
- Individuals under $200 ..............20%
- Other ...........................................15%

**Top Industries & Interest Groups**

Oil & Gas ....................................$46,025
Health Professionals .................$33,310
Lawyers & Lobbyists ..................$20,594
Misc Finance .............................$15,034
Misc Issues ...............................$10,700

Unidentified ...............................$15,678

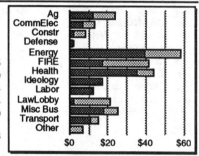

## 4. Dave McCurdy (D)

**1990 Committees:  Armed Services  Science**
**First elected: 1980**

1989-90 Total receipts: ............$342,376
1990 Year-end cash: ................$81,622

**Source of Funds**
- PACs ............................................42%
- Lg Individuals ($200+) ..............27%
- Individuals under $200 ..............22%
- Other ..............................................9%

**Top Industries & Interest Groups**

Defense Aerospace ...................$41,950
Oil & Gas ....................................$22,350
Defense Electronics ...................$19,750
General Contractors ...................$16,200
Lawyers & Lobbyists ..................$12,000

Unidentified ...............................$14,650

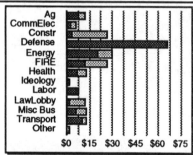

## 5. Mickey Edwards (R)

**1990 Committees:  Appropriations**
**First elected: 1976**

1989-90 Total receipts: ............$326,283
1990 Year-end cash: ................$13,371

**Source of Funds**
- PACs ............................................46%
- Lg Individuals ($200+) ..............33%
- Individuals under $200 ..............20%
- Other ..............................................2%

**Top Industries & Interest Groups**

Oil & Gas ....................................$49,950
Health Professionals .................$16,300
Insurance ...................................$13,950
Lawyers & Lobbyists ..................$12,700
Real Estate ................................$11,898

Unidentified ...............................$15,150

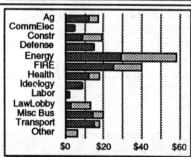

## 6. Glenn English (D)

**1990 Committees:  Agriculture  Govt Ops**
**First elected: 1974**

1989-90 Total receipts: ............$238,141
1990 Year-end cash: ..............$324,042

**Source of Funds**
- PACs ............................................59%
- Lg Individuals ($200+) ..............11%
- Individuals under $200 ..............10%
- Other ...........................................19%

**Top Industries & Interest Groups**

Oil & Gas ....................................$17,000
Crop Production/Processing ......$16,280
Telephone Utilities .....................$15,600
Agric Services/Products ............$13,200
Dairy ..............................................$9,200
Real Estate ...................................$9,200

Unidentified .................................$2,850

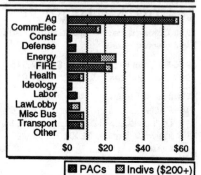

268

Key to committee & category abbreviations is on page 173

■ PACs   ⊠ Indivs ($200+)

# Oregon

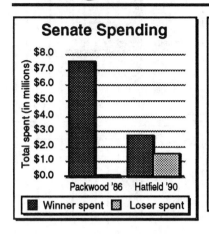

## Senate Spending

Total spent (in millions)

$8.0
$7.0
$6.0
$5.0
$4.0
$3.0
$2.0
$1.0
$0.0

Packwood '86    Hatfield '90

■ Winner spent    ▨ Loser spent

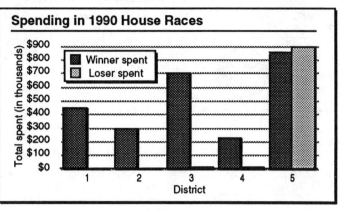

## Spending in 1990 House Races

Total spent (in thousands)

$900
$800
$700
$600
$500
$400
$300
$200
$100
$0

■ Winner spent
▨ Loser spent

1    2    3    4    5
District

## 1990 Elections at a Glance

| Dist | Name | Party | Vote Pct | Race Type |
|------|------|-------|----------|-----------|
| Sen | Mark O. Hatfield (1990) | Rep | 54% | Reelected |
| Sen | Bob Packwood (1986) | Rep | 63% | Reelected |
| 1 | Les AuCoin | Dem | 63% | Reelected |
| 2 | Bob Smith | Rep | 68% | Reelected |
| 3 | Ron Wyden | Dem | 81% | Reelected |
| 4 | Peter A. DeFazio | Dem | 86% | Reelected |
| 5 | Mike Kopetski | Dem | 55% | Beat Incumb |

*Totals in Thousands of Dollars*

## Sen. Mark O. Hatfield (R)

**1990 Committees: Appropriations  Energy  Rules**
**First elected: 1966**

1985-90 Total Rcpts: ............$2,518,181
1990 Year-end cash: ..................$4,332

### Source of Funds

■ PACs..................................................38%
▨ Lg Individuals ($200+) ...............33%
☐ Individuals under $200 ..............11%
▨ Other .............................................17%

### 1985-90

**Top  Industries & Interest Groups**

Forestry & Forest Products .....$175,100
Lawyers & Lobbyists ................$121,356
Oil & Gas ....................................$83,957
Securities & Investment ............$70,650
Health Professionals ..................$68,150

Unidentified .............................$183,767

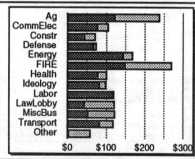

Ag
CommElec
Constr
Defense
Energy
FIRE
Health
Ideology
Labor
LawLobby
MiscBus
Transport
Other

$0    $100    $200    $300

## Sen. Bob Packwood (R)

**1990 Committees: Commerce  Finance**
**First elected: 1968**

1985-90 Total Rcpts: ............$9,148,907
1990 Year-end cash: ............$1,164,483

### Source of Funds

■ PACs.................................................11%
▨ Lg Individuals ($200+) ...............26%
☐ Individuals under $200 ..............54%
▨ Other .............................................10%

### 1985-90 (PACs only)

**Top  Industries & Interest Groups**

Insurance ..................................$113,543
Bldg/Indust/Misc Unions ............$74,430
Commercial Banks ......................$53,110
Securities & Investment .............$42,500
Telephone Utilities ......................$40,900

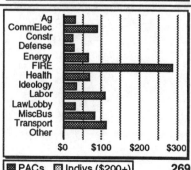

Ag
CommElec
Constr
Defense
Energy
FIRE
Health
Ideology
Labor
LawLobby
MiscBus
Transport
Other

$0    $100    $200    $300

▨ PACs    ▨ Indivs ($200+)

269

# 1. Les AuCoin (D)

**1990 Committees: Appropriations**
**First elected: 1974**

1989-90 Total receipts: ...........$599,295
1990 Year-end cash: ..............$361,578

**Source of Funds**
- PACs..................................................52%
- Lg Individuals ($200+) ...............33%
- Individuals under $200 ................7%
- Other.................................................8%

**Top Industries & Interest Groups**

Bldg/Indust/Misc Unions ............$45,850
Lawyers & Lobbyists ..................$42,260
Forestry & Forest Products .......$37,834
Transportation Unions ...............$34,250
Defense Aerospace ...................$27,500

Unidentified ...............................$24,900

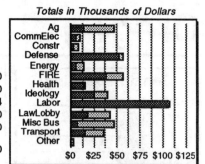

# 2. Bob Smith (R)

**1990 Committees: Agriculture  Interior**
**First elected: 1982**

1989-90 Total receipts: ...........$374,114
1990 Year-end cash: ..............$179,736

**Source of Funds**
- PACs..................................................43%
- Lg Individuals ($200+) ...............18%
- Individuals under $200 .............36%
- Other.................................................3%

**Top Industries & Interest Groups**

Forestry & Forest Products .......$37,047
Real Estate .................................$12,100
Agric Services/Products ...........$11,450
Livestock ....................................$10,930
Crop Production/Processing......$10,800

Unidentified ...............................$11,000

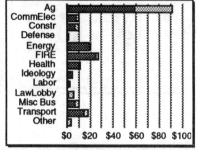

# 3. Ron Wyden (D)

**1990 Committees: Energy & Commerce  Sm Business**
**First elected: 1980**

1989-90 Total receipts: ...........$708,598
1990 Year-end cash: ..............$451,751

**Source of Funds**
- PACs..................................................47%
- Lg Individuals ($200+) ...............30%
- Individuals under $200 .............11%
- Other...............................................12%

**Top Industries & Interest Groups**

Health Professionals ..................$63,828
Pro-Israel ....................................$58,090
Lawyers & Lobbyists ..................$41,551
Insurance ....................................$36,589
Real Estate .................................$27,345

Unidentified ...............................$35,084

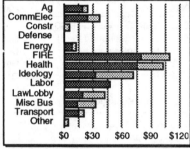

# 4. Peter A. DeFazio (D)

**1990 Committees: Interior  Public Works**
**First elected: 1986**

1989-90 Total receipts: ...........$257,547
1990 Year-end cash: ................$95,794

**Source of Funds**
- PACs..................................................66%
- Lg Individuals ($200+) .................6%
- Individuals under $200 .............23%
- Other.................................................6%

**Top Industries & Interest Groups**

Bldg/Indust/Misc Unions ............$41,500
Transportation Unions ...............$29,750
Public Sector Unions .................$23,855
Air Transport ..............................$11,600
Health Professionals ..................$11,300

Unidentified .................................$1,300

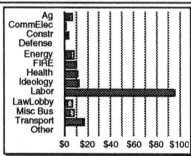

# 5. Mike Kopetski (D)

**1991-92 Committees: Agriculture  Judiciary  Science**
**First elected: 1990**

1989-90 Total receipts: ...........$849,729
1990 Year-end cash: ..................$5,949

**Source of Funds**
- PACs..................................................43%
- Lg Individuals ($200+) ...............13%
- Individuals under $200 .............37%
- Other.................................................7%

**Top Industries & Interest Groups**

Bldg/Indust/Misc Unions ..........$108,600
Public Sector Unions ................$54,499
Transportation Unions ...............$38,650
Lawyers & Lobbyists ..................$32,300
Pro-Israel ....................................$31,250

Unidentified ...............................$21,116

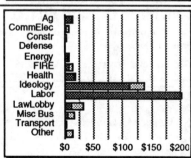

☒ PACs  ☒ Indivs ($200+)

# Pennsylvania

## Spending in 1990 House Races

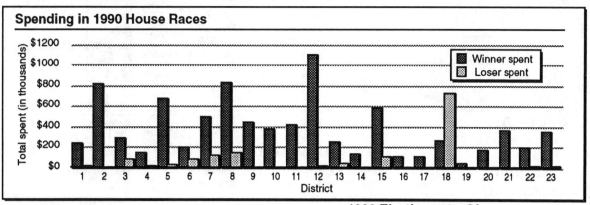

Total spent (in thousands) — by District

- Winner spent
- Loser spent

## Senate Spending

Total spent (in millions)

- Winner spent
- Loser spent

Specter '86    Heinz '88

## 1990 Elections at a Glance

| Dist | Name | Party | Vote Pct | Race Type |
|---|---|---|---|---|
| Sen | John Heinz (1988) | Rep | 66% | Reelected |
| Sen | Arlen Specter (1986) | Rep | 56% | Reelected |
| 1 | Thomas M. Foglietta | Dem | 79% | Reelected |
| 2 | William H. Gray III | Dem | 92% | Reelected |
| 3 | Robert A. Borski | Dem | 60% | Reelected |
| 4 | Joe Kolter | Dem | 56% | Reelected |
| 5 | Dick Schulze | Rep | 57% | Reelected |
| 6 | Gus Yatron | Dem | 57% | Reelected |
| 7 | Curt Weldon | Rep | 65% | Reelected |
| 8 | Peter H. Kostmayer | Dem | 57% | Reelected |
| 9 | Bud Shuster | Rep | 100% | Reelected |
| 10 | Joseph M. McDade | Rep | 100% | Reelected |
| 11 | Paul E. Kanjorski | Dem | 100% | Reelected |
| 12 | John P. Murtha | Dem | 62% | Reelected |
| 13 | Lawrence Coughlin | Rep | 60% | Reelected |
| 14 | William J. Coyne | Dem | 72% | Reelected |
| 15 | Don Ritter | Rep | 61% | Reelected |
| 16 | Robert S. Walker | Rep | 66% | Reelected |
| 17 | George W. Gekas | Rep | 100% | Reelected |
| 18 | Rick Santorum | Rep | 51% | Beat Incumb |
| 19 | Bill Goodling | Rep | 100% | Reelected |
| 20 | Joseph M. Gaydos | Dem | 66% | Reelected |
| 21 | Tom Ridge | Rep | 100% | Reelected |
| 22 | Austin J. Murphy | Dem | 63% | Reelected |
| 23 | William F. Clinger Jr. | Rep | 59% | Reelected |

*Totals in Thousands of Dollars*

## Sen. John Heinz (R)

**1990 Committees: Banking  Finance   Govt Affairs**
**First elected: 1976**

1985-90 Total Rcpts: ..........$6,290,693
1990 Year-end cash: ...........$1,122,168

### Source of Funds
- ■ PACs ....................................22%
- ▨ Lg Individuals ($200+) ..............32%
- □ Individuals under $200 ..............31%
- ▧ Other ..................................15%

### 1985-90 (PACs only)

**Top  Industries & Interest Groups**

| | |
|---|---|
| Insurance | $135,607 |
| Securities & Investment | $93,707 |
| Commercial Banks | $75,351 |
| Misc Manufacturing & Distrib | $66,049 |
| Oil & Gas | $55,685 |

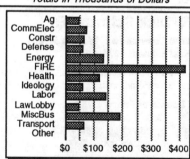

Ag, CommElec, Constr, Defense, Energy, FIRE, Health, Ideology, Labor, LawLobby, MiscBus, Transport, Other — $0  $100  $200  $300  $400

## Sen. Arlen Specter (R)

**1990 Committees: Appropriations  Judiciary  Vet Affairs**
**First elected: 1980**

1985-90 Total Rcpts: ...........$9,032,615
1990 Year-end cash: ...........$2,023,884

### Source of Funds
- ■ PACs ....................................19%
- ▨ Lg Individuals ($200+) ..............21%
- □ Individuals under $200 ..............47%
- ▧ Other ..................................13%

### 1985-90 (PACs only)

**Top  Industries & Interest Groups**

| | |
|---|---|
| Pro-Israel | $166,023 |
| Insurance | $135,077 |
| Bldg/Indust/Misc Unions | $120,657 |
| Lawyers & Lobbyists | $86,050 |
| Defense Aerospace | $83,950 |

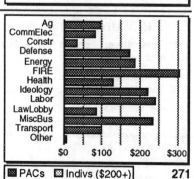

Ag, CommElec, Constr, Defense, Energy, FIRE, Health, Ideology, Labor, LawLobby, MiscBus, Transport, Other — $0  $100  $200  $300

- ■ PACs
- ▨ Indivs ($200+)

271

# 1. Thomas M. Foglietta (D)

**1990 Committees: Armed Services  Merchant Marine**
First elected: 1980

1989-90 Total receipts: ............ $593,914
1990 Year-end cash: ............... $366,322

**Source of Funds**

| | |
|---|---|
| ■ PACs | 47% |
| ▨ Lg Individuals ($200+) | 42% |
| ☐ Individuals under $200 | 5% |
| ▩ Other | 7% |

**Top Industries & Interest Groups**

Bldg/Indust/Misc Unions ............ $67,568
Lawyers & Lobbyists ................. $43,450
Public Sector Unions ................ $25,250
Transportation Unions .............. $22,750
Real Estate ....................... $20,994

Unidentified ...................... $39,266

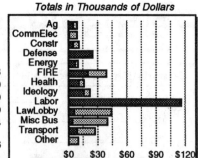

# 2. William H. Gray III (D)

**1990 Committees: Appropriations  DC**
First elected: 1978

1989-90 Total receipts: ............ $725,717
1990 Year-end cash: ................ $57,559

**Source of Funds**

| | |
|---|---|
| ■ PACs | 70% |
| ▨ Lg Individuals ($200+) | 20% |
| ☐ Individuals under $200 | 5% |
| ▩ Other | 5% |

**Top Industries & Interest Groups**

Lawyers & Lobbyists ................. $58,600
Public Sector Unions ................ $53,750
Bldg/Indust/Misc Unions ............ $49,245
Transportation Unions .............. $49,000
Health Professionals ................ $40,750

Unidentified ...................... $34,500

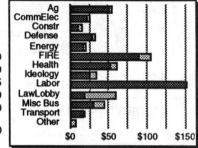

# 3. Robert A. Borski (D)

**1990 Committees: Merchant Marine  Public Works**
First elected: 1982

1989-90 Total receipts: ............ $325,222
1990 Year-end cash: ............... $155,234

**Source of Funds**

| | |
|---|---|
| ■ PACs | 47% |
| ▨ Lg Individuals ($200+) | 30% |
| ☐ Individuals under $200 | 16% |
| ▩ Other | 6% |

**Top Industries & Interest Groups**

Bldg/Indust/Misc Unions ............ $38,000
Public Sector Unions ................ $29,700
Transportation Unions .............. $23,750
Real Estate ....................... $21,200
Lawyers & Lobbyists ................. $16,450

Unidentified ...................... $23,148

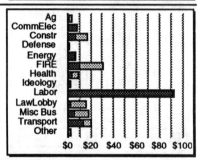

# 4. Joe Kolter (D)

**1990 Committees: Admin  Public Works**
First elected: 1982

1989-90 Total receipts: ............ $199,605
1990 Year-end cash: ............... $215,765

**Source of Funds**

| | |
|---|---|
| ■ PACs | 81% |
| ▨ Lg Individuals ($200+) | 6% |
| ☐ Individuals under $200 | 2% |
| ▩ Other | 11% |

**Top Industries & Interest Groups**

Bldg/Indust/Misc Unions ............ $38,570
Transportation Unions .............. $32,050
Public Sector Unions ................ $18,450
Health Professionals ................ $10,250
Air Transport ..................... $8,000

Unidentified ...................... $2,750

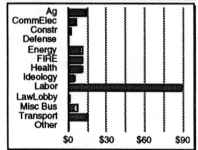

# 5. Dick Schulze (R)

**1990 Committees: Ways & Means**
First elected: 1974

1989-90 Total receipts: ............ $578,161
1990 Year-end cash: ............... $182,353

**Source of Funds**

| | |
|---|---|
| ■ PACs | 63% |
| ▨ Lg Individuals ($200+) | 20% |
| ☐ Individuals under $200 | 8% |
| ▩ Other | 9% |

**Top Industries & Interest Groups**

Insurance ......................... $59,718
Lawyers & Lobbyists ................. $37,030
Oil & Gas ......................... $24,300
Electric Utilities .................. $23,676
Real Estate ....................... $21,750

Unidentified ...................... $26,775

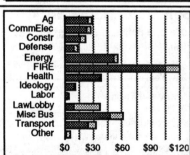

# 6. Gus Yatron (D)

**1990 Committees: Foreign Affairs  Post Office**
First elected: 1968

1989-90 Total receipts: ............ $212,729
1990 Year-end cash: ............... $157,501

**Source of Funds**

| | |
|---|---|
| ■ PACs | 54% |
| ▨ Lg Individuals ($200+) | 16% |
| ☐ Individuals under $200 | 10% |
| ▩ Other | 20% |

**Top Industries & Interest Groups**

Bldg/Indust/Misc Unions ............ $33,350
Public Sector Unions ................ $25,400
Transportation Unions .............. $21,250
Real Estate ....................... $13,500
Pro-Israel ........................ $13,500

Unidentified ...................... $7,550

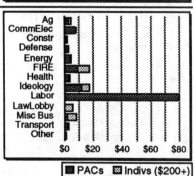

Key to committee & category abbreviations is on page 173

■ PACs   ▩ Indivs ($200+)

## 7. Curt Weldon (R)

**1990 Committees: Armed Services  Merchant Marine**
**First elected: 1986**

1989-90 Total receipts: ...........$505,644
1990 Year-end cash: ...............$135,364

**Source of Funds**
- PACs ........................................41%
- Lg Individuals ($200+) .............29%
- Individuals under $200 .............23%
- Other ........................................7%

**Top Industries & Interest Groups**

Defense Aerospace ..................$23,800
Bldg/Indust/Misc Unions ...........$23,025
Real Estate ............................$22,750
Lawyers & Lobbyists ................$21,027
Health Professionals ................$18,850

Unidentified .............................$42,150

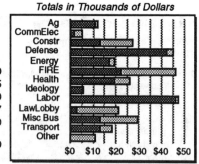

## 8. Peter H. Kostmayer (D)

**1990 Committees: Foreign Affairs  Interior**
**First elected: 1978 (did not serve 1981-83)**

1989-90 Total receipts: ...........$768,157
1990 Year-end cash: .................$10,140

**Source of Funds**
- PACs ........................................38%
- Lg Individuals ($200+) .............29%
- Individuals under $200 ............28%
- Other ........................................5%

**Top Industries & Interest Groups**

Bldg/Indust/Misc Unions ...........$85,000
Lawyers & Lobbyists .................$51,985
Public Sector Unions ................$42,652
Transportation Unions ..............$28,100
Real Estate ..............................$27,350

Unidentified .............................$53,950

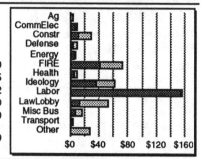

## 9. Bud Shuster (R)

**1990 Committees: Public Works**
**First elected: 1972**

1989-90 Total receipts: ...........$417,658
1990 Year-end cash: ...............$102,101

**Source of Funds**
- PACs ........................................46%
- Lg Individuals ($200+) .............51%
- Individuals under $200 .............2%
- Other ........................................1%

**Top Industries & Interest Groups**

General Contractors ..................$43,119
Building Materials & Equip.........$31,700
Trucking ..................................$24,350
Business Services .....................$22,955
Real Estate ..............................$21,750

Unidentified .............................$36,250

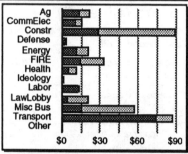

## 10. Joseph M. McDade (R)

**1990 Committees: Appropriations  Sm Business**
**First elected: 1962**

1989-90 Total receipts: ...........$383,030
1990 Year-end cash: ...............$335,857

**Source of Funds**
- PACs ........................................60%
- Lg Individuals ($200+) .............22%
- Individuals under $200 .............1%
- Other ......................................17%

**Top Industries & Interest Groups**

Defense Aerospace ...................$54,000
Defense Electronics ..................$39,250
Lawyers & Lobbyists .................$24,000
Bldg/Indust/Misc Unions ...........$15,750
Transportation Unions ..............$15,500

Unidentified .............................$22,500

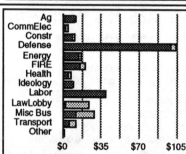

## 11. Paul E. Kanjorski (D)

**1990 Committees: Banking  Post Office**
**First elected: 1984**

1989-90 Total receipts: ...........$383,951
1990 Year-end cash: .................$94,480

**Source of Funds**
- PACs ........................................72%
- Lg Individuals ($200+) .............17%
- Individuals under $200 .............5%
- Other ........................................6%

**Top Industries & Interest Groups**

Insurance ................................$40,802
Public Sector Unions ................$34,350
Bldg/Indust/Misc Unions ...........$30,000
Commercial Banks ....................$23,650
Transportation Unions ..............$17,500

Unidentified .............................$14,550

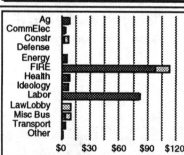

## 12. John P. Murtha (D)

**1990 Committees: Appropriations**
**First elected: 1974**

1989-90 Total receipts: ...........$878,887
1990 Year-end cash: .................$33,122

**Source of Funds**
- PACs ........................................57%
- Lg Individuals ($200+) .............29%
- Individuals under $200 .............2%
- Other ......................................12%

**Top Industries & Interest Groups**

Defense Aerospace .................$108,200
Defense Electronics ....................$69,600
Lawyers & Lobbyists .................$68,500
Bldg/Indust/Misc Unions ...........$55,950
Steel/Smelting..........................$49,225

Unidentified .............................$50,087

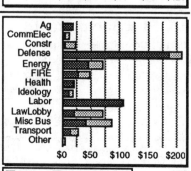

■ PACs  ▨ Indivs ($200+)

273

## 13. Lawrence Coughlin (R)

**1990 Committees: Appropriations**
**First elected: 1968**

1989-90 Total receipts: ............ $373,205
1990 Year-end cash: .............. $356,517

**Source of Funds**
- PACs ........................................... 43%
- Lg Individuals ($200+) ............... 27%
- Individuals under $200 .............. 19%
- Other .......................................... 11%

**Top Industries & Interest Groups**

| | |
|---|---|
| Air Transport ......................... | $27,350 |
| Lawyers & Lobbyists ............. | $22,750 |
| Real Estate ........................... | $16,338 |
| Defense Aerospace ................ | $13,000 |
| Defense Electronics .............. | $10,100 |
| Unidentified .......................... | $28,750 |

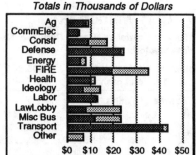

## 14. William J. Coyne (D)

**1990 Committees: Ways & Means**
**First elected: 1980**

1989-90 Total receipts: ............ $155,192
1990 Year-end cash: .............. $227,957

**Source of Funds**
- PACs ........................................... 89%
- Lg Individuals ($200+) ................. 4%
- Individuals under $200 ................ 1%
- Other ............................................ 6%

**Top Industries & Interest Groups**

| | |
|---|---|
| Public Sector Unions ............. | $18,000 |
| Insurance .............................. | $17,500 |
| Bldg/Indust/Misc Unions .......... | $17,500 |
| Health Professionals ............... | $11,800 |
| Lawyers & Lobbyists ............... | $8,750 |
| Unidentified .......................... | $1,000 |

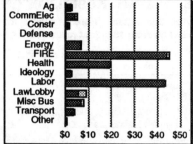

## 15. Don Ritter (R)

**1990 Committees: Energy & Commerce Science**
**First elected: 1978**

1989-90 Total receipts: ............ $560,729
1990 Year-end cash: ................. $25,821

**Source of Funds**
- PACs ........................................... 49%
- Lg Individuals ($200+) ............... 32%
- Individuals under $200 .............. 17%
- Other ............................................ 2%

**Top Industries & Interest Groups**

| | |
|---|---|
| Telephone Utilities .................... | $38,100 |
| Insurance ............................... | $33,150 |
| Health Professionals ................ | $27,300 |
| Misc Manufacturing & Distrib ..... | $20,362 |
| Chemicals .............................. | $17,250 |
| Unidentified .......................... | $59,537 |

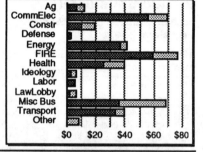

## 16. Robert S. Walker (R)

**1990 Committees: Science**
**First elected: 1976**

1989-90 Total receipts: .............. $96,737
1990 Year-end cash: ................. $35,408

**Source of Funds**
- PACs ........................................... 41%
- Lg Individuals ($200+) ............... 29%
- Individuals under $200 .............. 19%
- Other .......................................... 10%

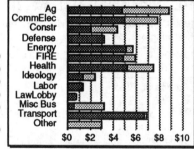

**Top Industries & Interest Groups**

| | |
|---|---|
| Air Transport ......................... | $3,600 |
| Lawyers & Lobbyists ............. | $3,200 |
| Retired .................................. | $2,950 |
| Retail Sales .......................... | $2,550 |
| Defense Aerospace ................ | $2,400 |
| Unidentified .......................... | $8,250 |

## 17. George W. Gekas (R)

**1990 Committees: Judiciary**
**First elected: 1982**

1989-90 Total receipts: ............ $128,438
1990 Year-end cash: .............. $141,544

**Source of Funds**
- PACs ........................................... 55%
- Lg Individuals ($200+) ................. 7%
- Individuals under $200 .............. 23%
- Other .......................................... 15%

**Top Industries & Interest Groups**

| | |
|---|---|
| Telephone Utilities .................... | $8,600 |
| Accountants ........................... | $8,300 |
| Real Estate ........................... | $7,590 |
| Health Professionals ................ | $6,100 |
| Home Builders ........................ | $5,500 |
| Unidentified .......................... | $3,830 |

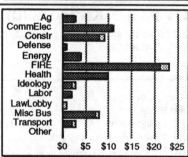

## 18. Rick Santorum (R)

**1991-92 Committees: Budget Vet Affairs**
**First elected: 1990**

1989-90 Total receipts: ............ $257,786
1990 Year-end cash: .................. $6,289

**Source of Funds**
- PACs ........................................... 10%
- Lg Individuals ($200+) ............... 54%
- Individuals under $200 .............. 28%
- Other ............................................ 8%

**Top Industries & Interest Groups**

| | |
|---|---|
| Lawyers & Lobbyists ................. | $21,854 |
| Retired .................................. | $11,730 |
| Securities & Investment ............. | $8,250 |
| Health Professionals ................ | $7,750 |
| Oil & Gas .............................. | $6,950 |
| Unidentified .......................... | $35,802 |

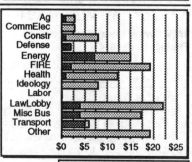

Key to committee & category abbreviations is on page 173

☐ PACs  ☒ Indivs ($200+)

## 19.  Bill Goodling (R)

**1990 Committees:  Budget  Educ/Labor**
**First elected: 1974**

1989-90 Total receipts: .............$41,011
1990 Year-end cash: ..................$6,251

| Source of Funds | |
| --- | --- |
| ■ PACs.................................9% | |
| ▨ Lg Individuals ($200+) .............20% | |
| ☐ Individuals under $200 ............71% | |
| ▧ Other.................................0% | |

**Top Industries & Interest Groups**

Food & Beverage .........................$4,000
Commercial Banks ....................$1,062
Human Rights ................................$900

Unidentified .................................$5,525

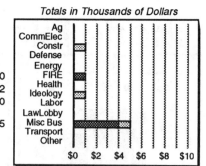

## 20.  Joseph M. Gaydos (D)

**1990 Committees:  Admin  Educ/Labor**
**First elected: 1968**

1989-90 Total receipts: ............$191,541
1990 Year-end cash: ...............$123,222

| Source of Funds | |
| --- | --- |
| ■ PACs.................................83% | |
| ▨ Lg Individuals ($200+) .............7% | |
| ☐ Individuals under $200 .............2% | |
| ▧ Other.................................8% | |

**Top Industries & Interest Groups**

Bldg/Indust/Misc Unions ............$46,800
Transportation Unions ...............$25,000
Public Sector Unions .................$16,550
Education .................................$12,450
Telephone Utilities .......................$6,000
Real Estate .................................$6,000

Unidentified .................................$2,000

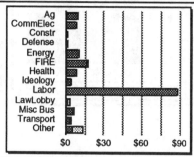

## 21.  Tom Ridge (R)

**1990 Committees:  Banking  Post Office  Vet Affairs**
**First elected: 1982**

1989-90 Total receipts: ............$454,349
1990 Year-end cash: ...............$226,719

| Source of Funds | |
| --- | --- |
| ■ PACs.................................53% | |
| ▨ Lg Individuals ($200+) .............24% | |
| ☐ Individuals under $200 ............17% | |
| ▧ Other.................................7% | |

**Top Industries & Interest Groups**

Commercial Banks ....................$66,300
Transportation Unions ...............$23,200
Lawyers & Lobbyists .................$21,750
Public Sector Unions .................$18,590
Insurance .................................$17,950

Unidentified .................................$30,710

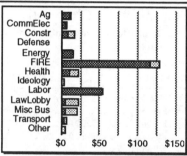

## 22.  Austin J. Murphy (D)

**1990 Committees:  Educ/Labor  Interior**
**First elected: 1976**

1989-90 Total receipts: ............$199,802
1990 Year-end cash: ...............$111,254

| Source of Funds | |
| --- | --- |
| ■ PACs.................................72% | |
| ▨ Lg Individuals ($200+) .............6% | |
| ☐ Individuals under $200 ............19% | |
| ▧ Other.................................3% | |

**Top Industries & Interest Groups**

Bldg/Indust/Misc Unions ............$35,510
Public Sector Unions .................$16,050
Transportation Unions ...............$14,700
Food & Beverage .......................$12,000
Health Professionals ...................$8,650

Unidentified .................................$3,450

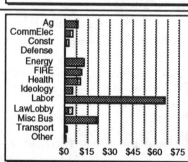

## 23.  William F. Clinger Jr. (R)

**1990 Committees:  Govt Ops  Public Works**
**First elected: 1978**

1989-90 Total receipts: ............$349,208
1990 Year-end cash: ................$84,577

| Source of Funds | |
| --- | --- |
| ■ PACs.................................55% | |
| ▨ Lg Individuals ($200+) .............12% | |
| ☐ Individuals under $200 ............29% | |
| ▧ Other.................................5% | |

**Top Industries & Interest Groups**

Air Transport .............................$42,200
Transportation Unions ...............$18,850
Oil & Gas .................................$16,600
General Contractors .................$11,002
Lawyers & Lobbyists ...................$8,450

Unidentified .................................$11,225

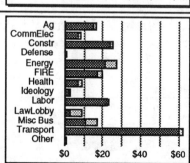

▨ PACs  ▧ Indivs ($200+)

# Rhode Island

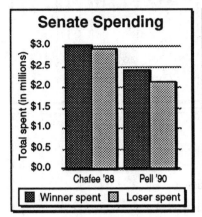

**Senate Spending**

Total spent (in millions)

$3.0, $2.5, $2.0, $1.5, $1.0, $0.5, $0.0

Chafee '88    Pell '90

▨ Winner spent    ▨ Loser spent

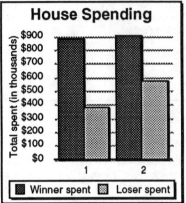

**House Spending**

Total spent (in thousands)

$900, $800, $700, $600, $500, $400, $300, $200, $100, $0

1    2

▨ Winner spent    ▨ Loser spent

## 1990 Elections at a Glance

| Dist | Name | Party | Vote Pct | Race Type |
|------|------|-------|----------|-----------|
| Sen | John H. Chafee (1988) | Rep | 55% | Reelected |
| Sen | Claiborne Pell (1990) | Dem | 62% | Reelected |
| 1 | Ronald K. Machtley | Rep | 55% | Reelected |
| 2 | John F. Reed | Dem | 59% | Open Seat |

*Totals in Thousands of Dollars*

## Sen. John H. Chafee (R)

**1990 Committees:** Envir/Public Works  Finance
**First elected:** 1976

1985-90 Total Rcpts: ............ $3,036,477
1990 Year-end cash: .............. $103,693

**Source of Funds**

- ■ PACs ............................................. 38%
- ▨ Lg Individuals ($200+) .............. 21%
- □ Individuals under $200 ............. 30%
- ▨ Other ........................................... 10%

**1985-90 (PACs only)**

**Top Industries & Interest Groups**

Insurance ................................. $127,433
Commercial Banks ................... $95,933
Securities & Investment ........... $76,234
Health Professionals ................ $72,300
Defense Aerospace .................. $46,861

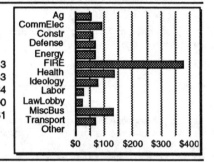

Ag, CommElec, Constr, Defense, Energy, FIRE, Health, Ideology, Labor, LawLobby, MiscBus, Transport, Other

$0  $100  $200  $300  $400

## Sen. Claiborne Pell (D)

**1990 Committees:** Foreign Relations  Labor  Rules
**First elected:** 1960

1985-90 Total Rcpts: ............ $2,261,423
1990 Year-end cash: .............. $216,256

**Source of Funds**

- ■ PACs ............................................. 38%
- ▨ Lg Individuals ($200+) .............. 41%
- □ Individuals under $200 ............... 8%
- ▨ Other ........................................... 13%

**1985-90**

**Top Industries & Interest Groups**

Pro-Israel ................................. $229,911
Bldg/Indust/Misc Unions .......... $148,950
Lawyers & Lobbyists ................ $130,960
Real Estate ................................ $81,100
Public Sector Unions ................ $74,850

Unidentified ............................. $206,500

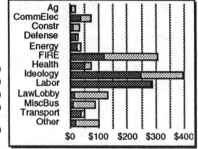

Ag, CommElec, Constr, Defense, Energy, FIRE, Health, Ideology, Labor, LawLobby, MiscBus, Transport, Other

$0  $100  $200  $300  $400

## 1. Ronald K. Machtley (R)

**1990 Committees:** Armed Services  Sm Business
**First elected:** 1988

1989-90 Total receipts: ............ $857,775
1990 Year-end cash: ................. $10,355

**Source of Funds**
- ■ PACs ............................................. 35%
- ▨ Lg Individuals ($200+) .............. 28%
- □ Individuals under $200 ............. 28%
- ▨ Other ............................................. 8%

**Top Industries & Interest Groups**

Health Professionals ................. $34,706
Misc Manufacturing & Distrib ..... $31,000
Public Sector Unions ................ $26,150
Defense Electronics .................. $25,200
Defense Aerospace .................. $22,300

Unidentified ............................... $86,122

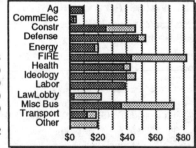

Ag, CommElec, Constr, Defense, Energy, FIRE, Health, Ideology, Labor, LawLobby, Misc Bus, Transport, Other

$0  $20  $40  $60  $80

## 2. John F. Reed (D)

**1991-92 Committees:** Educ/Labor  Judiciary  Merch Marine
**First elected:** 1990

1989-90 Total receipts: ............ $902,877
1990 Year-end cash: ................... $6,152

**Source of Funds**
- ■ PACs ............................................. 30%
- ▨ Lg Individuals ($200+) .............. 17%
- □ Individuals under $200 ............. 15%
- ▨ Other ........................................... 37%

**Top Industries & Interest Groups**

Bldg/Indust/Misc Unions ............ $85,750
Public Sector Unions ................ $51,250
Lawyers & Lobbyists ................ $43,885
Health Professionals ................ $31,170
Transportation Unions .............. $26,875

Unidentified ............................... $39,605

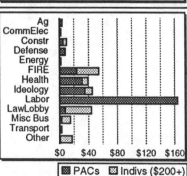

Ag, CommElec, Constr, Defense, Energy, FIRE, Health, Ideology, Labor, LawLobby, Misc Bus, Transport, Other

$0  $40  $80  $120  $160

▨ PACs  ▨ Indivs ($200+)

Key to committee & category abbreviations is on page 173

# South Carolina

## Senate Spending

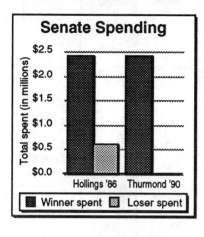

Total spent (in millions)

Winner spent   Loser spent

## Spending in 1990 House Races

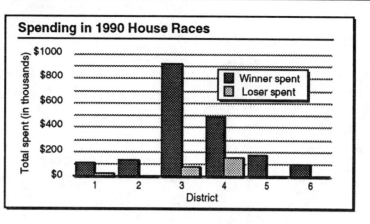

Total spent (in thousands)

Winner spent
Loser spent

District

## 1990 Elections at a Glance

| Dist | Name | Party | Vote Pct | Race Type |
|------|------|-------|----------|-----------|
| Sen | Ernest F. Hollings (1986) | Dem | 63% | Reelected |
| Sen | Strom Thurmond (1990) | Rep | 64% | Reelected |
| 1 | Arthur Ravenel Jr. | Rep | 66% | Reelected |
| 2 | Floyd D. Spence | Rep | 89% | Reelected |
| 3 | Butler Derrick | Dem | 58% | Reelected |
| 4 | Liz J. Patterson | Dem | 61% | Reelected |
| 5 | John M. Spratt Jr. | Dem | 100% | Reelected |
| 6 | Robin Tallon | Dem | 100% | Reelected |

*Totals in Thousands of Dollars*

## Sen. Ernest F. Hollings (D)

**1990 Committees: Appropriations  Budget  Commerce**
**First elected: 1966**

1985-90 Total Rcpts: ............$3,675,050
1990 Year-end cash: ..............$930,489

**Source of Funds**
- PACs .................................... 40%
- Lg Individuals ($200+) ............. 23%
- Individuals under $200 ............. 30%
- Other .................................... 7%

### 1985-90 (PACs only)
**Top Industries & Interest Groups**

Insurance ...................................$92,500
Telephone Utilities ....................$74,636
Transportation Unions ..............$74,250
Misc Manufacturing & Distrib .....$73,892
Air Transport .............................$62,800

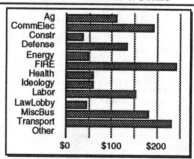

## Sen. Strom Thurmond (R)

**1990 Committees: ArmServ  Judiciary  Labor  VetAff**
**First elected: 1954**

1985-90 Total Rcpts: ............$2,207,157
1990 Year-end cash: ..............$221,092

**Source of Funds**
- PACs .................................... 27%
- Lg Individuals ($200+) ............. 25%
- Individuals under $200 ............. 32%
- Other .................................... 16%

### 1985-90
**Top Industries & Interest Groups**

Lawyers & Lobbyists ................$110,600
Insurance ..................................$80,357
Republican/Conservative ..........$69,234
Health Professionals .................$65,250
Misc Manufacturing & Distrib .....$63,500

Unidentified ..............................$112,739

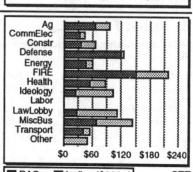

PACs   Indivs ($200+)

277

# 1. Arthur Ravenel Jr. (R)

**1990 Committees: Armed Services  Merchant Marine**
**First elected: 1986**

1989-90 Total receipts: ............$221,611
1990 Year-end cash: .............$284,458

**Source of Funds**
- PACs ...................................50%
- Lg Individuals ($200+) ..............19%
- Individuals under $200 ............15%
- Other ...................................15%

**Top Industries & Interest Groups**

Health Professionals ..................$18,300
Real Estate .................................$11,600
Steel/Smelting ............................$9,500
Public Sector Unions ...................$6,300
Automotive .................................$6,200

Unidentified .................................$2,900

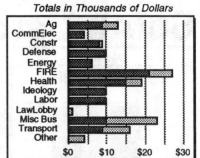

---

# 2. Floyd D. Spence (R)

**1990 Committees: Armed Services**
**First elected: 1970**

1989-90 Total receipts: ............$188,988
1990 Year-end cash: ................$62,190

**Source of Funds**
- PACs ...................................54%
- Lg Individuals ($200+) ..............12%
- Individuals under $200 ............29%
- Other .....................................4%

**Top Industries & Interest Groups**

Defense Aerospace ...................$16,350
Health Professionals ....................$9,900
Real Estate ..................................$8,989
Defense Electronics .....................$8,525
Misc Manufacturing & Distrib .......$6,500

Unidentified .................................$3,250

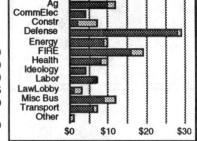

---

# 3. Butler Derrick (D)

**1990 Committees: Rules**
**First elected: 1974**

1989-90 Total receipts: ............$849,338
1990 Year-end cash: ..............$106,192

**Source of Funds**
- PACs ...................................62%
- Lg Individuals ($200+) ..............17%
- Individuals under $200 ............9%
- Other ...................................13%

**Top Industries & Interest Groups**

Lawyers & Lobbyists .................$52,703
Insurance ..................................$45,050
Commercial Banks ....................$43,850
Health Professionals .................$32,750
Misc Manufacturing & Distrib .....$27,450

Unidentified ...............................$26,280

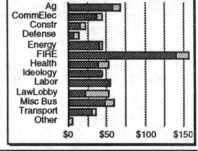

---

# 4. Liz J. Patterson (D)

**1990 Committees: Banking  Vet Affairs**
**First elected: 1986**

1989-90 Total receipts: ............$624,171
1990 Year-end cash: ..................$2,730

**Source of Funds**
- PACs ...................................61%
- Lg Individuals ($200+) ..............13%
- Individuals under $200 ............20%
- Other .....................................5%

**Top Industries & Interest Groups**

Commercial Banks ....................$56,250
Misc Manufacturing & Distrib .....$28,500
Health Professionals .................$26,290
Public Sector Unions ................$18,900
Real Estate ...............................$17,010

Unidentified ...............................$10,784

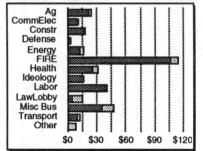

---

# 5. John M. Spratt Jr. (D)

**1990 Committees: Armed Services  Budget**
**First elected: 1982**

1989-90 Total receipts: ............$110,158
1990 Year-end cash: ..............$153,025

**Source of Funds**
- PACs ...................................73%
- Lg Individuals ($200+) ..............4%
- Individuals under $200 ............1%
- Other ...................................23%

**Top Industries & Interest Groups**

Defense Aerospace .....................$7,900
Defense Electronics .....................$7,500
Real Estate ..................................$6,350
Health Professionals ....................$6,350
Misc Defense ...............................$6,100

Unidentified .................................$1,250

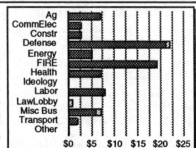

---

# 6. Robin Tallon (D)

**1990 Committees: Agriculture  Merchant Marine**
**First elected: 1982**

1989-90 Total receipts: ...........$231,293
1990 Year-end cash: ..............$350,780

**Source of Funds**
- PACs ...................................63%
- Lg Individuals ($200+) ..............13%
- Individuals under $200 ............13%
- Other ...................................12%

**Top Industries & Interest Groups**

Health Professionals ..................$14,350
Tobacco .....................................$13,000
Agric Services/Products ............$12,350
Crop Production/Processing ......$10,300
Securities & Investment ............$10,000

Unidentified .................................$4,550

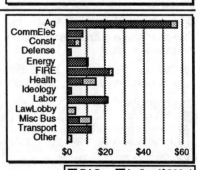

278   Key to committee & category abbreviations is on page 173

# South Dakota

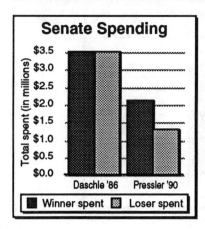

## Senate Spending

Total spent (in millions)

$3.5
$3.0
$2.5
$2.0
$1.5
$1.0
$0.5
$0.0

Daschle '86    Pressler '90

■ Winner spent  ▨ Loser spent

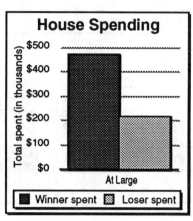

## House Spending

Total spent (in thousands)

$500
$400
$300
$200
$100
$0

At Large

■ Winner spent  ▨ Loser spent

## 1990 Elections at a Glance

| Dist | Name | Party | Vote Pct | Race Type |
|------|------|-------|----------|-----------|
| Sen | Tom Daschle (1986) | Dem | 52% | Beat Incumb |
| Sen | Larry Pressler (1990) | Rep | 52% | Reelected |
| 1 | Tim Johnson | Dem | 68% | Reelected |

*Totals in Thousands of Dollars*

## Sen. Tom Daschle (D)

**1990 Committees: Agriculture   Finance**
**First elected: 1986**

1985-90 Total Rcpts: ............$4,802,957
1990 Year-end cash: ..............$220,846

**Source of Funds**
■ PACs ..............................................35%
▨ Lg Individuals ($200+) ..............16%
☐ Individuals under $200 ..............44%
▨ Other ............................................6%

### 1985-90 (PACs only)
**Top Industries & Interest Groups**

Pro-Israel ...................................$231,230
Bldg/Indust/Misc Unions .........$208,799
Public Sector Unions ..............$119,400
Transportation Unions ............$104,150
Insurance ...................................$96,899

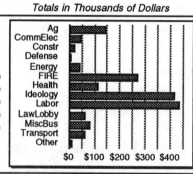

Ag
CommElec
Constr
Defense
Energy
FIRE
Health
Ideology
Labor
LawLobby
MiscBus
Transport
Other

$0  $100  $200  $300  $400

## Sen. Larry Pressler (R)

**1990 Committees: Banking   Commerce   ForRel   SmBus**
**First elected: 1978**

1985-90 Total Rcpts: ............$2,368,218
1990 Year-end cash: ..............$556,585

**Source of Funds**
■ PACs ..................................................41%
▨ Lg Individuals ($200+) ..................35%
☐ Individuals under $200 ..................8%
▨ Other ................................................17%

### 1985-90
**Top Industries & Interest Groups**

Pro-Israel ...................................$125,345
Insurance ...................................$122,698
Securities & Investment ............$85,434
Lawyers & Lobbyists .................$82,800
Real Estate ................................$79,400

Unidentified .............................$146,465

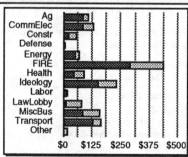

Ag
CommElec
Constr
Defense
Energy
FIRE
Health
Ideology
Labor
LawLobby
MiscBus
Transport
Other

$0  $125  $250  $375  $500

## 1.  Tim Johnson (D)

**1990 Committees: Agriculture   Interior   Vet Affairs**
**First elected: 1986**

1989-90 Total receipts: ............$516,816
1990 Year-end cash: ..............$104,643

**Source of Funds**
■ PACs ..................................................47%
▨ Lg Individuals ($200+) ..................11%
☐ Individuals under $200 ..................32%
▨ Other ................................................10%

### Top Industries & Interest Groups

Bldg/Indust/Misc Unions ............$50,450
Public Sector Unions .................$37,000
Transportation Unions ...............$22,800
Crop Production/Processing ......$19,050
Commercial Banks ....................$18,500
Health Professionals ..................$18,500

Unidentified ...............................$13,790

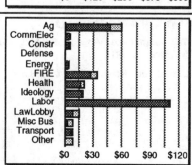

Ag
CommElec
Constr
Defense
Energy
FIRE
Health
Ideology
Labor
LawLobby
Misc Bus
Transport
Other

$0  $30  $60  $90  $120

■ PACs  ▨ Indivs ($200+)

**279**

# Tennessee

## Senate Spending

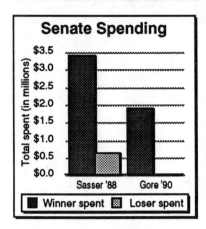

Total spent (in millions)

Winner spent  Loser spent

## Spending in 1990 House Races

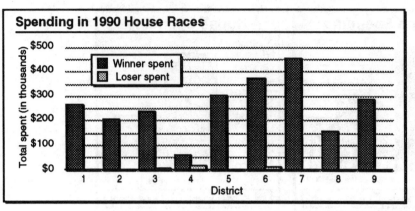

Total spent (in thousands)

Winner spent
Loser spent

District

## 1990 Elections at a Glance

| Dist | Name | Party | Vote Pct | Race Type |
|------|------|-------|----------|-----------|
| Sen | Al Gore (1990) | Dem | 68% | Reelected |
| Sen | Jim Sasser (1988) | Dem | 65% | Reelected |
| 1 | James H. Quillen | Rep | 100% | Reelected |
| 2 | John J. "Jimmy" Duncan Jr. | Rep | 81% | Reelected |
| 3 | Marilyn Lloyd | Dem | 53% | Reelected |
| 4 | Jim Cooper | Dem | 67% | Reelected |
| 5 | Bob Clement | Dem | 72% | Reelected |
| 6 | Bart Gordon | Dem | 67% | Reelected |
| 7 | Don Sundquist | Rep | 62% | Reelected |
| 8 | John Tanner | Dem | 100% | Reelected |
| 9 | Harold E. Ford | Dem | 58% | Reelected |

*Totals in Thousands of Dollars*

## Sen. Al Gore (D)

**1990 Committees: ArmServ  Commerce  Rules**
**First elected: 1984**

1985-90 Total Rcpts: ............$2,645,326
1990 Year-end cash: ..............$708,043

**Source of Funds**
- PACs ...................................43%
- Lg Individuals ($200+) ............40%
- Individuals under $200 ...............9%
- Other ....................................8%

### 1985-90

**Top Industries & Interest Groups**

Lawyers & Lobbyists ...............$307,868
Bldg/Indust/Misc Unions .........$219,387
Pro-Israel ..............................$113,905
Insurance ...............................$109,076
Public Sector Unions ..............$108,050

Unidentified ............................$248,624

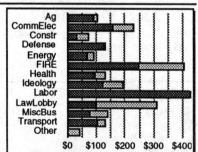

## Sen. Jim Sasser (D)

**1990 Committees: Approp  Banking  Budget  GovAff**
**First elected: 1976**

1985-90 Total Rcpts: ............$3,608,290
1990 Year-end cash: ..............$248,244

**Source of Funds**
- PACs ...................................43%
- Lg Individuals ($200+) ............32%
- Individuals under $200 .............19%
- Other ....................................5%

### 1985-90 (PACs only)

**Top Industries & Interest Groups**

Bldg/Indust/Misc Unions ..........$131,850
Insurance ...............................$108,050
Commercial Banks ..................$101,440
Defense Aerospace ..................$98,400
Public Sector Unions ................$87,000

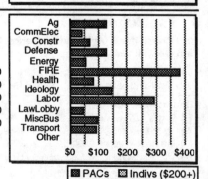

PACs  Indivs ($200+)

280  Key to committee & category abbreviations is on page 173

# 1. James H. Quillen (R)

**1990 Committees: Rules**
**First elected: 1962**

1989-90 Total receipts: ...........$596,536
1990 Year-end cash: ..........$1,044,255

**Source of Funds**
- PACs .............................................61%
- Lg Individuals ($200+) ...............14%
- Individuals under $200 .................1%
- Other ...........................................25%

**Top Industries & Interest Groups**

Lawyers & Lobbyists ................$28,800
Insurance ...................................$27,779
Public Sector Unions ................$26,000
Transportation Unions .............$25,000
Air Transport ............................$21,000

Unidentified .............................$18,400

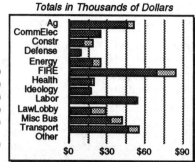

# 2. John J. "Jimmy" Duncan Jr. (R)

**1990 Committees: Interior  Public Works**
**First elected: 1988**

1989-90 Total receipts: ...........$325,691
1990 Year-end cash: ...........$137,716

**Source of Funds**
- PACs .............................................49%
- Lg Individuals ($200+) ...............27%
- Individuals under $200 ...............20%
- Other .............................................4%

**Top Industries & Interest Groups**

Health Professionals .................$34,419
Transportation Unions .............$20,000
Air Transport ............................$18,600
Real Estate ...............................$12,655
Lawyers & Lobbyists .................$10,550

Unidentified .............................$15,800

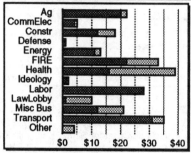

# 3. Marilyn Lloyd (D)

**1990 Committees: Armed Services  Science**
**First elected: 1974**

1989-90 Total receipts: ...........$415,056
1990 Year-end cash: ...............$184,618

**Source of Funds**
- PACs .............................................55%
- Lg Individuals ($200+) ...............19%
- Individuals under $200 ...............12%
- Other ...........................................14%

**Top Industries & Interest Groups**

Bldg/Indust/Misc Unions ...........$46,500
Defense Aerospace ...................$27,500
Health Professionals .................$19,250
Misc Manufacturing & Distrib .....$19,000
Public Sector Unions ................$16,500

Unidentified .............................$21,700

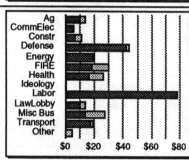

# 4. Jim Cooper (D)

**1990 Committees: Energy & Commerce  Sm Business**
**First elected: 1982**

1989-90 Total receipts: ...........$183,494
1990 Year-end cash: ...............$205,616

**Source of Funds**
- PACs .............................................59%
- Lg Individuals ($200+) ...............21%
- Individuals under $200 ...............14%
- Other .............................................6%

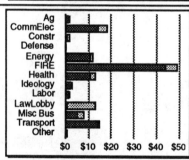

**Top Industries & Interest Groups**

Commercial Banks ....................$22,050
Lawyers & Lobbyists .................$12,350
Telephone Utilities .....................$10,500
Accountants ..............................$10,500
Air Transport ............................$10,000

Unidentified ...............................$6,450

# 5. Bob Clement (D)

**1990 Committees: Merchant Marine  Public Works**
**First elected: 1988**

1989-90 Total receipts: ...........$449,833
1990 Year-end cash: ...............$164,023

**Source of Funds**
- PACs .............................................64%
- Lg Individuals ($200+) ...............26%
- Individuals under $200 .................5%
- Other .............................................5%

**Top Industries & Interest Groups**

Bldg/Indust/Misc Unions ...........$43,350
Air Transport ............................$26,450
Transportation Unions .............$26,150
Public Sector Unions ................$25,200
Health Professionals .................$17,950

Unidentified .............................$21,300

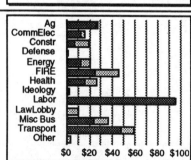

# 6. Bart Gordon (D)

**1990 Committees: Rules**
**First elected: 1984**

1989-90 Total receipts: ...........$620,052
1990 Year-end cash: ...............$535,072

**Source of Funds**
- PACs .............................................56%
- Lg Individuals ($200+) .................3%
- Individuals under $200 ...............26%
- Other ...........................................15%

**Top Industries & Interest Groups**

Bldg/Indust/Misc Unions ...........$50,200
Commercial Banks ....................$31,200
Public Sector Unions ................$29,650
Insurance ...................................$20,500
Transportation Unions .............$20,100

Unidentified ...............................$2,550

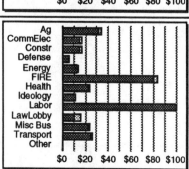

■ PACs  ⊠ Indivs ($200+)

281

## 7. Don Sundquist (R)

**1990 Committees:** Ways & Means
**First elected:** 1982

1989-90 Total receipts: ............$648,472
1990 Year-end cash: ..............$471,904

**Source of Funds**
■ PACs.......................................55%
▩ Lg Individuals ($200+)..............22%
□ Individuals under $200 ............16%
▨ Other .....................................7%

**Top Industries & Interest Groups**

Insurance ....................................$77,899
Tobacco .....................................$25,700
Real Estate ................................$25,122
Health Professionals ..................$21,100
Commercial Banks ....................$17,250

Unidentified ................................$26,825

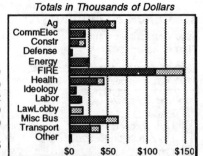

## 8. John Tanner (D)

**1990 Committees:** Armed Services  Science
**First elected:** 1988

1989-90 Total receipts: ............$314,094
1990 Year-end cash: ..............$228,267

**Source of Funds**
■ PACs.......................................42%
▩ Lg Individuals ($200+)..............31%
□ Individuals under $200 ............18%
▨ Other.......................................8%

**Top Industries & Interest Groups**

Insurance ....................................$15,275
Lawyers & Lobbyists ..................$12,550
Public Sector Unions ..................$12,300
General Contractors ...................$11,650
Air Transport ..............................$11,600

Unidentified ................................$15,435

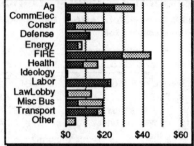

## 9. Harold E. Ford (D)

**1990 Committees:** Ways & Means
**First elected:** 1974

1989-90 Total receipts: ...........$283,587
1990 Year-end cash: .....................$126

**Source of Funds**
■ PACs.......................................55%
▩ Lg Individuals ($200+)..............32%
□ Individuals under $200 ..............3%
▨ Other.......................................9%

**Top Industries & Interest Groups**

Air Transport ..............................$24,100
Bldg/Indust/Misc Unions ...........$23,000
Lawyers & Lobbyists ..................$22,650
Health Professionals ..................$20,700
Public Sector Unions ................$20,250

Unidentified ................................$25,660

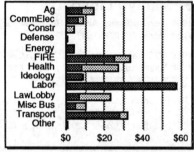

■ PACs  ▨ Indivs ($200+)

# Texas

## Spending in 1990 House Races

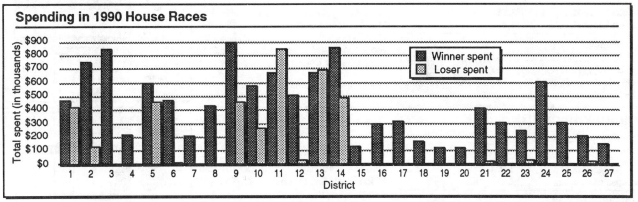

## 1990 Elections at a Glance

| Dist | Name | Party | Vote Pct | Race Type |
|------|------|-------|----------|-----------|
| Sen | Lloyd Bentsen (1988) | Dem | 59% | Reelected |
| Sen | Phil Gramm (1990) | Rep | 60% | Reelected |
| 1 | Jim Chapman | Dem | 61% | Reelected |
| 2 | Charles Wilson | Dem | 56% | Reelected |
| 3 | Steve Bartlett | Rep | 100% | Reelected |
| 4 | Ralph M. Hall | Dem | 100% | Reelected |
| 5 | John Bryant | Dem | 60% | Reelected |
| 6 | Joe L. Barton | Rep | 66% | Reelected |
| 7 | Bill Archer | Rep | 100% | Reelected |
| 8 | Jack Fields | Rep | 100% | Reelected |
| 9 | Jack Brooks | Dem | 58% | Reelected |
| 10 | J. J. Pickle | Dem | 65% | Reelected |
| 11 | Chet Edwards | Dem | 54% | Open Seat |
| 12 | Pete Geren | Dem | 71% | Reelected |
| 13 | Bill Sarpalius | Dem | 56% | Reelected |
| 14 | Greg Laughlin | Dem | 54% | Reelected |
| 15 | E. "Kika" de la Garza | Dem | 100% | Reelected |
| 16 | Ronald D. Coleman | Dem | 96% | Reelected |
| 17 | Charles W. Stenholm | Dem | 100% | Reelected |
| 18 | Craig Washington | Dem | 100% | Reelected |
| 19 | Larry Combest | Rep | 100% | Reelected |
| 20 | Henry B. Gonzalez | Dem | 100% | Reelected |
| 21 | Lamar Smith | Rep | 75% | Reelected |
| 22 | Tom DeLay | Rep | 71% | Reelected |

## Senate Spending

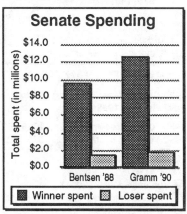

| Dist | Name | Party | Vote Pct | Race Type |
|------|------|-------|----------|-----------|
| 23 | Albert G. Bustamante | Dem | 64% | Reelected |
| 24 | Martin Frost | Dem | 100% | Reelected |
| 25 | Michael A. Andrews | Dem | 100% | Reelected |
| 26 | Dick Armey | Rep | 70% | Reelected |
| 27 | Solomon P. Ortiz | Dem | 100% | Reelected |

*Totals in Thousands of Dollars*

## Sen. Lloyd Bentsen (D)

**1990 Committees: Commerce  Finance**
**First elected: 1970**

1985-90 Total Rcpts: ............$9,550,410
1990 Year-end cash: ..............$147,979

**Source of Funds**
- PACs .................................................25%
- Lg Individuals ($200+) ...............45%
- Individuals under $200 ..............18%
- Other ................................................11%

### 1985-90 (PACs only)

**Top Industries & Interest Groups**

Oil & Gas .................................$246,987
Insurance ................................$216,650
Lawyers & Lobbyists...............$156,536
Securities & Investment..........$143,350
Commercial Banks .................$134,175

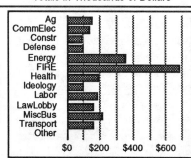

## Sen. Phil Gramm (R)

**1990 Committees: Appropriations  Banking  Budget**
**First elected: 1984**

1985-90 Total Rcpts: .........$16,268,341
1990 Year-end cash: ...........$4,147,378

**Source of Funds**
- PACs....................................................10%
- Lg Individuals ($200+) ...............44%
- Individuals under $200 ...............31%
- Other .................................................15%

### 1985-90

**Top Industries & Interest Groups**

Oil & Gas .................................$715,874
Lawyers & Lobbyists...............$634,550
Health Professionals................$386,949
Commercial Banks ..................$264,121
Real Estate ..............................$233,530

Unidentified...........................$1,863,023

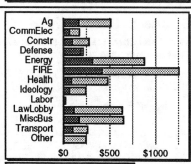

283

## 1. Jim Chapman (D)

**1990 Committees:** Appropriations
**First elected:** 1986

1989-90 Total receipts: ............$533,989
1990 Year-end cash: ..............$126,440

**Source of Funds**
PACs.............................................54%
Lg Individuals ($200+) ...............27%
Individuals under $200 ..............15%
Other..............................................4%

**Top Industries & Interest Groups**

Lawyers & Lobbyists .................$44,400
Health Professionals ................$32,057
Oil & Gas ...................................$28,700
Bldg/Indust/Misc Unions ...........$26,300
Public Sector Unions ................$24,000

Unidentified ...............................$13,149

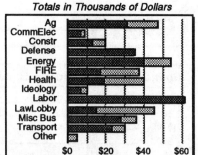

## 2. Charles Wilson (D)

**1990 Committees:** Appropriations
**First elected:** 1972

1989-90 Total receipts: ............$663,504
1990 Year-end cash: .......................$860

**Source of Funds**
PACs.............................................64%
Lg Individuals ($200+) ...............19%
Individuals under $200 ................9%
Other..............................................8%

**Top Industries & Interest Groups**

Defense Aerospace .................$107,250
Bldg/Indust/Misc Unions ...........$58,100
Defense Electronics ..................$53,550
Lawyers & Lobbyists .................$45,667
Oil & Gas ...................................$37,950

Unidentified ...............................$17,500

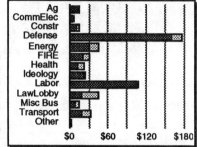

## 3. Steve Bartlett (R)

**1990 Committees:** Banking Educ/Labor
**First elected:** 1982

1989-90 Total receipts: ............$798,555
1990 Year-end cash: ..............$167,323

**Source of Funds**
PACs.............................................34%
Lg Individuals ($200+) ...............41%
Individuals under $200 ..............20%
Other..............................................5%

**Top Industries & Interest Groups**

Real Estate ...............................$69,510
Commercial Banks ...................$52,400
Oil & Gas ...................................$43,625
Lawyers & Lobbyists .................$42,675
Food & Beverage ......................$23,600

Unidentified ...............................$72,400

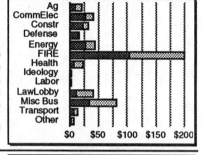

## 4. Ralph M. Hall (D)

**1990 Committees:** Energy & Commerce Science
**First elected:** 1980

1989-90 Total receipts: ............$261,431
1990 Year-end cash: ..............$212,938

**Source of Funds**
PACs.............................................76%
Lg Individuals ($200+) .................8%
Individuals under $200 ................6%
Other............................................10%

**Top Industries & Interest Groups**

Commercial Banks ....................$27,450
Oil & Gas ...................................$24,761
Health Professionals ................$22,380
Electric Utilities .........................$21,600
Telephone Utilities ....................$14,850

Unidentified .................................$2,450

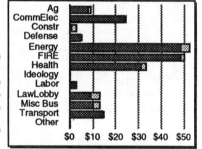

## 5. John Bryant (D)

**1990 Committees:** Budget Energy & Comm Judiciary
**First elected:** 1982

1989-90 Total receipts: .........$1,248,858
1990 Year-end cash: ..............$257,837

**Source of Funds**
PACs.............................................31%
Lg Individuals ($200+) ...............22%
Individuals under $200 ..............12%
Other............................................35%

**Top Industries & Interest Groups**

Lawyers & Lobbyists ...............$153,157
Bldg/Indust/Misc Unions ...........$73,550
Oil & Gas ...................................$30,264
Public Sector Unions ................$27,800
Health Professionals ................$27,000

Unidentified ...............................$59,450

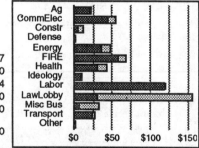

## 6. Joe L. Barton (R)

**1990 Committees:** Energy & Commerce
**First elected:** 1984

1989-90 Total receipts: ............$770,957
1990 Year-end cash: ..............$412,069

**Source of Funds**
PACs.............................................34%
Lg Individuals ($200+) ...............35%
Individuals under $200 ..............19%
Other............................................12%

**Top Industries & Interest Groups**

Oil & Gas ...................................$77,407
Electric Utilities .........................$36,000
Lawyers & Lobbyists .................$24,599
Telephone Utilities ....................$23,989
Retired .......................................$20,400

Unidentified ...............................$35,513

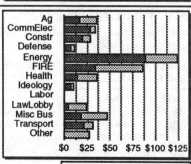

Key to committee & category abbreviations is on page 173

PACs    Indivs ($200+)

## 7. Bill Archer (R)

**1990 Committees: Ways & Means**
**First elected: 1970**

1989-90 Total receipts: ............ $241,863
1990 Year-end cash: .............. $670,901

**Source of Funds**
- ■ PACs ................................................... 0%
- ▨ Lg Individuals ($200+) ............. 36%
- □ Individuals under $200 ............ 18%
- ▨ Other ............................................... 46%

**Top Industries & Interest Groups**

Insurance ...................... $14,683
Lawyers & Lobbyists ................. $13,750
Oil & Gas ............................. $5,185
Misc Finance .......................... $4,500
Poultry & Eggs ....................... $4,000

Unidentified .......................... $16,096

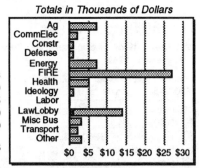

## 8. Jack Fields (R)

**1990 Committees: Energy & Comm  Merchant Marine**
**First elected: 1980**

1989-90 Total receipts: ............ $385,273
1990 Year-end cash: ................. $34,447

**Source of Funds**
- ■ PACs ................................................. 69%
- ▨ Lg Individuals ($200+) ............. 23%
- □ Individuals under $200 .............. 3%
- ▨ Other ................................................. 6%

**Top Industries & Interest Groups**

Oil & Gas ............................ $48,400
Health Professionals ................ $24,400
Transportation Unions .............. $21,500
Telephone Utilities ................. $21,350
Lawyers & Lobbyists ................ $20,600

Unidentified .......................... $13,225

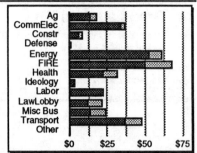

## 9. Jack Brooks (D)

**1990 Committees: Judiciary**
**First elected: 1952**

1989-90 Total receipts: ............ $775,167
1990 Year-end cash: ............... $330,424

**Source of Funds**
- ■ PACs ................................................. 58%
- ▨ Lg Individuals ($200+) ............. 25%
- □ Individuals under $200 .............. 5%
- ▨ Other ............................................... 12%

**Top Industries & Interest Groups**

Lawyers & Lobbyists ................. $83,567
Bldg/Indust/Misc Unions ........... $38,750
TV & Movies .......................... $38,741
Oil & Gas ............................ $33,700
Beer, Wine & Liquor ................. $33,100

Unidentified .......................... $23,333

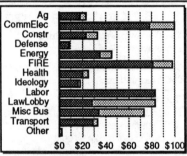

## 10. J. J. Pickle (D)

**1990 Committees: Ways & Means**
**First elected: 1963**

1989-90 Total receipts: ............ $491,649
1990 Year-end cash: ................. $66,442

**Source of Funds**
- ■ PACs ................................................. 50%
- ▨ Lg Individuals ($200+) ............. 32%
- □ Individuals under $200 ............ 13%
- ▨ Other ................................................. 6%

**Top Industries & Interest Groups**

Lawyers & Lobbyists ................. $63,900
Insurance ............................ $38,991
Health Professionals ................ $36,500
Oil & Gas ............................ $17,250
Real Estate .......................... $16,300

Unidentified .......................... $19,396

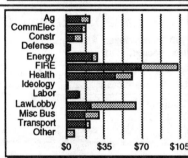

## 11. Chet Edwards (D)

**1991-92 Committees: Armed Services  Vet Affairs**
**First elected: 1990**

1989-90 Total receipts: ............ $672,399
1990 Year-end cash: ................... $3,460

**Source of Funds**
- ■ PACs ................................................. 48%
- ▨ Lg Individuals ($200+) ............. 34%
- □ Individuals under $200 .............. 4%
- ▨ Other ............................................... 13%

**Top Industries & Interest Groups**

Bldg/Indust/Misc Unions ........... $71,300
Lawyers & Lobbyists ................. $55,440
Real Estate .......................... $42,850
Public Sector Unions ............... $37,100
Insurance ............................ $29,050

Unidentified .......................... $41,450

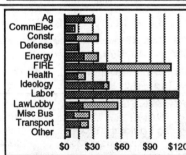

## 12. Pete Geren (D)

**1990 Committees: Public Works  Vet Affairs**
**First elected: 1989**

1989-90 Total receipts: ......... $1,434,684
1990 Year-end cash: ................. $18,132

**Source of Funds**
- ■ PACs ................................................. 38%
- ▨ Lg Individuals ($200+) ............. 46%
- □ Individuals under $200 .............. 6%
- ▨ Other ................................................. 9%

**Top Industries & Interest Groups**

Lawyers & Lobbyists ............... $193,288
Oil & Gas ........................... $175,800
Bldg/Indust/Misc Unions ........... $88,050
Public Sector Unions ............... $58,650
Real Estate .......................... $57,366

Unidentified ......................... $110,559

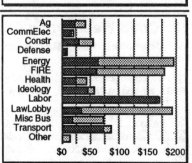

■ PACs  ▨ Indivs ($200+)

285

## 13. Bill Sarpalius (D)

**1990 Committees: Agriculture  Sm Business**
**First elected: 1988**

1989-90 Total receipts: ............$685,311
1990 Year-end cash: .................$17,542

**Source of Funds**
| | |
|---|---|
| ■ PACs .................................... | 54% |
| ▨ Lg Individuals ($200+) ............. | 14% |
| ☐ Individuals under $200 ............. | 12% |
| ▩ Other .................................. | 21% |

**Top Industries & Interest Groups**

Bldg/Indust/Misc Unions ............$35,800
Lawyers & Lobbyists ..................$34,600
Transportation Unions ..............$29,270
Public Sector Unions ................$28,550
Crop Production/Processing ......$24,380

Unidentified ..............................$25,555

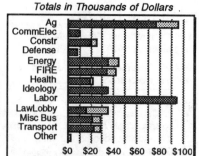

## 14. Greg Laughlin (D)

**1990 Committees: Merchant Marine  Public Works**
**First elected: 1988**

1989-90 Total receipts: ............$829,150
1990 Year-end cash: ...................$1,820

**Source of Funds**
| | |
|---|---|
| ■ PACs .................................... | 49% |
| ▨ Lg Individuals ($200+) ............. | 30% |
| ☐ Individuals under $200 ............. | 15% |
| ▩ Other .................................. | 6% |

**Top Industries & Interest Groups**

Lawyers & Lobbyists ...............$100,857
Oil & Gas .................................$49,598
Transportation Unions ..............$41,246
Air Transport ............................$35,600
Bldg/Indust/Misc Unions ...........$34,050

Unidentified ..............................$56,433

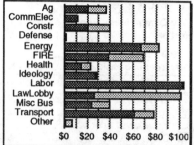

## 15. E. "Kika" de la Garza (D)

**1990 Committees: Agriculture**
**First elected: 1964**

1989-90 Total receipts: .............$86,524
1990 Year-end cash: ...............$137,477

**Source of Funds**
| | |
|---|---|
| ■ PACs .................................... | 68% |
| ▨ Lg Individuals ($200+) ............. | 21% |
| ☐ Individuals under $200 ............. | 11% |
| ▩ Other .................................. | 1% |

**Top Industries & Interest Groups**

Livestock .................................$15,900
Public Sector Unions ..................$9,500
Crop Production/Processing ........$9,250
Agric Services/Products .............$7,500
Commercial Banks .....................$6,500

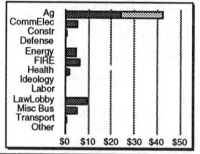

## 16. Ronald D. Coleman (D)

**1990 Committees: Appropriations**
**First elected: 1982**

1989-90 Total receipts: ............$279,452
1990 Year-end cash: ...................$9,538

**Source of Funds**
| | |
|---|---|
| ■ PACs .................................... | 58% |
| ▨ Lg Individuals ($200+) ............. | 30% |
| ☐ Individuals under $200 ............. | 12% |
| ▩ Other .................................. | 1% |

**Top Industries & Interest Groups**

Lawyers & Lobbyists ..................$29,660
Bldg/Indust/Misc Unions ............$19,300
Public Sector Unions ................$17,050
Transportation Unions ..............$15,950
Real Estate ...............................$13,000

Unidentified ................................$9,200

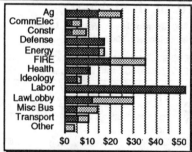

## 17. Charles W. Stenholm (D)

**1990 Committees: Agriculture  Vet Affairs**
**First elected: 1978**

1989-90 Total receipts: ............$254,175
1990 Year-end cash: .................$89,736

**Source of Funds**
| | |
|---|---|
| ■ PACs .................................... | 40% |
| ▨ Lg Individuals ($200+) ............. | 20% |
| ☐ Individuals under $200 ............. | 33% |
| ▩ Other .................................. | 7% |

**Top Industries & Interest Groups**

Livestock .................................$20,050
Agric Services/Products ............$15,300
Crop Production/Processing ......$12,250
Oil & Gas .................................$11,750
Health Professionals ...................$9,750

Unidentified ................................$2,750

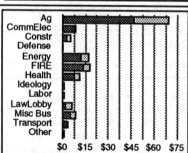

## 18. Craig Washington (D)

**1990 Committees: Educ/Labor  Judiciary**
**First elected: 1989**

1989-90 Total receipts: ............$789,126
1990 Year-end cash: .................$13,250

**Source of Funds**
| | |
|---|---|
| ■ PACs .................................... | 36% |
| ▨ Lg Individuals ($200+) ............. | 43% |
| ☐ Individuals under $200 ............. | 13% |
| ▩ Other .................................. | 8% |

**Top Industries & Interest Groups**

Lawyers & Lobbyists ...............$183,860
Public Sector Unions ................$53,950
Bldg/Indust/Misc Unions ...........$49,500
Transportation Unions ..............$35,750
Health Professionals .................$18,850

Unidentified ..............................$66,495

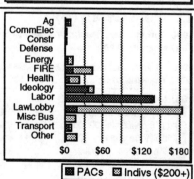

Key to committee & category abbreviations is on page 173

■ PACs  ▨ Indivs ($200+)

## 19. Larry Combest (R)

**1990 Committees:** Agriculture DC Sm Business
**First elected:** 1984

1989-90 Total receipts: ...........$201,299
1990 Year-end cash: ..............$129,221

**Source of Funds**
- PACs.............................................44%
- Lg Individuals ($200+) ................28%
- Individuals under $200 ...............26%
- Other..............................................2%

### Top Industries & Interest Groups

Crop Production/Processing ......$11,175
Health Professionals ..................$10,200
Agric Services/Products .............$9,000
Livestock .......................................$8,450
Commercial Banks .......................$7,925

Unidentified ...............................$18,950

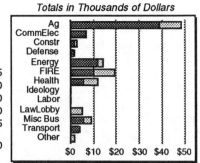

Totals in Thousands of Dollars

## 20. Henry B. Gonzalez (D)

**1990 Committees:** Banking
**First elected:** 1961

1989-90 Total receipts: ...........$142,661
1990 Year-end cash: .................$35,482

**Source of Funds**
- PACs............................................59%
- Lg Individuals ($200+) ................27%
- Individuals under $200 ...............14%
- Other..............................................0%

### Top Industries & Interest Groups

Public Sector Unions .................$15,900
Commercial Banks ....................$13,650
Real Estate .................................$13,200
Lawyers & Lobbyists .................$10,780
Bldg/Indust/Misc Unions ............$8,700

Unidentified ...............................$11,530

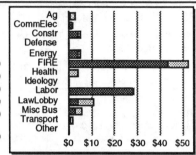

## 21. Lamar Smith (R)

**1990 Committees:** Judiciary Science
**First elected:** 1986

1989-90 Total receipts: ...........$609,914
1990 Year-end cash: ..............$352,846

**Source of Funds**
- PACs............................................22%
- Lg Individuals ($200+) ................42%
- Individuals under $200 ...............29%
- Other..............................................7%

### Top Industries & Interest Groups

Oil & Gas ....................................$56,602
Misc Finance .............................$40,000
Livestock .....................................$27,400
Health Professionals .................$26,400
Lawyers & Lobbyists .................$24,684

Unidentified ...............................$33,750

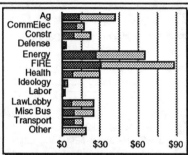

## 22. Tom DeLay (R)

**1990 Committees:** Appropriations
**First elected:** 1984

1989-90 Total receipts: ...........$324,134
1990 Year-end cash: .................$76,314

**Source of Funds**
- PACs............................................55%
- Lg Individuals ($200+) ................29%
- Individuals under $200 ...............16%
- Other..............................................0%

### Top Industries & Interest Groups

Air Transport ..............................$21,650
Oil & Gas ....................................$20,700
Health Professionals .................$15,050
Real Estate .................................$13,350
Chemicals ...................................$12,950

Unidentified ...............................$32,075

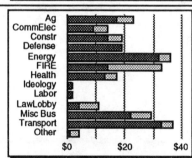

## 23. Albert G. Bustamante (D)

**1990 Committees:** Armed Services Govt Ops
**First elected:** 1984

1989-90 Total receipts: ...........$370,750
1990 Year-end cash: ..............$294,345

**Source of Funds**
- PACs............................................52%
- Lg Individuals ($200+) ................33%
- Individuals under $200 ...............3%
- Other............................................12%

### Top Industries & Interest Groups

Bldg/Indust/Misc Unions ...........$27,500
Lawyers & Lobbyists .................$26,950
Public Sector Unions ................$22,700
Defense Aerospace ...................$21,800
Oil & Gas ....................................$20,375

Unidentified ...............................$12,050

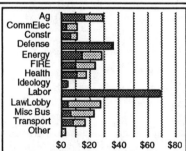

## 24. Martin Frost (D)

**1990 Committees:** Admin Rules
**First elected:** 1978

1989-90 Total receipts: ...........$679,688
1990 Year-end cash: ..............$316,106

**Source of Funds**
- PACs............................................61%
- Lg Individuals ($200+) ................24%
- Individuals under $200 ...............9%
- Other..............................................6%

### Top Industries & Interest Groups

Lawyers & Lobbyists .................$71,425
Bldg/Indust/Misc Unions ...........$55,750
Oil & Gas ....................................$54,350
Public Sector Unions ................$34,255
Defense Aerospace ...................$28,000

Unidentified ...............................$16,700

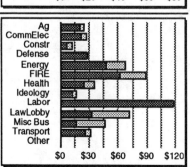

■ PACs ▨ Indivs ($200+)

287

## 25. Michael A. Andrews (D)

**1990 Committees: Ways & Means**
**First elected: 1982**

1989-90 Total receipts: ............$539,864
1990 Year-end cash: ..............$811,150

**Source of Funds**
■ PACs.....................................60%
▨ Lg Individuals ($200+) .............12%
□ Individuals under $200 .............7%
▧ Other ...................................20%

**Top Industries & Interest Groups**

Insurance ...................................$53,850
Lawyers & Lobbyists .................$46,550
Oil & Gas ..................................$43,435
Commercial Banks ...................$22,200
Real Estate ..............................$21,000

Unidentified ..............................$9,075

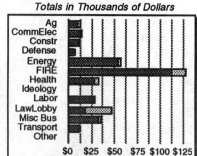

## 26. Dick Armey (R)

**1990 Committees: Budget Govt Ops**
**First elected: 1984**

1989-90 Total receipts: ............$440,375
1990 Year-end cash: ..............$362,311

**Source of Funds**
■ PACs....................................35%
▨ Lg Individuals ($200+) .............34%
□ Individuals under $200 .............20%
▧ Other ...................................11%

**Top Industries & Interest Groups**

Oil & Gas ..................................$31,000
Real Estate ...............................$25,600
Misc Manufacturing & Distrib .....$20,250
Health Professionals .................$19,850
Lawyers & Lobbyists .................$17,150

Unidentified ..............................$60,450

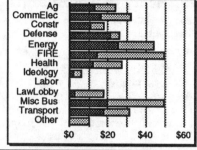

## 27. Solomon P. Ortiz (D)

**1990 Committees: Armed Services  Merchant Marine**
**First elected: 1982**

1989-90 Total receipts: ............$236,123
1990 Year-end cash: ..............$266,352

**Source of Funds**
■ PACs....................................44%
▨ Lg Individuals ($200+) .............31%
□ Individuals under $200 .............12%
▧ Other ...................................13%

**Top Industries & Interest Groups**

Defense Aerospace ...................$14,750
Real Estate ...............................$12,700
Public Sector Unions ................$12,400
Oil & Gas ..................................$11,650
Transportation Unions ..............$11,500

Unidentified ..............................$16,500

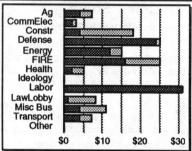

■ PACs  ▨ Indivs ($200+)

Key to committee & category abbreviations is on page 173

# Utah

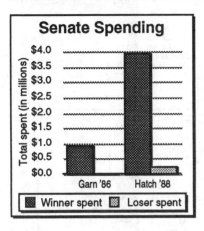

## Senate Spending

## Spending in 1990 House Races

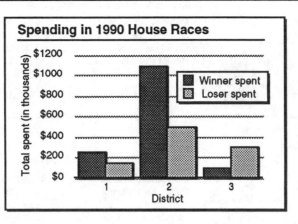

## 1990 Elections at a Glance

| Dist | Name | Party | Vote Pct | Race Type |
|------|------|-------|----------|-----------|
| Sen | Jake Garn (1986) | Rep | 72% | Reelected |
| Sen | Orrin G. Hatch (1988) | Rep | 67% | Reelected |
| 1 | James V. Hansen | Rep | 52% | Reelected |
| 2 | Wayne Owens | Dem | 58% | Reelected |
| 3 | Bill Orton | Dem | 58% | Open Seat |

*Totals in Thousands of Dollars*

## Sen. Jake Garn (R)

**1990 Committees: Approp Banking Energy Rules**
**First elected: 1974**

1985-90 Total Rcpts: ............$1,189,229
1990 Year-end cash: ................$86,391

**Source of Funds**

- PACs.............................................56%
- Lg Individuals ($200+) ................23%
- Individuals under $200 .............12%
- Other .........................................9%

### 1985-90 (PACs only)

**Top Industries & Interest Groups**

Commercial Banks .................$131,375
Defense Aerospace ...................$54,486
Oil & Gas ..................................$37,321
Insurance ..................................$35,166
Savings & Loans ......................$35,050

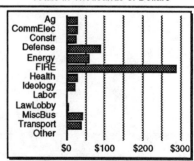

## Sen. Orrin G. Hatch (R)

**1990 Committees: Judiciary Labor**
**First elected: 1976**

1985-90 Total Rcpts: ............$4,462,008
1990 Year-end cash: ..............$238,935

**Source of Funds**

- PACs.............................................29%
- Lg Individuals ($200+) ................27%
- Individuals under $200 .............36%
- Other .........................................9%

### 1985-90 (PACs only)

**Top Industries & Interest Groups**

Insurance ..................................$86,492
Pharmaceuticals/Health Prod ....$76,300
Oil & Gas ..................................$73,850
Health Professionals .................$62,800
Misc Manufacturing & Distrib .....$51,090

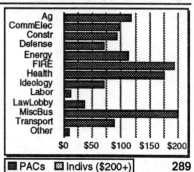

PACs   Indivs ($200+)    **289**

# 1. James V. Hansen (R)

**1990 Committees: Armed Services  Interior**
**First elected: 1980**

1989-90 Total receipts: ............$271,159
1990 Year-end cash: ................$41,944

**Source of Funds**

■ PACs............................................65%
▨ Lg Individuals ($200+)..............17%
☐ Individuals under $200..............16%
▨ Other..............................................3%

**Top  Industries & Interest Groups**

Defense Aerospace ...................$31,200
Defense Electronics...................$17,813
Oil & Gas ...................................$16,600
Health Professionals .................$15,200
Real Estate ................................$10,000

Unidentified................................$8,888

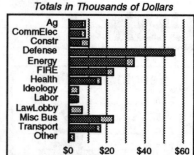

# 2. Wayne Owens (D)

**1990 Committees:  Foreign Affairs  Interior**
**First elected: 1986**

1989-90 Total receipts: .........$1,019,411
1990 Year-end cash: ...................$9,239

**Source of Funds**

■ PACs............................................50%
▨ Lg Individuals ($200+)..............30%
☐ Individuals under $200..............14%
▨ Other..............................................6%

**Top  Industries & Interest Groups**

Bldg/Indust/Misc Unions ..........$116,800
Public Sector Unions ................$65,550
Pro-Israel ..................................$52,700
Lawyers & Lobbyists .................$49,824
Transportation Unions .............$45,500

Unidentified................................$83,197

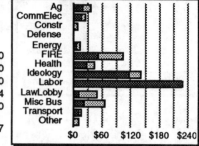

# 3. Bill Orton (D)

**1991-92 Committees:  Banking  Foreign Affairs  Sm Bus**
**First elected: 1990**

1989-90 Total receipts: ..............$86,601
1990 Year-end cash: ..................$-1,874

**Source of Funds**

■ PACs............................................37%
▨ Lg Individuals ($200+)................8%
☐ Individuals under $200................5%
▨ Other............................................49%

**Top  Industries & Interest Groups**

Bldg/Indust/Misc Unions ...........$19,000
Real Estate .................................$6,000
Transportation Unions ................$5,000
Democratic/Liberal......................$2,500
Electric Utilities ..........................$2,000

Unidentified................................$3,200

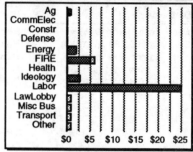

■ PACs   ▨ Indivs ($200+)

Key to committee & category abbreviations is on page 173

# Vermont

## Senate Spending

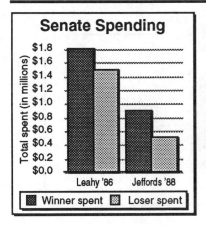

Total spent (in millions)

| | | |
|---|---|---|
| $1.8 | | |
| $1.6 | | |
| $1.4 | | |
| $1.2 | | |
| $1.0 | | |
| $0.8 | | |
| $0.6 | | |
| $0.4 | | |
| $0.2 | | |
| $0.0 | Leahy '86 | Jeffords '88 |

▨ Winner spent  ▨ Loser spent

## House Spending

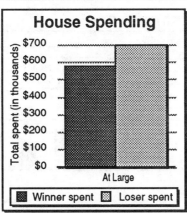

Total spent (in thousands)

| | |
|---|---|
| $700 | |
| $600 | |
| $500 | |
| $400 | |
| $300 | |
| $200 | |
| $100 | |
| $0 | At Large |

▨ Winner spent  ▨ Loser spent

## 1990 Elections at a Glance

| Dist | Name | Party | Vote Pct | Race Type |
|---|---|---|---|---|
| Sen | James M. Jeffords (1988) | Rep | 68% | Open Seat |
| Sen | Patrick J. Leahy (1986) | Dem | 63% | Reelected |
| 1 | Bernard Sanders | Oth | 56% | Beat Incumb |

*Totals in Thousands of Dollars*

## Sen. James M. Jeffords (R)

**1990 Committees: Envir/Public Works  Labor  Vet Affairs**
**First elected: 1988**

1987-90 Total Rcpts: ............$1,059,704
1990 Year-end cash: ..............$327,510

**Source of Funds**
- ■ PACs ..................................... 60%
- ▨ Lg Individuals ($200+) ............. 10%
- ☐ Individuals under $200 .............. 9%
- ▨ Other ..................................... 21%

### 1987-90 (PACs only)

**Top Industries & Interest Groups**

| | |
|---|---|
| Public Sector Unions ................. | $52,500 |
| Dairy ...................................... | $39,800 |
| Insurance ................................. | $36,158 |
| Health Professionals .................. | $35,733 |
| Transportation Unions .............. | $34,350 |

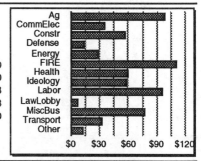

## Sen. Patrick J. Leahy (D)

**1990 Committees: Agriculture  Appropriations  Judiciary**
**First elected: 1974**

1985-90 Total Rcpts: ............$2,130,989
1990 Year-end cash: ..............$286,901

**Source of Funds**
- ■ PACs ..................................... 41%
- ▨ Lg Individuals ($200+) ............. 20%
- ☐ Individuals under $200 ............. 30%
- ▨ Other ...................................... 9%

### 1985-90 (PACs only)

**Top Industries & Interest Groups**

| | |
|---|---|
| Bldg/Indust/Misc Unions .......... | $130,500 |
| Pro-Israel ................................ | $92,200 |
| Public Sector Unions ................ | $64,054 |
| Transportation Unions .............. | $38,000 |
| Securities & Investment ............ | $35,250 |

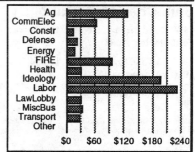

## 1. Bernard Sanders (I)

**1991-92 Committees: Banking  Govt Ops**
**First elected: 1990**

1989-90 Total receipts: ............$571,556
1990 Year-end cash: ...................$3,216

**Source of Funds**
- ■ PACs ..................................... 12%
- ▨ Lg Individuals ($200+) ............. 18%
- ☐ Individuals under $200 ............. 58%
- ▨ Other ..................................... 12%

### Top Industries & Interest Groups

| | |
|---|---|
| Bldg/Indust/Misc Unions ............ | $48,307 |
| Education ................................ | $12,191 |
| Foreign & Defense Policy .......... | $10,150 |
| Retired ................................... | $8,400 |
| Democratic/Liberal .................... | $8,000 |
| Unidentified ............................. | $28,040 |

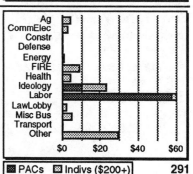

▨ PACs  ▨ Indivs ($200+)

291

# Virginia

## Senate Spending

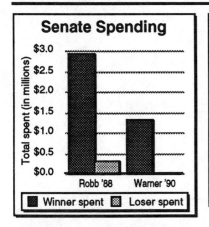

Total spent (in millions)

$3.0
$2.5
$2.0
$1.5
$1.0
$0.5
$0.0

Robb '88    Warner '90

■ Winner spent    ▨ Loser spent

## Spending in 1990 House Races

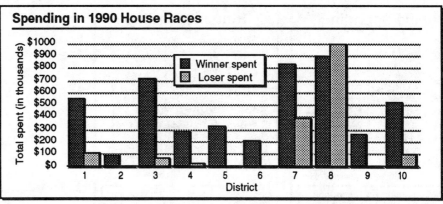

Total spent (in thousands)

$1000
$900
$800
$700
$600
$500
$400
$300
$200
$100
$0

1  2  3  4  5  6  7  8  9  10

District

■ Winner spent
▨ Loser spent

## 1990 Elections at a Glance

| Dist | Name | Party | Vote Pct | Race Type |
|------|------|-------|----------|-----------|
| Sen | Charles S. Robb (1988) | Dem | 71% | Open Seat |
| Sen | John W. Warner (1990) | Rep | 81% | Reelected |
| 1 | Herbert H. Bateman | Rep | 51% | Reelected |
| 2 | Owen B. Pickett | Dem | 75% | Reelected |
| 3 | Thomas J. Bliley Jr. | Rep | 65% | Reelected |
| 4 | Norman Sisisky | Dem | 78% | Reelected |
| 5 | Lewis F. Payne Jr. | Dem | 99% | Reelected |
| 6 | Jim Olin | Dem | 83% | Reelected |
| 7 | D. French Slaughter Jr. | Rep | 58% | Reelected |
| 8 | James P. Moran Jr. | Dem | 52% | Beat Incumb |
| 9 | Rick Boucher | Dem | 97% | Reelected |
| 10 | Frank R. Wolf | Rep | 62% | Reelected |

*Totals in Thousands of Dollars*

## Sen. Charles S. Robb (D)

**1990 Committees: Budget Commerce Foreign Relations**
**First elected: 1988**

1987-90 Total Rcpts: ..........$3,294,306
1990 Year-end cash: ...............$76,441

**Source of Funds**
■ PACs................................27%
▨ Lg Individuals ($200+)..............52%
□ Individuals under $200.............12%
▨ Other.................................8%

### 1987-90 (PACs only)

**Top Industries & Interest Groups**

Insurance ...................................$56,753
Oil & Gas ...................................$55,847
Transportation Unions ..............$47,050
Bldg/Indust/Misc Unions ............$46,450
Health Professionals .................$39,584

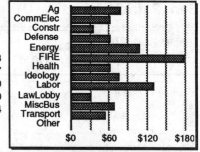

Ag
CommElec
Constr
Defense
Energy
FIRE
Health
Ideology
Labor
LawLobby
MiscBus
Transport
Other

$0    $60    $120    $180

## Sen. John W. Warner (R)

**1990 Committees: Armed Services Envir/Public Works**
**First elected: 1978**

1985-90 Total Rcpts: ...........$1,892,830
1990 Year-end cash: ..............$622,138

**Source of Funds**
■ PACs................................39%
▨ Lg Individuals ($200+)..............41%
□ Individuals under $200...............1%
▨ Other................................18%

### 1985-90

**Top Industries & Interest Groups**

Real Estate ............................$124,725
Lawyers & Lobbyists ...............$118,620
Defense Aerospace ..................$74,982
Defense Electronics .................$66,435
Misc Defense ...........................$64,000

Unidentified .............................$185,885

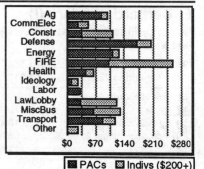

Ag
CommElec
Constr
Defense
Energy
FIRE
Health
Ideology
Labor
LawLobby
MiscBus
Transport
Other

$0    $70    $140    $210    $280

■ PACs    ▨ Indivs ($200+)

Key to committee & category abbreviations is on page 173

## 1. Herbert H. Bateman (R)

**1990 Committees:** Armed Services  Merchant Marine
**First elected:** 1982

1989-90 Total receipts: ............$525,199
1990 Year-end cash: ................$14,917

**Source of Funds**
- PACs .................................................41%
- Lg Individuals ($200+) ...............28%
- Individuals under $200 .............19%
- Other ...............................................12%

**Top Industries & Interest Groups**

Defense Aerospace ..................$34,700
Misc Defense .............................$31,000
Defense Electronics ...................$28,650
Health Professionals ..................$19,850
Real Estate .................................$18,200

Unidentified .................................$37,625

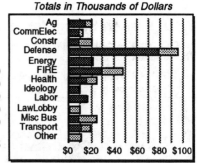

## 2. Owen B. Pickett (D)

**1990 Committees:** Armed Services  Merchant Marine
**First elected:** 1986

1989-90 Total receipts: ............$240,133
1990 Year-end cash: ..............$185,854

**Source of Funds**
- PACs .................................................59%
- Lg Individuals ($200+) ...............38%
- Individuals under $200 .............0%
- Other .................................................3%

**Top Industries & Interest Groups**

Real Estate .................................$22,000
Transportation Unions ................$21,200
Public Sector Unions .................$15,200
Lawyers & Lobbyists .................$14,200
Health Professionals ..................$12,600

Unidentified .................................$18,200

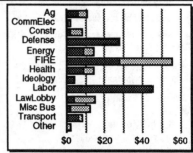

## 3. Thomas J. Bliley Jr. (R)

**1990 Committees:** DC  Energy & Commerce
**First elected:** 1980

1989-90 Total receipts: ............$632,395
1990 Year-end cash: .................$30,293

**Source of Funds**
- PACs .................................................63%
- Lg Individuals ($200+) ...............14%
- Individuals under $200 .............21%
- Other .................................................2%

**Top Industries & Interest Groups**

Tobacco ......................................$32,699
Health Professionals ..................$28,550
Accountants ................................$27,722
Oil & Gas ....................................$26,700
Pharmaceuticals/Health Prod ....$25,818

Unidentified .................................$24,700

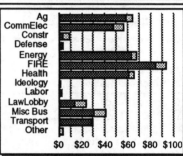

## 4. Norman Sisisky (D)

**1990 Committees:** Armed Services  Sm Business
**First elected:** 1982

1989-90 Total receipts: ............$240,553
1990 Year-end cash: ..............$281,644

**Source of Funds**
- PACs .................................................65%
- Lg Individuals ($200+) .................9%
- Individuals under $200 .............3%
- Other ...............................................23%

**Top Industries & Interest Groups**

Public Sector Unions .................$16,750
Defense Aerospace ...................$14,000
Tobacco ......................................$11,500
Misc Defense .............................$11,250
Defense Electronics ...................$10,350

Unidentified ...................................$5,250

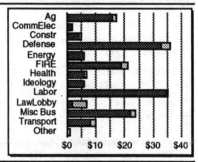

## 5. Lewis F. Payne Jr. (D)

**1990 Committees:** Public Works  Vet Affairs
**First elected:** 1988

1989-90 Total receipts: ............$317,828
1990 Year-end cash: ...................$9,594

**Source of Funds**
- PACs .................................................62%
- Lg Individuals ($200+) ...............29%
- Individuals under $200 .............9%
- Other .................................................0%

**Top Industries & Interest Groups**

Real Estate .................................$22,500
Health Professionals ..................$22,087
Transportation Unions ..............$19,750
Misc Manufacturing & Distrib .....$12,150
Lawyers & Lobbyists .................$11,900

Unidentified .................................$33,675

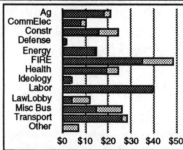

## 6. Jim Olin (D)

**1990 Committees:** Agriculture  Sm Business
**First elected:** 1982

1989-90 Total receipts: ............$254,058
1990 Year-end cash: .................$63,273

**Source of Funds**
- PACs .................................................53%
- Lg Individuals ($200+) ...............16%
- Individuals under $200 .............18%
- Other ...............................................12%

**Top Industries & Interest Groups**

Transportation Unions ..............$15,300
Public Sector Unions .................$14,050
Bldg/Indust/Misc Unions ............$11,375
Crop Production/Processing ........$9,100
Commercial Banks ......................$9,000

Unidentified .................................$13,350

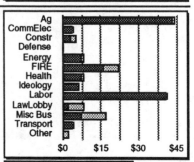

PACs  Indivs ($200+)

293

## 7. D. French Slaughter Jr. (R)

**1990 Committees: Judiciary Science Sm Business**
**First elected: 1984**

1989-90 Total receipts: ........... $649,588
1990 Year-end cash: .................. $2,857

**Source of Funds**
- ■ PACs ........................... 21%
- ▨ Lg Individuals ($200+) ............. 24%
- □ Individuals under $200 ........... 24%
- ▧ Other ............................ 31%

**Top Industries & Interest Groups**

Retired ........................................ $19,900
Real Estate ................................. $19,500
Insurance ................................... $16,500
Lawyers & Lobbyists .................. $14,200
Health Professionals ................. $12,850

Unidentified ............................... $39,900

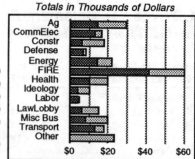

## 8. James P. Moran Jr. (D)

**1991-92 Committees: Banking Post Office**
**First elected: 1990**

1989-90 Total receipts: ........... $883,236
1990 Year-end cash: ...................... $20

**Source of Funds**
- ■ PACs ........................... 30%
- ▨ Lg Individuals ($200+) ............. 42%
- □ Individuals under $200 ........... 23%
- ▧ Other ............................. 4%

**Top Industries & Interest Groups**

Bldg/Indust/Misc Unions .......... $119,957
Lawyers & Lobbyists ................. $70,900
Real Estate ................................. $63,000
Public Sector Unions ............... $31,800
Health Professionals ................. $22,300

Unidentified ............................. $101,542

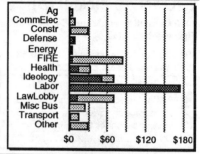

## 9. Rick Boucher (D)

**1990 Committees: Energy & Comm Judiciary Science**
**First elected: 1982**

1989-90 Total receipts: ........... $524,268
1990 Year-end cash: .............. $401,838

**Source of Funds**
- ■ PACs ........................... 69%
- ▨ Lg Individuals ($200+) ............. 14%
- □ Individuals under $200 ............. 9%
- ▧ Other ............................. 8%

**Top Industries & Interest Groups**

Telephone Utilities .................... $34,500
Commercial Banks .................... $31,650
Bldg/Indust/Misc Unions ........... $27,900
Accountants .............................. $27,375
Health Professionals ................. $19,800

Unidentified ............................... $14,550

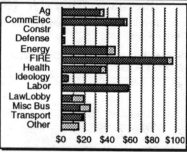

## 10. Frank R. Wolf (R)

**1990 Committees: Appropriations**
**First elected: 1980**

1989-90 Total receipts: ........... $514,240
1990 Year-end cash: ................. $59,412

**Source of Funds**
- ■ PACs ........................... 36%
- ▨ Lg Individuals ($200+) ............. 31%
- □ Individuals under $200 ............. 28%
- ▧ Other ............................. 5%

**Top Industries & Interest Groups**

Real Estate ................................. $47,085
Lawyers & Lobbyists ................. $17,750
Health Professionals ................. $16,350
Commercial Banks .................... $16,100
General Contractors ................. $15,400

Unidentified ............................... $50,510

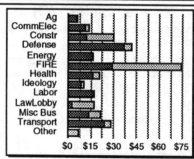

▨ PACs   ▧ Indivs ($200+)

Key to committee & category abbreviations is on page 173

# Washington

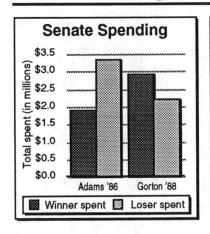

## Senate Spending

Total spent (in millions)

$3.5
$3.0
$2.5
$2.0
$1.5
$1.0
$0.5
$0.0

Adams '86    Gorton '88

▨ Winner spent    ▨ Loser spent

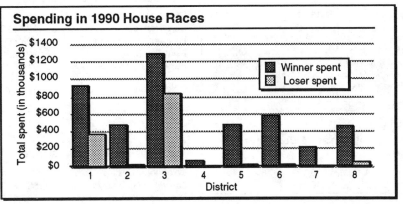

## Spending in 1990 House Races

Total spent (in thousands)

$1400
$1200
$1000
$800
$600
$400
$200
$0

1   2   3   4   5   6   7   8
District

■ Winner spent
▨ Loser spent

## 1990 Elections at a Glance

| Dist | Name | Party | Vote Pct | Race Type |
|------|------|-------|----------|-----------|
| Sen | Brock Adams (1986) | Dem | 51% | Beat Incumb |
| Sen | Slade Gorton (1988) | Rep | 51% | Open Seat |
| 1 | John Miller | Rep | 52% | Reelected |
| 2 | Al Swift | Dem | 50% | Reelected |
| 3 | Jolene Unsoeld | Dem | 54% | Reelected |
| 4 | Sid Morrison | Rep | 71% | Reelected |
| 5 | Thomas S. Foley | Dem | 69% | Reelected |
| 6 | Norm Dicks | Dem | 61% | Reelected |
| 7 | Jim McDermott | Dem | 72% | Reelected |
| 8 | Rod Chandler | Rep | 56% | Reelected |

*Totals in Thousands of Dollars*

## Sen. Brock Adams (D)

**1990 Committees: Appropriations  Labor  Rules**
**First elected: 1986**

1985-90 Total Rcpts: ...........$2,475,355
1990 Year-end cash: ...............$133,813

**Source of Funds**
■ PACs............................................35%
▨ Lg Individuals ($200+) ..............19%
□ Individuals under $200 ..............30%
▨ Other ...........................................17%

### 1985-90 (PACs only)

**Top  Industries & Interest Groups**

Bldg/Indust/Misc Unions ..........$214,856
Transportation Unions ...............$88,250
Public Sector Unions .................$87,250
Insurance ...................................$57,000
Leadership PACs ......................$52,762

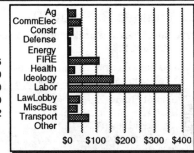

Ag
CommElec
Constr
Defense
Energy
FIRE
Health
Ideology
Labor
LawLobby
MiscBus
Transport
Other

$0   $100   $200   $300   $400

## Sen. Slade Gorton (R)

**1990 Committees: Agriculture  ArmServ  Commerce**
**First elected: 1988** *(also served 1981-87)*

1987-90 Total Rcpts: ...........$3,012,444
1990 Year-end cash: ..................$8,550

**Source of Funds**
■ PACs............................................33%
▨ Lg Individuals ($200+) ..............27%
□ Individuals under $200 ..............27%
▨ Other ...........................................14%

### 1987-90 (PACs only)

**Top  Industries & Interest Groups**

Commercial Banks ..................$150,756
Oil & Gas ................................$144,237
Insurance ................................$113,645
Forestry & Forest Products .....$102,683
Leadership PACs .....................$101,255

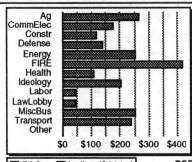

Ag
CommElec
Constr
Defense
Energy
FIRE
Health
Ideology
Labor
LawLobby
MiscBus
Transport
Other

$0   $100   $200   $300   $400

■ PACs   ▨ Indivs ($200+)

**295**

# 1. John Miller (R)

**1990 Committees: Foreign Affairs  Merchant Marine**
**First elected: 1984**

1989-90 Total receipts: ............$913,715
1990 Year-end cash: ................$11,196

**Source of Funds**
- PACs....................................27%
- Lg Individuals ($200+) ............27%
- Individuals under $200 ............26%
- Other..................................20%

**Top  Industries & Interest Groups**

Pro-Israel ....................................$30,115
Sea Transport ............................$27,523
Lawyers & Lobbyists ..................$25,850
Real Estate ................................$21,825
Forestry & Forest Products .......$18,772

Unidentified ................................$64,272

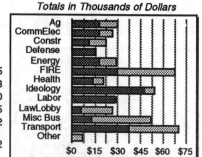

# 2. Al Swift (D)

**1990 Committees: Admin  Energy & Commerce**
**First elected: 1978**

1989-90 Total receipts: ............$503,123
1990 Year-end cash: ...............$168,462

**Source of Funds**
- PACs....................................67%
- Lg Individuals ($200+) ............14%
- Individuals under $200 ............11%
- Other....................................7%

**Top  Industries & Interest Groups**

Telephone Utilities ....................$34,850
Lawyers & Lobbyists ..................$33,375
Bldg/Indust/Misc Unions ............$27,575
Commercial Banks ......................$23,595
Transportation Unions ...............$21,650

Unidentified ................................$14,225

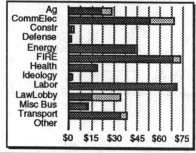

# 3. Jolene Unsoeld (D)

**1990 Committees: Educ/Labor  Merchant Marine**
**First elected: 1988**

1989-90 Total receipts: .........$1,304,200
1990 Year-end cash: ..................$5,610

**Source of Funds**
- PACs....................................44%
- Lg Individuals ($200+) ............14%
- Individuals under $200 ............28%
- Other..................................13%

**Top  Industries & Interest Groups**

Bldg/Indust/Misc Unions ..........$141,926
Human Rights ..........................$129,045
Public Sector Unions ................$73,950
Transportation Unions ..............$67,750
Misc Issues ..............................$45,989

Unidentified ................................$28,000

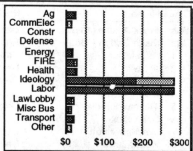

# 4. Sid Morrison (R)

**1990 Committees: Agriculture  Science**
**First elected: 1980**

1989-90 Total receipts: ............$111,572
1990 Year-end cash: ...............$218,634

**Source of Funds**
- PACs....................................36%
- Lg Individuals ($200+) ..............8%
- Individuals under $200 ............32%
- Other..................................24%

**Top  Industries & Interest Groups**

Crop Production/Processing........$6,700
Commercial Banks ......................$6,250
Telephone Utilities ......................$5,500
Health Professionals ..................$3,450
Real Estate ................................$3,000

Unidentified ................................$2,690

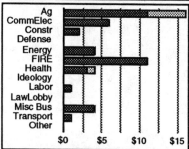

# 5. Thomas S. Foley (D)

**1990 Committees: Speaker of the House**
**First elected: 1964**

1989-90 Total receipts: ............$467,084
1990 Year-end cash: ...............$596,708

**Source of Funds**
- PACs....................................74%
- Lg Individuals ($200+) ............14%
- Individuals under $200 ..............1%
- Other..................................12%

**Top  Industries & Interest Groups**

Commercial Banks ....................$36,750
Oil & Gas ..................................$28,625
Insurance ..................................$27,537
Lawyers & Lobbyists ..................$21,397
Food Processing & Sales .........$21,000

Unidentified ................................$6,700

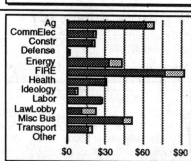

# 6. Norm Dicks (D)

**1990 Committees: Appropriations**
**First elected: 1976**

1989-90 Total receipts: ............$399,113
1990 Year-end cash: ...............$107,175

**Source of Funds**
- PACs....................................58%
- Lg Individuals ($200+) ............24%
- Individuals under $200 ..............5%
- Other..................................13%

**Top  Industries & Interest Groups**

Defense Aerospace ..................$30,602
Lawyers & Lobbyists ..................$29,150
Bldg/Indust/Misc Unions ............$28,600
Public Sector Unions ................$25,050
Defense Electronics..................$24,150

Unidentified ................................$34,250

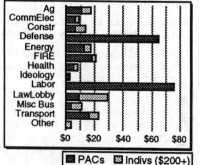

Key to committee & category abbreviations is on page 173

PACs  Indivs ($200+)

## 7. Jim McDermott (D)

**1990 Committees: Banking  DC  Interior**
**First elected: 1988**

1989-90 Total receipts: ............$232,919
1990 Year-end cash: .................$39,680

**Source of Funds**
- PACs ........................................83%
- Lg Individuals ($200+) ...............7%
- Individuals under $200 ................6%
- Other .........................................4%

**Top  Industries & Interest Groups**

Bldg/Indust/Misc Unions ............$26,600
Transportation Unions ...............$21,350
Commercial Banks ....................$20,700
Public Sector Unions ................$20,000
Health Professionals .................$19,750

Unidentified .................................$4,050

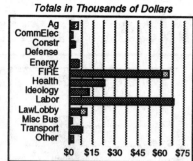

## 8. Rod Chandler (R)

**1990 Committees:  Post Office  Ways & Means**
**First elected: 1982**

1989-90 Total receipts: ............$472,433
1990 Year-end cash: ..............$128,864

**Source of Funds**
- PACs .........................................64%
- Lg Individuals ($200+) ..............14%
- Individuals under $200 ..............18%
- Other .........................................5%

**Top  Industries & Interest Groups**

Insurance ...................................$54,350
Health Professionals .................$27,525
Commercial Banks ....................$24,350
Telephone Utilities ....................$20,900
Air Transport .............................$18,490

Unidentified ...............................$30,392

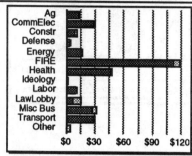

PACs    Indivs ($200+)

# West Virginia

## Senate Spending

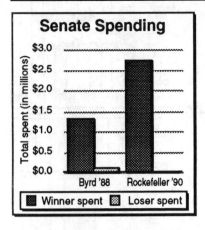

## Spending in 1990 House Races

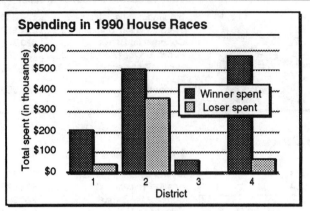

## 1990 Elections at a Glance

| Dist | Name | Party | Vote Pct | Race Type |
|------|------|-------|----------|-----------|
| Sen | Robert C. Byrd (1988) | Dem | 65% | Reelected |
| Sen | John D. Rockefeller IV (1990) | Dem | 68% | Reelected |
| 1 | Alan B. Mollohan | Dem | 67% | Reelected |
| 2 | Harley O. Staggers Jr. | Dem | 56% | Reelected |
| 3 | Bob Wise | Dem | 100% | Reelected |
| 4 | Nick J. Rahall II | Dem | 52% | Reelected |

*Totals in Thousands of Dollars*

## Sen. Robert C. Byrd (D)

**1990 Committees: Appropriations Arm Serv Rules**
**First elected: 1958**

1985-90 Total Rcpts: ............$1,586,772
1990 Year-end cash: ...............$535,853

**Source of Funds**

- ■ PACs .................................................63%
- Lg Individuals ($200+) ..............17%
- □ Individuals under $200 ................5%
- ▨ Other ..................................................14%

### 1985-90 (PACs only)

**Top Industries & Interest Groups**

Bldg/Indust/Misc Unions ............$96,800
Public Sector Unions .................$71,550
Transportation Unions ..............$71,200
Defense Aerospace ...................$63,000
Oil & Gas ...................................$61,350

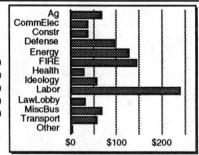

## Sen. John D. Rockefeller IV (D)

**1990 Committees: Commerce Energy Finance VetAff**
**First elected: 1984**

1985-90 Total Rcpts: ............$3,597,376
1990 Year-end cash: ..............$902,198

**Source of Funds**

- ■ PACs ..................................................39%
- Lg Individuals ($200+) ..............46%
- □ Individuals under $200 ...............8%
- ▨ Other ...................................................7%

### 1985-90

**Top Industries & Interest Groups**

Lawyers & Lobbyists ................$271,720
Health Professionals ................$251,102
Real Estate ..............................$162,775
Insurance .................................$161,350
Securities & Investment ..........$138,850

Unidentified ..............................$282,151

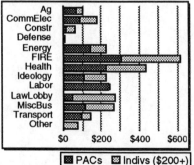

298      Key to committee & category abbreviations is on page 173

# 1. Alan B. Mollohan (D)

**1990 Committees:** Appropriations
**First elected:** 1982

1989-90 Total receipts: ............$247,797
1990 Year-end cash: ..............$136,457

**Source of Funds**
- ■ PACs ............................................54%
- ▨ Lg Individuals ($200+) ..............15%
- □ Individuals under $200 .................6%
- ▩ Other ...........................................24%

**Top Industries & Interest Groups**

Bldg/Indust/Misc Unions ............$22,850
Defense Aerospace ..................$12,300
Transportation Unions ..............$11,500
Misc Issues ................................$10,950
Public Sector Unions ................$10,300

Unidentified ..................................$5,400

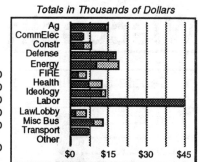

# 2. Harley O. Staggers Jr. (D)

**1990 Committees:** Agriculture  Judiciary  Vet Affairs
**First elected:** 1982

1989-90 Total receipts: ............$419,859
1990 Year-end cash: ..................$1,646

**Source of Funds**
- ■ PACs ............................................63%
- ▨ Lg Individuals ($200+) ..............11%
- □ Individuals under $200 .................8%
- ▩ Other ...........................................18%

**Top Industries & Interest Groups**

Bldg/Indust/Misc Unions ............$82,200
Public Sector Unions ................$33,800
Transportation Unions ..............$28,650
Lawyers & Lobbyists ..................$26,150
Health Professionals ................$16,750

Unidentified ..................................$4,400

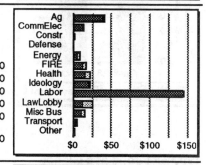

# 3. Bob Wise (D)

**1990 Committees:** Budget  Govt Ops
**First elected:** 1982

1989-90 Total receipts: ............$182,913
1990 Year-end cash: ..............$179,230

**Source of Funds**
- ■ PACs ............................................70%
- ▨ Lg Individuals ($200+) ................9%
- □ Individuals under $200 ..............14%
- ▩ Other .............................................7%

**Top Industries & Interest Groups**

Bldg/Indust/Misc Unions ............$24,750
Transportation Unions ..............$23,000
Public Sector Unions ................$11,700
Oil & Gas ....................................$8,250
Lawyers & Lobbyists ..................$7,200

Unidentified .....................................$950

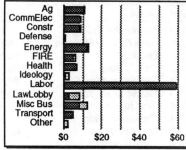

# 4. Nick J. Rahall II (D)

**1990 Committees:** Interior  Public Works
**First elected:** 1976

1989-90 Total receipts: ............$536,855
1990 Year-end cash: ..............$365,513

**Source of Funds**
- ■ PACs ............................................50%
- ▨ Lg Individuals ($200+) ..............20%
- □ Individuals under $200 ..............13%
- ▩ Other ...........................................17%

**Top Industries & Interest Groups**

Bldg/Indust/Misc Unions ............$60,600
Transportation Unions ..............$42,550
Public Sector Unions ................$30,325
Lawyers & Lobbyists ................$22,108
Mining ......................................$21,500

Unidentified ................................$19,275

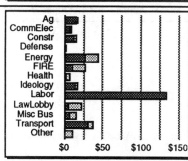

■ PACs  ▩ Indivs ($200+)

# Wisconsin

## Senate Spending

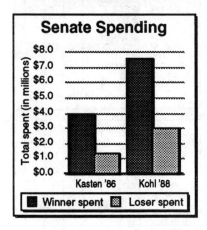

## Spending in 1990 House Races

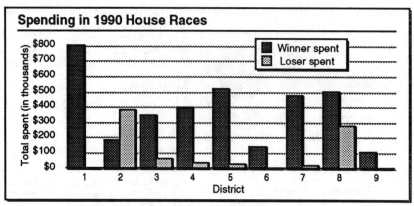

## 1990 Elections at a Glance

| Dist | Name | Party | Vote Pct | Race Type |
|------|------|-------|----------|-----------|
| Sen | Bob Kasten (1986) | Rep | 51% | Reelected |
| Sen | Herb Kohl (1988) | Dem | 52% | Open Seat |
| 1 | Les Aspin | Dem | 99% | Reelected |
| 2 | Scott L. Klug | Rep | 53% | Beat Incumb |
| 3 | Steve Gunderson | Rep | 61% | Reelected |
| 4 | Gerald D. Kleczka | Dem | 69% | Reelected |
| 5 | Jim Moody | Dem | 68% | Reelected |
| 6 | Thomas E. Petri | Rep | 100% | Reelected |
| 7 | David R. Obey | Dem | 62% | Reelected |
| 8 | Toby Roth | Rep | 54% | Reelected |
| 9 | F. James Sensenbrenner Jr. | Rep | 100% | Reelected |

## Sen. Bob Kasten (R)

**1990 Committees: Approp Budget Commerce SmBus**
**First elected: 1980**

1985-90 Total Rcpts: ............ $4,061,472
1990 Year-end cash: .............. $326,244

**Source of Funds**
- ■ PACs ....................................... 28%
- ▨ Lg Individuals ($200+) ............... 21%
- □ Individuals under $200 .............. 37%
- ▨ Other ....................................... 14%

### 1985-90 (PACs only)

**Top Industries & Interest Groups**

| | |
|---|---|
| Pro-Israel | $131,300 |
| Defense Aerospace | $71,264 |
| Misc Manufacturing & Distrib | $61,444 |
| Insurance | $53,578 |
| Commercial Banks | $50,223 |

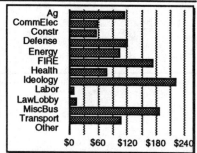

## Sen. Herb Kohl (D)

**1990 Committees: Govt Affairs Judiciary**
**First elected: 1988**

1987-90 Total Rcpts: ............ $8,035,208
1990 Year-end cash: ................. $18,591

**Source of Funds**
- ■ PACs ........................................ 0%
- ▨ Lg Individuals ($200+) ................ 5%
- □ Individuals under $200 ............... 3%
- ▨ Other ........................................ 92%

### 1987-90

**Top Industries & Interest Groups**

NOTE: Kohl reported receiving no PAC money in his 1990 campaign. He spent $7 million of his own money in the race.

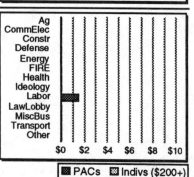

Key to committee & category abbreviations is on page 173

## 1. Les Aspin (D)

**1990 Committees: Armed Services**
First elected: 1970

1989-90 Total receipts: ............ $892,153
1990 Year-end cash: .............. $162,669

**Source of Funds**

- PACs ............................................. 37%
- Lg Individuals ($200+) ............. 29%
- Individuals under $200 ............ 32%
- Other ............................................. 2%

**Top Industries & Interest Groups**

Pro-Israel ..................................... $53,455
Lawyers & Lobbyists ................. $53,120
Defense Aerospace .................... $51,535
Defense Electronics ................... $46,350
Bldg/Indust/Misc Unions ........... $34,350

Unidentified ................................. $65,604

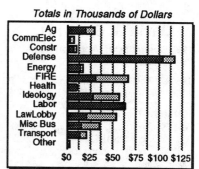

## 2. Scott L. Klug (R)

**1991-92 Committees: Educ/Labor Govt Ops**
First elected: 1990

1989-90 Total receipts: ............ $183,789
1990 Year-end cash: .................. $5,660

**Source of Funds**

- PACs ............................................. 18%
- Lg Individuals ($200+) ............. 30%
- Individuals under $200 ............ 41%
- Other ............................................. 10%

**Top Industries & Interest Groups**

Misc Manufacturing & Distrib ....... $9,500
Commercial Banks ....................... $6,683
Health Professionals .................... $6,603
Food & Beverage ......................... $6,217
Dairy .............................................. $3,700

Unidentified ................................. $18,321

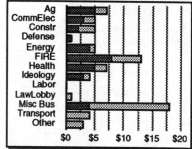

## 3. Steve Gunderson (R)

**1990 Committees: Agriculture Educ/Labor**
First elected: 1980

1989-90 Total receipts: ............ $388,310
1990 Year-end cash: ................. $98,169

**Source of Funds**

- PACs ............................................. 50%
- Lg Individuals ($200+) ............. 23%
- Individuals under $200 ............ 24%
- Other ............................................. 3%

**Top Industries & Interest Groups**

Agric Services/Products ............ $22,200
Misc Manufacturing & Distrib ..... $17,800
Dairy ............................................ $17,650
Crop Production/Processing ...... $16,900
Health Professionals ................. $15,340

Unidentified ................................. $19,670

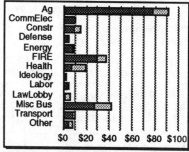

## 4. Gerald D. Kleczka (D)

**1990 Committees: Banking Govt Ops**
First elected: 1984

1989-90 Total receipts: ............ $304,440
1990 Year-end cash: ................. $86,327

**Source of Funds**

- PACs ............................................. 60%
- Lg Individuals ($200+) ............... 9%
- Individuals under $200 ............ 19%
- Other ............................................. 11%

**Top Industries & Interest Groups**

Bldg/Indust/Misc Unions ............ $29,900
Public Sector Unions ................. $23,350
Transportation Unions ............... $22,450
Commercial Banks .................... $21,750
Real Estate ................................ $13,600

Unidentified ................................... $4,750

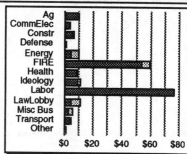

## 5. Jim Moody (D)

**1990 Committees: Ways & Means**
First elected: 1982

1989-90 Total receipts: ............ $735,212
1990 Year-end cash: ............... $237,639

**Source of Funds**

- PACs ............................................. 62%
- Lg Individuals ($200+) ............. 20%
- Individuals under $200 ............ 14%
- Other ............................................. 4%

**Top Industries & Interest Groups**

Insurance .................................... $68,850
Health Professionals ................. $53,550
Public Sector Unions ................. $53,450
Lawyers & Lobbyists ................. $53,300
Bldg/Indust/Misc Unions ........... $47,550

Unidentified ................................. $24,850

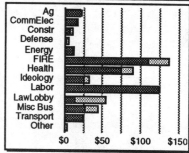

## 6. Thomas E. Petri (R)

**1990 Committees: Educ/Labor Public Works**
First elected: 1979

1989-90 Total receipts: ............ $240,501
1990 Year-end cash: ............... $397,666

**Source of Funds**

- PACs ............................................. 40%
- Lg Individuals ($200+) ............... 4%
- Individuals under $200 ............ 33%
- Other ............................................. 22%

**Top Industries & Interest Groups**

Insurance ...................................... $7,750
Air Transport ................................ $6,700
General Contractors ................... $6,300
Dairy ............................................. $5,650
Automotive ................................... $5,070

Unidentified ................................... $3,310

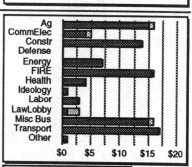

PACs    Indivs ($200+)

301

## 7. David R. Obey (D)

**1990 Committees: Appropriations**
**First elected: 1969**

1989-90 Total receipts: ............$620,219
1990 Year-end cash: ..............$334,565

### Source of Funds

| | |
|---|---|
| ■ PACs...........................................48% | |
| ▨ Lg Individuals ($200+)................21% | |
| ▢ Individuals under $200 ..............19% | |
| ▧ Other.......................................11% | |

### Top Industries & Interest Groups

Bldg/Indust/Misc Unions ............$64,100
Pro-Israel .................................$58,699
Public Sector Unions .................$39,500
Lawyers & Lobbyists .................$39,298
Real Estate ..............................$25,400

Unidentified ..............................$18,044

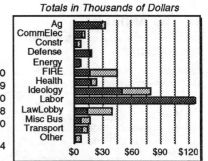

## 8. Toby Roth (R)

**1990 Committees: Banking  Foreign Affairs**
**First elected: 1978**

1989-90 Total receipts: ............$390,432
1990 Year-end cash: .................$93,841

### Source of Funds

| | |
|---|---|
| ■ PACs...........................................51% | |
| ▨ Lg Individuals ($200+)................14% | |
| ▢ Individuals under $200 ..............23% | |
| ▧ Other.......................................11% | |

### Top Industries & Interest Groups

Commercial Banks ....................$38,800
Insurance ..................................$19,000
Real Estate ..............................$14,250
Misc Issues ..............................$11,000
Trucking ......................................$9,950

Unidentified ..............................$15,550

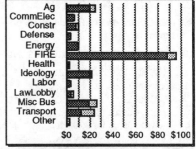

## 9. F. James Sensenbrenner Jr. (R)

**1990 Committees: Judiciary  Science**
**First elected: 1978**

1989-90 Total receipts: ............$266,285
1990 Year-end cash: ..............$312,478

### Source of Funds

| | |
|---|---|
| ■ PACs...........................................37% | |
| ▨ Lg Individuals ($200+)................16% | |
| ▢ Individuals under $200 ..............35% | |
| ▧ Other.......................................12% | |

### Top Industries & Interest Groups

Insurance ..................................$17,633
Dairy ..........................................$11,350
Telephone Utilities ......................$9,200
Air Transport ..............................$6,935
Automotive ..................................$6,850

Unidentified ..............................$15,500

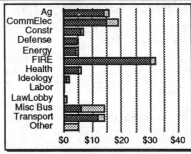

▨ PACs  ▨ Indivs ($200+)

Key to committee & category abbreviations is on page 173

# Wyoming

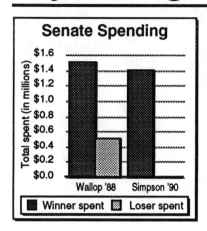

**Senate Spending**

Total spent (in millions)

| | Wallop '88 | Simpson '90 |

■ Winner spent  ▨ Loser spent

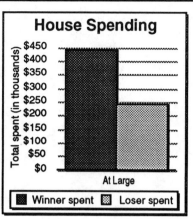

**House Spending**

Total spent (in thousands)

At Large

■ Winner spent  ▨ Loser spent

## 1990 Elections at a Glance

| Dist | Name | Party | Vote Pct | Race Type |
|------|------|-------|----------|-----------|
| Sen | Alan K. Simpson (1990) | Rep | 64% | Reelected |
| Sen | Malcolm Wallop (1988) | Rep | 50% | Reelected |
| 1 | Craig Thomas | Rep | 55% | Reelected |

*Totals in Thousands of Dollars*

## Sen. Alan K. Simpson (R)

**1990 Committees: Envir/Public Works  Judiciary  VetAff**
**First elected: 1978**

1985-90 Total Rcpts: ............$1,670,927
1990 Year-end cash: ..............$433,246

**Source of Funds**
- ■ PACs ................................................45%
- ▨ Lg Individuals ($200+) .............27%
- ☐ Individuals under $200 .............2%
- ▨ Other ............................................25%

**1985-90**

**Top Industries & Interest Groups**

| | |
|---|---|
| Insurance | $112,050 |
| Oil & Gas | $111,450 |
| Lawyers & Lobbyists | $59,825 |
| Health Professionals | $39,200 |
| Real Estate | $37,000 |
| Unidentified | $69,944 |

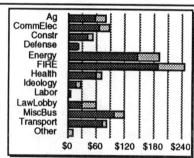

## Sen. Malcolm Wallop (R)

**1990 Committees: Armed Services  Energy  SmBus**
**First elected: 1976**

1985-90 Total Rcpts: ...........$1,684,657
1990 Year-end cash: ..............$157,308

**Source of Funds**
- ■ PACs ................................................58%
- ▨ Lg Individuals ($200+) ..............21%
- ☐ Individuals under $200 ..............8%
- ▨ Other ............................................14%

**1985-90 (PACs only)**

**Top Industries & Interest Groups**

| | |
|---|---|
| Oil & Gas | $155,967 |
| Insurance | $79,693 |
| Defense Aerospace | $51,861 |
| Securities & Investment | $48,667 |
| Leadership PACs | $34,297 |

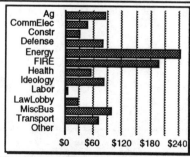

## 1. Craig Thomas (R)

**1990 Committees: Govt Ops  Interior**
**First elected: 1989**

1989-90 Total receipts: ............$968,450
1990 Year-end cash: ....................$4,531

**Source of Funds**
- ■ PACs ................................................33%
- ▨ Lg Individuals ($200+) ..............23%
- ☐ Individuals under $200 ..............17%
- ▨ Other ............................................26%

**Top Industries & Interest Groups**

| | |
|---|---|
| Oil & Gas | $94,300 |
| Livestock | $25,032 |
| Health Professionals | $24,030 |
| Electric Utilities | $22,500 |
| Insurance | $21,650 |
| Unidentified | $61,282 |

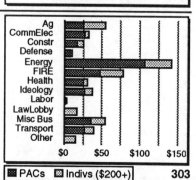

■ PACs  ▨ Indivs ($200+)

# 5.

# PAC Profiles

Cash Constituents of Congress

# Introduction to the PAC Profiles

The final section of *Csh Constituents* provides a directory of every political action committee that gave $20,000 or more in the 1989-90 election cycle. In all, these PACs contributed $148.6 million to congressional candidates — 93.4 percent of the total given by all PACs in the 1990 elections.

The PACs are listed alphabetically by the name of the PAC sponsor, or the name of the PAC itself where there is no other sponsor.

## What's included in the PAC profiles:

**Short name of the PAC or PAC sponsor.** This is the name used elsewhere in the book to identify the PAC. The term "sponsor" is used simply to identify the group whose members contribute to the PAC, and does not imply a formal relationship between the PAC and the organization. Many PACs are officially connected with their sponsoring organization; others operate independently, even though the PAC's contributors all work for the same company or belong to the same trade association, labor union, or other organization.

**Official name of the PAC.** The only abbreviation is the use of "PAC" for "Political Action Committee"

**Total contributions** in the 1989-90 election cycle.

| Alabama Power Co | $114,275 | 179 Candidates | Dems: | 54.4% |
|---|---|---|---|---|
| Alabama Power Co Employees Federal PAC (APC Employees Federal PAC) | | Avg House: $619 | House: | 78.0% |
| Birmingham, AL | Southern Co | Electric Utilities | Avg Sen: $720 | Incumb: 77.9% |

**Location** of the PAC's headquarters.

**Category or thumbnail description.** See Appendix A for the complete list of categories used to classify the PACs and other contributors in this book.

**Affiliated organization.** When an organization is listed here, it means the PAC is one of several affiliated with the parent group. In the case of leadership PACs operated by members of Congress or other political figures, the name of the PAC's sponsor is listed here.

**Percentage of total dollars that went to Democratic or Republican candidates**. Whichever party got more than 50 percent is listed.

**Number of federal candidates** receiving contributions from the PAC in 1989-90.

| Alabama Farm Bureau Federation | $86,511 | 72 Candidates | Dems: | 61.2% |
|---|---|---|---|---|
| ELECT - the PAC of Alabama Farm Bureau Federation | | Avg House: $1,239 | House: | 63.0% |
| Montgomery, AL | Farm Orgs | Avg Sen: $1,143 | Incumb: 84.3% | |

**Average contribution** to House candidates in 1989-90.

**Average contribution** to Senate candidates in 1989-90.

**Percentage of dollars that went to incumbents.**

**Percentage of dollars that went to House or Senate candidates**. The group that got the biggest share is listed.

**24th Congr Dist of California PAC**
24th Congressional District of California PAC
Beverly Hills, CA     Rep Henry Waxman (D-Calif)     Dem Leaders

| $110,000 | 26 Candidates | Dems: 100.0% |
| | Avg House: $4,200 | House: 95.5% |
| | Avg Sen: $5,000 | Incumb: 74.5% |

**Abbott Laboratories**
Abbott Laboratories Better Government Fund
Abbott Park, IL     Pharmaceuticals†

| $168,950 | 170 Candidates | Repubs: 71.0% |
| | Avg House: $656 | House: 51.6% |
| | Avg Sen: $2,209 | Incumb: 94.0% |

**ACRE (Action Committee for Rural Electrification)**
Action Committee for Rural Electrification (ACRE)
Washington, DC     Rural Electric

| $598,675 | 381 Candidates | Dems: 69.8% |
| | Avg House: $1,258 | House: 71.5% |
| | Avg Sen: $4,166 | Incumb: 88.3% |

**Aetna Life & Casualty**
Aetna Life and Casualty Company PAC
Hartford, CT     Insurance

| $195,029 | 125 Candidates | Repubs: 58.5% |
| | Avg House: $878 | Senate: 58.6% |
| | Avg Sen: $3,463 | Incumb: 98.7% |

**AFL-CIO**
AFL-CIO Committee on Political Education/Political Contributions Committee
Washington, DC     AFL-CIO     Labor Unions

| $827,927 | 296 Candidates | Dems: 99.0% |
| | Avg House: $2,451 | House: 79.0% |
| | Avg Sen: $5,981 | Incumb: 51.7% |

**AFL-CIO Bldg/Construction Trades Dept**
Political Educational Fund of the Building and Construction Trades Department
Washington, DC     AFL-CIO     Constr Unions

| $197,455 | 202 Candidates | Dems: 91.5% |
| | Avg House: $914 | House: 86.1% |
| | Avg Sen: $1,718 | Incumb: 94.8% |

**Air Line Pilots Assn**
Air Line Pilots Association PAC
Washington, DC     Air Transport Unions

| $1,167,797 | 298 Candidates | Dems: 81.2% |
| | Avg House: $3,550 | House: 78.4% |
| | Avg Sen: $6,300 | Incumb: 85.9% |

**Air Products & Chemicals Inc**
Air Products and Chemicals Inc Political Alliance
Trexlertown, PA     Chemicals†

| $54,800 | 57 Candidates | Repubs: 71.5% |
| | Avg House: $754 | House: 59.1% |
| | Avg Sen: $1,600 | Incumb: 97.6% |

**Aircraft Owners & Pilots Assn**
Aircraft Owners and Pilots Association PAC
Frederick, MD     General Aviation

| $513,900 | 149 Candidates | Repubs: 50.6% |
| | Avg House: $3,141 | House: 70.9% |
| | Avg Sen: $4,533 | Incumb: 97.4% |

**Akin, Gump, Hauer & Feld**
Akin, Gump, Strauss, Hauer & Feld Civic Action Committee
Washington, DC     Lawyers

| $267,602 | 204 Candidates | Dems: 76.9% |
| | Avg House: $1,123 | House: 67.1% |
| | Avg Sen: $1,999 | Incumb: 97.0% |

**Alabama Farm Bureau Federation**
ELECT - the PAC of Alabama Farm Bureau Federation
Montgomery, AL     Farm Orgs

| $86,511 | 72 Candidates | Dems: 61.2% |
| | Avg House: $1,239 | House: 63.0% |
| | Avg Sen: $1,143 | Incumb: 84.3% |

**Alabama Power Co**
Alabama Power Co Employees Federal PAC (APC Employees Federal PAC)
Birmingham, AL     Southern Co     Electric Utilities

| $114,275 | 179 Candidates | Dems: 54.4% |
| | Avg House: $619 | House: 78.0% |
| | Avg Sen: $720 | Incumb: 77.9% |

**Alcoa**
Alcoa Employees Political Fund
Pittsburgh, PA     Metal Mining/Process†

| $55,050 | 53 Candidates | Dems: 54.5% |
| | Avg House: $826 | House: 55.5% |
| | Avg Sen: $1,531 | Incumb: 96.4% |

**Allied-Signal**
Allied-Signal PAC
Morristown, NJ     Air Defense†

| $225,800 | 214 Candidates | Repubs: 54.1% |
| | Avg House: $684 | House: 52.4% |
| | Avg Sen: $2,623 | Incumb: 94.6% |

**Allstate Insurance**
Allstate Insurance Company PAC
Northbrook, IL     Sears     Insurance

| $67,200 | 69 Candidates | Repubs: 58.7% |
| | Avg House: $669 | Senate: 56.2% |
| | Avg Sen: $1,510 | Incumb: 97.6% |

**Alltel Corp**
Alltel Corporation PAC (APAC)
Hudson, OH     Phone Utilities

| $67,025 | 75 Candidates | Dems: 60.8% |
| | Avg House: $750 | House: 64.9% |
| | Avg Sen: $1,382 | Incumb: 93.5% |

**Amalgamated Clothing & Textile Workers**
Amalgamated Clothing and Textile Workers Union - PAC (ACTWU-PAC)
New York, NY     Clothing/Textile Workers     Manufacturing Unions

| $256,355 | 235 Candidates | Dems: 93.9% |
| | Avg House: $813 | House: 66.6% |
| | Avg Sen: $3,423 | Incumb: 78.2% |

**Amalgamated Transit Union**
Amalgamated Transit Union-COPE
Washington, DC     Transport Unions

| $512,630 | 222 Candidates | Dems: 94.9% |
| | Avg House: $1,970 | House: 72.2% |
| | Avg Sen: $4,187 | Incumb: 70.1% |

**America's Leaders' Fund**
America's Leaders' Fund (aka Chicago Campaign Committee)
Chicago, IL     Rep Dan Rostenkowski (D-Ill)     Dem Leaders

| $121,350 | 84 Candidates | Dems: 100.0% |
| | Avg House: $1,450 | House: 99.2% |
| | Avg Sen: $1,000 | Incumb: 64.1% |

† PAC sponsor has other major interests in addition to this primary category

| Sponsor / PAC / Location | Affiliate | 1989-90 Total | Candidates / Avg | % |
|---|---|---|---|---|
| **American Academy of Ophthalmology**<br>American Academy of Ophthalmology Inc Political Committee ("OPHTHPAC")<br>San Francisco, CA | Eye Doctors | $961,411 | 289 Candidates<br>Avg House: $3,039<br>Avg Sen: $5,224 | Dems: 51.7%<br>House: 79.4%<br>Incumb: 79.3% |
| **American Airlines**<br>American Airlines PAC<br>Washington, DC | Airlines | $141,519 | 114 Candidates<br>Avg House: $1,106<br>Avg Sen: $1,843 | Dems: 76.1%<br>House: 72.6%<br>Incumb: 91.6% |
| **American Assn of Crop Insurers**<br>American Association of Crop Insurers PAC (AACI PAC)<br>Washington, DC | Ag Services | $145,900 | 73 Candidates<br>Avg House: $1,568<br>Avg Sen: $3,224 | Dems: 59.1%<br>House: 58.0%<br>Incumb: 98.3% |
| **American Assn of Equipment Lessors**<br>AAEL Lease-PAC fka Amer Assoc of Equip Lessors Cap Invest-Lease PAC<br>Arlington, VA | Rentals | $57,700 | 37 Candidates<br>Avg House: $1,450<br>Avg Sen: $1,818 | Dems: 60.7%<br>House: 65.3%<br>Incumb: 97.4% |
| **American Assn of Nurse Anesthetists**<br>American Association of Nurse Anesthetists Separate Segregated Fund (CRNA-PAC)<br>Park Ridge, IL | Nurses | $64,100 | 54 Candidates<br>Avg House: $1,072<br>Avg Sen: $1,355 | Dems: 67.9%<br>House: 53.5%<br>Incumb: 99.6% |
| **American Bankers Assn**<br>American Bankers Association BankPAC<br>Washington, DC   American Bankers Assn | Commercial Banks | $1,323,659 | 404 Candidates<br>Avg House: $2,833<br>Avg Sen: $6,031 | Dems: 55.4%<br>House: 74.5%<br>Incumb: 95.6% |
| **American Bus Assn**<br>BusPAC-PAC of the American Bus Association<br>Washington, DC | Bus Services | $53,892 | 52 Candidates<br>Avg House: $985<br>Avg Sen: $1,208 | Dems: 67.2%<br>House: 73.1%<br>Incumb: 100.0% |
| **American Chiropractic Assn**<br>American Chiropractic Association PAC<br>Arlington, VA   American Chiropractic Assn | Chiropractors | $173,350 | 108 Candidates<br>Avg House: $1,200<br>Avg Sen: $2,950 | Dems: 72.9%<br>House: 57.5%<br>Incumb: 89.0% |
| **American College of Emergency Physicians**<br>National Emergency Medicine PAC of the American College of Emergency Physicians<br>Irving, TX | Doctors | $130,340 | 105 Candidates<br>Avg House: $1,142<br>Avg Sen: $1,564 | Dems: 75.0%<br>House: 69.2%<br>Incumb: 93.2% |
| **American Consulting Engineers Council**<br>American Consulting Engineers PAC (ACE/PAC)<br>Washington, DC | Engineers | $91,875 | 111 Candidates<br>Avg House: $594<br>Avg Sen: $1,490 | Repubs: 63.7%<br>House: 53.0%<br>Incumb: 95.8% |
| **American Council of Life Insurance**<br>American Council of Life Insurance, Life Insurance PAC<br>Washington, DC | Life Insurance | $692,493 | 316 Candidates<br>Avg House: $2,109<br>Avg Sen: $2,408 | Dems: 57.8%<br>House: 69.8%<br>Incumb: 97.3% |
| **American Crystal Sugar Corp**<br>American Crystal Sugar PAC<br>Moorhead, MN | Sugar | $408,125 | 326 Candidates<br>Avg House: $1,042<br>Avg Sen: $2,597 | Dems: 62.5%<br>House: 72.0%<br>Incumb: 95.6% |
| **American Dental Assn**<br>American Dental PAC<br>Washington, DC | Dentists | $817,428 | 349 Candidates<br>Avg House: $2,083<br>Avg Sen: $4,186 | Dems: 54.3%<br>House: 78.0%<br>Incumb: 91.5% |
| **American Electric Power**<br>American Electric Power Committee for Responsible Government; The<br>Columbus, OH | Electric Utilities | $81,300 | 107 Candidates<br>Avg House: $666<br>Avg Sen: $1,083 | Repubs: 56.7%<br>House: 68.0%<br>Incumb: 96.3% |
| **American Express**<br>American Express Company Committee for Responsible Government<br>Washington, DC   American Express | Securities Invest† | $80,850 | 95 Candidates<br>Avg House: $715<br>Avg Sen: $1,360 | Dems: 74.5%<br>House: 66.4%<br>Incumb: 96.9% |
| **American Family Corp**<br>American Family Corporation PAC<br>Washington, DC | Health Insurance | $430,250 | 164 Candidates<br>Avg House: $2,139<br>Avg Sen: $4,125 | Dems: 55.0%<br>House: 61.7%<br>Incumb: 84.4% |
| **American Federation of Govt Employees**<br>American Federation of Government Employees' PAC<br>Washington, DC | Federal Workers | $164,624 | 156 Candidates<br>Avg House: $752<br>Avg Sen: $2,277 | Dems: 92.6%<br>House: 57.1%<br>Incumb: 68.0% |
| **American Federation of State, County & Munic Employees**<br>American Federation of State County & Municipal Employees - PEOPLE, Qualified<br>Washington, DC | Local Govt Union | $1,548,970 | 325 Candidates<br>Avg House: $4,631<br>Avg Sen: $6,003 | Dems: 97.5%<br>House: 86.4%<br>Incumb: 69.2% |
| **American Federation of Teachers**<br>American Federation of Teachers Committee on Political Education<br>Washington, DC | Teachers | $1,026,550 | 253 Candidates<br>Avg House: $3,640<br>Avg Sen: $7,183 | Dems: 97.4%<br>House: 78.7%<br>Incumb: 69.1% |

| PAC Sponsor or Related Group/PAC Name | Affiliate | 1989-90 Total | Where the money went... | | |
|---|---|---|---|---|---|
| **American Financial Services Assn**<br>American Financial Services Assn PAC (formerly- National Consumer Finance Assn PAC)<br>Washington, DC | Credit/Loans | $81,797 | 72 Candidates<br>Avg House: $907<br>Avg Sen: $1,938 | Dems: 56.0%<br>House: 62.1%<br>Incumb: 97.5% | |
| **American Furniture Manufacturers Assn**<br>American Furniture Manufacturers Association PAC<br>High Point, NC | Furniture | $85,350 | 72 Candidates<br>Avg House: $881<br>Avg Sen: $1,978 | Repubs: 79.1%<br>House: 53.7%<br>Incumb: 94.3% | |
| **American Gas Assn**<br>Gas Employees PAC<br>Arlington, VA | Natural Gas | $72,350 | 125 Candidates<br>Avg House: $395<br>Avg Sen: $1,354 | Repubs: 53.3%<br>House: 55.1%<br>Incumb: 94.5% | |
| **American Health Care Assn**<br>American Health Care Association PAC (AHCA-PAC)<br>Washington, DC | Nursing Homes | $263,130 | 197 Candidates<br>Avg House: $1,150<br>Avg Sen: $2,139 | Dems: 68.0%<br>House: 69.9%<br>Incumb: 94.2% | |
| **American Home Products Corp**<br>American Home Products Corporation-AHP Good Government Fund<br>New York, NY | Pharmaceuticals† | $56,875 | 68 Candidates<br>Avg House: $662<br>Avg Sen: $1,156 | Repubs: 54.4%<br>House: 51.2%<br>Incumb: 99.5% | |
| **American Hospital Assn**<br>PAC of the American Hospital Association<br>Chicago, IL | Hospitals | $502,689 | 305 Candidates<br>Avg House: $1,313<br>Avg Sen: $3,343 | Dems: 68.2%<br>House: 66.4%<br>Incumb: 92.0% | |
| **American Hotel & Motel Assn**<br>American Hotel Motel PAC<br>Washington, DC | Hotels/Motels | $140,800 | 178 Candidates<br>Avg House: $655<br>Avg Sen: $1,311 | Dems: 51.0%<br>House: 65.5%<br>Incumb: 94.1% | |
| **American Institute of Architects**<br>American Institute of Architect's Quality Government Fund<br>Washington, DC | Architects | $63,000 | 49 Candidates<br>Avg House: $944<br>Avg Sen: $2,231 | Dems: 64.3%<br>House: 54.0%<br>Incumb: 54.0% | |
| **American Institute of CPA's**<br>American Institute of Certified Public Accountants Effective Legislation Committee (AICPA)<br>New York, NY | Accountants | $1,087,044 | 319 Candidates<br>Avg House: $2,972<br>Avg Sen: $5,750 | Dems: 56.2%<br>House: 73.5%<br>Incumb: 92.7% | |
| **American Insurance Assn**<br>American Insurance Association PAC<br>Washington, DC | Insurance | $108,940 | 151 Candidates<br>Avg House: $568<br>Avg Sen: $1,426 | Dems: 62.1%<br>House: 64.7%<br>Incumb: 94.9% | |
| **American International Group Inc**<br>American International Group Inc Employee PAC<br>New York, NY | Insurance | $149,450 | 112 Candidates<br>Avg House: $1,130<br>Avg Sen: $1,639 | Dems: 61.8%<br>House: 50.6%<br>Incumb: 91.1% | |
| **American Land Title Assn**<br>Title Industry PAC<br>Washington, DC | Title Insurance | $65,300 | 78 Candidates<br>Avg House: $751<br>Avg Sen: $1,200 | Repubs: 51.5%<br>House: 72.4%<br>Incumb: 94.6% | |
| **American Meat Institute**<br>American Meat Institute PAC<br>Arlington, VA | Meat Processing | $133,471 | 134 Candidates<br>Avg House: $778<br>Avg Sen: $1,527 | Repubs: 58.3%<br>House: 55.4%<br>Incumb: 97.6% | |
| **American Medical Assn**<br>American Medical Association PAC<br>Washington, DC | American Medical Assn | $2,375,537 | 482 Candidates<br>Avg House: $4,828<br>Avg Sen: $5,952 | Repubs: 50.7%<br>House: 89.2%<br>Incumb: 84.6% | Doctors |
| **American Nurses Assn**<br>American Nurses' Association PAC (ANA-PAC)<br>Washington, DC | Nurses | $289,860 | 192 Candidates<br>Avg House: $1,270<br>Avg Sen: $2,912 | Dems: 92.8%<br>House: 71.9%<br>Incumb: 57.2% | |
| **American Occupational Therapy Assn**<br>American Occupational Therapy Association PAC<br>Rockville, MD | Health Practitioners | $64,552 | 63 Candidates<br>Avg House: $729<br>Avg Sen: $1,660 | Dems: 86.0%<br>Senate: 51.4%<br>Incumb: 85.0% | |
| **American Optometric Assn**<br>American Optometric Association PAC<br>Alexandria, VA | Eye Doctors | $330,600 | 223 Candidates<br>Avg House: $1,236<br>Avg Sen: $3,068 | Dems: 63.1%<br>House: 72.2%<br>Incumb: 85.9% | |
| **American Pharmaceutical Assn**<br>American Pharmaceutical Association PAC<br>Washington, DC | Pharmacists | $70,500 | 80 Candidates<br>Avg House: $706<br>Avg Sen: $1,246 | Dems: 69.7%<br>House: 54.0%<br>Incumb: 88.8% | |
| **American Physical Therapy Assn**<br>American Physical Therapy Congressional Action Committee<br>Alexandria, VA | Health Practitioners | $149,750 | 109 Candidates<br>Avg House: $994<br>Avg Sen: $2,329 | Dems: 62.9%<br>House: 51.8%<br>Incumb: 86.7% | |

† PAC sponsor has other major interests in addition to this primary category

| PAC Sponsor or Related Group/PAC Name  Affiliate | 1989-90 Total | Where the money went... | | |
|---|---|---|---|---|
| **American Podiatry Assn**<br>Podiatry PAC<br>Bethesda, MD<br><br>MD Specialists | $256,750 | 159 Candidates<br>Avg House: $1,293<br>Avg Sen: $3,056 | Dems:<br>House:<br>Incumb: | 70.7%<br>65.5%<br>92.8% |
| **American Postal Workers Union**<br>Political Fund Committee of the American Postal Workers Union, AFL-CIO<br>Washington, DC<br><br>Postal Workers | $969,828 | 363 Candidates<br>Avg House: $2,417<br>Avg Sen: $4,194 | Dems:<br>House:<br>Incumb: | 91.9%<br>77.5%<br>76.1% |
| **American President Lines**<br>American President Lines Ltd PAC (APL/PAC)<br>Oakland, CA<br><br>Sea Transport | $121,119 | 108 Candidates<br>Avg House: $820<br>Avg Sen: $2,123 | Dems:<br>House:<br>Incumb: | 69.3%<br>56.2%<br>99.6% |
| **American Resort & Residential Development Assn**<br>American Resort & Residential Development Assn PAC<br>Washington, DC<br><br>Real Estate† | $62,050 | 52 Candidates<br>Avg House: $757<br>Avg Sen: $2,818 | Repubs:<br>House:<br>Incumb: | 62.1%<br>50.0%<br>95.9% |
| **American Society of Cataract & Refractive Surgery**<br>American Society of Cataract & Refractive Surgery PAC (aka EyePAC)<br>Fairfax, VA<br><br>Eye Doctors | $56,950 | 36 Candidates<br>Avg House: $910<br>Avg Sen: $2,925 | Dems:<br>Senate:<br>Incumb: | 88.9%<br>61.6%<br>87.2% |
| **American Society of Travel Agents**<br>American Society of Travel Agents PAC<br>Alexandria, VA<br><br>Travel Agents | $84,265 | 160 Candidates<br>Avg House: $447<br>Avg Sen: $911 | Dems:<br>House:<br>Incumb: | 52.5%<br>69.6%<br>97.5% |
| **American Sugar Cane League**<br>American Sugar Cane League PAC<br>Thibodaux, LA<br><br>Sugar | $197,315 | 271 Candidates<br>Avg House: $611<br>Avg Sen: $1,447 | Dems:<br>House:<br>Incumb: | 63.1%<br>72.1%<br>97.0% |
| **American Sugarbeet Growers Assn**<br>American Sugarbeet Growers Association PAC<br>Washington, DC<br><br>Sugar | $327,057 | 293 Candidates<br>Avg House: $906<br>Avg Sen: $2,371 | Dems:<br>House:<br>Incumb: | 58.7%<br>69.5%<br>96.5% |
| **American Supply Assn**<br>American Supply Association PAC<br>Chicago, IL<br><br>Pipe Products† | $78,200 | 88 Candidates<br>Avg House: $583<br>Avg Sen: $1,807 | Repubs:<br>Senate:<br>Incumb: | 83.0%<br>50.8%<br>83.4% |
| **American Textile Manufacturers Institute**<br>American Textile Manufacturers Institute, Inc Committee for Good Government<br>Washington, DC<br><br>Textiles | $139,900 | 138 Candidates<br>Avg House: $864<br>Avg Sen: $1,761 | Dems:<br>House:<br>Incumb: | 54.8%<br>71.0%<br>98.9% |
| **American Trucking Assns**<br>Trucking PAC of the American Trucking Associations' Inc<br>Washington, DC<br><br>Trucking Companies | $299,540 | 285 Candidates<br>Avg House: $847<br>Avg Sen: $2,231 | Dems:<br>House:<br>Incumb: | 55.7%<br>68.7%<br>95.1% |
| **American Veterinary Medical Assn**<br>American Veterinary Medical Association PAC (AVMAPAC)<br>Washington, DC<br><br>Veterinary | $235,000 | 209 Candidates<br>Avg House: $1,003<br>Avg Sen: $1,689 | Dems:<br>House:<br>Incumb: | 53.6%<br>73.4%<br>86.0% |
| **Americans for Good Government**<br>Americans for Good Government Inc<br>Jasper, AL<br><br>Pro-Israel | $147,250 | 75 Candidates<br>Avg House: $1,158<br>Avg Sen: $3,241 | Dems:<br>Senate:<br>Incumb: | 57.1%<br>63.8%<br>85.9% |
| **Ameritech Corp**<br>American Information Technologies Corporation PAC (Ameritech PAC)<br>Chicago, IL  Ameritech<br><br>Phone Utilities | $84,600 | 57 Candidates<br>Avg House: $1,153<br>Avg Sen: $2,052 | Repubs:<br>Senate:<br>Incumb: | 52.5%<br>50.9%<br>92.3% |
| **Amoco Corp**<br>Amoco PAC<br>Chicago, IL<br><br>Oil & Gas Prod† | $322,923 | 243 Candidates<br>Avg House: $812<br>Avg Sen: $5,463 | Repubs:<br>House:<br>Incumb: | 80.7%<br>54.3%<br>84.3% |
| **Anheuser-Busch**<br>Anheuser-Busch Companies Inc PAC (AB-PAC)<br>St. Louis, MO<br><br>Beer† | $133,770 | 110 Candidates<br>Avg House: $1,080<br>Avg Sen: $1,703 | Dems:<br>House:<br>Incumb: | 63.6%<br>69.5%<br>97.5% |
| **Archer-Daniels-Midland Corp**<br>Archer Daniels Midland Company-ADM PAC<br>Decatur, IL<br><br>Grain Traders† | $243,000 | 98 Candidates<br>Avg House: $1,528<br>Avg Sen: $3,859 | Dems:<br>Senate:<br>Incumb: | 57.0%<br>63.5%<br>93.7% |
| **Arnold & Porter**<br>Arnold & Porter Partners PAC<br>Washington, DC  Arnold & Porter<br><br>Lawyers/Lobbyists | $74,575 | 89 Candidates<br>Avg House: $711<br>Avg Sen: $1,114 | Dems:<br>House:<br>Incumb: | 87.7%<br>58.2%<br>97.4% |
| **Arthur Andersen & Co**<br>Arthur Andersen/Andersen Consulting PAC (Arthur Andersen & fka-CO PAC)<br>Washington, DC<br><br>Accountants | $124,475 | 109 Candidates<br>Avg House: $861<br>Avg Sen: $2,039 | Dems:<br>House:<br>Incumb: | 56.9%<br>57.4%<br>97.2% |

**ASCAP**
ASCAP Legislative Fund for the Arts
New York, NY — Music Production — $141,750

| 109 Candidates | Dems: 86.8% |
| Avg House: $1,139 | House: 65.1% |
| Avg Sen: $1,768 | Incumb: 99.6% |

**Ashland Oil**
Ashland Oil PAC for Employees (PACE)
Russell, KY — Oil Refining/Mktg† — $158,100

| 150 Candidates | Repubs: 64.4% |
| Avg House: $800 | House: 63.8% |
| Avg Sen: $2,388 | Incumb: 85.9% |

**Associated Builders & Contractors**
Associated Builders and Contractors PAC (ABC/PAC)
Washington, DC — Builders — $146,712

| 169 Candidates | Repubs: 92.5% |
| Avg House: $597 | House: 58.6% |
| Avg Sen: $2,428 | Incumb: 79.0% |

**Associated Credit Bureaus**
Associated Credit Bureaus PAC
Houston, TX — Credit/Loans — $51,550

| 61 Candidates | Dems: 57.5% |
| Avg House: $793 | House: 80.0% |
| Avg Sen: $1,145 | Incumb: 99.0% |

**Associated General Contractors**
Associated General Contractors PAC
Washington, DC — Comml Construction — $625,594

| 310 Candidates | Repubs: 78.5% |
| Avg House: $1,561 | House: 70.4% |
| Avg Sen: $6,625 | Incumb: 83.2% |

**Associated Milk Producers**
Committee for Thorough Agricultural Political Education of Associated Milk Producers
San Antonio, TX — Dairy — $769,800

| 270 Candidates | Dems: 66.6% |
| Avg House: $2,738 | House: 87.5% |
| Avg Sen: $4,013 | Incumb: 86.3% |

**Assn for the Advancement of Psychology**
Association for the Advancement of Psychology Inc Psychologists for Leg Action Now (PLAN)
Colorado Springs, CO — Psychol — $168,283

| 108 Candidates | Dems: 88.2% |
| Avg House: $1,287 | House: 57.4% |
| Avg Sen: $2,174 | Incumb: 97.0% |

**Assn of Flight Attendants**
Association of Flight Attendants PAC ("Flight PAC")
Washington, DC — Air Transport Unions — $171,950

| 157 Candidates | Dems: 98.0% |
| Avg House: $611 | Senate: 51.7% |
| Avg Sen: $4,231 | Incumb: 79.9% |

**Assn of Independent Colleges & Schools**
Association of Independent Colleges and Schools PAC
Washington, DC — Voc Tech Schools — $80,850

| 41 Candidates | Dems: 63.5% |
| Avg House: $1,584 | House: 54.9% |
| Avg Sen: $2,808 | Incumb: 98.8% |

**Assn of Trial Lawyers of America**
Association of Trial Lawyers of America PAC
Washington, DC — Lawyers — $1,533,550

| 318 Candidates | Dems: 86.9% |
| Avg House: $4,599 | House: 83.4% |
| Avg Sen: $6,375 | Incumb: 75.1% |

**AT&T**
American Telephone & Telegraph Company Inc PAC (AT&T PAC)
New York, NY — Long Distance† — $1,452,360

| 531 Candidates | Dems: 57.2% |
| Avg House: $2,611 | House: 81.4% |
| Avg Sen: $3,500 | Incumb: 93.8% |

**Atlantic Richfield**
Atlantic Richfield Company, Arco PAC
Los Angeles, CA — Oil & Gas Prod† — $300,264

| 207 Candidates | Repubs: 60.9% |
| Avg House: $1,074 | House: 63.6% |
| Avg Sen: $3,900 | Incumb: 90.9% |

**Auto Dealers & Drivers for Free Trade**
Auto Dealers and Drivers for Free Trade PAC
Jamaica, NY — Japanese Auto Dealers — $644,450

| 269 Candidates | Repubs: 67.5% |
| Avg House: $2,054 | House: 64.7% |
| Avg Sen: $3,447 | Incumb: 86.9% |

**Baker & Botts**
Bluebonnet Fund (Baker & Botts), The
Houston, TX — Lawyers — $56,050

| 44 Candidates | Dems: 50.5% |
| Avg House: $865 | Senate: 58.3% |
| Avg Sen: $1,924 | Incumb: 93.3% |

**Bakery, Confectionery & Tobacco Workers**
Bakery, Confectionery and Tobacco Workers International Union PAC
Kensington, MD — Food Service Unions — $105,800

| 78 Candidates | Dems: 100.0% |
| Avg House: $1,215 | House: 71.2% |
| Avg Sen: $1,906 | Incumb: 42.8% |

**Baltimore Gas & Electric**
Baltimore Gas and Electric Company PAC (BG&E PAC)
Baltimore, MD — Gas & Electric Util — $68,050

| 56 Candidates | Repubs: 61.8% |
| Avg House: $1,187 | House: 75.0% |
| Avg Sen: $1,308 | Incumb: 94.6% |

**Banc One Corp**
Banc One PAC
Columbus, OH — Commercial Banks — $58,110

| 73 Candidates | Dems: 55.6% |
| Avg House: $765 | House: 77.6% |
| Avg Sen: $923 | Incumb: 90.1% |

**BankAmerica**
BankAmerica Federal Election Fund
San Francisco, CA — Commercial Banks — $125,478

| 128 Candidates | Repubs: 50.1% |
| Avg House: $893 | House: 64.8% |
| Avg Sen: $1,195 | Incumb: 95.0% |

**Bankers Trust**
Bankers Trust New York Corporation PAC
New York, NY — Commercial Banks — $158,050

| 76 Candidates | Dems: 66.4% |
| Avg House: $1,858 | House: 65.8% |
| Avg Sen: $2,700 | Incumb: 98.4% |

† PAC sponsor has other major interests in addition to this primary category

| **Barnett Banks of Florida** Barnett People for Better Government Inc - Federal a PAC of Barnett Banks Inc Jacksonville, FL | | Commercial Banks | **$462,050** | 222 Candidates Avg House: $1,794 Avg Sen: $3,211 | Repubs: 55.5% House: 68.7% Incumb: 92.4% |
|---|---|---|---|---|---|
| **Bath Iron Works** Bath Iron Works Corp PAC (fka Congoleum Corp PAC) Arlington, VA | | Naval Ships† | **$52,800** | 40 Candidates Avg House: $1,071 Avg Sen: $2,178 | Dems: 53.7% House: 62.9% Incumb: 100.0% |
| **BDM International** BDM International, Inc. PAC (BDM-PAC) McLean, VA | Ford Motor Co (until Oct 90) | Defense R&D | **$126,970** | 81 Candidates Avg House: $1,343 Avg Sen: $2,100 | Repubs: 60.8% House: 60.3% Incumb: 98.5% |
| **Bechtel Corp** Bechtel Group, Inc PAC San Francisco, CA | | Power Plant Equipt† | **$106,329** | 60 Candidates Avg House: $1,593 Avg Sen: $2,159 | Dems: 50.1% House: 61.4% Incumb: 99.3% |
| **Bell Atlantic** Bell Atlantic Corporation PAC Philadelphia, PA | Bell Atlantic | Phone Utilities† | **$161,872** | 126 Candidates Avg House: $843 Avg Sen: $2,761 | Dems: 57.6% House: 50.5% Incumb: 96.3% |
| **BellSouth Corp** BellSouth Corporation Federal PAC Atlanta, GA | BellSouth | Phone Utilities | **$181,500** | 139 Candidates Avg House: $1,010 Avg Sen: $2,186 | Dems: 54.1% House: 57.9% Incumb: 93.6% |
| **BellSouth Services** BellSouth Services Incorporated Federal PAC Birmingham, AL | BellSouth | Phone Utilities | **$116,500** | 116 Candidates Avg House: $842 Avg Sen: $1,431 | Repubs: 65.9% House: 60.7% Incumb: 97.4% |
| **Beneficial Management Corp** Beneficial Management Corporation and Affiliated Corporations PAC Peapack, NJ | | Credit/Loans† | **$129,775** | 107 Candidates Avg House: $1,141 Avg Sen: $1,569 | Dems: 65.6% House: 78.2% Incumb: 92.8% |
| **Bethlehem Steel** Bethlehem Steel Good Government Committee Bethlehem, PA | | Steel | **$76,900** | 78 Candidates Avg House: $833 Avg Sen: $1,750 | Dems: 59.0% House: 70.4% Incumb: 97.1% |
| **Blue Cross/Blue Shield** CarePAC, the Blue Cross and Blue Shield Association PAC Washington, DC | | Health Insurance | **$168,568** | 170 Candidates Avg House: $792 Avg Sen: $1,619 | Dems: 66.5% House: 60.6% Incumb: 95.7% |
| **Blue Diamond Growers** Blue Diamond Growers PAC (fka Calif Almond Growers Exchange PAC) Sacramento, CA | | Fruit/Veg | **$89,989** | 57 Candidates Avg House: $1,648 Avg Sen: $659 | Dems: 58.2% House: 97.1% Incumb: 83.3% |
| **Boeing Co** Boeing Company PAC (BPAC) Seattle, WA | | Aircraft† | **$275,507** | 156 Candidates Avg House: $1,536 Avg Sen: $2,692 | Dems: 53.2% House: 69.7% Incumb: 97.1% |
| **Boilermakers Union** International Brotherhood of Boilermakers, In Sp Bldrs, Bkmths, Frgrs & Hlprs-Leg Ed Fund Kansas City, KS     Boilermakers Union | | Mfg Unions† | **$235,650** | 188 Candidates Avg House: $990 Avg Sen: $3,243 | Dems: 95.2% House: 69.7% Incumb: 77.5% |
| **Boise Cascade** Boise Cascade Political Fund Boise, ID | | Forest Products | **$84,000** | 31 Candidates Avg House: $2,000 Avg Sen: $4,000 | Repubs: 91.7% Senate: 52.4% Incumb: 82.7% |
| **Bowling Proprietors Assn** Bowling Proprietors Assn of America PAC Arlington, TX | | Amusement Centers | **$63,075** | 83 Candidates Avg House: $644 Avg Sen: $1,332 | Repubs: 81.5% House: 70.4% Incumb: 94.5% |
| **BP America** BPA-PAC (the BP America PAC) Cleveland, OH | | Oil & Gas Prod† | **$121,250** | 118 Candidates Avg House: $848 Avg Sen: $1,578 | Repubs: 58.3% House: 62.3% Incumb: 96.5% |
| **Bricklayers Union** International Union of Bricklayers and Allied Craftsmen PAC Washington, DC | | Constr Unions | **$248,175** | 130 Candidates Avg House: $1,505 Avg Sen: $3,648 | Dems: 98.3% House: 63.1% Incumb: 74.9% |
| **Bristol-Myers Squibb** Bristol-Myers Squibb Company PAC New York, NY | Bristol-Myers Squibb | Pharmaceuticals† | **$105,300** | 133 Candidates Avg House: $561 Avg Sen: $2,024 | Repubs: 60.6% House: 59.6% Incumb: 90.9% |
| **Brotherhood of Railroad Signalmen** Brotherhood of Railroad Signalmen PAC Mt. Prospect, IL | | Railroad Unions | **$85,770** | 115 Candidates Avg House: $646 Avg Sen: $1,411 | Dems: 95.2% House: 75.3% Incumb: 92.4% |

| --- | --- | --- | --- | --- | --- |
| **Brotherhood of Locomotive Engineers** Brotherhood of Locomotive Engineers Legislative League Cleveland, OH | Railroad Unions | $237,300 | 257 Candidates Avg House: $808 Avg Sen: $1,731 | Dems: 94.8% House: 76.6% Incumb: 83.7% | |
| **Brown & Root** Brownbuilders PAC of Brown & Root, Inc Employees Houston, TX | Halliburton Co / Comml Construction† | $61,800 | 78 Candidates Avg House: $613 Avg Sen: $1,392 | Repubs: 62.0% House: 59.5% Incumb: 94.3% | |
| **Brown & Williamson Tobacco** Brown & Williamson Tobacco Corporation Employee PAC Aka EMPAC Louisville, KY | Batus Inc / Tobacco | $59,700 | 83 Candidates Avg House: $543 Avg Sen: $1,180 | Repubs: 51.6% House: 54.5% Incumb: 94.1% | |
| **Brown-Forman Distillers** Brown-Forman Corporation Non-Partisan Committee for Responsible Government Louisville, KY | Wine & Liquor† | $84,000 | 83 Candidates Avg House: $703 Avg Sen: $1,730 | Repubs: 75.6% Senate: 51.5% Incumb: 90.5% | |
| **Browning-Ferris Industries** Browning-Ferris Industries PAC (BFI PAC) Houston, TX | Waste Mgmt | $170,789 | 170 Candidates Avg House: $872 Avg Sen: $1,709 | Dems: 67.1% House: 73.0% Incumb: 86.5% | |
| **Burlington Industries** Burlington Industries Good Government Committee Greensboro, NC | Burlington Industries / Textiles† | $219,029 | 143 Candidates Avg House: $1,343 Avg Sen: $2,162 | Dems: 56.8% House: 67.4% Incumb: 97.0% | |
| **Burlington Northern Railroad** Burlington Northern Railroad RailPAC (BN RailPAC) Fort Worth, TX | Burlington Northern / Railroads | $202,346 | 155 Candidates Avg House: $878 Avg Sen: $2,534 | Repubs: 51.3% House: 49.9% Incumb: 94.5% | |
| **Burlington Resources** Burlington Resources Inc PAC (fka: Burlington Northern Employees Vol Good Govt Fund) Seattle, WA | Burlington Northern / Railroads | $79,950 | 105 Candidates Avg House: $553 Avg Sen: $1,548 | Dems: 51.4% House: 57.4% Incumb: 95.6% | |
| **Business Industry PAC** Business Industry PAC Washington, DC | Pro-Business Assn | $110,632 | 75 Candidates Avg House: $1,241 Avg Sen: $2,497 | Repubs: 93.3% House: 68.4% Incumb: 43.1% | |
| **C&S/Sovran Corp** C&S/Sovran Corporation PAC (C&S/Sovran PAC) Norfolk, VA | C&S/Sovran Corp / Commercial Banks | $70,600 | 62 Candidates Avg House: $1,198 Avg Sen: $969 | Dems: 52.6% House: 78.0% Incumb: 98.3% | |
| **Campaign America** Campaign America Washington, DC | Sen Bob Dole (R-Kan) / Repub Leaders | $302,497 | 107 Candidates Avg House: $1,449 Avg Sen: $5,560 | Repubs: 99.9% Senate: 64.3% Incumb: 64.7% | |
| **Capital Holding Corp** Capital Holding PAC - Cap*PAC Louisville, KY | Insurance | $75,824 | 71 Candidates Avg House: $797 Avg Sen: $1,714 | Dems: 55.4% House: 52.5% Incumb: 97.4% | |
| **Cargill Inc** Cargill, Incorporated, PAC Minneapolis, MN | Crop Production† | $60,000 | 38 Candidates Avg House: $1,138 Avg Sen: $3,000 | Repubs: 90.0% House: 55.0% Incumb: 70.0% | |
| **Carolina Power & Light** Employees Federal PAC - Carolina Power & Light Co Raleigh, NC | Electric Utilities | $76,400 | 82 Candidates Avg House: $846 Avg Sen: $1,198 | Repubs: 56.6% House: 68.6% Incumb: 95.9% | |
| **Carpenters & Joiners Union** Carpenters Legislative Improvement Comm, United Brotherhood of Carpenters & Joiners of Amer Washington, DC | Constr Unions | $1,489,520 | 378 Candidates Avg House: $3,784 Avg Sen: $5,161 | Dems: 96.3% House: 84.3% Incumb: 68.3% | |
| **Casualty & Surety Agents Assn** National Association of Casualty & Surety Agents PAC (NACSAPAC) Bethesda, MD | Insurance | $224,883 | 180 Candidates Avg House: $1,003 Avg Sen: $2,113 | Repubs: 50.5% House: 62.4% Incumb: 90.9% | |
| **Caterpillar Tractor** Caterpillar Tractor Co Committee for Effective Government Peoria, IL | Constr Equipment† | $109,695 | 83 Candidates Avg House: $924 Avg Sen: $2,575 | Repubs: 89.9% House: 53.1% Incumb: 79.7% | |
| **Centel Corp** Centel Corporation Good Government Fund Washington, DC | Phone Utilities† | $69,970 | 83 Candidates Avg House: $578 Avg Sen: $1,954 | Repubs: 63.1% House: 55.3% Incumb: 97.6% | |
| **Century 21 Real Estate** Century 21 Political Action Committee (CEN-PAC) Washington, DC | Metropolitan Life / Real Estate | $113,400 | 55 Candidates Avg House: $1,461 Avg Sen: $3,821 | Dems: 54.5% House: 52.8% Incumb: 98.7% | |

† PAC sponsor has other major interests in addition to this primary category

| PAC Sponsor or Related Group / PAC Name | Affiliate | 1989-90 Total | Where the money went... | | |
|---|---|---|---|---|---|
| **CF Industries**<br>CF Industries Employees' Good Government Fund<br>Long Grove, IL | Ag Chemicals† | $68,700 | 93 Candidates<br>Avg House: $574<br>Avg Sen: $1,188 | Dems: 54.8%<br>House: 56.8%<br>Incumb: 94.2% | |
| **CH2M Hill**<br>CH2M Hill PAC Inc<br>Corvallis, OR | Engineers† | $103,907 | 136 Candidates<br>Avg House: $578<br>Avg Sen: $1,452 | Repubs: 63.8%<br>House: 59.5%<br>Incumb: 94.3% | |
| **Champion International Corp**<br>Champion International Corporation PAC<br>Stamford, CT | Paper/Forest Prod | $99,517 | 96 Candidates<br>Avg House: $699<br>Avg Sen: $1,780 | Repubs: 63.0%<br>Senate: 53.7%<br>Incumb: 94.3% | |
| **Chase Manhattan**<br>Chase Manhattan Corporation PAC - (ChasePAC)<br>New York, NY | Commercial Banks | $152,400 | 109 Candidates<br>Avg House: $1,202<br>Avg Sen: $2,058 | Dems: 53.8%<br>House: 66.2%<br>Incumb: 92.4% | |
| **Chemical Bank**<br>Chemical Bank Fund for Good Government<br>New York, NY | Commercial Banks | $101,300 | 99 Candidates<br>Avg House: $953<br>Avg Sen: $1,300 | Dems: 71.9%<br>House: 74.3%<br>Incumb: 96.2% | |
| **Chevron Corp**<br>Chevron Employees PAC<br>San Francisco, CA | Oil & Gas Prod† | $312,393 | 229 Candidates<br>Avg House: $898<br>Avg Sen: $4,231 | Repubs: 73.0%<br>House: 56.7%<br>Incumb: 83.5% | |
| **Chicago & North Western Transport**<br>North Western Officers Trust Account - Chicago & North Western Transportation Co<br>Chicago, IL | Railroads | $50,150 | 46 Candidates<br>Avg House: $652<br>Avg Sen: $1,913 | Repubs: 52.9%<br>Senate: 61.0%<br>Incumb: 95.3% | |
| **Chicago Board of Trade**<br>Auction Markets PAC of the Chicago Board of Trade a/k/a AMPAC/CBT<br>Chicago, IL | Commodity Trading | $371,311 | 195 Candidates<br>Avg House: $1,505<br>Avg Sen: $3,405 | Dems: 67.8%<br>House: 62.4%<br>Incumb: 97.7% | |
| **Chicago Mercantile Exchange**<br>Commodity Futures Political Fund of the Chicago Mercantile Exchange<br>Chicago, IL | Commodity Trading | $459,500 | 233 Candidates<br>Avg House: $1,328<br>Avg Sen: $4,330 | Dems: 65.0%<br>House: 52.9%<br>Incumb: 93.5% | |
| **Chrysler Corp**<br>Chrysler Corporation Political Support Committee a/k/a Chrysler Political Support Cmte<br>Highland Park, MI | Auto Mfrs† | $218,900 | 212 Candidates<br>Avg House: $826<br>Avg Sen: $2,075 | Dems: 70.8%<br>House: 66.8%<br>Incumb: 97.9% | |
| **Chubb Corp**<br>Chubb Corporation PAC "ChubbPAC"<br>Warren, NJ | Insurance | $52,850 | 35 Candidates<br>Avg House: $1,294<br>Avg Sen: $2,050 | Repubs: 62.4%<br>House: 61.2%<br>Incumb: 87.3% | |
| **Ciba-Geigy Corp**<br>Ciba-Geigy Employee Good Government Fund<br>Ardsley, NY | Pharmaceuticals† | $120,775 | 138 Candidates<br>Avg House: $705<br>Avg Sen: $1,418 | Repubs: 53.1%<br>House: 61.3%<br>Incumb: 97.4% | |
| **Cigna Corp**<br>Cigna Corporation PAC<br>Philadelphia, PA | Insurance | $171,225 | 165 Candidates<br>Avg House: $721<br>Avg Sen: $2,259 | Repubs: 62.1%<br>House: 55.2%<br>Incumb: 95.1% | |
| **Circus Circus Enterprises**<br>Circus Circus Enterprises Inc PAC (aka CC-PAC)<br>San Francisco, CA | Casinos/Gambling† | $58,136 | 19 Candidates<br>Avg House: $2,497<br>Avg Sen: $3,204 | Dems: 95.7%<br>Senate: 71.6%<br>Incumb: 99.1% | |
| **Citicorp**<br>Citicorp Voluntary Political Fund Federal<br>Washington, DC | Commercial Banks | $383,828 | 206 Candidates<br>Avg House: $1,661<br>Avg Sen: $2,962 | Dems: 59.2%<br>House: 75.3%<br>Incumb: 96.8% | |
| **Citizens & Southern National Bank**<br>C&S/Sovran Corporation Better Government Committee<br>Atlanta, GA | C&S/Sovran Corp<br>Commercial Banks | $106,700 | 78 Candidates<br>Avg House: $1,218<br>Avg Sen: $1,867 | Dems: 66.7%<br>House: 68.5%<br>Incumb: 97.1% | |
| **Citizens for the Republic**<br>Citizens for the Republic<br>Santa Monica, CA | Ronald Reagan<br>Repub Leaders | $53,500 | 24 Candidates<br>Avg House: $1,842<br>Avg Sen: $3,700 | Repubs: 100.0%<br>House: 65.4%<br>Incumb: 26.2% | |
| **Citizens Organized PAC**<br>Citizens Organized PAC<br>Los Angeles, CA | Pro-Israel | $191,000 | 27 Candidates<br>Avg House: $5,000<br>Avg Sen: $7,947 | Dems: 76.4%<br>Senate: 79.1%<br>Incumb: 93.2% | |
| **City PAC**<br>City PAC<br>Deerfield, IL | Pro-Israel | $70,500 | 41 Candidates<br>Avg House: $1,000<br>Avg Sen: $3,950 | Dems: 85.1%<br>Senate: 56.0%<br>Incumb: 77.3% | |

| PAC Sponsor or Related Group/PAC Name | Affiliate | 1989-90 Total | Candidates / Avg | Party | Where |
|---|---|---|---|---|---|
| **Coastal Corp** <br> Coastal Corp. Employee Action Fund <br> Houston, TX | Natural Gas† | $233,000 | 145 Candidates <br> Avg House: $1,387 <br> Avg Sen: $2,527 | Dems: 74.3% <br> House: 69.6% <br> Incumb: 94.7% | |
| **Coca-Cola Co** <br> Coca-Cola Company Nonpartisan Committee for Good Government <br> Atlanta, GA | Soft Drinks† | $183,120 | 199 Candidates <br> Avg House: $758 <br> Avg Sen: $1,474 | Dems: 60.6% <br> House: 63.8% <br> Incumb: 92.9% | |
| **Colt Industries** <br> Coltec Industries Voluntary Political Committee (fka-Colt Industries Voluntary Pol Cmte) <br> New York, NY | Air Defense† | $62,300 | 69 Candidates <br> Avg House: $722 <br> Avg Sen: $1,417 | Repubs: 55.5% <br> House: 59.1% <br> Incumb: 94.4% | |
| **Columbia Gas System** <br> Columbia Gas Employees Political Action Fund <br> Wilmington, DE | Columbia Gas System <br> Natural Gas | $136,725 | 116 Candidates <br> Avg House: $1,025 <br> Avg Sen: $1,712 | Dems: 51.0% <br> House: 67.5% <br> Incumb: 95.0% | |
| **Columbia Natural Resources** <br> Columbia Employees Political Action Fund <br> Charleston, WV | Columbia Gas System <br> Oil & Gas Prod | $116,835 | 93 Candidates <br> Avg House: $1,060 <br> Avg Sen: $1,931 | Repubs: 51.8% <br> House: 65.3% <br> Incumb: 93.7% | |
| **Combustion Engineering** <br> Asea Brown Boveri Employees' Fund for Effective Government (fka COMPAC) <br> Stamford, CT | Power Plant Equip | $55,028 | 53 Candidates <br> Avg House: $798 <br> Avg Sen: $1,506 | Dems: 52.3% <br> House: 50.8% <br> Incumb: 99.1% | |
| **Committee for America's Future** <br> Committee for America's Future <br> Washington, DC | Sen Robert Byrd (D-WVa) <br> Dem Leaders | $65,000 | 12 Candidates <br> Avg House: $4,000 <br> Avg Sen: $5,700 | Dems: 100.0% <br> Senate: 87.7% <br> Incumb: 92.3% | |
| **Committee for a Democratic Consensus** <br> Committee for a Democratic Consensus; The <br> Washington, DC | Sen Alan Cranston (D-Calif) <br> Dem Leaders | $99,500 | 25 Candidates <br> Avg House: $1,750 <br> Avg Sen: $4,684 | Dems: 100.0% <br> Senate: 89.5% <br> Incumb: 68.8% | |
| **Committee for Democratic Opportunity** <br> Committee for Democratic Opportunity <br> Washington, DC | Rep William Gray III (D-Pa) <br> Dem Leaders | $155,785 | 78 Candidates <br> Avg House: $2,038 <br> Avg Sen: $443 | Dems: 99.1% <br> House: 99.4% <br> Incumb: 64.7% | |
| **Committee for Quality Orthopaedic Health Care** <br> Committee for Quality Orthopaedic Health Care Inc <br> Washington, DC | MD Specialists | $121,782 | 139 Candidates <br> Avg House: $744 <br> Avg Sen: $1,299 | Repubs: 53.1% <br> House: 64.8% <br> Incumb: 89.9% | |
| **Commodity Exchange Inc** <br> Commodity Exchange , Inc. PAC (COMPAC) <br> Washington, DC | Commodity Trading | $53,250 | 54 Candidates <br> Avg House: $815 <br> Avg Sen: $1,583 | Dems: 70.6% <br> House: 64.3% <br> Incumb: 100.0% | |
| **Communications Workers of America** <br> CWA-COPE Political Contributions Committee <br> Washington, DC | Communic Unions | $789,537 | 251 Candidates <br> Avg House: $2,766 <br> Avg Sen: $5,743 | Dems: 99.2% <br> House: 76.7% <br> Incumb: 57.0% | |
| **Computer Sciences Corp** <br> Computer Sciences Corporation PAC (CSC PAC) <br> El Segundo, CA | Computer Services† | $138,300 | 120 Candidates <br> Avg House: $936 <br> Avg Sen: $1,774 | Repubs: 56.4% <br> House: 60.2% <br> Incumb: 99.6% | |
| **Comsat** <br> Communications Satellite Corporation (Comsat) ComsatPAC <br> Washington, DC | Satellite Communic† | $98,700 | 86 Candidates <br> Avg House: $718 <br> Avg Sen: $2,476 | Dems: 53.1% <br> Senate: 52.7% <br> Incumb: 98.8% | |
| **ConAgra Inc** <br> ConAgra, Inc. Good Government Association <br> Omaha, NE | Food Processing† | $204,949 | 106 Candidates <br> Avg House: $1,334 <br> Avg Sen: $3,007 | Repubs: 78.0% <br> Senate: 55.8% <br> Incumb: 82.4% | |
| **Connecticut Mutual Life Insurance** <br> Connecticut Mutual Life Insurance Co-PAC (CM-PAC;/CM PAC;CML PAC) <br> Hartford, CT | Life Insurance | $85,500 | 65 Candidates <br> Avg House: $1,174 <br> Avg Sen: $1,591 | Repubs: 52.1% <br> House: 59.1% <br> Incumb: 89.5% | |
| **Conservative Victory Committee** <br> Conservative Victory Committee <br> Alexandria, VA | Repub/Conservative | $97,262 | 53 Candidates <br> Avg House: $1,509 <br> Avg Sen: $2,839 | Repubs: 100.0% <br> House: 62.1% <br> Incumb: 51.4% | |
| **Consolidated Freightways** <br> Consolidated Freightways Inc PAC <br> Menlo Park, CA | Trucking Companies | $101,050 | 85 Candidates <br> Avg House: $955 <br> Avg Sen: $1,664 | Dems: 60.5% <br> House: 53.9% <br> Incumb: 94.5% | |
| **Consolidated Rail Corp** <br> Consolidated Rail Corporation Good Government Fund (Conrail Good Government Fund) <br> Philadelphia, PA | Railroads | $54,775 | 80 Candidates <br> Avg House: $556 <br> Avg Sen: $1,293 | Dems: 63.9% <br> House: 67.0% <br> Incumb: 100.0% | |

† PAC sponsor has other major interests in addition to this primary category

| | | | |
|---|---|---|---|
| **Consumer Bankers Assn**<br>Consumer Bankers Association PAC, The<br>Arlington, VA<br><br>Banks | **$53,985** | 61 Candidates<br>Avg House: $866<br>Avg Sen: $954 | Dems: 63.1%<br>House: 77.0%<br>Incumb: 100.9% |
| **Consumers Power Co**<br>Consumers Power Company Employees for Better Government - Federal<br>Jackson, MI     CMS Energy Corp     Gas & Electric Util† | **$103,188** | 83 Candidates<br>Avg House: $1,164<br>Avg Sen: $1,552 | Dems: 50.5%<br>House: 74.4%<br>Incumb: 87.4% |
| **Contel**<br>Contel Corporation PAC (ContelPAC)<br>Washington, DC<br><br>Phone Utilities† | **$280,620** | 182 Candidates<br>Avg House: $1,347<br>Avg Sen: $2,421 | Repubs: 71.3%<br>House: 71.5%<br>Incumb: 84.8% |
| **Continental Illinois Corp**<br>Political Participation Fund of Continental Illinois Corp<br>Chicago, IL<br><br>Commercial Banks | **$119,550** | 77 Candidates<br>Avg House: $1,282<br>Avg Sen: $2,379 | Dems: 70.0%<br>House: 62.2%<br>Incumb: 97.5% |
| **Cooper Industries**<br>Cooper Industries PAC (CIPAC)<br>Houston, TX<br><br>Power Plant Equip† | **$230,550** | 126 Candidates<br>Avg House: $1,283<br>Avg Sen: $4,040 | Repubs: 95.5%<br>House: 56.2%<br>Incumb: 61.4% |
| **Cooperative of American Physicians**<br>Cooperative of American Physicians Federal Action Committee (CAP/FAC)<br>Los Angeles, CA<br><br>Doctors | **$77,650** | 55 Candidates<br>Avg House: $1,321<br>Avg Sen: $1,679 | Dems: 77.2%<br>House: 69.7%<br>Incumb: 97.4% |
| **Coopers & Lybrand**<br>Coopers & Lybrand PAC<br>Washington, DC<br><br>Accountants | **$146,786** | 142 Candidates<br>Avg House: $933<br>Avg Sen: $1,485 | Dems: 59.8%<br>House: 73.7%<br>Incumb: 97.5% |
| **Corning Glass Works**<br>Corning Employees PAC<br>Corning, NY<br><br>Communications Equip† | **$164,460** | 109 Candidates<br>Avg House: $1,282<br>Avg Sen: $2,735 | Dems: 51.2%<br>House: 71.7%<br>Incumb: 89.3% |
| **Corp for the Advancement of Psychiatry**<br>Corporation for the Advancement of Psychiatry PAC (CAPPAC)<br>Washington, DC<br><br>Psychol | **$117,426** | 124 Candidates<br>Avg House: $851<br>Avg Sen: $1,291 | Dems: 84.9%<br>House: 70.3%<br>Incumb: 81.8% |
| **Council for a Livable World**<br>Council for a Livable World<br>Boston, MA     Council for Livable World     Pro-Peace | **$83,893** | 17 Candidates<br>Avg House: $761<br>Avg Sen: $5,196 | Dems: 93.5%<br>Senate: 99.1%<br>Incumb: 57.7% |
| **Council for National Defense**<br>Conservative Republican Committee<br>Springfield, VA<br><br>Pro-Defense | **$95,294** | 28 Candidates<br>Avg House: $3,520<br>Avg Sen: $250 | Repubs: 100.0%<br>House: 99.7%<br>Incumb: 24.0% |
| **Credit Union National Assn**<br>Credit Union Legislative Action Council<br>Washington, DC<br><br>Credit Unions | **$475,493** | 254 Candidates<br>Avg House: $1,649<br>Avg Sen: $3,063 | Dems: 56.8%<br>House: 74.2%<br>Incumb: 87.3% |
| **CSX Transportation Inc**<br>CSX Transportation Inc PAC (fka Seaboard System Railroad PAC)<br>Washington, DC     CSX Corp     Railroads† | **$130,458** | 152 Candidates<br>Avg House: $617<br>Avg Sen: $1,883 | Dems: 64.5%<br>House: 58.1%<br>Incumb: 97.1% |
| **Cyprus Minerals Co**<br>Cyprus Minerals Company PAC/Cyprus PAC<br>Englewood, CO<br><br>Metal Mining/Process† | **$92,412** | 56 Candidates<br>Avg House: $891<br>Avg Sen: $2,740 | Repubs: 71.6%<br>Senate: 68.2%<br>Incumb: 95.4% |
| **Dairymen Inc**<br>Dairymen Inc-Special Political Agricultural Community Education (DI-SPACE)<br>Louisville, KY     Dairymen Inc     Dairy | **$119,501** | 121 Candidates<br>Avg House: $846<br>Avg Sen: $1,506 | Dems: 66.4%<br>House: 67.2%<br>Incumb: 96.9% |
| **Dallas Entrepreneurial PAC**<br>Dallas Entrepreneurial PAC (fka: Dallas Energy PAC)<br>Dallas, TX<br><br>Oil & Gas Prod | **$89,000** | 20 Candidates<br>Avg House: $2,188<br>Avg Sen: $5,958 | Repubs: 100.0%<br>Senate: 80.3%<br>Incumb: 81.5% |
| **Dean Witter Reynolds**<br>Dean Witter Financial Services Group Inc PAC (aka) Dean Witter PAC<br>New York, NY     Sears     Securities Invest | **$94,549** | 83 Candidates<br>Avg House: $1,155<br>Avg Sen: $1,084 | Repubs: 51.7%<br>House: 78.2%<br>Incumb: 82.5% |
| **Deere & Co**<br>Deere & Company Civic Action Fund<br>Moline, IL<br><br>Farm Equip† | **$110,300** | 86 Candidates<br>Avg House: $1,049<br>Avg Sen: $2,167 | Repubs: 89.5%<br>House: 64.6%<br>Incumb: 68.6% |
| **Delaware Valley PAC**<br>Delaware Valley PAC<br>Bensalem, PA<br><br>Pro-Israel | **$157,250** | 74 Candidates<br>Avg House: $1,077<br>Avg Sen: $4,180 | Dems: 73.9%<br>Senate: 66.5%<br>Incumb: 87.9% |

| PAC Sponsor or Related Group/PAC Name | Affiliate | 1989-90 Total | Where the money went... | | |
|---|---|---|---|---|---|
| **Deloitte & Touche** <br> Deloitte & Touche Federal PAC (aka-Touche Ross Partners Fed PAC) <br> Washington, DC | Accountants | $101,561 | 90 Candidates <br> Avg House: $1,035 <br> Avg Sen: $1,479 | Dems: 57.4% <br> House: 72.3% <br> Incumb: 94.6% | |
| **Delta Airlines** <br> Delta Airlines Inc PAC <br> Atlanta, GA | Airlines | $82,700 | 83 Candidates <br> Avg House: $823 <br> Avg Sen: $1,477 | Dems: 64.6% <br> House: 60.7% <br> Incumb: 98.1% | |
| **Democrats for the 90's** <br> Democrats for the 90's <br> Washington, DC | Dem/Liberal | $117,750 | 20 Candidates <br> Avg House: $2,375 <br> Avg Sen: $6,278 | Dems: 100.0% <br> Senate: 96.0% <br> Incumb: 60.3% | |
| **Desert Caucus** <br> Desert Caucus <br> Tucson, AZ | Pro-Israel | $166,379 | 36 Candidates <br> Avg House: $1,967 <br> Avg Sen: $7,588 | Dems: 64.8% <br> Senate: 77.5% <br> Incumb: 93.2% | |
| **Detroit Edison** <br> Detroit Edison PAC-EDPAC-Federal <br> Detroit, MI | Electric Utilities | $61,400 | 51 Candidates <br> Avg House: $1,094 <br> Avg Sen: $1,655 | Dems: 62.0% <br> House: 73.0% <br> Incumb: 93.0% | |
| **Dickstein, Shapiro & Morin** <br> Dickstein, Shapiro & Morin PAC <br> Washington, DC | Lawyers | $104,425 | 143 Candidates <br> Avg House: $625 <br> Avg Sen: $975 | Dems: 58.2% <br> House: 59.9% <br> Incumb: 97.6% | |
| **Distilled Spirits Council** <br> Distilled Spirits Council PAC <br> Washington, DC | Wine & Liquor | $66,838 | 83 Candidates <br> Avg House: $641 <br> Avg Sen: $1,360 | Dems: 67.7% <br> House: 61.3% <br> Incumb: 90.3% | |
| **Dominion Resources Inc** <br> Committee for Responsible Government-Dominion Resources Inc (formerly Va Elec & Power) <br> Richmond, VA | Electric Utilities | $72,100 | 83 Candidates <br> Avg House: $758 <br> Avg Sen: $1,175 | Repubs: 53.0% <br> House: 64.1% <br> Incumb: 91.1% | |
| **Dow Chemical** <br> Dow Chemical Company Employees' PAC <br> Freeport, TX | Dow Chemical <br> Chemicals† | $105,750 | 54 Candidates <br> Avg House: $1,750 <br> Avg Sen: $3,357 | Repubs: 88.4% <br> House: 77.8% <br> Incumb: 61.2% | |
| **Dow Chemical/HQ Unit** <br> Dow Chemical Company-Headquarters Unit Employees PAC; The <br> Midland, MI | Dow Chemical <br> Chemicals† | $67,600 | 54 Candidates <br> Avg House: $1,069 <br> Avg Sen: $2,167 | Repubs: 94.8% <br> House: 71.1% <br> Incumb: 53.4% | |
| **Dresser Industries** <br> Dresser Industries PAC (DIPAC) <br> Dallas, TX | Oilfield Services | $66,500 | 74 Candidates <br> Avg House: $630 <br> Avg Sen: $1,576 | Repubs: 81.5% <br> House: 50.2% <br> Incumb: 95.6% | |
| **Duke Power Co** <br> Employees Federal PAC - Duke Power Company <br> Charlotte, NC | Electric Utilities | $66,960 | 57 Candidates <br> Avg House: $992 <br> Avg Sen: $2,150 | Repubs: 65.4% <br> House: 71.1% <br> Incumb: 86.9% | |
| **Dun & Bradstreet** <br> PAC of the Dun & Bradstreet Corporation <br> Washington, DC | Market Research† | $152,198 | 117 Candidates <br> Avg House: $697 <br> Avg Sen: $2,508 | Repubs: 65.8% <br> Senate: 64.3% <br> Incumb: 93.6% | |
| **Dyncorp** <br> Dyncorp Federal PAC (fka Dynalectron Corporation Fed PAC) <br> Reston, VA | Air Defense† | $56,300 | 47 Candidates <br> Avg House: $1,008 <br> Avg Sen: $1,818 | Repubs: 55.1% <br> House: 64.5% <br> Incumb: 96.9% | |
| **E-Systems/Corporate Div** <br> E-Systems Corporate Division PAC <br> Dallas, TX | E-Systems <br> Defense | $110,361 | 128 Candidates <br> Avg House: $804 <br> Avg Sen: $1,226 | Repubs: 64.5% <br> House: 76.5% <br> Incumb: 90.4% | |
| **Eastern Airlines** <br> Eastern Airlines PAC <br> Miami, FL | Continental Airlines <br> Airlines | $63,190 | 53 Candidates <br> Avg House: $983 <br> Avg Sen: $1,599 | Dems: 54.6% <br> House: 54.4% <br> Incumb: 95.3% | |
| **Eaton Corp** <br> Eaton Corporation Public Policy Association <br> Cleveland, OH | Auto Equipment† | $158,700 | 88 Candidates <br> Avg House: $1,443 <br> Avg Sen: $3,885 | Repubs: 92.3% <br> House: 68.2% <br> Incumb: 49.9% | |
| **Edison Electric Institute** <br> Power PAC of the Edison Electric Institute <br> Washington, DC | Electric Utilities | $65,600 | 137 Candidates <br> Avg House: $446 <br> Avg Sen: $694 | Repubs: 59.1% <br> House: 81.0% <br> Incumb: 96.3% | |
| **Effective Government Committee** <br> Effective Government Committee <br> Washington, DC | Rep Richard Gephardt (D-Mo) <br> Dem Leaders | $252,000 | 75 Candidates <br> Avg House: $3,310 <br> Avg Sen: $4,250 | Dems: 100.0% <br> House: 93.3% <br> Incumb: 42.9% | |

† PAC sponsor has other major interests in addition to this primary category

317

**Electron Mach Furn Workers**
IUE Cmte on Pol Educ Int'l Union/Electronic Electrical Tech Salaried Mach Workers AFL-CIO
Washington, DC

| | |
|---|---|
| Communic Unions† | |

$226,648

| | | |
|---|---|---|
| 140 Candidates | Dems: | 98.6% |
| Avg House: $1,285 | House: | 69.7% |
| Avg Sen: $4,035 | Incumb: | 62.3% |

**Electronic Data Systems**
Electronic Data Systems Employees' PAC
Washington, DC     General Motors     Computer Services

$85,341

| | | |
|---|---|---|
| 98 Candidates | Dems: | 50.4% |
| Avg House: $738 | House: | 67.5% |
| Avg Sen: $1,388 | Incumb: | 93.8% |

**Eli Lilly & Co**
Eli Lilly and Company PAC
Indianapolis, IN     Pharmaceuticals†

$175,740

| | | |
|---|---|---|
| 145 Candidates | Repubs: | 68.9% |
| Avg House: $787 | House: | 51.1% |
| Avg Sen: $2,774 | Incumb: | 92.0% |

**Emerson Electric**
Emerson Electric Co. PAC ("EMPAC")
St. Louis, MO     Industrial Equipment†

$63,000

| | | |
|---|---|---|
| 68 Candidates | Repubs: | 54.3% |
| Avg House: $682 | House: | 59.5% |
| Avg Sen: $1,962 | Incumb: | 99.6% |

**Emily's List**
Emily's List
Washington, DC     Womens Issues

$71,013

| | | |
|---|---|---|
| 14 Candidates | Dems: | 100.0% |
| Avg House: $4,894 | House: | 89.6% |
| Avg Sen: $7,392 | Incumb: | 26.5% |

**Employee Stock Ownership Assn**
Employee Stock Ownership Association Inc PAC
Washington, DC     Financial Services

$56,275

| | | |
|---|---|---|
| 64 Candidates | Repubs: | 51.7% |
| Avg House: $703 | House: | 65.0% |
| Avg Sen: $1,642 | Incumb: | 99.1% |

**Enserch Corp**
Enserch Corporation Employees Political Support Association
Dallas, TX     Natural Gas†

$110,528

| | | |
|---|---|---|
| 101 Candidates | Dems: | 64.2% |
| Avg House: $786 | House: | 53.3% |
| Avg Sen: $1,985 | Incumb: | 93.3% |

**Equitable Financial Services**
Equitable Financial Services PAC (EQUI-PAC)
New York, NY     Equitable Life     Insurance†

$175,550

| | | |
|---|---|---|
| 112 Candidates | Dems: | 67.5% |
| Avg House: $1,227 | Senate: | 50.4% |
| Avg Sen: $2,156 | Incumb: | 97.6% |

**Ernst & Young**
Ernst & Young PAC
Washington, DC     Ernst & Young     Accountants

$81,611

| | | |
|---|---|---|
| 96 Candidates | Dems: | 59.0% |
| Avg House: $758 | House: | 74.3% |
| Avg Sen: $1,313 | Incumb: | 95.7% |

**Ernst & Young**
Federal Arthur Young & Company PAC
New York, NY     Ernst & Young     Accountants

$53,050

| | | |
|---|---|---|
| 47 Candidates | Dems: | 59.5% |
| Avg House: $971 | House: | 53.1% |
| Avg Sen: $1,383 | Incumb: | 97.2% |

**Exxon Corp**
Exxon Corporation PAC (EXPAC)
Houston, TX     Oil & Gas Prod†

$188,660

| | | |
|---|---|---|
| 209 Candidates | Repubs: | 75.7% |
| Avg House: $572 | House: | 55.8% |
| Avg Sen: $3,479 | Incumb: | 86.7% |

**Family Health Program Inc**
FHP Healthcare PAC
Fountain Valley, CA     HMOs

$52,700

| | | |
|---|---|---|
| 46 Candidates | Dems: | 55.9% |
| Avg House: $1,025 | House: | 73.9% |
| Avg Sen: $1,719 | Incumb: | 98.1% |

**Farm Credit Council**
Farm Credit PAC
Washington, DC     Ag Services

$105,107

| | | |
|---|---|---|
| 160 Candidates | Dems: | 55.2% |
| Avg House: $579 | House: | 74.9% |
| Avg Sen: $1,098 | Incumb: | 98.6% |

**Farmland Industries**
Farmland Industries PAC (Farmland/PAC)
Kansas City, MO     Ag Services†

$50,200

| | | |
|---|---|---|
| 50 Candidates | Repubs: | 57.9% |
| Avg House: $954 | House: | 64.6% |
| Avg Sen: $1,109 | Incumb: | 99.5% |

**Federal Express Corp**
Federal Express Corporation PAC "FEPAC"
Memphis, TN     Express Delivery

$757,150

| | | |
|---|---|---|
| 221 Candidates | Dems: | 63.2% |
| Avg House: $3,113 | House: | 62.9% |
| Avg Sen: $4,129 | Incumb: | 98.0% |

**Federal Managers' Assn**
Federal Managers' Association PAC
Washington, DC     Federal Workers

$64,325

| | | |
|---|---|---|
| 86 Candidates | Dems: | 72.4% |
| Avg House: $673 | House: | 71.2% |
| Avg Sen: $1,031 | Incumb: | 94.9% |

**Federal National Mortgage Assn**
Federal National Mortgage Association PAC ("Fannie PAC")
Washington, DC     Mortgage Banking

$51,950

| | | |
|---|---|---|
| 58 Candidates | Dems: | 82.4% |
| Avg House: $871 | House: | 72.1% |
| Avg Sen: $967 | Incumb: | 98.3% |

**Federation of American Hospitals**
Federation of American Health Systems PAC
Washington, DC     Hospitals

$174,350

| | | |
|---|---|---|
| 130 Candidates | Dems: | 67.9% |
| Avg House: $998 | House: | 55.0% |
| Avg Sen: $2,309 | Incumb: | 94.2% |

**First Boston Corp**
First Boston Corporation PAC (FB-PAC)
New York, NY     Investment Banking

$84,500

| | | |
|---|---|---|
| 57 Candidates | Dems: | 72.2% |
| Avg House: $1,571 | House: | 78.1% |
| Avg Sen: $1,233 | Incumb: | 95.3% |

| PAC Sponsor or Related Group/PAC Name | Affiliate | 1989-90 Total | Where the money went... | | |
|---|---|---|---|---|---|

**First Chicago Corp**
First Chicago Corp Government Affairs c/o the First National Bank of Chicago
Chicago, IL — Commercial Banks — **$149,121**

| 119 Candidates | Dems: 62.0% |
|---|---|
| Avg House: $1,057 | House: 63.8% |
| Avg Sen: $1,863 | Incumb: 95.7% |

**First Union Corp**
First Union Corporation Employees Good Government "F" Fund
Charlotte, NC — Mortgage Banking — **$61,700**

| 40 Candidates | Dems: 78.8% |
|---|---|
| Avg House: $845 | Senate: 57.5% |
| Avg Sen: $3,945 | Incumb: 54.9% |

**Florida Congressional Committee**
Florida Congressional Committee
Miami, FL — Pro-Israel — **$130,000**

| 53 Candidates | Dems: 60.8% |
|---|---|
| Avg House: $970 | Senate: 75.4% |
| Avg Sen: $4,900 | Incumb: 91.4% |

**Florida Medical Assn**
Florida Medical PAC
Jacksonville, FL — American Medical Assn — Doctors — **$57,825**

| 21 Candidates | Repubs: 63.4% |
|---|---|
| Avg House: $2,909 | House: 100.6% |
| Avg Sen: $-350 | Incumb: 68.4% |

**Florida Power & Light**
Good Government Management Assn Florida Power & Light Company Employee's PAC
Juno Beach, FL — Electric Utilities† — **$57,750**

| 83 Candidates | Repubs: 51.6% |
|---|---|
| Avg House: $577 | House: 66.9% |
| Avg Sen: $1,194 | Incumb: 89.5% |

**Florida Sugar Cane League**
Florida Sugar Cane League PAC
Clewiston, FL — Sugar — **$175,650**

| 236 Candidates | Dems: 63.1% |
|---|---|
| Avg House: $668 | House: 77.6% |
| Avg Sen: $1,230 | Incumb: 97.2% |

**Flowers Industries**
Flowers Industries Inc PAC
Thomasville, GA — Food Processing — **$128,500**

| 31 Candidates | Repubs: 98.0% |
|---|---|
| Avg House: $3,167 | Senate: 63.0% |
| Avg Sen: $5,063 | Incumb: 65.8% |

**Fluor Corp**
Fluor Corporation Public Affairs Committee (Fluor PAC)
Irvine, CA — Comml Construction† — **$305,843**

| 141 Candidates | Repubs: 60.7% |
|---|---|
| Avg House: $1,530 | House: 51.5% |
| Avg Sen: $3,901 | Incumb: 96.0% |

**FMC Corp**
FMC Corporation Good Government Program
Chicago, IL — Chemicals† — **$336,540**

| 231 Candidates | Repubs: 73.8% |
|---|---|
| Avg House: $1,020 | House: 59.1% |
| Avg Sen: $3,825 | Incumb: 86.3% |

**Food & Commercial Workers Union**
Active Ballot Club, a Dept of United Food & Commercial Workers Int'l Union
Washington, DC — Retail Unions† — **$935,281**

| 347 Candidates | Dems: 97.6% |
|---|---|
| Avg House: $2,419 | House: 80.2% |
| Avg Sen: $5,086 | Incumb: 61.7% |

**Food Marketing Institute**
Food Marketing Institute PAC (FOOD PAC)
Washington, DC — Food Stores — **$376,572**

| 288 Candidates | Repubs: 64.6% |
|---|---|
| Avg House: $1,098 | House: 72.6% |
| Avg Sen: $2,648 | Incumb: 91.2% |

**Ford Motor Co**
Ford Motor Company Civic Action Fund
Detroit, MI — Ford Motor Co — Auto Mfrs† — **$231,350**

| 223 Candidates | Dems: 53.3% |
|---|---|
| Avg House: $848 | House: 72.2% |
| Avg Sen: $2,471 | Incumb: 99.2% |

**Fox Inc**
FoxPAC (Fox Inc and Subsidiaries) (fka Twentieth Century Fox PAC)
Beverly Hills, CA — Movies/TV — **$50,650**

| 45 Candidates | Dems: 85.3% |
|---|---|
| Avg House: $1,152 | House: 54.6% |
| Avg Sen: $1,095 | Incumb: 97.0% |

**Free Cuba PAC**
Free Cuba PAC Inc
Miami, FL — Anti-Castro — **$114,127**

| 49 Candidates | Dems: 59.3% |
|---|---|
| Avg House: $1,548 | Senate: 58.0% |
| Avg Sen: $3,675 | Incumb: 90.9% |

**Freeport-McMoRan Inc**
Freeport-McMoRan Inc Citizenship Committee
Washington, DC — Metal Mining/Process† — **$148,650**

| 128 Candidates | Dems: 50.6% |
|---|---|
| Avg House: $885 | Senate: 50.6% |
| Avg Sen: $1,671 | Incumb: 95.6% |

**Fulbright & Jaworski**
Freedom Fund; The
Houston, TX — Lawyers — **$53,050**

| 51 Candidates | Dems: 68.8% |
|---|---|
| Avg House: $959 | House: 61.5% |
| Avg Sen: $1,203 | Incumb: 80.2% |

**Fund for a Democratic Majority**
Fund for a Democratic Majority
Washington, DC — Sen Edward Kennedy (D-Mass) — Dem Leaders — **$117,000**

| 24 Candidates | Dems: 100.0% |
|---|---|
| Avg House: $1,438 | Senate: 90.2% |
| Avg Sen: $6,594 | Incumb: 67.5% |

**Garden State PAC**
Garden State PAC
Roseland, NJ — Pro-Israel — **$87,450**

| 57 Candidates | Dems: 58.9% |
|---|---|
| Avg House: $846 | Senate: 64.2% |
| Avg Sen: $2,808 | Incumb: 93.5% |

**GenCorp Inc**
GenCorp Inc PAC (GENPAC)
Fairlawn, OH — Air Defense† — **$94,075**

| 86 Candidates | Dems: 61.7% |
|---|---|
| Avg House: $964 | House: 68.6% |
| Avg Sen: $1,553 | Incumb: 95.9% |

† PAC sponsor has other major interests in addition to this primary category

319

| | | | | |
|---|---|---|---|---|
| **General American Life Insurance**<br>General American Life Insurance Co Associates Federal PAC<br>St. Louis, MO | Insurance | **$53,800** | 32 Candidates<br>Avg House: $1,822<br>Avg Sen: $1,500 | Dems: 56.3%<br>House: 61.0%<br>Incumb: 100.0% |
| **General Atomics**<br>General Atomics PAC<br>San Diego, CA | Nuclear Power Equip† | **$97,000** | 56 Candidates<br>Avg House: $1,577<br>Avg Sen: $2,088 | Dems: 58.6%<br>House: 63.4%<br>Incumb: 92.5% |
| **General Dynamics**<br>General Dynamics Corporation Voluntary Political Contribution Plan<br>St. Louis, MO | Air Defense† | **$370,631** | 197 Candidates<br>Avg House: $1,518<br>Avg Sen: $3,686 | Dems: 57.9%<br>House: 67.2%<br>Incumb: 96.2% |
| **General Electric**<br>Non-Partisan Political Support Committee for General Electric Company Employees<br>Fairfield, CT      General Electric | Manufacturing† | **$360,825** | 310 Candidates<br>Avg House: $846<br>Avg Sen: $2,361 | Dems: 60.1%<br>House: 57.5%<br>Incumb: 96.1% |
| **General Mills**<br>General Mills Inc PAC (GM PAC)<br>Minneapolis, MN      General Mills | Food Processing† | **$97,250** | 72 Candidates<br>Avg House: $967<br>Avg Sen: $2,029 | Repubs: 66.6%<br>Senate: 54.2%<br>Incumb: 79.4% |
| **General Mills Restaurants**<br>General Mills Restaurants, Inc Employees Good Govt Fund (aka) Red Lobster Emp Govt Fd<br>Orlando, FL      General Mills | Restaurants | **$76,249** | 79 Candidates<br>Avg House: $776<br>Avg Sen: $1,455 | Repubs: 62.0%<br>House: 58.0%<br>Incumb: 83.6% |
| **General Motors**<br>Civic Involvement Program/General Motors Corporation<br>Detroit, MI      General Motors | Auto Mfrs† | **$259,900** | 239 Candidates<br>Avg House: $723<br>Avg Sen: $3,140 | Repubs: 64.3%<br>House: 56.5%<br>Incumb: 96.9% |
| **General Public Utilities**<br>General Public Utilities Political Participation Association<br>Washington, DC | Electric Utilities | **$56,326** | 70 Candidates<br>Avg House: $743<br>Avg Sen: $1,104 | Dems: 51.2%<br>House: 76.5%<br>Incumb: 96.5% |
| **Georgia Power Co**<br>Georgia Power Company Federal PAC Inc<br>Atlanta, GA      Southern Co | Electric Utilities | **$58,800** | 102 Candidates<br>Avg House: $560<br>Avg Sen: $645 | Dems: 69.2%<br>House: 78.1%<br>Incumb: 93.9% |
| **Georgia-Pacific Corp**<br>G-P Employees Fund of Georgia-Pacific Corporation<br>Washington, DC | Forest Products | **$109,147** | 96 Candidates<br>Avg House: $653<br>Avg Sen: $2,313 | Repubs: 64.2%<br>Senate: 59.3%<br>Incumb: 95.1% |
| **Glaxo Inc**<br>Glaxo Inc Democracy Fund<br>Research Triangle, NC | Pharmaceuticals | **$105,850** | 82 Candidates<br>Avg House: $970<br>Avg Sen: $2,355 | Dems: 54.3%<br>House: 57.7%<br>Incumb: 97.6% |
| **Goldman, Sachs & Co**<br>GSMMI Holdings Inc PAC aka Goldman Sachs PAC<br>Washington, DC | Investment Banking | **$169,800** | 120 Candidates<br>Avg House: $1,181<br>Avg Sen: $2,222 | Dems: 67.4%<br>House: 64.7%<br>Incumb: 93.9% |
| **WR Grace & Co**<br>W R Grace & Co PAC (GracePAC)<br>New York, NY | Chemicals† | **$116,547** | 122 Candidates<br>Avg House: $758<br>Avg Sen: $1,851 | Repubs: 55.0%<br>House: 65.1%<br>Incumb: 97.0% |
| **Graphic Communications Union**<br>Graphic Communications International Union Political Contributions Committee<br>Washington, DC | Communic. Unions | **$59,600** | 69 Candidates<br>Avg House: $759<br>Avg Sen: $1,480 | Dems: 99.2%<br>House: 75.2%<br>Incumb: 71.1% |
| **Great Western Financial Corp**<br>Great Western Financial Corporation Good Government Committee<br>Beverly Hills, CA | Savings & Loans | **$87,850** | 69 Candidates<br>Avg House: $1,315<br>Avg Sen: $1,107 | Dems: 58.2%<br>House: 82.4%<br>Incumb: 97.7% |
| **Greater Washington Board of Trade**<br>Greater Washington Board of Trade Federal PAC<br>Washington, DC | Chamber of Commerce | **$55,400** | 26 Candidates<br>Avg House: $1,970<br>Avg Sen: $2,667 | Dems: 56.7%<br>House: 71.1%<br>Incumb: 90.3% |
| **Greyhound Dial**<br>Greyhound Dial Good Government Project<br>Phoenix, AZ | Household Chemicals† | **$120,175** | 134 Candidates<br>Avg House: $690<br>Avg Sen: $1,717 | Repubs: 70.4%<br>House: 61.4%<br>Incumb: 89.2% |
| **Grumman Corp**<br>Grumman PAC<br>Bethpage, NY | Air Defense† | **$264,075** | 205 Candidates<br>Avg House: $1,101<br>Avg Sen: $1,995 | Dems: 59.5%<br>House: 67.5%<br>Incumb: 98.2% |
| **GTE Corp**<br>GTE Corporation Political Action Club (GTE PAC)<br>Washington, DC      GTE | Phone Utilities† | **$369,430** | 310 Candidates<br>Avg House: $1,018<br>Avg Sen: $2,366 | Repubs: 51.1%<br>House: 74.4%<br>Incumb: 90.0% |

**Hallmark Cards**
Hallmark PAC-Federal HallPAC-Federal
Kansas City, MO
Greeting Cards
$74,250

| 46 Candidates | | Repubs: 84.9% |
| Avg House: $769 | | Senate: 72.0% |
| Avg Sen: $2,816 | | Incumb: 97.0% |

**Handgun Control Inc**
Handgun Control Voter Education Fund
Washington, DC
Anti-Guns
$149,968

| 157 Candidates | | Dems: 87.1% |
| Avg House: $765 | | House: 72.4% |
| Avg Sen: $2,760 | | Incumb: 82.3% |

**Hardee's Food Systems**
Hardee's Food Systems Inc Good Government Fund
Rocky Mount, NC
Restaurants
$55,300

| 62 Candidates | | Repubs: 71.1% |
| Avg House: $732 | | House: 70.2% |
| Avg Sen: $1,833 | | Incumb: 75.6% |

**Harris Corp**
Harris Corporation-Federal PAC
Melbourne, FL
Electronics†
$226,500

| 113 Candidates | | Repubs: 96.9% |
| Avg House: $1,220 | | Senate: 51.0% |
| Avg Sen: $5,250 | | Incumb: 78.1% |

**Harsco Corp**
Harsco Corporation PAC
Camp Hill, PA
Weapons†
$51,900

| 69 Candidates | | Dems: 61.8% |
| Avg House: $688 | | House: 75.5% |
| Avg Sen: $1,058 | | Incumb: 99.0% |

**Hartford Insurance**
Hartford Insurance Group - PAC
Hartford, CT — ITT Corp
Insurance
$73,900

| 71 Candidates | | Dems: 64.8% |
| Avg House: $853 | | House: 56.6% |
| Avg Sen: $1,459 | | Incumb: 94.3% |

**Hawaiian Sugar Planters Assn**
Hawaiian Sugar Planters' Association-PAC (Hawaiian Sugar-PAC)
Aiea, HI
Sugar
$81,975

| 165 Candidates | | Dems: 62.8% |
| Avg House: $417 | | House: 70.2% |
| Avg Sen: $904 | | Incumb: 96.3% |

**Health Insurance Assn of America**
Health Insurance PAC of the Health Insurance Association
Washington, DC
Health Insurance
$156,125

| 175 Candidates | | Dems: 51.8% |
| Avg House: $698 | | House: 58.5% |
| Avg Sen: $1,472 | | Incumb: 98.2% |

**Heartland PAC**
Heartland PAC Fka: Youngstown PAC
Washington, DC
Pro-Israel
$73,250

| 42 Candidates | | Dems: 69.3% |
| Avg House: $679 | | Senate: 80.5% |
| Avg Sen: $2,810 | | Incumb: 89.8% |

**Henley Group Inc**
Henley Group Inc Employees Committee for Sensible Government
Hampton, NH
Medical Supplies†
$98,750

| 50 Candidates | | Dems: 58.8% |
| Avg House: $1,602 | | House: 51.9% |
| Avg Sen: $2,639 | | Incumb: 90.9% |

**Hoechst Celanese Corp**
Hoechst Celanese Corporation PAC (Hoechst Celanese PAC)
Somerville, NJ
Synthetic Fibers†
$137,800

| 106 Candidates | | Repubs: 63.0% |
| Avg House: $1,004 | | House: 61.9% |
| Avg Sen: $2,500 | | Incumb: 89.6% |

**Hoffmann-La Roche**
Hoffmann-La Roche Inc Good Government Committee
Nutley, NJ
Pharmaceuticals†
$57,750

| 62 Candidates | | Repubs: 58.4% |
| Avg House: $780 | | House: 67.5% |
| Avg Sen: $1,563 | | Incumb: 98.4% |

**Holiday Inns**
Inn/PAC Int'l Assn of Holiday Inns Inc PAC
Memphis, TN — Bass PLC
Hotels/Motels
$59,000

| 81 Candidates | | Repubs: 72.0% |
| Avg House: $629 | | House: 74.6% |
| Avg Sen: $1,364 | | Incumb: 89.5% |

**Holland & Knight**
Holland & Knight Committee for Effective Government
Washington, DC
Lawyers/Lobbyists
$82,200

| 68 Candidates | | Dems: 68.1% |
| Avg House: $947 | | House: 55.3% |
| Avg Sen: $1,838 | | Incumb: 88.3% |

**Hollywood Women's Political Committee**
Hollywood Women's Political Committee
Culver City, CA
Dem/Liberal†
$107,000

| 35 Candidates | | Dems: 99.1% |
| Avg House: $2,288 | | House: 55.6% |
| Avg Sen: $5,278 | | Incumb: 53.7% |

**Home Shopping Network Inc**
Home Shopping Network Inc PAC (HSN PAC)
Clearwater, FL
Cable TV
$80,000

| 28 Candidates | | Dems: 59.4% |
| Avg House: $2,500 | | Senate: 53.1% |
| Avg Sen: $3,269 | | Incumb: 96.3% |

**Honeywell Inc**
Honeywell Employee Citizenship Fund
Minneapolis, MN
Aerospace/Electronics†
$51,126

| 47 Candidates | | Repubs: 75.8% |
| Avg House: $853 | | Senate: 53.3% |
| Avg Sen: $1,434 | | Incumb: 91.2% |

**Hotel/Restaurant Employees Union**
Hotel Employees & Restaurant Employees Int'l Union T I P - "To Insure Progress"
Washington, DC
Food Service Unions
$230,225

| 213 Candidates | | Dems: 92.6% |
| Avg House: $952 | | House: 72.8% |
| Avg Sen: $1,692 | | Incumb: 88.0% |

**House Leadership Fund**
House Leadership Fund; The
Washington, DC — Rep Thomas Foley (D-Wash)
Dem Leaders
$204,719

| 65 Candidates | | Dems: 98.5% |
| Avg House: $3,202 | | House: 98.5% |
| Avg Sen: $1,500 | | Incumb: 46.0% |

† PAC sponsor has other major interests in addition to this primary category

| PAC Sponsor or Related Group / PAC Name / Location | Affiliate | 1989-90 Total | Where the money went... | | |
|---|---|---|---|---|---|
| **Household International**<br>Household International Inc & Subsidiary Companies PAC (HousePAC)<br>Prospect Heights, IL | Credit/Loans† | $129,350 | 90 Candidates<br>Avg House: $1,035<br>Avg Sen: $2,758 | Dems: 53.2%<br>House: 55.2%<br>Incumb: 89.5% | |
| **Houston Industries**<br>Houston Industries PAC<br>Houston, TX | Electric Utilities† | $76,500 | 31 Candidates<br>Avg House: $2,328<br>Avg Sen: $4,500 | Dems: 60.1%<br>House: 88.2%<br>Incumb: 81.0% | |
| **Hudson Valley PAC**<br>Hudson Valley PAC<br>Spring Valley, NY | Pro-Israel | $231,254 | 126 Candidates<br>Avg House: $1,066<br>Avg Sen: $4,527 | Dems: 56.8%<br>Senate: 54.8%<br>Incumb: 88.6% | |
| **Hughes Aircraft**<br>Hughes Aircraft Company Active Citizenship Fund (aka Hughes Active Citizenship Fund)<br>Los Angeles, CA  General Motors | Defense† | $272,650 | 202 Candidates<br>Avg House: $1,098<br>Avg Sen: $2,852 | Repubs: 50.7%<br>House: 69.7%<br>Incumb: 98.6% | |
| **Human Rights Campaign Fund**<br>Human Rights Campaign Fund PAC<br>Washington, DC | Gay/Lesbian | $475,621 | 133 Candidates<br>Avg House: $3,337<br>Avg Sen: $5,984 | Dems: 83.6%<br>House: 84.9%<br>Incumb: 63.8% | |
| **ICI Americas Inc**<br>ICI Americas Inc PAC<br>Wilmington, DE | Pharmaceuticals† | $79,925 | 125 Candidates<br>Avg House: $562<br>Avg Sen: $1,000 | Dems: 57.3%<br>House: 72.5%<br>Incumb: 100.0% | |
| **Illinois Bell Telephone**<br>Illinois Bell Citizenship Responsibility Committee<br>Chicago, IL  Ameritech | Phone Utilities | $63,250 | 19 Candidates<br>Avg House: $3,484<br>Avg Sen: $2,500 | Repubs: 61.3%<br>House: 88.1%<br>Incumb: 89.4% | |
| **Independent Action**<br>Independent Action Inc<br>Washington, DC | Dem/Liberal | $180,490 | 75 Candidates<br>Avg House: $1,784<br>Avg Sen: $4,008 | Dems: 99.5%<br>House: 53.4%<br>Incumb: 26.6% | |
| **Independent Bankers Assn**<br>Independent Bankers Association of America PAC (IBAA PAC)<br>Washington, DC | Commercial Banks | $238,080 | 207 Candidates<br>Avg House: $963<br>Avg Sen: $1,826 | Dems: 56.4%<br>House: 65.5%<br>Incumb: 93.3% | |
| **Independent Insurance Agents of America**<br>Independent Insurance Agents of America Inc PAC (INSURPAC)<br>Washington, DC | Insurance | $676,335 | 317 Candidates<br>Avg House: $1,812<br>Avg Sen: $3,432 | Dems: 58.5%<br>House: 68.0%<br>Incumb: 89.8% | |
| **International Assn of Drilling Contractors**<br>International Association of Drilling Contractors PAC<br>Houston, TX | Oilfield Services | $50,150 | 34 Candidates<br>Avg House: $1,115<br>Avg Sen: $2,227 | Repubs: 71.4%<br>House: 51.1%<br>Incumb: 92.2% | |
| **International Assn of Firefighters**<br>International Association of Firefighters Interested in Registration and Education PAC<br>Washington, DC | Public Safety Union | $206,380 | 220 Candidates<br>Avg House: $843<br>Avg Sen: $1,616 | Dems: 92.7%<br>House: 78.9%<br>Incumb: 72.3% | |
| **International Brotherhood of Electrical Workers (IBEW)**<br>International Brotherhood of Electrical Workers Committee on Political Education<br>Washington, DC | IBEW | $1,214,410 | 322 Candidates<br>Avg House: $3,517<br>Avg Sen: $5,564 | Dems: 97.5%<br>House: 81.7%<br>Incumb: 61.3% | |
| **International Council of Shopping Centers**<br>International Council of Shopping Centers Inc PAC (ICSC PAC)<br>Alexandria, VA | Retail | $198,800 | 122 Candidates<br>Avg House: $1,219<br>Avg Sen: $3,074 | Repubs: 62.0%<br>House: 58.3%<br>Incumb: 94.2% | |
| **International Longshoremen & Warehousemen's Union**<br>International Longshoremen's & Warehousemen's Union - Political Action Fund<br>San Francisco, CA | Sea Transport Unions | $72,050 | 45 Candidates<br>Avg House: $1,453<br>Avg Sen: $2,195 | Dems: 97.9%<br>House: 72.6%<br>Incumb: 76.5% | |
| **International Longshoremen's Assn**<br>International Longshoremen's Association AFL-CIO Committee on Political Education ILA-COPE<br>New York, NY | Sea Transport Unions | $138,870 | 71 Candidates<br>Avg House: $1,923<br>Avg Sen: $2,136 | Dems: 84.4%<br>House: 83.1%<br>Incumb: 88.1% | |
| **International Paper Co**<br>Voluntary Contributors for Better Government: Employees of International Paper Company<br>Washington, DC | Paper/Forest Prod | $224,190 | 91 Candidates<br>Avg House: $1,319<br>Avg Sen: $5,848 | Repubs: 81.6%<br>Senate: 60.0%<br>Incumb: 85.0% | |
| **Internorth Inc**<br>Enron PAC (fka HNG/Internorth PAC)<br>Houston, TX | Natural Gas† | $128,750 | 140 Candidates<br>Avg House: $660<br>Avg Sen: $1,834 | Repubs: 58.3%<br>House: 55.8%<br>Incumb: 92.6% | |
| **Interstate Natural Gas Assn**<br>Interstate Natural Gas Association of America PAC<br>Washington, DC | Natural Gas | $71,717 | 79 Candidates<br>Avg House: $635<br>Avg Sen: $1,496 | Dems: 64.5%<br>Senate: 52.2%<br>Incumb: 97.2% | |

| PAC Sponsor or Related Group/PAC Name | Affiliate | 1989-90 Total | Candidates | | Where the money went |
|---|---|---|---|---|---|
| **Investment Company Institute**<br>Investment Management Political Action Cmte of the Investment Company Institute (IMPAC)<br>Washington, DC | Securities Invest | $117,750 | 70 Candidates<br>Avg House: $1,522<br>Avg Sen: $2,458 | Dems: 84.3%<br>House: 75.0%<br>Incumb: 99.1% | |
| **Ironworkers Union**<br>Ironworkers Political Action League<br>Washington, DC | Constr Unions | $410,349 | 154 Candidates<br>Avg House: $2,506<br>Avg Sen: $3,671 | Dems: 95.9%<br>House: 81.2%<br>Incumb: 63.3% | |
| **ITEL Corp**<br>ITEL Corporation PAC<br>Chicago, IL | Railroad Services† | $80,916 | 53 Candidates<br>Avg House: $1,055<br>Avg Sen: $2,617 | Dems: 72.1%<br>Senate: 51.7%<br>Incumb: 98.8% | |
| **ITT Corp**<br>Corporate Citizenship Committee (ITT)<br>New York, NY | ITT Corp / Insurance† | $92,150 | 141 Candidates<br>Avg House: $510<br>Avg Sen: $1,320 | Repubs: 65.4%<br>House: 64.2%<br>Incumb: 94.9% | |
| **Johnson & Johnson**<br>Johnson & Johnson Employees' Good Government Fund<br>New Brunswick, NJ | Health Care Products† | $72,325 | 76 Candidates<br>Avg House: $800<br>Avg Sen: $1,479 | Dems: 54.3%<br>House: 65.2%<br>Incumb: 95.2% | |
| **Joint Action Committee for Political Affairs**<br>Joint Action Committee for Political Affairs<br>Highland Park, IL | Pro-Israel | $206,000 | 101 Candidates<br>Avg House: $1,475<br>Avg Sen: $4,191 | Dems: 94.2%<br>House: 57.3%<br>Incumb: 71.0% | |
| **Jones, Day, Reavis & Pogue**<br>Jones, Day, Reavis & Pogue Good Government Fund<br>Cleveland, OH | Lawyers/Lobbyists | $102,712 | 103 Candidates<br>Avg House: $762<br>Avg Sen: $1,659 | Repubs: 53.4%<br>House: 56.4%<br>Incumb: 94.2% | |
| **K Mart Corp**<br>K Mart Corporation PAC<br>Troy, MI | Department Stores | $64,300 | 165 Candidates<br>Avg House: $309<br>Avg Sen: $1,141 | Repubs: 87.7%<br>House: 71.6%<br>Incumb: 80.3% | |
| **Kansas City Southern**<br>Kansas City Southern Employees PAC<br>Kansas City, MO | Railroads† | $106,470 | 114 Candidates<br>Avg House: $694<br>Avg Sen: $1,637 | Dems: 64.0%<br>House: 55.4%<br>Incumb: 92.4% | |
| **Kellogg Co**<br>Kellogg Better Government Committee<br>Battle Creek, MI | Food Processing | $63,625 | 84 Candidates<br>Avg House: $692<br>Avg Sen: $983 | Dems: 60.8%<br>House: 70.6%<br>Incumb: 96.9% | |
| **KidsPAC**<br>KidsPAC<br>Cambridge, MA | Health/Welfare | $334,350 | 157 Candidates<br>Avg House: $1,295<br>Avg Sen: $5,391 | Dems: 87.7%<br>Senate: 51.6%<br>Incumb: 81.8% | |
| **Kirkland & Ellis**<br>Kirkland & Ellis PAC (fka WSS PAC)<br>Chicago, IL | Lawyers/Lobbyists | $55,832 | 42 Candidates<br>Avg House: $860<br>Avg Sen: $2,020 | Dems: 90.6%<br>Senate: 61.5%<br>Incumb: 98.2% | |
| **Kirkpatrick & Lockhart**<br>Kirkpatrick & Lockhart PAC<br>Pittsburgh, PA | Lawyers/Lobbyists | $56,450 | 55 Candidates<br>Avg House: $827<br>Avg Sen: $1,375 | Dems: 69.9%<br>House: 51.3%<br>Incumb: 94.7% | |
| **Kutak, Rock & Campbell**<br>Kutak Rock & Campbell PAC<br>Washington, DC | Lawyers/Lobbyists | $71,900 | 60 Candidates<br>Avg House: $948<br>Avg Sen: $1,700 | Dems: 80.3%<br>House: 52.7%<br>Incumb: 81.1% | |
| **Laborers' Political League**<br>Laborers' Political League of Laborers' International Union of N A<br>Washington, DC | Laborers Union / Constr Unions | $1,170,215 | 327 Candidates<br>Avg House: $3,292<br>Avg Sen: $5,332 | Dems: 90.9%<br>House: 79.0%<br>Incumb: 73.4% | |
| **Laborers' Western Political League**<br>Laborers' Western Political League<br>Sacramento, CA | Laborers Union / Constr Unions | $179,450 | 41 Candidates<br>Avg House: $4,281<br>Avg Sen: $6,250 | Dems: 100.0%<br>House: 93.0%<br>Incumb: 69.9% | |
| **Ladies Garment Workers Union**<br>International Ladies Garment Workers Union Campaign Committee<br>New York, NY | Manufacturing Unions | $290,140 | 285 Candidates<br>Avg House: $868<br>Avg Sen: $2,167 | Dems: 94.3%<br>House: 75.4%<br>Incumb: 82.2% | |
| **Land O'Lakes Inc**<br>Land O'Lake Inc PAC<br>Minneapolis, MN | Ag Chemicals/Dairy† | $92,200 | 57 Candidates<br>Avg House: $1,480<br>Avg Sen: $1,941 | Dems: 58.0%<br>House: 64.2%<br>Incumb: 94.0% | |
| **League of Conservation Voters**<br>League of Conservation Voters<br>Washington, DC | Environment | $152,216 | 81 Candidates<br>Avg House: $1,845<br>Avg Sen: $1,982 | Dems: 88.2%<br>House: 74.0%<br>Incumb: 40.1% | |

† PAC sponsor has other major interests in addition to this primary category

**Liberty Mutual Insurance**
Liberty Mutual Insurance Company PAC
Boston, MA — Property Insurance — **$50,950**

| 34 Candidates | Repubs: 85.4% |
| Avg House: $1,028 | Senate: 67.7% |
| Avg Sen: $1,917 | Incumb: 87.2% |

**Litton Industries**
Litton Industries Inc Employees Political Assistance Committee (LEPAC)
Beverly Hills, CA — Defense† — **$175,350**

| 136 Candidates | Repubs: 68.2% |
| Avg House: $1,102 | House: 66.0% |
| Avg Sen: $1,923 | Incumb: 94.3% |

**Lockheed Corp**
Lockheed Employees' PAC
Calabasas, CA — Air Defense† — **$424,909**

| 227 Candidates | Repubs: 57.9% |
| Avg House: $1,502 | House: 67.1% |
| Avg Sen: $3,773 | Incumb: 91.1% |

**Loral Corp**
Civic Action Fund - Loral Systems Group (fka Goodyear Aerospace Corp PAC)
Akron, OH — Defense† — **$81,800**

| 73 Candidates | Dems: 62.2% |
| Avg House: $963 | House: 57.7% |
| Avg Sen: $1,442 | Incumb: 98.7% |

**LTV Aerospace & Defense Co**
LTV Aerospace and Defense Company Active Citizenship Campaign
Dallas, TX — LTV Corp — Air Defense† — **$196,025**

| 137 Candidates | Dems: 64.9% |
| Avg House: $1,216 | House: 68.8% |
| Avg Sen: $2,350 | Incumb: 97.3% |

**Machinists/Aerospace Workers Union**
Machinists Non-partisan Political League
Washington, DC — Machinists/Aerospace Workers — Mfg Unions — **$1,454,595**

| 332 Candidates | Dems: 98.1% |
| Avg House: $4,224 | House: 88.0% |
| Avg Sen: $6,026 | Incumb: 64.7% |

**Maintenance of Way Employees**
Maintenance of Way Political League
Detroit, MI — Railroad Unions — **$177,141**

| 145 Candidates | Dems: 95.7% |
| Avg House: $831 | House: 56.3% |
| Avg Sen: $3,098 | Incumb: 78.8% |

**Malone & Hyde Inc**
Malone & Hyde Inc Committee for Responsible Government
Oklahoma City, OK — Fleming Companies — Food Wholesalers† — **$82,250**

| 57 Candidates | Repubs: 74.2% |
| Avg House: $1,046 | House: 62.3% |
| Avg Sen: $3,875 | Incumb: 82.7% |

**Manatt, Phelps et al**
Golden State PAC (fka Manatt, Phelps, Rothenberg & Tunney PAC)
Los Angeles, CA — Lawyers — **$55,650**

| 70 Candidates | Dems: 71.3% |
| Avg House: $596 | House: 54.6% |
| Avg Sen: $1,329 | Incumb: 99.1% |

**Manufacturers Hanover**
Manufacturers Hanover Association for Responsible Government Fund
New York, NY — Commercial Banks — **$110,825**

| 111 Candidates | Dems: 52.6% |
| Avg House: $872 | House: 64.5% |
| Avg Sen: $1,355 | Incumb: 94.3% |

**Manville Corp**
Manville Corporation PAC
Washington, DC — Forest Products† — **$93,250**

| 84 Candidates | Repubs: 62.7% |
| Avg House: $709 | Senate: 53.6% |
| Avg Sen: $2,174 | Incumb: 98.4% |

**Mapco Inc**
Mapco Employees PAC
Tulsa, OK — Oil Refining/Mktg† — **$102,830**

| 96 Candidates | Repubs: 93.0% |
| Avg House: $586 | Senate: 61.3% |
| Avg Sen: $2,250 | Incumb: 83.0% |

**Marathon Oil**
Marathon Oil Company Employees PAC (MEPAC)
Findlay, OH — USX Corp — Oil & Gas Prod† — **$60,250**

| 58 Candidates | Repubs: 50.5% |
| Avg House: $773 | House: 53.9% |
| Avg Sen: $1,738 | Incumb: 95.4% |

**Marine Engineers District 2 Maritime Officers**
District 2 Marine Engineers Beneficial Assn-Associated Maritime Officers, AFL-CIO PAF
Brooklyn, NY — Marine Engineers Union — Sea Transport Unions — **$603,750**

| 261 Candidates | Dems: 59.8% |
| Avg House: $2,276 | House: 89.0% |
| Avg Sen: $2,660 | Incumb: 94.7% |

**Marine Engineers District 2 Retirees**
District 2 Marine Engineers Beneficial Assn-Assoc Maritime Officers, AFL-CIO, Retirees AF
Brooklyn, NY — Marine Engineers Union — Sea Transport Unions — **$87,500**

| 46 Candidates | Repubs: 81.7% |
| Avg House: $1,663 | House: 76.0% |
| Avg Sen: $3,500 | Incumb: 91.4% |

**Marine Engineers Union**
Marine Engineers' Beneficial Association Political Action Fund Aka (MEBA Pol Action Fund)
Washington, DC — Marine Engineers Union — Sea Transport Unions — **$356,850**

| 167 Candidates | Dems: 75.1% |
| Avg House: $1,931 | House: 72.0% |
| Avg Sen: $2,941 | Incumb: 91.3% |

**Marine Midland Banks**
Marine Midland Banks Inc
Buffalo, NY — Commercial Banks — **$90,668**

| 122 Candidates | Repubs: 56.6% |
| Avg House: $677 | House: 73.2% |
| Avg Sen: $1,011 | Incumb: 83.9% |

**Marriott Corp**
Marriott Corporation PAC
Bethesda, MD — Hotels/Motels† — **$133,700**

| 119 Candidates | Repubs: 60.5% |
| Avg House: $915 | House: 58.9% |
| Avg Sen: $1,667 | Incumb: 91.0% |

**Martin Marietta Corp**
Martin Marietta Corporation PAC
Bethesda, MD — Air Defense† — **$378,760**

| 319 Candidates | Repubs: 54.5% |
| Avg House: $902 | House: 63.8% |
| Avg Sen: $2,689 | Incumb: 89.8% |

**Maryland Assn for Concerned Citizens**
Maryland Association for Concerned Citizens PAC
Pikesville, MD — Pro-Israel — **$90,200**

| 37 Candidates | | Dems: | 67.2% |
| Avg House: $1,248 | | Senate: | 68.2% |
| Avg Sen: $4,393 | | Incumb: | 92.2% |

**Massachusetts Mutual Life Insurance**
Massachusetts Mutual Life Insurance Company PAC
Springfield, MA — Life Insurance — **$199,075**

| 104 Candidates | | Dems: | 72.5% |
| Avg House: $1,750 | | House: | 67.7% |
| Avg Sen: $2,382 | | Incumb: | 94.9% |

**Masters, Mates & Pilots Union**
Masters, Mates and Pilots Political Contribution Fund
Linthicum Heights, MD — Sea Transport Unions — **$154,420**

| 117 Candidates | | Dems: | 77.1% |
| Avg House: $1,241 | | House: | 76.4% |
| Avg Sen: $1,659 | | Incumb: | 99.0% |

**May Department Stores**
May Department Stores Company PAC (MayPAC)
St. Louis, MO — Department Stores — **$127,800**

| 149 Candidates | | Repubs: | 73.5% |
| Avg House: $625 | | House: | 63.6% |
| Avg Sen: $2,447 | | Incumb: | 95.5% |

**Maytag Co**
Maytag Good Government Committee
Newton, IA — Appliances — **$69,100**

| 73 Candidates | | Repubs: | 93.0% |
| Avg House: $752 | | House: | 65.3% |
| Avg Sen: $1,846 | | Incumb: | 60.6% |

**MCA Inc**
MCA PAC
Universal City, CA — Movies† — **$183,400**

| 120 Candidates | | Dems: | 85.7% |
| Avg House: $833 | | Senate: | 61.4% |
| Avg Sen: $3,217 | | Incumb: | 97.5% |

**McDonald's Corp**
McDonald's Corporation PAC
Oak Brook, IL — Restaurants — **$191,500**

| 177 Candidates | | Repubs: | 70.5% |
| Avg House: $597 | | Senate: | 51.7% |
| Avg Sen: $4,500 | | Incumb: | 94.0% |

**McDonnell Douglas**
McDonnell Douglas Corporation Good Government Fund
St. Louis, MO — McDonnell Douglas — Air Defense† — **$295,850**

| 178 Candidates | | Dems: | 50.9% |
| Avg House: $1,438 | | House: | 71.4% |
| Avg Sen: $2,726 | | Incumb: | 98.3% |

**McDonnell Douglas Helicopter**
McDonnell Douglas Helicopter Company PAC
Mesa, AZ — McDonnell Douglas — Air Defense — **$77,250**

| 86 Candidates | | Dems: | 55.9% |
| Avg House: $765 | | House: | 64.3% |
| Avg Sen: $1,312 | | Incumb: | 99.6% |

**MCI Telecommunications**
MCI Telecommunications PAC (MCI PAC)
Washington, DC — Long Distance — **$77,300**

| 113 Candidates | | Dems: | 69.9% |
| Avg House: $535 | | House: | 63.7% |
| Avg Sen: $1,338 | | Incumb: | 97.4% |

**Mead Corp**
Mead Corporation Effective Citizenship Fund
Dayton, OH — Paper Prod† — **$76,000**

| 71 Candidates | | Repubs: | 69.7% |
| Avg House: $725 | | Senate: | 53.3% |
| Avg Sen: $1,841 | | Incumb: | 88.8% |

**Merck & Co**
Merck & Co, Inc PAC (Merck PAC)
Rahway, NJ — Pharmaceuticals† — **$87,900**

| 100 Candidates | | Repubs: | 58.2% |
| Avg House: $630 | | House: | 57.3% |
| Avg Sen: $1,875 | | Incumb: | 91.0% |

**Merrill Lynch**
Merrill Lynch PAC
Washington, DC — Securities Invest† — **$121,555**

| 111 Candidates | | Repubs: | 58.2% |
| Avg House: $767 | | Senate: | 51.4% |
| Avg Sen: $1,838 | | Incumb: | 97.2% |

**Metropolitan Life Insurance**
Metropolitan Life Insurance Company (MetLife) Employees' Political Participation Fund A
New York, NY — Metropolitan Life — Life Insurance† — **$258,812**

| 162 Candidates | | Dems: | 71.9% |
| Avg House: $1,519 | | House: | 72.8% |
| Avg Sen: $1,855 | | Incumb: | 91.6% |

**Michigan Bell Telephone**
Michigan Bell Telephone Company PAC (MICHBELLPAC)
Detroit, MI — Ameritech — Phone Utilities — **$70,080**

| 35 Candidates | | Dems: | 56.2% |
| Avg House: $2,088 | | House: | 83.4% |
| Avg Sen: $1,661 | | Incumb: | 87.7% |

**Michigan Consolidated Gas**
MCN Corporation/Michigan Consolidated Gas Company Federal PAC a/k/a MCN/MichCon
Detroit, MI — Natural Gas — **$67,095**

| 46 Candidates | | Dems: | 68.2% |
| Avg House: $1,138 | | House: | 56.0% |
| Avg Sen: $2,273 | | Incumb: | 95.2% |

**Mid Manhattan PAC**
Mid Manhattan PAC (Mid PAC)
New York, NY — Pro-Israel — **$75,250**

| 48 Candidates | | Dems: | 77.7% |
| Avg House: $680 | | Senate: | 71.1% |
| Avg Sen: $3,344 | | Incumb: | 84.4% |

**Mid-America Dairymen**
Mid-America Dairymen Inc Agricultural & Dairy Educational Political Trust ADEPT
Springfield, MO — Dairy — **$485,950**

| 277 Candidates | | Dems: | 71.1% |
| Avg House: $1,583 | | House: | 80.8% |
| Avg Sen: $3,217 | | Incumb: | 92.3% |

**Milk Industry Foundation**
Ice Cream & Milk PAC, PAC of the Int'l Ice Cream Association & Milk Industry Foundation
Washington, DC — Dairy — **$94,150**

| 77 Candidates | | Repubs: | 69.8% |
| Avg House: $811 | | Senate: | 55.2% |
| Avg Sen: $2,080 | | Incumb: | 99.8% |

† PAC sponsor has other major interests in addition to this primary category

**Milk Marketing Inc**
Milk Marketing Inc PAC
Strongsville, OH — Dairy — **$72,300**

| 68 Candidates | | Dems: | 61.9% |
| Avg House: | $1,059 | House: | 85.0% |
| Avg Sen: | $1,085 | Incumb: | 90.2% |

**Minn-Dak Farmers Co-op**
Minn-Dak Farmers Cooperative PAC (MDFPAC)
Wahpeton, ND — Sugar — **$57,355**

| 95 Candidates | | Dems: | 51.7% |
| Avg House: | $505 | House: | 64.3% |
| Avg Sen: | $931 | Incumb: | 92.9% |

**Minnesota Mining & Manufacturing (3M)**
Minnesota Mining & Manufacturing Company PAC (3M PAC)
St. Paul, MN — Industrial Equipment† — **$91,650**

| 91 Candidates | | Repubs: | 69.7% |
| Avg House: | $672 | House: | 55.7% |
| Avg Sen: | $2,707 | Incumb: | 84.7% |

**MNC Financial Inc**
MNC Financial PAC (MNPAC)
Washington, DC — Commercial Banks — **$58,525**

| 49 Candidates | | Dems: | 66.1% |
| Avg House: | $1,192 | House: | 69.2% |
| Avg Sen: | $1,200 | Incumb: | 91.0% |

**Mobil Oil**
Mobil Oil Corporation PAC (a/k/a Mobil PAC)
Fairfax, VA — Oil & Gas Prod† — **$209,800**

| 194 Candidates | | Repubs: | 86.5% |
| Avg House: | $607 | Senate: | 50.5% |
| Avg Sen: | $4,609 | Incumb: | 86.6% |

**Monsanto Co**
Monsanto Citizenship Fund
St. Louis, MO — Monsanto — Chemicals† — **$90,850**

| 87 Candidates | | Repubs: | 77.4% |
| Avg House: | $706 | House: | 52.0% |
| Avg Sen: | $2,179 | Incumb: | 89.5% |

**Montgomery Ward**
Montgomery Ward & Co Incorporated PAC a/k/a WardPAC
Chicago, IL — Department Stores† — **$79,700**

| 81 Candidates | | Dems: | 59.4% |
| Avg House: | $754 | Senate: | 50.8% |
| Avg Sen: | $1,397 | Incumb: | 95.0% |

**MOPAC**
MOPAC
Troy, MI — Pro-Israel — **$83,300**

| 38 Candidates | | Dems: | 100.0% |
| Avg House: | $839 | Senate: | 76.8% |
| Avg Sen: | $4,267 | Incumb: | 89.1% |

**Morgan Stanley & Co**
Morgan Stanley & Co Incorporated Better Government Fund
New York, NY — Investment Banking† — **$176,250**

| 101 Candidates | | Dems: | 58.6% |
| Avg House: | $1,641 | House: | 70.8% |
| Avg Sen: | $2,060 | Incumb: | 100.0% |

**JP Morgan & Co**
Morgan Companies PAC (MorganPAC)
New York, NY — Commercial Banks — **$403,525**

| 108 Candidates | | Dems: | 54.6% |
| Avg House: | $3,792 | House: | 73.3% |
| Avg Sen: | $3,592 | Incumb: | 99.8% |

**Morrison Inc**
Morrison's PAC
Mobile, AL — Food Services† — **$54,550**

| 86 Candidates | | Repubs: | 87.4% |
| Avg House: | $486 | House: | 62.4% |
| Avg Sen: | $1,281 | Incumb: | 79.3% |

**Mortgage Bankers Assn of America**
Mortgage Bankers Association of America PAC
Washington, DC — Mortgage Banking — **$235,000**

| 251 Candidates | | Repubs: | 50.3% |
| Avg House: | $796 | House: | 69.8% |
| Avg Sen: | $1,578 | Incumb: | 93.4% |

**Motorola Inc**
Motorola Employees Good Government Committee
Washington, DC — Communications Equip† — **$111,720**

| 114 Candidates | | Repubs: | 65.7% |
| Avg House: | $703 | House: | 54.1% |
| Avg Sen: | $1,830 | Incumb: | 88.5% |

**Multi-Issue PAC**
Multi-issue PAC (MI-PAC)
Highland Park, IL — Pro-Israel — **$106,300**

| 59 Candidates | | Dems: | 99.3% |
| Avg House: | $695 | Senate: | 73.2% |
| Avg Sen: | $4,322 | Incumb: | 68.0% |

**Mutual Life Insurance of New York**
Mutual Life Insurance Company of New York MONY PAC
New York, NY — Insurance — **$53,700**

| 40 Candidates | | Dems: | 72.7% |
| Avg House: | $1,231 | House: | 66.5% |
| Avg Sen: | $1,636 | Incumb: | 95.8% |

**Mutual of Omaha**
General Agents Association PAC (COMPAC)
Winston-Salem, NC — Mutual of Omaha — Insurance — **$52,500**

| 89 Candidates | | Repubs: | 81.0% |
| Avg House: | $444 | House: | 60.0% |
| Avg Sen: | $1,167 | Incumb: | 84.8% |

**Nabisco Brands Inc**
Nabisco Brands, Inc Program for Active Citizenship (NABPAC)
East Hanover, NJ — RJR Nabisco — Food Processing — **$83,500**

| 81 Candidates | | Repubs: | 59.6% |
| Avg House: | $847 | House: | 59.9% |
| Avg Sen: | $1,523 | Incumb: | 89.2% |

**National Abortion Rights Action League**
National Abortion Rights Action League - PAC NARAL-PAC
Washington, DC — Pro-Choice — **$384,295**

| 123 Candidates | | Dems: | 89.2% |
| Avg House: | $2,927 | House: | 80.0% |
| Avg Sen: | $4,278 | Incumb: | 49.6% |

**National Action Committee**
National Action Committee - NACPAC
Miami, FL — Pro-Israel — **$103,979**

| 54 Candidates | | Dems: | 70.7% |
| Avg House: | $736 | Senate: | 78.1% |
| Avg Sen: | $3,530 | Incumb: | 90.6% |

| PAC Sponsor or Related Group/PAC Name | Affiliate | 1989-90 Total | Where the money went... | | |
|---|---|---|---|---|---|

**National Albanian American PAC**
National Albanian American PAC
Palm Beach Gardens, FL — Ethnic Group — **$99,671**

| 16 Candidates | | Repubs: 71.4% |
|---|---|---|
| Avg House: $4,117 | Senate: 75.2% |
| Avg Sen: $7,497 | Incumb: 85.0% |

**National Assn of Broadcasters**
National Association of Broadcasters Television and Radio PAC
Washington, DC — TV/Radio — **$277,268**

| 177 Candidates | | Repubs: 53.4% |
|---|---|---|
| Avg House: $1,173 | House: 58.0% |
| Avg Sen: $2,914 | Incumb: 96.1% |

**National Assn of Federal Credit Unions**
National Association of Federal Credit Unions PAC (NAFCUPAC)
Arlington, VA — Credit Unions — **$63,400**

| 75 Candidates | | Dems: 66.6% |
|---|---|---|
| Avg House: $752 | House: 78.2% |
| Avg Sen: $1,533 | Incumb: 98.0% |

**National Assn of Home Builders**
Build PAC of the National Association of Home Builders
Washington, DC — Resid Construction — **$1,358,050**

| 459 Candidates | | Repubs: 51.5% |
|---|---|---|
| Avg House: $2,705 | House: 82.7% |
| Avg Sen: $5,348 | Incumb: 82.1% |

**National Assn of Independent Insurers**
National Association of Independent Insurers PAC
Des Plaines, IL — Insurance — **$254,797**

| 188 Candidates | | Repubs: 78.6% |
|---|---|---|
| Avg House: $710 | Senate: 59.3% |
| Avg Sen: $3,600 | Incumb: 94.4% |

**National Assn of Letter Carriers**
Committee on Letter Carriers Political Education (Letter Carriers Political Action Fund)
Washington, DC — Postal Workers — **$1,730,050**

| 397 Candidates | | Dems: 85.9% |
|---|---|---|
| Avg House: $4,284 | House: 85.2% |
| Avg Sen: $4,840 | Incumb: 80.9% |

**National Assn of Life Underwriters**
National Association of Life Underwriters PAC
Washington, DC — Life Insurance — **$1,487,800**

| 445 Candidates | | Dems: 51.0% |
|---|---|---|
| Avg House: $3,111 | House: 81.5% |
| Avg Sen: $4,991 | Incumb: 82.1% |

**National Assn of Pharmacists**
NARD PAC
Alexandria, VA — Pharmacists — **$163,810**

| 112 Candidates | | Dems: 67.7% |
|---|---|---|
| Avg House: $1,339 | House: 64.6% |
| Avg Sen: $1,758 | Incumb: 91.5% |

**National Assn of Postal Supervisors**
National Association of Postal Supervisors PAC
Washington, DC — Postal Workers — **$101,746**

| 123 Candidates | | Dems: 84.8% |
|---|---|---|
| Avg House: $726 | House: 70.0% |
| Avg Sen: $1,263 | Incumb: 90.7% |

**National Assn of Postmasters**
NAPUS PAC for Postmasters (fka Political Education for Postmasters)
Alexandria, VA — Postal Workers — **$319,551**

| 316 Candidates | | Dems: 81.5% |
|---|---|---|
| Avg House: $902 | House: 74.5% |
| Avg Sen: $1,565 | Incumb: 92.2% |

**National Assn of Private Psychiatric Hospitals**
National Association of Private Psychiatric Hospitals/PAC
Washington, DC — Hospitals — **$74,150**

| 43 Candidates | | Dems: 83.4% |
|---|---|---|
| Avg House: $1,139 | Senate: 58.5% |
| Avg Sen: $2,713 | Incumb: 97.3% |

**National Assn of Professional Insurance Agents**
Professional Insurance Agents PAC
Alexandria, VA — Insurance — **$271,778**

| 202 Candidates | | Repubs: 52.3% |
|---|---|---|
| Avg House: $920 | House: 52.8% |
| Avg Sen: $2,788 | Incumb: 91.6% |

**National Assn of Realtors**
Realtors PAC
Chicago, IL — Real Estate — **$3,094,228**

| 510 Candidates | | Dems: 55.7% |
|---|---|---|
| Avg House: $6,297 | House: 92.0% |
| Avg Sen: $4,277 | Incumb: 90.5% |

**National Assn of Retired Federal Employees**
National Association of Retired Federal Employees PAC (NARFE-PAC)
Washington, DC — Federal Workers — **$1,533,000**

| 410 Candidates | | Dems: 75.7% |
|---|---|---|
| Avg House: $3,698 | House: 87.8% |
| Avg Sen: $4,065 | Incumb: 85.8% |

**National Assn of Social Workers**
Political Action for Candidate Election
Silver Spring, MD — Social Workers — **$176,450**

| 116 Candidates | | Dems: 97.5% |
|---|---|---|
| Avg House: $962 | Senate: 50.4% |
| Avg Sen: $3,558 | Incumb: 54.6% |

**National Assn of Water Companies**
National Association of Water Companies PAC (NAWC - PAC)
Washington, DC — Water Utilities — **$66,400**

| 108 Candidates | | Repubs: 72.5% |
|---|---|---|
| Avg House: $481 | House: 62.4% |
| Avg Sen: $1,136 | Incumb: 98.3% |

**National Assn of Wholesale-Distributors**
Wholesaler-Distributor PAC of the National Association of Wholesale-Distributors
Washington, DC — Wholesale — **$128,172**

| 149 Candidates | | Repubs: 87.3% |
|---|---|---|
| Avg House: $567 | House: 52.7% |
| Avg Sen: $2,022 | Incumb: 84.9% |

**National Auto Dealers Assn**
Dealers Election Action Committee of the National Automobile Dealers Association (NADA)
McLean, VA — Auto Dealers — **$1,313,900**

| 374 Candidates | | Repubs: 62.2% |
|---|---|---|
| Avg House: $3,379 | House: 84.4% |
| Avg Sen: $4,470 | Incumb: 81.4% |

**National Beer Wholesalers Assn**
National Beer Wholesalers' Association PAC (NBWA PAC)
Falls Church, VA — Liquor Wholesalers — **$633,150**

| 323 Candidates | | Dems: 56.7% |
|---|---|---|
| Avg House: $1,594 | House: 67.7% |
| Avg Sen: $3,786 | Incumb: 97.4% |

† PAC sponsor has other major interests in addition to this primary category

| | | | | |
|---|---|---|---|---|
| **National Broiler Council**<br>National Broiler Council PAC<br>Washington, DC | | **$144,650**<br><br>Poultry/Egg | 145 Candidates<br>Avg House:  $851<br>Avg Sen:  $1,457 | Dems:  51.1%<br>House:  64.7%<br>Incumb:  96.1% |
| **National Cable Television Assn**<br>National Cable Television Association's PAC (Cable PAC)<br>Washington, DC | | **$570,475**<br><br>Cable TV | 160 Candidates<br>Avg House: $2,983<br>Avg Sen:  $5,724 | Dems:  63.0%<br>House:  65.9%<br>Incumb:  97.5% |
| **National Cattlemen's Assn**<br>National Cattlemen's Association PAC<br>Englewood, CO | Natl Cattlemens Assn<br>Livestock | **$215,384** | 246 Candidates<br>Avg House:  $750<br>Avg Sen:  $1,523 | Repubs:  61.9%<br>House:  71.7%<br>Incumb:  85.2% |
| **National Cmte to Preserve Social Security & Medicare**<br>National Committee to Preserve Social Security and Medicare - PAC<br>Washington, DC | | **$913,802**<br><br>Elderly/Soc Security | 286 Candidates<br>Avg House: $2,956<br>Avg Sen:  $5,402 | Dems:  90.7%<br>House:  83.5%<br>Incumb:  72.2% |
| **National Coal Assn**<br>CoalPAC - the PAC of the National Coal Association<br>Washington, DC | | **$139,374**<br><br>Coal | 168 Candidates<br>Avg House:  $581<br>Avg Sen:  $2,477 | Repubs:  63.3%<br>House:  60.9%<br>Incumb:  94.4% |
| **National Committee for an Effective Congress**<br>National Committee for an Effective Congress<br>Washington, DC | | **$598,575**<br><br>Dem/Liberal | 164 Candidates<br>Avg House: $3,250<br>Avg Sen:  $6,528 | Dems:  99.4%<br>House:  78.2%<br>Incumb:  54.2% |
| **National Community Action Foundation**<br>Community Action Program-PAC (SSF of National Community Action Foundation Inc)<br>Washington, DC | | **$72,500**<br><br>Health/Welfare | 36 Candidates<br>Avg House: $1,523<br>Avg Sen:  $2,786 | Dems:  89.0%<br>Senate:  53.8%<br>Incumb:  94.5% |
| **National Concrete Masonry Assn**<br>National Concrete Masonry Association PAC<br>Herndon, VA | | **$77,350**<br><br>Stone/Concrete | 122 Candidates<br>Avg House:  $547<br>Avg Sen:  $990 | Repubs:  67.4%<br>House:  69.3%<br>Incumb:  95.6% |
| **National Cotton Council**<br>National Cotton Council Committee for the Advancement of Cotton<br>Memphis, TN | | **$188,056**<br><br>Cotton | 163 Candidates<br>Avg House:  $907<br>Avg Sen:  $2,091 | Dems:  53.0%<br>House:  62.2%<br>Incumb:  98.9% |
| **National Council of Farmer Co-ops**<br>National Council of Farmer Cooperatives Political Action Committee (Co-op/PAC)<br>Washington, DC | | **$126,396**<br><br>Farm Orgs | 181 Candidates<br>Avg House:  $581<br>Avg Sen:  $1,266 | Dems:  66.2%<br>House:  69.0%<br>Incumb:  97.6% |
| **National Council of Savings Institutions**<br>National Council of Savings Institutions (ThriftPAC)<br>Washington, DC | | **$88,387**<br><br>Savings & Loans | 109 Candidates<br>Avg House:  $782<br>Avg Sen:  $1,046 | Dems:  60.3%<br>House:  85.8%<br>Incumb:  95.0% |
| **National Council of Senior Citizens**<br>National Council of Senior Citizens PAC<br>Washington, DC | | **$101,918**<br><br>Elderly/Soc Security | 53 Candidates<br>Avg House: $1,223<br>Avg Sen:  $3,542 | Dems:  100.0%<br>Senate:  55.6%<br>Incumb:  59.3% |
| **National Education Assn**<br>National Education Association PAC<br>Washington, DC | | **$2,324,480**<br><br>Teachers | 381 Candidates<br>Avg House: $6,201<br>Avg Sen:  $5,291 | Dems:  93.5%<br>House:  90.4%<br>Incumb:  71.5% |
| **National Electrical Contractors Assn**<br>Electrical Construction PAC-National Electrical Contractors Association, Inc (ECPAC)<br>Bethesda, MD | | **$201,000**<br><br>Electrical Contr | 107 Candidates<br>Avg House: $1,294<br>Avg Sen:  $4,136 | Repubs:  89.5%<br>House:  54.7%<br>Incumb:  89.5% |
| **National Federation of Independent Business**<br>National Federation of Independent Business Free Enterprise PAC<br>San Mateo, CA | | **$316,710**<br><br>Small Business Assn | 183 Candidates<br>Avg House: $1,281<br>Avg Sen:  $4,328 | Repubs:  89.4%<br>House:  63.1%<br>Incumb:  73.1% |
| **National Forest Products Assn**<br>Forest Industries PAC of NFPA<br>Washington, DC | | **$61,524**<br><br>Forest Products | 81 Candidates<br>Avg House:  $550<br>Avg Sen:  $1,322 | Repubs:  61.3%<br>House:  52.7%<br>Incumb:  92.4% |
| **National League of Postmasters**<br>National League of Postmasters PAC<br>Alexandria, VA | | **$156,666**<br><br>Postal Workers | 244 Candidates<br>Avg House:  $544<br>Avg Sen:  $1,015 | Dems:  69.0%<br>House:  67.0%<br>Incumb:  97.8% |
| **National Machine Tool Builders Assn**<br>NMTBA-The Association for Manufacturing Technology-Machine ToolPAC<br>McLean, VA | | **$65,737**<br><br>Industrial Equipment | 92 Candidates<br>Avg House:  $423<br>Avg Sen:  $1,380 | Repubs:  69.1%<br>Senate:  58.8%<br>Incumb:  96.4% |
| **National Medical Enterprises Inc**<br>National Medical Enterprises Inc PAC<br>Santa Monica, CA | | **$85,383**<br><br>Hospitals† | 89 Candidates<br>Avg House:  $845<br>Avg Sen:  $1,379 | Dems:  66.9%<br>House:  69.3%<br>Incumb:  84.2% |

| --- | --- | --- | --- | --- | --- |
| **National Multi Housing Council**<br>National Multi Housing Council PAC<br>Washington, DC | Resid Construction | $51,750 | 69 Candidates<br>Avg House: $685<br>Avg Sen: $950 | Dems: 54.6%<br>House: 68.8%<br>Incumb: 96.1% | |
| **National Organization for Women**<br>National Organization for Women PAC (NOW/PAC)<br>Washington, DC | Womens Issues† | $135,320 | 43 Candidates<br>Avg House: $2,726<br>Avg Sen: $6,344 | Dems: 87.1%<br>House: 76.6%<br>Incumb: 31.8% | |
| **National PAC**<br>National PAC<br>Washington, DC | Pro-Israel | $953,500 | 184 Candidates<br>Avg House: $4,881<br>Avg Sen: $6,857 | Dems: 61.0%<br>House: 79.9%<br>Incumb: 85.5% | |
| **National Pest Control Assn**<br>National Pest Control Association PAC<br>Dun Loring, VA | Pest Control | $59,800 | 98 Candidates<br>Avg House: $596<br>Avg Sen: $657 | Repubs: 62.7%<br>House: 74.8%<br>Incumb: 91.1% | |
| **National Pork Producers Council**<br>National Pork Producers Council Pork PAC<br>Des Moines, IA | Livestock | $84,575 | 126 Candidates<br>Avg House: $560<br>Avg Sen: $939 | Dems: 56.9%<br>House: 58.9%<br>Incumb: 99.4% | |
| **National Restaurant Assn**<br>National Restaurant Association PAC<br>Washington, DC | Restaurants | $571,642 | 203 Candidates<br>Avg House: $2,616<br>Avg Sen: $3,743 | Repubs: 80.3%<br>House: 76.4%<br>Incumb: 67.6% | |
| **National Rifle Assn**<br>NRA Political Victory Fund<br>Washington, DC | Pro-Guns | $749,493 | 221 Candidates<br>Avg House: $2,962<br>Avg Sen: $5,926 | Repubs: 60.9%<br>House: 74.7%<br>Incumb: 82.1% | |
| **National Right to Life PAC**<br>National Right to Life PAC<br>Washington, DC | Pro-Life | $112,177 | 66 Candidates<br>Avg House: $1,516<br>Avg Sen: $2,526 | Repubs: 89.0%<br>House: 73.0%<br>Incumb: 62.4% | |
| **National Rural Letter Carriers Assn**<br>National Rural Letter Carriers' Association PAC<br>Alexandria, VA | Postal Workers | $430,875 | 293 Candidates<br>Avg House: $1,105<br>Avg Sen: $3,781 | Dems: 87.5%<br>House: 64.9%<br>Incumb: 85.9% | |
| **National Society of Professional Engineers**<br>National Society of Professional Engineers - PAC (NSPE-PAC)<br>Alexandria, VA | Engineers | $54,202 | 80 Candidates<br>Avg House: $616<br>Avg Sen: $922 | Repubs: 67.3%<br>House: 72.8%<br>Incumb: 85.7% | |
| **National Telephone Cooperative Assn**<br>National Telephone Cooperative Association Telephone Education Committee Organization<br>Washington, DC | Phone Utilities | $50,358 | 118 Candidates<br>Avg House: $403<br>Avg Sen: $512 | Dems: 68.4%<br>House: 73.6%<br>Incumb: 98.3% | |
| **National Tooling & Machining Assn**<br>Tooling & Machining PAC of the National Tooling and Machining Association<br>Ft Washington, MD | Industrial Equipment | $83,425 | 104 Candidates<br>Avg House: $633<br>Avg Sen: $1,398 | Repubs: 76.1%<br>House: 61.5%<br>Incumb: 97.2% | |
| **National Treasury Employees Union**<br>National Treasury Employees Union PAC (TEPAC)<br>Washington, DC | Federal Workers | $192,531 | 136 Candidates<br>Avg House: $971<br>Avg Sen: $2,923 | Dems: 90.0%<br>House: 52.9%<br>Incumb: 86.9% | |
| **National Utility Contractors Assn**<br>National Utility Contractors Assn Legislative Information & Action Committee<br>Arlington, VA | Comml Construction | $331,768 | 163 Candidates<br>Avg House: $1,797<br>Avg Sen: $3,186 | Repubs: 59.1%<br>House: 73.1%<br>Incumb: 98.2% | |
| **National Venture Capital Assn**<br>National Venture Capital Association PAC (NVCA PAC)<br>Washington, DC | Venture Capital | $296,226 | 128 Candidates<br>Avg House: $1,587<br>Avg Sen: $4,691 | Dems: 63.5%<br>House: 52.5%<br>Incumb: 98.2% | |
| **National Wholesale Grocers Assn**<br>National American Wholesale Grocers' Association PAC: NAWGAPAC<br>Falls Church, VA | Food Wholesalers | $77,400 | 111 Candidates<br>Avg House: $537<br>Avg Sen: $1,425 | Repubs: 90.4%<br>House: 63.2%<br>Incumb: 92.4% | |
| **Navistar International**<br>Navistar International Transportation Corp Good Govt Cmte (fka International Harvester)<br>Chicago, IL | Farm Equip | $57,500 | 35 Candidates<br>Avg House: $891<br>Avg Sen: $3,083 | Repubs: 80.4%<br>Senate: 64.4%<br>Incumb: 83.5% | |
| **NCNB Corp**<br>NCNB Corporation PAC (NCNB PAC)<br>Charlotte, NC | NCNB Corp | Commercial Banks | $66,450 | 84 Candidates<br>Avg House: $616<br>Avg Sen: $1,390 | Dems: 69.3%<br>House: 60.3%<br>Incumb: 80.9% |
| **NCNB Texas**<br>NCNB Texas PAC Fka First Republic Bank (FRB)<br>Dallas, TX | NCNB Corp | Commercial Banks | $76,900 | 50 Candidates<br>Avg House: $1,479<br>Avg Sen: $1,775 | Dems: 73.7%<br>House: 76.9%<br>Incumb: 90.5% |

† PAC sponsor has other major interests in addition to this primary category

| | | | | |
|---|---|---|---|---|
| **Nestle Enterprises Inc** | | $61,681 | 133 Candidates | Repubs: 94.8% |
| Nestle Enterprises Inc PAC | | | Avg House:  $428 | House:  84.6% |
| Solon, OH | Food & Beverage | | Avg Sen:  $864 | Incumb:  74.9% |
| **New England Mutual Life** | | $84,100 | 73 Candidates | Dems:  61.4% |
| New England Mutual Life Insurance Company PAC/New England Life PAC (NELPAC) | | | Avg House:  $1,076 | House:  69.1% |
| Boston, MA | Life Insurance | | Avg Sen:  $1,368 | Incumb:  95.2% |
| **New York Life** | | $74,900 | 51 Candidates | Dems:  82.6% |
| New York Life Insurance Company PAC | | | Avg House:  $1,312 | House:  68.3% |
| New York, NY | Life Insurance | | Avg Sen:  $1,979 | Incumb:  97.7% |
| **New York Medical Assn** | | $66,591 | 27 Candidates | Dems:  59.6% |
| New York Medical PAC | | | Avg House:  $2,392 | House:  93.4% |
| Lake Success, NY | American Medical Assn | Doctors | Avg Sen:  $4,400 | Incumb:  88.7% |
| **New York Telephone** | | $64,887 | 43 Candidates | Dems:  55.2% |
| New York Telephone Federal PAC | | | Avg House:  $1,537 | House:  90.0% |
| New York, NY | NYNEX | Phone Utilities | Avg Sen:  $1,295 | Incumb:  99.7% |
| **Norfolk Southern Corp** | | $141,550 | 173 Candidates | Dems:  60.8% |
| Norfolk Southern Corporation Good Government Fund | | | Avg House:  $704 | House:  69.7% |
| Norfolk, VA | Norfolk Southern | Railroads† | Avg Sen:  $1,302 | Incumb:  97.9% |
| **Norstar Bancorp** | | $56,760 | 53 Candidates | Dems:  55.5% |
| Fleet/Norstar Federal PAC | | | Avg House:  $797 | House:  56.1% |
| Providence, RI | Fleet/Norstar Financial Group | Comml Banks | Avg Sen:  $1,915 | Incumb:  84.9% |
| **North American Van Lines** | | $62,200 | 66 Candidates | Dems:  62.2% |
| North American Van Lines Inc PAC (NAPAC)/Norfolk Southern Corp Good Government Fund | | | Avg House:  $832 | House:  80.2% |
| Fort Wayne, IN | Norfolk Southern | Trucking Companies | Avg Sen:  $2,050 | Incumb:  93.1% |
| **Northern States Power Co** | | $51,570 | 68 Candidates | Dems:  52.2% |
| Northern States Power Employee Political Interest Committee | | | Avg House:  $564 | House:  54.7% |
| Minneapolis, MN | Gas & Electric Util† | | Avg Sen:  $1,297 | Incumb:  95.2% |
| **Northrop Corp** | | $411,775 | 257 Candidates | Repubs:  62.8% |
| Northrop Employees PAC (aka NEPAC) | | | Avg House:  $1,262 | House:  65.9% |
| San Francisco, CA | Air Defense† | | Avg Sen:  $3,342 | Incumb:  96.0% |
| **Northwest Airlines** | | $79,098 | 66 Candidates | Dems:  70.7% |
| Northwest Airlines PAC (fka Republic Airlines PAC) | | | Avg House:  $903 | House:  54.8% |
| St. Paul, MN | Airlines | | Avg Sen:  $1,986 | Incumb:  97.7% |
| **Northwestern Mutual Life** | | $86,000 | 60 Candidates | Dems:  52.6% |
| Northwestern Mutual Life Insurance Company Federal PAC (NML FEDPAC) | | | Avg House:  $1,396 | House:  60.1% |
| Milwaukee, WI | Life Insurance | | Avg Sen:  $1,494 | Incumb:  95.0% |
| **Norwest Corp** | | $53,450 | 58 Candidates | Dems:  63.6% |
| Norwest Corporation PAC (Norwest PAC) | | | Avg House:  $750 | House:  67.4% |
| Minneapolis, MN | Commercial Banks | | Avg Sen:  $1,745 | Incumb:  93.9% |
| **NYNEX Corp** | | $106,999 | 92 Candidates | Repubs:  62.2% |
| NYNEX Employees' Federal PAC | | | Avg House:  $733 | Senate:  58.0% |
| New York, NY | NYNEX | Phone Utilities† | Avg Sen:  $2,068 | Incumb:  96.4% |
| **Occidental Oil & Gas** | | $68,100 | 105 Candidates | Repubs:  87.6% |
| Occidental Oil & Gas Corporation PAC (OOGPAC) (aka Cities Service Oil & Gas Corp PAC) | | | Avg House:  $547 | House:  70.6% |
| Tulsa, OK | Occidental Petroleum | Oil & Gas Prod† | Avg Sen:  $1,177 | Incumb:  75.6% |
| **Occidental Petroleum** | | $123,600 | 86 Candidates | Dems:  65.7% |
| Occidental Petroleum Corporation PAC | | | Avg House:  $956 | Senate:  56.7% |
| Los Angeles, CA | Occidental Petroleum | Oil & Gas Prod† | Avg Sen:  $2,335 | Incumb:  96.4% |
| **Ocean Spray Cranberries Inc** | | $118,782 | 87 Candidates | Dems:  53.5% |
| Ocean Spray Cranberries Inc PAC | | | Avg House:  $1,080 | Senate:  52.7% |
| Lakeville-Middleboro, MA | Fruit/Veg | | Avg Sen:  $1,789 | Incumb: 100.0% |
| **Office & Professional Employees Union** | | $82,940 | 42 Candidates | Dems:  99.4% |
| Office and Professional Employees International Union-Voice of the Electorate | | | Avg House:  $1,598 | House:  57.8% |
| Washington, DC | Misc Unions | | Avg Sen:  $2,917 | Incumb:  74.1% |
| **Operating Engineers Union** | | $696,750 | 268 Candidates | Dems:  95.1% |
| Engineers Political Education Committee (EPEC)/International Union of Operating Engineers | | | Avg House:  $2,263 | House:  76.6% |
| Washington, DC | Operating Engineers Union | Constr Unions | Avg Sen:  $5,086 | Incumb:  83.4% |

**Oral & Maxillofacial Surgeons**
Oral and Maxillofacial Surgery PAC (OMSPAC)
Rosemont, IL — Dentists — **$108,500**
39 Candidates — Repubs: 52.1%
Avg House: $1,944 — Senate: 51.6%
Avg Sen: $4,667 — Incumb: 88.9%

**Outdoor Advertising Assn of America**
Outdoor Advertising Association of America PAC
Washington, DC — Billboards — **$82,000**
82 Candidates — Repubs: 50.7%
Avg House: $730 — House: 49.9%
Avg Sen: $1,581 — Incumb: 91.6%

**Owens-Corning Fiberglas**
Owens-Corning Fiberglas Corporation Employees' Better Government Fund
Toledo, OH — Bldg Materials† — **$78,945**
56 Candidates — Repubs: 83.1%
Avg House: $786 — Senate: 62.2%
Avg Sen: $2,728 — Incumb: 92.4%

**Owens-Illinois**
Owens-Illinois Inc Employees Good Citizenship Fund
Toledo, OH — Kohlberg, Kravis & Roberts — Glass Products† — **$81,301**
59 Candidates — Dems: 54.4%
Avg House: $1,279 — House: 73.9%
Avg Sen: $1,767 — Incumb: 96.3%

**Pacific Enterprises**
Pacific Enterprises Political Assistance Committee
Los Angeles, CA — Natural Gas† — **$151,199**
121 Candidates — Dems: 56.2%
Avg House: $1,057 — House: 64.3%
Avg Sen: $1,862 — Incumb: 95.0%

**Pacific Gas & Electric**
Pacific Gas and Electric Company Employees' Federal PAC
San Francisco, CA — Gas & Electric Util† — **$191,415**
119 Candidates — Dems: 54.0%
Avg House: $1,381 — House: 64.2%
Avg Sen: $2,283 — Incumb: 98.1%

**Pacific Mutual Life**
Pacific Mutual Life Insurance Company PAC (PMPAC)
Newport Beach, CA — Life Insurance — **$88,800**
67 Candidates — Dems: 56.1%
Avg House: $1,175 — House: 70.2%
Avg Sen: $1,893 — Incumb: 98.3%

**Pacific Telesis Group**
Pacific Telesis Group PAC (Federal Account)
San Francisco, CA — Phone Utilities† — **$239,054**
170 Candidates — Dems: 61.6%
Avg House: $1,220 — House: 67.9%
Avg Sen: $2,074 — Incumb: 98.3%

**PaineWebber**
PaineWebber Fund for Better Government
New York, NY — Securities Invest — **$79,688**
53 Candidates — Dems: 71.5%
Avg House: $667 — Senate: 76.5%
Avg Sen: $2,440 — Incumb: 83.9%

**Painters & Allied Trades Union**
International Brotherhood of Painters & Allied Trades Political Action Together
Washington, DC — Constr Unions — **$127,700**
109 Candidates — Dems: 96.0%
Avg House: $975 — House: 70.2%
Avg Sen: $2,235 — Incumb: 71.9%

**Panhandle Eastern Corp**
Panhandle Eastern Corp PAC (fka Texas Eastern PAC)
Houston, TX — Natural Gas† — **$85,828**
118 Candidates — Dems: 52.9%
Avg House: $565 — House: 63.9%
Avg Sen: $1,476 — Incumb: 88.6%

**Paramount Communications**
Paramount Communications Inc PAC
New York, NY — TV/Movies† — **$114,050**
56 Candidates — Dems: 73.9%
Avg House: $1,090 — Senate: 67.5%
Avg Sen: $3,500 — Incumb: 98.3%

**Peabody Coal**
Peabody PAC
St. Louis, MO — Coal — **$100,250**
74 Candidates — Repubs: 54.5%
Avg House: $840 — Senate: 56.4%
Avg Sen: $2,570 — Incumb: 98.7%

**Peace PAC**
Peace PAC
Boston, MA — Council for Livable World — Pro-Peace — **$66,757**
35 Candidates — Dems: 98.4%
Avg House: $1,907 — House: 100.0%
Avg Sen: $0 — Incumb: 28.0%

**Pelican PAC**
Pelican PAC
Seattle, WA — Sen J Bennett Johnston (D-La) — Dem Leaders — **$61,886**
18 Candidates — Dems: 100.0%
Avg House: $4,094 — House: 52.9%
Avg Sen: $2,914 — Incumb: 47.1%

**JC Penney Co**
J C Penney Company PAC (Penney PAC)
Dallas, TX — Department Stores† — **$266,975**
256 Candidates — Dems: 60.7%
Avg House: $876 — House: 64.3%
Avg Sen: $1,589 — Incumb: 93.1%

**Pepsico Inc**
Pepsico Concerned Citizens Fund
Purchase, NY — Food & Beverage — **$264,377**
182 Candidates — Repubs: 73.8%
Avg House: $1,177 — House: 69.9%
Avg Sen: $3,184 — Incumb: 77.3%

**Petroleum Marketers Assn**
Petroleum Marketers Association of America Small Businessmen's Committee
Washington, DC — Gas Stations† — **$193,325**
202 Candidates — Repubs: 68.1%
Avg House: $776 — House: 70.3%
Avg Sen: $2,130 — Incumb: 77.7%

**Pfizer Inc**
Pfizer PAC
New York, NY — Pharmaceuticals† — **$137,300**
160 Candidates — Dems: 52.2%
Avg House: $619 — House: 58.2%
Avg Sen: $1,853 — Incumb: 96.1%

† PAC sponsor has other major interests in addition to this primary category

| PAC Sponsor or Related Group/PAC Name | Affiliate | 1989-90 Total | Where the money went... | | | |
|---|---|---|---|---|---|---|
| **Philip Morris**<br>Philip Morris PAC (aka PHIL-PAC)<br>New York, NY | Philip Morris<br>Tobacco/Food Prod† | $572,410 | 329 Candidates<br>Avg House: $1,497<br>Avg Sen: $2,952 | Dems: 54.1%<br>House: 71.6%<br>Incumb: 92.7% | | |
| **Phillips Petroleum**<br>Phillips Petroleum Company PAC<br>Bartlesville, OK | Oil & Gas Prod† | $216,052 | 172 Candidates<br>Avg House: $1,099<br>Avg Sen: $2,180 | Repubs: 73.8%<br>House: 74.8%<br>Incumb: 68.3% | | |
| **Pittston Co**<br>Pittston Company PAC<br>Greenwich, CT | Air Freight/Coal† | $55,000 | 71 Candidates<br>Avg House: $644<br>Avg Sen: $1,132 | Dems: 54.9%<br>House: 60.9%<br>Incumb: 97.3% | | |
| **Planning Research Corp**<br>Planning Research Corp PAC (fka-Emhart Corporation PAC)<br>McLean, VA | Black & Decker<br>Computers† | $57,350 | 53 Candidates<br>Avg House: $946<br>Avg Sen: $1,500 | Repubs: 56.9%<br>House: 66.0%<br>Incumb: 99.6% | | |
| **Plumbers/Pipefitters Union**<br>United Association of Journeymen and Apprentices of the Plumbing and Pipefitters Industry<br>Washington, DC | Constr Unions | $615,134 | 299 Candidates<br>Avg House: $1,807<br>Avg Sen: $4,390 | Dems: 93.2%<br>House: 79.3%<br>Incumb: 76.4% | | |
| **Powell, Goldstein, Frazer & Murphy**<br>Powell, Goldstein, Frazer & Murphy PAC<br>Atlanta, GA | Lawyers | $131,790 | 167 Candidates<br>Avg House: $624<br>Avg Sen: $1,236 | Dems: 89.9%<br>House: 57.8%<br>Incumb: 93.6% | | |
| **Precision Metalforming Assn**<br>Precision Metalforming Association PAC (fka American Metal Stamping Assn PAC)<br>Richmond Heights, OH | Metal Products | $64,000 | 48 Candidates<br>Avg House: $1,054<br>Avg Sen: $2,273 | Repubs: 98.4%<br>House: 60.9%<br>Incumb: 54.7% | | |
| **Preston, Gates et al**<br>Preston Gates Ellis & Rouvelas Meeds PAC (fka-Preston, Thorgrimson, Ellis & Holm)<br>Washington, DC | Lawyers/Lobbyists | $91,106 | 142 Candidates<br>Avg House: $579<br>Avg Sen: $910 | Dems: 69.0%<br>House: 73.0%<br>Incumb: 99.0% | | |
| **Price Waterhouse**<br>Price Waterhouse Partners' PAC<br>Washington, DC | Accountants | $55,650 | 48 Candidates<br>Avg House: $1,175<br>Avg Sen: $1,100 | Dems: 62.4%<br>House: 80.2%<br>Incumb: 98.2% | | |
| **Principal Mutual Life Insurance**<br>Principal Mutual Life Insurance Company - Federal PAC<br>Des Moines, IA | Insurance | $76,559 | 78 Candidates<br>Avg House: $708<br>Avg Sen: $1,596 | Dems: 59.6%<br>House: 50.0%<br>Incumb: 98.0% | | |
| **Printing Industries of America**<br>Printing Industries of America PAC (Print PAC)<br>Arlington, VA | Printing | $94,900 | 74 Candidates<br>Avg House: $707<br>Avg Sen: $2,410 | Repubs: 91.4%<br>Senate: 63.5%<br>Incumb: 79.7% | | |
| **Prudential Insurance**<br>Prudential Insurance Company of America Federal PAC ("Prudential PAC")<br>Newark, NJ | Prudential Insurance<br>Insurance† | $207,170 | 155 Candidates<br>Avg House: $1,046<br>Avg Sen: $2,200 | Dems: 61.4%<br>House: 58.6%<br>Incumb: 91.3% | | |
| **Prudential-Bache Securities**<br>Prudential-Bache Securities Inc PAC<br>New York, NY | Prudential Insurance<br>Securities Invest | $60,245 | 61 Candidates<br>Avg House: $890<br>Avg Sen: $1,187 | Dems: 55.1%<br>House: 60.6%<br>Incumb: 94.2% | | |
| **Public Securities Assn**<br>Public Securities Association PAC<br>Washington, DC | Securities Invest | $101,370 | 127 Candidates<br>Avg House: $686<br>Avg Sen: $1,400 | Dems: 70.2%<br>House: 72.4%<br>Incumb: 92.8% | | |
| **Public Service Electric & Gas**<br>Public Service Electric and Gas Company PAC (PEGPAC)<br>Newark, NJ | Gas & Electric Util | $101,835 | 95 Candidates<br>Avg House: $1,044<br>Avg Sen: $1,166 | Repubs: 50.2%<br>House: 74.8%<br>Incumb: 92.1% | | |
| **Public Service Research Council**<br>Public Service PAC<br>Reston, VA | Anti-Union | $239,575 | 170 Candidates<br>Avg House: $984<br>Avg Sen: $3,996 | Repubs: 98.9%<br>House: 60.0%<br>Incumb: 58.6% | | |
| **Raytheon**<br>Raytheon Company PAC<br>Lexington, MA | Defense† | $245,700 | 149 Candidates<br>Avg House: $1,472<br>Avg Sen: $2,133 | Dems: 52.3%<br>House: 65.3%<br>Incumb: 97.6% | | |
| **Recording Industry Assn**<br>Recording Industry Assoc of America Inc PAC (fka Recording Arts PAC)<br>Washington, DC | Music Production | $60,100 | 68 Candidates<br>Avg House: $680<br>Avg Sen: $1,547 | Dems: 88.9%<br>House: 58.8%<br>Incumb: 92.8% | | |
| **Religion and Tolerance PAC**<br>Religion and Tolerance PAC (RATPAC)<br>Washington, DC | Dem/Liberal | $82,000 | 16 Candidates<br>Avg House: $1,500<br>Avg Sen: $5,643 | Dems: 100.0%<br>Senate: 96.3%<br>Incumb: 80.5% | | |

| PAC Sponsor or Related Group/PAC Name | Affiliate | 1989-90 Total | Where the money went... | | |
|---|---|---|---|---|---|

**Republican Leader's Fund**
Republican Leader's Fund
Washington, DC — Rep Bob Michel (R-Ill) — Repub Leaders — **$163,500**

| 58 Candidates | Repubs: 100.0% |
|---|---|
| Avg House: $2,819 | House: 100.0% |
| Avg Sen: $0 | Incumb: 29.4% |

**Republican Majority Fund**
Republican Majority Fund
Washington, DC — Sen Richard Lugar (R-Ind) — Repub Leaders — **$59,150**

| 26 Candidates | Repubs: 100.0% |
|---|---|
| Avg House: $1,334 | Senate: 93.2% |
| Avg Sen: $2,398 | Incumb: 93.2% |

**Reynolds Metals**
Reynolds Metals Company Political Participation Program Fund (RAPPP)
Richmond, VA — Metal Mining/Process — **$76,101**

| 70 Candidates | Repubs: 69.5% |
|---|---|
| Avg House: $798 | Senate: 50.7% |
| Avg Sen: $1,678 | Incumb: 92.7% |

**Rhone-Poulenc Inc**
Rhone-Poulenc Inc PAC (RPAC)
Princeton, NJ — Ag Chemicals† — **$64,700**

| 60 Candidates | Repubs: 74.7% |
|---|---|
| Avg House: $783 | Senate: 56.4% |
| Avg Sen: $1,521 | Incumb: 89.2% |

**Right to Work PAC**
Right to Work PAC
Springfield, VA — Anti-Union — **$197,904**

| 97 Candidates | Repubs: 97.2% |
|---|---|
| Avg House: $1,900 | House: 79.7% |
| Avg Sen: $2,872 | Incumb: 42.7% |

**RJR Nabisco**
RJR PAC/RJR Nabisco Inc
Winston-Salem, NC — RJR Nabisco — Tobacco/Food Prod† — **$720,000**

| 359 Candidates | Dems: 51.2% |
|---|---|
| Avg House: $1,857 | House: 82.8% |
| Avg Sen: $3,263 | Incumb: 92.4% |

**Roadway Services Inc**
Roadway Services Inc REXPAC
Akron, OH — Roadway Services — Trucking Companies — **$59,400**

| 76 Candidates | Dems: 55.8% |
|---|---|
| Avg House: $712 | House: 74.3% |
| Avg Sen: $1,089 | Incumb: 98.7% |

**Rockwell International**
Rockwell International Corporation
Pittsburgh, PA — Air Defense† — **$365,585**

| 254 Candidates | Repubs: 62.3% |
|---|---|
| Avg House: $1,073 | House: 64.0% |
| Avg Sen: $3,750 | Incumb: 94.3% |

**Rubber Cork Linoleum & Plastic Workers Union**
Cope Committee of the United Rubber Cork Linoleum and Plastic Workers of America AFL-CIO
Akron, OH — Manufacturing Unions — **$193,375**

| 86 Candidates | Dems: 100.0% |
|---|---|
| Avg House: $2,020 | House: 71.0% |
| Avg Sen: $3,118 | Incumb: 55.5% |

**Ruff PAC**
Ruff PAC (Ruff-PAC)
Washington, DC — Tax Policy — **$65,457**

| 73 Candidates | Repubs: 98.4% |
|---|---|
| Avg House: $853 | House: 87.3% |
| Avg Sen: $1,383 | Incumb: 31.7% |

**S&A Restaurant Corp**
S & A Restaurant Corporation Employees PAC
Dallas, TX — Restaurants — **$160,000**

| 49 Candidates | Repubs: 94.1% |
|---|---|
| Avg House: $2,662 | House: 56.6% |
| Avg Sen: $4,633 | Incumb: 71.3% |

**St Louisans for Better Government**
St Louisans for Better Government
St. Louis, MO — Pro-Israel — **$107,750**

| 39 Candidates | Dems: 71.0% |
|---|---|
| Avg House: $1,337 | Senate: 67.8% |
| Avg Sen: $5,615 | Incumb: 90.0% |

**Salomon Brothers**
Salomon Brothers Inc PAC
New York, NY — Securities Invest — **$152,150**

| 100 Candidates | Repubs: 60.3% |
|---|---|
| Avg House: $642 | Senate: 71.3% |
| Avg Sen: $3,391 | Incumb: 94.9% |

**San Franciscans for Good Government**
San Franciscans for Good Government
San Francisco, CA — Pro-Israel — **$76,000**

| 18 Candidates | Dems: 82.2% |
|---|---|
| Avg House: $2,500 | Senate: 90.1% |
| Avg Sen: $4,567 | Incumb: 100.0% |

**Santa Fe Southern Pacific**
Santa Fe Southern Pacific Corporation PAC
Chicago, IL — Railroads† — **$76,200**

| 95 Candidates | Repubs: 69.3% |
|---|---|
| Avg House: $619 | House: 59.3% |
| Avg Sen: $1,411 | Incumb: 96.7% |

**Schering-Plough Corp**
Schering - Plough Corporation Better Government Fund
Madison, NJ — Pharmaceuticals† — **$127,934**

| 90 Candidates | Repubs: 58.8% |
|---|---|
| Avg House: $1,009 | House: 53.6% |
| Avg Sen: $2,698 | Incumb: 92.5% |

**Sea-Land Corp**
Sea-land Service Inc Employees Good Govt Fund, aka Sea-Land Employees Good Govt Fund
Washington, DC — CSX Corp — Sea Transport† — **$114,413**

| 102 Candidates | Dems: 53.0% |
|---|---|
| Avg House: $927 | House: 60.0% |
| Avg Sen: $1,636 | Incumb: 98.7% |

**Seafarers International Union**
Seafarers Political Activity Donation (SPAD)
Camp Springs, MD — Sea Transport Unions — **$946,246**

| 314 Candidates | Dems: 85.3% |
|---|---|
| Avg House: $2,609 | House: 76.9% |
| Avg Sen: $6,234 | Incumb: 81.7% |

**Joseph E Seagram & Sons**
Joseph E Seagram & Sons, Inc PAC
New York, NY — Wine & Liquor† — **$124,025**

| 111 Candidates | Dems: 74.9% |
|---|---|
| Avg House: $798 | House: 57.9% |
| Avg Sen: $2,486 | Incumb: 90.7% |

† PAC sponsor has other major interests in addition to this primary category

333

| | | | | | |
|---|---|---|---|---|---|
| **Sears**<br>Sears PAC<br>Chicago, IL | Sears | $68,950<br><br>Retail† | 116 Candidates<br>Avg House: $441<br>Avg Sen: $1,485 | Repubs: 83.6%<br>House: 63.4%<br>Incumb: 75.9% | |
| **Securities Industry Assn**<br>Securities Industry PAC<br>Washington, DC | | $81,244<br><br>Securities Invest | 90 Candidates<br>Avg House: $806<br>Avg Sen: $1,289 | Dems: 70.6%<br>House: 71.5%<br>Incumb: 97.9% | |
| **Security Pacific Corp**<br>Security Pacific Corporation Active Citizenship Today Committee (SPACT)<br>Los Angeles, CA | | $129,400<br><br>Commercial Banks | 111 Candidates<br>Avg House: $1,096<br>Avg Sen: $1,362 | Dems: 64.3%<br>House: 69.5%<br>Incumb: 98.1% | |
| **Senate Victory Fund**<br>Senate Victory Fund PAC (fka Cochran Committee)<br>Jackson, MS | Sen Thad Cochran (R-Miss) | $62,500<br><br>Repub Leaders | 15 Candidates<br>Avg House: $0<br>Avg Sen: $4,167 | Repubs: 100.0%<br>Senate: 100.0%<br>Incumb: 98.4% | |
| **Service Employees Intl Union**<br>Service Employees Int'l Union Committee on Political Education Political Campaign<br>Washington, DC | | $303,146<br><br>Misc Unions | 161 Candidates<br>Avg House: $1,470<br>Avg Sen: $4,489 | Dems: 97.3%<br>House: 67.4%<br>Incumb: 69.8% | |
| **Shearson Lehman Hutton**<br>Action Fund of Shearson Lehman Brothers Inc<br>New York, NY | American Express | $124,675<br><br>Securities Invest | 118 Candidates<br>Avg House: $765<br>Avg Sen: $1,625 | Dems: 61.4%<br>Senate: 52.1%<br>Incumb: 95.8% | |
| **Sheet Metal & Air Conditioning Contractors**<br>Sheet Metal and Air Conditioning Contractors' PAC<br>Vienna, VA | | $195,560<br><br>Plumbing/AirCon | 106 Candidates<br>Avg House: $1,365<br>Avg Sen: $3,786 | Repubs: 91.4%<br>House: 59.4%<br>Incumb: 78.3% | |
| **Sheet Metal Workers Union**<br>Sheet Metal Workers International Association Political Action League (PAL)<br>Washington, DC | | $672,358<br><br>Constr Unions | 182 Candidates<br>Avg House: $3,532<br>Avg Sen: $4,517 | Dems: 98.1%<br>House: 79.9%<br>Incumb: 60.6% | |
| **Shell Oil**<br>Shell Oil Company Employees' Political Awareness Committee<br>Houston, TX | | $143,400<br><br>Oil & Gas Prod† | 165 Candidates<br>Avg House: $613<br>Avg Sen: $2,023 | Repubs: 66.8%<br>House: 57.7%<br>Incumb: 95.6% | |
| **Sierra Club**<br>Sierra Club Political Committee<br>San Francisco, CA | | $408,210<br><br>Environment | 221 Candidates<br>Avg House: $1,711<br>Avg Sen: $2,967 | Dems: 91.2%<br>House: 82.6%<br>Incumb: 60.4% | |
| **Simpson Investment Co**<br>Simpson Investment Company PAC (aka Simpson Pol Act Cmte/SIMPAC)<br>Seattle, WA | | $58,640<br><br>Forest Products | 38 Candidates<br>Avg House: $1,540<br>Avg Sen: $1,547 | Repubs: 78.8%<br>House: 57.8%<br>Incumb: 80.6% | |
| **Skadden, Arps et al**<br>Skadden Arps PAC<br>Washington, DC | | $80,350<br><br>Lawyers | 87 Candidates<br>Avg House: $621<br>Avg Sen: $1,635 | Dems: 66.4%<br>Senate: 52.9%<br>Incumb: 95.1% | |
| **SmithKline Beckman**<br>SmithKline Beckman PAC (SB-PAC)<br>Philadelphia, PA | | $117,350<br><br>Pharmaceuticals† | 90 Candidates<br>Avg House: $1,080<br>Avg Sen: $1,957 | Repubs: 62.3%<br>House: 61.7%<br>Incumb: 99.1% | |
| **Society of American Florists**<br>Society of American Florists PAC (SAF-PAC)<br>Alexandria, VA | | $55,289<br><br>Florists | 92 Candidates<br>Avg House: $549<br>Avg Sen: $869 | Repubs: 82.5%<br>House: 76.4%<br>Incumb: 99.5% | |
| **Society of Indep Gasoline Marketers of America**<br>Society of Independent Gasoline Marketers of America<br>Reston, VA | | $70,125<br><br>Gas Stations | 79 Candidates<br>Avg House: $879<br>Avg Sen: $918 | Dems: 61.5%<br>House: 76.4%<br>Incumb: 97.5% | |
| **South Central Bell Telephone**<br>South Central Bell Telephone Company Federal PAC (SCB FPAC)<br>Birmingham, AL | BellSouth | $103,800<br><br>Phone Utilities | 48 Candidates<br>Avg House: $1,939<br>Avg Sen: $3,281 | Dems: 77.1%<br>House: 74.7%<br>Incumb: 84.4% | |
| **Southern Bell**<br>Southern Bell Telephone & Telegraph Co Federal PAC (SOBELL FED-PAC)<br>Birmingham, AL | BellSouth | $213,700<br><br>Phone Utilities | 61 Candidates<br>Avg House: $3,496<br>Avg Sen: $3,550 | Dems: 55.8%<br>House: 86.7%<br>Incumb: 93.8% | |
| **Southern California Edison**<br>Federal Citizenship Responsibility Group of the Employees of So Ca Edison Co - A Vol Assoc<br>Rosemead, CA | | $187,700<br><br>Electric Utilities | 158 Candidates<br>Avg House: $949<br>Avg Sen: $2,130 | Dems: 65.3%<br>House: 63.7%<br>Incumb: 94.3% | |
| **Southern Co**<br>Southern Company Services PAC<br>Atlanta, GA | Southern Co | $76,800<br><br>Electric Utilities | 162 Candidates<br>Avg House: $400<br>Avg Sen: $751 | Repubs: 52.4%<br>House: 66.7%<br>Incumb: 89.6% | |

334

**Southern Minnesota Sugar Cooperative** — $215,825
Southern Minnesota Sugar Cooperative PAC
Renville, MN     Sugar

| 235 Candidates | Dems: 51.6% |
| Avg House: $807 | House: 66.6% |
| Avg Sen: $1,265 | Incumb: 96.9% |

**Southern Natural Resources** — $57,150
Sonat Inc PAC
Birmingham, AL     Natural Gas†

| 52 Candidates | Dems: 71.9% |
| Avg House: $699 | Senate: 56.0% |
| Avg Sen: $2,000 | Incumb: 97.4% |

**Southwest Peanut Membership Organization** — $82,000
Southwest Peanut PAC
Washington, DC     Misc Crops

| 80 Candidates | Dems: 67.8% |
| Avg House: $865 | House: 58.1% |
| Avg Sen: $1,376 | Incumb: 94.7% |

**Southwestern Bell** — $193,250
Southwestern Bell Corporation Employee Federal PAC (SWB EMPAC or EMPAC)
St. Louis, MO     Phone Utilities†

| 130 Candidates | Dems: 51.0% |
| Avg House: $1,353 | House: 71.4% |
| Avg Sen: $1,974 | Incumb: 95.5% |

**AE Staley Manufacturing Co** — $59,661
Staley PAC of A E Staley Manufacturing Company
Decatur, IL     Tate & Lyle PLC     Food Processing†

| 47 Candidates | Dems: 61.6% |
| Avg House: $1,005 | Senate: 61.3% |
| Avg Sen: $1,523 | Incumb: 98.3% |

**Stephens Overseas Services** — $53,250
Stephens Overseas Services PAC
Little Rock, AR     Financial Services

| 20 Candidates | Dems: 56.7% |
| Avg House: $2,117 | House: 59.6% |
| Avg Sen: $4,300 | Incumb: 63.5% |

**Stone & Webster** — $61,100
Stone & Webster PAC
New York, NY     Engineers†

| 90 Candidates | Dems: 59.0% |
| Avg House: $606 | House: 74.4% |
| Avg Sen: $1,043 | Incumb: 97.4% |

**Stone Container Corp** — $134,000
Stone Container Corporation PAC
Chicago, IL     Paper Packaging†

| 74 Candidates | Repubs: 79.5% |
| Avg House: $1,518 | House: 62.3% |
| Avg Sen: $2,658 | Incumb: 81.7% |

**Sun Co** — $115,000
Sun Company Inc PAC
Radnor, PA     Oil Refining/Mktg†

| 115 Candidates | Repubs: 89.6% |
| Avg House: $760 | House: 63.5% |
| Avg Sen: $2,211 | Incumb: 74.8% |

**Sunkist Growers** — $56,100
Sunkist Growers, Inc PAC
Sherman Oaks, CA     Fruit/Veg

| 62 Candidates | Dems: 58.4% |
| Avg House: $879 | House: 83.1% |
| Avg Sen: $1,056 | Incumb: 89.3% |

**Teamsters Union** — $2,353,475
Democratic Republican Independent Voter Education Committee
Washington, DC     Teamsters Union     Teamsters

| 359 Candidates | Dems: 92.9% |
| Avg House: $6,565 | House: 89.3% |
| Avg Sen: $6,476 | Incumb: 69.7% |

**Tele-Communications Inc** — $103,568
Tele-Communications, Inc PAC (TCI PAC)
Denver, CO     Cable TV

| 33 Candidates | Dems: 65.5% |
| Avg House: $2,141 | Senate: 60.7% |
| Avg Sen: $4,492 | Incumb: 85.3% |

**Tenneco Inc** — $217,750
Tenneco Inc. Employees Good Government Fund (aka Tenneco Employees Good Govt Fund)
Houston, TX     Naval Ships/Nat Gas†

| 125 Candidates | Repubs: 88.4% |
| Avg House: $1,341 | House: 64.1% |
| Avg Sen: $3,726 | Incumb: 70.3% |

**Texaco** — $149,825
Texaco Political Involvement Committee
White Plains, NY     Oil & Gas Prod†

| 168 Candidates | Repubs: 73.6% |
| Avg House: $653 | House: 61.9% |
| Avg Sen: $2,198 | Incumb: 92.8% |

**Texas Air** — $317,850
Continental Airlines Inc Employee Fund for a Better America (fka Continental Holdings PAC)
Houston, TX     Airlines

| 160 Candidates | Repubs: 69.6% |
| Avg House: $1,489 | House: 57.2% |
| Avg Sen: $3,584 | Incumb: 93.7% |

**Texas Cattle Feeders Assn** — $81,900
Beef-PAC (Beef PAC of Texas Cattle Feeders Association)
Amarillo, TX     Natl Cattlemens Assn     Feedlots

| 59 Candidates | Repubs: 67.0% |
| Avg House: $1,176 | House: 64.6% |
| Avg Sen: $2,071 | Incumb: 79.6% |

**Texas Instruments** — $94,850
Constructive Citizenship Program of Texas Instruments
Dallas, TX     Computer Equip†

| 88 Candidates | Dems: 53.2% |
| Avg House: $957 | House: 64.6% |
| Avg Sen: $1,400 | Incumb: 97.4% |

**Texas Utilities Electric Co** — $86,900
Texas Utilities Company PAC
Dallas, TX     Texas Utilities     Electric Utilities

| 100 Candidates | Repubs: 61.3% |
| Avg House: $756 | House: 72.2% |
| Avg Sen: $1,421 | Incumb: 95.0% |

**Texas Utilities Electric Co** — $50,300
Texas Utilities Electric Company TP&L Division Employee PAC
Dallas, TX     Texas Utilities     Electric Utilities

| 35 Candidates | Repubs: 55.8% |
| Avg House: $1,617 | House: 83.6% |
| Avg Sen: $917 | Incumb: 86.4% |

† PAC sponsor has other major interests in addition to this primary category

| PAC Sponsor or Related Group/PAC Name / Affiliate | 1989-90 Total | Where the money went... | | |
|---|---|---|---|---|
| **Textron Inc**<br>Textron Inc PAC<br>Providence, RI — Air Defense† | $373,625 | 208 Candidates<br>Avg House: $1,413<br>Avg Sen: $3,513 | Dems: 56.1%<br>House: 64.3%<br>Incumb: 94.1% | |
| **Thiokol**<br>Thiokol PAC<br>Ogden, UT — Air Defense† | $62,800 | 71 Candidates<br>Avg House: $758<br>Avg Sen: $1,186 | Repubs: 54.6%<br>House: 60.4%<br>Incumb: 95.9% | |
| **Tobacco Institute**<br>Tobacco Institute PAC<br>Washington, DC — Tobacco | $204,525 | 259 Candidates<br>Avg House: $719<br>Avg Sen: $1,452 | Repubs: 58.1%<br>House: 82.3%<br>Incumb: 94.9% | |
| **Torchmark Corp**<br>Torchmark Corporation Political Action Committee (Torch-PAC)<br>Birmingham, AL — Insurance | $149,890 | 86 Candidates<br>Avg House: $1,366<br>Avg Sen: $2,293 | Repubs: 62.3%<br>Senate: 53.5%<br>Incumb: 90.8% | |
| **Trans Comm Intl Union**<br>Responsible Citizens Political League-a Project of the Trans Comm Intl Union(TCU)<br>Rockville, MD — Transport Unions | $377,401 | 320 Candidates<br>Avg House: $866<br>Avg Sen: $3,446 | Dems: 97.0%<br>House: 64.2%<br>Incumb: 74.6% | |
| **TransAmerica Life Companies**<br>TransAmerica Life Companies PAC "TALCPAC"<br>Los Angeles, CA — TransAmerica — Life Insurance | $51,750 | 51 Candidates<br>Avg House: $1,063<br>Avg Sen: $841 | Dems: 69.0%<br>House: 82.1%<br>Incumb: 98.1% | |
| **Transport Workers Union**<br>Transport Workers Union Political Contributions Committee<br>New York, NY — Transport Unions | $332,665 | 178 Candidates<br>Avg House: $1,575<br>Avg Sen: $3,515 | Dems: 96.5%<br>House: 71.5%<br>Incumb: 76.4% | |
| **Travelers Corp**<br>Travelers Corporation PAC (T-PAC); The<br>Hartford, CT — Insurance† | $260,200 | 119 Candidates<br>Avg House: $1,751<br>Avg Sen: $3,231 | Repubs: 59.2%<br>House: 56.5%<br>Incumb: 96.9% | |
| **TRW Inc**<br>TRW Good Government Fund<br>Lyndhurst, OH — Defense† | $169,100 | 182 Candidates<br>Avg House: $774<br>Avg Sen: $1,780 | Repubs: 54.5%<br>House: 70.5%<br>Incumb: 96.2% | |
| **Turner Broadcasting System**<br>Turner Broadcasting System PAC Inc<br>Atlanta, GA — Cable TV Prod | $56,458 | 56 Candidates<br>Avg House: $488<br>Avg Sen: $1,812 | Dems: 79.7%<br>Senate: 70.6%<br>Incumb: 98.2% | |
| **Tyson Foods**<br>Tyson Foods Inc PAC (TYPAC)<br>Springdale, AR — Poultry† | $126,950 | 79 Candidates<br>Avg House: $1,178<br>Avg Sen: $2,481 | Dems: 79.0%<br>Senate: 50.8%<br>Incumb: 88.3% | |
| **Union Camp Corp**<br>Union Camp Corporation PAC<br>Wayne, NJ — Paper/Forest Prod† | $122,500 | 58 Candidates<br>Avg House: $583<br>Avg Sen: $4,614 | Repubs: 83.3%<br>Senate: 82.9%<br>Incumb: 94.5% | |
| **Union Oil**<br>Union Oil (Unocal) Political Awareness Fund<br>Los Angeles, CA — Oil & Gas Prod† | $137,884 | 153 Candidates<br>Avg House: $576<br>Avg Sen: $2,648 | Repubs: 64.1%<br>House: 53.9%<br>Incumb: 86.5% | |
| **Union Pacific Corp**<br>Union Pacific Fund for Effective Government<br>Washington, DC — Railroads† | $512,614 | 275 Candidates<br>Avg House: $1,201<br>Avg Sen: $4,576 | Repubs: 62.7%<br>House: 51.8%<br>Incumb: 89.0% | |
| **Unisys Corp**<br>Unisys Corporation Employees PAC<br>Washington, DC — Computer Equip† | $83,275 | 124 Candidates<br>Avg House: $588<br>Avg Sen: $988 | Repubs: 55.9%<br>House: 69.1%<br>Incumb: 97.5% | |
| **United Airlines**<br>United Airlines PAC<br>Chicago, IL — Airlines | $165,200 | 158 Candidates<br>Avg House: $893<br>Avg Sen: $1,754 | Dems: 54.2%<br>House: 70.3%<br>Incumb: 100.0% | |
| **United Auto Workers**<br>UAW - V - CAP (UAW Voluntary Community Action Program)<br>Detroit, MI — Manufacturing Unions | $1,795,912 | 345 Candidates<br>Avg House: $5,151<br>Avg Sen: $5,724 | Dems: 99.1%<br>House: 89.5%<br>Incumb: 64.8% | |
| **United Mine Workers**<br>United Mine Workers of America - Coal Miners PAC<br>Washington, DC — Mine Workers | $313,415 | 233 Candidates<br>Avg House: $1,124<br>Avg Sen: $2,638 | Dems: 94.4%<br>House: 71.4%<br>Incumb: 78.2% | |
| **United Paperworkers**<br>United Paperworkers International Union Political Education Program<br>Washington, DC — Manufacturing Unions | $79,000 | 64 Candidates<br>Avg House: $1,078<br>Avg Sen: $1,605 | Dems: 97.7%<br>House: 61.4%<br>Incumb: 51.3% | |

| PAC Sponsor or Related Group/PAC Name | Affiliate | 1989-90 Total | Where the money went... | | |
|---|---|---|---|---|---|
| **United Parcel Service** <br> UPSPAC <br> Greenwich, CT | Express Delivery† | $658,332 | 404 Candidates <br> Avg House: $1,421 <br> Avg Sen: $2,759 | Dems: 60.3% <br> House: 73.6% <br> Incumb: 97.9% | |
| **United States Tobacco Co** <br> U S Tobacco Executives, Administrators and Managers PAC (USTEAM PAC) <br> Greenwich, CT | Tobacco | $306,900 | 123 Candidates <br> Avg House: $2,010 <br> Avg Sen: $4,069 | Repubs: 68.9% <br> House: 61.6% <br> Incumb: 85.7% | |
| **United Steelworkers** <br> United Steelworkers of America Political Action Fund <br> Pittsburgh, PA | Manufacturing Unions | $897,675 | 181 Candidates <br> Avg House: $4,627 <br> Avg Sen: $6,942 | Dems: 99.7% <br> House: 79.9% <br> Incumb: 56.7% | |
| **United Technologies** <br> United Technologies Corporation, PAC <br> Washington, DC | Air Defense† | $323,475 | 188 Candidates <br> Avg House: $1,301 <br> Avg Sen: $3,492 | Repubs: 54.3% <br> House: 61.1% <br> Incumb: 97.0% | |
| **United Telecommunications** <br> United Telecommunications, Inc PAC (UNIPAC) <br> Westwood, KS | Phone Utilities† | $215,502 | 188 Candidates <br> Avg House: $930 <br> Avg Sen: $2,287 | Repubs: 63.7% <br> House: 68.2% <br> Incumb: 87.7% | |
| **United Transportation Union** <br> Transportation Political Education League <br> Cleveland, OH | Railroad Unions | $709,300 | 325 Candidates <br> Avg House: $1,989 <br> Avg Sen: $3,486 | Dems: 92.4% <br> House: 79.4% <br> Incumb: 82.5% | |
| **Upjohn Co** <br> Upjohn Employees PAC <br> Kalamazoo, MI | Pharmaceuticals | $111,000 | 118 Candidates <br> Avg House: $786 <br> Avg Sen: $1,432 | Dems: 63.5% <br> House: 60.9% <br> Incumb: 97.9% | |
| **US League of Savings Assns** <br> US League-Savings Association Political Elections Committee <br> Washington, DC | Savings & Loans | $249,699 | 209 Candidates <br> Avg House: $1,025 <br> Avg Sen: $1,813 | Dems: 64.8% <br> House: 67.3% <br> Incumb: 98.4% | |
| **US Telephone Assn** <br> United States Telephone Assn PAC <br> Washington, DC | Phone Utilities | $156,833 | 139 Candidates <br> Avg House: $762 <br> Avg Sen: $2,353 | Dems: 54.0% <br> House: 52.0% <br> Incumb: 98.2% | |
| **US West Inc** <br> US West Inc PAC <br> Denver, CO | Phone Utilities | $334,657 | 148 Candidates <br> Avg House: $1,997 <br> Avg Sen: $3,148 | Repubs: 56.0% <br> House: 68.0% <br> Incumb: 81.1% | |
| **USX Corp** <br> USX Corporation PAC <br> Washington, DC | USX Corp | Oil & Gas Prod† | $103,700 | 97 Candidates <br> Avg House: $842 <br> Avg Sen: $2,067 | Dems: 62.8% <br> House: 64.1% <br> Incumb: 92.4% |
| **Valley Education Fund** <br> Valley Education Fund <br> Washington, DC | ex-Rep Tony Coelho (D-Calif) | Dem Leaders | $70,740 | 55 Candidates <br> Avg House: $1,217 <br> Avg Sen: $5,000 | Dems: 100.0% <br> House: 92.9% <br> Incumb: 74.5% |
| **Van Ness, Feldman & Curtis** <br> Van Ness, Feldman & Curtis, PC PAC <br> Washington, DC | Lawyers | $50,684 | 72 Candidates <br> Avg House: $576 <br> Avg Sen: $1,015 | Dems: 70.8% <br> House: 58.0% <br> Incumb: 95.6% | |
| **Verner, Liipfert et al** <br> Verner, Liipfert, Bernhard, McPherson & Hand PAC <br> Washington, DC | Lawyers/Lobbyists | $122,769 | 85 Candidates <br> Avg House: $799 <br> Avg Sen: $2,831 | Dems: 78.7% <br> Senate: 62.3% <br> Incumb: 95.7% | |
| **Veterans of Foreign Wars** <br> Veterans of Foreign Wars PAC Inc <br> Washington, DC | Pro-Defense | $84,250 | 136 Candidates <br> Avg House: $623 <br> Avg Sen: $583 | Repubs: 57.6% <br> House: 91.7% <br> Incumb: 97.0% | |
| **Vinson, Elkins, Searls et al** <br> National Good Government Fund; The <br> Houston, TX | Lawyers/Lobbyists | $91,666 | 59 Candidates <br> Avg House: $1,634 <br> Avg Sen: $1,452 | Dems: 72.7% <br> House: 58.8% <br> Incumb: 85.5% | |
| **Voters for Choice/Friends of Family Planning** <br> Voters for Choice/Friends of Family Planning <br> Washington, DC | Pro-Choice | $173,263 | 95 Candidates <br> Avg House: $1,663 <br> Avg Sen: $2,560 | Dems: 91.7% <br> House: 74.9% <br> Incumb: 54.5% | |
| **Wall & Ceiling/Gypsum Drywall Contractors** <br> Wall and Ceiling PAC <br> Alexandria, VA | Subcontractors | $57,550 | 74 Candidates <br> Avg House: $532 <br> Avg Sen: $1,542 | Repubs: 95.1% <br> House: 51.8% <br> Incumb: 86.4% | |
| **Walt Disney Co** <br> Walt Disney Company Employees' PAC <br> Burbank, CA | Movies/Resorts† | $86,519 | 59 Candidates <br> Avg House: $1,192 <br> Avg Sen: $2,436 | Dems: 61.5% <br> House: 63.4% <br> Incumb: 96.0% | |

† PAC sponsor has other major interests in addition to this primary category

| **Warner Communications**<br>Warner Communications Inc PAC<br>New York, NY | Time Warner | **$129,350**<br><br>Broadcasting† | 65 Candidates<br>Avg House: $1,219<br>Avg Sen: $2,611 | Dems: 89.1%<br>Senate: 72.7%<br>Incumb: 89.6% |
|---|---|---|---|---|
| **Warner-Lambert**<br>Warner-Lambert PAC ("WALPAC")<br>Morris Plains, NJ | | **$61,450**<br><br>Health Products† | 40 Candidates<br>Avg House: $1,331<br>Avg Sen: $1,844 | Dems: 55.0%<br>House: 52.0%<br>Incumb: 89.1% |
| **Washington PAC**<br>Washington PAC<br>Washington, DC | | **$262,375**<br><br>Pro-Israel | 172 Candidates<br>Avg House: $854<br>Avg Sen: $3,671 | Dems: 75.2%<br>Senate: 57.4%<br>Incumb: 91.5% |
| **Waste Management Inc**<br>Waste Management Inc Employees' Better Government Fund ("WMI PAC")<br>Oak Brook, IL | Waste Mgmt | **$392,380**<br><br> | 320 Candidates<br>Avg House: $981<br>Avg Sen: $2,268 | Dems: 56.9%<br>House: 64.7%<br>Incumb: 91.1% |
| **West Publishing**<br>West Publishing Company PAC (West Publishing PAC)<br>Minneapolis, MN | | **$74,700**<br><br>Books & Mags | 45 Candidates<br>Avg House: $1,216<br>Avg Sen: $2,643 | Dems: 71.6%<br>House: 50.5%<br>Incumb: 98.7% |
| **Westinghouse Electric**<br>Westinghouse Electric Corporation Employees Political Participation Program<br>Pittsburgh, PA | | **$270,975**<br><br>Electronics† | 246 Candidates<br>Avg House: $889<br>Avg Sen: $2,076 | Dems: 57.8%<br>House: 66.3%<br>Incumb: 96.9% |
| **Westvaco Corp**<br>Westvaco Corporation Political Participation Program<br>New York, NY | | **$235,500**<br><br>Paper/Forest Prod† | 75 Candidates<br>Avg House: $2,588<br>Avg Sen: $4,889 | Repubs: 78.6%<br>House: 62.6%<br>Incumb: 90.2% |
| **Wexler Group**<br>Wexler, Reynolds, Fuller, Harrison & Schule, Inc PAC<br>Washington, DC | Hill & Knowlton | **$79,234**<br><br>Lobbyist/PR | 123 Candidates<br>Avg House: $527<br>Avg Sen: $952 | Dems: 70.6%<br>House: 59.2%<br>Incumb: 98.4% |
| **Weyerhaeuser Co**<br>Weyerhaeuser Company Special Shareholders PAC<br>St. Paul, MN | Weyerhaeuser | **$78,000**<br><br>Paper/Forest Prod† | 62 Candidates<br>Avg House: $793<br>Avg Sen: $2,167 | Repubs: 82.6%<br>Senate: 58.3%<br>Incumb: 88.5% |
| **Willamette Industries**<br>WILPAC Willamette Industries Inc PAC<br>Portland, OR | | **$54,000**<br><br>Forest Products† | 27 Candidates<br>Avg House: $1,525<br>Avg Sen: $3,357 | Repubs: 95.4%<br>House: 56.5%<br>Incumb: 68.5% |
| **Williams & Jensen**<br>Williams & Jensen PC PAC (W & J PAC)<br>Washington, DC | | **$79,211**<br><br>Lawyers/Lobbyists | 129 Candidates<br>Avg House: $553<br>Avg Sen: $1,075 | Dems: 54.9%<br>House: 79.6%<br>Incumb: 92.2% |
| **Wine and Spirits Wholesalers of America**<br>Wine and Spirits Wholesalers of America PAC<br>Washington, DC | | **$160,450**<br><br>Liquor Wholesalers | 111 Candidates<br>Avg House: $1,198<br>Avg Sen: $2,391 | Dems: 59.8%<br>House: 65.7%<br>Incumb: 96.0% |
| **Winn-Dixie Stores**<br>Sunbelt Good Government Committee of Winn-Dixie Stores, Inc.<br>Jacksonville, FL | | **$133,500**<br><br>Food Stores† | 73 Candidates<br>Avg House: $1,490<br>Avg Sen: $2,667 | Repubs: 58.1%<br>House: 58.1%<br>Incumb: 86.9% |
| **Women's Alliance for Israel**<br>Women's Alliance for Israel<br>Beverly Hills, CA | | **$151,500**<br><br>Pro-Israel | 53 Candidates<br>Avg House: $1,618<br>Avg Sen: $5,079 | Dems: 79.2%<br>Senate: 63.7%<br>Incumb: 81.2% |
| **Women's Campaign Fund**<br>Women's Campaign Fund Inc<br>Washington, DC | | **$122,355**<br><br>Womens Issues† | 34 Candidates<br>Avg House: $3,334<br>Avg Sen: $4,833 | Dems: 61.0%<br>House: 76.3%<br>Incumb: 38.0% |
| **Women's Pro-Israel National PAC**<br>Women's Pro-Israel National PAC ("WIN PAC")<br>Washington, DC | | **$122,416**<br><br>Pro-Israel | 71 Candidates<br>Avg House: $867<br>Avg Sen: $3,208 | Dems: 51.8%<br>Senate: 68.1%<br>Incumb: 94.1% |
| **Xerox Corp**<br>Team Xerox PAC ("TXP")<br>Stamford, CT | | **$79,500**<br><br>Office Machines† | 88 Candidates<br>Avg House: $863<br>Avg Sen: $1,100 | Repubs: 59.1%<br>House: 79.3%<br>Incumb: 89.9% |
| **Yellow Freight System**<br>Yellow Freight System Inc PAC<br>Shawnee Mission, KS | | **$124,475**<br><br>Trucking Companies | 131 Candidates<br>Avg House: $762<br>Avg Sen: $1,676 | Dems: 64.1%<br>House: 63.7%<br>Incumb: 94.1% |

# Appendix: Industry & Interest Group Categories

This is a listing of the detailed categories used in classifying all the contributors that gave money to federal candidates in the 1990 elections. Included are the category name, the total in 1989-90 contributions, and a breakdown of the totals by PACs and political parties.

Classification of contributors is not always a straightforward matter, particularly when the contributor has multiple interests or multiple sources of revenue. Many corporate PACs have been assigned multiple categories — a primary code based on their single largest source of income, and as many as six alternate codes encompassing smaller, but significant revenue sources. Throughout this book, and in the listings below, the category assigned to a particular contribution depends both on the interests of the contributor *and the congressional committee assignments of the recipient.* This is particularly relevant in the defense sector, as many defense contractors earn the majority of their revenues from non-defense activities. In such cases, the contributions are classified as defense-related *only when they are made to a member who sits on a defense-related committee.* (For that reason, totals in the defense sector can be considered very conservative.) A similar procedure was used for all other diversified companies.

In most cases, individual contributors are classified according to the economic interests of their employer. Contributions from non-income earning spouses and children are classified according to the economic interest of the income earner within the family. Thus a bank president, his wife and children would all be classified under "commercial banking" unless the wife had a job as well, in which case she would be classified separately.

Individual contributors are classified under the ideological/single-issue categories only if they contributed to an ideological or single-issue PAC. Even then, the contribution is considered ideological only if the candidate who received the contribution also drew money from an ideological PAC with similar interests. The following example illustrates the procedure used: If a real estate developer contributes both to a pro-Israel PAC and to a candidate who received direct contributions from pro-Israel PACs, the contribution would be classified under "pro-Israel." If the donor gave to someone who got no money from pro-Israel PACs, it would be classified under "real estate." In the case of ideological contributors, non-income earning spouses and children are *not* classified as ideological givers unless they themselves have contributed to an ideological PAC.

Detailed profiles of the spending patterns of each major industry group can be found in the "Industry Profile" section of this book, on pages 41-93.

## Agriculture

|  | Total | PAC Pct | Dem Pct | Repub Pct |
|---|---|---|---|---|
| ***Crop Production & Basic Processing*** | | | | |
| Sugar cane & sugar beets | $1,855,632 | 90% | 60% | 40% |
| Vegetables, fruits and tree nuts | $705,120 | 80% | 49% | 51% |
| Cotton | $402,649 | 78% | 51% | 49% |
| Wheat, corn, soybeans and cash grain | $153,524 | 86% | 55% | 45% |
| Other commodities (incl rice, peanuts, honey) | $334,253 | 77% | 68% | 32% |
| Farmers, crop unspecified | $708,122 | 7% | 47% | 53% |
| ***Tobacco*** | | | | |
| Tobacco & tobacco products | $2,126,974 | 95% | 47% | 53% |
| ***Dairy*** | | | | |
| Milk & dairy producers | $1,887,117 | 94% | 63% | 37% |
| ***Livestock & Poultry*** | | | | |
| Livestock | $947,903 | 44% | 34% | 66% |
| Feedlots & related livestock services | $202,505 | 83% | 39% | 61% |
| Poultry & eggs | $554,975 | 61% | 63% | 37% |
| Sheep & wool producers | $49,850 | 81% | 55% | 45% |
| ***Agricultural Services & Products*** | | | | |
| Agricultural services, diversified | $433,711 | 84% | 54% | 46% |
| Agricultural chemicals (fertilizers & pesticides) | $612,425 | 94% | 41% | 59% |
| Animal feed & health products | $78,735 | 69% | 40% | 60% |
| Veterinarians | $281,583 | 84% | 52% | 48% |
| Grain traders & terminals | $337,300 | 68% | 62% | 38% |
| Farm organizations & cooperatives | $506,815 | 100% | 55% | 45% |
| Farm machinery & equipment | $259,925 | 79% | 22% | 78% |
| Florists & nursery services | $155,275 | 48% | 32% | 68% |

### Food Processing & Sales

| | Total | PAC Pct | Dem Pct | Repub Pct |
|---|---|---|---|---|
| Food & beverage products and services, diversified | $437,103 | 75% | 31% | 69% |
| Food and kindred products manufacturing | $1,166,128 | 80% | 33% | 67% |
| Meat processing & products | $149,627 | 56% | 34% | 66% |
| Food stores | $930,169 | 67% | 39% | 61% |
| Food wholesalers | $295,877 | 60% | 34% | 66% |

### Forestry & Forest Products

| | Total | PAC Pct | Dem Pct | Repub Pct |
|---|---|---|---|---|
| Forestry & forest products | $961,661 | 61% | 28% | 72% |
| Paper & pulp mills and paper manufacturing | $1,046,899 | 92% | 25% | 75% |

### Commodity Trading

| | Total | PAC Pct | Dem Pct | Repub Pct |
|---|---|---|---|---|
| Commodity brokers/dealers | $1,323,500 | 82% | 67% | 33% |

### Other & Unclassified

| | Total | PAC Pct | Dem Pct | Repub Pct |
|---|---|---|---|---|
| Misc Agriculture | $254,434 | 0% | 42% | 58% |

## Communications & Electronics

| | Total | PAC Pct | Dem Pct | Repub Pct |
|---|---|---|---|---|
| **Printing & Publishing** | | | | |
| Book, newspaper & periodical publishing | $672,197 | 17% | 72% | 27% |
| Commercial printing & typesetting | $266,587 | 38% | 37% | 63% |
| Greeting card publishing | $92,550 | 80% | 24% | 76% |
| Misc printing & publishing | $73,050 | 49% | 28% | 72% |
| **Broadcasting, Motion Pictures & Entertainment** | | | | |
| Broadcasting & motion pictures, diversified | $364,875 | 38% | 84% | 16% |
| Motion picture production & distribution | $1,303,815 | 27% | 89% | 11% |
| Television production | $374,025 | 39% | 85% | 15% |
| Commercial TV & radio stations | $566,113 | 55% | 55% | 45% |
| Cable & satellite TV operators | $1,366,326 | 70% | 66% | 34% |
| Recorded music & music production | $334,000 | 60% | 90% | 10% |
| **Telephone Utilities** | | | | |
| Local & regional telephone utilities | $3,504,071 | 95% | 50% | 50% |
| Long-distance telephone utilities | $1,213,409 | 96% | 58% | 42% |
| **Telecommunications Services & Equipment** | | | | |
| Telephone & communications equipment | $470,397 | 82% | 46% | 54% |
| Satellite communications | $129,300 | 83% | 59% | 41% |
| Paging & cellular phones & services | $46,650 | 43% | 76% | 24% |
| Other communications services | $7,125 | 86% | 41% | 59% |
| Telecommunications, unclassified | $53,750 | 0% | 62% | 38% |
| **Electronics Manufacturing & Services** | | | | |
| Electronics manufacturing & services | $488,201 | 69% | 37% | 63% |
| **Computer Equipment & Services** | | | | |
| Computer manufacture & services, diversified | $229,420 | 29% | 56% | 44% |
| Computers, components & accessories | $341,330 | 58% | 43% | 57% |
| Data processing & computer services | $270,392 | 68% | 51% | 48% |
| Computer software | $86,827 | 9% | 22% | 78% |
| **Other & Unclassified** | | | | |
| Misc communications & electronics | $20,700 | 0% | 60% | 40% |

## Construction

| | Total | PAC Pct | Dem Pct | Repub Pct |
|---|---|---|---|---|
| **General Contractors** | | | | |
| Builders associations | $107,412 | 100% | 6% | 94% |
| Public works, industrial & commercial construction | $2,219,773 | 67% | 38% | 62% |
| Construction, unclassified or diversified | $1,486,680 | 0% | 50% | 50% |
| **Home Builders** | | | | |
| Residential construction | $1,816,180 | 80% | 48% | 52% |
| Mobile home construction | $120,500 | 74% | 36% | 64% |
| **Special Trade Contractors** | | | | |
| Special trade contractors, diversified | $335,682 | 31% | 36% | 64% |
| Electrical contractors | $312,570 | 64% | 31% | 69% |

| | | | |
|---|---|---|---|
| Plumbing, heating & air conditioning | $310,447 | 72% | 20% | 80% |
| Landscaping & excavation services | $48,541 | 0% | 41% | 59% |

### Construction Services

| | | | |
|---|---|---|---|
| Engineering, architecture & construction mgmt, diversified | $945,451 | 46% | 62% | 38% |
| Architectural services | $291,056 | 23% | 73% | 27% |
| Surveying | $50,330 | 59% | 43% | 57% |

### Building Materials & Equipment

| | | | |
|---|---|---|---|
| Building materials, diversified | $335,789 | 49% | 44% | 56% |
| Stone, clay, glass & concrete products | $514,935 | 48% | 26% | 74% |
| Lumber & wood products | $185,284 | 10% | 41% | 59% |
| Plumbing & pipe products | $150,711 | 52% | 39% | 61% |
| Electrical supply dealers | $30,015 | 0% | 53% | 47% |
| Construction equipment | $155,695 | 59% | 22% | 78% |
| Other construction-related products | $59,700 | 26% | 42% | 58% |

## Defense

| | Total | PAC Pct | Dem Pct | Repub Pct |
|---|---|---|---|---|

### Defense Aerospace

| | | | | |
|---|---|---|---|---|
| Defense aerospace contractors | $4,424,015 | 96% | 50% | 50% |

### Defense Electronics

| | | | | |
|---|---|---|---|---|
| Defense electronic contractors | $2,444,906 | 94% | 49% | 51% |

### Misc Defense

| | | | | |
|---|---|---|---|---|
| Defense research & development | $262,350 | 89% | 44% | 56% |
| Defense shipbuilders | $270,000 | 82% | 27% | 73% |
| Defense nuclear contractors | $21,450 | 0% | 86% | 14% |
| Ground-based & other weapons systems | $249,200 | 96% | 49% | 51% |
| Defense-related services | $188,663 | 73% | 53% | 47% |
| Defense, unclassified | $21,800 | 0% | 50% | 50% |

## Energy & Natural Resources

| | Total | PAC Pct | Dem Pct | Repub Pct |
|---|---|---|---|---|

### Oil & Gas

| | | | | |
|---|---|---|---|---|
| Oil & gas, diversified | $945,811 | 29% | 46% | 54% |
| Major (multinational) oil & gas producers | $2,412,151 | 90% | 30% | 70% |
| Independent oil & gas producers | $1,501,245 | 38% | 41% | 59% |
| Natural gas transmission & distribution | $1,935,226 | 88% | 59% | 41% |
| Oilfield service, equipment & exploration | $777,212 | 52% | 38% | 62% |
| Petroleum refining & marketing | $807,441 | 70% | 37% | 63% |
| Gasoline service stations | $401,784 | 77% | 47% | 53% |
| Fuel oil dealers | $47,990 | 15% | 72% | 28% |
| LPG/liquid propane dealers & producers | $42,050 | 67% | 31% | 69% |

### Mining

| | | | | |
|---|---|---|---|---|
| Mining, diversified | $81,153 | 43% | 40% | 60% |
| Coal mining | $552,040 | 66% | 46% | 54% |
| Metal mining & processing | $680,578 | 90% | 38% | 62% |
| Non-metallic mining | $39,475 | 81% | 57% | 43% |
| Mining services & equipment | $17,400 | 3% | 53% | 47% |

### Misc Energy

| | | | | |
|---|---|---|---|---|
| Power plant construction & equipment | $489,701 | 93% | 33% | 67% |
| Nuclear plant construction, equipment & services | $207,150 | 90% | 57% | 43% |
| Energy production & distribution | $85,856 | 20% | 42% | 58% |
| Alternate energy production & services | $27,400 | 41% | 68% | 32% |
| Misc energy | $51,651 | 91% | 67% | 33% |

### Electric Utilities

| | | | | |
|---|---|---|---|---|
| Electric power utilities | $2,071,279 | 93% | 51% | 49% |
| Gas & electric utilities | $990,911 | 95% | 48% | 52% |
| Rural electric cooperatives | $674,139 | 97% | 69% | 31% |

### Environmental Services

| | | | | |
|---|---|---|---|---|
| Environmental services, equipment & consulting | $82,708 | 12% | 71% | 29% |

### Waste Management
Waste management ...................................................................... $809,854 ............... 79% ............... 63% ............... 37%

### Commercial Fishing
Fishing ........................................................................................ $119,892 ............... 51% ............... 49% ............... 51%

### Other & Unclassified
Hunting & wildlife ......................................................................... $250 ............... 0% ............ 100% ................. 0%
Water Utilities ............................................................................. $89,825 ............... 93% ............... 35% ............... 65%
Misc energy, natural resources and environment ...................... $48,765 ................. 0% ............... 27% ............... 73%

## Fire, Insurance & Real Estate

| | Total | PAC Pct | Dem Pct | Repub Pct |
|---|---|---|---|---|

### Commercial Banks
Commercial banks & bank holding companies ....................... $7,775,819 ............... 81% ............... 56% ............... 44%

### Savings & Loans
Savings banks and savings & loans ...................................... $1,284,666 ............... 76% ............... 57% ............... 43%

### Credit Unions
Credit unions ....................................................................... $597,848 ............... 96% ............... 58% ............... 42%

### Misc Banks
Banks & lending institutions, diversified ................................ $259,827 ............... 25% ............... 51% ............... 49%

### Finance/Credit Companies
Credit agencies & finance companies ................................... $687,310 ............... 79% ............... 59% ............... 41%

### Securities & Investment
Securities, commodities & investment, diversified .................. $130,110 ................. 0% ............... 57% ............... 43%
Security brokers & investment companies .......................... $3,775,778 ............... 33% ............... 64% ............... 35%
Investment banking .......................................................... $1,392,356 ............... 35% ............... 74% ............... 26%
Stock exchanges ................................................................ $77,613 ............... 72% ............... 70% ............... 30%
Venture capital .................................................................. $499,030 ............... 59% ............... 59% ............... 41%

### Commodity Trading
Commodity brokers & dealers ........................................... $1,323,500 ............... 82% ............... 67% ............... 33%

### Insurance
Insurance companies, brokers & agents, diversified ............. $6,126,838 ............... 75% ............... 50% ............... 50%
Accident & health insurance ............................................... $887,185 ............... 95% ............... 58% ............... 42%
Life insurance ................................................................... $3,654,834 ............... 93% ............... 57% ............... 43%
Property & casualty insurance ............................................ $149,650 ............... 67% ............... 37% ............... 63%
Insurance, unclassified ....................................................... $38,800 ............... 55% ............... 59% ............... 41%

### Real Estate
Real estate, diversified .................................................... $1,823,656 ................. 0% ............... 62% ............... 38%
Real estate developers & subdividers ............................... $2,369,556 ............... 13% ............... 63% ............... 37%
Real estate agents & managers ....................................... $4,265,904 ............... 76% ............... 56% ............... 44%
Building operators & managers ........................................... $741,455 ................. 3% ............... 69% ............... 31%
Mortgage bankers & brokers .............................................. $541,370 ............... 65% ............... 64% ............... 36%
Title insurance & title abstract offices ................................ $132,975 ............... 58% ............... 52% ............... 47%
Mobile home dealers & parks ................................................ $8,150 ................. 0% ............... 48% ............... 52%
Other real estate services .................................................. $73,450 ............... 69% ............... 61% ............... 39%

### Accountants
Accountants ...................................................................... $2,550,917 ............... 67% ............... 57% ............... 43%

### Misc Finance
Credit reporting services & collection agencies ..................... $127,449 ............... 70% ............... 36% ............... 64%
Misc financial services & consulting ...................................... $71,550 ............... 39% ............... 50% ............... 50%
Tax return services ............................................................. $23,175 ............... 71% ............... 52% ............... 48%
Other financial services .................................................... $165,575 ............... 86% ............... 59% ............... 41%
Other finance, diversified or unclassified ........................... $1,604,229 ................. 0% ............... 51% ............... 49%

# Health

| | Total | PAC Pct | Dem Pct | Repub Pct |
|---|---|---|---|---|
| **Health Professionals** | | | | |
| Physicians | $5,947,306 | 48% | 51% | 49% |
| Optometrists & ophthalmologists | $1,521,417 | 89% | 55% | 45% |
| Psychiatrists & psychologists | $389,254 | 76% | 85% | 15% |
| Other physician specialists | $688,744 | 71% | 60% | 40% |
| Dentists | $1,131,900 | 82% | 52% | 48% |
| Nurses | $377,749 | 94% | 85% | 15% |
| Chiropractors | $301,103 | 83% | 69% | 31% |
| Pharmacists | $298,280 | 88% | 68% | 32% |
| Other non-physician health practitioners | $375,357 | 94% | 73% | 27% |
| **Hospitals/Nursing Homes** | | | | |
| Hospitals | $1,333,078 | 74% | 70% | 30% |
| Nursing homes | $535,212 | 66% | 72% | 28% |
| Health care institutions, diversified | $21,275 | 3% | 58% | 42% |
| **Health Services** | | | | |
| Health care services | $91,340 | 56% | 68% | 32% |
| Home care services | $68,202 | 50% | 76% | 24% |
| HMOs | $106,190 | 73% | 64% | 36% |
| Outpatient health services (incl drug & alcohol) | $63,100 | 66% | 98% | 2% |
| Medical laboratories | $37,960 | 37% | 54% | 46% |
| Optical services (glasses & contact lenses) | $9,700 | 30% | 57% | 43% |
| **Pharmaceuticals/Health Products** | | | | |
| Health care products, diversified | $110,975 | 57% | 61% | 39% |
| Medical supplies manufacturing & sales | $372,819 | 62% | 58% | 42% |
| Personal health care products | $118,225 | 81% | 45% | 55% |
| Pharmaceutical manufacturing | $2,008,511 | 88% | 46% | 54% |
| Pharmaceutical wholesale/retail | $79,701 | 67% | 46% | 54% |
| **Other & Unclassified** | | | | |
| Health, education & human resources, unclassified | $306,214 | 0% | 66% | 34% |

# Lawyers & Lobbyists

| | Total | PAC Pct | Dem Pct | Repub Pct |
|---|---|---|---|---|
| **Lawyers** | | | | |
| Attorneys & law firms | $15,426,424 | 28% | 75% | 25% |
| **Lobbyists** | | | | |
| Lobbyists & public relations | $3,168,285 | 7% | 74% | 26% |

# Miscellaneous Business

| | Total | PAC Pct | Dem Pct | Repub Pct |
|---|---|---|---|---|
| **Business Associations** | | | | |
| General business associations | $75,846 | 99% | 67% | 34% |
| Chambers of commerce | $80,552 | 78% | 54% | 46% |
| Small business organizations | $382,452 | 100% | 17% | 83% |
| Pro-business organizations | $113,731 | 100% | 7% | 93% |
| General commerce, unclassified or diversified | $153,238 | 0% | 47% | 53% |
| **Food & Beverage** | | | | |
| *NOTE: Food manufacturers are listed under Agriculture* | | | | |
| Restaurants & drinking establishments | $1,760,397 | 68% | 31% | 69% |
| Food catering & food services | $93,603 | 63% | 34% | 66% |
| Confectionery processors & manufacturers | $64,829 | 63% | 48% | 52% |
| Artificial sweeteners and food additives | $24,000 | 89% | 75% | 25% |
| Fish processing | $68,834 | 21% | 60% | 40% |
| Non-alcoholic beverages | $253,374 | 88% | 57% | 43% |
| Beverage bottling & distribution | $132,330 | 54% | 44% | 56% |
| **Beer, Wine & Liquor** | | | | |
| Alcohol | $9,900 | 0% | 73% | 27% |
| Beer | $246,536 | 71% | 59% | 41% |
| Wine & distilled spirits manufacturing | $642,136 | 67% | 69% | 31% |

| | | | | |
|---|---|---|---|---|
| Beer & liquor wholesalers | $1,291,280 | 63% | 61% | 39% |
| Liquor stores | $40,548 | 1% | 82% | 18% |

### Retail Sales

| | | | | |
|---|---|---|---|---|
| Retail trade, diversified | $411,013 | 70% | 43% | 57% |
| Department, variety & convenience stores | $730,295 | 88% | 46% | 54% |
| Apparel & accessory stores | $215,990 | 16% | 65% | 35% |
| Consumer electronics & computer stores | $96,412 | 39% | 51% | 49% |
| Furniture & appliance stores | $127,961 | 0% | 58% | 42% |
| Hardware & building materials stores | $73,462 | 0% | 59% | 41% |
| Miscellaneous retail stores | $339,744 | 2% | 62% | 37% |
| Catalog & mail order houses | $83,950 | 70% | 71% | 29% |
| Direct sales | $62,555 | 79% | 39% | 61% |
| Vending machine sales & services | $34,154 | 0% | 48% | 52% |
| Drug stores | $195,784 | 62% | 53% | 47% |

### Misc Services

| | | | | |
|---|---|---|---|---|
| Equipment rental & leasing | $168,047 | 54% | 47% | 53% |
| Funeral services | $139,154 | 20% | 62% | 38% |
| Laundries & dry cleaners | $61,475 | 0% | 69% | 31% |
| Miscellaneous repair services | $7,540 | 0% | 40% | 60% |
| Pest control | $98,947 | 68% | 45% | 55% |
| Physical fitness centers | $30,850 | 0% | 71% | 29% |
| Video tape rental | $13,450 | 0% | 6% | 94% |
| Other services | $120,864 | 0% | 53% | 47% |

### Business Services

| | | | | |
|---|---|---|---|---|
| Beauty & barber shops | $20,235 | 0% | 42% | 58% |
| Advertising & public relations | $397,810 | 10% | 70% | 30% |
| Direct mail advertising | $95,800 | 67% | 21% | 79% |
| Outdoor advertising | $242,277 | 46% | 57% | 43% |
| Commercial photography, art & graphic design | $56,730 | 0% | 75% | 24% |
| Employment agencies | $125,325 | 39% | 44% | 56% |
| Management consultants & services | $184,353 | 0% | 65% | 35% |
| Marketing research services | $189,228 | 71% | 44% | 56% |
| Security services | $123,634 | 42% | 49% | 51% |
| Warehousing | $47,125 | 0% | 64% | 36% |
| Other business services | $782,069 | 8% | 63% | 37% |

### Recreation & Live Entertainment

| | | | | |
|---|---|---|---|---|
| Casinos, racetracks & gambling | $268,419 | 67% | 75% | 25% |
| Amusement/recreation centers & movie theaters | $133,766 | 54% | 38% | 62% |
| Professional sports, arenas & related equip & svcs | $84,939 | 2% | 62% | 38% |
| Bands, orchestras & other live music production | $37,500 | 0% | 87% | 7% |
| Amusement parks | $15,700 | 0% | 13% | 87% |
| Misc recreation/entertainment | $41,257 | 17% | 65% | 34% |

### Lodging & Tourism

| | | | | |
|---|---|---|---|---|
| Hotels & motels | $678,681 | 52% | 49% | 51% |
| Travel agents | $184,532 | 54% | 58% | 42% |
| Resorts | $46,616 | 34% | 55% | 45% |
| Lodging & tourism, diversified | $63,119 | 21% | 40% | 60% |

### Chemical & Related Manufacturing

| | | | | |
|---|---|---|---|---|
| Chemical manufacturing | $1,438,832 | 72% | 28% | 72% |
| Household cleansers & chemicals | $97,475 | 89% | 31% | 69% |
| Plastics & Rubber processing & products | $197,639 | 36% | 33% | 67% |
| Paints, Solvents and Coatings | $53,775 | 33% | 54% | 46% |
| Explosives | $13,800 | 44% | 66% | 34% |
| Adhesives & Sealants | $10,500 | 0% | 0% | 100% |

### Steel/Smelting

| | | | | |
|---|---|---|---|---|
| Steel | $600,636 | 44% | 57% | 43% |
| Smelting and non-petroleum refining | $28,250 | 0% | 65% | 35% |

### Misc Manufacturing & Distributing

| | | | | |
|---|---|---|---|---|
| Wholesale trade | $276,153 | 52% | 33% | 67% |
| Manufacturing, diversified | $327,036 | 34% | 51% | 49% |
| Manmade fibers | $124,650 | 98% | 38% | 62% |
| Misc heavy industrial manufacturing | $17,190 | 0% | 57% | 43% |
| Industrial/commercial equipment & materials | $1,019,022 | 48% | 29% | 71% |
| Recycling of metal, paper, plastics, etc. | $141,442 | 35% | 58% | 42% |

| | Total | PAC Pct | Dem Pct | Repub Pct |
|---|---|---|---|---|
| Personal products manufacturing, diversified | $67,950 | 0% | 55% | 45% |
| Clothing & accessories | $298,766 | 3% | 71% | 29% |
| Shoes & leather products | $101,488 | 34% | 69% | 31% |
| Toiletries & cosmetics | $145,150 | 22% | 58% | 42% |
| Jewelry | $53,300 | 0% | 72% | 28% |
| Toys | $15,450 | 0% | 68% | 32% |
| Sporting goods sales & manufacturing | $10,150 | 10% | 43% | 57% |
| Household & office products | $97,893 | 29% | 47% | 53% |
| Furniture & wood products | $179,892 | 48% | 32% | 68% |
| Office machines | $101,630 | 87% | 39% | 61% |
| Household appliances | $124,990 | 89% | 14% | 86% |
| Fabricated metal products | $218,892 | 33% | 35% | 65% |
| Hardware & tools | $27,050 | 70% | 9% | 91% |
| Electroplating, polishing & related services | $37,280 | 7% | 50% | 50% |
| Small arms & ammunition | $19,174 | 5% | 18% | 82% |
| Electrical lighting products | $6,750 | 0% | 15% | 85% |
| Paper, glass & packaging materials, diversified | $103,702 | 35% | 43% | 57% |
| Paper packaging materials | $196,200 | 60% | 48% | 52% |
| Glass products | $186,376 | 84% | 40% | 60% |
| Metal cans & containers | $20,000 | 48% | 36% | 64% |
| Textiles & fabrics | $789,657 | 62% | 46% | 54% |
| Precision instruments | $9,701 | 8% | 77% | 23% |
| Optical instruments & lenses | $3,000 | 0% | 100% | 0% |
| Photographic equipment & supplies | $10,749 | 0% | 64% | 36% |
| Clocks & watches | $24,100 | 14% | 77% | 23% |

## Transportation

| | Total | PAC Pct | Dem Pct | Repub Pct |
|---|---|---|---|---|
| **Air Transport** | | | | |
| Airlines | $1,066,538 | 90% | 52% | 48% |
| Express delivery services | $1,175,737 | 98% | 61% | 39% |
| Air freight | $338,220 | 95% | 60% | 38% |
| General aviation (private pilots) | $518,500 | 100% | 49% | 51% |
| Aircraft manufacturers | $220,693 | 92% | 58% | 42% |
| Aircraft parts & equipment | $248,954 | 78% | 47% | 53% |
| Aviation services & airports | $121,650 | 48% | 53% | 47% |
| Space vehicles & components | $203,171 | 92% | 52% | 48% |
| Air transport, diversified | $71,175 | 14% | 29% | 71% |
| **Automotive** | | | | |
| Auto manufacturers | $512,945 | 85% | 56% | 44% |
| Auto dealers, new & used | $1,944,025 | 68% | 38% | 62% |
| Auto dealers, Japanese imports | $747,496 | 86% | 33% | 67% |
| Automotive/truck parts & accessories | $575,969 | 65% | 33% | 67% |
| Auto repair | $26,205 | 7% | 69% | 31% |
| Car & truck rental agencies | $142,478 | 39% | 67% | 33% |
| Misc automotive | $27,559 | 0% | 50% | 50% |
| **Trucking** | | | | |
| Trucking companies & services | $1,194,519 | 74% | 56% | 44% |
| Truck & trailer manufacturers | $52,960 | 58% | 23% | 76% |
| Misc trucking | $22,000 | 5% | 30% | 70% |
| **Railroads** | | | | |
| Railroads | $1,450,464 | 92% | 51% | 49% |
| Railroad services | $103,266 | 95% | 71% | 29% |
| Manufacturers of railroad equipment | $44,100 | 67% | 32% | 68% |
| Misc railroad transportation | $6,650 | 0% | 70% | 30% |
| **Sea Transport** | | | | |
| Ship building & repair | $259,631 | 50% | 36% | 64% |
| Sea freight & passenger services | $817,728 | 68% | 55% | 45% |
| Sea transport, diversified | $144,000 | 0% | 44% | 56% |
| **Misc Transport** | | | | |
| Bus services | $109,042 | 80% | 66% | 34% |
| Taxicabs | $42,100 | 37% | 45% | 55% |
| Buses & taxis, diversified | $24,300 | 60% | 34% | 66% |
| Local freight & delivery services | $39,836 | 18% | 32% | 68% |

| | Total | PAC Pct | Dem Pct | Repub Pct |
|---|---|---|---|---|
| Motorcycles, snowmobiles & other motorized vehicle | $53,310 | 90% | 29% | 71% |
| Motor homes & camper trailers | $10,050 | 12% | 12% | 88% |
| Pleasure boats | $62,045 | 87% | 58% | 42% |
| Bicycles & other non-motorized recreational transport | $19,980 | 98% | 14% | 86% |
| Recreational transport, diversified | $2,750 | 0% | 0% | 100% |
| Other transportation | $104,958 | 0% | 56% | 44% |

## Labor

| | Total | PAC Pct | Dem Pct | Repub Pct |
|---|---|---|---|---|
| **Public Sector Unions** | | | | |
| Federal employees unions | $1,992,127 | 100% | 79% | 21% |
| State & local government employee unions | $1,554,220 | 100% | 97% | 2% |
| Police & firefighters unions & associations | $219,190 | 99% | 92% | 8% |
| US Postal Service unions & associations | $3,785,819 | 100% | 86% | 14% |
| Teachers unions | $3,384,691 | 100% | 95% | 5% |
| **Bldg Trades, Industrial & Misc Unions** | | | | |
| Construction unions | $6,295,554 | 99% | 94% | 6% |
| Manufacturing unions | $5,363,157 | 100% | 98% | 1% |
| Intl Brotherhood of Electrical Workers (IBEW) | $1,257,920 | 100% | 97% | 2% |
| Communications & hi-tech unions | $1,119,985 | 100% | 99% | 1% |
| **Transportation Unions** | | | | |
| Air transport unions | $1,365,492 | 100% | 83% | 17% |
| Teamsters Union | $2,438,434 | 100% | 92% | 8% |
| Railroad unions | $1,214,311 | 100% | 94% | 6% |
| Merchant marine & longshoremen unions | $2,463,481 | 100% | 74% | 26% |
| Other transportation unions | $1,225,646 | 100% | 96% | 4% |
| **Other Unions** | | | | |
| Labor unions, diversified | $838,852 | 99% | 99% | 1% |
| Retail trade unions | $948,131 | 100% | 97% | 2% |
| Food service & related unions | $346,275 | 100% | 95% | 5% |
| Entertainment unions | $29,612 | 91% | 99% | 1% |
| Other commercial unions | $307,571 | 100% | 97% | 3% |
| Health worker unions | $9,200 | 100% | 98% | 2% |
| Mining unions | $317,515 | 99% | 95% | 5% |
| Energy-related unions (non-mining) | $38,825 | 99% | 96% | 1% |
| Other unions | $84,540 | 100% | 99% | 1% |

## Ideological/Single-Issue

| | Total | PAC Pct | Dem Pct | Repub Pct |
|---|---|---|---|---|
| **Republican/Conservative** | | | | |
| Conservative/Republican | $1,351,283 | 30% | 1% | 98% |
| **Democratic/Liberal** | | | | |
| Liberal/Democrat | $2,202,277 | 60% | 99% | 1% |
| **Leadership PACs** | | | | |
| Democratic leadership PACs | $1,491,998 | 100% | 99% | 1% |
| Republican leadership PACs | $860,962 | 100% | 0% | 99% |
| Democratic officials, candidates & former members | $48,044 | 100% | 100% | 0% |
| Republican officials, candidates & former members | $61,691 | 100% | 1% | 99% |
| State & local candidate committees | $20,218 | 99% | 100% | 0% |
| **Foreign & Defense Policy** | | | | |
| Foreign policy | $174,374 | 83% | 64% | 35% |
| Anti-Castro | $57,400 | 0% | 33% | 67% |
| Defense policy, pro-military | $246,304 | 89% | 15% | 85% |
| Defense policy, pro-peace | $338,641 | 61% | 95% | 3% |
| **Pro-Israel** | | | | |
| Pro-Israel | $6,747,554 | 60% | 75% | 25% |
| **Abortion Policy** | | | | |
| Pro-Choice | $701,858 | 81% | 90% | 10% |
| Pro-Life | $198,260 | 92% | 22% | 78% |

### Human Rights

| | | | | |
|---|---|---|---|---|
| Women's issues | $779,068 | 48% | 85% | 15% |
| Gay & lesbian rights & issues | $528,395 | 91% | 85% | 15% |
| Health & welfare policy | $553,724 | 77% | 90% | 10% |
| Minority/ethnic Groups | $374,889 | 62% | 51% | 49% |
| Other human rights | $23,344 | 43% | 100% | 0% |

### Misc Issues

| | | | | |
|---|---|---|---|---|
| Anti-gun control | $803,808 | 99% | 37% | 63% |
| Pro-gun control | $151,418 | 99% | 87% | 13% |
| Elderly issues/social security & medicare | $1,016,420 | 100% | 92% | 8% |
| Environmental policy | $802,267 | 81% | 89% | 10% |
| Labor, anti-union | $455,128 | 96% | 2% | 98% |
| Fiscal & tax policy | $74,757 | 89% | 2% | 98% |
| Animal rights | $5,200 | 4% | 81% | 19% |
| Consumer groups | $7,950 | 85% | 100% | 0% |
| Other single-issue or ideological groups | $114,045 | 84% | 40% | 60% |

## Other & Unknown

| | Total | PAC Pct | Dem Pct | Repub Pct |
|---|---|---|---|---|
| **Other** | | | | |
| Military personnel & employees | $24,340 | 0% | 42% | 58% |
| Other | $296,179 | 8% | 65% | 34% |
| **Non-Profit Institutions** | | | | |
| Non-profit foundations | $64,154 | 0% | 75% | 25% |
| Museums, art galleries, libraries, etc. | $38,627 | 0% | 89% | 11% |
| Other non-profit organizations | $15,580 | 0% | 66% | 34% |
| **Civil Servants & Public Officials** | | | | |
| Civil servant/public employee | $623,745 | 0% | 63% | 36% |
| Public official (elected or appointed) | $112,787 | 0% | 51% | 48% |
| Courts & justice system officials & employees | $63,970 | 0% | 57% | 42% |
| **Education** | | | | |
| Schools & colleges | $581,973 | 1% | 72% | 27% |
| Medical schools | $54,700 | 0% | 74% | 26% |
| Law schools | $21,100 | 0% | 86% | 14% |
| Technical, business and vocational schools & svcs | $294,388 | 47% | 76% | 24% |
| Public school teachers, administrators & officials | $146,645 | 0% | 68% | 32% |
| Education, unclassified | $164,214 | 0% | 71% | 27% |
| **Welfare & Social Work** | | | | |
| Welfare & social work | $210,942 | 84% | 96% | 4% |
| **Retired** | | | | |
| Retired | $2,660,255 | 0% | 41% | 59% |
| **Homemakers & Other Non-Income Earners** | | | | |
| Homemakers, students & other non-income earners | $3,861,602 | 0% | 57% | 43% |
| **Unknown** | | | | |
| No employer listed or discovered | $8,527,036 | 0% | 41% | 59% |
| Generic occupation - unable to assign category | $969,740 | 0% | 55% | 45% |
| Employer listed but category unknown | $11,629,388 | 0% | 57% | 43% |

# Index

## Symbols

Amoco Corp 25, 60, 62, 108, 110, 151, 154, 310
Anderson, Glenn M. (D-Calif) 81, 83, 158, 181, 187
Andrews, Michael A. (D-Texas) 168, 283, 288
Andrews, Robert E. (D-NJ) 55, 57, 245, 246
Andrews, Thomas H. (D-Maine) 221
Anheuser-Busch 27, 29, 76, 78, 310
Annunzio, Frank (D-Ill) 65, 128, 136, 204, 206
Anthony, Beryl Jr. (D-Ark) 168, 179, 180
Applegate, Douglas (D-Ohio) 158, 166, 262, 265
Appropriations Committee, House 130-131
Appropriations Committee, Senate 98-99
Archer, Bill (R-Texas) 19, 168, 283, 285
Archer-Daniels-Midland Corp 27, 29, 46, 49, 96, 124, 310
Arizona delegation 177-178
Arizona Leadership for America 91
Arkansas Best Corp 83
Arkansas delegation 179-180
Arkla Inc 27, 28, 62, 108
Armed Services Committee, House 132-133
Armed Services Committee, Senate 98-99
Armey, Dick (R-Texas) 35, 91, 138, 148, 283, 288
Armstrong, William L. 104, 112
Arnold & Porter 74, 310
Arthur Andersen & Co 27, 310
ASCAP 311
Ashland Oil 60, 62, 63, 108, 311
Aspin, Les (D-Wis) 34, 35, 59, 134, 300, 301
Assn for the Advancement of Psychology 70, 72, 311
Assn of American Publishers 52
Assn of Flight Attendants 311
Assn of Independent Colleges & Schools 311
Assn of Trial Lawyers of America 24, 29, 44, 74, 112, 116, 118,
    120, 126, 128, 138, 140, 142, 145, 146, 148, 152, 160, 163,
    164, 166, 168, 311
Associated Builders & Contractors 54, 56, 311
Associated Credit Bureaus 311
Associated General Contractors 24, 44, 54, 56, 122, 159, 311
Associated Milk Producers 24, 44, 46, 48, 96, 130, 133, 311
AT&T 24, 44, 50, 53, 58, 98, 100, 104, 114, 116, 118, 122, 124,
    128, 133, 135, 138, 140, 145, 146, 148, 152, 156, 160, 163,
    164, 166, 168, 311
Atkins, Chester G. (D-Mass) 52, 132, 225, 226
Atlantic Richfield 25, 27, 60, 62, 108, 151, 154, 311
AuCoin, Les (D-Ore) 49, 132, 269, 270
Auto Dealers & Drivers for Free Trade 24, 80, 82, 98, 104, 110,
    114, 120, 122, 159, 311
Automotive industry contributions 80, 81, 82

# B

Bacchus, Jim (D-Fla) 75, 195, 197
Baker & Botts 28, 311
Baker, Richard H. (R-La) 136, 164, 218, 219
Bakery, Confectionery & Tobacco Workers 311
Ballenger, Cass (R-NC) 79, 142, 158, 258, 260
Baltimore Gas & Electric 311
Banc One Corp 311
BankAmerica 137, 311
Bankers Trust 66, 137, 311
Banking, Finance & Urban Affairs Committee, House 134-135
Banking, Housing & Urban Affairs Committee, Senate 100-101
Barnard, Doug Jr. (D-Ga) 65, 66, 136, 148, 199, 201
Barnett Banks of Florida 25, 64, 66, 102, 137, 312
Barrett, Bill (R-Neb) 49, 241
Bartlett, Steve (R-Texas) 65, 78, 136, 142, 283, 284

Barton, Joe L. (R-Texas) 57, 61, 63, 144, 283, 284
Bass Brothers Enterprises/Bass International 29
Bateman, Herbert H. (R-Va) 59, 134, 154, 292, 293
Bates, Jim 128, 144, 148
Bath Iron Works 312
Batus Inc 48
Baucus, Max (D-Mont) 19, 71, 78, 83, 89, 96, 110, 112, 124, 240
BDM International 58, 100, 135, 312
Bear Stearns & Co 112
Bear, Stearns & Co 27, 28, 67
Bechtel Corp 312
Beilenson, Anthony C. (D-Calif) 19, 138, 160, 181, 186
Bell Atlantic 50, 53, 145, 312
BellSouth 24, 27, 44, 50, 53
BellSouth Corp 106, 122, 145, 312
BellSouth Services 312
Beneficial Management Corp 27, 312
Bennett, Charles E. (D-Fla) 134, 154, 195, 196
Bentley, Helen Delich (R-Md) 35, 83, 138, 154, 222, 223
Bentsen, Lloyd (D-Texas) 19, 106, 112, 283
Bereuter, Doug (R-Neb) 136, 146, 241, 242
Berman, Howard L. (D-Calif) 52, 66, 138, 146, 152, 181, 186
Bethlehem Steel 312
Beverly Enterprises 73
Bevill, Tom (D-Ala) 132, 174, 175
Biden, Joseph R. Jr. (D-Del) 34, 85, 114, 118, 194
Bilbray, James (D-Nev) 134, 164, 243
Bilirakis, Michael (R-Fla) 71, 144, 166, 195, 197
Bingaman, Jeff (D-NM) 100, 108, 120, 249
Blaz, Ben (R-Guam) 134, 146, 150
Bliley, Thomas J. Jr. (R-Va) 48, 140, 144, 292, 293
Blue Cross/Blue Shield 27, 68, 312
Blue Diamond Growers 312
Bluegrass Committee 91
Boehlert, Sherwood (R-NY) 158, 162, 251, 256
Boehner, John A. (R-Ohio) 5, 77, 262, 264
Boeing Co 58, 80, 82, 100, 135, 312
Boggs, Lindy 132
Boilermakers Union 154, 312
Boise Cascade 49, 312
Bond, Christopher S. (R-Mo) 91, 96, 102, 104, 124, 237
Bonior, David E. (D-Mich) 19, 53, 85, 91, 160, 228, 230
Boren, David L. (D-Okla) 19, 61, 96, 112, 124, 267
Borski, Robert A. (D-Pa) 154, 158, 271, 272
Boschwitz, Rudy 47, 48, 49, 96, 104, 114, 124
Bosco, Douglas H. 146, 154, 158
Boucher, Rick (D-Va) 144, 152, 162, 292, 294
Bowling Proprietors Assn 312
Boxer, Barbara (D-Calif) 138, 148, 181, 183
BP America 151, 154, 312
Bradley, Bill (D-NJ) 28, 29, 51, 52, 55, 56, 65, 66, 67, 68, 69, 71,
    73, 75, 77, 78, 79, 81, 89, 108, 112, 245
Breaux, John B. (D-La) 106, 110, 112, 218
Brennan, Joseph E. 134, 154
Brewster, Bill (D-Okla) 267, 268
Bricklayers Union 312
Bristol-Myers Squibb 70, 73, 312
Brooks, Jack (D-Texas) 51, 78, 152, 283, 285
Broomfield, William S. (R-Mich) 146, 164, 228, 231
Brotherhood of Locomotive Engineers 86, 313
Brotherhood of Railroad Signalmen 312
Browder, Glen (D-Ala) 28, 29, 85, 87, 134, 162, 174, 175
Brown & Root 54, 56, 313
Brown & Williamson Tobacco 313
Brown, George E. Jr. (D-Calif) 49, 89, 90, 91, 130, 162, 181, 188

## E

E&J Gallo Winery  27, 29, 78
E-Systems  135
E-Systems/Corporate Div  317
Eagle Forum  92
Early, Joseph D. (D-Mass)  132, 225, 226
Eastern Airlines  82, 317
Eaton Corp  80, 82, 317
Eckart, Dennis E. (D-Ohio)  144, 148, 164, 262, 264
Edison Electric Institute  317
Education & Labor Committee, House  140-141
Edwards, Chet (D-Texas)  283, 285
Edwards, Don (D-Calif)  152, 166, 181, 183
Edwards, Mickey (R-Okla)  132, 267, 268
Effective Government Committee  88, 90, 91, 317
Electron Mach Furn Workers  318
Electronic Data Systems  318
Eli Lilly & Co  27, 28, 70, 73, 120, 318
Emerson, Bill (R-Mo)  47, 49, 130, 158, 237, 239
Emerson Electric  318
Emily's List  27, 29, 93, 318
Empire Leadership Fund  91
Employee Stock Ownership Assn  318
Energy & Commerce Committee, House  142-143
Energy & Natural Resources Committee, Senate  106-107
Energy & Natural Resources industry contributions  42, 44, 45, 60-63; Targeting House committees  38
Engel, Eliot L. (D-NY)  136, 146, 164, 251, 255
English, Glenn (D-Okla)  130, 148, 267, 268
Enserch Corp  62, 318
Entergy Corp  63
Environment & Public Works Committee, Senate  108-109
Environmental issue PACs  93
Equitable Financial Services  318
Equitable Life  27
Erdreich, Ben (D-Ala)  136, 148, 174, 175
Ernst & Young  27, 318
Espy, Mike (D-Miss)  47, 130, 138, 235, 236
Evans, Lane (D-Ill)  134, 166, 204, 207
Exon, Jim (D-Neb)  19, 28, 48, 51, 53, 59, 81, 82, 83, 85, 86, 90, 100, 104, 106, 241
Exxon Corp  60, 62, 108, 151, 154, 318

## F

Faleomavaega, Eni F. H. (D-American Samoa)  146, 150
Family Health Program Inc  318
Farm Credit Council  49, 318
Farmland Industries  318
Fascell, Dante B. (D-Fla)  146, 195, 198
Fauntroy, Walter E.  136, 140
Fawell, Harris W. (R-Ill)  142, 162, 204, 207
Fazio, Vic (D-Calif)  132, 181, 182
Federal Election Commission  10-14
Federal Express Corp  24, 29, 44, 80, 82, 98, 104, 106, 112, 114, 116, 120, 122, 124, 126, 159, 160, 168, 318
Federal Managers' Assn  318
Federal National Mortgage Assn  69, 318
Federation of American Hospitals  70, 73, 318
Feighan, Edward F. (D-Ohio)  146, 152, 262, 266
Ferraro, Geraldine  91
Fields, Jack (R-Texas)  144, 154, 283, 285
Finance Committee, Senate  110-111
Finance, Insurance & Real Estate industry contributions  43, 44, 45, 64-69; Targeting House committees  38
First Boston Corp  27, 28, 67, 318
First Chicago Corp  66, 137, 319
First City Bancorp/Texas  28, 102
First Union Corp  69, 319
Fish, Hamilton Jr. (R-NY)  152, 251, 255
Flake, Floyd H. (D-NY)  136, 164, 251, 252
Fleetwood Enterprises  56
Flippo, Ronnie (D-Ala)  91
Flippo, Ronnie G.  128, 168
Florida Congressional Committee  90, 319
Florida delegation  195-198
Florida Medical Assn  319
Florida Power & Light  319
Florida Sugar Cane League  48, 319
Florio, James J.  144, 166
Flowers Industries  49, 319
Fluor Corp  54, 56, 108, 110, 126, 319
FMC Corp  25, 76, 79, 110, 135, 151, 319
Foglietta, Thomas M. (D-Pa)  134, 154, 271, 272
Foley, Thomas S. (D-Wash)  34, 90, 91, 295, 296
Food & beverage industry contributions  76, 77, 78
Food & Commercial Workers Union  24, 84, 87, 142, 319
Food Marketing Institute  25, 46, 49, 96, 130, 319
Ford, Harold E. (D-Tenn)  28, 29, 168, 280, 282
Ford Motor Co  25, 27, 80, 82, 100, 135, 319
Ford, Wendell H. (D-Ky)  19, 106, 108, 122, 216
Ford, William D. (D-Mich)  34, 86, 142, 156, 228, 231
Foreign Affairs Committee, House  144-145
Foreign Relations Committee, Senate  112-113
Forest City Enterprises Inc  69
Forest Electric Corp  57
Forest products industry contributions  46, 47, 49
Fowler, Wyche Jr. (D-Ga)  96, 98, 104, 199
Fox Inc  52, 319
Frank, Barney (D-Mass)  136, 148, 152, 225, 226
Franks, Gary (R-Conn)  35, 192, 193
Free Cuba PAC  319
Freeport-McMoRan Inc  63, 319
Frenzel, Bill  138, 168
Frost, Martin (D-Texas)  62, 128, 160, 283, 287
Fullbright & Jaworski  319
Fund for a Democratic Majority  90, 91, 319
Fund for a Republican Majority  91
Fund for Effective Leadership  91
Fund for the Future Committee  91
Fuster, Jaime B. (D-Puerto Rico)  142, 146, 150

## G

Gallegly, Elton (R-Calif)  146, 150, 181, 185
Gallo, Dean A. (R-NJ)  35, 55, 56, 132, 138, 245, 247
Gantt, Harvey  85, 90
Garcia, Robert  136, 156
Garden State PAC  319
Garn, Jake (R-Utah)  19, 98, 102, 108, 122, 289
Gay & lesbian rights PACs  93
Gaydos, Joseph M. (D-Pa)  19, 128, 142, 271, 275
Gejdenson, Sam (D-Conn)  128, 146, 150, 192, 193
Gekas, George W. (R-Pa)  152, 271, 274
GenCorp Inc  319
General American Life Insurance  320
General Atomics  320
General Dynamics  25, 58, 100, 135, 320
General Electric  25, 27, 58, 76, 79, 98, 100, 108, 122, 135, 320

Tele-Communications Inc 53, 106, 335
Telephone utility contributions 50, 51, 53
Television industry contributions 50, 51, 52, 53
Tenneco Inc 58, 100, 135, 154, 335
Tennessee delegation 280-282
Texaco 335
Texas Air 80, 82, 335
Texas Cattle Feeders Assn 335
Texas delegation 283-288
Texas Instruments 335
Texas Utilities 60, 63
Texas Utilities Electric Co 151, 335
Textron Inc 25, 58, 100, 122, 135, 336
Thiokol 336
Thomas, Bill (R-Calif) 128, 138, 168, 181, 185
Thomas, Craig (R-Wyo) 61, 62, 63, 148, 150, 303
Thomas, Lindsay (D-Ga) 132, 199, 200
Thompson & Mitchell 29, 138
Thornton, Ray (D-Ark) 29, 179, 180
Thurmond, Strom (R-SC) 59, 100, 118, 120, 126, 277
Time Warner 25, 27, 28, 50, 52, 106, 112, 114, 118, 124
Tobacco industry contributions 46, 47, 48
Tobacco Institute 46, 48, 336
Torchmark Corp 336
Torres, Esteban E. (D-Calif) 136, 164, 181, 187
Torricelli, Robert G. (D-NJ) 146, 162, 245, 247
Towns, Edolphus (D-NY) 144, 148, 158, 251, 253
Traficant, James A. Jr. (D-Ohio) 158, 162, 262, 265
Trammell Crow Co 69
Trans Comm Intl Union *see Transportation Communication Inil Union*
TransAmerica Life Companies 336
Transport Workers Union 25, 86, 159, 336
Transportation Communication Intl Union 25, 86, 336
Transportation industry contributions 43, 44, 45, 80-83; Targeting House committees 39
Transportation union contributions 84, 85, 86
Travelers Corp 68, 336
Traxler, Bob (D-Mich) 132, 228, 230
Trucking industry contributions 80, 81, 83
TRW Inc 58, 336
Turner Broadcasting System 53, 336
Tyson Foods 27, 336

## U

Udall, Morris K. (D-Ariz) 19, 146, 150, 156, 177, 178
Unidentified contributors, members with highest proportion 35
Union Camp Corp 49, 336
Union Oil 151, 336
Union Pacific Corp 25, 27, 80, 83, 98, 104, 106, 108, 151, 159, 336
Union Pacific Railroad 28
Unisys Corp 336
United Airlines 80, 82, 159, 336
United Auto Workers 24, 29, 84, 87, 128, 133, 138, 140, 142, 146, 148, 152, 156, 160, 163, 164, 166, 336
United Mine Workers 151, 336
United Paperworkers 336
United Parcel Service 24, 44, 80, 82, 104, 122, 159, 337
United States Tobacco Co 46, 48, 96, 337
United Steelworkers 24, 84, 87, 337
United Technologies 58, 100, 135, 337
United Telecommunications 50, 53, 337
United Transportation Union 24, 86, 110, 145, 159, 337

Unsoeld, Jolene (D-Wash) 19, 28, 29, 85, 86, 89, 142, 154, 295, 296
Upjohn Co 73, 337
Upton, Fred (R-Mich) 158, 164, 228, 229
US League of Savings Assns 25, 64, 66, 102, 137, 337
US Telephone Assn 337
US Tobacco Co *see United States Tobacco Co*
US West 25, 50, 53
US West Inc 337
USA Committee 91
USX Corp 27, 60, 62, 108, 337
USX Corp* 29
Utah delegation 289-290

## V

Valentine, Tim (D-NC) 158, 162, 258, 259
Valley Education Fund 90, 91, 337
Valmont Industries 78
Van Ness, Feldman & Curtis 337
Vander Jagt, Guy (R-Mich) 168, 228, 230
Vento, Bruce F. (D-Minn) 136, 150, 232, 233
Vermont delegation 291
Verner, Liipfert et al 74, 337
Veterans' Affairs Committee, House 164-165
Veterans' Affairs Committee, Senate 124-125
Veterans of Foreign Wars 93, 337
Viacom International 53
Vinson, Elkins, Searls et al 74, 337
Virginia delegation 292-294
Visclosky, Peter J. (D-Ind) 150, 158, 209, 210
Volkmer, Harold L. (D-Mo) 130, 162, 237, 239
Voluntary Hospitals of America 73
Voters for Choice/Friends of Family Planning 88, 92, 337
Vucanovich, Barbara F. (R-Nev) 63, 128, 150, 243
Vulcan Materials Co 57

## W

Walgren, Doug 144, 162
Walker, Robert S. (R-Pa) 162, 271, 274
Wall & Ceiling/Gypsum Drywall Contractors 54, 57, 337
Wallop, Malcolm (R-Wyo) 19, 100, 108, 124, 303
Walsh, James T. (R-NY) 128, 130, 251, 256
Walt Disney Co 27, 28, 50, 52, 106, 112, 114, 152, 337
Walter Industries 56
Warner Communications 116, 338
Warner, John W. (R-Va) 55, 59, 81, 82, 100, 110, 292
Warner-Lambert 28, 338
Washington, Craig (D-Texas) 28, 29, 75, 142, 152, 283, 286
Washington delegation 295-297
Washington PAC 88, 90, 114, 122, 124, 338
Waste Management Inc 25, 27, 60, 108, 110, 114, 338
Waterfield, Richard Allen 5
Waters, Maxine (D-Calif) 35, 91, 181, 187
Watkins, Wes 132
Waxman, Henry A. (D-Calif) 71, 72, 73, 90, 91, 144, 148, 181, 186
Ways and Means Committee, House 166-167; Top insurance industry recipients 68
Weber, Vin (R-Minn) 91, 132, 232, 233
Weiss, Ted (D-NY) 136, 146, 148, 251, 254
Weldon, Curt (R-Pa) 134, 154, 271, 273
Wellstone, Paul (D-Minn) 35, 232
West Publishing 52, 118, 338

# X

# Y

# Z

## DATE DUE

| | |
|---|---|
| JUN 1 5 '93 | |
| | |
| | |
| | |
| | |
| | |
| | |
| | |
| | |
| | |
| | |
| | |
| | |
| | |
| | |

BRODART                                    Cat. No. 23-2